D0083167

British Playwrights, 1956–1995

British Playwrights, 1956–1995

A RESEARCH AND PRODUCTION SOURCEBOOK

Edited by WILLIAM W. DEMASTES

GREENWOOD PRESS
Westport, Connecticut • London

Library of Congress Cataloging-in-Publication Data

British playwrights, 1956–1995 : a research and production sourcebook /
  edited by William W. Demastes.
    p. cm.
  Includes bibliographical references and indexes.
  ISBN 0–313–28759–7 (alk. paper)
  1. English drama—20th century—History and criticism.
2. Theater—Great Britain—History—20th century. 3. English
drama—20th century—Bibliography. I. Demastes, William W.
PR736.B75   1996
822'.91409—dc20   95–25609

British Library Cataloguing in Publication Data is available.

Library of Congress Catalog Card Number: 95–25609
ISBN: 0–313–28759–7

First published in 1996

Greenwood Press, 88 Post Road West, Westport, CT 06881
An imprint of Greenwood Publishing Group, Inc.

Printed in the United States of America

The paper used in this book complies with the
Permanent Paper Standard issued by the National
Information Standards Organization (Z39.48–1984).

10 9 8 7 6 5 4 3 2 1

Contents

Preface

May 8, 1956, stands out in modern British drama as the day the modern stage changed. The premiere of John Osborne's *Look Back in Anger* marked the turning point, a moment wherein the genteel comedy of manners that had dominated the stage for decades would be replaced by a radical social consciousness that challenged both the previous aesthetic preferences and the social order that supported the aesthetic. Social consciousness, combined with voices from an underclass that demanded an audience, took over the British stage and in its many forms has held court ever since.

The dominating upper-class, genteel voice of the past was replaced by a din of new voices from a variety of sources. The ''other'' England was being heard. Osborne opened the way for other voices, for Arnold Wesker and Harold Pinter, and for a social realism in general that clearly moved the theatre beyond its former function as a medium primarily of entertainment. It was now a medium of confrontation, of challenge, controlled by the Angry Young Men formerly ignored by theatre and society, and by a kitchen sink realism that could not be ignored.

Lest we forget, an allied revolutionary moment occurred slightly before May 1956, on August 3, 1955, to be precise, when Samuel Beckett's *Waiting for Godot* found its way to the London stage. If social disruption was the key to kitchen sink realism, philosophical disruptions were key to Beckett's theatre of the absurd. And toward the end of the decade Pinter would come along to unite the two, infusing absurdist disruptions into his bleak realist drama.

What followed the turbulent 1950s has been nearly thirty-five years of social confrontation. Voices have changed and diversified. Women have found a voice in the theatre; ethnic minorities have likewise increasingly found a place. The National and Royal Shakespeare theatres have embraced the new playwrights, incorporating them into their repertoires along with the masters of the past. And sparks continually ignite new bursts of energy, from those early years to a "second wave" in the 1970s through to various rejuvenations since those years.

The implication above is that the British stage has become the exclusive forum of a single, leftist vision. But it must be emphasized that the threat of monolithic, countercultural stagnation has rarely been a serious concern. The numerous voices of this "movement" would alone very likely prevent such an occurrence. There is also, in the midst of this varied and various social confrontation, highly theatrical relatives to the social realists. The theatre of Tom Stoppard comes immediately to mind, more indebted to Beckett than Osborne, but equally confrontational and challenging on another plane than the social realists inhabit. And if this new mainstream theatre of revolt becomes too complacent, reactionary, or safe, there's always the writers for the Fringe warning against complacency.

Generally speaking, it could be—and has been—argued that the period since 1956 is as theatrically vital a period as ever existed on the stage, the Elizabethan stage included. While the youthful enthusiasm of the 1950s has perhaps subsided, there seems little significant evidence that the British stage is in danger of dying. That is not to say that crises in the theatre—economic, creative, and others—have not and do not threaten the life of the British theatre; rather, there seems every hope that the theatre is currently strong enough to withstand any number of future crises with the energy that it has survived past crises.

What is clearly and decidedly evident is that so much has occurred and continues to occur that scholars and students may never tire of mining the genre and the period. The purpose of this reference book is to assist those who are interested in studying this period, either for the sake of interpretation on the page or reinterpretation on the stage. The playwrights included in this volume are by no means the only worthy candidates for review. They are, however, a reasonably representative compilation of established playwrights and more recent voices on the British stage. They attest to the diversity of the British theatre and very likely will encourage study of numerous colleagues not included in this volume. The playwrights chosen include the "canonized" and recognized figures of the period as well as voices perhaps worthy of greater attention.

Each essay includes the following components, designed to allow the flexibility necessary to accommodate the range of artists included while providing a unified structure to allow the reader easiest access to the referred materials:

1. *Biographical Overview:* A thumbnail sketch of significant events in the playwright's life, generally to be considered a basic introduction to the playwright. In parentheses following the overview is "Selected Biographical Sources," references available for gathering further biographical information.

2. *Major Plays, Premieres, and Significant Revivals: Theatrical Reception:* A selective list, includes dates and runs of significant productions, including important revivals.

Summaries of the published critical receptions of these productions (generally from newspaper and magazine reviews) follow.

3. *Additional Plays, Adaptations, and Productions:* Includes theatrical events that were less significant in the playwright's career.

4. *Assessment of the Playwright's Career:* Includes general assessments from the essay's author; also significantly incorporates summarized references to published evaluations from critics and/or scholars writing in magazines, journals, dissertations, and books.

5. *Archival Sources:* A listing of locations housing unpublished materials.

6. *Primary Bibliography:* A selective locator of the playwright's published plays and essays and articles by the playwright relevant to the theatre and/or the playwriter's career.

7. *Secondary Bibliography:* A selected list of materials relevant to the playwright's life and career, including materials referenced in the sections above.

8. *Bibliographies:* If available, bibliographies concentrating on the playwright are listed, for further referral to material not included in the above selected *Secondary Bibliography.*

The essayists in this volume have striven to select materials most significant to future scholarship on their respective playwrights, but few if any of the essays should be viewed as comprehensive in their bibliographic references. For further sources of material, especially for those playwrights who have not yet received individualized bibliographic attention beyond this volume, two works are of general value:

Charles A. Carpenter. *Modern Drama Scholarship and Criticism, 1966–1980: An International Bibliography.* Toronto: University of Toronto Press, 1986.

Kimball King. *Twenty Modern British Playwrights: A Bibliography, 1956 to 1976.* New York: Garland, 1977.

For a current annual bibliography of scholarly materials, refer to issue 2 (June) of each annual volume of the journal *Modern Drama,* issues concentrating on listing recent publications on modern drama. These issues are actually complements to Carpenter's work above.

Many newspapers are difficult to locate in most libraries. Unfortunately beginning only in 1980, the periodical publication *London Theatre Record* compiles reviews of significant productions. An index to *The Times* of London is helpful in retrieving reviews of that influential newspaper, and there is an index to the *New York Times* as well for New York premieres of British plays. An annually produced collection of New York reviews, available since 1940, is the *New York Theatre Critics Reviews* (New York: Critics Theatre Reviews). Also available is a bibliography of *New York Times* theatre reviews: *New York Times Theatre Reviews, 1920–1980,* 15 vols. (New York: Random House).

William W. Demastes

John Arden
(1930–)

MICHAEL L. COUNTS

John Arden was born on 26 October 1930, in Barnsley, Yorkshire. Unlike his working-class contemporaries, John Osborne, Harold Pinter, and Arnold Wesker, Arden was born into the middle class. His father, Charles Alwyn Arden, was a manager of a glass factory and his mother, Annie Elizabeth Layland Arden, a former school teacher. Arden attended school in Barnsley until the outbreak of World War II and then finished at a public school in Sedbergh.

After graduating from public school, Arden served in the military from 1949 to 1950. He then entered Kings College, Cambridge University, and received a B.A. in architecture in 1953. Arden continued his studies in architecture at the Edinburgh College. It was at Edinburgh that his first play, *All Fall Down*, a Victorian romantic comedy, was performed by the student drama group, with Arden in the cast.

Arden received his diploma in 1955 and then worked for two years as an assistant architect in London. He continued to write plays during this period. In 1956 his radio play *The Life of Man* won a British Broadcasting Corporation (BBC) Northern Region Prize. In 1957 the Royal Court Theatre gave a Sunday night performance of *The Waters of Babylon*. The Royal Court was sufficiently impressed to offer him a job as a script reader and commission Arden to write another play. On 1 May 1957, Arden married Margaretta D'Arcy, an Irish actress-playwright.

The commissioned play *Live Like Pigs* was produced by the Royal Court on 30 September 1958. Although this play about a group of gypsies battling with the establishment failed to impress the critics, Arden was recognized as a promising playwright. The Royal Court produced his next play, *Serjeant Musgrave's Dance*, on 22 October 1959. The critics were largely mystified by this play depicting four British army deserters arriving at a northern English town in the 1880s seeking revenge for the death of a comrade.

Arden received a fellowship in playwriting from Bristol University for 1959–1960. He also received the *Evening Standard* Award for most promising playwright during this period. His television play *Soldier, Soldier: A Comic Song for Television* was presented by the BBC in 1960 and won the Trieste Festival Award in 1961. It was during this period that he began collaborating with his wife, Margaretta D'Arcy. Their first play, *The Happy Haven*, was produced by the Royal Court on 14 September 1960. Their next play, *The Business of Good Government: A Christmas Play*, was the first of several plays designed specifically to be produced as community theatre with a cast of amateurs.

Arden's next solo effort was *The Workhouse Donkey: A Vulgar Melodrama*, produced at the Chichester Festival on 8 July 1963. Although received coolly by the critics, it is now regarded as one of his finest plays. An Aristophanic-styled comedy, it depicts petty political corruption in a northern English industrial town. Arden's next play, *Armstrong's Last Goodnight*, became his first unqualified success. It was first presented at the Glasgow Citizen's Theatre and then moved to the Old Vic at the National Theatre in October 1965. Set in sixteenth-century Scotland, the play portrays the struggles of James V to impose order in his kingdom.

Arden was then commissioned by the City of London to write a play celebrating the 750th anniversary of the signing of Magna Carta. The play, *Left Handed Liberty: A Play about Magna Carta*, was performed at the Mermaid Theatre on 14 June 1965. It was well received by the critics. His next major play was another collaboration with D'Arcy, *The Hero Rises Up*. The play lampoons the English naval hero Admiral Horatio Nelson. It was roundly dismissed by the critics. Their next play, *The Island of the Mighty*, was presented by the Royal Shakespeare Company at the Aldwych 5 December 1972. It marked a turning point in Arden's career. He and D'Arcy had become more politically committed since a 1969-1970 visit to India, where they were imprisoned for political activity. This, the Ardens' distress over the troubles in Northern Ireland, and dissatisfaction with the conditions of production in commercial theatre precipitated a series of events that overshadowed the play. Arden walked out of rehearsals, D'Arcy fought with the director and attempted to disrupt rehearsals, and the pair picketed the theatre during performances.

Ironically, Arden, who unlike his contemporaries Osborne, Wesker, and Pinter never took sides in his early plays, now became increasingly committed to leftist politics in his work, as the others moved to the center or right. The Ardens began to devote more effort to a true "people's theatre." Although the majority of their efforts were minor, they did manage to produce two major works: *The Ballygombeen Bequest* (aka *The Little Gray Home in the West*) in 1972 and *The Non-Stop Connolly Show* in 1975.

Arden and D'Arcy continue to write plays intended solely for amateur production. Arden has continued to write radio plays because he feels he has more control over their production. In 1982 his career took another turn as his first novel, *Silence among the Weapons*, was published. Although interest in his plays remains high with revivals, especially of *Serjeant Musgrave's Dance* and *Live Like Pigs*, Arden gives no indication of a return to commercial theatre.

Selected Biographical Sources: Anderson; Hayman; Leeming; Trussler [1].

MAJOR PLAYS, PREMIERES, AND SIGNIFICANT REVIVALS: THEATRICAL RECEPTION

Live Like Pigs. 1958. Opened 30 September at the Royal Court Theatre, London, directed by Anthony Page and George Devine. Actors Playhouse (NY), 7 June 1965, directed by David Wheeler. Theatre Upstairs, London, 19 February 1972, Pam Brighton director.

The play is set in a public housing development and pits a group of gypsies, and their freewheeling lifestyle, against their respectable neighbors. Arden employs the Brechtian device of ballads to intercut the naturalistic dialogue. Several critics agreed with Hastings [1], who felt the ballads should be cut and the play was too long. It received somewhat better notices in the United States, mostly for the ensemble work. However, Thompson and Gottfried were among a small group of critics who recognized the play's merit. Gottfried stated what a "very impressive, very original, and very important debut it was."

Serjeant Musgrave's Dance. 1959. Opened 22 October at the Royal Court Theatre, London, directed by Lindsay Anderson. Théâtre de l'Athenée 1963, directed by Peter Brook. Royal Court, London, 1965, directed by Jane Howell. National Theatre, London, 1981, directed by John Burgess. Old Vic, London, 1984, directed by Albert Finney. American productions: Actors Company of San Francisco, 1961, directed by Herbert Blau. Arena Theater (NY), 1966, directed by Ed Sherrin. Theatre de Lys (NY), 1966, directed by Stuart Burge. Tyrone Guthrie Theatre, Minneapolis, 1968, Mel Shapiro director. CSC Repertory 1977, directed by John Shannon.

A group of deserters from the late-nineteenth-century British army, led by Black Jack Musgrave, invade a northern English town determined to seek revenge for the murder of one of their comrades. This play also uses Brechtian-style ballads interpolated into the flow of the dramatic action. Although it established Arden as a major playwright, critics found the play confusing and irritating.

However, as the revivals increased, so did critical praise. Hobson [12] admitted that he had underrated the play in his original review. In 1966 Brown wrote that the play "has come to be regarded as one of the seminal plays of the new English drama." Gordon stated that the play is "the most considerable play to have been written in this country since George Devine established the English Stage Company."

The Happy Haven (with D'Arcy). 1960. Premiered at the Drama Studio, Bristol, then moved to the Royal Court, London, on 14 September; William Gaskill directed both productions. Encompass Theatre (NY), 31 March 1977, directed by Peter Clough.

The play, set in an old age home, depicts the insensitive and demeaning manner in which the elderly are treated by society. The elderly are played by young actors who, in commedia masks, do not attempt a naturalistic portrayal but comment on old age in Brechtian fashion. Gussow [2] expressed the view of most critics: "far less ambitious than his weightier efforts." However, Hunt cautioned, "But the fact that *The Happy Haven* is very funny doesn't prevent it from also being very serious."

The Workhouse Donkey: A Vulgar Melodrama. 1963. Chichester Festival Theatre, Sussex, 8 July, directed by Stuart Burge. Brandeis University, 1967, directed by Howard Bay.

Arden's Brechtian influence is most obvious here, as the play borrows heavily from *In the Jungle of Cities*. In a northern English town Butterthwaite, the corrupt, Napoleonic municipal leader is locked in battle with the moralist Feng. The two destroy each other in their fight for control of the town.

Most critics were once again confused by Arden's dramaturgy and his refusal to take a political or moral stance.

Armstrong's Last Goodnight. 1964. Glasgow Citizens Theatre, 5 May, directed by Dennis Carey. Chichester Festival Theatre, 6 July 1965, directors John Dexter and William Gaskill; moved to the National Theatre, London, at the Old Vic.

Set in sixteenthth-century Scotland, the play presents the political struggle between John Armstrong, a tribal chieftain, and the young King James V. Johnny Armstrong's raids across the border with England threaten war between the two nations. Armstrong is lured into a trap and hanged. Arden uses archaic Scottish dialect, incidental music, and occasional verse.

Although critics expressed reservations about the use of Scottish dialect, the play was unanimously praised. Nightingale [2] refers to the play as "his masterpiece . . . a rich, complex piece"(135).

Left Handed Liberty: A Play about Magna Carta. 1965. Mermaid Theatre, London, 14 June, directed by David Williams. Theatre Company of Boston, February 1968.

Commissioned by the City of London to celebrate the 750th anniversary of Magna Carta, the play utilizes a presentational dramaturgy. Arden's characters address the audience both in the historical context and in the present. Once again Arden uses song and rhymed verse.

Although the play is seldom produced, several critics consider *Left Handed Liberty* to be one of Arden's better efforts. Trussler [1] believes it is underrated and "succeeds, and does so not least in its recognition and turning to account of its own limitations." Hunt writes, "Here we are at the point where Arden's struggle with theatre form and his political commitment come together."

The Hero Rises Up (with D'Arcy). 1968. Round House Theatre, London, 6 November, directed by Bill Hayes. Nottingham Playhouse Company, 8 September 1969, directed by Bill Hayes.

The play is a demythologizing of the British naval hero Lord Nelson. It is structured in pure Brechtian style with placards, street ballads, baroque arias, third-person narrative, and episodic structure. The production was not well received. However, after the Ardens reworked it, critics reversed themselves. Bryden [3], who disliked the original, felt the new work was "in some ways the most theatrical [Arden's] yet written." Hobson [9], who also dismissed the original, wrote that the new production "gives more vivid flashes of historical insight than do most solemn costume plays."

The Island of the Mighty (with D'Arcy). 1972. Royal Shakespeare Company, London, at the Aldwych, 5 December, directed by David Jones.

The play reworks the legend of King Arthur: there is no Lancelot, no Round Table, no Holy Grail. It concentrates on King Arthur's attempts to unite the kings and princes of England against a common enemy.

The production became a cause célèbre as the Ardens fought with the director, attempted to interrupt rehearsals, picketed the performances, and attacked the production in the press. Critical reception was mixed, but most agreed that it was a good thing that Arden and D'Arcy were not able to halt production. Nightingale [3] stated, "Thank goodness he failed. As it is, we don't only get an intellectually challenging (and marvelously spectacular) play, but also a curiously stirring one." Kingston felt that "Arden's play comes near to being a masterwork" (100).

The Ballygombeen Bequest (aka *The Little Gray Home in the West*, with D'Arcy). 1972. St. Mary's College, Belfast, May, directed by John McGrath. Shepard's Bush Theatre, London, 7:84 Company, directed by Brian McAvera. St. Clements (NY), December 1976, directed by Omar Shapli.

The play depicts the oppression of the rural Irish poor by British businessmen. The original, based upon historical fact, used actual names. This led to a lawsuit, forcing the Ardens to change character names and retitle the play. Critical reception was sharply divided; several critics dismissed it as mere "agitprop." However, Lewsen felt the play was "a thoroughgoing statement of an extremely complex political situation." Lahr [1] addressed the issue of agitprop, calling the play "a gorgeous exception, mixing politics with theatrical panache"(104). Whale combined both views, declaring that "as theatre it is rough but compelling"(187).

The Non-Stop Connolly Show (with D'Arcy). 1975. Liberty Hall, Dublin, 29 March, directed by Arden and D'Arcy. Almost Free Theatre, London, rehearsed readings, 1976. Washington Square United Methodist Church (NY), Easter Weekend 1980.

The Irish Trades Union leader James Connolly, who was shot for his part in the Irish Easter 1916 uprising, is the central character in this lengthy (six parts, 10-plus hours) socialist drama. The play is structured much like a medieval cycle drama, employing over 100 actors. Cohen calls it "probably the most ambitious attempt in English to dramatize working-class and socialist history." Even though the play has received critical praise, it has seldom been produced, never by a major professional company. The Ardens never intended the play to be produced by a commercial company. With its huge cast and political stance, the play will most likely continue to put off commercial producers.

ADDITIONAL PLAYS

All Fall Down (1955); *The Waters of Babylon* (1957); *When Is a Door Not a Door?* (1958); *The Business of Good Government: A Christmas Play* (1960); *Ironhand* (1963); *Ars Longa, Vita Brevis* (with D'Arcy, 1964); *Fidelio* (1965); *Friday's Hiding* (with D'Arcy, 1965); *Play without Words* (1965); *The Royal Pardon; or, The Soldier Who Became an Actor* (with D'Arcy, 1966); *The True History of Squire Jonathan and His Unfortunate Treasure* (1968); *Harold Muggins Is a Martyr* (with D'Arcy, 1968); *The Soldier's Tale* (1968); *Granny Welfare and the Wolf* (with D'Arcy, 1971); *My Old Man's a Tory* (with D'Arcy, 1971); *Two Hundred Years of Labour History* (with D'Arcy, 1971); *Rudi Dutschke Must Stay* (with D'Arcy, 1971); *Serjeant Musgrave Dances On* (with John McGrath, 1972); *The Devil and the Parish Pump* (with D'Arcy, 1974); *The Crown Strike Play* (with D'Arcy, 1975); *Sean O'Scrudu* (with D'Arcy, 1976); *The Mongrel Fox* (with D'Arcy, 1976); *No Room at the Inn* (with D'Arcy, 1976); *Silence* (with D'Arcy, 1977); *Mary's Name* (with D'Arcy, 1977); *Blow-in Chorus for Liam Cosgrave* (with D'Arcy, 1977); *Vandaleur's Folly* (with D'Arcy, 1978).

ASSESSMENT OF ARDEN'S CAREER

The title of a 1978 article by Clinton, "John Arden, The Promise Unfulfilled," captures the view of Arden's career shared by many critics. Clinton cites early praise of Arden's work, which saw the playwright providing a fresh, invigorating voice in British theatre. Arden brought forth this hope with the production of *Serjeant Musgrave's Dance* in 1959. While the critics were not overwhelming in their praise, some were frankly confused by the play, and most were aware that a major talent was emerging upon the English stage.

Hunt discusses the confusion surrounding Arden and the critics. It is twofold: confusion over individual plays and confusion over the manner in which Arden chooses to conduct his career. Hunt writes that Arden's political position has always been clear in his plays. The playwright "is a revolutionary, who instinctively and intellectually rejects authority" (21). Hunt faults those who go to Arden's productions expecting one type of play and come away disappointed or confused because he did not give it to them. Roy covers the same issue, as do several critics of Arden's work.

It is the proprietary interest audiences and critics alike take in playwrights that has led to feelings of disappointment in Arden's career. However, it is important to note that the turns Arden has taken in his career are entirely his own choice. Since the beginning of his playwriting, he has experimented with many forms, including medieval cycle dramas, Elizabethan and Jacobean drama, music hall ballads, Brechtian distancing, and fragmentary writing. These efforts do not win universal acceptance or acclaim for playwrights. However, Arden has had his champions from the early stages of his career. In 1973 Corrigan referred to Arden as "one of the most vital and significant playwrights of the contemporary British theatre" (324). As early as 1962 Hatch [2] cautioned that by experimenting in a variety of styles, unlike contemporaries Pinter and Wesker, Arden "is paying a price for the experience gained" (92).

Hatch's words of warning were prophetic because Arden eventually became disenchanted with the world of commercial theatre. His last commercial production was *The Island of the Mighty* (with D'Arcy) produced by the Royal Shakespeare Company in 1974. His collaboration with Margaretta D'Arcy began in 1960 with *The Happy Haven*. Arden continued to alternate between solo efforts and collaborations with D'Arcy until the mid-1970s. He then devoted his playwriting efforts to collaboration with her. Their efforts have been deliberately noncommercial. Arden and D'Arcy are devoted to community, or more accurately, communal theatre. Some of their work has been done with amateur casts and some with semiprofessional companies committed, as Arden and D'Arcy are, to leftist plays.

The impact and influence Margaretta D'Arcy has had upon John Arden as a playwright has been assessed varyingly from critic to critic, with some, quite frankly, often taking on a misogynist tone. Many of the daily reviewers of Arden's plays deride D'Arcy's influence, citing it as harmful. However, she does have supporters. Several critics note how she assisted Arden in his development as a playwright. Hayman obliquely credits D'Arcy's influence. He praises the play *Ars Longa, Vita Brevis* but fails to mention D'Arcy as a collaborator. She tackles this issue in the introduction to *Arden/D'Arcy Plays: One*. D'Arcy states that the publisher insisted upon placing Arden's name first on the cover. However, she and Arden worked out the question of influence by placing the major contributor's name first. Thus, *Ars Longa, Vita Brevis* is listed MD'A/JA, as are others, including the impressive *Non-Stop Connolly Show*.

Arden's career is divided roughly into three stages. First are the early years with *The Waters of Babylon*, *Live Like Pigs*, *Serjeant Musgrave's Dance*, *The Workhouse Donkey*, and *Armstrong's Last Goodnight*. These plays are marked by a decidedly nonpolitical stance. This is the period when Arden was content to experiment with styles and innovations. Collaborations with D'Arcy and a growing commitment to socialist ideals constitute the second phase of Arden's career. This is the period of the *The Royal Pardon*, *The Hero Rises Up*, *The Ballygombeen Bequest* (a.k.a. *The Little Gray Home in the West*), *The Island of the Mighty*, and *The Non-Stop Connolly Show*. The current phase of Arden's career has been devoted to writing novels, radio plays, and communal theatre.

There is no indication that Arden will ever return to commercial theatre. Critics fault Arden for this decision because he has yet to write his great play. Others point out that just as Arden's major influences—Bertolt Brecht, Ben Jonson, and George Bernard Shaw—are not faulted for never producing a great play, neither should Arden be. These writers are praised for their body of work, so should Arden be praised. Just as a *Galileo*, or a *Volpone*, or a *Saint Joan* appears in compilations of influential drama, so does *Serjeant Musgrave's Dance*. The plays of Brecht, Jonson, and Shaw are constantly produced, as are Arden's. Arden is in a self-imposed exile from commercial theatre. On the subject of a possibility of his return, Hayman writes: "He certainly has the stuff of greatness in him; whether it ever comes out may depend more on the way English theatre treats him than on anything within his own control"(77).

ARCHIVAL SOURCES

There is an extensive collection of clippings files on John Arden and the individual plays in the Billy Rose Collection of the New York Public Library at Lincoln Center.

PRIMARY BIBLIOGRAPHY

Plays

Armstrong's Last Goodnight. New York: Grove Press, 1965.
The Ballygombeen Bequest (with D'Arcy). *Scripts 1* (Sept. 1972).
The Business of Good Government: A Christmas Play (with D'Arcy). London: Methuen, 1963.
The Hero Rises Up: A Romantic Melodrama (with D'Arcy). London: Methuen, 1960.
Ironhand. London: Methuen, 1965.
The Island of the Mighty: A Play on a Traditional British Theme (with D'Arcy). London: Eyre Methuen, 1974.
Left Handed Liberty: A Play about Magna Carta. London: Methuen, 1965; New York: Grove Press, 1966.
Live Like Pigs. New York: Grove Press, 1964.
The Non-Stop Connolly Show (with D'Arcy). London: Pluto, 1978.
The Royal Pardon; or, The Soldier Who Became an Actor (with D'Arcy). London: Methuen, 1967.
Serjeant Musgrave's Dance. London: Methuen, 1960.
The True History of Squire Jonathan and His Unfortunate Treasure. *Plays and Players* (Aug. 1968): 60–64.
The Workhouse Donkey: A Vulgar Melodrama. London: Methuen, 1964.

Anthologies

Arden/D'Arcy Plays: One. (*Ars Longa, Vita Brevis, The Business of Good Government, Friday's Hiding, Immediate Rough Theatre, The Little Gray Home in the West, The Royal Pardon, Vandaleur's Folly*). London: Methuen, 1991. *Plays*. (*Armstrong's Last Goodnight, Serjeant Musgrave's Dance, The Workhouse Donkey: A Vulgar Melodrama*). New York: Grove Press, 1977.

Soldier, Soldier and Other Plays. (*Friday's Hiding, Wet Fish: A Professional Reminiscence for Television, When Is a Door Not a Door?*). London: Methuen, 1967.

Three Plays. (*The Happy Haven*, with D'Arcy; *Live Like Pigs*; *Vandaleur's Folly*). New York: Grove Press, 1964.

Two Autobiographical Plays. (*The Bagman; or, The Impromptu of Muswell Hill*; *The True History of Squire Jonathan and His Unfortunate Treasure*). London: Methuen, 1971.

Essays and Interviews

"Art, Politics, and John Arden" (interview with Ira Peck). *New York Times* (10 July 1966).

Awkward Corners (with D'Arcy). London: Methuen, 1988.

"Delusions of Grandeur." *The Twentieth Century* 169 (Feb. 1961): 200–206.

"The *Island* Controversy at the Aldwych." *Performance* (fall 1973):11–20.

"The Island of the Ardens" (interview with Pam Gems). *Plays and Players* (Jan. 1973): 16–19.

"Telling a True Tale." In *New Theatre Voices of the Fifties and Sixties*, ed. Charles Marowitz et al. London: Eyre Methuen, 1965, 1981.

To Present the Pretence. London: Eyre Methuen, 1977.

"Who's for a Revolution? Two Interviews with John Arden."(with Walter Wager). *Tulane Drama Review* 11.34 (winter 1966): 41–48.

"Verse in the Theatre." *New Theatre Magazine* 11.3 (Apr. 1961):12–17.

SECONDARY BIBLIOGRAPHY

Anderson, Michael. *Anger and Detachment: A Study of Arden, Osborne, and Pinter*. London: Pitman, 1976.

Bannister, Winifred. "Armstrong's Last Goodnight." *Theatre World* (July 1964): 26.

Barker, Felix. "Drama and Poetry—But, Oh It's So Difficult." *Evening News* (7 July 1965).

Bernheimer, Martin. "Promising but Angry." *Christian Science Monitor* (12 June 1965).

Blindheim, Joan Tindale. "John Arden's Use of the Stage." *Modern Drama* 11.3 (Dec. 1968): 306–16.

Bolton, Whitney. "Arden Has Promise for Future." *New York Morning Telegraph* (9 Jan. 1965).

Brahms, Caryl. "Lines of Communication." *Plays and Players* (Dec. 1959): 11.

Brian, Alan. "Alan Brian's Diary." *Sunday Times* (10 Dec. 1972).

Brown, E. Martin. "Serjeant Musgrave's Dance." *Drama Survey* 5 (spring 1966): 87–88.

Brustein, Robert [1]. "The Ballygombeen Bequest." *The Observer* (24 Sept. 1972): 36.
———— [2]. "Better the Censor than the Eavesdropper." *New York Times* (12 Nov. 1972).
———— [3]. "Picketing His Own Play." *New York Times* (7 Jan. 1973).
———— [4]. "Subjects of Scandal." *The Observer* (17 Dec. 1972): 31.
———— [5]. "Subjects of Scandal and Concern." *New Republic* (6 and 13 Jan. 1973): 25–26.
Bryden, Ronald [1]. "Deep as England." *New Statesman* (17 Dec. 1965): 979.
———— [2]. "The Hero Rises Up." *The Observer* (10 Nov. 1968).
———— [3]. "The Hero Rises Up." *The Observer* (14 Sept. 1969).
———— [4]. "Romantic Muggins." *The Observer* (16 June 1968).
Chapin, Louis. "Musgrave's Dance in Double Bow." *Christian Science Monitor* (24 Mar. 1966).
Clinton, Craig. "John Arden: The Promise Unfulfilled." *Modern Drama* 21.1 (Mar. 1977): 47–57.
Cohen, Michael. "A Defence of D'Arcy and Arden's *Non-Stop Connolly Show*." *Theatre Research International* 15.1 (spring 1990): 78–88.
Corrigan, Robert W. *The Theatre in Search of a Fix*. New York: Delacorte Press, 1973.
Darlington, W. A. "Historical Play Suits Open Stage." *Daily Telegraph* (7 July 1965).
Dawson, Helen. "*Live Like Pigs*." *The Observer* (20 Feb. 1972): 27.
Elsom, John. *Post-war British Theatre*. London: Routledge & Kegan Paul, 1976.
Feingold, Michael. "Lost in the Forest of Arden." *Village Voice* (2 Mar. 1972): 49.
Gascoigne, Bamber [1]. "Arden's Border Manoeuvres." *The Observer* (10 May 1964).
———— [2]. "Musgrave in Paris." *The Observer* (13 Oct. 1963).
———— [3]. "The Scandals of Arden's Borough." *The Observer* (14 July 1963).
Gillespie, Elgy. "Vandaleur's Folly." *Sunday Times* (22 Oct. 1978).
Gilliat, Penelope. "Adjusting the Focus of History." *The Observer* (11 July 1965).
Gilman, Richard. "Arden's Unsteady Ground." *Tulane Drama Review* 2 (winter 1966): 54–62.
Gordon, Giles. "*Serjeant Musgrave's Dance*." *The Spectator* (2 June 1984).
Gottfried, Martin. "*Live Like Pigs*." *Women's Wear Daily* (8 June 1965): 75.
Gussow, Mel [1]. "Arden's Mock-Heroic at AMDA." *New York Times* (24 Dec. 1974): 10.
———— [2]. "The Happy Haven." *New York Times* (5 Apr. 1977): 38.
Hastings, Ronald [1]. "Cavemen in a Council House." *Daily Telegraph* (1 Oct. 1958).
———— [2]. "A Second Look for Critics." *Daily Telegraph* (27 Nov. 1965).
Hatch, Robert [1]. "Arden." *Nation* (21 June 1965): 681–82.
———— [2]. "A Coming Talent Cast Its Shadow Before." *Horizon* (July 1962): 91–94.
Hayman, Ronald. *John Arden*. London: Heinemann, 1968.
Hewes, Henry [1]. "Broadway Postscript." *Saturday Review* (23 Apr. 1966): 43.
———— [2]. "Here's Mud in Your Sty." *Saturday Review* (26 June 1965): 45.
———— [3]. "Journey into a North Wind." *Saturday Review* (26 Mar. 1966): 45.
Hobson, Harold [1]. "The Hero Rises Up." *Sunday Times* (10 Nov. 1968).
———— [2]. "Horatio Hits the Deck." *Sunday Times* (14 Sept. 1969).
———— [3]. "The Island of the Mighty." *Sunday Times* (10 Dec. 1972): 36.
———— [4]. "John Arden's True History of Squire Jonathan." *Sunday Times* (15 July 1973).

———— [5]. "Mercury Rises for Serjeant Musgrave." *Christian Science Monitor* (18 Oct. 1963).

———— [6]. "One up from the Gorillas." *Sunday Times* (11 July 1965).

———— [7]. "Pattern of Protest vs. Director Domination." *Christian Science Monitor* (8 Dec. 1972): 4.

———— [8]. "The Pursuit of Happiness." *Sunday Times* (8 Nov. 1959).

———— [9]. "Restaged Arden Play Topples a British Hero." *Christian Science Monitor* (26 Sept. 1969).

———— [10]. "Rough Waters for Arden, Osborne Plays." *Christian Science Monitor* (6 Dec. 1972).

———— [11]. "Scots Scoot out of Past." *Christian Science Monitor* (11 May 1964).

———— [12]. "*Serjeant Musgrave's Dance.*" *Christian Science Monitor* (15 Dec. 1965).

———— [13]. "The Soldier's Tale." *Sunday Times* (18 Dec. 1965).

———— [14]. "The True History of Squire Jonathan." *Sunday Times* (23 June 1968).

Hope-Wallace, Philip. "Something Short of a Great Play." *The Guardian* (24 Oct. 1959).

Hunt, Albert. *Arden: A Study of His Plays.* London: Eyre Methuen, 1974.

Itzin, Catherine. *Stages in the Revolution.* London: Eyre Methuen, 1980.

Jenkins, Alan. "Delivering the Word." *Times Literary Supplement* (15 June 1981).

Kauffmann, Stanley [1]. "The Art of John Arden." *New York Times* (20 Mar. 1966): 11.

———— [2]. "Colicos in Title Role of John Arden's Play." *New York Times* (9 Mar. 1966): 44.

Kennedy, Andrew K. *Six Dramatists in Search of a Language: Studies in Dramatic Literature.* Cambridge: Cambridge University Press, 1975.

Kingston, Jeremy. "Theatre." *Punch* (13 Dec. 1972): 100.

Lahr, John [1]. "Acting out the Protest." *New Statesman* (22 Sept. 1972): 408.

———— [2]. "On Stage." *Village Voice* (18 Nov. 1973): 62.

Lambert, J. W. "Rooted in Dishonor." *Sunday Times* (17 Oct. 1965).

Leeming, Glenda. *John Arden.* London: Longmans, 1974.

Lewis, Peter. "Serjeant Jack Shows His Mettle." *Daily Mail* (12 Oct. 1965).

Lewsen, Charles. "The Ballygombeen Bequest." *The Times* (29 Aug. 1972): 6.

Manchester, Victoria. "Let's Do Some Undressing: The 'War Carnival' at New York University." *Educational Theatre Journal* 19.4 (Dec. 1967): 502–10.

Marcus, Frank [1]. "Alas, How the Mighty Have Fallen." *Sunday Telegraph* (28 June 1968).

———— [2]. "The Hero Rises Up." *Sunday Telegraph* (10 Nov. 1968).

———— [3]. "The True History of Squire Jonathan." *Sunday Telegraph* (23 June 1968).

Mills, John. "Love and Anarchy in *Serjeant Musgrave's Dance.*" *Drama Survey* 7.1 and 2 (winter 1968–69): 45–51.

Nadel, Norman. "Wild and Gamy, *Pigs* Is Superbly Acted Play." *New York World-Telegram and Sun* (8 June 1965).

Nightingale, Benedict [1]. "Armstrong's Last Goodnight." *The Guardian* (7 July 1965).

———— [2]. *Reader's Guide to Fifty Modern British Plays.* London: Heinemann, 1982.

———— [3]. "The True Voice of Liberty." *New Statesman* (15 Dec. 1972): 915–16.

O'Hanlon, Redmond. "The Theatrical Values of John Arden." *Theatre Research International* 3 (autumn 1980): 218–36.

Oliver, Edith. "Doleful Drama." *The New Yorker* (19 Mar. 1966).

Page, Malcolm. ''The Motives of Pacifists: John Arden's 'Serjeant Musgrave's Dance.' ''
   Drama Survey (spring-summer 1967): 67–72.
Panter-Downes, Molly. ''The Workhouse Donkey.'' *The New Yorker* (3 Aug. 1963).
Prideaux, Tom. ''Serjeant Musgrave's Dance.'' *Life* (1 Apr. 1966): 12.
Roy, Emil. *British Drama since Shaw.* Carbondale: Southern Illinois University Press,
   1972.
Sainer, Arthur [1]. ''The Ballygombeen Bequest.'' *Village Voice* (6 Dec. 1976): 99.
———— [2]. ''Jesus Christ, Super-Englishman.'' *Village Voice* (31 Dec. 1970): 34.
———— [3]. ''War Dances.'' *Village Voice* (26 Dec. 1977): 77.
Silver, Lee. '' 'Live Like Pigs' Gets Good Performances.'' *New York Daily News* (8 June
   1965).
Steinberg, M. W. ''Violence in 'Serjeant Musgrave's Dance': A Study in Tragic Anti-
   theses.'' *Dalhousie Review* 57.3 (autumn 1977): 437–52.
Sullivan, Dan. ''The Theater: Musgrave.'' *New York Times* (16 June 1968): 52.
Taylor, John Russell [1]. *Anger and After: A Guide to New British Drama.* London:
   Methuen, 1962.
———— [2]. ''What's Happened to the New Dramatists?'' *Plays and Players* (Aug. 1964):
   8–9.
Thompson, Jack. ''A Good Gypsy Drama.'' *New York Journal American* (8 June 1965):
   18.
Todd, Susan. ''*Serjeant Musgrave's Dance.*'' *New Statesman* (1 June 1984).
Trilling, Ossia. ''The Young British Drama.'' *Modern Drama* 3.2 (Sept. 1960): 168–77.
Trussler, Simon [1]. *John Arden.* New York: Columbia University Press, 1973.
———— [2]. ''Postscript on Arden.'' *The Observer* (13 June 1968).
Wardle, Irving. ''New Play by Arden Celebrates Nelson.'' *New York Times* (9 Nov.
   1968): 26.
Washburn, Martin. ''Theatre: The Business of Good Government.'' *Village Voice* (1 Jan.
   1970): 40.
Watts, Richard, Jr. ''The Family That Lived Like Pigs.'' *New York Post* (8 June 1965).
Weinraub, Bernard. ''London: Power Play for Center Stage.'' *New York Times* (18 Dec.
   1972): 52.
Wellwarth, George. *The Theatre of Protest and Paradox.* New York: New York Uni-
   versity Press, 1964.
Whale, John. ''Cottage Industries.'' *Sunday Times* (5 May 1972): 187.
Williams, Raymond. *Drama from Ibsen to Brecht.* Oxford: Oxford University Press,
   1969.
Worsley, T. C. [1]. ''Chichester Offers Satire on England as 3rd Production.'' *New York
   Times* (9 July 1963): 26.
———— [2]. ''Triumph at Chichester.'' *New York Times* (15 Sept. 1963).

BIBLIOGRAPHY

King, Kimball. ''John Arden.'' *Twenty Modern British Playwrights: A Bibliography,
   1956 to 1976.* New York: Garland, 1977.

Alan Ayckbourn
(1939–)

JAMES FISHER

Alan Ayckbourn, undoubtedly England's most prolific comic playwright of the past three decades, has been most celebrated for his satiric portraits of middle-class British social mores and relationships.

Ayckbourn was born in London 12 April 1939, the son of Horace Ayckbourn, first violinist with the London Symphony Orchestra, and Irene Worley, a novelist and short story writer who published under the pseudonym Mary James. He was educated at Haileybury, Hertford (1952-1956) on a Barclay Bank scholarship until the age of seventeen, when he entered the theatre with a school drama group tour of Holland, the United States, and Canada. In the summer of 1956 he joined Sir Donald Wolfit's company at the Edinburgh Festival as an assistant stage manager and in bit roles. Later that year he became a member of a weekly repertory company at Worthing as assistant stage manager. Over the next few years he worked variously in stage management, acting, and the technical aspects of theatre for various companies, including a repertory company at Leatherhead, the Studio Theatre Company at Scarborough, and the Oxford Playhouse.

For Ayckbourn, 1959 was a watershed year: he married actress Christine Roland, fathered a son, Steven Paul (another son, Philip Nicholas, was born in 1961), and saw the production of his first play, *The Square Cat*, at the theatre-in-the-round at Scarborough, under the direction of Stephen Joseph. *The Square Cat*, and Ayckbourn's next few plays, *Love after All* (1959), *Dad's Tale* (1960), and *Standing Room Only* (1961) were all produced under the pseudonym Roland Allen (a combination of his name and his wife's). Ayckbourn continued to act during this time in such roles as Vladimir in *Waiting for Godot*, Stanley in *The Birthday Party*, Sir Thomas More in *A Man for All Seasons*, and Starbuck in *The Rainmaker*.

Ayckbourn's fruitful collaboration with Joseph's theatre at Scarborough as both a playwright and a director (often of his own plays) has continued to the present, despite Joseph's untimely death in 1967 and Ayckbourn's numerous productions in the West End, beginning with *Relatively Speaking* in 1967, and at the National Theatre, beginning with *Bedroom Farce* in 1977. Ayckbourn assumed the artistic directorship at Scarborough in 1970. Between 1965 and 1970, while continuing with his playwriting, Ayckbourn also worked as a drama producer for BBC Radio in Leeds.

Since *How the Other Half Loves* in 1969, Ayckbourn has produced a steady flow of acclaimed plays, including *Absurd Person Singular* (1972), *The Norman Conquests* (1973), *Just between Ourselves* (1976), *A Chorus of Disapproval* (1985), *Woman in Mind* (1985), *Man of the Moment* (1988), *Body Language* (1990), *Time of My Life* (1992), and *Communicating Doors* (1994). His plays have won many prestigious awards, leading to a series of honorary degrees and the 1987 appointment by Queen Elizabeth as C.B.E. (Commander of the Order of the British Empire). In 1988 Ayckbourn collaborated with director Michael Winner on the screenplay of *A Chorus of Disapproval*, the first of his plays made into a film, although there have been numerous television treatments of his plays.

Ayckbourn has continued to direct at Scarborough over the years. In 1986, at the invitation of Sir Peter Hall, he led a group of actors, including Michael Gambon, at the Royal National Theatre, directing his own *A Small Family Business* (1986), as well as the 1920s farce *Tons of Money* and highly acclaimed productions of Arthur Miller's *A View from the Bridge* and the Jacobean drama *'Tis Pity She's a Whore*.

In recent years Ayckbourn has also written plays for children, including *Invisible Friends* (1991), which had a sold-out run at the Royal National Theatre, and *Mr. A's Amazing Maze Plays* (1988), which was also produced in March 1993 at the Royal National Theatre after a successful run in Scarborough.

In 1992 Ayckbourn was named the Cameron Mackintosh Professor of Contemporary Theatre at St. Catherine's College, Oxford.

Selected Biographical Sources: Billington [1]; Gussow; Kalson [1]; Page [2]; Watson [3]; White.

MAJOR PLAYS, PREMIERES, AND SIGNIFICANT REVIVALS: THEATRICAL RECEPTION

Relatively Speaking (earlier title: *Meet My Father*). Opened 8 July 1965, at the Library Theatre, Scarborough. London production: 29 March 1967, Duke of York's Theatre; closed 3 February 1968. American production: 17 June 1974, Arena Stage, Washington, D.C. Revival: 7 April 1986, at the Greenwich Theatre. Television: 2 March 1969, BBC-TV; 24 December 1989, BBC-TV.

This two-act romantic farce involves a younger and an older couple. The wife of the younger couple has had an affair with the husband of the older couple, but after a change of heart, she wants to end the relationship. She goes to the older couple's country home, where she is met by her husband, who makes the assumption that the older couple are her parents. Wardle saw the play as a thin "house of cards" but notes that Ayckbourn has played it out as "brilliantly as possible." Other critics largely agreed with Wardle's view, including American critics like Novick, who acknowledged the play's humor but found it "fatuous." Over the years, however, critics have been more appreciative of the play's farcical elements. Benedictus wrote admiringly of the acclaimed 1986 Greenwich Theatre revival, proclaiming that "the moral is that Ayckbourn was, is, and will remain the most accurate and the funniest archivist of middle-class England during the farcical years since Macmillan came to power."

How the Other Half Loves. 1969. Opened 31 July at the Library Theatre, Scarborough. London production: 5 August 1970, Lyric Theatre; closed 30 September 1972. American production: 29 March 1971, Royale Theatre (NY). Revival: 8 June 1988, Duke of York's Theatre, London.

A two-act farce, among the most produced of Ayckbourn's plays, *How the Other Half Loves* involves two business associates, Bob Phillips and Frank Foster. Frank's American wife, Fiona, is having an affair with Bob. This simple situation is given a particularly Ayckbournian spin by showing the audience, simultaneously, the living rooms of both couples. This ingenious scenic effect affords Ayckbourn the opportunity of doubling the farcical possibilities from the start of the play. This widely applauded comedy is best summed up by Billington [1], who has explained that the "dazzling technique is not there as an end in itself but to service an idea; and one indicated by the punning title which obliquely refers both to one's marital partner and the class system. The play is very much about different styles of loving amongst the employers and the employed."

Absurd Person Singular. 1972. Opened 26 June at the Library Theatre, Scarborough. London production: 4 July 1973, Criterion Theatre (transferred to Vaudeville Theatre, where it closed 1 November 1975). American production: 8 October 1974, Music Box Theatre, New York. Television: 1 January 1985, BBC-TV. Revival: 15 May, 1990, Whitehall Theatre, London; closed 16 March 1991. *Evening Standard* Award for best comedy, 1973.

In this acclaimed three-act comedy Ayckbourn has set each act on successive Christmas Eves in the three quite different kitchens of three couples. The play begins in an initially farcical mood, but in each subsequent act the characters' peccadilloes take on an increasingly tragic air as a tradesman, Sidney, seen in the first act becomes a real estate developer in the fast track to big money. As the other characters sink into various failures, from career setbacks to alcoholism, the real estate man rises in what Lambert [2] called "a gruesomely funny demonstration of the power of money." As Nightingale [3] has noted, *Absurd Person Singular* is "very much a piece of its time. Sidney is that success-symbol of the 1960s and early 1970s, the property speculator, complete with a suitably ugly philosophy about dog-eats-dog and you-scratch-my-back-I'll-scratch-yours.

His rise is accompanied by the fall of those representing more traditional status, wealth, and power.'' Kerr, recalling the first New York production and cogently capturing the play's mood, wrote that it "had one of the funniest second acts I have ever seen; and death was the joke.''

The Norman Conquests. 1973. Opened 18 June and 9 July at the Library Theatre, Scarborough. London production: 9, 21 May, and 6 June, 1974, Greenwich Theatre; transferred 1 August 1974, Globe Theatre London; closed 13 March 1976. American production: 7 December 1975, Morosco Theatre (NY). Television: 5, 12, 19, October 1977, Thames TV. Awards: *Evening Standard* award for best play, 1974; *Plays and Players*, Award for best play, 1974.

The Norman Conquests is a trilogy including three related plays, each in two acts: *Table Manners*, *Living Together*, and *Round and Round the Garden*. All the plays examine the same situation and characters; in each play, Norman, a libidinous assistant librarian, pursues relationships with his two sisters-in-law (Annie and Sarah) and his wife, Ruth. The plays do not occur consecutively but are simultaneous: each play is another layer of the preceding one. Pontac described the play as offering "a pleasing richness of comedy characterization, perceptively observed by Mr. Ayckbourn, lucid, intelligent and funny.'' Noting that Ayckbourn might be striking a slight blow for "men's lib,'' other critics compared the work favorably to the Don Juan legend and Henrik Ibsen's dramas. Billington [2] stated that "like all good comedy, the plays are about something important,'' and Rich, writing of the television production, regarded the play as "not only funny but impossibly wise about sex, marriage, love and loneliness. [The characters] are doomed by circumstance and social convention to a defeated middle age.''

Bedroom Farce. 1975. Opened 6 June at the Library Theatre, Scarborough. London production: 14 March 1977, Lyttleton Theatre; transferred to the Prince of Wales's Theatre, where it closed 29 September 1979. American production: 29 March 1979, Brooks Atkinson Theatre (NY). Television: Granada ITV, 28 September 1980.

This two-act play set simultaneously in three bedrooms peopled at various times by four couples is not at all about sex, but about the desperation Ayckbourn sees in middle-class marriage. As Simon [2] wrote of the New York production, "The hotbed of errant eroticism has become the cold bed of marriages settled into routines and gamesmanship that can all too easily be disrupted by the most inconsequential turmoil from without.'' The play was well received on all fronts, with the play's London director, Peter Hall, eloquently writing that the play is "about the fact that if you give yourself to somebody you are vulnerable. So it's safer not to give, but you are then lonely and unhappy.''

Way Upstream. 1981. Opened 2 October at the Stephen Joyce Theatre-in-the-Round, Scarborough. London production: 5 October 1982, Lyttleton Theatre (closed 19 April 1983). American production: 24 February 1982, Alley Theatre,

Houston, Texas. Television: BBC-TV, 31 December 1987; repeated 17 August 1989.

In searching for a new location for his suburban couples, Ayckbourn has set this two-act play on a boat cruising up the River Orb. One aggressive couple, Keith and June, and one passive couple, Alistair and Emma, partners in a fancy goods company, are distressed to discover that while they are away on vacation their employees have taken over their factory. When a vicious tough, Vince, and his girlfriend, Fleur, try a similar takeover on the boat, the passive couple, caught between the aggressive greed of Keith and June and the violent brutality of Vince, are forced to assert themselves. Less naturalistic than most Ayckbourn plays, *Way Upstream* has a strikingly mystical quality when it becomes apparent that the characters are on the Ship of Life for a trip on which meek and repressed characters emerge stronger. Critics were generally negative, with some, like Fenton, noting that the play "is more of a technical curiosity than a stage play," while others, including Nightingale [2] found it a case of a "comic dramatist getting out of his depth." Among the few approving reviews, King called the play "nothing short of masterly."

A Chorus of Disapproval. 1984. Opened 2 May at the Stephen Joyce Theatre-in-the-Round, Scarborough. London production: 1 August 1985, Olivier Theatre; transferred to the Lyric Theatre, where it closed 7 March 1987. American production: 14 July 1988, Contemporary Theatre, Seattle, Washington. Film: 1988, screenplay (with Michael Winner; film released in 1989). *Evening Standard* Award for best comedy 1985; Olivier Award for best comedy, 1985; DRAMA Award for best comedy, 1985.

A comedy in two acts, this "brilliantly imaginative and funny comedy of life, sex and sadness in a small town amateur operatic society during rehearsals for *The Beggar's Opera*" (Ratcliffe), is among the most acclaimed and successful of Ayckbourn's later works. Timid Guy Jones rises from the chorus to the lead and becomes an unwitting victim of the marital and sexual frustrations of a typically Ayckbournian collection of suburban stereotypes, as well as a ferocious Welsh stage director. Critical response was uniformly positive, with Wilson wondering if the first-night audience "would find it so funny if they looked beneath the comical surface and realized exactly who and what they were laughing at?" Most praise was lavished on Ayckbourn's characterizations, with Peter stating that *A Chorus of Disapproval* "is moral comedy in the best sense: Ayckbourn is not afraid to like his creation," and Hoyle noting that the "complexity of the characters hearteningly illustrates Ayckbourn's constantly ripening gifts."

Woman in Mind. 1985. Opened 30 May at the Stephen Joyce Theatre-in-the-Round, Scarborough. London production: 3 September 1986, Vaudeville Theatre; closed 4 July 1987. American production: 7 February 1988, Manhattan Theatre Club (NY).

Subtitled "December Bee," this "bilious, raw, strange and surreal account of a married woman's dissatisfactions and hallucinated family counterparts after she has knocked herself out on the garden rake" (Coveney), has been widely acclaimed in both England and America, featuring a strong leading female character, Susan, played in London by Julia McKenzie and in America by Stockard Channing. Cushman [2] was ambivalent about the play, stating that its strength "is its concentration on Susan," but the majority of critics found, as Thornber [2] did, that as Ayckbourn "digs relentlessly deeper into her psyche the farce becomes more bizarre, so the volume of laughter increases to block out pain until the last, lingering moment as she sinks into incoherence. Who else has the nerve, the assurance, and the accomplishment to leave us on such a downbeat of despair, by way of such merriment? Who else could turn the dramatic cliché of a knock on the head into such a compassionate study of the damage we unthinkingly, unfeelingly, do to each other?" Of the notable American production, Simon [1] wrote that "*Woman in Mind* teaches us to shed our facile certainties."

A Small Family Business. 1987. Opened 21 May at the Olivier Theatre, London; closed 10 September 1988. American production: June 1992, Music Box Theater (NY). *Evening Standard* Award for best play, 1987.

With this play Ayckbourn created his first work outside of the nurturing environment of his Scarborough theatre. *A Small Family Business*, written for production at the Royal National Theatre's Olivier stage, is a dark farce in two acts concerning corruption inside the family of a furniture mogul. When Jack McCracken steps in to take over management of the business from his ill father-in-law, he innocently speaks of creating an atmosphere of "basic trust" in the company. Within a short time, however, he is pulled into the depths of a truly corrupt organization. The play was popular with audiences, but critics were guarded. Among the dissenting voices, Cushman [1] believed that Ayckbourn "seems to have run out of grisly suburban types, and has to re-cycle them from earlier plays." Disch wrote of the American production that the eccentric characters and farcical action "are the stock in trade of all writers of farce, who keep their machinery running with tics. You either enjoy that sort of thing or you sniff and complain of artificiality. Myself, I love it."

Man of the Moment. 1988. Opened 10 August at the Stephen Joyce Theatre-in-the-Round, Scarborough. London production: 14 February 1990, Globe Theatre; closed 12 January 1991. *Evening Standard* Award for best comedy, 1990.

Set at a Mediterranean villa, this grim comedy concerns Vic Parks, a convicted criminal who has been transformed by the media into a TV personality. Ayckbourn examines the paradox that a villain may achieve fame and fortune via media hype, whereas the victim's life is ruined. As with *Way Upstream*, Ayckbourn's protagonist is a decent, mild-mannered nonentity forced into action. The meek do not exactly inherit the earth, although they may at least become aware of society's ills. Acclaimed by critics, who noted that although it lacked the fantastical elements of *Way Upstream* and *Woman in Mind*, and the farcical lunacies of *A Small Family Business*, its darker reality continued themes introduced by Ayckbourn in those plays. Hoyle wrote that Ayckbourn "constantly cajoles us into laughter only to freeze the smile on our lips at the realization of the cruelty we so easily accept."

ADDITIONAL PLAYS, ADAPTATIONS, AND PRODUCTIONS

Alan Ayckbourn's four earliest plays, *The Square Cat* (opened 30 July 1959), *Love after All* (opened 21 December 1959), *Dad's Tale* (opened 19 December 1960), and *Standing Room Only* (opened 13 July 1961), were all written under the pseudonym Roland Allen and produced at the Library Theatre, Scarborough. Other early plays include *Mr. Whatnot* (opened 12 November 1963), *The Sparrow* (opened 10 July 1967), and *Countdown* (opened 6 February 1969). Ayckbourn's other major plays include *Family Circles* (earlier titles: *The Story So Far* and *Me Times Me Times Me*; opened 20 August 1970), *Time and Time Again* (opened 8 July 1971), *Absent Friends* (opened 17 June 1974), *Confusions* (opened 30 September 1974), *Just between Ourselves* (opened 28 January 1976), *Ten Times Table* (opened 18 January 1977), *Joking Apart* (opened 11 January 1978), *Sisterly Feelings* (opened 11 January 1979), *Taking Steps* (opened 27 September 1979), *Season's Greetings* (opened 25 September 1980), *Intimate Exchanges* (opened 3 June 1982), *A Trip to Scarborough* (variations on the play by Richard Brinsley Sheridan; opened 8 December 1982), *It Could Be Any One of Us* (opened 5 October 1983), *Henceforward . . .* (opened 30 July 1987), *The Revengers' Comedies* (opened 13 June 1989). Ayckbourn's most recent works include: *The Inside Outside Slide Show* (opened 22 July 1989), *Body Language* (opened 21 May 1990), *Wildest Dreams* (opened 6 May 1991), *My Very Own Story* (1991), *Time of My Life* (1992), *Dreams from a Summerhouse* (opened 1992, with music by John Pattison), and *Communicating Doors* (1994). His adaptations include *The Wolf at the Door*, from David Walker's translation of *Les Corbeaux* by Henri Becque (opened 3 October 1989). Plays for children have occupied Ayckbourn from the beginning of his playwriting career. These include *Xmas v Mastermind* (opened 26 December 1962), *Ernie's Incredible Illucinations* (opened 17 September 1971), *Mr. A's Amazing Maze Plays* (opened 30 November 1988), *Invisible Friends* (opened 23 November 1989), *This Is Where We Came In* (opened 11 August 1990), and *Callisto 5* (opened 12 December 1990). Aside from television adaptations of his stage plays, Ayckbourn's additional television works include *Service Not Included* (broadcast on BBC2, 1974), a half-hour play produced as part of the *Masquerade* series; and *A Cut in the Rates* (27 January 1984), a short play written for the BBC-TV "English File" series. Ayckbourn's forays into musical theatre include the musical comedy *Jeeves* (music by Andrew Lloyd Webber; opened 22 April 1975) and, in collaboration with Paul Todd, several musical revues or entertainments, including *Men on Women on Men* (opened 17 June 1978), *First Course* (opened 8 July 1980), *Second Helping* (opened 5 August 1980), *Suburban Strains* (opened 18 January 1980), *Me, Myself and I* (opened 2 June and 8, 9 July 1981),

Ayckbourn's strength is in his creation of the characters that fill these light situations and premises with greater significance. Some critics have pointed out that his plays are at their best when the least action is happening, providing the opportunity for the darker shadings of human nature to emerge. Ayckbourn may indeed begin with stereotypes representing familiar images of contemporary society, a traditional device of farcical comedy, but at his best he elevates these familiar characters by illuminating their individuality and the depth of emotions and desires. Although the style and themes of his plays may vary (some of the plays are clearly more serious, even frankly grim), there is a continual trend in virtually all his works: his characters are in a struggle with the mere act of living. They are filled with fear and mistrust of each other, and Ayckbourn sees both humor and tragedy in the sad fact that people may do nice things, but life may not work out for them anyway. As he has stated himself, "A lot of the worst things that happen in life are the result of well-meaning actions" (qtd. in Foster). He is most effective at finding new ways to chart the complicated relationships of men and women. As he himself has put it, he remains fascinated by "the fact that members of each sex are like Martians to the other" (qtd. in Lawson). In recent years critics have sensed that in plays like *A Small Family Business* and *A Chorus of Disapproval*, his characters are becoming nasty; but Ayckbourn believes that they are instead becoming sadder: "It seems to me that the deeper you go into a character, the sadder the play must inevitably become" (qtd. in Connolly).

The full recognition of his status as a major dramatist emerged clearly during the 1980s, perhaps most significantly with the much-praised *Woman in Mind*. In the past, critics have tended to find his women characters little more than stereotypes, with the more-dimensioned male characters driving the action on stage. With Susan in *Woman in Mind*, and, indeed, with occasional other female characters in some preceding plays, he has successfully overcome such criticism. Neither an obvious feminist or an antifeminist, Ayckbourn has steadily ripened as a dramatist, finding new and eloquently simpler ways of revealing his characters, male and female. In *Woman in Mind* Ayckbourn uses a remarkably simple device (Susan is struck on the head with a rake, permitting the audience a chance to "see" what she dreams) to expose the many layers of her highly individual and complex personality. It has been the most acclaimed of his plays in recent years, and one of his few plays to find the critical and commercial success in the United States that he has become accustomed to in England. As he continues to experiment with the bounds of the comic genre, there is ample reason to believe that Ayckbourn will continue to prosper as the leading comic chronicler of the angst-ridden lives of the late-twentieth-century English-speaking people.

PRIMARY BIBLIOGRAPHY

Plays

Absent Friends. London: Samuel French, 1975.
Absurd Person Singular. London: Samuel French, 1977.

Bedroom Farce. London: Samuel French, 1977.
A Chorus of Disapproval. London: Samuel French, 1985.
Confusions. London: Samuel French, 1977; London: Methuen, 1983.
Countdown, published in *Mixed Doubles.* London: Samuel French, 1977.
Ernie's Incredible Illucinations. London: Samuel French, 1969.
Henceforward . . . London: Faber & Faber, 1988.
How the Other Half Loves. London: Evans Plays, 1971.
Intimate Exchanges. 2 vols. London: Samuel French, 1986.
Invisible Friends. London: Faber & Faber, 1991.
Joking Apart. London: Samuel French, 1979.
Just between Ourselves. London: Samuel French, 1978.
Man of the Moment. London: Faber & Faber, 1990.
Mr A's Amazing Maze Plays. London: Faber & Faber, 1990.
The Norman Conquests. London: Samuel French, 1975.
Relatively Speaking. London: Evans Plays, 1968.
The Revengers' Comedies. London: Faber & Faber, 1991.
Season's Greetings. London: Samuel French, 1982.
Sisterly Feelings. London: Samuel French, 1981.
A Small Family Business. London: Samuel French, 1987.
Suburban Strains. London: Samuel French, 1982.
Taking Steps. London: Samuel French, 1981; Chatto & Windus, 1981.
Ten Times Table. London: Samuel French, 1978.
Time and Time Again. London: Samuel French, 1973.
Way Upstream. London: Samuel French, 1983.
Woman in Mind. London: Samuel French, 1986.

Anthologies

Joking Apart and Other Plays. London: Chatto & Windus, 1979, 1982.
Three Plays. London: Chatto & Windus, 1977; New York: Grove Press, 1977, 1989.
Three Plays. London: Penguin, 1979.

Essays and Articles on Drama and Theatre

"Alan Ayckbourn."*Drama* 1 (1988): 5–7.
"Provincial Playwriting." *The Author* 81 (spring 1970): 25–28.

SECONDARY BIBLIOGRAPHY

Bartsch, Uta. *Alan Ayckbourns Dramenfiguren: Charakterisierung und Charakterisika.* Anglistische und Amerikanistische Texte und Studien, Band 1. Hildesheim: Georg Olms Verlag, 1986.
Becker, Peter von. "Der Fall Ayckbourn."In *Theater 1987,* edited by Peter von Becker, Michael Merschmeier, and Henning Rischbieter. Zurich: Orell Fussli & Friedrich Verlag, 1987.
Benedictus, David. Review of *Relatively Speaking. Plays International* (June 1986): 23–24.
Billington, Michael [1]. *Alan Ayckbourn.* London: Macmillan, 1983; New York: Grove Press, 1984.

————[2]. Review of *The Norman Conquests. The Guardian* (29 May 1974).

Blistein, Elmer M. "Alan Ayckbourn: Few Jokes, Much Comedy." *Modern Drama* 26.1 (Mar. 1983): 26–35.

Cave, Richard Allen. *New British Drama in Performance on the London Stage, 1970 to 1985*. Gerrards Cross: Colin Smythe, 1987.

Church, Michael. "Shakespeare of the South Bank." *Sunday Times* (1 June 1986): 41–42.

Connell, Brian. "Playing for Laughs to a Lady Typist." *The Times* (5 Jan. 1976): 5.

Connolly, Ray. "Ayckbourn, with Music." *Sunday Times* (8 Feb. 1981): 32.

Coveney, Michael. Review of *Woman in Mind. Financial Times* (4 Sept. 1986).

Cushman, Robert [1]. Review of *A Small Family Business. Plays International* (July 1987): 26.

————[2]. Review of *Woman in Mind. Plays International* (Oct. 1986): 23.

Danziger, Danny, ed. "Interview with Alan Ayckbourn." *All in a Day's Work*. London: Fontana, 1987.

Disch, Thomas M. "A Small Family Business." *Nation* (8 June 1992): 799.

Dukore, Bernard. *Alan Ayckbourn: A Casebook*. New York: Garland, 1991.

Elsom, John. *Post-War British Theatre*. London: Routledge & Kegan Paul, 1976.

Fenton, James. "Why All That Glitters Is Not Gold." *Sunday Times* (10 Oct. 1982): 43.

Foster, William. "Playwright in the Round." *In Britain* 35 (May 1980): 22–24.

Glaap, Albert-Reiner, ed. *Alan Ayckbourn: Denkwurdiges und Merkwurdiges zum funfzigsten Geburtstag*. Hamburg: Rowholt Theater Verlag, 1989.

Gussow, Mel [1]. "Ayckbourn, Ex-Actor, Now Plays Singular Writer of Comedies." *New York Times* (11 Oct. 1974): 30.

————[2]. "Bard of the British Bourgeoisie." *New York Times Magazine* (28 Jan. 1990): 23–24, 26–27, 84.

Hall, Peter. *Diaries*. London: Hamish Hamilton, 1983.

Hayman, Ronald [1]. "Alan Ayckbourn." *The Times* (4 July 1973): 13.

————[2]. *British Theatre since 1955*. Oxford: Oxford University Press, 1979.

Henry, William A. "Review of *Wildest Dreams*." *Time* (7 Feb. 1994): 73.

Hickling, Michael. "Absolutely Farcical." *Yorkshire Post* (5 May 1984).

Hirschhorn, Clive. Review of *Wildest Dreams. Theatre Week* (7–13 Mar. 1994): 29–30.

Hobson, Harold. "Alan Ayckbourn—Playwright of Ineradicable Sadness." *Drama* (winter 1982): 4–6.

Holt, Hazel. "Grasped the Essential Ayckbourn." *The Stage* (27 May 1976): 15.

Hoyle, Martin. Review of *Man of the Moment. Plays and Players* (Oct. 1988): 30.

Joseph, Stephen. *Theatre in the Round*. London: Barrie & Rockliff, 1967.

Kalson, Albert E. [1]. "Alan Ayckbourn." In *British Drama since World War II, Part I: A Dictionary of Literary Biography*, vol. 13, ed. Stanley Weintraub. Detroit: Gale Research 1982: 15–32.

———— [2]. *Laughter in the Dark: The Plays of Alan Ayckbourn*. Cranbury, NJ: Fairleigh Dickinson University Press, 1993.

————[3]. "On Stage, off Stage, and Backstage with Alan Ayckbourn." In *Themes in Drama 10: Farce*, ed. J. Redmond. Cambridge: Cambridge University Press, 1988: 251–58.

Kerensky, Oleg. *The New British Drama: Fourteen Playwrights since Osborne and Pinter*. London: Hamish Hamilton, 1977; New York: Taplinger, 1979.

Kerr, Walter. *Journey to the Center of the Theater*. New York: Alfred A. Knopf, 1979.

King, Francis. "The Sins of the Forefathers." *Sunday Telegraph* (10 Oct. 1982): 18.

Lambert, J. W. [1]. "Plays in Performance." *Drama* (winter 1972): 15–16.

———[2]. "Plays in Performance." *Drama* (autumn 1973): 20–21.

Lawson, Mark. "A Nation of Shoplifters." *The Independent* (20 May 1987): 13.

Morley, Sheridan [1]. "British Farce, from Travers to Ayckbourn." *The Times* (20 Nov. 1979): 17.

———[2]. "Tour de Force." *Punch* (10 Feb. 1982): 241.

Nightingale, Benedict [1]. "Ayckbourn—Comic Laureate of Britain's Middle Class." *New York Times* (25 Mar. 1979): 2:1, 4.

———[2]. "All in the Same Boat." *New Statesman* (8 Oct. 1982): 27–28.

———[3]. *An Introduction to Fifty Modern British Plays*. London: Pan Books, 1982.

Novick, Julius. "Two Plays at Washington's Arena Stage." *New York Times* (14 July 1974): 2:3.

Page, Malcolm [1]. "Ayckbourn, Alan." In *Contemporary Dramatists*, ed. D. L. Kirkpatrick. Chicago: St. James Press, 1988.

———[2]. *File on Ayckbourn*. London: Methuen, 1989.

———[3]. "The Serious Side of Alan Ayckbourn." *Modern Drama* 26 (Mar. 1983): 36–46.

Peter, John. "The Art of Survival." *Sunday Times* (4 Aug. 1985): 43.

Pontac, Perry. Review of *The Norman Conquests*. *Plays and Players* (July 1974): 42–43.

Ratcliffe, Michael. "Beggaring Neighbours." *The Observer* (4 Aug. 1985): 19.

Rich, Frank. "Ménage à Six." (19 June 1978): 49.

Simon, John [1]. "British Twilight, American Fog." *New York* (29 Feb. 1988): 120–21.

———[2]. "From Top to Botho." *New York* (16 Apr. 1979): 88.

Thornber, Robin [1]. "A Farceur, Relatively Speaking." *The Guardian* (7 Aug. 1970).

———[2]. "Savage Spirit of the Family." *The Guardian* (1 June 1985).

Wardle, Irving. "Fun down to the Last Drop." *The Times* (30 Mar. 1967): 10.

Watson, Ian [1]. *Alan Ayckbourn: Bibliography, Biography, Playography*. Theatre Checklist No. 21. London: TQ Publications, 1980.

———[2]. "Ayckbourn of Scarborough." *Municipal Entertainment* (5 May 1978): 7–17.

———[3]. *Conversations with Ayckbourn*. London: Macdonald Futura, 1981; London: Faber & Faber, 1988.

White, Sidney Howard. *Alan Ayckbourn*. English Author Series. Boston: Twayne, 1984: 384.

Wilson, Sandy. Review of *A Chorus of Disapproval*. *Plays International* (July 1986): 28–29.

Wolf, Matt. "What Makes Ayckbourn Run?" *American Theatre* (Jan. 1990): 29–31, 60–61.

BIBLIOGRAPHY

King, Kimball. "Alan Ayckbourn." *Twenty Modern British Playwrights: A Bibliography, 1956 to 1976*. New York: Garland, 1977: 27–30.

Howard Barker

(1946–)

DAVID IAN RABEY

The son of Sydney Charles and Georgia Irene Carter Barker, Howard Barker was born in London on 28 June 1946. He married Sandra Mary Law in 1972. Barker read history at Sussex University from 1964 to 1968 and gained an M.A.

In 1970 his first stage play, *Cheek*, was staged at the Royal Court Theatre Upstairs, and his first radio play, *One Afternoon on the 63rd Level of the North Face of the Pyramid of Cheops the Great,* was broadcast by the BBC. His radio play *Scenes from an Execution* was awarded the Prix Italia in 1985. That same year three of his plays (*Downchild*, *Crimes in Hot Countries*, *The Castle*) were staged by the Royal Shakespeare Company at the Barbican Pit Theatre, London, as a special season, ''Barker at the Pit.'' The Wrestling School Theatre Company was formed to produce Barker's plays: its first production was *The Last Supper* in 1988, followed by *Seven Lears* and *Golgo* in 1989, a revival of the 1983 Barker play *Victory* in 1990, and the British premiere of *The Europeans* (written 1987) in 1993. His work was the subject of a British television documentary, *Refuse to Dance: The Theatre of Howard Barker*, on Channel 4 in 1986. His first collection of essays, *Arguments for a Theatre*, was published in 1989 and relaunched in a second, expanded edition in 1993.

Selected Biographical Sources: Grant; Klotz; Rabey [3,6].

MAJOR PLAYS, PREMIERES, AND SIGNIFICANT REVIVALS: THEATRICAL RECEPTION

The Castle. 1985. Opened 14 October at The Barbican Pit Theatre, London, for 15 performances. A Royal Shakespeare Company production, directed by Nick Hamm. Revived by Lurking Truth Theatre Company (Cwmni'r Gwir Sy'n Llechu) at the Castle Theatre, Aberystwyth, 1986; by Moving Being at St. Stephen's Theatre, Cardiff, 1990; and by the Wrestling School for its European tour, 1995.

The play was acclaimed by critics as political drama in the widest sense, wherein Barker's characters have to deal with extremes of emotion and where the writing achieves psychological power. Along with Howard Brenton and David Hare's *Pravda* it was declared by many to be one of the two best new plays of the year. While critics summarized the play in polarized and sentimental terms as a prescription for political correctness, this does the play and its characters a disservice, given their intrinsic resistance to facile circumscription; Rabey [2, 3] emphasizes the specifically "metaphorical" power of Barker's "treatment of contemporary perils" and notes how the characters, of whatever gender, are "self-conscious obsessives" who will not have their worlds or selves "divided in the name of supposedly resolving contradictions"[1].

The Bite of the Night. 1988 (written 1986). Opened September at the Barbican Pit Theatre, London. A Royal Shakespeare Company production, directed by Danny Boyle.

Ratcliffe commented, "Mr Barker, one of our most gifted, most uncompromising playwrights, has knowingly spawned a monster of the stage." Several critics, such as Peter, objected to the length, range, variety, and demands of the play: "The immense length of his play (the evening lasts four and a half hours) is made up of short phrases: venomous asides, grim aphorisms, cosmic wisecracks." Peter deduced from his own experience that "the constant cracking of whiplash wit reduces you to incomprehension and mental fatigue." Wardle was also made uncomfortable by stylistic variety: "Wild plotting apart, what scuppers the play for me are its cascades of dense rhetoric, and Barker's coldly manipulative returns to comic banality at the moments of greatest horror." Tinker objected to Barker's method and objectives: "Yet simply to say, as Mr Barker does, that each person must take away something different from this arduous evening's unstructured ramblings of quasi-history and high rhetoric, is simply to opt out of the artist's basic responsibilities." Hiley noted the tone of his fellow critics' responses and deduced that Barker "has committed the sin of ambition—acceptable in dead playwrights, less often so in living ones. And he claims, most discomforting of all, to be building his new theatre in the ruins of once-common assumptions. Liberal pundits don't like to be reminded of the collapse of the liberal concensus." Hiley preferred to conclude, "He recasts classical myth with resonant skill, to evoke the shifting moral sands of our own society. In particular, he charts the ever more sophisticated manipulation of passion, freedom and political spectacle. This is a major work, intelligent and commanding."

Seven Lears. 1989. Opened October at Sheffield Crucible, touring to Leicester Haymarket and the Royal Court Theatre. A Wrestling School production, directed by Kenny Ireland.

The less-jaded critical faculties of regional critics seemed more amenable to the challenges of Barker's work than the London journalistic establishment. Reviewing at Sheffield, Thornber wrote: "Barker uses the pre-history of the Lear family as the framework for a debate on the same issues as Shakespeare's: the possibility of goodness and its application to government. The difference is that Barker's twentieth century argument is necessarily inconclusive, open-ended."

Reviewing at Leicester, Kellaway also thought the play strong in both ambition and execution: "Barker is unafraid of launching universal questions and asks most intently about waste."

The Europeans. 1988 (written 1987). First staged in Toronto by the Necessary Angel Theatre Company, directed by Richard Rose. Presented as a rehearsed reading by the Wrestling School at Leicester Haymarket, 1990. European premiere production by Aberystwyth University Drama Department, 1991, directed by John O'Brien and David Ian Rabey. English professional premiere of a full production, 1993, at Glasgow Tramway, touring to Leicester Haymarket, Sheffield Crucible, and Greenwich Theatre; a Wrestling School production, directed by Kenny Ireland. Revived 1995, Luxembourg Municipal Theatre, directed and translated by Eric Schneider.

The mixed impulses and frustrated paternalism of liberal response depicted in the play are manifested most informatively by McMillan: "It captures the sour, brutal and nihilistic mood of Europe in 1993 with uncanny precision and force." She remarked how play and director worked against "a more humanistic flavour" to invite us to sympathize with Katrin and Starhemberg. To Barker, this no doubt represents creative disruption of a bland liberal. But the fashionable little sniggers of complicity with which his Glasgow audience responds to this strand of nihilism should tell him that this is not so."

ASSESSMENT OF BARKER'S CAREER

It lent critics an obvious facility to group Barker with his generational peers, Brenton, Hare, David Edgar, and Snoo Wilson, as political dramatists who emerged to notice and notoriety in the 1970s. Indeed, these dramatists initially shared a thematic sense of disgust at the invasive internalization of capitalist conformities, on the one hand, and a contempt for the self-debilitating ingratiation of social democratic posturing on the other. These dramatists initially identified intrinsically ephemeral revelations of truth or faith with the disruptive individual experiences of sexual gratification or dislocation; however, their writing led them increasingly toward dramatized debates of conflicting ideas, appealing primarily to people who dealt in ideas; an unfortunate response to the political climate of Britain in the 1980s, where debate became less of an index to intellectual virility, more a futile and ultimately impotent bid for self-reassurance, when the government ethos and edicts of so-called popular resistance both geared themselves toward collective ideological prescription and the devaluation of the individual imagination.

Compared to his fellow dramatists, Barker has often been less obviously timely but more deeply prophetic. His work has become increasingly and deliberately complex in a time when both left- and right-wing critics and ideologues have located value in the readily reducible statements of linear narratives and messages couched in documentary form. With characteristic willed perversity and defiance of aesthetic limitations, Barker's work has refused infiltration by transatlantic or televisual paradigms (promoting the neoutilitarian courting of "accessibility," usually expressed in terms of recognizable bankability). Rather, his initiatives have become more European in their spirit of classical and existential austerity, and more determinedly painful in their explorations of sexuality and its conflictive relationship with state authorities.

I use the term "painful" with reference to Elaine Scarry's analysis of feeling, *The Body in Pain*, which characterizes pain as an unsharable certainty, which according to perspective cannot be denied or cannot be confirmed, principally because of its resistance to language. Barker seems drawn toward the apparently impossible task—not least because of its apparent impossibility—of reversing the deobjectifying effects of pain by forcing pain into forms of articulation, even so far as the poetic and the operatic, in order to demonstrate the practical and ethical consequences of unique experience and expression. When the reflexes of state power are concerned to deny even the imaginative possibility of "otherness," pain might yet beget a paradoxical freedom through its effects of isolation and absolute dislocation from other contexts. The expressed poetics of pain might expose the statements, interpretations and rationalizations of authority as the ultimately flawed attempts at comprehensive control that they fundamentally represent. Scarry pertinently observes how a person in pain "typically moves through a handful of descriptive words" to an "as if" clause or construction "that has a weapon on the other side" (172). This is an essential trope for many Barker characters, who discover, through ostensible disempowerment, a paradoxical power, both to expose the (sometimes implicit) weapons of their torturers, and the mental and material culture they represent, and to invent new terms of self-description and new imaginative modes of self-definition, which oppose the exclusive limits of the vocabulary of description and determinism that forms the basis of political power. This restoration of primacy to the language of individual expression seeks to explode both the ironic displacement of conventional imprecisions and the veneration of the terms of social and critical theory as prescriptive because both of these reflexes seek to obviate and dismiss individual uniqueness and complexity.

As is probably already apparent, some of the most revealing facets of Barker's work are the terms on which they irritate commentators, exposing dominant presumptions. In the early 1980s his use of "obscene" words or images provoked denouncements, which often protested that such use bespoke a failure of imagination in the dramatist. Barker explicitly and argumentatively challenged such conclusions and their own bids to limit the imagination to literally descriptive and socially prescriptive functions (see "On Language in Drama," in Barker's *Arguments for a Theatre*). Later in the decade detractors more frequently complained about Barker's "arrogance" in refusing to write in ways that accorded with prevalent impulses toward the current terms of consumerist art: commercial appeal, accessibility, recognizable classical naturalism, normative sexual orthodoxy, and political correctness. In response Barker opposed the ideal of "popular theatre," on any combination of these terms, with his own objective of a "radical elitist" theatre, which would deliberately avoid instant comprehensibility. This was, of course, a consciously provocative identification, since Barker acknowledged, "An artist uses imagination to speculate about life as it is lived, and proposes, consciously or unconsciously, life as it might be lived. The more daringly he dreams, therefore, the more subversive he becomes" (33).

Barker's preferred theatre shares some qualities with those which Stephen Greenblatt identifies in Shakespeare's: "an institution which calls forth what is not, that signifies absence, that transforms the literal into the metaphorical, that evacuates everything it represents" (127).

In Barker's work the poetic is inevitably political. This is because socially ratified models of the imagination restrict people to thinking in terms of opposites (such as "past and future," "good and evil"). Barker's writing creates some of its most startling effects by destabilizing conventional oppositions; and his protagonists seek apotheoses of demonic integrity, which include all supposedly opposing facets of the self. This location of possibilities for renewal, not in mass movements, but in the passionate search for individual regeneration, links Barker in spirit rather than in form with the European expressionist dramatists of the early twentieth century; they similarly rejected naturalism's innate antitheatricality in favor of a drive to reestablish the theatre as a crucible of intensities, of boldness in both cruelty and love.

Barker is also the most compulsively prolific major British dramatist of his generation, with a canon of over sixty works of drama and collected poems and essays, within which I will attempt to identify some major achievements and turning points.

Fair Slaughter (staged 1977) follows a characteristic course, that of an odyssey of discovery, yielding exhaustive experience that forges unexpected collusion between former enemies. However, the spirit of enquiry is not reconciliatory, more a relentless questioning of the terms of (self-)betrayal. England's oldest living murderer, Gocher, excites the curiosity of his jailer by harboring the startling talisman of a severed hand, which once belonged to Trotsky's engine driver. Gocher enlists the jailer in a quest to invent a suitable ritual to assimilate this appalling icon of European history into English soil. The play's depiction of a struggle for possession and interpretation of disintegrated physicality initiates a theme for many of Barker's later plays.

No End of Blame (staged 1981) and *Scenes from an Execution* (broadcast 1984, staged 1990) both demonstrate the social reflexes that seek to control and limit the expression of artists immediately after a war, and both develop Barker's version of the protagonist as questionable existential hero (pitched irreverently somewhere between Bertolt Brecht's Galileo and Mother Courage).

Barker's early series of plays considering the continuing failure of British social democracy is represented most pungently by the dour dystopia *That Good between Us* (staged 1977), which draws a direct correlation between the hypocritical stances on private sexuality and the warping fictions of public political power. This sequence is concluded with a vicious flourish in the haunting, savage comedy-thriller *Downchild* (written 1977, staged 1985); and by a final, uniquely pained and painful, uneasy inside perspective on Labour party politics, *A Passion in Six Days*, which focuses on the ways in which political theory and sexual experience tend to break open on each other, resisting the stasis of either idealism or expediency.

Victory (staged 1983) marks Barker's breakthrough to his own invention of a particularly demanding form of tragedy, in which the *Choices in Reaction* of the play's subtitle are referred to the audience without the restoration of pre-existent moral values. The refusal of an identifiable message challenges audience members to discover personal meaning, thus defining individual differences rather than celebrating solidarity. This presages Barker's public identification of his theory and form, ''Theatre of Catastrophe,'' for which his collection of essays *Arguments for a Theatre* serves as an exposition. In this drama social catastrophe forces the abolition of existing life and with it a rupturing of conventional pieties, permitting the release of new selves for characters, even as they reel in exploration of their own dislocation. The widely performed series of ten short plays, *The Possibilities* (staged 1988), continues this experience of flux and fragmentation, demonstrating what Barker terms ''the suspension of moral predictability'' through the dramatization of various responses to different forms of political oppression. The plays aspire not to indicate ''correct'' action or analysis but, rather, to ''divide the audience into its individual components'' (60). Thus, in both theme and intended theatrical effect Barker's drama seeks to force back the territory conventionally owed to collective morality.

Thematically, *Crimes in Hot Countries* (written 1980, first full production 1983, revised for 1985) is Barker's early broaching of the increasingly important subject of sexual desire. A wild and poignant derailment of comedy of manners into existential tragedy, *Crimes* fully addresses the potentially fatal pains of sexual longing and loss, subsequently explored to their most explosive ramifications in *The Castle* (staged 1985) and *Women Beware Women* (staged 1986). *The Castle* pursues negotiations of power, gender, and sexuality in the shadow of an armed bastion that grows as a near animate, self-perpetuating metaphor for its owner's mingled pain, hysteria, and hubris. *Women Beware Women* ''hijacks'' the form and characters of Thomas Middleton's Jacobean tragedy and impels the story to less conventional, more radical social disruptions, in terms of both violence and eroticism.

Barker's reinventions of the dramatic monologue (*Don't Exaggerate, The*

Breath of the Crowd, and *Gary the Thief/Gary Upright* grow from his poetry's restless divinings of the masquerade and decay of European history, as touchstones for contemporary retrenchments; the foregrounding of the individual against the crowd in reciprocal relationships of revelation and avoidance; the drives toward personal knowledge and regeneration that prompt collisions of interpenetrative love and cruelty in defiance of all forms of prescription. This latter trajectory also informs his most recent and innovative phase of drama, commenced by *The Bite of the Night* and *The Europeans*. *The Bite* is a mythic exploration of transgression, in which form, space, chronology, and character become disturbingly fluid as part of the "education" of a university lecturer, Savage. Awash amidst tides of classical mythology, personal history, sexual possession, and the vortices of state authority, Savage determines to defy exhaustion and steer a course through them, an effort of will that involves him in acknowledging the satisfactions within cruelty, until he confronts the essential isolation that follows on discovery itself. *The Europeans* questions the terms and senses of the word "love" (as *The Bite* did, of the word "knowledge") in the aftermath of a Christian-Islamic war. The wily Hapsburg emperor Leopold seeks to establish a cohesive culture but finds his initiatives resisted by his principal war hero, Starhemberg, who has become obsessed with a victim of atrocity, Katrin; nevertheless, Leopold bids to annex her into the iconograph of a new order of reconciliation. Katrin thwarts this by allying with Starhemberg in a joint project of self-realization and cultural subversion to outperform the would-be writers of history. Their love and actions testify to what Barker has termed "the individual's right to chaos," the right to elude conditioning, understanding, and comprehension through experience beyond control, interpretation, or incorporation by social repression.

Thus, in Barker's work courage is increasingly identified with characters' will to search for unborn selves, which involves self-exposure to potential damage but prefers the experience of successive tensions to the social routine and platitudinous habitual morality that a productive society demands. The transgressive protagonists are often banished, but they discover or form an outlaw society predicated on existential performance, the demands of which heighten imaginative life. *The Last Supper* (staged 1988) features a messiah figure, Lvov, who commands his disciples to break connections with society by acts of unforgivable rebellion, although this is also a means of creating an addiction and binding his followers to himself and each other. It is wryly apt that the disciples are finally granted the martyrdom they seek to confirm some form of status and deliver them from dissipation and the impotence of rigor. Lvov's power is based on the absence of desire, whereas the less assimilable and more profound shatterings of social discipline in Barker's work tend to be generated by the collaborations of lovers in acts of desire involving mutual suffering, mutually inflicted, mutually endured, which create ruthless new asocial loyalties, centralizing mayhem and pursuit rather than the order that social collections demand.

Hence, Barker's recent drama emanates from the crucial proposition that morality must be invented by each individual for him- or herself. His characters' will is a defiance of determinism; they are impelled into this defiance by a catastrophe ignited by social crisis rather than self-invention; thereafter, they choose to confront—or even force themselves into—new crises, which entail and demonstrate risk to public and private moral structures (there is a parallel here with the relentless output of their compulsively disaffected creator, always seeking to shift ground at the limits of tolerance, his own and others'). Characters who demonstrate their uniqueness often derive a resistant and aptly unstable following from so doing, as does, for example, the pope Park in *Rome* (written 1988). This epic play develops the interwoven narratives, interludes, and digressive form of *The Bite*, reflecting accumulation beyond exhaustion (this dramatic meditation on siege, pride, and sacrifice has proved prophetic of European self-evisceration, as was *The Europeans* of cultural conflicts and rituals of attempted reintegration). Sleen—a fictional version of the French author Céline—is another such thorny charismatic, who appears in the plays *The Early Hours of a Reviled Man* and *Ego in Arcadia*. Sleen compulsively poeticizes transgression and isolation in the ruins of calamitous love; his manic abject defiance drives him to draw out the moral disdain of his witnesses, only to puncture their prejudices and presumptions, until like several of Barker's apostles of irresistible speech, he is returned to a final silence.

Self-invention and self-expression in terms other than those provided by the stage often involves characters in seeking to preserve the erotic as problematic, where *eros* owes nothing to the socially decorative (one of the themes in the dramatic meditations on disfigurement, *Wounds to the Face*). Indeed, however artificially prolonged, desire exposes the opposing notion of "the harmonious erotic" as a specious socially ordained fallacy. The drive to discover or create space within or beyond the edicts of a congested and intrusive mass society is a frequently dramatized feature of Barker's work; but so is the personal variety and difference of its citizens, relished as a source of dignity, excitement, and hope.

Two recent "renegotiations"—*Uncle Vanya* (proceeding from Anton Chekhov's play) and *Minna* (from Gotthold Lessing's *Minna von Barnhelm*)—are particularly powerful reinvestments of characters who are sprung from the matrix of determinism represented by the purposefully twinned social and dramatic conventions governing their original invention. In Barker's version Vanya's pistol shot at Serebryakov strikes home; thereupon committed to a vindication of "wrong action," Vanya leads a rebellion of his fellow characters against the coercive necessitarianisms of naturalism. This extends even to a confrontation with their creator, Chekhov, and a continuing drive beyond the boundaries of socially justified existence. *Minna* and *Ten Dilemmas in the Life of a God* are Barker's most anguished and tragic portraits of love as an attraction of conventionally opposed impulses and propositions, and of the collective wrath it provokes.

In 1994 Barker proved himself an accomplished director with a production, for the Wrestling School, of impressive visual invention and taut verbal precision. As well as being animated with clear, tensile unsentimentality, the new play *Hated Nightfall* was a literally classical example of his work: a figure usually submerged by history—the tutor of the Romanoff children—pursues his own triumph of absolute play, murderous abandon, and vengeful erotic dedication with comic but lethal disregard for the agents of ideological discipline and historical order who attempt to interrupt him. *The Gaoler's Ache for the Nearly Dead* in some ways reverses the perspectives to focus on the viewpoints of a mother and child—Marie Antoinette and her son—menaced by forces of a new order. Barker's restoration of persuasive articulacy to characters imaginatively disenfranchised by political censoriousness and glib populist celebrations is characteristically assured; so is his sympathetic depiction of an incestuous relationship in defiance of general imaginative recoil. For Barker, as for Giambattista Vico, ''The criterion of truth is to have invented it for oneself''; but then to reinvent it anew, *ad infinitum*.

PRIMARY BIBLIOGRAPHY

Plays

The Bite of the Night. London: John Calder, 1988.
The Breath of the Crowd. London: John Calder, 1986.
The Castle and *Scenes from an Execution*. London: John Calder, 1985.
Cheek. London: Methuen, 1971.
Crimes in Hot Countries and *Fair Slaughter*. London: John Calder, 1984.
Don't Exaggerate (Desire and Abuse). London: John Calder, 1985.
The Europeans and *Judith*. London: John Calder, 1990.
Fair Slaughter. London: John Calder, 1978.
Gary the Thief/Gary Upright. London: John Calder, 1987.
The Hang of the Gaol and *Heaven*. London: John Calder, 1982.
A Hard Heart and *The Early Hours of a Reviled Man*. London: John Calder, 1992.
Hated Nightfall and *Wounds to the Face*. New York: Riverrun/Calder Publications, 1994.
The Last Supper. London: John Calder, 1988.
The Love of a Good Man and *All Bleeding*. London: John Calder, 1980.
No End of Blame. London: John Calder, 1981.
A Passion in Six Days and *Downchild*. London: John Calder, 1985.
The Possibilities. London: John Calder, 1988.
Seven Lears and *Golgo*. London: John Calder, 1990.
Stripwell and *Claw*. London: John Calder, 1977.
That Good between Us and *Credentials of a Sympathiser*. London: John Calder, 1980.
Victory. London: John Calder, 1983.
Women Beware Women (with Thomas Middleton). London: John Calder, 1986.

Anthologies

Collected Plays. Vol. 2: *The Love of a Good Man*, *The Possibilities*, *Brutopia*, *Rome*, *Uncle Vanya*, *Ten Dilemmas*. New York: Riverrun/Calder Publications, 1993.

Two Plays for the Right. (The Loud Boy's Life, Birth on a Hard Shoulder). London: John Calder, 1982.

Essays and Articles on Drama and Theatre

Arguments for a Theatre. London: John Calder, 1989; 2nd ed., expanded, Manchester: Manchester University Press, 1993.
"Barker & McDiarmid" (interview). *City Limits* (18–24 Oct. 1985): 78–79.
"On *The Hang of the Gaol*." *RSC Warehouse Writers 1*. Undated (probably 1978).
"On *The Loud Boy's Life*." *RSC Warehouse Writers 9*. Undated (probably 1980).
"On *The Love of a Good Man*." *RSC Publication*. Undated (probably 1978).
Note: *Gambit* 41 (London: John Calder, 1984) contains the text of *Pity in History*, Barker interview with Tony Dunn, and articles by Eric Mottram, Tony Dunn, Ian McDiarmid, and Ruth Shade. The television documentaries *A Play for Bridport* (BBC Arena, 1982) and *Refuse to Dance: The Theatre of Howard Barker* (Channel 4, 1986) are also noteworthy, particularly the latter.

SECONDARY BIBLIOGRAPHY

Bell, Leslie, ed. *Contradictory Theatres*. Essex University Press, 1984.
Carver, Robert. "Theatre of the Catastrophic." *Times Higher Educational Supplement* (23 Mar. 1990): 136.
Cooper, Ian. *Images of Englishness in the Plays of Bond, Brenton and Barker*. M.Phil. thesis, University of Birmingham, 1993.
Craig, Sandy, ed. *Dreams and Deconstructions*. London: Amber Lane Press, 1980.
Donesky, Finlay. "Oppression, Resistance and the Writer's Testament" (unauthorized interview). *New Theatre Quarterly* 2. 8 (Nov. 1986): 336–44.
Dunn, Tony. "Howard Barker." *In Contemporary British Dramatists*, ed. K. A. Berney. Detroit: St. James Press, 1994: 38–42.
Grant, Steve. "Barker's Bite." *Plays and Players* 23.3 (Dec. 1975): 36–39.
Greenblatt, Stephen. *Shakespearian Negotiations*. Oxford: Clarendon Press, 1988.
Hiley, Jim. "The Trojan Mores." *The Listener* (15 Sept. 1988): 42.
Imran, Mamdouh [1]. "A Study of the Plays of Howard Barker, with Special Reference to the Artist Figures." Ph.D. thesis, University of Kent at Canterbury, 1989.
——— [2]. "Undoing Whole Cliffs of Discipline: A Study of Barker's Version of Middleton's *Women Beware Women*." *Essays in Theatre/Etudes Théâtrales* 12.2 (May 1994): 169–78.
Itzin, Catherine. *Stages in the Revolution*. London: Methuen, 1980.
Jellicoe, Ann. *Community Plays*. London: Methuen, 1987.
Kellaway, Kate. "Caged Birds and Torn Kites." *The Observer* (5 Nov. 1989).
Kerensky, Oleg. *The New British Drama*. London: Hamish Hamilton, 1977.
Klotz, Gunther. "Howard Barker: Paradigm of Postmodernism." *New Theatre Quarterly* 7.25 (Feb. 1991): 20–26.
Knapp, Richard. "The Impact of Thatcherism upon the Work of Selected English Dramatists of the Left in the 1980's." M.Phil. Thesis, University of Wales, Aberystwyth, 1994.
Lamb, Charles. "Irrational Theatre: Seduction in the Theatre of Howard Barker." Ph.D. thesis, University of Warwick, 1993.

Littlewood, Kate. "Production Commentary on 'The Barker Plays'." In *Royal Shakespeare Company 1985/86, 1986/87*, ed. Peter Harlock. London: RSC Publications, 1987: 78.

Lucas, Paul. "Normality, Democracy and Realism in British Theatre Post 1990." M.Phil. thesis, University of Wales, Aberystwyth, 1993.

McMillan, Joyce. "The Europeans." *The Guardian* (5 Feb. 1993).

Page, Adrian, ed. *The Death of the Playwright?* London: Macmillan, 1992.

Peter, John. "The Difficult Art of Turning Tragedy into an Obsession with Trivia." *Sunday Times* (Sept. 1988).

Rabey, David Ian [1]. "RSC's Howard Barker Season." *Plays And Players* (Dec. 1985): 29–30.

———— [2]. *British and Irish Political Drama in the Twentieth Century*. London: Macmillan, 1986.

———— [3]. *Howard Barker: Politics and Desire*. London: Macmillan, 1989.

———— [4]. "For the Absent Truth Erect: Impotence and Potency in Howard Barker's Recent Drama." *Essays in Theatre/Etudes Théâtrales* 10.1 (Nov. 1991): 31–38.

———— [5]. " 'What Do You See?' Howard Barker's *The Europeans*: A Director's Perspective." *Studies in Theatre Production* 6 (Dec. 1992): 23–34.

———— [6]. "Howard Barker." In *International Dictionary of Theatre Vol. 2: Playwrights*, ed. Mark Hawkins-Dady. Detroit: St. James Press, 1994: 57–59.

Ratcliffe, Michael. "A Tale of Twelve Cities." *The Observer* (11 Sept. 1988): 38.

Reedman, Rosalind, "Classical Tragic Vision in the Work of Howard Barker." M.Phil. thesis, University of Wales, Aberystwyth, 1991.

Scarry, Elaine. *The Body in Pain*. New York: Oxford University Press, 1985.

Shaughnessy, Robert. "The Making of a Heavyweight: Howard Barker, The Wrestling School and the Cult of the Author." *New Theatre Quarterly* 5.19 (Aug. 1989): 264–71.

Thornber, Robin. "Roller-Coaster of the Soul." *The Guardian* (19 Oct. 1989): 29.

Tinker, Jack. "Barker's Bite Is the Pits." *Daily Mail* (15 Sept. 1988).

Trussler, Simon. "The Small Rediscovery of Dignity" (interview). In *New Theatre Voices of the Seventies*, ed. S. Trussler. London: Methuen, 1980.

Wardle, Irving. "Bloody Troytown." *The Times* (7 Sept. 1988).

Peter Barnes
(1931–)

STEPHEN WEEKS

Peter Barnes made an indelible impression on Britain's postwar theatrical scene with the 1968 production of *The Ruling Class* at the Nottingham Playhouse. Acclaimed by Hobson [1] as one of four plays in his twenty years of reviewing to announce "an entirely new talent of a very high order," it is still the work for which he is best known, not only because of its distinctive blend of black comedy, social satire, and triumphant theatricality, but also because of its reincarnation as a film starring Peter O'Toole in 1972. Since *The Ruling Class*, however, Barnes has had legendary difficulties getting plays into production, and only six more original plays (including two one-acts) have appeared on stage. He has had a rather more prolific career as an adaptor, screenwriter, and radio and television dramatist.

Barnes was born 10 January 1931, in London's East End to Frederick and Martha Miller Barnes. Prior to World War II, the family moved to the seaside resort of Clacton-on-Sea where the parents operated amusement stalls and other businesses. At age seventeen Barnes passed a civil service exam and left school to work for the Greater London Council (GLC). He served a year of military service with the Royal Air Force, 1949–1950 and then returned to the GLC. He began to write film reviews for the GLC's monthly magazine but quit shortly thereafter for freelance reviewing, including work for *Films and Filming*. In 1956, at age twenty-five, he became story editor for Warwick Films. He married Charlotte Beck in 1961.

Barnes began his writing career with a series of screenplays in the late 1950s and early 1960s. His work for film appeared infrequently after this early period, but in 1990 he wrote the screenplay for the Oscar-nominated film *Enchanted April*. Barnes also turned to television early on with a script called *The Man with a Feather in His Hat*. He did not return to the medium until 1989. Barnes turned to playwrighting as early as 1963, and his first success was with a one-act satire called *Sclerosis*, which opened at the Traverse Theatre in Edinburgh in June 1965. *The Ruling Class* opened at the Nottingham Playhouse on 6 November 1968, directed by Stuart Burge. It transferred to London 26 February 1969. The play was controversial but garnered two major awards: the John Whiting and the *Evening Standard* (for most promising playwright).

Noonday Demons and *Leonardo's Last Supper*, two one-acts, directed by Charles Marowitz, premiered at the Open Space Theatre in London in 1969. *The Bewitched*, directed by Terry Hands, was presented by the Royal Shakespeare Company at the Aldwych Theatre in 1974. *Laughter!* directed by Marowitz, opened at the Royal Court in 1978. *Red Noses*, directed by Hands, premiered at the Royal Shakespeare Company Barbican in 1985. *Sunsets and Glories*, directed by Burge, opened at West Yorkshire Playhouse in 1990.

Barnes's career as a radio dramatist began in 1973 and has continued to the present. In 1983 he wrote "I began my literary career writing epic plays. Effectively barred from the theatre for the last few years I have had the time, like a professional golfer, to take my game to pieces and redefine certain basic techniques—correct my stance, swing and grip. The truth probably is that unable to exercise a natural bent for large-scale work I have had to adjust to miniatures."("Introduction,"*Barnes'People II*). This adjustment has brought its own rewards. The "Barnes' People" series created a ready outlet for his work that the theatre has not always provided.

Adaptation has been a significant element in Barnes's creative achievement. He has been the foremost champion of the Jacobeans in the contemporary English theatre and has edited or adapted many of their plays, particularly Ben Jonson's, for radio and for the stage. Barnes also had early success with *Lulu*, his adaptation of two plays by Frank Wedekind, and with *The Frontiers of Farce*, an adaptation of two one-acts, one by Wedekind and one by Georges Feydeau. He remains active in this area. In 1990 he adapted the screenplay of *Enchanted April* from the novel by Elizabeth von Arnim. In 1991 he adapted *Tango at the End of Winter* from the play by Kunio Shimizu.

Barnes also directs many of his own adaptations and revues. Recently he has added television drama. It is only his original stage work that he prefers to leave to others.

Well-known for his regular work routine, Barnes writes six days a week, from ten to five, in the Reading Room of the British Museum. As many have pointed out, it is there that Barnes does his part to change the world, just as Karl Marx had done, in the same room, before him.

Selected Biographical Sources: Dukore [5, 9]; Barnes interviews, see especially "On Class, Christianity, and Questions of Comedy."

MAJOR PLAYS, PREMIERES, AND SIGNIFICANT
REVIVALS: THEATRICAL RECEPTION

The Ruling Class. 1968. Opened 6 November at the Nottingham Playhouse, Nottingham; moved 26 Feb. 1969 to Piccadilly Theatre, London, directed by Stuart Burge. American production: January 1971, Arena Stage Company, Washington, D.C., at the Kreeger Theatre.

The play addresses many of the themes with which Barnes would be concerned throughout his career: the folly of class-based society; the putative English habit of servility; the mysteries of belief; the role of organized religion, particularly Christianity, in an apparently godless universe; the malignity of power and authority and the countering force of love. In addition, the play establishes many ''Barnesian'' stylistic elements: extravagant theatricality, striking visual imagery, a mixing of tones and effects, an antinaturalistic approach to language and character, a grandness of scale, and a zeal for vaudevillean humor. Although some critics faulted the play for its apparently Victorian and antiquated view of the ruling class, major voices rallied to its defense. Esslin [7] called it ''an exhilaratingly talented play, the work of an exuberantly baroque, grotesque imagination.'' Similarly, Hobson [4] noted Barnes's ''zest'' and his ''power of outrageous caricature and extravagant fantastication,'' while Wardle [1] praised Barnes's ''volcanic powers of comic invention.'' Novick found Barnes's visceral loathing of the class system striking but claimed the writing was ''second-rate.''

Noonday Demons and ***Leonardo's Last Supper.*** 1969. Opened 25 November at the Open Space Theatre, London. Directed by Charles Marowitz.

Noonday Demons pits two holy men against each other with violent results— a favorite motif Barnes first tested in *The Ruling Class*. *Leonardo's Last Supper* explores the contradictions between humanism and capitalism during the Italian Renaissance. Hobson [3] found both plays a letdown after *The Ruling Class*: ''There is not in all this conscientiously researched coprology the life that so gloriously abounded in *The Ruling Class*.'' Wardle [3], on other hand, took them as a confirmation of Barnes's stature: ''one of the most original and biting comic writers working in Britain.''

The Bewitched. 1974. Opened on 7 May at the Aldwych Theatre, London; produced by the Royal Shakespeare Company and directed by Terry Hands.

An excursion into the absurdities of authority during the reign of the impotent and deformed Spanish Hapsburg king Carlos II, *The Bewitched* elicited perhaps the most effusive praise of all Barnes's work. Hobson [2] called it ''one of the most important plays of the modern generation'' and cited its ''mastery of language varying incessantly and vertiginously from the sheerly magnificent and poetic to the deliberately banal and obscene.'' Esslin's encomium [4] marked it as ''a masterpiece, a work of true genius.'' Bryden [1] called *The Bewitched* ''the finest modern play I'd read in years.'' On the negative side, Nightingale [1] found it all much ado about nothing: "It is all means and no end." Spurling took the tack that the end was only too apparent: "Like Shaw he cannot allow audiences to approach the play at any point on their own terms. . . . [This] play strives too hard to be significant." Still, *The Bewitched* has to be accounted a major work, one of the most extraordinary to appear in Britain during the 1970s.

Laughter! 1975. Opened at the Royal Court Theatre, London, on 25 January. Directed by Charles Marowitz.

Laughter! consists of two thematically related acts set in different historical periods: the first in the tsarist Russia of Ivan the Terrible; the second in Berlin of 1942, in an office charged with the administration of Auschwitz. The play contrasts the personal brand of terror practiced by Ivan with the bureaucratization of death perfected by the Nazis. It also assesses the value of humor as a weapon against injustice, a theme to which Barnes would return in *Red Noses*. Again, the play drew mixed reviews, with most critics favoring Part Two, "Auschwitz." Levin faulted even this section for its lack of originality: "For the Auschwitz section Mr. Barnes appears in turn to have discovered Hannah Arendt's phrase 'the banality of evil' and been much impressed by it." What was praised in *The Bewitched*—Barnes's creation of an extravagant and multi-faceted theatrical language—Levin condemned in *Laughter!* as an impossible "pastiche-archaic" idiom that gives the actors difficulty. Billington [1] dismissed the play as "a clumsy experiment that just doesn't come off." Wardle [2] came to the play's defense, neatly summarizing the kind of response a Barnes play frequently evokes in its admirers: "Nothing is more exciting in the theatre than a moment of genuine stylistic change: when the old dramatic categories crack apart under pressure of new experience and one sees a playwright not merely writing a play but reinventing what a play ought to be."

Red Noses. 1985. Opened at the Barbican Theatre, London, 2 July. Produced by the Royal Shakespeare Company, directed by Terry Hands. American productions include the Goodman Theatre, Chicago, 1987; San Diego Repertory, 1988; A Contemporary Theatre, Seattle, 1989. Trinity Square Repertory, Providence, 1989.

Red Noses concerns a ragtag band of comedians led by Father Flote during the plague years of the fourteenth century in France. Appearing after a lapse of seven years between major plays, it was welcomed by most critics as a sign of the continued vitality of Barnes's theatrical powers. Nightingale [2] this time articulated the minority view by calling the "gloomy musings" of the play "mostly unexceptionable, but also unexceptional." Moreover, as Billington had done in his review of *Laughter!* Nightingale cited Trevor Griffiths's *Comedians* as a play offering a more sophisticated treatment of the "politics of humour." Billington [2] himself, however, praised the play as "brilliant" and as "something rare in modern drama"—a play that presents us with an unsentimental "vision of love and hope." Coveney [1] rejoiced in "the re-establishment of

Peter Barnes as one of our major dramatists'' and called *Red Noses* an ''extraordinary morality play.'' Both Esslin [6] and Rabey commented on the play's analysis of comedy. Rabey noted that the play is ''centrally an exploration and celebration of the power of theatre, particularly comedy.'' Gary Seibert wrote that ''amoral greed and the built-in tendency of those in power to prolong their administrations at the cost of human lives are his real targets.''

Sunsets and Glories. 1990. Opened at the West Yorkshire Playhouse 28 June; directed by Stuart Burge. American production: A Contemporary Theatre, Seattle, 1992.

This meditation on power and goodness, inspired by the story of Celestine V, a thirteenth-century pope who resigned the papacy, generated a less enthusiastic response than *Red Noses*. At least among the critics, the play did little to make either new converts or enemies. Coveney [2] felt that the play deserved ''grim chuckling admiration if not exactly unadulterated rejoicing,'' but he noted that the play's director had to ''cope with the ludicrous incongruities of Barnes's inchoate style.'' Nightingale [3], never much impressed by Barnes, accused the playwright of tendentiousness: ''The characters finally matter to him only as illustrations of his theme . . . that may be the root reason why the evening, ambitious though it is, seems so unsatisfactory.'' Cherry, however, called the play ''a journey as eventful as any he has made'' and praised the characters' attempt to ''make sense of what Barnes suggests is a universe governed by a chill wind.'' Predictably, Wardle [5] praised the play as ''a work of the highest and most thrilling theatrical energy.''

ADDITIONAL PLAYS, ADAPTATIONS, AND PRODUCTIONS

The Alchemist, edited version of Ben Jonson's play, 9 February 1970, Nottingham Playhouse; revised version, 23 May 1977, Other Place Theatre, Stratford-upon-Avon; 14 December 1977, Aldwych Theatre, London. *Lulu*, adapted from Frank Wedekind's *Earth Spirit* and *Pandora's Box*, 7 October 1970, Nottingham Playhouse; 8 December 1970, Royal Court Theatre, London. *The Devil Is an Ass*, adapted from Jonson's play, 14 March 1973, Nottingham Playhouse; revised version, October 1976, Edinburgh Festival; 2 May 1977, Lyttleton Theatre, London. *For All Those Who Get Despondent*, adapted from Bertolt Brecht and Wedekind's poems and songs, March 1976, Royal Court Theatre Upstairs, London; revised as *The Two Hangmen: Brecht and Wedekind*, 20 December 1978, BBC Radio. *Frontiers of Farce*, adapted from Wedekind's *The Singer* and Georges Feydeau's *The Purging*, 11 October 1976, Old Vic Theatre, London. *The Purging* produced in New York in 1980; Virginia Stage Company, 1987. *Antonio*, adapted from John Marston's *Antonio and Mellida* and *Antonio's Revenge*, 1977, BBC Radio; revised version, 20 September 1979, Nottingham Playhouse. *Bartholomew Fair*, edited version of Jonson's play, 3 August 1978, Round House Theatre, London; 1 June 1987, Open Air, Regent's Park, London.

The Devil Himself, adapted from Wedekind's songs and sketches, 28 April 1980, Lyric Theatre, Hammersmith, London. *Sommersaults* (revue), October 1981, Haymarket Theatre, Leicester. *Scenes from a Marriage*, adaptation of a play by Georges Feydeau, 1986, Royal Shakespeare Company, Barbican. *Tango at the End of Winter*, adapted from the play by Kunio Shimizu, 10 August 1991, Edinburgh Festival; 28 August 1991, Piccadilly Theatre, London.

RADIO DRAMA

My Ben Jonson, 1973. *Eastward Ho!*, adaptation of the play by Jonson, Chapman, and Marston, 1973. *Lulu*, adaptation of Wedekind's *Earth Spirit* and *Pandora's Box*, 1975. *Antonio*, adaptation of the plays *Antonio and Mellida* and *Antonio's Revenge*, by Marston, 1977. *The Two Hangmen: Brecht and Wedekind*, revision of *For All Those Who Get Despondent*, 1978. *A Chaste Maid in Cheapside*, adaptation of the play by Thomas Middleton, 1979. *Eulogy on Baldness*, from the essay by Synesius of Cyrene, 1980. *For the Conveyance of Oysters*, adaptation of a work by Maxim Gorky, 1981. *The Soldier's Fortune*, adaptation of the play by Thomas Otway, 1981. *The Singer*, adaptation of the play by Frank Wedekind, 1981. *The Atheist*, adaptation of the play by Thomas Otway, 1981. *Barnes' People* (seven monologues), 1981. *The Dutch Courtesan*, adaptation of the play by John Marston, 1982. *Actors*, adaptation of Lope de Vega, 1983. *A Mad World, My Masters*, adaptation of the play by Thomas Middleton, 1983. *Barnes' People II* (seven duologues), 1984. *The Primrose Path*, adaptation of a play by Feydeau, 1984. *A Trick to Catch the Old One*, adaptation of a play by Thomas Middleton, 1985. *The Old Law*, adaptation of a play by Middleton and Rowley, 1986. *Woman of Paris*, adaptation of a work by Henri Becque, 1986. *Barnes' People III* (eight triologues), published as *The Real Long John Silver and Other Plays*, 1986. *The Magician*, adaptation of a work by Gorky, 1982. *The Magnetic Lady*, adaptation of the play by Jonson, 1987. *The Devil Is an Ass*, adaptation of the play by Jonson, 1987. *No End to Dreaming*, 1988. *Don Juan and Faust*, adaptation of the play by Christian Grabbe, 1987. *More Barnes' People*, 1989 and 1990.

ASSESSMENT OF BARNES'S CAREER

From the beginning of his career Peter Barnes's vision of the theatre has been demanding and expansive. His major plays require large casts, frequent changes of scene and mood, extraordinary stage effects, unusual linguistic (and often physical) agility in the acting, and costuming appropriate to the distant epochs he favors. In addition, they are dense with horrific imagery: stabbings, burnings, impalements, disfigurement, excreta, blood, disease, and squalor. There is no need to imagine a hell, Barnes suggests, as this world is overflowing with torment and injustice. The need for change is obvious, but the means to produce change is not: the power of goodness is all but overwhelmed by the machinations of authority and even the anodyne of laughter may be another means of collusion. Given the dark extremity of his imagery, the seemingly obscure historical subject matter, and the heavy demands on theatrical resources, it is perhaps not surprising that Barnes has been infrequently seen on Britain's stages. Nor has his work, when it has appeared, been particularly successful with the public. With the exception of *The Ruling Class*, none of his plays has transferred to the commercial stage, and there have been no significant revivals. Despite these difficulties, Barnes has attracted ardent admirers. These insist on the strength and originality of his voice and make claims of particular brilliance for *The Ruling Class*, *The Bewitched*, and *Red Noses*.

Barnes has not been the subject of extensive academic commentary. Bernard Dukore has written the only full-length study of Barnes's work, and that in 1981. He continues to be Barnes's chief academic interpreter. Dukore has identified and commented upon major stylistic and thematic features of Barnes's work: his innovative use of language; his debt to Jonson and the Jacobeans, to Brecht, and to Artaud; his reiterative meditations on goodness and power, his animus against class distinctions, capitalism, and organized religion; his concern with the uses of laughter; and his juxtaposition of contrasting modes—the historical with the contemporary, the erudite with the popular, the brutal with the sublime, and so on. Dukore's solid analyses and continuing interest provide a strong basis for additional research.

A question that hovers over Barnes's career is whether he has fulfilled the promise signaled by the appearance of *The Ruling Class*. In 1981 Dukore revisited Hobson's well-known assertion that *The Ruling Class* had to be ranked alongside *Waiting for Godot*, *Look Back in Anger*, and *The Birthday Party* as one of the most significant events of his twenty-year reviewing career. Dukore concludes that, whereas John Osborne may have faded, both Harold Pinter and Peter Barnes had grown in stature: "They tower above all other contemporary English dramatists." It may be more difficult to cleave to that assessment in the 1990s. Although *Red Noses* is certainly one of the major plays of the 1980s, and Barnes's voice is as distinctive as ever, his theatrical style has not evolved significantly—that is to say, unexpectedly—since *The Bewitched*. Although his most recent play, *Sunsets and Glories*, is an important work, it does recycle a number of motifs: the battle of the two archangel Gabriels is reminiscent of the warring "gods" in *The Ruling Class* or the warring saints in *Noonday Demons*; the anomalous presence of goodness in a corrupt world (act 1), followed by the inexorable return of power and the status quo (act 2) is a theme (and a structure) also pursued in *The Ruling Class* and *Red Noses*; the moment in which the cardinals all mimic the speech impediment of Jacopone has an analogue in the courtiers' spastic homage to Carlos II in *The Bewitched*, and so on. Thematic or stylistic reiteration is not necessarily a failing, and the complexity of Barnes's major plays has been insufficiently explored; nonetheless, the solidification of a "Barnesian" style combined with the infrequency of production has contributed to a certain stalemate in the critical debate and perhaps a reduction of interest. While Barnes remains a vital force in the British theatre, the preeminence attributed to him by Hobson and by Dukore is by no means self-evident. If the nature of his contributions to postwar theatre are to be more clearly grasped, he will need the kind of serious and sustained critical discussion that has already been accorded to Samuel Beckett, Harold Pinter, and even John Osborne.

Reassessment, then, is overdue. Barnes has produced two major stage plays and a significant number of original radio plays, television dramas, and adaptations during the twelve years since Dukore's full-length study was published. Christopher Innes's 1992 summary essay is useful, but it is perhaps too dismissive of Barnes's vision, which he finds so "extreme" (a term frequently used by Barnes, and applied to him, that should itself be reexamined) that it "reduces itself to pure theatre," on the one hand, and alienates the audience on the other. Other avenues of exploration suggest themselves. Barnes may be the playwright, for example, whose work most clearly demonstrates the intensity of Britain's postwar affair with the European masters—particularly Brecht, Beckett, and Artaud. Through their influence the British theatre moved quickly beyond the kitchen sink realism of the 1950s, and through Barnes their separate styles were enlisted in a full-bodied, uniquely British theatrical idiom. As a related issue, Barnes's work as a stage imagist has been inadequately explored. To an unusual degree his plays work as much through the boldness of their visual imagery as through the inventiveness of their language. Whether considered semiotically, historically, or psychologically, the nature and use of Barnes's imagery offers a rich field of study. Paradoxically, perhaps, Barnes has also become a notable dramatist for radio, and this aspect of his career is similarly understudied.

PRIMARY BIBLIOGRAPHY

Stage Plays, Adaptations, Radio Drama, and Teleplays

Barnes' People (seven monologues). In *Collected Plays*. London: Heinemann, 1981.
Barnes' People II (seven duologues). London: Heinemann, 1984.
Barnes: Plays One. London: Heinemann, 1990.
The Bewitched. London: Heinemann, 1974.
Collected Plays. London: Heinemann, 1981.
Frontiers of Farce. London: Heinemann, 1977.
Laughter! London: Heinemann, 1978.
Leonardo's Last Supper and *Noonday Demons*. London: Heinemann, 1970.
Lulu. London: Heinemann, 1971.
The Real Long John Silver and Other Plays. London: Faber & Faber, 1986.
Red Noses. London: Faber & Faber, 1985.
Revolutionary Witness and *Nobody Here but Us Chickens*. London: Methuen, 1989.
The Ruling Class. London: Heinemann, 1969. New York: Grove Press, 1972. Also in
        Landmarks of British Drama: The Sixties. London: Methuen, 1985.
The Spirit of Man and *More Barnes' People*. London: Methuen, 1990.

Sunsets and Glories. London: Methuen, 1990.

"Author's Note." In *Revolutionary Witness* and *Nobody Here but Us Chickens.* London: Methuen, 1989.

"Ben Jonson and the Modern Stage." *Gambit* 6.22 (1972): 5–30.

"Hands off the Classics—Asses and Devilry." Barnes et al. *The Listener* 99 (5 Jan. 1978): 17–19.

Introduction to *Barnes' People*; *Barnes' People II* (seven duologues); *The Collected Plays*; *The Frontiers of Farce*; *Leonardo's Last Supper* and *Noonday Demons*; *The Real Long John Silver* and *Other Plays*; *The Spirit of Man* and *More Barnes' People*; *Sunsets and Glories.*

"Notes." *The Real Long John Silver and Other Plays.* London: Faber & Faber, 1986.

"Staging Jonson." In *Jonson and Shakespeare*, ed. Ian Donaldson. London: Macmillan, 1983: 156–62.

"Still Standing Upright: Ben Jonson, 350 Years Alive." *New Theatre Quarterly* 3 (August 1987): 202–6.

Interviews

"Barnes Stormer" (with Nick Curtis). *Plays and Players* 440 (July, 1990): 11–13.

"Center Stage: Peter Barnes and the Theatre of Disturbance" (with Yvonne Shafer). *Theatre News* 9 (Dec. 1982): 7–9.

"Desperate Acts on a Large Scale" (with Angela Wilkes). *Sunday Times* (30 June 1985).

"Liberating Laughter: Peter Barnes and Peter Nichols" (with Jim Hiley). *Plays and Players* 25 (Mar. 1978): 17.

"On Class, Christianity, and Questions of Comedy" (with Clive Barker). *New Theatre Quarterly* 6 (Feb. 1990): 5–24.

"Peter Barnes" (with Brendan Hennessy). *Transatlantic Review*, 37–38 (autumn-winter 1970–71): 118–24.

"Peter Barnes" (with Yvonne Shafer). *Journal of Dramatic Theory and Criticism* 2.1 (fall 1987): 87–94.

"Peter Barnes" (with Adolf Wimmer). *Pessimistisches Theater: eine Studie zur Entfremdung in englischen Drama 1955–1975.* Salz: IAA, 1979.

"Peter Barnes on American Drama" (with Bernard F. Dukore). *Journal of Dramatic Theory and Criticism* 7.1 (fall 1992): 163–73.

"Plays and Playing: Conversations at Leeds" (with Bernard F. Dukore). *Theatre Topics* 2.1 (Sept. 1991): 99–116.

"The Playwright Who Can't Find a Stage." *The Guardian* (18 Sept. 1979): 10.

"Theatre of the Extreme" (with Mark Bly and Doug Wager). *Theater* 12 (spring 1981): 43–48.

SECONDARY BIBLIOGRAPHY

Barker, Felix. "It's Not Funny." *Evening News* (25 Jan. 1978): 15.

Billington, Michael [1]. Review of *Laughter! The Guardian* (25 Jan. 1978): 10.

———— [2]. Review of *Red Noses. The Guardian* (4 July 1985).

Bryden, Ronald [1]. Introduction to *The Bewitched.* London: Heinemann, 1974.

———— [2]. Review of *The Bewitched. The Observer* (2 Mar. 1969).

———— [3]. Review of *The Ruling Class. The Observer* (17 Nov. 1968).

Blumenfeld, Yorick. Review of *The Ruling Class. Atlantic Monthly* (Aug. 1969): 99–101.

Bull, John. "Peter Barnes." In *Contemporary Dramatists*, ed. D. L. Kirkpatrick, 4th ed. London: St. James Press, 1988: 37–39.

Carlson, Susan. "Comic Collisions: Convention, Rage, and Order." *New Theatre Quarterly* 3 (Nov. 1987): 303–15.

Cave, Richard Allen. *New British Drama in Performance on the London Stage: 1970–1985.* Gerrards Cross: Colin Smythe, 1987.

Cerny, Lothar. "Peter Barnes, *The Bewitched.*"In *Englische Literatur der Gegenwart, 1971–1975*, ed. Lengeler and Rainer. Dusseldorf: Bagel, 1977.

Cherry, Simon. Review of *Sunsets and Glories. Plays and Players* 442 (Sept. 1990): 31.

Christiansen, Richard. Review of *Red Noses. Chicago Tribune* (6 Oct. 1987): 12.

Cornish, Roger, and Violet Ketels. "Peter Barnes." *Landmarks of British Drama: The Sixties.* London: Methuen, 1985.

Coveney, Michael. [1]. Review of *Red Noses. Financial Times* (3 July 1985).

———— [2]. Review of *Sunsets and Glories. The Observer* (8 July 1990).

Cushman, Robert. "Bewitched, Bewildered." *The Observer* (12 May 1974).

Dukore, Bernard [1]. "The Author's Play: From Red Noses, Black Death to Red Noses." *Twentieth-Century Literature* 33.2 (summer 1987): 159–78.

———— [2]. "Lope Discovered: Barnes's *Actors.*" *Theatre History Studies* 7 (1987): 12–27.

———— [3]. "Newer Peter Barnes, with Links to the Past." *Essays in Theatre* 5 (Nov. 1986): 47–59.

———— [4]. "People Like You and Me: The Auschwitz Plays of Peter Barnes and C. P. Taylor." *Essays in Theatre* 3 (May 1985): 108–24.

———— [5]. "Peter Barnes." In *British Dramatists Since World War II: A Dictionary of Literary Biography.* Vol. 13, Part 1. Ed. Stanley Weintraub. Detroit, MI: Gale Research, 1982: 47–52.

———— [6]. "Peter Barnes."In *Essays on Contemporary British Drama*, ed. Hedwig Bock and Albert Wertheim. Munich: Max Hueber Verlag, 1981: 97–116.

———— [7]. "Peter Barnes and the Problem of Goodness." In *Around the Absurd: Essays on Modern and Postmodern Drama*, ed. Enoch Brater and Ruby Cohn. Ann Arbor: University of Michigan Press, 1990: 155–74.

———— [8]. "*Red Noses* and *Saint Joan.*" *Modern Drama* 30.3 (Sept. 1987): 340–51.

———— [9]. *The Theatre of Peter Barnes.* London: Heinemann, 1981.

Esslin, Martin [1]. "Green Room." *Plays and Players* 21 (Aug. 1974): 12–13.

———— [2]. Introduction to *Lulu.* London: Heinemann, 1971.

———— [3]. *Jenseits des Absurden: Aufsatze zum modernen Drama.* Vienna: Europaverlag, 1972.

———— [4]. Review of *The Bewitched. Plays and Players* 21 (June 1974): 36–37.

———— [5]. Review of *Leonardo's Last Supper* and *Noonday Demons. Plays and Players* 17 (Jan. 1970): 51.

———— [6]. Review of *Red Noses. Plays International* 1 (Aug. 1985): 28.

———— [7]. Review of *The Ruling Class. Plays and Players* 16 (Jan. 1969): 53.

Elsom, John. *Post-war British Theatre.* London: Routledge & Kegan Paul, 1976.

Feldman, Peter. "Notes for an Open Theatre Production." *Tulane Drama Review* 10 (summer 1966): 200–208.

Friedman, Arthur. Review of *Red Noses. Boston Herald* (17 May 1989).

Hammond, James. "Barnes, Peter." In *Contemporary Dramatists*, ed. James Vinson. 3rd ed. London: St. Martin's Press, 1982: 71–73.

Hands, Terry. "*Red Noses* at the Barbican." *Plays International* 1 (Aug. 1985): 14–17.

Hinchliffe, Arnold. *British Theatre, 1950–70*, Oxford: Basil Blackwell, 1974.

Hobson, Harold [1]. "Introduction." *The Ruling Class*. London: Heinemann, 1969.

———— [2]. Review of *The Bewitched. Sunday Times* (12 May 1974): 38.

———— [3]. Review of *Leonardo's Last Supper* and *Noonday Demons. Sunday Times* (7 Dec. 1969): 53.

———— [4]. Review of *The Ruling Class. Sunday Times* (10 Nov. 1968).

———— [5]. Review of *The Ruling Class. Sunday Times* (2 Mar. 1969).

Innes, Christopher. "Peter Barnes and Trevor Griffiths: The Politics of Comedy." *Modern British Drama, 1890–1990*. Cambridge: Cambridge University Press, 1992.

Inverso, Marybeth. *The Gothic Impulse in Contemporary Drama*. Ann Arbor, MI: UMI Research Press, 1990.

Jones, Welton. Review of *Red Noses. San Diego Union* (11 Aug. 1988): D4.

Kalem, T. E. Review of *The Ruling Class. Time* (15 Feb. 1971): 60–61.

Lahr, John. Review of *Laughter! Plays and Players* 25 (Mar. 1978): 26–27.

Levin, Bernard. Review of *Laughter! Sunday Times* (5 Feb. 1978): 35.

Lob, Ladislaus. "Don Juan und Faust: Grabbes Drama in einer englischen Radiobearbeitung von Peter Barnes." *Grabbe—Jhrb* 8 (1989): 87–95.

Nightingale, Benedict [1]. "Green Room." *Plays and Players* 21 (July 1974): 12–13.

———— [2]. Review of *Red Noses. New Statesman* (12 July 1985): 32–33.

———— [3]. Review of *Sunsets and Glories. The Times* (5 July 1990).

Review of *Nobody Here but Us Chickens. Washington (D.C.) Times* (29 Nov. 1991).

Novick, Julius. Review of *The Ruling Class. New York Times* (31 Jan. 1971): 16–17.

Rabey, David Ian. Review of *Red Noses. Plays and Players* 384 (Sept. 1985): 20–21.

Review of *Red Noses. Juneau (Alaska) Empire* (5 May 1989).

Seibert, Gary. "*Red Noses* in Chicago." *America* (28 Nov. 1987): 411.

Simon, John. Review of *The Bewitched. New York Magazine* (2 Sept. 1974): 56.

———— [2]. Review of *Red Noses. New York Magazine* (29 Aug. 1988): 59–60.

Spurling, John. Review of *The Bewitched. Encounter* (Jan. 1975).

Sullivan, Dan. Review of *Red Noses. Los Angeles Times* (12 Aug. 1988): 27–28.

Taylor, John Russell. *The Second Wave*. New York: Hill & Wang, 1971.

Wardle, Irving [1]. "*The Ruling Class*: A Satire on Violence, Staged in London." *New York Times* (28 Feb. 1969): 31.

———— [2]. Review of *Laughter! The Times* (25 Jan. 1978): 13.

———— [3]. Review of *Leonardo's Last Supper* and *Noonday Demons. The Times* (5 Dec. 1969): 7.

———— [4]. "Overloaded with Good Material." *The Times* (27 Feb. 1969): 7.

———— [5]. Review of *Sunsets and Glories. Independent on Sunday* (8 July 1990).

Weeks, Jerome. Review of *Laughter! Dallas Morning News* (12 Feb. 1992).

Weiss, Hedy. "Stinker of a Script Plagues Goodman's *Red Noses*." *Chicago Sun Times* (7 Oct. 1987).

Winkler, Elizabeth Hale. *The Function of Song in Contemporary British Drama*. Newark: University of Delaware Press, 1990.

Worth, Katharine J. *Revolutions in Modern English Drama*. London: Bell, 1972.

Young, B. A. Review of *The Bewitched*. *Financial Times* (9 May 1974): 3.

BIBLIOGRAPHY

King, Kimball. ''Peter Barnes.'' *Twenty Modern British Playwrights: A Bibliography, 1956 to 1976*. New York: Garland, 1977: 31–34.

Samuel Beckett

(1906–1989)

WILLIAM HUTCHINGS

With the possible exception of William Shakespeare, no playwright has transformed both the form and content of drama as radically and as profoundly as Samuel Beckett.

Samuel Beckett was born in Foxrock, an affluent suburb of Dublin, Ireland, in 1906; he was the second son of May Roe Beckett, a former hospital nurse, and William Frank Beckett, a civil engineer. Although his birth certificate lists the date as 13 May Beckett insisted that he was born exactly one month earlier— on Good Friday the Thirteenth. His education was typical of affluent Protestant boys of the time; he attended the Earlsfort House School in Dublin, and in 1920 the Portora Royal School in the province of Ulster (now Northern Ireland), where he distinguished himself as an athlete (cricket, swimming, and rugby) more than as a scholar.

In 1923 Beckett enrolled at Trinity College, Dublin, where he studied fine arts and modern languages. When he left college in 1927, a prize student, he received the coveted appointment as Trinity's *lecteur d'anglais* at the École Normale Supérieure in Paris. Prior to assuming these duties, he spent nine months teaching French at Campbell College, Belfast.

In Paris from 1928 to 1930, Beckett was much attracted to the works of surrealists and other experimental writers who were publishing in little magazines as well as avant-garde theatre and highly innovative painting—all of which were works of a kind unavailable in Dublin. Even more important, however, was the presence in Paris of James Joyce, for whom Beckett became a major resource and aide, as Joyce, with failing eyesight and ill health, continued to work on *Finnegans Wake* (then known as *Work in Progress*). Lucia, Joyce's emotionally precarious daughter, liked to believe that Beckett came to the apartment to see her rather than her father, although Beckett felt obliged to tell her otherwise; he was at the time being pursued by Peggy Guggenheim, though he remained a loyal friend to Lucia Joyce until her death in 1982.

In 1929 his essay on *Finnegans Wake*—entitled "Dante . . . Bruno. Vico . . Joyce" (each period representing one century)—appeared in a book that Joyce titled *Our Exagimation Round His Factification for Incamination of Work in Progress*. "Whoroscope," his first published poem, had won a competition sponsored by the Hours Press; it is a parody based on the philosophy of Descartes and is accompanied by documentation that is more obscure than the notes published with T. S. Eliot's *The Waste Land*. In 1930 Beckett returned to Dublin, where under contract, he was to teach for three years at Trinity College after completing the two-year appointment in Paris; he completed an M.A. thesis on Marcel Proust's *A la recherche du temps perdu*. While at Trinity he also made his only known stage appearance in a skit known as *Le Kid*, whose title was both a burlesque of Pierre Corneille's *Le Cid* (1637) and an allusion to Charlie Chaplin's popular 1921 film *The Kid*. The play received the first of Beckett's many negative and/or uncomprehending theatre reviews, from the student newspaper. Beckett received his degree in 1931 but decided not to pursue an academic career, intending to become a poet and novelist instead.

After a brief self-imposed exile during which he worked as a translator of verse and wrote his first novel, *Dream of Fair to Middling Women* (published posthumously), Beckett moved to England briefly and then returned to Dublin, residing in a garret above his father's business. There he reshaped parts of his novel into *More Pricks than Kicks*, a collection of short stories published in 1934. The book was banned in Ireland, though it received a guardedly favorable review in the *Times Literary Supplement*.

With an annuity received from his father's estate (Beckett's father died in 1933), Beckett returned to London. There, following the deaths of several other close relatives, he suffered an emotional breakdown and consulted W. R. Bion, a pioneer of the group therapy process for the rehabilitation of Royal Air Force flyers and later a noted psychoanalyst. During this period he worked on but did not complete his novel *Murphy*, which is in part set in a mental hospital. Following a series of moves between London, Dublin, and the continent, he settled permanently in Paris in 1937, although unlike Joyce he occasionally returned to Ireland for visits.

After a series of rejections *Murphy* was published by Routledge in January 1938. The same month, Beckett was attacked in the streets of Paris by a pimp named Prudent, who demanded money from him and plunged a knife into his chest when Beckett refused. Beckett later confronted the imprisoned assailant and asked him why he had been selected as the victim, the reply was simply "*Je ne sais pas*"—an unmistakable example of the absurdity and arbitrariness that would later become a preoccupation in *Waiting for Godot* (in which the line is assigned to the Boy) and in other works as well. While recovering from this wound, he was visited by the woman who would later become his wife,

Suzanne Dumesnil, a pianist at the Paris Conservatoire; they were officially married in 1962.

Beckett chose to remain in Paris during World War II, working for the French Resistance as a microphotographer and translator of captured documents—service that later won him the Croix de Guerre. Of the more than eighty members of his Resistance unit, only thirty were to survive the war. He escaped occupied Paris to the south, for the remainder of the war remaining in Vaucluse, where he continued to work actively for the Resistance. Following the Normandy invasion, he was among the first to volunteer for the Irish Red Cross. In 1946 he returned to Paris, where his apartment and books had been left intact. During his time in Roussillon, Beckett wrote *Watt*, a novel in English in whose third part the rudiments of language—word order and then the words themselves—break down. The novel was not published until 1953.

Convinced that there was nothing more to be done in the novel genre after *Finnegans Wake*, with its densely "packed" text, puns, allusions, and all-inclusiveness, Beckett began a series of radical subtractions in both the form and content of fiction and, later, drama. He also began writing in French, reportedly to write "*sans style.*" He sometimes translated his works into English (as with *Waiting for Godot*) and sometimes had them translated by others. Between 1946 and 1950 he wrote *En attendant Godot*, a trilogy of novels (known in English as *Molloy, Malone Dies*, and *The Unnamable*), three short stories ("The End," "The Calmative," and "The Expelled"), a longer prose work "First Love," a prose tale *Mercier and Camier*, a series of *Texts for Nothing*, and a still-unpublished three-act play titled *Eleuthéria* (the Greek word for freedom). His novels became progressively more solipsistic, interior, and self-reflexive; increasingly their subject is the quest for the narrating self as exterior events and, indeed, the exterior world itself becomes less important—and less evident—in each novel. It is, as Brater [4] has aptly termed, a "work in regress," written in a style resembling stream of consciousness but having little referentiality to the exterior world and even less epistemological certainty about virtually anything other than the Cartesian thinking (speaking) self. *The Unnamable* is apparently narrated from a dark and unchanging realm of the afterdeath, where the speaker yearns for an unattainable oblivion, a cessation of consciousness, an end to the obligation to speak about itself.

In the interval between *Malone Dies* (whose narrator is in the process of writing himself to death) and *The Unnamable*, Beckett wrote *En attendant Godot*, turning to the open space of the stage as a relief from the increasingly hermetic world of his prose. Suzanne showed the script to several directors who turned it down before it was accepted by the then virtually unknown Roger Blin. Beset by production delays, the play was published before it was produced, brought out by Jerome Lindon in 1952; Lindon also offered Beckett the imprint of Les Éditions de Minuit for his novels, and he has remained the French publisher for all of Beckett's works in French. With a government agency grant and support from the actress Delphine Seyrig, *En attendant Godot* had its world premiere at the Théâtre de Babylone on 5 January 1953, and ran for 100 performances. Blin himself played Pozzo; Lucien Raimbourg was Vladimir, Pierre Latour was Estragon, and Jean Martin was Lucky. The play attracted mostly favorable reviews, including one from playwright Jean Anouilh, who likened its impact to the opening night of Luigi Pirandello's *Six Characters in Search of an Author*. The production toured Germany in 1953, and a translated version was produced there by the end of the year. The first London production, by Peter Hall, opened at the Arts Theatre Club on 3 August 1955, and was later transferred later to the Criterion; it was vigorously championed by two particularly influential reviewers, Harold Hobson of the *Sunday Times* and Kenneth Tynan of *The Observer*.

In 1956 the director Alan Schneider brought *Waiting for Godot* to the United States, where producer Michael Myerberg wanted to stage it on Broadway as a vehicle for actors Bert Lahr and Tom Ewell. Myerberg opened the play at the Coconut Grove in Miami on 3 January 1956, billing it as a "laugh sensation on two continents." The outraged first-night audience, including newspaper columnist Walter Winchell, walked out in droves, although playwrights Tennessee Williams and William Saroyan stayed and applauded vigorously. When the play arrived at the John Golden Theater on Broadway on 19 April, E. G. Marshall replaced Ewell as Vladimir and Herbert Berghof had taken over directorial responsibilities. Kurt Kasznar and Alvin Epstein played Pozzo and Lucky, respectively. Despite some positive reviews, the Broadway production never achieved the success of its English and European counterparts.

Throughout the heated critical controversies and despite the myriad conflicting interpretations of what *Waiting for Godot* meant, who Godot is, and whether he "really" exists, Beckett maintained a resolute refusal to elaborate on what he had written or provide an exegesis, apart from occasional denials of certainty: " 'If by Godot I had meant God I would have said God, and not Godot,' Beckett told Ralph Richardson" (qtd. in Brater [4]). The play's central enigma, its irreconcilable allusiveness, its lyric simplicity and eloquent silences, its minimalist staging, its tragicomic blend of pathos and vaudevillian humor, and its resistance to any single totalizing or "definitive" interpretation led to seemingly endless explications, arguments, and revaluations.

His next play was *Fin de partie*, known as *Endgame* in English, produced in French in London on 3 April 1957. It was dedicated to Roger Blin, who directed it and played Hamm. Alan Schneider directed *Endgame* in New York at the Cherry Lane Theatre in Greenwich Village on 28 January 1958; the English premiere of the English version was produced at the Royal Court Theatre by George Devine, who played Hamm. This production was initially denied a license for public performance by the Lord Chancellor's Office unless changes were made in certain "obscene" and "blasphemous" passages; Beckett insisted on "a firm stand" against changes, and the play was produced only after lengthy negotiations between Beckett, Devine, and the Lord Chamberlain's Office.

In the summer of 1956 Beckett approached the BBC about the possibility of developing a script for the Radio Drama Department; the result was *All That Fall*, broadcast on 13 January 1957, directed by Donald McWhinnie. *Krapp's Last Tape* was written early in 1958 for the Irish actor Patrick Magee; it opened the following October at the Royal Court Theatre on a double bill with George Devine's *Endgame*. The French version, *La dernière bande*, was directed by Roger Blin and opened in Paris in 1960. Its remarkable yet simple use of technology—the tape recorder—juxtaposes the present and (recorded) past selves of the central character, providing a new perspective on the familiar Beckettian preoccupation with the effects of time. It is also the first of his plays to utilize a sharply delimited acting space of light within a large stage darkness—a visual style that would increasingly be used in his later plays.

Happy Days, written in English (as were his subsequent plays into the 1980s), had its world premiere in New York at the Cherry Lane Theatre on 17 September 1961; it was produced at the Royal Court in 1962 and in Paris in 1963. Like *Waiting for Godot*, it is built around a stunningly simple yet evocative visual image: its central character, Winnie, is buried up to her waist in a mound of earth, on a brightly lit stage that seems to stretch to the horizon; in the second act, she is buried up to her neck. Her husband, Willie, puts in only brief appearances; although not confined as she is, like the characters in *Endgame*, he is unable to leave. Whereas *Godot* had removed all vestiges of traditional plot, *Happy Days* dispensed with almost all physical movement.

The three ashen-gray characters in *Play* can move only their mouths, endlessly narrating their individual stories (parts of a tale of adultery) as a single spotlight alternates among them; like *The Unnamable*, they are confined in what appear to be burial urns in the darkness of the afterdeath. The play was first performed in German (titled *Spiel*) at the Ulmer Theater, Ulm-Donau, on 14 June 1963. Its first English production was at the Old Vic in London, by the National Theatre Company—the first of Beckett's plays to have been produced there.

During the mid-1960s, Beckett wrote works for both film and video, demonstrating an uncanny mastery of the capabilities and unique demands of each medium, as he had done earlier with radio. *Film*, a twenty-four-minute film directed by Alan Schneider in the summer of 1965, provided silent film comedian Buster Keaton with one of his last screen roles; *Eh Joe*, a teleplay written for the Irish actor Jack MacGowran, was first broadcast on the BBC on 4 July 1966.

In his writings for the stage, however, Beckett continued his edulcoration of theatrical forms, as his later plays became even more austere—and even briefer—presentations of intensely poetic, yet uniquely theatrical, images of minimal existences amid the darkness of the void. Beckett coined the term "dramaticules" for these works, which rely ever-increasingly on meticulously accurate adherence to technically precise, remarkably detailed directions for dialogue, costuming, and (often minimal) actions. Thus, for example, *Not I* (produced in 1972) consists of an endlessly speaking mouth that is illuminated with a pinpoint spotlight so that the rest of the face is in total darkness; a dimly lit, cowled Auditor listens and occasionally shrugs. *That Time* (produced in 1976) features a disembodied head hanging in a proscenium frame ten feet above the stage, listening as three prerecorded voices broadcast memories from three fixed positions in the dark void.

The "most minimal" of all of Beckett's works is *Breath*, a thirty-five-second dramaticule consisting solely of a stage setting of scattered rubbish, a series of recorded sounds, and a single visual effect of lighting. Sent to Kenneth Tynan, it was included as the prologue to the U.S. production of his then controversial erotic revue *Oh! Calcutta!* in 1969, though Beckett was enraged to learn that nude bodies had been added to the pile of rubbish on stage. Typically adamant that no unauthorized changes be made in the staging of his works, Beckett discovered that he could not stop the U.S. production but could prevent such versions elsewhere. He also engaged in a quarrel with Tynan, who threatened a libel suit against him and claimed that the alterations were due to others (see Bair).

On 23 October 1969, Beckett was notified that he had won the Nobel Prize for literature. He was cited for his "body of work that, in new forms of fiction and the theatre, has transmuted the destitution of modern man into his exalta-tion" (qtd. in Bair). As intensely private as ever, he did not attend the award ceremonies and did not publicly address the academy, as is traditional. He also sent word that he did not want the prize to be accepted by the Irish ambassador; the gold medal, diploma, and check in the amount of $73,000 were presented by King Gustaf Adolf and received by Jerome Lindon on Beckett's behalf.

In 1971 Deirdre Bair, a doctoral candidate in search of a dissertation topic, wrote to Beckett asking to write his biography; although he doubted it would be worth her while, he replied that he "would neither help nor hinder" her research. The resulting biography was published in 1978.

Beckett's stage plays of the 1970s and 1980s continue his fascination with mechanical aspects of the theatrical medium and his minimalist exploration of time, memory, loss, and the void. *Footfalls* (1976) was written for actress Billie Whitelaw and directed by Beckett himself when it opened at the Royal Court Theatre in London. Later works, including *Ghost Trio* (1977), *Quad* (1982), and *. . . but the clouds . . .* (1977) approximate and incorporate the precision of math-ematics and music in achieving their effects. *Catastrophe* (1982), dedicated to dissident Czech playwright Václav Havel, is Beckett's only overtly political play, as a tyrannical director rehearses and represses his Protagonist, an emblem of suffering, oppressed, and brutalized humanity.

Beckett's fiction after the trilogy underwent a similar process of edulcoration and stylistic innovation, from the unpunctuated *Comment c'est* (1961), translated by Beckett as *How It Is* (1964), through such prose texts as *Company* (1980), *Mal vu mal dit* (1981), and *Worstward Ho* (1983), his last work of fiction. A stage version of *Company* was produced at the National Theatre in London in 1980, and another version was produced in London in 1987.

Samuel Beckett died on 22 December 1989, and was buried in the Montpar-nasse Cemetery. Suzanne Beckett had died the previous July.

Selected Biographical Sources: Bair; Bergreen; Brater [4]; Driver; Esslin [3]; O'Brien; Schneider [2]; Shenker. The authorized biography is now being written by James Knowlson.

MAJOR PLAYS, PREMIERES, AND SIGNIFICANT REVIVALS: THEATRICAL RECEPTION

Waiting for Godot. 1953. Written in French as *En attendant Godot.* Opened 5 January at Theatre de Babylone, Paris, for 100 performances. Directed by Roger Blin. English premiere at the Arts Theatre Club, London, 3 August 1955. Directed by Peter Hall. First U.S. performance was at the Coconut Grove Playhouse, Miami, Florida, on 3 January 1956. Directed by Alan Schneider. The New York premiere was at the John Golden Theatre, 19 April 1956. Directed by Herbert Berghof. Numerous revivals have been staged throughout the world in English, French, and German. Among the most notable are the San Francisco Actors Workshop production at San Quentin prison on 19 November 1957, directed by Herbert Blau; a second production by the San Quentin Drama Workshop was staged by convict Rick Cluchey in 1961. The "first unexpurgated version" in London opened on 30 December 1964 for sixty-nine performances at the Royal Court Theatre, directed by Anthony Page; the German production at the Schiller Theater, Berlin, in April 1975, directed by Beckett; the National Theatre of Great Britain production, opened on 15 November 1987, directed by Michael Rudman and based on the Actors Workshop and Schiller Theater productions; the New York production at Lincoln Center, opened in November 1988, directed by Mike Nichols; the Dublin production at the Gate Theatre opened 30 August 1988, directed by Walter Asmus. The first Chinese production, entitled *Dengdai Geduo*, was staged by the Yangtze Theatre in 1987, given by students at the Shanghai Drama Institute. Two all-female productions were produced in 1988, against Beckett's explicit wishes: one at the Haarlem Toneelschuur Theatre and the other at the Denver Center Theatre Company.

Controversial from the outset, *Waiting for Godot* has generated more critical commentary—and more diverse interpretations—than any other play in modern drama. Initial French reviews were mixed, though it was defended by Anouilh, Audiberti, and Robbe-Grillet. The first London production was widely derided in the daily press and termed "this odd mass of nonsense" by Barker; however, it was defended by Hobson [3] and by Tynan [3]. The first explicitly Christian review of it was by Gray. Selected key reviews are reprinted in Cohn [3]; Butler [2]; Graver and Federman; and Elsom [1].

All That Fall (radio play). 1957. Written in English. First performed on the BBC Third Programme, January 13. Translated into French by Beckett and Robert Pinget as *Tous ceux qui tombent.*

Critics quickly recognized that radio was an effective medium for Beckett's unique combination of words, sounds, and silence. The anonymous reviewer for the *Times Literary Supplement* praised its "rich local flavour, . . . rhetorical zest, a rhythmical extravagance, and a melancholy humour" (Review of *All That Fall*). Davie praised its originality but disliked its "trick ending" and "derivative slapstick."

Endgame (one act). 1957. Written in French as *Fin de partie*. First performed in French at the Royal Court Theatre, London, 3 April, where it was given six performances, accompanied by the afterpiece *Acte sans paroles* (see below). First performed in Paris at Studio des Champs-Élysées, 26 April 1957. First performed in New York at the Cherry Lane Theatre, 28 January 1958, directed by Alan Schneider. First performed in London in English, translated by Beckett himself, at the Royal Court Theatre, 28 October 1958, where it had thirty-eight performances on a double bill with *Krapp's Last Tape*; both were directed by George Devine and Donald McWhinnie. Significant revivals, in which Beckett worked with the directors, include a London production by the Royal Shakespeare Company at the Aldwych Theatre in 1964 and the Royal Court's "Beckett Season" production in 1976, directed by Donald McWhinnie. Beckett himself directed the German *Endspiel* at the Schiller Theater in Berlin in 1967 and the San Quentin Drama Workshop production at the Peacock Theatre, Dublin, in 1980. Noteworthy U.S. productions include one directed by Joseph Chaikin in 1977 at the Manhattan Theatre Club (NY), which was later produced in Paris. A production by JoAnne Akalaitis, which set the action in an abandoned New York subway car, opened in December 1984 at the American Repertory Theatre in Cambridge, Massachusetts, and was threatened with legal action because of supposed liberties taken with Beckett's "explicit" stage directions.

Hobson [1] remarked that *Endgame* had "outraged the Philistines, earned the contempt of halfwits and filled those who are capable of telling the difference between a theatre and a bawdy-house with a profound and sombre and paradoxical joy," adding that "its presentation is among the greatest of the services that the English Stage Company has rendered to the British public." Tynan [1] considered it "an analysis of the power-complex" in which Beckett contends that "man is a pygmy who connives at his own inevitable degradation"—a message that Tynan found both "disagreeable and forced down [his] throat." Atkinson found it "impressive in the macabre intensity of the mood," which "deals in tones and perversities of expression" but "never comes precisely to the point" of its "unearthly" theme. For a selection of early reviews and interpretive essays, see Chevigny.

Act without Words I (mime). 1957. Written in French as *Acte sans paroles* with music by John Beckett, the author's cousin. First performed at the Royal Court Theatre, London, 3 April, as an afterpiece with *Fin de partie*; there were six performances.

Tynan [1] deplored its "facile pessimism" as "not only the projection of a personal sickness, but a conclusion reached on inadequate evidence." Hobson [1], however, contended that "its last thirty seconds are especially fine."

Krapp's Last Tape (dramatic monologue). 1958. Written in English. First performed at the Royal Court Theatre, London, 28 October, on a double bill with *Endgame*, for thirty-eight performances; directed by Donald McWhinnie and starred Patrick Magee, the Northern Irish actor for whom the part was written. First performed in New York at the Provincetown Playhouse, 14 January 1960. Translated into French by Beckett and Pierre Leyris as *La dernière bande* and first performed in Paris at Théâtre Récamier, 22 March 1960. Beckett directed the Schiller Theater production of *Das letzte Bande* in 1969 and directed an English version at the *Academie der Kunste* in Berlin in 1977, starring Rick Cluchey, the former convict who had staged *Godot* in San Quentin in 1961. A television production was first shown as *Thirty Minute Theatre* on BBC2, 29 November 1972; it was directed by Donald McWhinnie and starred Patrick Magee. Beckett directed Pierre Chabert in *La dernière bande* at the Petit Théâtre d'Orsay in 1975, and Rick Cluchey appeared in the San Quentin Drama Workshop production at the Peacock Theatre in Dublin in 1980, directed by Beckett. A revival was directed by Antoni Libera at Riverside Studios in London in 1990, paired with *Catastrophe*.

Brustein [2] praised the play as a "dramatic poem about the old age of the world," showing more compassion than Beckett's earlier works though "still obsessed with the alienation, vacuity, and decay of life upon a planet devoid of God and hope." The anonymous reviewer of the *Times Literary Supplement* found it "psychological rather than philosophical" in its interest, presenting "a terrifying image of individual misery and loneliness" ("The Dying of the Light"). Tynan's review [2] is a parody titled "Slamm's Lask Knock."

Act without Words II (mime). 1960. Written in French at about the same time as *Act without Words I* (i.e., 1956). First performed (probably) at the Institute of Contemporary Arts, London, 25 January. Revival produced by Charles Marowitz at In-Stage, London, 1962.

This mime has attracted relatively little detailed critical attention. In his review of *Happy Days*, Marowitz described the mime "bolder and more economical"—though less subtle and nuanced—than the longer play.

Happy Days. 1961. Written in English. First performed at the Cherry Lane Theatre (NY) 17 September; directed by Alan Schneider. First performed in London at the Royal Court Theatre, 1 November 1962, for thirty-five performances; directed by George Devine. Translated into French by Beckett as *Oh les beaux jours* and first performed in Paris at Odéon-Théâtre de France, 15 November 1963. Beckett directed the Schiller Theater production of *Glückliche Tage* in 1971 and the Royal Court production starring Billie Whitelaw in 1979. Peggy Ashcroft played Winnie in the National Theatre production that opened at the Liverpool Playhouse on 26 November 1974, and joined the National Theatre London repertory at the Old Vic in March 1975, directed by Peter Hall. An American revival starring Irene Worth was directed by Andrei Serban at the Public Theatre in New York in 1976.

Knowlson and Pilling rightly contend that "if one looks at the challenge offered to the dramatist by the setting, situation, and characters in *Happy Days*, it undoubtedly appears as Beckett's boldest piece of dramatic writing to date," and they consider it "widely underestimated" but "eventually . . . to be regarded as one of his finest pieces of writing for the theatre'" (108–9). Brustein [1] considered it "the least of his dramatic efforts," its language lacking the poetic intensity of *Godot* and *Krapp's Last Tape* and its symbols "almost nude in their unambiguousness." Dennis commended it for bringing to the fore Beckett's first major female character and praised his ability to "present the ludicrous so frankly and get back such a heart-rending groan"; he also considered it "the tightest and best-managed of Mr. Beckett's plays." Simon termed it "tragedy degree zero," showing Beckett's "great and cruel" artistry; he contended that there are "few tragic moments, even among the greatest dramatists, that can compare" with Winnie's "sudden awareness of truth." Hewes [2], however, found the play "somewhat remote and artificial," as its characters were "waiting for Heaven in an earthly Hell." Marowitz considered it to be "about the rollicking decomposition of all of us," showing "how blithely we can convert death-rattles into chortles and with what desperate cunning we transform pain into pleasure."

Play. 1963. Written in English. First performed in German translation, *Spiel*, at the Ulmer Theater, Ulm-Donau, 14 June (translated by Erika and Elmar Tophoven). First New York performance at the Cherry Lane Theatre, 4 January 1964, directed by Alan Schneider on a double bill with Harold Pinter's *The Lover*. First London performance at the Old Vic Theatre by the National Theatre Company, 7 April 1964, directed by George Devine. Translated into French by Beckett as *Comédie*. First French performance at Pavillon de Marsan, Paris, 11 June 1964. Revival at the Royal Court in London in 1976, directed by Donald McWhinnie.

Clurman [1] admired the fifteen-minute play as "the essentialized comic-tragedy (or 'metadrama') of adultery" and said it was "like a statement of the polygamous sex-agony inscribed in sure short-hand strokes." Gascoigne complained that the characters' words were nearly unintelligible but praised the precision of the spotlight and the actors' timing; noting rather disparagingly that "there is still plenty to be done away with," he predicted that "the live actor will be the next victim" of Beckett's minimalist reductionism—although that prophecy was not actually fulfilled until *Breath* was produced five years later. Brustein [3] considered *Play* "more like a spasm" but found it "a strangely moving experience."

Come and Go. 1966. Written in English. First produced in German translation by Elmar Tophoven, *Kommen und Gehen*, in a triple bill with *Act without Words II* and *All That Fall*, 14 January, Schiller Theater Werkstatt, Berlin. First produced in English at the Peacock Theatre, Dublin, 28 February 1968. First produced in England, 9 December 1968, Royal Festival Hall, London.

First play to be designated a "dramaticule," a term coined by Beckett meaning a "little play" or "playlet." Knowlson and Pilling offer the most detailed analysis of this work, noting its echoes of Eliot's "Prufrock," *Macbeth*, and the Bible, among other sources, adding that it "can seem almost as compelling in performance as some of Beckett's longer, and thematically more complex, plays" (125).

Breath. 1969. Written in English. Sent to Kenneth Tynan in response to his request for a contribution to his erotic revue *Oh! Calcutta!*. First performed in New York at the Eden Theatre, 16 June, as a prologue to *Oh! Calcutta!*; although the work was not specifically attributed to him, the style made it virtually unmistakeable, and his name was listed alongside those of the other writers (including Sam Shepard and Joe Orton) whose skits comprise Tynan's renowned, long-running, and controversial "evening of elegant erotica." Beckett's specifications for the play's setting were not respected: nude bodies were added to the onstage decor, lending a wholly unauthorized significance to the "breath." *Breath* was withdrawn from the London production of *Oh! Calcutta!* at Beckett's insistence. First production of the unaltered version (and first British production) occurred at the Close Theatre Club, Glasgow, October 1969. Also produced at the Oxford Playhouse, 8 March 1970.

For details of the controversy surrounding the alteration of the text for this thirty-five-second dramaticule when included in *Oh! Calcutta!*, see Bair. Knowlson and Pilling contend that "however admirably shaped *Breath* may be, its dramatic interest and impact must be judged as severely limited" (128). The most detailed analysis of it is by Hutchings, who views it as the culmination of Beckett's radical subtractions in the theatre and traces its imagery to Shakespeare's *Measure for Measure*, the Venerable Bede, and the New Testament.

Not I. 1972. Written in English. First performed at the Forum Theatre of Lincoln Center (NY), 22 November 1972. First performed in London at the Royal Court Theatre, 15 January 1973, for forty performances, paired with *Krapp's Last Tape* with both directed by Anthony Page; it was also produced there in 1975, again directed by Anthony Page, for twenty-seven performances (on a double bill with Athol Fugard's *Statements after an Arrest under the Immorality Act*). The French translation, *Pas moi*, premiered at the Théâtre d'Orsay, Petite salle, in 1975; Beckett restaged the play there in 1978, restoring the role of the Auditor, who had been omitted from his first French production. A television adaptation starring Billie Whitelaw, who originated the role at the Royal Court, was broadcast by the BBC in 1977.

This fifteen-minute monologue by a seemingly disembodied mouth was praised by Nightingale [2] for challenging the assumption "that a play should necessarily strip and show its all (or even much of itself) at first encounter," adding that it "is, I suspect, capable of giving growing satisfaction with each hearing." Oliver [1] described it as "an aural mosaic of words, which come pell-mell but not always helter-skelter'' so that it has ''a literally stunning impact upon the audience.''

That Time. 1976. Written in English. First performed at the Royal Court Theatre, 20 May, directed by Donald McWhinnie for sixty-one performances as part of a triple bill with *Play* and *Footfalls*. First performed in the United States at the Arena Stage, Washington, D.C., 8 December 1976.

Wardle described *That Time* as ''an unpunctuated set of free-associations'' in which ''details do not matter'' in this portrayal of ''obsessive memory,'' but Cushman dismissed the play as ''a re-run of 'Krapp's Last Tape' without the props'' and characterized all three plays on this triple bill ''compulsive vomitings of the human voice and brain.'' Elsom [2], however, considered ''each play . . . a full experience, distilled to its concentrated essence, requiring no further development.''

Footfalls. 1976. Written in English. First performed at the Royal Court Theatre, 20 May, directed by Samuel Beckett; it was part of a triple bill with *Play* and *That Time*, both directed by Donald McWhinnie. First performed in the United States at the Arena Stage, Washington, D.C., 8 December 1976. The French version, *Pas*, was directed by Beckett at the Théâtre d'Orsay in Paris in 1978. ''Restaged'' in London at Riverside Studios in observance of Beckett's eightieth birthday in 1986 (paired with *Rockaby* and a staged reading of the short prose text ''Enough'').

Cushman praised *Footfalls* as ''the nearest thing to a full-length portrait Mr Beckett has painted in years'' and considered the relationship between Billie Whitelaw's character and her unseen (but heard) mother ''terrifyingly evoked.'' Wardle admitted, ''I do not understand this play . . . but simply in terms of stage imagery, and the sense of an indefinable, unassuageable grief, the impression is as potent as that . . . in 'Not I.' '' Elsom [2] contended that ''the ties of an endless childhood, stretching on to a premature senility, have never been for me so graphically and compellingly expressed.''

Rockaby. 1981. Written in English. First performed in Buffalo (NY), directed by Alan Schneider; revived in 1984 at the Samuel Beckett Theatre (NY). The French version, *Berceuse*, was directed by Pierre Chabert at the Théâtre du Rond-Point in Paris, 1983.

Praising Billie Whitelaw's ability to perform ''daredevil isometric exercises of the soul,'' Corliss cited this play, *Ohio Impromptu*, and *Footfalls* as embodiments of ''the human need to keep replaying our own life stories, no matter how hopeless the tales.'' Oliver [2] also praised Whitelaw and remarked that ''the monologue becomes a litany and then a lullaby.'' Gee termed the play ''unforgettable,'' noting the palpable ''sense of relief . . . as the whole elaborate edifice of will and ritual gently slips away.''

Ohio Impromptu. 1981. Written in English. First performed in the Drake Union, Stadium 2 Theatre, in association with Ohio State University, on 9 May, directed by Alan Schneider; the first New York performance was at the Harold Clurman Theatre, on 15 June 1983, directed by Alan Schneider with the same cast as in Ohio (part of a triple bill with *Catastrophe* and *What Where*).

Jenkins [1] noted that the play's two characters dramatize "the self split between speech and listening . . . and, in its relation with language, between words as torment and as relief—of a kind." He added that "the piece might almost be, in miniature . . . an episode from Dante."

Catastrophe. 1982. First performed at the Avignon Festival in Avignon, France, on 21 July, directed by Stephan Meldegg. First produced in the United States at the Harold Clurman Theatre (NY) on 15 June 1983, directed by Alan Schneider (on a triple bill with *What Where* and *Ohio Impromptu*) also produced at Donmar Warehouse in London in 1984. French version directed by Pierre Chabert at the Théâtre du Rond-Point in Paris, 1983. Revival directed by Antoni Libera at Riverside Studios in London, 1990 (on a double bill with *Krapp's Last Tape*).

Dedicated to dissident Czech playwright Václav Havel, this is Beckett's "most overtly 'public' utterance," depicting what Jenkins [2] accurately described as "the painstaking humiliation of a person by other more powerful persons, in other words a brief, banal and terrible history of tyrant and victim, master and slave." In reviewing the original London production, Jenkins [1] more explicitly equated it with "the silencing of the artist by the totalitarian state" but found its ending "Beckett's most direct elaboration of that compassion [that is] his irreducible, enduring theme."

What Where. 1983. Written in French as *Quoi où*. First produced at the Harold Clurman Theatre (NY), on 15 June, directed by Alan Schneider (on a triple bill with *Catastrophe* and *Ohio Impromptu*). Revised stage version directed by S. E. Gontarski at the Magic Theatre, San Francisco, 1986.

Jenkins [1] described *What Where* as "another Dantean piece" in which "the mathematically choreographed comings and goings of four figures . . . enact a recurring cycle of interrogation and cruelty."

ADDITIONAL PLAYS, ADAPTATIONS, AND PRODUCTIONS

Other stage plays included in *The Collected Shorter Plays of Samuel Beckett* are *Rough for Theatre I* and *Rough for Theatre II*, both written in French in the late 1950s; *The Old Tune*, an adaptation of a radio play by Robert Pinget entitled *La Manivelle*; and *A Piece of Monologue*, written for actor David Warrilow in 1979 and performed by him in New York in 1980. In 1984 Beckett adapted Pierre Chabert's *Compagnie* as *Company*, which was directed by S. E. Gontarski at the Los Angeles Actors Theatre in 1985. A dramatic fragment entitled *Human Wishes* was published in *Disjecta: Miscellaneous Writings and a Dramatic Fragment* in 1984.

Following his success with the radio play *All That Fall* in 1960, Beckett wrote a number of works for *recorded* performance during the next twenty-five years; they display both a remarkable versatility and a mastery of the unique demands of the various media. The radio plays include *Embers*, first broadcast on the BBC on 24 June 1959; *Words and Music*, first broadcast on the BBC on 13 November 1962, with a musical score composed by his cousin John Beckett; *Cascando*, first broadcast on ORFT-Paris on 13 October 1963, with a musical score by Marcel Mihalovici, his opus 86 (the English version was first broadcast on the BBC on 6 October 1964); *Radio I*, unproduced; *Radio II*, first broadcast on the BBC as "Rough for Radio," on 13 April 1976. For a detailed account of these works, see Esslin [3] and Zilliacus. In 1986 *All That Fall*, *Embers*, *Words and Music*, *Cascando*, and *Rough for Radio II* were produced as the *Beckett Festival of Radio Plays*, directed by Everett C. Frost and distributed by National Public Radio in the United States; each was the U.S. national premiere of the work and was accompanied by a documentary about the play and its place in the context of Beckett's works. The documentaries included interviews with many distinguished Beckett scholars and with actors associated with the series.

Film, produced in 1964 by Evergreen Theatre, Inc., is a twenty-four-minute black-and-white film starring silent film comedian Buster Keaton in one of his last screen roles; it was directed by Alan Schneider. A version starring Max Wall was directed by David Clark in 1979.

Eh Joe, first broadcast on the BBC on 4 July 1966, was Beckett's first work written for television; Beckett and Alan Gibson were the directors. *Ghost Trio* was written in 1975 for BBC-TV and first broadcast on BBC2 on 17 April 1977, directed by Donald McWhinnie (though Beckett attended rehearsals and closely supervised the taping). It was shown with . . . *but the clouds* . . . and the television version of *Not I*; this triple bill was known as "Shades." Beckett directed a German version of *Ghost Trio*, known as *Die Geister Trio*, which was broadcast on SDR in 1977. *Quadrat 1 + 2*, a television mime play with percussion, was recorded in color and was transmitted by Suddeutscher Rundfunk in 1982; the BBC version, known as *Quad*, was first broadcast by BBC2 on 16 December 1982. *Nacht und Träume* was directed by Beckett in Stuttgart in 1982 and transmitted on German television on 19 May 1983.

There have also been numerous staged readings and/or adaptations of various prose texts under their own names: *The Lost Ones* in 1972 with David Warrilow, directed by Lee Breuer with music by Philip Glass; *Enough* by Billie Whitelaw in 1986; *Lessness*, performed by the Rohan Theatre Group, directed by Lucy Bailey, at the Oxford Playhouse, Oxford, in 1982; and *Company*, directed by John Russell Brown at the National Theatre in September 1980, which was also produced in New York in 1983 (directed by Frederick Newman) and again in London (directed by Tim Piggott-Smith) in 1987. Steven Kent directed an adaptation of *Texts for Nothing* at the Public Theatre in New York in 1981; Joseph Chaikin directed it at New York's Joseph Papp Public Theatre in November 1992.

Barry McGovern, Jack MacGowran, and Chris O'Neill have performed separate one-man shows based on readings from Beckett's works, including the trilogy of novels. McGovern's revue was entitled *I'll Go On*, originally presented at the Gate Theatre in Dublin. MacGowran's *End of Day* played in Dublin for one week before opening at the New Arts Theatre in London on October 16, 1961; *Beginning to End*, a television adaptation, was broadcast by BBC's *Monitor* program on 23 February 1965. O'Neill's *Endwords* was produced in 1991.

ASSESSMENT OF BECKETT'S CAREER

More than any other modern playwright, Samuel Beckett has reshaped the content and form of drama in the twentieth century. His plays are remarkable for their expression of existential angst through eloquent yet austere stage images, their inimitably bleak humor, their resonant yet seemingly simple language (often punctuated with equally resonant silences), their technical virtuosity (and the demands that they make on actors, directors, designers, and technicians), and their innovative use of stage resources and modern media. Remaining indifferent to public controversy and critical attention alike, Beckett maintained an uncompromising fidelity to his unique creative vision, ever refusing to "explain" what his works are "meant to be." His influence extended worldwide and has been acknowledged by countless younger playwrights, whose styles are as different as Harold Pinter, Tom Stoppard, Edward Albee, Sam Shepard, David Mamet, Caryl Churchill, and Athol Fugard. In effect, Beckett single-handedly redefined what theater is and what theatre can do in the (post)modern world.

In much the same way that Sophocles' *Oedipus Rex* underlies the definition of tragedy in Aristotle's *Poetics*, Beckett's *Waiting for Godot* embodies the "theatre of the absurd," a term coined by Martin Esslin [4] in reference to "works that are essentially concerned with conveying the author's sense of mystery, bewilderment, and anxiety when confronted with the human condition, and his despair at being unable to find a meaning in existence" (12). Though replete with Christian allusions and grounded in the philosophical tradition from Descartes to Nietzsche and Schopenhauer, Beckett's first play presented the complex ideas that Esslin lists but did so with a kind of radical simplicity, relying on fundamental and readily accessible images—a road, a tree, a rock or mound of earth, two friends waiting for an appointment, a few passers-by, a boy, and a seemingly endless expanse of time. Even more audaciously, the playwright disregarded—even defied—conventional expectations that an unsuspecting audience could be presumed to bring to the theatre: *Waiting for Godot* lacked any semblance of a "dramatic" plot, as if to repudiate the traditional standards of the "well-made play." Even one of the characters complained that "nothing happens, nobody comes, nobody goes, it's awful!" (27b) and remarked that "nothing is certain" (10b).

Such radical uncertainty is, in fact, the key to the play's innovativeness and its perennially tantalizing appeal. Apart from the fact of the characters' waiting and the occurrence of certain events during that time (the duration of which is itself uncertain), the only certainty is that *any* certainty about their plight is wrong. That is, any interpretation that purports to know who Godot is (or is not), whether he exists, whether he will ever come or never come, whether he has come, or even whether he may have come without being recognized (or possibly in disguise) is, if not demonstrably wrong, at least *not* demonstrably right. This revolutionary principle of literary uncertainty was brought to the stage for the first time in *Waiting for Godot* and accounts for the seemingly endless variety of interpretations that have been written since 1954 (second in volume and diversity only to those of Shakespeare's *Hamlet*). Although the play's images and Christian allusions (the crucified thieves, the sheep and the goats, etc.) seem to invite interpretation as symbols, they are in fact mere shards of a culture, used in the play for their suggestiveness but *without exact allegorical equation*. Among readers and audience members, as among the characters whom Beckett termed "non-knowers and non-can-ers" (Shenker), a disconcerting uncertainty about the "meaning" of the play is a crucial part of the experience of *Waiting for Godot* and any discussion of it.

In reviewing the first London production of *Waiting for Godot* in 1955, Tynan [3] noted how the work affected him and described the process that it would subsequently demand of every student, teacher, critic, audience member, and reader: "*Godot*," he said, "forced me to re-examine the rules that have hitherto governed the drama; and, having done so, to pronounce them not elastic enough." We must, in Davenport's phrase, "reeducate our eyes." This is, in effect, the basis of Beckett's minimalist aesthetic, which demands first and foremost a willingness to pay particular attention to the *absence* of what we are accustomed to inspect; instead of seeing only how little there is in the minimalist work that satisfies conventional expectations, the viewer or reader should consider how many familiar devices the artist can do *without* while still retaining meaningful, expressive, even eloquently poetic communication.

The importance of this way of seeing becomes clear within the context of Beckett's subsequent stage works: more and more, there's less and less—yet their eloquence, intensity, pathos, and humor remain astonishingly undiminished. *Waiting for Godot*, then, can be seen as the first in a series of plays that strip away inessential elements of drama but keep the "essentials" of theatrical form. Thus, *Play* removes all gesture and, with the exception of the actors' mouths, all movement; *Not I* further reduces the essential components of the genre to a seemingly disembodied mouth and a separate, mute, rarely gesturing, cowled body. Within the context of these ongoing radical subtractions, Beckett's mimes (*Act without Words I* and *II*) take on additional significance, since they necessarily excise language itself; the radio plays (*All That Fall*, *Embers*, etc.) confirm that—for a modern audience, unlike its counterparts in earlier times— neither the theatre itself, nor a stage, nor a setting of any kind is essential for the creation of drama, which can consist of broadcast (recorded) words and sounds. His most extreme excisions, however, occur in *Breath*, a thirty-five-second "dramaticule" that not only lacks a conventional plot but also has no characters, no language, no movement, and no actor in the theatre at the time of the performance. What remains is an austere, wordless, minimalist metaphor for human existence—a uniquely theatrical synchrony of sound and sight, an observed "event" in a trash-strewn space, its meaning not "bound" by any national, cultural, or linguistic considerations, as accessible as music. It is drama's ultimate *reductio* by the master of the absurd.

Concurrent with these radical excisions of theatrical form, there is in Beckett's plays an increasing interiority that parallels a similar progression in his fiction, in which exterior events—and, indeed, life in this world—are apparently left behind. The set of *Endgame*, for example, is often described as a "skullscape," with eyelike high windows outside which there is apparently only a wasteland of ravaged earth and few signs of life. In *Play* the three characters are confined in what appear to be burial urns in some dim realm of the afterdeath, endlessly recounting an earthly adulterous triangle but unaware of one another's proximity; memory alone persists for them—that most interior and intimate "voice" in the dark that is *not* oblivion. It is again evoked, with both comedy and pathos, in *Krapp's Last Tape*, wherein past and present selves "speak" in the present, ironically juxtaposed through modern technology. Even more austerely, but with no less theatrical power, memory and the ravages of time are the subject of a number of the late plays, including *Not I*, *That Time*, *Footfalls*, and *Rockaby*.

Fascinated by the capabilities of technology in the various media of modern communications, Beckett was remarkably adept at incorporating them into his works; no other modern playwright has shown such versatility, writing not only for the stage but also for radio, television, film, and mime. (*Quad* could be more accurately described as a work of choreography than as any form of drama.) Pioneered in *Krapp's Last Tape*, the use of the *recorded* voice figures prominently in *That Time* and *Rockaby*, emanating from an unseen otherwhere in the darkness of an onstage void.

That void—an absence that is always so palpable a presence in Beckett's works, so full of existential implications—is portrayed through a characteristically stark use of stage chiaroscuro. Although *Waiting for Godot* and *Happy Days* are played on fully lit stages, most of the other plays take place in a "mere-most minimum" of light, often precisely focused through pinpoint spots (as in *Not I* and *Play*) or an overhead source that precisely delimits a relatively small acting area outside of which there is no physical set but dark and seemingly empty space (as in *Krapp's Last Tape*, *Rockaby*, *Ohio Impromptu*, *Footfalls*, *Company*, and *What Where*). The characters who inhabit this space, especially in the later works, also have a characteristically Beckettian look: gaunt, dire, and spectral, ravaged by time and/or experience, almost (but never quite) unworldly or otherworldly, humanity *in extremis*.

Because these intense stage images are achieved with such economy of theatrical means but demand so much precision for their effects to be achieved,

Beckett consistently refused permission for substantive changes in his plays by directors and producers seeking the rights to stage his works. He repeatedly denied requests to permit casting women in *Waiting for Godot* (on grounds that "they have no prostate," from which one of the tramps suffers). When, in 1985, director JoAnne Akalaitis set her production of *Endgame* in a derelict New York subway station and added music composed by Philip Glass, Beckett threatened an injunction to block the production; just before opening night an agreement was reached whereby the show would go on provided that disclaimers from both Beckett and his American publisher, Barney Rosset, were attached to each program (along with a defense of the production by American Repertory Theater's artistic director Robert Brustein). The Beckett estate has proved equally vigilant about adherence to the text as written, most recently in a dispute with director Deborah Warner over a production of *Footfalls* at the Garrick Theatre in London in March 1994. The estate's position, as reported in the *Times Literary Supplement* of 1 April 1994 (quoting a letter to *The Guardian*), is that

when approached by a theatre or director for the rights to perform a Beckett play the estate's agents go through the contract and point out the clauses relating to the integrity of the text and stage directions and the fact that they must be adhered to . . . . There are more than 15 recordings of Beethoven's late string quartets in the catalogue, every interpretation different, one from the next, but they are all based on the same notes, tonalities, dynamic and tempo markings. We feel justified in asking the same measure of respect for Samuel Beckett's plays. (14)

Warner had changed the central character's name, altered stage directions, changed costuming, and otherwise altered the text; the production was denied permission to tour as planned. It should be noted, however, that when Beckett directed his own plays he often changed lines and stage directions to an extent that is only now being fully realized with the publication of his theatrical notebooks (Gontarski [5], Knowlson [2, 3, 4]) and studies based on them (see Macmillan and Fehsenfeld).

Amid the plethora of interpretive books and articles on Beckett's works (the products of the so-called "Beckett industry"), a surprising amount of scholarly work is also being done to establish definitive texts and an accurate biography. A new, revised and corrected edition of the *Complete Dramatic Works* has been announced by Faber and Faber, edited by S. E. Gontarski, and the authorized biography written by James Knowlson (Bair's biography appeared in a revised edition in 1990; an ongoing list of corrections to the first edition has been published in *The Beckett Circle*, the newsletter of the Samuel Beckett Society). A selection of Beckett's letters, projected to fill five volumes, is to be published by Grove Press, edited by Martha D. Fehsenfeld and Lois M. Overbeck. The aforementioned theatrical notebooks have been published as a series since 1992. All these resources will doubtless yield more insights, revisions, and controversies. Those seeking an introduction to Beckett studies could well begin with the pioneering works of Ruby Cohn and Hugh Kenner, as listed in the bibliography; for those interested specifically in Beckett's later plays, Brater [2] and Knowlson and Pilling provide especially insightful and reliable guides.

The *Journal of Beckett Studies* was founded by James Knowlson in 1976 and was published by John Calder, Beckett's English publisher, until 1991; it was virtually an anomaly among literary and academic journals in that it was issued by a commercial publishing house that was also committed to keeping all of Beckett's works in print as well as those of the impressive array of other controversial contemporary playwrights whose works were available under the Calder imprint. Accordingly, the eleven issues of the original series of the journal appeared irregularly during the fifteen-year period, and early issues are now eagerly sought by collectors but permanently out of print; as a result, a number of articles were reprinted in Gontarski [1]. The new series of the *Journal*, edited by Gontarski, appears semiannually under the aegis of Florida State University. *The Beckett Circle*, the newsletter of the international Samuel Beckett Society, is also published semiannually; it is particularly valuable for its detailed reviews of productions of Beckett's plays worldwide.

ARCHIVAL SOURCES

The Beckett Archive is maintained at the University of Reading in England and includes many items contributed by Beckett himself. The Humanities Research Center at the University of Texas at Austin and the library of Washington University in St. Louis also have major collections of Beckett materials. There is a Samuel Beckett Society and estate.

PRIMARY BIBLIOGRAPHY

Plays

All That Fall. New York: Grove Press, 1957; London: Faber & Faber, 1957.

Breath and Other Shorts. (*Breath, Come and Go, Act without Words I, Act without Words II*, and *From an Abandoned Work* [prose]). London: Faber & Faber, 1972.

. . . but the clouds . . . London: Faber & Faber, 1977.

Cascando. Evergreen Review (May/June 1963).

Cascando and Other Short Dramatic Pieces. (*Cascando, Words and Music, Eh Joe, Play, Come and Go, Film*). New York: Grove Press, 1969.

Come and Go. Paris: Éditions de Minuit, 1966; London: Calder & Boyars, 1967.

Comédie et actes divers. (*Comedie, Va et vient, Parole et Music, Dis Joe*, Acte sans paroles II). Trans. Samuel Beckett. Paris: Éditions de Minuit, 1966.

La dernière bande, suivi de Cendres. Trans. Samuel Beckett and Pierre Leyris. Paris: Éditions de Minuit, 1960.

Human Wishes. In *Disjecta: Miscellaneous Writings and a Dramatic Fragment*, ed. Ruby Cohn. New York: Grove Press, 1984.

Eh Joe and Other Writings. (*Eh Joe*, *Act without Words II*, and *Film*.) London: Faber & Faber, 1967.

Embers (a piece for radio). *Evergreen Review* (Nov./Dec. 1959).

En attendant Godot. Paris: Éditions de Minuit, 1952.

Endgame, Followed by Act without Words [1]. Trans. Samuel Beckett. New York: Grove Press, 1958; London: Faber & Faber, 1958.

Ends and Odds. (*Not I*, *That Time*, *Footfalls*, *Ghost Trio*, *Theatre I*, *Theatre II*, *Radio I*, *Radio II*). New York: Grove Press, 1976.

Film. London: Faber & Faber, 1967.

Film, suivi de Souffle. Trans. Samuel Beckett. Paris: Éditions de Minuit, 1972.

Fin de partie, suivi de Acte sans paroles. Paris: Éditions de Minuit, 1957.

Footfalls. London: Faber & Faber, 1976.

Happy Days. New York: Grove Press, 1961; London: Faber & Faber, 1962.

Krapp's Last Tape and Other Dramatic Pieces. (*Krapp's Last Tape*, *All That Fall*, *Embers*, *Act without Words I*, and *Act without Words II*). New York: Grove Press, 1960.

Not I. London: Faber & Faber, 1973.

Oh les beaux jours. Trans. Samuel Beckett. Paris: Éditions de Minuit, 1963.

Oh les beaux jours, suivi de Pas moi. Trans. Samuel Beckett. Paris: Éditions de Minuit, 1975.

Ohio Impromptu, Catastrophe, and What Where: Three Plays by Samuel Beckett. New York: Grove Press, 1984.

Play and Two Short Pieces for Radio. (*Play*, *Words and Music*, *Cascando*). London: Faber & Faber, 1964.

Quad. London: Faber & Faber, 1984.

Rockaby and Other Short Pieces. (*Rockaby*, *Ohio Impromptu*, *All Strange Away*, and *A Piece of Monologue*). New York: Grove Press. 1981.

That Time. London: Faber & Faber, 1976.

Tous ceux qui tombent. Trans. Samuel Beckett and Robert Pinget. Paris: Éditions de Minuit, 1957.

Waiting for Godot. Trans. Samuel Beckett. New York: Grove Press, 1954. London: Faber & Faber, 1956.

Words and Music (a piece for radio). *Evergreen Review* (Nov./Dec. 1962).

Anthologies

The Collected Shorter Plays of Samuel Beckett. New York: Grove Press, 1984.

I Can't Go On, I'll Go On: A Selection from Samuel Beckett's Work. Ed. Richard W. Seaver. New York: Grove Press, 1976.

Waiting for Godot, All That Fall, Endgame, From an Abandoned Work, Krapp's Last Tape, and *Embers.* London: Faber & Faber, 1959.

SECONDARY BIBLIOGRAPHY

Acheson, James, and Kateryna Arthur, eds. *Beckett's Later Fiction and Drama: Texts for Company.* London: Macmillan, 1987.

Admussen, Richard. *The Samuel Beckett Manuscripts: A Study.* Boston: G. K. Hall, 1979.

Adorno, Theodor W. "Trying to Understand *Endgame*." Trans. Michael T. Jones. *New German Critique* 26 (spring-summer 1982): 119–50.

Review of *All That Fall*. *Times Literary Supplement* (6 Sept. 1957): 528; rpt. in Graver & Federman: 150–52.

Andonian, Cathleen Carlotta. *Samuel Beckett: A Reference Guide*. Boston: G. K. Hall, 1989.

Anouilh, Jean. "*Godot* or The Music-Hall Sketch of Pascal's *Pensees* as Played by the Fratellini Clowns." Trans. Ruby Cohn. *Arts-Spectacles* 400 (27 Jan. 1953); rpt. in Cohn [3]: 12–13; and in Graver & Federman: 92.

Atkinson, Brooks. Review of *Endgame*. *New York Times* (29 Jan. 1958): 32; rpt. in Graver & Federman: 171–72.

Audiberti, Jacques. "At the Babylone: A Fortunate Move on the Theatre Checkerboard." Trans. Ruby Cohn. *Arts-Spectacles* no. 394 (16 Jan. 1953): 3; rpt. in Cohn [3]: 13–14.

Bair, Deirdre. *Samuel Beckett: A Biography*. New York: Harcourt, 1978; rev. ed., New York: Simon & Schuster, "Touchstone Books," 1990.

Barker, Ronald. "*Waiting for Godot*." *Plays and Players* (Sept. 1955): 18–19; rpt. in Butler [2]: 22–23.

Beja, Morris, S. E. Gontarski, and Pierre Astier, eds. *Samuel Beckett: Humanistic Perspectives*. Columbus: Ohio State University Press, 1983.

Ben-Zvi, Linda [1]. *Samuel Beckett*. Boston: Twayne, 1986.

———[2]. "Women in Godot." *The Beckett Circle* 10.1 (1988): 7.

———, ed. [3]. *Women in Beckett: Performance and Critical Perspectives*. Urbana: University of Illinois Press, 1990.

Bentley, Eric. "The Talent of Samuel Beckett." *New Republic* (14 May 1956): 20–21; rpt. in Butler [2]: 37–40; rpt. with 1967 postscript in Cohn [3]: 59–66; and in Graver & Federman: 104–11.

Bergreen, Laurence. "Beckett's Last Act." *Esquire* (May 1990): 87–98.

Bernard, Marc. Review of *Endgame*. Trans. Larysa Mykyta and Mark Schumacher. *Nouvelles Litteraires* (9 May 1957): 10; rpt. in Graver & Federman: 166–68.

Brater, Enoch, ed. [1]. *Beckett at 80/Beckett in Context*. New York: Oxford University Press, 1986.

———[2]. *Beyond Minimalism: Beckett's Late Style in the Theatre*. New York: Oxford University Press, 1987.

———, ed. [3]. (Special issue on Samuel Beckett). *Journal of Modern Literature* 6 (1977): 3–168.

———[4]. *Why Beckett*. London: Thames, 1989.

Brater, Enoch, and Ruby Cohn, eds. *Around the Absurd: Essays on Modern and Postmodern Drama*. Ann Arbor: University of Michigan Press, 1990.

Brink, Andrew. "Samuel Beckett's *Endgame* and the Schizoid Ego." *The Sphinx* 4 (1982): 87–93, 98–100; rpt. in Butler [2]: 262–70.

Brown, John Russell. "Beckett and the Art of Nonplus." In Brater [1]: 25–45.

Browne, Joseph. "The 'Crritic' [sic] and Samuel Beckett: A Bibliographic Essay." *College Literature* 8 (1981): 292–309.

Brustein, Robert [1]. Review of *Happy Days*. *New Republic* (2 Oct. 1961): 45–46; rpt. in Graver & Federman: 258–61.

———[2]. Review of *Krapp's Last Tape*. *New Republic* (22 Feb. 1960): 21; rpt. in Graver & Federman: 192–93.

————[3]. Review of *Play*. *New Republic* (1 Feb. 1964): 30; rpt. in Graver & Federman: 273–74.

Burghardt, Lori Hall. "Talking Heads: Samuel Beckett's *Play* as a Metaphor for the Schopenhauerian Will." *The Comparatist* (May 1988): 32–39; rpt. in Butler [2]: 354–61.

Burkman, Katherine H. [1]. *The Arrival of Godot: Ritual Patterns in Modern Drama*. Madison, NJ: Fairleigh Dickinson University Press, 1986.

————, ed. [2]. *Myth and Ritual in the Plays of Samuel Beckett*. Madison, NJ: Fairleigh Dickinson University Press, 1987.

Busi, Frederick. *The Transformations of Godot*. Lexington: University Press of Kentucky, 1980.

Butler, Lance St. John [1]. *Samuel Beckett and the Meaning of Being*. New York: St. Martin's Press, 1984.

————, ed. [2]. *Critical Essays on Samuel Beckett*. Critical Thought Series 4. Aldershot: Scholar Press, 1993.

Butler, Lance St. John, and Robin J. Davis, eds. *Rethinking Beckett: A Collection of Critical Essays*. London: Macmillan, 1990.

C. B. Review of *Waiting for Godot*. *San Quentin News* (28 Nov. 1957): 1, 3; rpt. in Graver & Federman: 111–13.

Calder, John, ed. [1]. *As No Other Dare Fail: A Tribute on Samuel Beckett's 80th Birthday by His Friends and Admirers*. London: John Calder, 1986; New York: Riverrun, 1986.

————[2]. *Beckett at Sixty*. London: Calder, 1967.

————[3]. "Samuel Beckett." *The Independent* (27 Dec. 1989); rpt. in Butler [2]: 374–76.

Chevigny, Bell Gale, ed. *Twentieth Century Interpretations of Endgame*. Englewood Cliffs, NJ: Prentice-Hall, 1969.

Clausius, Claudia. "Bad Habits While Waiting for Godot: The Demythification of Ritual." In Burkman [2].

Clurman, Harold [1]. Review of *Play*. *Nation* (27 Jan. 1954): 106–7; rpt. in Butler [2]: 124–25.

————[2]. Review of *Waiting for Godot*. *Nation* (5 May 1956): 487–90; rpt. in Butler [2]: 42–43.

Coe, Richard. *Samuel Beckett*. New York: Grove Press, 1964.

Cohn, Ruby [1]. "The Absurdly Absurd: Avatars of Godot." *Comparative Literature Studies* 3.2 (1965): 233–40.

————[2]. *Back to Beckett*. Princeton, NJ: Princeton University Press, 1973.

————, ed. [3]. *Casebook on Waiting for Godot*. New York: Grove Press, 1967.

————[4]. "Growing (up?) with Godot." In Brater [1].

————[5]. *Just Play: Beckett's Theatre*. Princeton, NJ: Princeton University Press, 1980.

————, ed. [6]. (Special issue on Samuel Beckett). *Modern Drama* 9.4 (Dec. 1966): 237–346.

————, ed.]7]. (Special issue on Samuel Beckett). *Perspective* 11 (autumn 1959): 119–96.

————, ed. [8]. *Samuel Beckett: A Collection of Criticism*. New York: McGraw Hill, 1975.

————[9]. *Samuel Beckett: The Comic Gamut*. New Brunswick, NJ: Rutgers University Press, 1962.

————[10]. "Waiting Is All." *Modern Drama* 3.3 (Sept. 1960): 162–67.

Corliss, Richard. "Spook Sonatas." *Time* (27 Feb. 1984): 101.

Cousineau, Thomas. *Waiting for Godot: Form in Movement*. Boston: Twayne, 1990.

Cushman, Robert. Review of *That Time* and *Footfalls*. *The Observer* (26 May 1976): 30; rpt. in Graver & Federman: 342–44.

Davie, Donald. Review of *All That Fall*. *Spectrum* (winter 1958): 25–31; rpt. in Graver & Federman: 153–60.

Dearlove, J. E. *Accommodating the Chaos: Samuel Beckett's Nonrelational Art*. Durham, NC: Duke University Press, 1982.

Dennis, Nigel. Review of *Happy Days*. *Encounter* (Jan. 1963): 37–39; rpt. in Graver & Federman: 261–66.

Doll, Mary A. *Beckett and Myth: An Archetypal Approach*. Syracuse, NY: Syracuse University Press, 1988.

Drew, Anne-Marie, ed. *Past Crimson, Past Woe: The Shakespeare-Beckett Connection*. New York: Garland Press, 1993.

Driver, Tom F. "Beckett by the Madeleine." *Columbia University Forum* 4.3 (1961): 21–25; rpt. in Graver & Federman: 217–23.

Duckworth, Colin [1]. *Angels of Darkness: Dramatic Effect in Samuel Beckett with Special Reference to Eugene Ionesco*. London: Allen, 1972.

————[2]. "Beckett's *Educations Sentimentales*: From *Premier Amour* to *La Derniere Bande* and *Ohio Impromptu*." *Australian Journal of French Studies* (Jan.-Apr. 1983): 61–69; rpt. in Butler [2]: 293–301.

————[3]. "The Making of *Godot*." In Cohn [3]: 89–100.

Dukore, Bernard. "Gogo, Didi, and the Absent Godot." *Drama Survey* (winter 1962): 301–7.

"The Dying of the Light." *Times Literary Supplement* (8 Jan. 1960): 20; rpt. in Butler [2]: 93.

Elam, Keir. "Dead Heads: Damnation-Narration in the 'Dramaticules.' " In Pilling [2]: 145–66.

Elsom, John, ed. [1]. *Post-war British Theatre Criticism*. London: Routledge, 1981.

————[2]. Review of *That Time* and *Footfalls*. *The Listener* (27 May 1976): 681; rpt. in Graver & Federman: 344–46.

"*Endgame*." *Theatre Arts* (Apr.1958): 26; rpt. in Butler [2]: 63–64.

Esslin, Martin [1]. "Godot and His Children." In *Experimental Drama*, ed. William A. Armstrong. London: G. Bell & Sons, 1963: 128–46.

————, ed. [2]. *Samuel Beckett: A Collection of Critical Essays*. Englewood Cliffs, NJ: Prentice-Hall, 1965.

————[3]. "Samuel Beckett and the Art of Broadcasting." *Encounter* 45.3 (Sept. 1975): 38–46.

————[4]. *The Theatre of the Absurd*. New York: Doubleday, 1961.

Federman, Raymond, and John Fletcher. *Samuel Beckett: His Works and His Critics*. Berkeley: University of California Press, 1970.

Fischer, Eileen. "The Discourse of The Other in *Not I*: A Confluence of Beckett and Lacan." *Theatre* 10.3 (summer 1979): 101–3; rpt. in Butler [2]: 230–32.

Fletcher, Beryl S., John Fletcher, Barry Smith, and Walter Bachen, eds. *A Student's Guide to the Plays of Samuel Beckett*. 1978. 2nd ed., London: Faber & Faber, 1985.

Fletcher, John. *Samuel Beckett's Art*. London: Chatto & Windus, 1971.

Fletcher, John, and John Spurling. *Beckett: A Study of His Plays.* London: Methuen; New York: Hill, 1972.

Francis, Richard Lee. "Beckett's Metaphysical Tragicomedy." *Modern Drama* 8.4 (Dec. 1965): 259–67.

Fraser, G. S. Review of *Waiting for Godot. Times Literary Supplement* (10 Feb. 1956): 84; rpt. in Graver & Federman: 97–104.

Friedman, Alan W., Charles Rossman, and Dina Sherzer, eds. *Beckett Translating/Translating Beckett.* University Park: Pennsylvania State University Press, 1987.

Friedman, Melvin J. [1]. "Crritic!" *Modern Drama* 9.4 (Dec. 1966): 300–308.

———, ed. [2]. *Samuel Beckett Now.* Chicago: University of Chicago Press, 1970.

Gascoigne, Bamber. "How Far Can Beckett Go?" *The Observer Weekend Review* (12 Apr. 1964): 24; rpt. in Butler [2]: 135–36.

Gee, Maggie. "The Voice Within." *Times Literary Supplement* (14 Feb. 1986): 166.

Gidal, Peter. *Understanding Beckett: A Study of Monologue and Gesture in the Works of Samuel Beckett.* New York: St. Martin's Press, 1986.

" 'Godot' Gets Around." *Theatre Arts* (July 1958): 73–74; rpt. in Butler [2]: 67–68.

Gold, Herbert. "Beckett: Style and Desire." *Nation* (10 Nov. 1956): 397–99.

Gontarski, S. E., ed. [1]. *The Beckett Studies Reader.* Gainesville: University Press of Florida, 1993.

———[2]. *The Intent of Undoing in Samuel Beckett's Dramatic Texts.* Bloomington: Indiana University Press, 1985.

———, ed. [3]. (Special issue on Samuel Beckett). *Modern Fiction Studies* 29 (1983): 3–152.

———, ed. [4]. *On Beckett: Essays and Criticism.* New York: Grove Press, 1986.

———, ed. [5]. *The Theatrical Notebooks of Samuel Beckett: Endgame.* New York: Grove Press, 1993.

Graver, Lawrence. *Samuel Beckett: Waiting for Godot.* Cambridge: Cambridge University Press, 1989.

Graver, Lawrence, and Raymond Federman, eds. *Samuel Beckett: The Critical Heritage.* London: Routledge & Kegan Paul, 1979.

Gray, Ronald. "*Waiting for Godot*: A Christian Interpretation." *The Listener* (24 Jan. 1957): 160–61; rpt. in Butler [2]: 44–48.

Hale, Jane Alison. *The Broken Window: Beckett's Dramatic Perspective.* West Lafayette, IN: Purdue University Press, 1987.

Hayman, David, ed. (Special issue on Samuel Beckett). *James Joyce Quarterly* 8 (1971): 275–424.

Henning, Sylvie Debevec. *Beckett's Critical Complicity: Carnival, Contestation, and Tradition.* Lexington: University Press of Kentucky, 1988.

Hewes, Henry [1]. "Mankind in Merdecluse." *Saturday Review* (5 May 1956); rpt. in Cohn [3]: 67–69.

———[2]. "Speak Your Wait." *Saturday Review of Literature* (7 Oct. 1961): 38; rpt. in Butler [2]: 116.

Hobson, Harold [1]. Review of *Fin de partie* and *Acte sans paroles. Sunday Times* (7 Apr. 1957): 15; rpt. in Graver & Federman: 161–64.

———[2]. "Samuel Beckett, Dramatist of the Year." *International Theatre Annual, No. 1.* London: John Calder, 1956: 153–55.

———[3]. "Tomorrow." *Sunday Times* (7 Aug. 1955): 11; rpt. in Cohn [3]: 27–29, and in Graver & Federman, 93–95.

Hoffman, Frederick J. *Samuel Beckett: The Language of Self.* Carbondale: Southern Illinois University Press, 1962.

Homan, Sidney. *Beckett's Theaters: Interpretations for Performance.* Lewisburg, PA: Bucknell University Press, 1984.

Hughes, Catherine. "Beckett and the Game of Life." *Catholic World* (June 1962): 163–68.

Hutchings, William. "Abated Drama: Samuel Beckett's Unbated *Breath.*" *Ariel: A Review of International English Literature* 17.1 (1986): 85–94.

Iser, Wolfgang. "Samuel Beckett's Dramatic Language." Trans. Ruby Cohn. *Modern Drama* 9.4 (Dec. 1966): 251–59; rpt. in Butler [2]: 145–53.

Jacobsen, Josephine, and William R. Mueller. *The Testament of Samuel Beckett.* New York: Hill & Wang, 1964.

Jenkins, Alan [1]. "Exactions of the Theatre." *Times Literary Supplement* (7 Sept. 1984): 997.

———[2]. "Invasions of Reality." *Times Literary Supplement* (19–25 Jan. 1990): 65.

Johnson, B. S. "Exploration." *The Spectator* (26 June 1964): 858; rpt. in Butler [2]: 139–40.

Johnston, Denis. "Waiting with Beckett." *Irish Writing* (spring 1956); rpt. in Cohn [3]: 31–38.

Kalb, Jonathan. *Beckett in Performance.* Cambridge: Cambridge University Press, 1989.

Kane, Leslie. *The Language of Silence: On the Unspoken and the Unspeakable in Modern Drama.* Madison, NJ: Fairleigh Dickinson University Press, 1984.

Kavanagh, Patrick. "Some Reflections on *Waiting for Godot.*" *Irish Times* (28 Jan. 1956): 17; rpt. in Butler [2]: 27–28.

Kennedy, Andrew. *Samuel Beckett.* Cambridge: Cambridge University Press, 1989.

Kenner, Hugh [1]. *A Reader's Guide to Samuel Beckett.* New York: Farrar, 1973.

———[2]. *Samuel Beckett: A Critical Study.* New York: Grove Press, 1961.

———[3]. *The Stoic Comedians: Flaubert, Joyce, and Beckett.* Berkeley: University of California Press, 1962.

Kern, Edith. "Drama Stripped for Inaction: Beckett's *Godot.*" *Yale French Studies* 14 (winter 1954–55): 41–47.

Knowlson, James [1]. *Light and Darkness in the Theatre of Samuel Beckett.* London: Turret, 1972.

———, ed. [2]. *Happy Days: The Production Notebook of Samuel Beckett.* New York: Grove Press, 1985.

———, ed. [3]. *Samuel Beckett's* Krapp's Last Tape: *A Theatre Workbook.* London: Brutus Books, 1980.

———, gen. ed. [4]. *Waiting for Godot: The Theatrical Notebooks of Samuel Beckett.* New York: Grove Press, 1994.

Knowlson, James, and John Pilling. *Frescoes of the Skull: The Later Prose and Drama of Samuel Beckett.* London: Calder, 1979.

Knowlson, James, S. E. Gontarski, and Dougald McMillan, eds. *The Theatrical Notebooks of Samuel Beckett.* London: Faber & Faber, 1992– .

Kott, Jan. "A Note on Beckett's Realism." *Tulane Drama Review* 10.3 (1966): 156–59; rpt. in Butler [2]: 141–43.

Lahr, John. "Waiting for Godot." *Notes on a Cowardly Lion: The Biography of Bert Lahr.* New York: Knopf, 1969: 253–82.

Lawley, Paul. "Stages of Identity: From *Krapp's Last Tape* to *Play.*" In Pilling [2]: 88–105.

Lee, Warren. "The Bitter Pill of Samuel Beckett." *Chicago Review* (winter 1957): 77–87.

LeMarchand, Jacques [1]. Review of *Endgame*. Trans. Jean M. Sommermeyer. *Figaro Litteraire* (11 May 1957): 14; rpt. in Graver & Federman: 168–71.

———[2]. Review of *Waiting for Godot*. Trans. Jean M. Sommermeyer. *Figaro Litteraire*, (17 Jan. 1953): 10; rpt. in Graver & Federman: 89–92.

Leventhal, A. J. "Mr. Beckett's *En attendant Godot*." *Dublin Magazine* (Apr.-June 1954): 11–16.

Levy, Alan. "The Long Wait for Godot." *Theatre Arts* (Aug. 1956): 33–35, 96; rpt. in Cohn [3]: 74–78.

Libera, Antoni. "Beckett's *Catastrophe*." *Modern Drama* 28.3 (Sept. 1985): 341–46; rpt. in Butler [2]: 332–37.

Logue, Christopher. "For Those Still Standing." *New Statesman* (14 Sept. 1957): 325; rpt. in Butler [2]: 52.

Lyons, Charles R. [1] "Beckett's Major Plays and the Trilogy." *Comparative Drama* 5.4 (winter 1971): 254–68.

———[2]. "Perceiving *Rockaby*—As a Text, As a Text by Samuel Beckett, As a Text for Performance." *Comparative Drama* 16.4 (winter 1982): 301–4; rpt. in Butler [2]: 282–85.

———[3]. *Samuel Beckett*. New York: Grove Press, 1983.

Mailer, Norman. "A Public Notice on *Waiting for Godot*." *Village Voice* (7 May 1966). Rpt. in *Advertisements for Myself*. New York: G. P. Putnam's Sons, 1959: 320–25; rpt. in Cohn [3]: 69–74.

Mannes, Marya. "Two Tramps." *The Reporter* (20 Oct. 1955); rpt. in Cohn [3]: 30–31.

Marinello, Leone J. "Samuel Beckett's *Waiting for Godot*." *Drama Critique* (spring 1963): 75–81.

Markus, Thomas B. "Bernard Dukore and *Waiting for Godot*." *Drama Survey* (Feb. 1963): 360–63.

Marowitz, Charles [C. M.]. "A View from the Gods." *Encore* (Jan.-Feb.1963): 6–7; rpt. in Butler [2]: 120–21.

McCandless, David. "Beckett and Tillich: Courage and Existence in *Waiting for Godot*." *Philosophy and Literature* (Apr. 1988): 48–57; rpt. in Butler [2]: 344–53.

McCarthy, Patrick A., ed. *Critical Essays on Samuel Beckett*. Boston: Hall, 1986.

McCoy, Charles. "*Waiting for Godot*: A Biblical Approach." *Florida Review* (spring 1958): 63–72.

McMillan, Dougald, and Martha Fehsenfeld. *Beckett in the Theatre: The Author as Practical Playwright and Director*. Vol. 1 *From* Waiting for Godot *to* Krapp's Last Tape. London: John Calder; New York: Riverrun, 1988.

Megged, Matti. *Dialogue in the Void: Beckett and Giacometti*. New York: Lumen, 1985.

Mercier, Vivian [1]. "A Pyrrhonian Eclogue." *The Hudson Review* 7.4 (winter 1955): 620–24.

———[2]. *Beckett/Beckett*. New York: Oxford University Press, 1974.

———[3]. "Samuel Beckett, Bible Reader." *Commonweal* 105 (1978): 266–68.

———[4]. "The Uneventful Event." *Irish Times* (18 Feb. 1956): 6; rpt. in Butler [2]: 29–30.

Moore, John R. "A Farewell to Something." *Tulane Drama Review* (Sept. 1960): 49–60.

Morrison, Kristin. *Canters and Chronicles: The Use of Narrative in the Plays of Samuel Beckett and Harold Pinter*. Chicago: University of Chicago Press, 1983.

Nightingale, Benedict [1]. Review of *That Time* and *Footfalls*. *New Statesman* (28 May 1976): 723; rpt. in Graver & Federman: 346–48.

———[2]. Review of *Not I*. *New Statesman* (26 Jan. 1973): 135–36; rpt. in Graver & Federman: 329–33.

O'Brien, Eoin. *The Beckett Country: Samuel Beckett's Ireland*. Dublin: Black Cat; London: Faber & Faber, 1986.

Oldsey, Bernard, ed. (Special issue on Samuel Beckett). *College Literature* 8 (1981): 209–312.

Oliver, Edith [1]. Review of *Not I*. *New Yorker* (2 Dec. 1972): 124; rpt. in Graver & Federman: 328–29.

———[2]. Review of *Rockaby*, *Footfalls*, and "Enough." *The New Yorker* (27 Feb. 1984): 114.

Peter, John. *Vladimir's Carrot: Modern Drama and the Modern Imagination*. Chicago: University of Chicago Press, 1987.

Pilling, John [1]. *Samuel Beckett*. London: Routledge, 1976.

———, ed. [2]. *The Cambridge Companion to Beckett*. Cambridge: Cambridge University Press, 1994.

Politzer, John R. "The Egghead Waits for Godot." *Christian Scholar* (Mar. 1959): 46–50.

Pountney, Rosemary. *Theatre of Shadows: Samuel Beckett's Drama, 1956–76*. Gerrards Cross: Colin Smythe, 1988; Totowa, NJ: Barnes, 1988.

Ratcliffe, Michael. Review of *Ghost Trio* and *. . . but the clouds . . . The Times* (18 Apr. 1977): 6; rpt. in Graver & Federman: 352–53.

Rechtien, Brother John, S. M. "Time and Eternity Meet in the Present." *Texas Studies in Language and Literature* (spring 1964): 5–21.

Reid, Alec [1]. *All I Can Manage, More than I Could: An Approach to the Plays of Samuel Beckett*. Dublin: Dolmen Press, 1968.

———[2]. "Beckett and the Drama of Unknowing." *Drama Survey* (Oct. 1962): 130–38.

———[3]. "Impact and Parable in Beckett: A First Encounter with *Not I*." *Hermathena, A TCD Review* (winter 1986): 13–18, 20; rpt. in Butler [2]: 338–43.

Rexroth, Kenneth. "The Point Is Irrelevance." *Nation* (14 Apr. 1956): 325–28.

Rhodes, S. A. "From Godeau to Godot." *French Review* (Jan. 1963): 260–65.

Ricks, Christopher. "Beckett and the Lobster." *New Statesman* (14 Feb. 1964): 254–55; rpt. in Butler [2]: 128–34.

Riva, Raymond T. "Beckett and Freud." *Criticism* 12.2 (1970): 120–27, 129–32; rpt. in Butler [2]: 159–68.

Robbe-Grillet, Alain. "Samuel Beckett or Presence on the Stage." *Critique* (Feb. 1953). Rev. version in *For a New Novel*. Trans. Richard Howard. New York: Grove Press, 1965: 111–25; rpt. in Cohn [3]: 15–21.

Robinson, Michael. *The Long Sonata of the Dead: A Study of Samuel Beckett*. London: Hart-David; New York: Grove Press, 1969.

Rosen, Steven. *Samuel Beckett and the Pessimistic Tradition*. New Brunswick, NJ: Rutgers University Press, 1976.

Salacrou, Armand. "It's Not an Accident but a Triumph." Trans. Ruby Cohn. *Arts-Spectacles* 400 (27 Jan. 1953); rpt. in Cohn [3]: 14–15.

Schlueter, June. *Metafictional Characters in Modern Drama*. New York: Columbia University Press, 1979.

Schlueter, June, and Enoch Brater, eds. *Approaches to Teaching Beckett's* Waiting for Godot. New York: Modern Language Association, 1991.

Schneider, Alan [1]. *Entrances: An American Director's Journey*. New York: Viking, 1986.

————[2]. "Waiting for Beckett: A Personal Chronicle." *Chelsea Review* 14.2 (1958): 3–13, 15–20; rpt. in Butler [2]: 69–83; rpt. as "Working with Beckett (1958)" in Graver & Federman: 173–88; Excerpt rpt. in Cohn [3]: 51–57.

Schneider, Pierre. "Play and Display." *The Listener* (28 Jan. 1954): 174–76.

Shenker, Israel. "Moody Man of Letters." *New York Times* (5 May 1956): 2: 1, 3; rpt. as "An Interview with Beckett (1956)" in Graver & Federman: 146–49.

Simon, Alfred. Review of *Happy Days*. *Esprit* (Dec. 1963): 905–9. Trans. by Jean M. Sommermeyer; rpt. in Graver & Federman: 266–71.

Simpson, Alan. "Producing *Godot* in Dublin." *Beckett and Behan*. London: Routledge, 1962: 62–137; excerpt rpt. in Cohn [3]: 45–49.

States, Bert O. *The Shape of Paradox: An Essay on Waiting for Godot*. Berkeley: University of California Press, 1978.

Takahashi, Yasunari. "The Theatre of Mind: Samuel Beckett & the Noh." *Encounter* (Apr. 1982): 66, 68–70; rpt. in Butler [2]: 257–61.

Tallmer, Jerry. "Godot on Broadway" and "Godot: Still Waiting"; rpt. in *Village Voice Reader*, ed. Daniel Wolf and Edwin Fancher. New York: Doubleday, 1962; rpt. New York: Grove Press, 1963: 60–66.

Tynan, Kenneth [1]. "A Philosophy of Despair." *The Observer* (7 Apr. 1957): 15; rpt. in Butler [2]: 49–50 and in Graver & Federman: 164–66.

————[2]. Review of *Krapp's Last Tape*. *The Observer* (2 Nov. 1958): 19; rpt. in Graver & Federman: 189–92.

————[3]. Review of *Waiting for Godot*. *The Observer* (7 Aug. 1955): 11; rpt. in Graver & Federman: 95–97, and in Butler [2]: 20–21.

Vahanian, Gabriel. "The Empty Cradle." *Theology Today* (4 Jan. 1957): 521–26.

Via, D. O., Jr. "*Waiting for Godot* and Man's Search for Community." *Journal of Bible and Religion* (Jan. 1962): 32–37.

Wardle, Irving. Review of *That Time* and *Footfalls*. *The Times* (21 May 1976): 13; rpt. in Graver & Federman: 340–42.

Webb, Eugene. *The Plays of Samuel Beckett*. Seattle: University of Washington Press, 1972.

Williams, Raymond. "Hope Deferred." *New Statesman* (19 May 1961): 802; rpt. in Butler [2]: 111–15.

Worsley, T. C. "Cactus Land." *New Statesman and Nation* (13 Aug. 1955): 184–85.

Worth, Katharine, ed. [1]. *Beckett the Shape Changer: A Symposium*. London: Routledge & Kegan Paul, 1975.

————[2]. *The Irish Drama of Europe: From Yeats to Beckett*. London: Athlone, 1978; Atlantic Highlands, NJ: Humanities, 1978.

Worton, Michael. "*Waiting for Godot* and *Endgame*: Theatre as Text." In Pilling [2]: 67–87.

Young, Jordan R. *The Beckett Actor*. Beverly Hills, CA: Moonstone, 1987.

Zegel, Sylvain. "At the Théâtre de Babylone: *Waiting for Godot* by Samuel Beckett.'' Trans. Ruby Cohn. *La Libération* (7 Jan. 1953); rpt. in Cohn [3]: 11–12, and in Graver & Federman: 88–89.

Zeifman, Hersh. ''The Alterable Whey of Words: The Texts of *Waiting for Godot*.'' *Educational Theatre Journal* 29.1 (1977): 77–84.

Zilliacus, Clas. *Beckett and Broadcasting*. Abo, Finland: Acta Academiae Aboensis, Ser. A. Humaniora, 51, no. 2, 1976.

BIBLIOGRAPHIES

Andonian, Cathleen Carlotta. *Samuel Beckett: A Reference Guide*. Boston: G. K. Hall, 1989.

Federman, Raymond, and John Fletcher. *Samuel Beckett: His Works and His Critics*. Berkeley: University of California Press, 1970.

Murphy, P. J., Konrad Schoell, Rolf Breuer, and Werner Huber. *Critique of Beckett Criticism: A Guide to Research in English, French, and German*. Columbia, SC: Camden House, 1994.

Tanner, J. F., and J. D. Vann. *Samuel Beckett: A Checklist*. Columbus: Ohio State University Press, 1969.

Edward Bond

(1934–)

WILLIAM J. FREE

Edward Bond was born in Holloway, North London, on 18 July 1934. His father was an agricultural worker who was forced to find employment in London during the Great Depression. Thus Bond identifies himself with the 75 percent of Englishmen who belong to the working class, a fact that has had a profound influence on his plays.

Like many London children, Bond was evacuated during the war, first to Cornwall and later to his grandparents' home near Ely in Cambridgeshire. His elementary school education occurred in those districts. After the war he attended Crouch End Secondary Modern School in London, but he was denied the opportunity to take 11-plus exams (the gateway to continuing in comprehensive school and at university), and his formal education ended at the age of fifteen. Bond believes that his being denied access to grammar school and university education was a positive force in his continuing intellectual development.

Bond was introduced to the theatre early in life. One of his sisters (he is one of five children) worked as a magician's assistant in a music hall, and he often stood backstage and watched her being sawed in two. This experience greatly influenced his understanding of theatrical imagery and timing. In 1948 he saw Donald Wolfit's *Macbeth* at the Bedford Theatre in Camden Town, a London working-class neighborhood. The performance awakened a sense of life and beauty in him that later caused him to turn naturally to dramatic writing.

After leaving school Bond worked at a variety of laboring jobs—paint mixer, insurance clerk, aircraft factory employee. Between 1953 and 1955 he served in the British army, fulfilling his national service obligation. His experience with the brutality and dehumanization of army life helped form his image of force as a controlling social instrument. During his army tour in Vienna, Bond first began to write short stories.

Upon returning from the army, Bond began a serious effort to become a playwright. Between 1956 and 1958 he wrote a stage play, *The Asses of Kish*, five radio plays, and a television play, all of which were rejected. In 1958 he submitted two plays, *Klaxon in Atreus' Place* and *The Fiery Tree*, to the English Stage Company at the Royal Court Theatre, which had been founded in 1956 by George Devine as a writers' theatre. Although the Court rejected the plays, Bond was invited to join its writers' group, newly formed to foster talented young playwrights. Director William Gaskill took a strong interest in Bond's work. Membership in the writers' group gave Bond the opportunity to see productions of original plays at the Royal Court and to see important visiting companies such as Bertolt Brecht's Berliner Ensemble.

Bond worked with the writers' group from 1958 until 1962 before his first work was accepted for performance. That play, *The Pope's Wedding*, appeared on 9 December 1962, for a single performance without decor on a Sunday night, the Court's normal process for introducing work by new playwrights. The play attracted positive critical attention and was nominated for an award. This success led George Devine to commission a second new play from Bond, whose career as a professional playwright now began to make rapid progress.

Saved, the second play, became one of the most important events in modern theatre history. At the time, performances of plays in London were subject to the approval of the Lord Chamberlain. The Royal Court management submitted the play for approval in June 1965. The Lord Chamberlain's office demanded cuts, which Bond refused. In November the Royal Court presented *Saved* as a private club performance not subject to censorship under the law. But in January 1966 the Royal Court managers were arrested and charged under the Theatres Act of 1843; they were convicted and fined in April. The notoriety of this action began a movement in both the House of Commons and the House of Lords to abolish theatre censorship. In November 1967 the Royal Court submitted another Bond play, *Early Morning*, which was rejected in its entirety. Planned performances of the play were closed by the police in the spring of 1968. In September 1968 the Lord Chamberlain's office was abolished by Parliament.

The legal action against the two plays and the resulting parliamentary action made Bond an important figure in the history of English drama. It also began his active involvement in political questions and in the legal rights of dramatists. Beginning with the teach-in organized to defend *Saved* in November 1965, Bond has participated in many public events, including speeches and teach-ins concerning his plays, the antiapartheid movement, the establishment of the Theatre Writers Union, lectures and fellowships at the Universities of Durham and Newcastle, and a continuing series of workshops, readings, and panels all over England. One of the highlights of these appearances was a three-day directing workshop at the National Theatre in spring 1982.

Bond has also written extensively about the theatre and about contemporary politics. His ''Theatre Poems'' have been collected in two volumes, and many of his published plays contain prefaces and essays. His most recent effort to date is an ambitious philosophical essay, "Notes on Post-Modernism," included in his 1990 *Two Post-Modern Plays*. His extensive appearances and writings in support of his plays, of the theatre generally, and of his political vision have reminded scholars and critics of the similar activities of George Bernard Shaw and Bertolt Brecht.

Since *Saved*, Bond has written and seen through production seventeen original plays and has produced highly acclaimed adaptations and translations of *The Cherry Orchard*, *A Chaste Maid of Cheapside*, *The White Devil*, and, most prominently, his and his wife Elisabeth Bond's translation of Frank Wedekind's *Spring Awakening*, which has become the standard performance text of that play in English. He has received numerous awards in England and in continental Europe and has received an honorary doctorate from Yale University.

Since the triumph of Thatcherism in the mid-1980s, Bond's plays have appeared less frequently on the London stage, but he has continued to work actively in and for the theatre. His plays both new and revived have continued to appear in university theatre departments, in regional theatres, on television, and throughout Europe. He has continued to write and speak on behalf of his sense of the truth about society and about drama. At age sixty-two his energy and enthusiasm continue unabated.

Selected Biographical Sources: Hay and Roberts [1, 2]; Roberts; Kerensky; Taylor.

MAJOR PLAYS, PREMIERES, AND SIGNIFICANT REVIVALS: THEATRICAL RECEPTION

The Pope's Wedding. 1962. Opened at the Royal Court Theatre, London, on 9 December, in a single Sunday night *sans decor* production. Directed by Keith Johnstone. Revived by the Northcott Theatre, Exeter, 13 June 1973. This production transferred to the Bush Theatre, Hammersmith, London, on 3 July 1973. The play was revived in Exeter and in London in July 1973.

Levin called the play a "bizarre and unclassifiable piece" that is at the same time a *tour de force*. Peter [1] and Elsom praised Bond's ability to create a believable sense of a small community and its alienation from the larger world.

Saved. 1965. Opened as a club performance at the Royal Court Theatre, London, 3 Nov. 1965. Directed by William Gaskill. Revived more than eighty times between 1965 and 1976, including productions in Munich and at Yale Repertory Theatre. Named best play and production of 1967 by the German theatre journal *Theater Heute*. Won first prize at the 1969 Belgrade Festival. Included in the Royal Court's "Bond Season" in February 1969. Filmed for television in 1984.

Bond characterized the reviews of *Saved* as "hysterical." Gilliatt reported that she spent the first act "shaking with claustrophobia and thinking I was going to be sick." Wardle [6] accused the play of degrading human beings. Kretzmer found the images in the play so horrible that they should not be allowed, even in the name of free speech. Laurence Olivier, on the other hand, insisted in a letter to *The Observer* that grownups should have the courage to look at the play and face what English society is doing to the young. In contrast to the London reviewers, Barnes in the *New York Times* described *Saved* as "incandescent." In spite of its structural flaws, he continued, the play "can lodge in the mind and expand in the imagination."

Early Morning. 1968. Opened at the Royal Court Theatre, London, on 31 March 1968. Directed by William Gaskill. Continued for thirteen performances. Revived as part of the "Bond Season" at the Royal Court in March 1969. Performed by La Mama Experimental Theatre Club in New York beginning 18 November 1970. Revived at the Royal Court in March 1969, at the Schauspielhaus in Zurich in October 1969, and at the Citizens Theatre, Glasgow, in May 1974.

Hobson [2] found the images of cannibalism in the play "unspeakably horrible." Bryden [2] also found the play's images to be horrible but justified the cannibalism as a metaphor for the consumer society and for the horrors perpetrated by the ruling classes of Victorian society. Wardle [2] complained, "We are confronted by savage events and dumb inert language." He regretted that the Royal Court's fight for free speech had been "conducted on a piece as muddled and untalented as this."

Narrow Road to the Deep North. 1968. Commissioned by Coventry Cathedral. Opened at the Belgrade Theatre, Coventry, on 24 June 1968. Transferred to the Royal Court Theatre, London, as part of the "Bond Season," 19 February 1969. Directed by Jane Howell. Played for eighteen performances to small audiences. Productions in Boston in October 1969, in Munich in September of that year, in Bristol in May 1971, and at 2nd Stage in Hollywood in 1993.

Wardle [5] praised the play, primarily on the grounds that unlike Bond's three previous plays, it contained nothing offensive. The *Boston Globe* (Review of *Narrow Road to the Deep North*) found the play's images beautiful and mysterious, "as simple and pure as a . . . haiku."

Lear. 1971. Opened at the Royal Court Theatre, London, on 29 September 1971. Directed by William Gaskill. Played for thirty-seven performances to relatively small houses. Produced at Yale Repertory in April 1973; at the Schiller Theater, Berlin, in June 1973, where it won first prize at the BITEF Festival; in Lyons, France, in April 1975; at the Other Place in Stratford in June 1982; transferred to the Barbican Pit May 1983.

Reviews of *Lear* were more positive than those greeting Bond's earlier plays. Although Wardle [4] wondered if Bond were lacking in common humanity, he also wondered if what passes for humanity in our society is lacking. Dawson recognized the violence and brutality of the play's images but she insisted that far from being a negative work, *Lear* is an indictment of the false values of its society. Marowitz believed the play to be of "inescapable magnitude" and saw it as a continuation of Bond's "finest writing." However, he found the ending forced and unconvincing because like much of the play, it was "subservient to [Bond's] dialectic." Masters, reviewing the 1983 revival, found the play more relevant to audiences in the 1980s than it had been to audiences originally, in the 1970s.

Black Mass. 1970. Opened at the Lyceum Theatre, London, on 22 March 1970. Directed by David Jones. Produced in Amsterdam in September 1971 and in Bonn in September 1972.

The play was not widely reviewed. Kustow called it "ghastly . . . a George Grosz picture come to life," but he admitted that perhaps the play contained the only form of imagery with which to describe such evil.

Passion. 1971. Opened at the Alexandra Park Racecourse in April 1971. Directed by Bill Bryden. Productions at Yale Repertory in February 1972 and in Wellington, New Zealand, in April 1976.

Although Dewhurst found the play to be a familiar kind of "symbolic nonsense," he also believed it to be more cunning than the average play of its sort.

The Sea. 1973. Opened at the Royal Court Theatre, London, on 22 May 1973. Directed by William Gaskill. Ran for forty performances, sold 60 percent of its seats, and closed with a small profit. Productions at the Goodman Theatre in Chicago in November 1974; the Marlowe Theatre, Canterbury, in July 1975; Teatro Duse in Genoa in December 1976; the Phoenix Theatre in Toronto in April 1977; and the National Theatre in London in December 1991. BBC-TV version broadcast in March 1978.

Esslin caught many analogies from *Lear* to *The Sea* while recognizing the smaller scale and more comic tone of the new play. Wardle, [7] on the other hand, found *The Sea* to be a striking departure from Bond's other plays. He praised Bond's newfound kindness to his characters and comments favorably on the playwright's "talent for hard, detailed satire and explosive incongruities." Walker compared Bond's wit to that of George Bernard Shaw and Oscar Wilde.

Bingo. 1973. Opened in Exeter on 14 November 1973. Transferred to the Royal Court on 14 August 1974. Directed by Jane Howell and John Dove. Played for fifty-four performances to almost full houses. Its profit of over £17,000 pounds made it the most lucrative investment in a Bond play in the history of the Royal Court. Productions in Cleveland, Ohio, on 31 October 1975; at the Yale Repertory Theatre in 1976; in Seattle on 22 February, 1977. The Yale production won a special citation at the Obie Awards for 1976. Revived by the Royal Shakespeare Company in its Other Place in Stratford-upon-Avon on 3 November 1976; transferred to the Warehouse Theatre in London on 8 August 1977. Royal Shakespeare production directed by Howard Davies.

Reviews centered around the critics' reaction to the image of Shakespeare as a rich, retired property owner who kills himself because his plays have failed to stem the evils of society, including his own complicity in the ruin of small landowners. To Billington [1] the play repeated a familiar Bond theme, the impotence of the artist in a world of institutionalized violence. Bryden [1] saw the same dilemma and believed Shakespeare could only kill himself in its face. Pam Gems contended that *Bingo* is a tender and affectionate portrayal of its subject. However, Hobson [1] believed Bond's "despair is total." He also believed that Bond had been unfair in dealing with Shakespeare's contributions to world culture.

The Fool. 1975. Opened at the Royal Court Theatre, London, on 18 November 1975. Directed by Peter Gill. Played for thirty-eight performances. Productions at the Folger Theatre group in Washington, D.C., 12 October 1976; the Other Place, Stratford-upon-Avon, 25 June 1980; transferred to London to the Warehouse on 22 September 1981. Royal Shakespeare Company production directed by Howard Davies.

Lahr called *The Fool* "a superb new play," and saw it as continuing Bond's theme of the artist who, finding himself a success in the marketplace, becomes a victim of it. Wardle [3] confessed that he had "no clear impression of what the play is saying." He could find little relationship between protagonist John Clare as social emblem and Bond's ending portrait of Clare as an "utterly withdrawn old man." Nightingale compared *The Fool* to *Bingo* in the sense that both plays show the "writer floundering in the yellow sludge of British society." John Clare, according to Nightingale, is caught between "the reading classes who do not feel and the feeling classes who do not read."

The Woman. 1978. Opened at the National Theatre, London, on 10 August 1978. Directed by Edward Bond.

Savona saw the play as a summation of Bond's work to date, but with the addition of sexism to the general political analysis. Wardle [8] praised Bond for showing how Greek myths imprison Western culture in a defeatist world view, and he remarked that Bond's play is in no way diminished by comparison to its origins. Peter [2] was less enthusiastic. Although he admitted the play "speaks like the bad conscience of our time," he thought Bond depended too much on character types and that the ending offered an easy way out, betraying Bond's beliefs about the horrifying nature of people and the wars in which they participate.

Restoration. 1981. Opened at the Royal Court Theatre, London, 21 July 1981. Directed by Edward Bond. Revived at the Barbican Pit in March 1989.

Billington [2] complained that the play contained too much material to be digested at one sitting, but he praised Bond for abandoning the agitprop form and making his points through laughter. Holland compared the play to *The Fool* in its unsentimental treatment of the misuse of justice in the hands of the powerful. He also praised Bond's use of poems and songs to create analogues and parallels to the play's action.

Summer. 1982. Opened at the National Theatre, London, on 27 January 1982. Directed by Edward Bond. Performance at the Manhattan Theatre Club in New

York on 19 February 1983. Adapted for BBC Radio 3 by Edward Bond; broadcast on 23 December 1982.

Bond told me in an unpublished interview that he thought the reviews that greeted *Summer* were as hysterical and uncomprehending as those that greeted *Saved*. Indeed, Fenton accused the play of being imprisoned in ideology and isolated in ''an Albanian quality of cretinism.'' Figes, on the other hand, saw *Summer* as among Bond's best work, but she questioned the political and moral impact of the play by contending that it demonstrates that horrors are ''all in people's heads,'' an idea that goes against the grain of Bond's entire career.

Red Black and Ignorant. 1984. Opened at the Barbican Theatre, London, on 19 January 1984. Directed by Nick Hamm.

Ratcliffe praised the play for taking the audience ''through the horrors of our own age reflected in those of worse to come.'' He observed that Bond's language was still effective and that the play provided ''precision, clarity, and clout.''

ADDITIONAL PLAYS AND PRODUCTIONS

A-A-America! (1976) opened by the fringe group Almost Free Theatre, on 26 October 1976, directed by Jack Emery. An evening of two one-act plays, the second of which, *The Swing*, was reviewed at the Theater de Freien Hansestadt in Bremen on 15 March 1977. *Stone* (1976) opened at the Gay Sweatshop, London, 8 June 1976, directed by Gerald Chapman. *The Bundle* (1978) opened at the Warehouse, London, 13 Jan. 1978, directed by Howard Davies. Cushman praised Bond's narrative skill and dynamic scene construction. *The Worlds* (1979) opened with an amateur cast at the Newcastle Playhouse, on 8 March 1979, directed by Edward Bond; remounted by the Activists Youth Theatre Club at the Royal Court Theatre Upstairs, on 21 November 1979. Its first professional production was at the New Half Moon Theatre, London, on 12 June 1981, directed by Nick Hamm. *Derek* (1982) opened at the Other Place, Stratford-upon-Avon, on 18 October 1982, directed by Nick Hamm. *The Tin Can People* (1984) opened at Bread and Circuses Theatre Company in Birmingham, England, on 4 May 1984, directed by Nick Philippou. *The War Plays* (1985) opened at the Barbican Pit, London, 29 May 1984, produced by the Royal Shakespeare Company, directed by Edward Bond and Nick Hamm. *Jackets* (1989) was produced by the Department of Theatre Studies, Lancaster University, 24 January 1989, directed by Keith Sturgess. Part II opened at the Leicester Haymarket, 28 November 1989, directed by Nick Philippou. *September* (1989) was first performed at Canterbury Cathedral, on 16 September 1989, directed by Greg Doran. *In the Company of Men* (1992) was produced in Paris.

ASSESSMENT OF EDWARD BOND'S CAREER

Any assessment of Edward Bond's achievement must begin with his place in the history of English drama. Bond wrote the last play to be closed by police action and the last play to be denied performance by censors in England. Although he did not write *Saved* and *Early Morning* for the purpose of attacking censorship, they became the focal points of political action that resulted in the abolition of a practice that went historically back to Shakespeare's time. Whatever fate his plays may have at the hands of the public and critics in the future, his name is forever linked to that momentous event in English history.

Although Bond's plays met with mixed critical and audience response at the time of their first presentation, his reputation as a major playwright of the last half of the twentieth century is secure. He has met with particular success in continental Europe and is esteemed by academic critics in both England and America. Three of his plays, *Saved*, *Lear*, and *Bingo*, have attracted a large body of commentary and are frequently taught at colleges and universities. These three and several others, most notably *The Sea*, *Restoration*, *A Narrow Road to the Deep North*, and *The Fool* have received professional revivals, and a number of Bond's plays have been telecast or broadcast.

Bond has, in the face of both admiration and criticism, maintained his view of the truth about life in our time. His convictions have two important anchoring points. First, he believes that humankind has a biological need for justice. Being treated fairly is as important to Bond as food, clothing, and shelter. Without justice there can be no tranquility or peace. Second, Bond believes that authority has historically created injustice. Society is composed of structures of authority. We live social roles that naturally implicate us in injustice. When Shakespeare becomes a wealthy landlord in *Bingo,* he is unjust to his tenants, one of whom he has hanged. Society must also act to protect and further its authority by both force and ideology. In *The Woman* Bond astutely alters the Trojan War myth to have the subject of the war not a living woman but a statue. Possession of the statue validates the authority of the possessor. The real gains from the war are less important than the validity of authority. That authority is maintained by organized violence—by war.

Critics have frequently accused Bond's plays of excessive, even gratuitous, violence. Certainly, the autopsy scene in *Lear*, the stoning of the baby in *Saved*, and the cannibalism in *Early Morning* challenge the composure of their viewers. Bond believes that violence is the natural consequence of injustice in our world. In his preface to *Saved*, he contends that the stoning to death of one baby is an understatement in comparison to the thousands of children whose lives are brutalized daily. His essay ''On Violence'' defends his thematic concern with violence by arguing that in a class society violence exists both to enforce the class system and as an expression of the frustration and aggression felt by members of society, especially in those who are too inarticulate to express their frustration in any other way. Violence can only be ended by making the world more just. Bond believes his plays are ways of creating understanding of that truth.

Some critics and scholars have, rightly, compared Bond's plays to those of Bertolt Brecht. But Bond is not just an English imitation of Brecht. His most immediate resemblance to Brecht is his choice to distance the story of many of his plays from contemporary life. Like Brecht, he has turned to oriental fable (as in *Narrow Road to the Deep North*), to various historical periods (as in *Restoration* or *The Fool*), and to past literary works (as in *Lear* or *The Woman*), all for the purpose of revealing the historical development of the nature of social injustice. All these plays exhibit qualities Brecht called ''epic.'' But unlike Brecht, Bond has another large body of work that deals with the present. *The Pope's Wedding*, *Saved*, *Summer*, and many of his plays of the 1980s and 1990s describe contemporary life with a simplicity and clarity that at times approach minimalist concerns.

Bond's artistry as a playwright in his better plays is unquestioned. Two things deserve mention. Bond is able to visually isolate meaningful elements on stage, thus giving them particular clarity and force. The rowboat or the baby pram on the bare stage in *Saved* provide examples that could be multiplied from many of his plays. A second form of artistic control concerns Bond's use of multiple events and his ability to engage the audience directly. The eventful stage compositions of *Restoration* and *Lear* come to mind.

Edward Bond is a dedicated playwright who has something to say about human societies and who has stuck by his vision over a fruitful career. He has never compromised his vision in the face of hostility from critics or audiences. His plays have made a lasting contribution to the debate about life in the last half of the twentieth century.

PRIMARY BIBLIOGRAPHY

Plays

A-A-America! and *Stone*. London: Eyre Methuen, 1976.

Bingo: Scenes of Money and Death. London: Eyre Methuen, 1974.

Black Mass. In *The Pope's Wedding*. London: Eyre Methuen, 1971; also in *Gambit* (17 Oct. 1970).

The Bundle: Scenes of Right and Evil or *New Narrow Road to the Deep North*. London: Eyre Methuen, 1978.

Derek; and *Chores after the Assassinations*. London: Methuen, 1983.

Early Morning. London: Calder & Boyars, 1968.

The Fool: Scenes of Bread and Love and *We Come to the River*. London: Eyre Methuen, 1976.

Human Cannon. London: Methuen, 1985.

Lear. London: Eyre Methuen, 1972.

Narrow Road to the Deep North: A Comedy. London: Eyre Methuen, 1968; also in *Plays and Players* (Sept. 1968).

Olly's Prison. London: Methuen, 1993.

Passion. In *Plays and Players* (June 1971).

Poems, 1978–1985. London: Methuen, 1987.

The Pope's Wedding. London: Eyre Methuen, 1971. Also in *Plays and Players* (April 1969).

Restoration and The Cat. London: Methuen, 1982.
Saved. London: Eyre Methuen, 1966; also in *Plays and Players* (Jan. 1966).
The Sea: A Comedy. London: Eyre Methuen, 1975.
Summer and *Fables*. London: Methuen, 1982.
Theatre Poems and Songs. London: Methuen, 1978.
Tuesday. London: Methuen, 1993.
Two Post-Modern Plays. (*Jackets, In the Company of Men*). London: Methuen, 1990.
The War Plays. London: Methuen, 1985.
We Come to the River. In *Gambit* 68 (1976) and *New Writing and Writers* 13. London: Calder, 1976.
The Woman. London: Eyre Methuen, 1978.
The Words and *The Activist Papers*. London: Methuen, 1980.

Anthologies

Plays: One. (*Saved, Early Morning, The Pope's Wedding*). London: Methuen, 1977.
Plays: Two. (*Narrow Road to the Deep North, Lear, The Sea, Black Mass, Passion*). London: Methuen, 1978.
Plays: Three. (*Bingo, The Fool, The Woman*). London: Methuen, 1983.
Plays: Four. (*The Worlds, The Activist Papers, Restoration, Summer*). London: Methuen, 1992.
Note: For an extensive list of interviews, published nonfiction, translations and adaptations, and published fiction before 1984, see Hay and Roberts [2] and Roberts [1].

Interview

''Edward Bond: An Interview (with Hilde Klein). *Modern Drama* 38.3 (fall 1995): 408–15.

SECONDARY BIBLIOGRAPHY

Arnold, A. ''Lines of Development in Bond's Plays.'' *Theatre Quarterly* 5 (1972): 15–19.
Babula, William. ''Scene Thirteen of Bond's *Saved*.'' *Modern Drama* 15.2 (June 1972): 147–49.
Barnes, Clive. Review of *Saved*. *New York Times* (29 Oct. 1970).
Barth, Adolf K. H. ''The Aggressive 'Theatrum Mundi' of Edward Bond: *Narrow Road to the Deep North*.'' *Modern Drama* 18.2 (June 1975): 189–200.
Billington, Michael [1]. Review of *Bingo*. *The Guardian* (15 Aug. 1974).
———[2]. Review of *Restoration*. *The Guardian* (22 July 1981).
Brown, Christy L. ''Edward Bond's *Bingo*: Shakespeare and the Ideology of Genius.'' *Iowa State Journal of Research* 50.3 (Feb. 1986): 343–54.
Brown, T. *Playwrights' Theatre: The English Stage Company at the Royal Court*. London: Pitman, 1975.
Bryce, J. ''Rehearsing Optimism.'' *The Leveller* 60 (July 1981): 10–24.

Bryden, Ronald [1]. Review of *Bingo*. *New York Times* (25 Aug. 1974).

———[2]. Review of *Early Morning*. *The Observer* (14 April 1968).

Bulman, James C. [1]. "Bond, Shakespeare, and the Absurd." *Modern Drama* 29.1 (Mar. 1986): 60–70.

———[2]. "*The Woman* and Greek Myth: Bond's Theatre of History." *Modern Drama* 29.4 (Dec. 1986): 505–15.

Burghardt, Lori Hall. "Beyond Realism: The Role of Arthur in Edward Bond's *Early Morning*." *Notes on Contemporary Literature* 18.3 (May 1988): 10–12.

Callow, Simon. *Being an Actor*. London: Methuen, 1984.

Castillo, Debra A. "Dehumanized or Inhuman: Doubles in Edward Bond." *South Central Review* 3.2 (summer 1986): 78–89.

Cardullo, Bert. "Bond's *Saved*." *The Explicator* 44.3 (spring 1986): 62, 64.

Cawood, Mal. "Whistling in the Wilderness: Edward Bond's Most Recent Plays." *Red Letters: A Journal of Cultural Politics* 19 (May 1986): 11–23.

Cohn, Ruby. "The Fabulous Theatre of Edward Bond." In *Essays on Contemporary British Drama*, ed. Hedwig Bock and Albert Wortheim. Munster: Heuber, 1981: 185–204.

Cohn, Ruby. *Modern Shakespeare Offshoots*. Princeton, NJ: Princeton University Press, 1976.

Coult, Tony [1]. Review of *A-A-America*. *Plays and Players* (Feb. 1977).

———[2]. "Bringing Light Back to the Earth: Edward Bond's *The Woman*." *Canadian Theatre Review* 24 (1979): 96–104.

———[3]. *The Plays of Edward Bond*. London: Methuen, 1979.

Cushman, Robert. Review of *The Bundle*. *The Observer* (22 Jan. 1978).

Dark, Gregory. "Production Casebook, No. 5: Edward Bond's *Lear* at the Royal Court." *Theatre Quarterly* 5 (1972): 20–31.

Dawson, Helen. *Lear*. *The Observer* (9 Oct. 1971).

Des Roches, Kay Unruh. "*The Sea*: Anarchy as Order." *Modern Drama* 30.4 (Dec. 1987): 480–95.

Dewhurst, Keith. Review of *Passion*. *The Guardian* (13 Apr. 1971).

Dohmen, William F. " 'Wise Fools' and Their Disciples in the Development of Edward Bond's Drama." *Kansas Quarterly* 12.4 (1980): 53–61.

Donohue, Walter. "Edward Bond's *The Fool* at the Royal Court Theatre." *Theatre Quarterly* 21 (1976): 12–44.

Duncan, Joseph E. "The Child and the Old Man in the Plays of Edward Bond." *Modern Drama* 19.1 (Mar. 1976): 1–10.

Durbach, Errol. "Herod in the Welfare State: *Kindermord* in the Plays of Edward Bond." *Educational Theatre Journal* 27 (1975): 480–87.

Eagleton, Terry. "Nature and Violence: The Prefaces of Edward Bond." *Critical Quarterly* 26.1 and 2 (spring and summer 1984): 127–35.

Elsom, John. Review of *The Pope's Wedding*. *The Listener* (19 July 1962).

Esslin, Martin [1]. Review of *The Sea*. *Play and Players* (July 1973).

———[2]. "The Theatre of Edward Bond." *Times Educational Supplement* (24 Sept. 1971).

Fenton, James. Review of *Summer*. *Sunday Times* (31 Jan. 1982).

Figes, Eva. Review of *Summer*. *Times Literary Supplement* (5 Feb. 1982).

Findlater, Richard, ed. *At the Royal Court*. New York: Grove Press, 1981.

Fitzpatrick, Peter. "Bond's *Lear*: A Study in Conventions." In *Page to Stage: Theatre as Translation*, ed. Ortrun Zuberr-Skerritt. Amsterdam: Rodopi, 1984: 137–44.

Gems, Pam. Review of *Bingo*. *Plays and Players* (Sept. 1974).

Gilliatt, Penelope. Review of *Saved*. *The Observer* (7 Nov. 1965).

Hay, Malcolm, and Philip Roberts [1]. *Bond: A Study of His Plays*. London: Methuen, 1980.

———[2]. *Edward Bond/A Companion to the Plays*. London: TQ Publications, 1978.

———[3]. "Edward Bond: Stages in a Life." *The Observer Magazine* (6 Aug. 1978).

Hayman, Ronald. *British Theatre since 1955*. Oxford: Oxford University Press, 1979.

Hobson, Harold [1]. Review of *Bingo*. *Sunday Times* (18 Nov. 1973).

———[2]. Review of *Early Morning*. *Sunday Times* (16 Mar. 1969).

Holland, Peter [1]. "Brecht, Bond, Gaskill, and the Practice of Political Theatre." *Theatre Quarterly* 30 (1978): 24–34.

———[2]. Review of *Restoration*. *Times Literary Supplement* (7 Aug. 1981).

Hunt, Albert. "A Writer's Theatre." *New Society* (11 Dec. 1975).

Hughes, G.E.H. "Edward Bond's *Restoration*." *Critical Quarterly* 25.4 (winter 1983): 77–81.

Hur, Myung-so. "Tom Stoppard's *Rosencrantz and Guildenstern Are Dead* and Edward Bond's *Lear*: Modern 'Contaminations' of Shakespeare's *Hamlet* and *King Lear*." *Journal of English Language and Literature* (Seoul, Korea) 38.4 (winter 1992): 783–99.

Iden, Peter. *Edward Bond*. Velber: Friedrich, 1973.

Innes, Christopher. "The Political Spectrum of Edward Bond: From Rationalism to Rhapsody." *Modern Drama* 25.2 (June 1982): 189–206.

Itzen, Catherine. *Stages in the Revolution*. London: Methuen, 1980.

Jellicoe, Ann. "Royal Court Theatre Writers' Group." *Gambit* 68 (1976): 61–64.

Jones, D.A.N. "A Unique Style of Theatre." *Nova* (July 1969).

Jones, Daniel R. "Edward Bond's 'Rational Theatre.' " *Theatre Journal* 32 (1980): 505–17.

Kerensky, Oleg. *The New British Drama*. London: Hamish Hamilton, 1977.

Khan, Naseem. Review of *Stone*. *Evening Standard* (11 June 1976).

Kretzmer, Herbert. Review of *Saved*. *Daily Express* (4 Nov. 1965).

Kustow, Michael. Review of *Black Mass*. *The Listener* (23 Apr. 1970).

Lahr, John. Review of *The Fool*. *Plays and Players* (Jan. 1976).

Lappin, Lou [1]. *The Art and Politics of Edward Bond*. New York: Peter Lang, 1987.

———[2]. "The Artist in Society: Bond, Shakespeare, and *Bingo*." In *Before His Eyes: Essays in Honor of Stanley Kauffmann*, ed. Bert Cardullo. Lanham, MD: University Press of America, 1986: 57–70.

Levin, Bernard. Review of *The Pope's Wedding*. *Daily Mail* (10 Dec. 1962).

Marowitz, Charles. Review of *Lear*. *New York Times* (24 Oct. 1971).

Masters, Anthony. Review of *Lear*. *The Times* (20 May 1983).

Merchant, P. "The Theatre Poems and Bertolt Brecht, Edward Bond, and Howard Brenton." *Theatre Quarterly* 34 (1979): 49–51.

Review of *Narrow Road to the Deep North*. *Boston Globe* (3 Nov. 1969).

Nightingale, Benedict. Review of *The Fool*. *New Statesman* (28 Nov. 1965).

Nodelman, Perry. "Beyond Politics in Bond's *Lear*." *Modern Drama* 23.3 (Sept. 1980): 269–76.

Olivier, Lawrence. "Letter [*Saved*]." *The Observer* (28 Nov. 1965).

Oppel, H., and S. Christenson. *Edward Bond's Lear and Shakespeare's Lear*. Mainz: Akademie der Wissenschaften und der Literatur, 1974.

Parham, Sidney F. "Mythologizing Willie S.: *King Lear and Lear.*"In *To Hold a Mirror to Nature: Dramatic Images and Reflections*, ed. Karelisa V. Hartigan. Lanham, MD: University Press of America, 1982: 77–90.

Peter, John [1]. Review of *The Pope's Wedding. Sunday Times* (17 July 1962).

———[2]. Review of *The Woman. Sunday Times* (13 Aug. 1973).

Rademacher, Frances. "Violence and the Comic in the Plays of Edward Bond." *Modern Drama* 23.3 (Sept. 1980): 258–68.

Ratcliffe, Michael. Review of *Derek. The Observer* (22 Jan. 1984).

Roberts, Philip [1]. *Bond/Facts on File*. London: Methuen, 1985.

———[2]. "Edward Bond's *Summer*: 'A Voice from the Working Class.' " *Modern Drama* 26.2 (June 1983): 127–38.

———[3]. " 'Making the Two Words One'—the Plays of Edward Bond." *Critical Quarterly* 21.4 (1979): 80–88.

———[4]. "The Search for Epic Drama: Edward Bond's Recent Work." *Modern Drama* 24.4 (Dec. 1981): 458–78.

Robinson, Marc. "Breaking the Bond with Edward Bond." *Theater* 21.1–2 (winter-spring 1989–90): 23–28.

Savona, George. "Edward Bond's *The Woman.*" *Gambit* 36 (1980): 25–30.

Scharine, R. *The Plays of Edward Bond*. Lewisburg, PA: Bucknell University Press, 1976.

Sinfield, Alan. "Making Space: Appropriation and Confrontation in Recent British Plays." In *The Shakespearean Myth*. ed. Graham Holderness. Manchester: Manchester University Press, 1988: 128–44.

Smith, Leslie [1]. "Edward Bond's *Lear.*" *Comparative Drama* 13.1 (spring 1979): 65–85.

———[2]. "Edward Bond's Dramatic Strategies." In *Contemporary English Drama*, ed. C.W.E. Bigsby. London: Arnold, 1981.

———[3]. "Rewriting 'Classics': Edward Bond's *The Woman.*" *Modern Drama* 32.4 (Dec. 1989): 561–73.

Spencer, Jenny S. *Dramatic Strategies in the Plays of Edward Bond*. New York: Cambridge University Press, 1992.

Stuart, Ian. "Answering to the Dead: Edward Bond's *Jackets.*" *New Theatre Quarterly* 7.28 (May 1991): 171–83.

Taplin, Oliver. "What's Hecuba to Him?" *Times Literary Supplement* (18 Aug. 1978): 931.

Taylor, John Russell. *The Second Wave*. London: Methuen, 1971.

Tener, Robert L. "Edward Bond's Dialectic: Irony and Dramatic Metaphors." *Modern Drama* 25.4 (Dec. 1982): 423–34.

Trussler, Simon. *Edward Bond*. Harlow: Longmans, 1976.

Walker, John. Review of *The Sea. International Herald Tribune* (26 May 1973).

Wardle, Irving [1]. "The British Sixties." *Performance* (Dec. 1971): 174–81.

———[2]. Review of *Early Morning. The Times* (8 Apr. 1969).

———[3]. Review of *The Fool. The Times* (19 Nov. 1975).

———[4]. Review of *Lear. The Times* (30 Sept. 1971).

———[5]. Review of *Narrow Road to the Deep North. The Times* (20 Feb. 1969).

———[6]. Review of *Saved. The Times* (4 Nov. 1965).

———[7]. Review of *The Sea*. *The Times* (23 May 1973).

———[8]. Review of *The Woman*. *The Times* (11 Aug. 1978).

Worth, Katharine [1]. "Bond's *Restoration.*"*Modern Drama* 24.4 (Dec. 1981): 478–93.

———[2]. "Edward Bond," In *Essays on Contemporary British Drama*, ed. Hedwig Bock and Albert Wertheim. Munster: Hueber, 1981: 205–22.

———[3]. *Revolutions in Modern English Drama*. London: Bell, 1972.

Worthen, J. "Endings and Beginnings: Edward Bond and the Shock of Recognition." *Educational Theatre Journal* 27.4 (1975): 466–79.

von Ledebur, Ruth. "The Adaptation and Reception in Germany of Edward Bond's *Saved.*" In *The Play out of Context: Transferring Plays from Culture to Culture,* ed. Peter Holland. New York: Cambridge University Press, 1989: 199–213.

Zapf, Hubert. "Two Concepts of Society in Drama: Bertolt Brecht's *The Good Woman of Setzuan* and Edward Bond's *Lear.*" *Modern Drama* 31.3 (Sept. 1988), 352–64.

BIBLIOGRAPHY

King, Kimball. "Edward Bond." *Twenty Modern British Playwrights: A Bibliography, 1956 to 1976*. New York: Garland, 1977: 43–54.

Howard Brenton

(1942–)

JOHN E. O'CONNOR

Howard Brenton began writing for the theatre in 1965. In the three decades that have elapsed since then, he has produced a body of work that, even if it were not critically and historically significant, would be impressive simply because of its size. Brenton has written over fifty pieces for theatre and television, as well as a novel and two small volumes of poetry. He has adapted two works by Bertolt Brecht and one by Georg Büchner and has collaborated with other playwrights on eleven plays.

The stage plays range in size from short one-acts with small casts to large, sprawling works with many characters. The technical requirements may be as little as a bare playing space with no special lighting effects or props to large stages with every available theatrical resource exploited for dramatic effect. The stories told through these plays can be as simple as the portrayal of a man's search for faith, as in *Wesley*; or as complex as the depiction of Roman, Norman, and English imperialism seen in *The Romans in Britain*. Brenton is a socialist who writes to illustrate and support socialist ideology, but his plays are not about "the worker" and proletarian revolution. Instead, Brenton concerns himself with values and the nature of relationships between individuals and their society. All his work shares a common impulse, which he says is "trying to write truthfully about the society I'm in and trying to intervene to help the good in it and discourage the bad" ("Howard Brenton: *An Introduction and Interview*").

Howard Brenton was born in Portsmouth, England, in 1942. His mother was a shop worker and his father a policeman. When he was in his early teens the family moved to Yorkshire, where his father, having quit the police force to become a Methodist minister, had his first post. His father had a strong effect on Brenton's development as a playwright. Images of policemen abound in

Brenton's early plays, and he wrote *Wesley* as a kind of tribute to the working-class people of his father's congregations. His father was also active as a director in amateur theatre groups.

Brenton taught for a short time in secondary schools before entering St. Catherine's College, Cambridge, in 1962. He hated the university, particularly the insulated focus of the teaching of literature, which he felt had no connection with reality. He developed a decidedly anti-cultural bent and was soon spending more time acting and writing than attending classes. He left Cambridge in 1965 with a third-class degree and spent a few years working at odd jobs, including factory and kitchen work, to help support his writing. The combination of his experiences at Cambridge and his direct contact with working-class lifestyles and values affected his early works. Brenton's disdain for established culture, for example, can be seen in *The Education of Skinny Spew*; and *Weapons of Happiness* reflects his experiences in the factory.

While at Cambridge Brenton wrote four plays: *Ladder of Fools*, *Winter, Daddykins*, and *It's My Criminal*. The latter was produced at the Royal Court Theatre Upstairs in 1966. His work brought him to the attention of the Court's artistic director, William Gaskill, who helped Brenton find jobs both at the Court and in provincial theatre companies.

While working in the provinces Brenton joined forces with the Brighton Combination, a community theatre group devoted to producing new works for mixed audiences of students, professionals, the working class, and the unemployed. There he met Chris Parr, who subsequently joined the theatre faculty at the University of Bradford. Parr invited Brenton to work with his student actors in collaborative efforts. The outcome of his work with the Brighton Combination and the University of Bradford was three plays, all produced in 1969: *Gum and Goo*, *Heads*, and *The Education of Skinny Spew*.

Brenton spent the remainder of 1969 and 1970–1973 working with Parr at Bradford and with London fringe theatre groups. *Revenge* was produced at the Royal Court Theatre Upstairs and *Christie in Love* at the Oval House, London, both in 1969. The latter marks the beginning of Brenton's association with David Hare and the Portable Theatre. He worked with Bradford in 1970 on *Wesley*, written specifically to be produced in a Methodist church; and on *Scott of the Antarctic*, written to be performed in an indoor ice-skating arena. He returned to the Royal Court later in 1970 for *Fruit*. The Open Space Theatre, London, produced *A Sky Blue Life* in 1971 and *How Beautiful with Badges* in 1972. *Measure for Measure*, a contemporary adaptation of Shakespeare's play, was produced at the Nottingham Playhouse in 1972. Brenton served as the resident dramatist at the Royal Court for the 1972–1973 season. He also continued to experiment with the collaborative techniques he had utilized with Parr at Brighton and Bradford, working with Max Stafford-Clark and the Traverse Theatre Club, Edinburgh, to produce *Hitler Dances* in 1972. He also collaborated with fringe playwrights on a number of works: *Lay By* (1971), *England's Ireland* (1972), and *A Fart for Europe* (1973).

The year 1973 is significant in Brenton's career. Early in that year he worked with David Hare on *Brassneck*, produced at the Nottingham Playhouse. The play was the first of two significant collaborations with Hare. Brenton's growing reputation resulted in a commission from Max Stafford-Clark at the Royal Court Theatre. *Magnificence* was the first play written by a fringe playwright to be produced in the Royal Court's main theatre; it opened on 28 June 1973. The production is a landmark both in Brenton's career and in his development as a playwright, for it reflects his growing political sophistication and commitment to socialism; and it marks his break with the fringe theatres and his entry into the subsidized theatre establishment. The success of the production led to a commission from the Nottingham Playhouse in 1974 for a play to mark the centenary of Winston Churchill's birth. Brenton responded with *The Churchill Play*, which was successfully revived by the Royal Shakespeare Company in 1978 and 1988. The National Theatre gave him a commission in 1976, which Brenton filled with *Weapons of Happiness*, the first play to be produced in the National's new Lyttleton Auditorium and the winner of the *Evening Standard* Award for best play of 1976.

Brenton returned briefly to the fringe in 1977–1978, working with Foco Novo on *Epsom Downs* and in collaboration with Trevor Griffiths, Ken Campbell, and David Hare on *Deeds*. In 1979 he wrote the first of three "Utopia" plays, *Sore Throats*, which was produced by the Royal Shakespeare Company at their London venue, the Warehouse. The play was revived by the Royal Court in 1988 as a part of their "Three Plays for Utopia" season. He returned to the National Theatre in 1980 with an adaptation of Brecht's *The Life of Galileo* and the controversial *The Romans in Britain*. His adaptation of Büchner's *Danton's Death* was produced by the National in 1982. In addition to his work for the stage, Brenton also found time during the summer of 1982 to visit Beirut on behalf of the Bertrand Russell Peace Foundation to report on conditions there.

Brenton did not diminish his prolific output in the 1980s and early 1990s. He continued to experiment with collaborative writing: working with Tony Howard on *A Short Sharp Shock!* (1980); with Tunde Ikoli on *Sleeping Policemen* (1983); with David Hare on *Pravda*, produced by the National Theatre in 1985 and winner of both the London *Evening Standard* and City Limits Awards for best play; and with Tariq Ali on *Iranian Nights* (1989), a response to the controversy surrounding Salman Rushdie's *Satanic Verses*, and *Moscow Gold* (1990). Brenton returned to the Royal Shakespeare Company in 1981 with *Thirteenth Night* and in 1989 with *H.I.D. (Hess Is Dead)*. He renewed his relationship with Foco Novo in 1984 with *Bloody Poetry*, revived at the Royal Court in 1988 as a part of their "Utopia" season, and continued his work with the Royal Court with *The Genius* (1983), *Greenland* (1988), and *Berlin Bertie* (1992). During the 1980s Brenton also produced two major television scripts, *Desert of Lies* and *Dead Head*, and the novel *Diving for Pearls*.

Howard Brenton continues to work in London. Current projects include a second novel, a film version of *Diving for Pearls*, and the publication of his selected essays and diaries. His creative drive and passion for theatre show no signs of abating.

Selected Biographical Sources: "Caesar on the South Bank: An Interview with Howard Brenton"; "Disrupting the Spectacle: An Interview with Howard Brenton"; "Howard Brenton: An Introduction and Interview"; "The Man Behind the Lyttleton's First New Play: An Interview with Howard Brenton"; "Messages First: An Interview with Howard Brenton"; "Petrol Bombs through the Proscenium Arch: An Interview with Howard Brenton."

MAJOR PLAYS, PREMIERES, AND SIGNIFICANT REVIVALS: THEATRICAL RECEPTION

Magnificence. 1973. Opened 28 June at the Royal Court Theatre. Directed by Max Stafford-Clark.

The play marks Brenton's break with the fringe and his move into the establishment theatre. Brenton consciously used the tradition of kitchen sink realism, which the Court audience had come to expect, setting Act One in a grittily realistic abandoned tenement apartment. Brenton himself heard an audience member during intermission say, "Oh! It's another, Jimmy Porter, isn't it? . . . a sordid room" (Roberts [2]). Brenton reversed audience expectations by shifting stylistic gears and setting the remainder of the play on a bare stage. The mixture of styles confounded most critics. Hammond saw the play as a reflection of vaguely formed political beliefs and was confused by its stylistic incoherence. Some critics did appreciate the fresh political point of view and the play's theatricality. Bull would later see the play as "a hard-won rediscovery of the politics rejected by his [Brenton's] early works." The mixture of enthusiastic praise and vituperous criticism engendered by the production is typical of the critical response to the majority of Brenton's mature work.

The Churchill Play. 1974. Opened 8 May at the Nottingham Playhouse. Directed by Richard Eyre. Revised and revived: Royal Shakespeare Company, August 1978 and November 1988.

The play is both a doomsday vision of a fascist England of the future and a demythologizing of Winston Churchill. Some critics found Brenton's vision both paranoid and offensive (see Boon [1]). Billington's [5] review of the 1978 revival took the play to task for its "slightly alarmist" vision while grudgingly acknowledging Brenton as "a major talent." Hobson [2] found both "great aesthetic and intellectual power" in the production. Billington's attitude toward Brenton is not uncommon. Many critics appreciate his theatricality and the strength of his writing but cannot abide his politics. Sir Peter Hall, artistic director of the National Theatre, wrote in his diary after reading the play, "It is quite magnificent." Hall compares Brenton favorably with Samuel Beckett, John Osborne, and Harold Pinter.

Weapons of Happiness. 1976. Opened 14 July in the Lyttleton Auditorium of the National Theatre, London. Directed by David Hare.

Sir Peter Hall commissioned the play partly as a result of his positive response to *The Churchill Play*. The play investigates British socialism from the wider historical perspective of European socialism. Critics appreciated both the intellectual content and the theatricality of the piece. Coveney wrote of the play's "highly charged scenes"; Hobson [3] said, "This is indeed a relevant play" and called it "a great success." The play won the *Evening Standard* Award for best play of 1976.

Sore Throats. 1979. Opened 8 August at the Warehouse. Produced by the Royal Shakespeare Company. Directed by Barry Kyle. Revived: Royal Court Theatre, May 1988. American premiere: The Repertory Theatre of St. Louis, April 1983.

Subtitled "An Intimate Play in Two Acts," the play represents a departure from Brenton's exploration of history and society in the epic mode. It is the first of his three Utopia plays. Barber appreciated the change from Brenton's "usual violent political radicalism." Billington [10] did not react favorably, referring to the play as "a nasty, jagged-edged mirror" of nature. Kauffmann was effusive in his praise, calling the play "the strongest play about sex and marriage since Pinter's *Old Times*" and "a drama of exquisite compassion."

The Romans in Britain. 1980. Opened 16 October in the Olivier Theatre of the National Theatre, London. Directed by Michael Bogdanov.

The play is an indictment of imperialism, an epic of vast proportions that tells the story of the Roman and Norman conquests of Britain within the context of the English occupation of Ireland. The play generated an incredible controversy, owing to the graphic depiction in act 1, scene 3, of the rape and sodomy of a young Druid by a Roman soldier. The director was taken to court for "procuring an act of gross indecency" and the Greater London Council cut its subsidy to the National Theatre. The critical response to the production focused primarily on the presentation of Brenton's ideas, rather than on the ideas themselves or on how the presentation related to the ideas. Most critics dismissed the play as pornographic self-indulgence (see Roberts [1]). Billington [9] found "a vast disproportion between the extravagance of the form and the banality of the thesis." Very few critics could agree with Levin's [1] assessment that "*The Romans in Britain* is a very good play indeed." Later criticism has been more positive. Boon [1] cites the fact that many regard the play as Brenton's masterpiece and says that it is "a scandal" that it has received only one professional production.

Thirteenth Night. 1981. Opened 2 July at the Warehouse, London. Produced by the Royal Shakespeare Company. Directed by Barry Kyle.

After *The Romans in Britain* Brenton abandoned his exploration of political and social themes in an epic mode and began writing smaller plays that focus on the consequences of political action on individuals and their personal relationships. In *Thirteenth Night* he examines the fragmented state of the Labour party in the early 1980s, using *Macbeth* as a springboard. Boon [1] makes it clear that most critics were too wrapped up in the "game" of finding all the allusions to Shakespeare to be able to comment on the contemporary political issues in the play. Billington [3] was one of a few critics who appreciated the play, calling it "a sharp flinty piece of theatre."

The Genius. 1983. Opened 8 September at the Royal Court Theatre. Directed by Danny Boyle.

The impulse for this play about an American physicist's attempt to come to terms with the ethical and moral implications of his work came from Brenton's work on translating Brecht's *The Life of Galileo* for the National Theatre in 1980. Most critics agreed with Billington [6] that the piece lacked dramatic action, contained mouthpieces rather than characters, and was overcome by its passionate rhetoric. Boon [1] says that in spite of its flaws, "it is a rich and rewarding piece."

Bloody Poetry. 1984. Opened 1 October at the Haymarket Theatre, London. Produced by Foco Novo. Directed by Roland Rees. Revised and revived: Royal Court Theatre, May 1988. American Premiere: Manhattan Theatre Club (NY), January 1987.

The play takes its name from the life and writing of Percy Bysshe Shelley, whose work Brenton genuinely admires. The play is the second in the Utopia trilogy and is about the various sexual and emotional entanglements between Shelley, Lord Byron, Mary Shelley, and Claire Clairemont. Brenton uses their story to explore the relationships between art, revolution, and life. Most critics were not impressed with the play and were confused by the deliberate anachronisms Brenton employs to bring his characters and their ideas into the twentieth century (see Boon [1]). Some critics (including Billington [2] and Wardle [1]) did appreciate the play's bold theatricality and Brenton's honesty in trying to come to grips with his own role as an artist and socialist.

Greenland. 1988. Opened 26 May at the Royal Court Theatre, London. Directed by Simon Curtis.

The third of Brenton's Utopia plays, its setting moves from London in 1987 to a place called Greenland, 700 years in the future. *Greenland* is Brenton's attempt to portray what a Utopia might be like. Most critics were unimpressed, citing such problems as overblown emotions, ill-defined characters, and lack of dramatic conflict (see Boon [1]).

Berlin Bertie. 1992. Opened 9 April at the Royal Court Theatre, London. Directed by Danny Boyle.

In this play Brenton returns to the squalid interior he introduced to the Court audience in *Magnificence*, twenty years earlier. The play is about two sisters, one from London, the other from East Berlin, who attempt to put their lives in order after various psychological and emotionally traumatic experiences. The critics greeted the play with a lukewarm response. Everett felt that the play overheated onstage and that the dramatic action was not able to sustain the high pitch of the characters. He wrote that the actors "—uncomfortably—[were] people with problems and mouthpieces for problems."

ASSESSMENT OF BRENTON'S CAREER

Since he began writing for the theatre in 1965, Brenton's basic vision of the world has not changed: the Western world is controlled by a system that respects only money and power. His methods of presenting this vision and his responses to it have changed over the course of his career. His plays explore British society from many angles, historical, political, and social. He has experimented with a number of stylistic approaches, from naturalism to expressionism to surrealism. His characters include law enforcement officials and criminals, peers of the realm and illiterate factory workers, nineteenth-century poets and twenty-seventh-century artisans, and refugees from political as well as personal turmoil. Regardless of their differences in theme, style, or character, the plays all have one common impulse, a passionate commitment to the truth.

Brenton has been on a journey of discovery and exploration for the past thirty years. His plays reflect that journey. The early plays, written for fringe venues with limited means, are small and agitational. They explore the moral, social, and political decay of post–World War II England. Their themes include public corruption, a restrictive educational system, the nature of violence, sexual politics, the process of mythologizing history, and political terrorism. Most of the early plays are violent, morally ambivalent, and politically unsophisticated. They simply present the world as Brenton sees it and offer very little in the way of a solution.

With *Magnificence* Brenton came to believe that larger, epic plays written for establishment theatres were the best means for him to explore the ways in which a society in need of change might be changed. The plays of this stage in his career offer an investigation of the nature of revolution, both for himself and his audience. Brenton's purpose in these epic works is not to convert but simply to agitate, to strike out against complacency, acceptance, and decay. He analyzes problems he sees as inherent in capitalist society and explores traditions and myths. The plays have large casts, many scenes, and action moving freely among the past, present, and future. They combine tragic and comic elements and are seemingly incoherent stylistically.

Sore Throats marks the beginning of a new phase in Brenton's career in which he abandons the epic mode for a return to the simplicity of his fringe roots. The impulse for this shift is twofold: the changing economic conditions of the subsidized theatres, which mitigated against the production of large, potentially unpopular works; and Brenton's desire to explore the personal implications of revolutionary activity. His characters move from the public stage of world history to the private stages of the living room, patio and office. They no longer confront their historical, political, or social destiny but face, instead, their personal destiny in their relationships with spouses, relatives, lovers, and friends. They reflect Brenton's belief that social change must be preceded by personal reflection and growth, as well as by an understanding of our responsibility for ourselves and others.

The Utopia plays and *Berlin Bertie* explore the nature of the new society that might be formulated when personal change precedes political change. Their purpose is to show the world as it could be. They do not provide pat answers; in fact, they raise many questions that are unresolved. They do mark a departure for Brenton in that they move away from the bleak vision of a society impelled by money and power and toward a glimpse of humanity that is positive and hopeful.

The ambiguity in Brenton's work has confounded critics. They see no order in plot development and no consistency in characters. They decry the violence and the often obvious imagery and symbolism. Brenton himself acknowledges the critics' confusion in his introduction to *Plays: One*. He admits that right-wing critics find his plays "preachy," whereas left-wing critics conclude they are "not preachy enough."

Although most critics have taken him to task for the thematic content of his plays, they are consistent in their praise of Brenton's use of theatrical images, which are capable of condensing entire arguments into a single action or moment. His talent is evident even in the early plays. There is Skinny's birth in *The Education of Skinny Spew*, portrayed as a tug-o-war between two actors playing a doctor and a mother. The actor portraying Christie in *Christie in Love* rises like a ghoul out of a pile of crumpled newspapers in eerie lighting, combining images of tabloid news stories and the chills of a horror movie.

When he began writing for larger venues, Brenton continued to use all the resources at hand to forge striking and memorable moments. He creates the spectacle of a planetarium tour of the solar system in *Weapons of Happiness*; and *The Churchill Play* ends with the camp literally breaking into the audience with floodlights, sirens, and loudspeakers. Even the more personal plays are not without their moments of striking imagery: *Bloody Poetry* contains the brilliant shadow play; and *Greenland* ends with the image of a jewel shattering a single beam of light that splinters out into the audience.

Many of the images Brenton presents are extremely difficult to confront. There is the rape of the Druid in *The Romans in Britain* and the beating Judy endures in *Sore Throats*. Brenton forces these images on his audience because violence is a part of human nature that should not be ignored. He compels his audience to sink into the mire of life and feel its weight. The violence is never gratuitous. The Druid's rape is juxtaposed with the soldiers' flippant attitudes toward his suffering. Judy grows during the course of *Sore Throats*, and at the end of the play she hits Jack.

Many critics and audience members are offended by Brenton's work, saying it is too violent, too simplistic, too complex, or too naive. The real difficulty with his work is that it is all of these: violent, simplistic, complex, naive, sophisticated, and more. He seeks to portray truth on the stage, and truth is neither easy to define nor universally accepted. Brenton himself understands the polarization his work engenders in critics and is resigned to it, as he explained in a 1979 interview: "The message of a play that is true is very likely to be widely known, hated, ridiculed, but known" ("Howard Brenton: An Introduction and Interview").

Brenton's work has been consistently challenging and, in many cases, controversial. He has had a significant impact on the development of contemporary British theatre. His influence will continue to be felt for many years to come. The publication of his selected essays and diaries promises to provide additional insights into his writing and politics.

PRIMARY BIBLIOGRAPHY

Plays

Berlin Bertie. London: Nick Hern Books, 1992.
Bloody Poetry. London: Methuen, 1985.
The Churchill Play. London: Methuen, 1974.
Epsom Downs. London: Methuen, 1977.
The Genius. London: Methuen, 1983.
Greenland. London: Methuen, 1988.
H.I.D. (Hess is Dead). London: Nick Hern Books, 1989.
Hitler Dances. London: Methuen, 1982.
Magnificence. London: Methuen, 1973.
Revenge. London: Methuen, 1970.
The Romans in Britain. London: Methuen, 1980.
Thirteenth Night. London: Methuen, 1981.
Weapons of Happiness. London: Methuen, 1976.

Anthologies

Plays for the Poor Theatre. (*The Saliva Milkshake, Christie in Love, Gum and Goo, Heads, The Education of Skinny Spew*). London: Methuen, 1980.
Plays for Public Places. (*Gum and Goo, Wesley, Scott of the Antartic*). London: Methuen, 1972.
Plays: One. (*Christie in Love, Magnificence, The Churchill Play, Weapons of Happiness, Epsom Downs, Sore Throats*). London: Methuen, 1986.
Plays: Two. (*The Romans in Britain, Thirteenth Night, The Genius, Bloody Poetry, Greenland*). London: Methuen, 1989.
Three Plays. (*A Sky Blue Life, How Beautiful with Badges, Measure for Measure*). Sheffield: Sheffield Academic Press, 1989.

Collaborations

A Short Sharp Shock! (with Tony Howard). London: Methuen, 1981.
Brassneck (with David Hare) London: Methuen, 1974.
Deeds (with Trevor Griffiths et al.). In *Plays and Players* 25 (May 1978): 41–50; (June 1978): 43–50.
Iranian Nights (with Tariq Ali). London: Nick Hern Books, 1989.
Lay By (with David Hare et al). London: Calder & Boyars, 1972.
Moscow Gold (with Tariq Ali). London: Nick Hern Books, 1990.
Pravda: A Fleet Street Comedy (With David Hare). London: Methuen, 1985.
Sleeping Policemen (with Tunde Ikoli). London: Methuen, 1984.

Adaptations and Translations

Brecht, Bertolt. *Conversations in Exile.* Adapted from a translation by David Dollenmayer. *Theater* 17 (spring 1986): 8–18.
———. *The Life of Galileo.* London: Methuen, 1980.
Büchner, Georg. *Danton's Death.* London: Methuen, 1982.

Interviews

"Caesar on the South Bank: An Interview with Howard Brenton" (with Philip Oakes). *The Times,* (12 Oct. 1980): 39.
"Disrupting the Spectacle: An Interview with Howard Brenton" (with Peter Ansorge). *Plays and Players* 20 (July 1973): 22–23.
"History on Cue and a Massage for Gorbachev" (with Michael Coveney). *The Observer* (23 Sept. 1990).
"Howard Brenton: An Introduction and Interview" (with Malcolm Hay and Philip Roberts). *Performing Arts Journal* 3 (winter 1979): 132–41.
"Interview with Howard Brenton" (with Ronald Hayman). *The New Review* 3 (Aug. 1976): 56–58.
"Interview with Howard Brenton" (with Hugh Herbert). *The Guardian* (9 May 1974): 10.
"The Man behind the Lyttleton's First New Play: An Interview with Howard Brenton" (with Morley Sheridan). *The Times* (10 July 1976): 9.
"Messages First: An Interview with Howard Brenton" (with Jonathan Hammond). *Gambit* 6.23 (1973): 24–32.
"Petrol Bombs through the Proscenium Arch: An Interview with Howard Brenton" (with Catherine Itzin and Simon Trussler). *Theatre Quarterly* 5 (spring 1975): 4–20.
"The Red Theatre under the Bed: Interview with Howard Brenton" (with Tony Mitchell). *New Theatre Quarterly* 3 (Nov. 1987): 195–201.
"Still Slogging the Road to Utopia: An Interview with Howard Brenton" (with Hugh Herbert). *The Guardian* (9 Sept. 1983): 9.

Essays

Hot Irons. London: Nick Hern Books, 1995

SECONDARY BIBLIOGRAPHY

Ansorge, Peter. *Disrupting the Spectacle*. London: Pitman, 1975.

Auslander, Philip. "Toward a Concept of the Political in Postmodern Theatre." *Theatre Journal* 34 (Mar. 1987): 20–34.

Barber, John. "Rancid Story of a Failing Marriage." *Daily Telegraph* (29 Aug. 1979).

Beacham, Richard. "Brenton Invades Britain: *The Romans in Britain* Controversy." *Theater* 22 (spring 1981): 34–37.

Bigsby, C.W.E. [1]. "The Language of Crisis in English Theatre: The Drama of Cultural Pathology." In *Contemporary English Drama*, ed. C.W.E. Bigsby. London: Edward Arnold, 1981: 10–51.

———[2]. "The Politics of Anxiety: Contemporary Socialist Theatre in England." *Modern Drama* 34 (Dec. 1981): 393–403.

Billington, Michael [1]. "All Hell before the Heaven." *The Guardian* (27 Apr. 1988).

———[2]. "Blood Lines." *The Guardian* (14 Apr. 1988).

———[3]. "Brenton's Scary Monster State." *The Guardian* (3 July 1981).

———[4]. Review of *Christie in Love*. *Plays and Players* 17 (June 1970): 48.

———[5]. Review of *The Churchill Play*. *The Guardian* (22 Aug. 1978).

———[6]. Review of *The Genius*. *The Guardian* (14 Sept. 1983).

———[7]. Review of *Heads* and *The Education of Skinny Spew*. *Plays and Players* 17 (Apr. 1970): 51.

———[8]. "Paradise Lost." *The Guardian* (3 June 1988).

———[9]. Review of *The Romans in Britain*. *The Guardian* (17 Oct. 1980).

———[10]. Review of *Sore Throats*. *The Guardian* (29 Aug. 1979).

Bond, Edward. "The Romans and the Establishment's Fig Leaf." *Theater* 12 (spring 1981): 39–42.

Boon, Richard [1]. *Brenton: The Playwright*. London: Methuen, 1991.

———[2]. "Politics and Terror in the Plays of Howard Brenton." In *Terrorism and Modern Drama*, ed. Dragan Klaic and John Orr. Edinburgh: Edinburgh University Press, 1990.

———[3]. "Retreating to the Future: Brenton in the Eighties." *Modern Drama* 33 (Mar. 1990): 30–41.

———[4]. "Setting up the Scaffolding: Howard Brenton's *Hitler Dances*." *New Theatre Quarterly* 9 (Nov. 1988): 335–43.

———[5]. "Writers with Dirty Hands: Howard Brenton's *A Sky Blue Life: Scenes after Maxim Gorky*." *Modern Drama* 32 (June 1989): 183–91.

Boon, Richard, and Mangan, Mick. "Howard Brenton's *Hitler Dances* in Production." *Studies in Theatre Production* 1 (Jan. 1990): 23–43.

Brown, Mick. "Still Angry after All These Years." *Elle* (Dec. 1988): 40–45.

Bull, John. *New British Political Dramatists*. London: Macmillan, 1984.

Cameron, Ben. "Howard Brenton: The Privilege of Revolt." *Theater* 12 (spring 1981): 28–33.

Caplan, Betty. "Imagining No Possessions." *New Statesman and Society* (10 June 1988): 47.

Caulfield, Carl. "What the Bomb Does to Our Minds: Sewell's *Welcome the Bright World* and Brenton's *The Genius*." *Australasian Drama Studies* 14 (Apr. 1989): 19–32.

Caute, David. "*Iranian Nights.*" *New Statesman and Society* (28 Apr. 1989): 14–16.

Cave, Richard Allen. *New British Drama in Performance on the London Stage.* Gerrards Cross: Colin Smythe, 1987.

Chaillet, Ned. Review of *Epsom Downs.* *Plays and Players* 25 (Oct. 1977): 23.

Coveney, Michael. Review of *Sore Throats.* *Financial Times* (27 Apr. 1988).

Cushman, Robert [1]. Review of *The Genius.* *The Observer* (18 Sept. 1983).

———[2]. Review of *The Romans in Britain.* *The Observer* (19 Oct. 1980).

Dahl, Mary Karen. *Political Violence in Drama.* Ann Arbor, MI: UMI Research Press, 1987.

Davie, Michael. "Urban Ire." *Times Literary Supplement* (17 May 1985).

Dunn, Tony [1]. "The Play of Politics." *Drama* (summer 1985): 13–15.

———[2]. "The Truth about Truth." *Plays and Players* (June 1985): 18–20.

Edgar, David. "Ten Years of Political Theatre, 1968–1978." *Theatre Quarterly* 7 (winter 1979): 25–33.

Elsom, John [1]. "Commitment as a Form of Privilege." *Contemporary Review* (Aug. 1986): 83–88.

———[2]. *Post-war British Theatre.* London: Routledge & Kegan Paul, 1976.

———[3]. "The Well-Intentioned Subsidy: Theatre against Itself." *Encounter* 58 (May 1982): 70–75.

Everett, Barbara. Review of *Berlin Bertie.* *Times Literary Supplement* (24 Apr. 1992).

Fenton, James. Review of *The Romans in Britain.* *Sunday Times* (19 Oct.1980).

Gore-Langron, Robert. "Going for Glasnost Gold." *The Guardian* (8–9 Sept. 1990).

Hall, Peter. *Peter Hall's Diaries: The Story of a Dramatic Battle.* Ed. John Goodwin. London: Hamish Hamilton, 1983.

Hammond, Jonathan. Review of *Magnificence.* *Plays and Players* (July 1973).

Hayman, Ronald. *British Theatre since 1955: A Reassessment.* Oxford: Oxford University Press, 1976.

Hewison, Robert. "Mid-life Crisis for the Children of the Revolution." *Sunday Times* (17 Apr.1988).

Hiley, Jim. *Theatre at Work: The Story of the National Theatre's Production of Brecht's GALILEO.* London: Routledge & Kegan Paul, 1981.

Hobson, Harold [1]. "Bold as Brass." *Sunday Times* (23 Sept. 1973).

———[2]. Review of *The Churchill Play.* *Sunday Times* (2 June 1974).

———[3]. *Theatre in Britain.* Oxford: Phaidon Press, 1984.

Hunt, Albert [1]. "Avoiding Making Drama out of a Crisis." *New Statesman and Society* (1 July 1988): 45–46.

———[2]. "Theatre of Violence." *New Society* (Nov. 1976): 261–62.

Itzin, Catherine. *Stages in the Revolution.* London: Methuen, 1980.

Kauffmann, Stanley. "Small Scale, Large Scope." *Saturday Review* (July-Aug. 1983): 18–20.

Kennedy, Douglas. "Two Britains." *New Statesman and Society* (14 Oct. 1988): 36–37.

Kerensky, Oleg. *The New British Drama.* New York: Taplinger, 1977.

Kidd, Timothy. "Between Revolt and Rancour." *Encounter* (Jan. 1988): 62–68.

Levin, Bernard [1]. "Conquered by the Romans." *The Times* (11 Mar. 1981).

———[2]. "The Truth about This Play." *The Times* (29 Oct. 1985).

Marowitz, Charles. Review of *Weapons of Happiness.* *Plays and Players* (Sept. 1976): 18–19.

Merchant, Paul. "The Theatre Poems of Bertolt Brecht, Edward Bond, and Howard Brenton." *Theatre Quarterly* 9.34 (1979): 49–51.

Murray, Oswyn. Review of *The Romans in Britain*. *Times Literary Supplement* (24 Oct. 1980).

Nightingale, Benedict [1]. "Fair Partisans." *New Statesman* (6 Oct. 1972): 484–85.

———[2]. "Jed-Propelled." *New Statesman* (6 July 1973): 27.

Oliver, Cordelia. Review of *Hitler Dances*. *Plays and Players* (Mar. 1972): 53.

O'Connor, John E. *Revolution and the Society of the Spectacle: A Critical Analysis of Selected Plays by Howard Brenton*. Ann Arbor, MI: University Microfilms, 1989.

Peacock, Keith D. "Chronicles of Wasted Time." In *Historical Drama*. ed. James Redmond. Cambridge: Cambridge University Press, 1986: 195–212.

Peake, Catherine. Review of *Sore Throats*. *Theatre Australia* (Apr. 1980): 52.

Peter, John. "Finding a Language for Utopia." *Sunday Times* (5 June 1988).

Rabey, David Ian. *British and Irish Political Drama in the Twentieth Century*. London: Macmillan, 1986.

Ratcliffe, Michael. "Press Gangs." *Drama* (autumn 1985): 32–33.

Reinelt, Janelle. "Bertolt Brecht and Howard Brenton: The Common Task." *Pacific Coast Philology* 20 (Nov. 1985): 46–52.

Roberts, Philip [1]. "Howard Brenton's Romans." *Critical Quarterly* 23 (autumn 1981): 5–23.

———[2]. *The Royal Court Theatre: 1965–1972*. London: Routledge & Kegan Paul, 1986.

Soto-Morettini, Donna. "Disrupting the Spectacle: Brenton's *Magnificence*." *Theatre Journal* 38 (Mar. 1986): 82–95.

Taylor, John Russell [1]. "British Dramatists: The New Arrivals." *Plays and Players* (Feb. 1971): 24–27; (Mar. 1971): 16–18.

———[2]. *The Second Wave: British Drama for the Seventies*. London: Methuen, 1970.

Taylor, Paul. "A Winnie of Despair." *The Independent* (2 Dec. 1988).

Thornber, Robin. Review of *Bloody Poetry*. *The Guardian* (9 Oct. 1984).

Treglown, Jeremy. "Cambridgeshire Drippers." *Times Literary Supplement* (10 July 1981).

Veitch, Andrew. "How a Bitch Was Ditched in the Name of Satire." *The Guardian* (20 June 1980).

Wardle, Irving [1]. "Life with the Lions." *The Times* (15 Apr. 1988).

———[2]. "The Pink and Promised Land." *The Times* (2 June 1988).

———[3]. Review of *Sore Throats*. *The Times* (27 Apr. 1988).

Weiner, Bernard. "*The Romans in Britain* Controversy." *Drama Review* 25.1 (1981): 57–68.

Wilcher, Robert. "*Pravda*: A Morality Play for the 1980s." *Modern Drama* 33 (Mar. 1990): 42–56.

Wu, Duncan [1]. "In Search of Utopia." *Times Literary Supplement* (17–23 June 1988).

———[2]. "Realistic Revolutions." *Times Literary Supplement* (22–28 Apr. 1988).

Zelenak, Michael X. "The Politics of History: Howard Brenton's Adaptations." *Theater* 18 (winter 1988): 52–55.

BIBLIOGRAPHIES

Mitchell, Tony [1]. "Theatre Checklist No. 5: Howard Brenton." *Theatrefacts* 2.1 (1975): 2–9.

———[2]. *File on Brenton*. London: Methuen, 1988.

Caryl Churchill

(1938–)

AMELIA HOWE KRITZER

Caryl Churchill emerged in the 1980s as one of the most important British dramatists of the late twentieth century. Her plays focus on social criticism and philosophical questioning while rejecting the realism associated with the problem play tradition in favor of theatrical inventiveness and subversive comedy. Churchill is best known for works focusing on gender issues, but recent plays address a broad range of contemporary political topics.

Churchill was born in London 3 September 1938, and grew up in London and Montreal, Quebec. She completed a degree in English literature at Oxford University in 1960. Becoming involved in theatre at Oxford, Churchill had three plays produced while she was a student. *Easy Death*, produced by the Oxford Playhouse in 1961, brought Churchill to the attention of agent Margaret Ramsay. With Ramsay's encouragement, Churchill began to write for radio, finding immediate success with *The Ants,* broadcast by the BBC in 1962. She became a regular contributor to BBC Radio drama from that point through the early 1970s.

Churchill's transition to writing primarily for the stage occurred in 1972, when *Owners* was performed at the Royal Court. The play's enthusiastic reception proved her potential and introduced her to what is generally seen as London's most serious theatre constituency. Over the next several years Churchill's association with the Royal Court solidified as she became its resident dramatist—the first woman to hold the position—and saw several of her plays produced there.

The year 1976 has been identified by Churchill as a watershed in her career. She became involved in collaborative projects with two companies: Monstrous Regiment, formed by a group of socialist feminists committed to expanding the range of theatrical roles available to women, and Joint Stock, a fringe collective founded to provide an alternative to the usually brief rehearsal period for a professional theatre production. Joint Stock's distinctive, three-phase process— consisting of a workshop in which all participants engage in research, discussion, and improvisation, a writing period during which the playwright drafts the play using ideas generated in the workshop, and the rehearsal period during which the play is reworked into its final form—proved particularly well suited to Churchill's interests. She became the playwright most closely associated with Joint Stock, and in recent years she has participated in collaborative workshops with other groups.

Churchill continued to write for radio and television until the early 1980s but encountered resistance to the politically charged tone of some work. A television dramatization of the trial of a teenager accused of planting a bomb in Northern Ireland brought Churchill into direct conflict with the BBC when it rewrote a voice-over prologue to the action and cut the epilogue without consulting her. Although her fight to retain the original script generated a great deal of public sympathy, the program was broadcast in its altered form. Churchill and the play's director removed their names from the credits in protest.

Churchill's most important stage successes, encompassing a remarkable range of subjects, offering provocative viewpoints, and demonstrating continual experiment with theatrical form, occurred in the 1980s. Four of the plays she premiered during this time brought her critical acclaim, international recognition, and major awards. Three additional plays, including one cowritten with David Lan, enjoyed more limited success. During the 1980s Churchill also contributed to two performance art works.

Churchill continues active as a playwright. Her most recently produced work is *Mad Forest* (1990), created with a workshop group from the Central School of Speech and Drama in London. It has played successfully in London, Bucharest, and New York and in regional theatres across the United States. Fourteen of Churchill's full-length stage plays are currently in print, and a volume of short plays, including work for both radio and stage, was recently published.

Selected Biographical Sources: Betsko and Koenig; Cousin; Fitzsimmons; Kritzer [2]; Randall.

MAJOR PLAYS, PREMIERES, AND SIGNIFICANT REVIVALS: THEATRICAL RECEPTION

Owners. 1972. Commissioned by Michael Codron. Opened 6 December at the Royal Court Theatre Upstairs, London. Directed by Nicholas Wright. First New York production: Mercer-Shaw Theatre, May 1973. Revivals: Young Vic Theatre, London, April 1987, directed by Annie Castledine; New York Theatre Workshop, March 1993, directed by Mark Wing-Davey.

This play pits an aggressive female real estate developer against a male who refuses to fight in a dispute over a house that subjects the institution of property ownership to critical questioning. Its initial reception indicated strong interest in Churchill's potential: Esslin, for example, asked whether the play points to "a higher order of love than the striving for mere possession of the other person," but he concluded that the play need not answer the question because it "poses it and starts one on such trains of thinking." Of the 1987 revival, Vidal alluded to the correspondence between the central character of *Owners* and Margaret Thatcher, stating that the play "has become starkly relevant, whereas once it was a more philosophical debate on the nature of individual power-sharing."

Objections to Sex and Violence. 1975. Opened 2 January at the Royal Court Theatre, London. Directed by John Tydeman.

Set on a beach at a seaside resort, the play shows a young, sexually liberated would-be revolutionary clashing with her sister, ex-husband, and various friends over principles concerning sex and violence. Most reviewers found the structure and characters deficient in dramatic value, and Lambert called the work "something of a morality play without a moral."

Light Shining in Buckinghamshire. 1976. Produced by Joint Stock Theatre Company. Opened 7 September at the Traverse Theatre, Edinburgh. Music by Colin Sell. Directed by Max Stafford-Clark. First London performance 27 September at the Royal Court Theatre Upstairs; second run at the Theatre Upstairs, January 1977. Revival: Perry Street Theater, New York, February 1991; directed by Lisa Peterson.

This reexamination of the English civil war of the seventeenth century uses a Brechtian theatrical framework. Churchill worked with Joint Stock on the play, participating in a workshop that found immediacy in the historical material through singing psalms, ad libbing sermons based on randomly chosen biblical passages, and observing street people. These explorations propelled Churchill into the nine-week writing period "crammed with ideas and seizing on structure, character, incidents that might contain them" (Ritchie, 119). The play was well received in Edinburgh and London: Wardle [2], for example, pointed to its paradoxical ability to "belong to another century" while maintaining "contact with ours," and Billington [2] praised its "austere eloquence."

Vinegar Tom. 1976. Produced by Monstrous Regiment. Opened 12 October at the Humberside Theatre, Hull. Music by Helen Glavin. Directed by Pam Brighton. First London performance: 14 December at the Institute of Contemporary Art; transferred to the Half Moon Theatre, January 1977.

The play analyzes the oppression of women and the misogynist ideology that undergirds this oppression. It was written for Monstrous Regiment, with whom Churchill agreed upon a subject—witchcraft—and a form that would include the entire company. The play's action, which dramatizes a witch-hunt in a seventeenth-century village, proceeds in brief episodes alternating with contemporary songs. Its formal experimentation and undisguised rejection of male privilege led to a mixed reception, with Mairowitz, for example, complaining of the "graphic" nature of the songs and resulting "estrangement" but acknowledging "Churchill's writing strength" and ability to "leave sharp scars."

Traps. 1977. Opened 27 January at the Royal Court Theatre Upstairs, London. Directed by John Ashford. Revival: New York Theater Workshop, March 1993, directed by Lisa Peterson.

A play about choices and limitations, *Traps* experiments with an open concept of time that Churchill described in the play's preface as "like an impossible object . . . the characters can be thought of as living many of their possibilities at once." A number of critics complained of its "trick" quality. Gilbert, however, found the play "fascinating" and called it Churchill's "most confident and creative deployment of stagecraft to date."

Cloud Nine. 1979. Produced by Joint Stock. Opened at Dartington College, 14 February. Music by Andy Roberts. Directed by Max Stafford-Clark. Revived: Royal Court Theatre, 1980; directed by Max Stafford-Clark and Les Waters. First New York production (with altered text): Theatre de Lys (Lucille Lortel Theatre), 18 May 1981; directed by Tommy Tune. New York production won Obie Award.

This comedic dissection of traditional attitudes and contemporary dilemmas regarding sex and gender was developed through a workshop with participants representing different sexual orientations and experiences. The play is remarkable in its use of theatricality, including cross-gender and cross-racial roles and a time shift of one hundred years that ages the characters only twenty-five years. Several versions exist because the original text was altered by the New York production but then reinstated, with minor alterations, for many subsequent productions.

Reception for the London premiere was fairly negative, with Young deriding its message as "old news by now," and Billington [1] calling the play "a superficial jog around the . . . territory of sexual relations." The tone changed, however, for the 1980 production: Wardle [1], while expressing reservations about the slower pace of the second act, found that "the real dramatic interest lies in the double approach to character as a fixed or fluid thing"; Coveney [1] called the writing "compassionate, witty, and economic." Reviews of the New York production tended to focus on whether Tommy Tune's reshaping enhanced or detracted from the original. The play was subsequently produced in many countries, and its international success gave Churchill a secure base from which to continue her work.

Top Girls. 1982. Opened at the Royal Court Theatre 28 August. Directed by Max Stafford-Clark. Transferred to the Public Theater, New York, 21 December. Second run at the Royal Court, February 1983. Won Obie Award for New York run. Revival: Royal Court Theatre, April 1991, directed by Max Stafford-Clark.

An all-female exploration of work, *Top Girls* moves on two planes—the imaginative one of the first act's dinner party, which brings together an array of women from history and myth, and the realistic one of the second act, in which an ambitious businesswoman deals with personal and career choices. Critics, although divided on the play's merits, warmed to the play in its second London run and responded with notable thoughtfulness. Coveney [5] wrote that the play "seems at first to be a piece written on the small scale, but . . . takes flight as great arcs of interconnecting incident and observation light up the scenario." Nightingale [2] felt the play demonstrated "audacity and assurance" in its questioning of whether "feminism consist[s] in aggressively adopting the very values that have for centuries oppressed your sex." Billington [4] praised Churchill for her "downright passion." Although some American critics failed to relate to the play's socialist feminism, Munk declared: "I'd say the play is, among other things, a critique of bourgeois feminism; that the motor of its harshness is compassion; that Churchill writes mothers and children better than anyone else around; and that sentimentality has rarely been so remote." *Top Girls*, like *Cloud Nine*, has been produced in many countries. When it received a major London revival in 1991, *Sunday Times* critic John Peter wrote of the play: "I was gripped and shocked by the accuracy of its dark prescience. Churchill's forecast for the 1980s has proved hideously accurate."

Fen. 1983. Joint Stock production. Opened at the University of Essex on 20 January. Music by Ilona Sekacz. Directed by Les Waters. First London performance: Almeida Theatre, 16 February. Transferred to the Public Theater, New York, 29 May. Transferred to the Royal Court Theatre, 29 July. Re-cast and produced at the Public Theater in New York, February 1984. Won Susan Smith Blackburn Prize.

This play about rural workers originated with a Joint Stock workshop that involved a week of residence in a village in the fens area of England. It juxtaposes documentarylike scenes with nonrealistic moments in which ghosts appear and an argument between a boss and a worker is enacted by a single actor. To the surprise of its Joint Stock originators, who had worried that a play about farm laborers would not interest urban audiences, *Fen* was an immediate popular and critical success. Critics seemed even to appreciate the roughness evident in the production, which occurred in a partially remodeled theatre with "bare walls, freezing temperatures, and a mist that slowly engulfed the auditorium" (Ritchie, 28). Coveney [2], for example, noted that this play lacked "the high gloss" of *Cloud Nine* and *Top Girls* while praising its "dialogue of impressive vigour and economy" and the "brooding rural atmosphere." Barnes, reviewing the New York production, wrote that *Fen* presented "a rich, complex, tragic picture, often very funny." It was with *Fen* that critics began to view Churchill as a major contemporary playwright: Radin [1] expressed a general view in her judgment that *Fen* "shows that Caryl Churchill is one of our weightiest and most robustly original writers for the stage."

Softcops. 1984. Royal Shakespeare Company production. Opened at the Barbican Center's Pit, London, on 2 January. Directed by Howard Davies.

This revue-style examination of various methods of social control, inspired by Michel Foucault's *Discipline and Punish*, received an elaborate production that included onstage music by the Medici String Quartet. Reviewers tended to find the play unsatisfying, with Chaillet acknowledging the "power" of Churchill's "broad strokes of . . . theatrical imagery" but deploring the play's lack of "any sense of direction." Wardle's [3] characterization of the play as "more an animated argument than an act of story-telling" was representative of the critical reception.

A Mouthful of Birds. 1986. Cowritten with David Lan. Joint Stock production. Opened at Birmingham Repertory Theatre, 29 August. Directed by Ian Spink and Les Waters. First London performance 26 November at the Royal Court Theatre.

For this play the Joint Stock workshop took as its starting point *The Bacchae of Euripides.* The action, which incorporates dance and choreographed movement, interweaves the dramas of seven characters who become possessed by some violent passion that changes their lives. Radin's [2] mixed response was typical of critical reaction: while acknowledging "patches of obscurity," she described it as "visually beautiful."

Serious Money. 1987. Opened at the Royal Court Theatre, London, 21 March. Songs by Ian Dury; music by Micky Gallagher and Chaz Jankel. Directed by Max Stafford-Clark. Transferred to Wyndham's Theatre, 6 July. First New York performance, the Public Theater, 22 November. Won Olivier Award for best new play and Susan Smith Blackburn Prize.

The most acclaimed of Churchill's plays to date, *Serious Money* originated in a Royal Court workshop centered on London's financial center. While the play was being researched and written, financial scandals, Thatcherite privatization, and deregulation of the London stock exchange made headlines; the play, therefore, served to define a period of unusual activity and change. Its satirical style and rhyming dialogue delighted even the brokers, jobbers, and financial manipulators who were its target. Most reviewers were enthusiastic. It was described by Collins as "pure genius," and by Ratcliffe as "a vigorous, aggressive, funny, and much-needed attack on British values." Wardle [3] found it "a piece in the great Royal Court tradition: an angry, witty front-line report." A few reviewers, such as Hoyle, who feared that "outsiders" to the world of London finance would experience "numbing boredom" and Radin [3], who praised the play's "freshness" but did not think it would be "a lasting work," expressed more equivocal views. With some cast changes the play transferred to a West End theatre—the first Churchill play to do so—and continued to play to full houses. After the London production was greeted enthusiastically in a brief run at the Public Theater (NY), it was recast with American actors and moved to Broadway's Royale Theatre but ran for less than two weeks there.

Ice Cream. 1989. Opened 11 April at the Royal Court Theatre, London. Directed by Max Stafford-Clark. A rehearsed reading of the short companion piece "Hot Fudge" was added to the bill several weeks into the play's initial run. First New York performance (which included "Hot Fudge") 2 May 1990, at the Public Theater; directed by Les Waters.

A blackly comedic examination of relations between the United States and Great Britain seen through the perspectives of a middle-aged, middle-class American couple and a young brother and sister from Britain's working class, this play attracted generally favorable notices in London. Coveney [3] called it "an explosive allegory of the historical transatlantic alliance" that "encourages a rare sense of theatrical and aesthetic experimentation," and Hiley found it "a bleak but not misanthropic farce, which haunts the mind long after the curtain falls," adding that "once again, our most inquisitive dramatist has reinvented her own talent." American reviewers were less favorably impressed: Rich [2], for example, declared that the scenes set in the United States "seem to have been culled from old Dennis Hopper road movies and television reruns."

Mad Forest. 1990. Central School of Speech and Drama production. Opened at the Embassy Theatre, London, 25 June. Directed by Mark Wing-Davey. Performed at the Teatrul National, Bucharest, 17–22 September. Transferred to the Royal Court Theatre 9 October. First New York production opened 4 December 1991, at the New York Theater Workshop, directed by Mark Wing-Davey.

Developed after a research period during which Churchill, the director, and a student workshop group visited Romania, the play deals with the overthrow of the dictatorship of Nicolae Ceaușescu. It has played to sold-out houses in England, Romania, and the United States. The play was greeted with substantial critical praise, Morley noting its "immediacy and potency," while Coveney [4] called it a "triumph." Billington [3] found it "in the best Joint Stock tradition" and wrote that what it does, "brilliantly in places, is to evoke the mood of a country through snapshot images." New York reviewers were even more enthusiastic: Richards, typically, described the play as "an intensely vivid . . . defiantly theatrical experience."

ADDITIONAL PLAYS, ADAPTATIONS, AND PRODUCTIONS

Other produced stage plays include *Easy Death* (1962, Oxford Playhouse), *Moving Clocks Go Slow* (1975, Royal Court Theatre Upstairs), *Floorshow*, co-written with Michelene Wandor, Bryony Lavery, and David Bradford for Monstrous Regiment (1975, Theatre Royal, Stratford East), and *Three More Sleepless Nights* (1980, Soho Poly). Performance art pieces to which Churchill has contributed include *Midday Sun* (Institute for Contemporary Arts, 1984) and *Fugue* (BBC-TV, 1988). Short plays written for radio and broadcast by the BBC include *The Ants* (1962), *Lovesick* (1967), *Identical Twins* (1968), *Abortive* (1971),

Not . . . Not . . . Not . . . Not . . . Not Enough Oxygen (1971), *Schreber's Nervous Illness* (1972), *Henry's Past* (1972), and *Perfect Happiness* (1973). Two of the radio plays, *Schreber's Nervous Illness* and *Perfect Happiness,* were adapted for stage; the former was produced by the King's Head lunchtime theatre in 1972, the latter by Soho Poly in 1975. Plays for television produced by BBC-TV include *The Judge's Wife* (1972), *Turkish Delight* (1974), *Save It for the Minister,* cowritten with Mary O'Malley and Cherry Potter (1975), *The After-Dinner Joke* (1978), *The Legion Hall Bombing* (1978), and *Crimes* (1982). Two published works, *The Hospital at the Time of the Revolution* (1972) and *Seagulls* (1978), have not been produced.

ASSESSMENT OF CHURCHILL'S CAREER

In her work to date Churchill has addressed an expansive range of subjects and ideas. As a politically oriented playwright who identifies herself as a socialist-feminist, Churchill has approached specifically feminist, specifically socialist, and more broadly defined social issues with a passionate honesty that does not bend to ideological orthodoxies or harden into predictable arguments. Her work thus stands out as more interesting, and perhaps more enduring, than those dramatists whose political terrain is narrower and more overtly polemical.

What most distinguishes Churchill from her peers among twentieth-century British playwrights, however, is her insistent experimentation with dramatic form. This experimentation intensifies the questioning of power relations and exploration of alternatives that form the basis of Churchill's drama. Questions that unsettle habitual perceptions and thought patterns are presented in forms that challenge habitual patterns of reception. Churchill's plays typically conclude with the central question resolutely left unanswered. This open-ended format, evidence of a continually evolving engagement with Brechtian dramaturgy, challenges and invigorates audiences to think about answers rather than simply identifying with or against an idea generated by the playwright.

Churchill has, furthermore, extended her experiments with form to the process of creating a play. In doing so she has herself been challenged and her viewpoint enlarged by the collaborative workshops in which she has engaged. The workshops' research periods have provided Churchill access to previously unfamiliar areas of knowledge and experience. As she writes, she condenses her own learning experience, sharing it with audiences in a drama that presents a process as well as a finished work. In addition, the improvisation and exercises of the workshops have given Churchill vital contact with the playful aspect of theatre; the energy of play has thus infused her dramas with the theatricality for which they are so well known.

Critics began, as if by common agreement, to view Churchill as a major contemporary playwright in 1983, when productions of *Fen* and *Top Girls* ran in London and New York. Benedict Nightingale [1] made one of the first general assessments of Churchill's work, asserting that she ''must surely be rated among the half-dozen best now writing.'' Frank Rich [1], writing at about the same time, saw *Fen* as ''yet another confirmation that its author possesses one of the boldest theatrical imaginations to emerge in this decade.'' Brustein described Churchill as ''a model of honesty, intelligence and compassion'' and praised her ''theatrical originality.'' Recent assessments confirm Churchill's place as a dramatist with an established international reputation who nevertheless, as Bloom notes, embraces ''an expanding range'' as she deals with ''far-flung subject matter.'' Churchill has been accorded considerable attention by academic specialists, with numerous articles and four full-length volumes devoted to her work.

One of the first women dramatists to gain international recognition, Churchill is cited as an influence more often than any other person by those interviewed in a study of contemporary women playwrights. Tina Howe, for example, says, ''Caryl Churchill comes the closest to the kind of theatrical originality I love,'' while Wendy Wasserstein admires ''the way she took the larger political scope and then looked at the personal'' (qtd. in Betsko and Koenig, 235, 431). With her 1960 call for theatre that was ''not ordinary, not safe,'' Churchill entered the theatrical arena as an agent of change. Her works to date stand out as a new kind of drama that not only has entered the mainstream but has at least the potential to change the course of that stream.

ARCHIVAL SOURCES

Manuscripts of radio plays are held at the BBC Play Library, Broadcasting House, London. Tape recordings of radio plays are held in the BBC Sound Archives, Broadcasting House, London. Tape recordings of stage plays and radio plays are held at the National Sound Archive, Division of the British Library, London. Video recording of *The Legion Hall Bombing* is held by the National Film Archive, London. Videotapes of other television plays are held by BBC-TV, London. Manuscripts of unpublished plays are held by the Women's Theatre Archive, Department of Drama, University of Bristol.

PRIMARY BIBLIOGRAPHY

Plays

The Ants. New English Dramatists 12. Harmondsworth: Penguin, 1969.

Cloud Nine. London: Pluto Press and Joint Stock Theatre Group, 1979 London: Samuel French, 1979. Rev. ed., London: Methuen, 1984. London: Nick Hern Books, 1990.

Fen. London: Methuen, 1983. Rev. ed., London: Methuen (*Softcops* and *Fen*), 1986.

Ice Cream. London: Nick Hern Books, 1989.

Light Shining in Buckinghamshire. London: Pluto Press, 1978. London: Nick Hern Books, 1990.

Mad Forest. London: Nick Hern Books, 1990.

A Mouthful of Birds (with David Lan). London: Methuen, 1986.

Objections to Sex and Violence. In Plays by Women 4. London: Methuen, 1985.
Owners. London: Eyre Methuen, 1973. London: Methuen, 1985.
Serious Money. London: Methuen, 1987.
Softcops. London: Methuen, 1984. London: Methuen (*Softcops* and *Fen*), 1986.
Top Girls. London: Methuen, 1982.
Traps. London: Pluto Press, 1978. London: Methuen, 1985. London: Nick Hern Books, 1990.
Vinegar Tom. London: TQ Publications, 1978. *In Plays by Women* 1. London: Methuen, 1978.

Anthologies

Plays: One. (*Owners*, *Traps*, *Vinegar Tom*, *Light Shining in Buckinghamshire*, *Cloud Nine.*) London: Methuen, 1985.
Plays: Two. (*Softcops*, *Top Girls*, *Fen*, *Serious Money*). London: Metheun, 1990.
Shorts. ("Three More Sleepless Nights," "Lovesick," "The After-Dinner Joke," "Abortive," "Schreber's Nervous Illness," "The Judge's Wife," "The Hospital at the Time of the Revolution," "Hot Fudge," "Not . . . Not . . . Not . . . Not . . . Not Enough Oxygen," and "Seagulls."). London: Nick Hern Books, 1990.

Essays and Articles on Drama and Theatre

"The Common Imagination and the Individual Voice" (interview with Geraldine Cousin). *New Theatre Quarterly* 4.13 (Feb. 1988): 3–16.
"Driven by Greed and Fear." *New Statesman* (17 July 1987): 10–11.
"Fear and Loathing in the City." *City Limits* (16 July 1987): 12–13.
"Not Ordinary, Not Safe." *The Twentieth Century* (1960): 446.

SECONDARY BIBLIOGRAPHY

Barnes, Clive. Review of *Fen. New York Post* (31 May 1983).
Betsko, Kathleen, and Rachel Koenig. *Interviews with Contemporary Women Play-wrights.* New York: Beech Tree Books, 1987.
Billington, Michael [1]. Review of *Cloud Nine. Manchester Guardian* (30 Mar. 1979).
———[2]. Review of *Light Shining in Buckinghamshire. Manchester Guardian* (28 Sept. 1976).
———[3]. Review of *Mad Forest. Manchester Guardian* (27 June 1990).
———[4]. Review of *Top Girls. Mancheser Guardian.* (9 Feb. 1983).
Bloom, Michael. "International Flavors Spice Churchill's Works." *Plays and Players* 6.8 (Nov. 1990): 64–65.
Brustein, Robert. "Theater with a Public Dimension." *New Republic*, Feb. 14, 1983: 23–24, 27.
Carlson, Susan [1]. "Comic Collisions: Convention, Rage, and Order." *New Theatre Quarterly* 3.12 (Nov. 1987): 303–16.
———[2]. *Women and Comedy: Rewriting the British Theatrical Tradition.* Ann Arbor: University of Michigan Press, 1991.
Chaillet, Ned. Review of *Softcops. Wall Street Journal* (27 Jan. 1984).

Collins, Neil. Review of *Serious Money*. *Daily Telegraph* (30 Mar. 1987).

Cousin, Geraldine. *Churchill the Playwright*. London: Methuen, 1990.

Coveney, Michael [1]. Review of *Cloud Nine*. *Financial Times* (5 Sept. 1980).

————[2]. Review of *Fen*. *Financial Times* (17 Feb. 1983).

————[3]. Review of *Ice Cream*. *Financial Times* (12 Apr. 1989).

————[4]. Review of *Mad Forest*. *The Observer* (7 Aug. 1990).

————[5]. Review of *Top Girls*. *Financial Times* (8 Feb. 1983).

Diamond, Elin [1]. "(In)Visible Bodies in Churchill's Theater." *Making a Spectacle: Feminist Essays on Contemporary Women's Theatre*. Ann Arbor: University of Michigan Press, 1989.

————[2]. "Narrative Interventions in Churchill, Benmussa, Duras." *Theatre Journal* 37.3 (Oct. 1985): 273–86.

Esslin, Martin. Review of *Owners*. *Plays and Players* (Feb. 1973): 41–42.

Fitzsimmons, Linda [1]. *File on Churchill*. London: Methuen, 1989.

————[2]. " 'I Won't Turn Back for You or Anyone': Caryl Churchill's Socialist-Feminist Theatre." *Essays in Theatre* 6.1 (Nov. 1987): 19–29.

Gilbert, W. Stephen. Review of *Traps*. *Plays and Players* 24.6 (Mar. 1977): 32–33.

Henderson, Liza. "Serious Money and Critical Cost: Language in the Material World." *Theater* 19.3 (summer-fall 1988): 87–88.

Hiley, Jim. Review of *Ice Cream*. *The Listener* (20 Apr. 1989).

Hoyle, Martin. Review of *Serious Money*. *Financial Times* (7 July 1987).

Itzin, Catherine. *Stages in the Revolution*. London: Methuen, 1980.

Keyssar, Helene. *Feminist Theatre*. London: Macmillan, 1984.

Kritzer, Amelia Howe [1]. "Madness and Political Change in the Plays of Caryl Churchill." *Themes in Drama* 15 (1992): 203–16.

————[2]. *The Plays of Caryl Churchill: Theatre of Empowerment*. London: Macmillan, 1991; New York: St. Martin's Press, 1991.

————[3]. "Theatricality and Empowerment in the Plays of Caryl Churchill." *Journal of Dramatic Theory and Criticism* 4.1 (1989): 125–31.

Lambert, J. W. Review of *Objections to Sex and Violence*. *Drama* (spring 1975): 43–45.

Mairowitz, David Zane. "God and the Devil." *Plays and Players* 24.5 (Feb. 1977): 24–25.

Marohl, Joseph. "De-realized Women: Performance and Identity in *Top Girls*." *Modern Drama* 30.3 (Sept. 1987): 376–88.

Morley, Sheridan. Review of *Mad Forest*. *Herald Tribune* (17 Oct. 1990).

Muller, Klaus Peter. "A Serious City Comedy: Fe-/Male History and Value Judgments in Caryl Churchill's *Serious Money*." *Modern Drama* 33.3 (Sept. 1990): 347–62.

Munk, Erika. "Making It." *Village Voice* (11 Jan. 1983).

Nightingale, Benedict [1]. "Hard Labour." *New Statesman* (25 Feb. 1983): 30.

————[2]. "Women's Playtime." *New Statesman* (10 Sept. 1982): 27.

Peter, John. Review of *Top Girls*. *Sunday Times* (21 Apr. 1991).

Radin, Victoria [1]. Review of *Fen*. *The Observer* (30 July 1983).

————[2]. Review of *A Mouthful of Birds*. *New Statesman* (5 Dec. 1986).

————[3]. Review of *Serious Money*. *New Statesman* (3 Apr. 1987).

Randall, Phyllis, ed. *Churchill: A Casebook*. New York: Garland, 1990.

Ratcliffe, Michael. Review of *Serious Money*. *The Observer* (29 Mar. 1987).

Reinelt, Janelle [1]. "Beyond Brecht: Britain's New Feminist Drama," *Theatre Journal* 38.2 (May 1986): 154–63.

————[2]. "Elaborating Brecht: Churchill's Domestic Drama." *Communications from the International Brecht Society* 14.2 (Apr. 1985): 49–56.

Rich, Frank [1]. Review of *Fen. New York Times* (31 May 1983).

————[2]. Review of *Ice Cream with Hot Fudge. New York Times* (4 May 1990): C5.

Richards, David. "Into the Woods, Where the Ancient Passions Lurk." *New York Times* (22 Dec. 1991): H5, H26.

Ritchie, Rob, ed. *The Joint Stock Book: The Making of a Theatre Collective.* London: Methuen, 1987.

Solomon, Alisa. "Witches, Ranters, and the Middle Class: The Plays of Caryl Churchill." *Theatre* 12.2 (spring 1981): 49–55.

Swanson, Michael. "Mother/Daughter Relationships in Three Plays by Caryl Churchill." *Theatre Studies* 31–32 (1986): 49–66.

Thomsen, Christian W. "Three Socialist Playwrights: John McGrath, Caryl Churchill, Trevor Griffiths." *Contemporary English Drama.* Stratford-upon-Avon Studies 19. London: Edward Arnold, 1981.

Troxel, Patricia. "Making Serious Money: Caryl Churchill and Post-modernist Comedy." *Text and Representation.* Lanham, MD: University Press of America, 1989.

Vidal, John. "Power and the Woman." *The Guardian* (9 Apr. 1987).

Wardle, Irving [1]. Review of *Cloud Nine. The Times* (10 Sept. 1980).

————[2]. Review of *Light Shining in Buckinghamshire. The Times* (28 Sept. 1976).

————[3]. Review of *Serious Money* in "Vigorous Drama of a New Elite." *The Times* (30 Mar. 1987).

————[4]. Review of *Softcops. The Times* (11 Jan. 1984).

Young, B. A. Review of *Cloud Nine. Financial Times* (30 Mar. 1979).

Shelagh Delaney

(1939–)

COLETTE LINDROTH

Shelagh Delaney took the theater world by storm in 1958 when her first play, *A Taste of Honey*, became a hit and an instant subject of controversy. Her youth—she was just nineteen—and her working-class background—she was born in industrial Lancashire and had left school by the time she was seventeen—immediately caught the attention of the press, and for several years Delaney was never far from the public eye and ear. This rush of attention did not last, however, and by 1970 some critics were wondering whether she would fulfill her early promise. That question is still being raised.

Of Irish ancestry, Delaney was born in 1939 in Salford, near Manchester, the daughter of Elsie and Joseph Delaney, a bus inspector who died in 1958, a few months after *A Taste of Honey* opened in London. Numerous interviews attest to Delaney's intellectual independence from her early youth. She always loved stories, remembering with special enthusiasm her father's tales of his life as a soldier with the Lancashire Fusiliers in North Africa, but she was a rebellious and often bored student who had attended several schools before she was fifteen. She gained a passing grade in her General Certificate of Education but was uninterested in further formal education and left school at seventeen for a series of uninteresting jobs: salesgirl, usherette, clerk, and assistant in the research photography department of Metro-Vickers, a large industrial firm.

School was not entirely meaningless for Delaney, however; while at Broughton Secondary School she was encouraged by the headmistress, Miss Leek, who gained Delaney's approval by accepting her casual approach to grammar. She also praised Delaney's ability to make her characters sound the way real people do, especially the people in the working-class neighborhoods of Salford. Miss Leek was responsible for introducing Delaney to serious theater when she took the twelve-year-old to a school production of *Othello*, an experience that confirmed Delaney's ambition to write for the stage.

And write she did, winning success at nineteen with an exploit dear to interviewers' hearts. Details of the story vary—sometimes the play is given as Terence Rattigan's *Parade Ground*, sometimes his *Variations on a Theme*—but always the significance is the same. At eighteen Delaney saw Margaret Leighton in a fashionable West End play that gave the actress nothing to do but parade around showing off lavish costumes and mouthing inane lines. Disgusted at this waste of talent, Delaney said, she vowed she could do better. She went home and started to work on material that she had intended for a novel but decided to turn into a play. She produced *A Taste of Honey* in less than a month.

Having launched this challenge to the dramatic establishment Delaney was excited to hear of another theatrical rebel. She read a newspaper account of a dispute between Joan Littlewood's experimental Theatre Workshop and the Lord Chamberlain, England's official censorship office. Hoping that this challenge to tradition and rules meant that Littlewood would have a sympathetic ear for her material, Delaney sent her play to Littlewood for commentary. It was received with enthusiasm, and *A Taste of Honey* was in rehearsal at the Theatre Workshop under Littlewood's direction within a month. It opened on 27 May 1958, at the Theatre Royal, Stratford East, where it ran until 28 June of that year. It was restaged and moved to Wyndham's Theatre in the West End of London on 10 February 1959.

The reaction was overwhelming. Some critics hailed Delaney's brash, gritty, often comic realism as a breath of fresh air for a theater that was stifling, predictable, and conformist; others found it disgusting, a self-indulgent wallow in pessimism and degradation. No one was uninterested, however, and the play was produced at the Lyceum Theatre in New York City on 4 October 1960. On 20 February 1961, it moved to the Booth Theatre, New York, where it played nearly 400 performances. By the age of twenty-one Delaney had assured herself of a place in the theatrical history of both London and New York. Her play also launched the careers of Joan Plowright, who played Jo on the New York stage, and Rita Tushingham, who played the role in the movie, as well as providing Angela Lansbury, who played the mother in New York, with one of her strongest stage roles.

A Taste of Honey won many awards, including the Charles Henry Foyle New Play Award in 1958, an Arts Council Bursary Award in 1959, and the New York Drama Critics Circle Award for best foreign play in 1961. Delaney and cowriter Tony Richardson won an Academy Award for best screenplay for the filmed version in 1962. The film also won awards for best film and best screenplay from the British Film Academy as well as an award for best actress for Dora Bryan and most promising new star for Rita Tushingham. In the United States the play toured extensively, and productions were also mounted in Denmark, Hungary, France, and Sweden. The play was revived in New York in 1978, 1979, and 1981, and in England in 1989, each time to general critical approval. It was produced for British television in 1979, with Diana Dors playing the mother's role.

This success was a hard act to follow. Delaney's second play, *The Lion in Love*, was unsuccessful in a provincial run in 1960, although it was successfully produced in London at the Royal Court Theatre, where it opened 29 December 1960. Although it won some critical praise, especially from Ann Giudici, who directed it off-Broadway in New York, it was generally found to be much less interesting than *Honey*, lacking in focus and too loosely structured. New York received it more enthusiastically, however, and it won the Brittanica Award for Playwrights in 1963.

A book of autobiographical stories and sketches, *Sweetly Sings the Donkey*, won critical praise in 1963. Delaney became a director at Granada Television and from the mid-1960s on most of her work was for films and television.

On screen as on the stage Delaney was never satisfied with ordinary or conventional material, and she always challenged established social ideas. In *Dance with a Stranger* (1985) she dealt with the factual story of Ruth Ellis, who in 1955 became the last woman in England to be hanged (Ellis was hanged for the murder of her lover). Delaney stated that she was initially dubious about the material, especially since she had always created her own fictional world to work with. What won her over, she said, were the social implications of the story, especially what it said about the lack of choices open to a lower-class woman in postwar England.

Delaney's social concerns were also evident in her personal life. Like Littlewood and dramatist Arnold Wesker she spoke frequently on the subject of the need for a realistic, working-class theatre, criticizing the safe, fashionable productions for which the West End was famous. During the 1960s she was active in the British movement for nuclear disarmament and was once arrested with several other artists, including Vanessa Redgrave and John Osborne, at an antinuclear sit-in in London's Trafalgar Square.

Delaney lives in London, where she continues to work on film and television projects. She was awarded the Writers Guild Award for screenplay in 1969, and the Cannes Film Festival Award in 1985, and she was made a fellow of the Royal Society of Literature in 1985.

Selected Biographical Sources: Berney; Connors; Fields.

MAJOR PLAYS, PREMIERES, AND SIGNIFICANT REVIVALS: THEATRICAL RECEPTION

A Taste of Honey. Opened at the Theatre Royal, Stratford East, London, 27 May 1958, directed by Joan Littlewood. Music was provided by the Apex Jazz Trio. Moved to Wyndham's Theatre in the West End of London on 10 February 1959, produced by Donald Albery and Oscar Lowenstein. Littlewood again directed. Opened at the Lyceum Theatre, New York, 4 October 1960, directed by Tony Tanner and George Devine. Produced by David Merrick.

Revived at the Priory Theatre in New York in 1978, Robert Dorman director; by the Counterpoint Theater Company in New York in 1979, Terry Walker director; and at the Roundabout Theatre, New York, 28 April 1981, Tony Tanner director. Revived at the Royal Exchange Theatre, Manchester, England, from 2 March to 1 April 1989, directed by Ian Hastings.

The freshness and originality of this play won praise from the first, although its bleak outlook and sardonic humor also offended many viewers. As Brien phrased it, the production split the critics into two camps. One camp included the "posh" papers and literary publications that "frothed and lathered with excitement." Newspapers with a more conservative readership "reacted with baffled, suspicious shrugs," finding in the short-lived sexual liaisons, the inter-racial romance, the incipient alcoholism and the contentious mother-daughter relationship another degrading example of the kitchen sink school of drama. Many critics found that its candid, ungrammatical dialogue did a disservice to Delaney's native Salford, and even critics who were impressed, like Stephens, wondered if the characters were more suited to "the anonymity of a seamy section of a great metropolis" than to a small provincial town.

Others, especially the London critics, praised the accurate and unromanticized picture of modern life and morals. Anderson called it a "real escape from the middlebrow middle-class vacuum of the West End," and Brien pronounced it a "minor triumph." Everyone commented on Delaney's astonishing youth, and even reviewers who were not pleased by this play predicted that she would have a lasting effect on the English theatrical scene. London critics also had almost universal praise for Littlewood and the Theatre Workshop, but some wondered if the play's impact was really the result of Delaney's writing or of Littlewood's forceful directing. All the reviewers commented on the staging, especially the combination of realistic and surreal effects, including the use of the jazz trio on stage.

In New York the critics were also sharply divided. Kerr [2] commented that Delaney "leaves you breathless" with her "slam-bang sentences" and words that fly "like tracer bullets." "Patience is gone, kindness is gone, the forms of adult civilization have flown the coop," Kerr asserted, but the play is undeniably forceful, funny, fresh, and wistful. It would not, he warned, "be to everyone's taste." Chapman praised the acting and directing and found that Delaney had "a natural gift for theater," praising her fast-paced action and "swift, salty humor." He found the play effective but slight, wondering if Delaney has "any other aim than to give a thick slice of life." Coleman, on the other hand, found the play "unpalatable," a work "penned by a snarling, cynical" young woman who was too young to be so bitter.

Like many critics Coleman compared Delaney to Britain's "angry young men," a phrase rather loosely applied to novelists and playwrights like John Wain, Kingsley Amis, John Braine, and John Osborne who found much to criticize in postwar England. This label stuck to Delaney for years, but it was a link and an attitude she denied, insisting that her aims and interests were quite different from theirs.

The revivals of *A Taste of Honey* were also given critical commendation. The Roundabout Theatre production in 1981 was especially enthusiastically received, with praise for the direction of Tony Tanner and for all the actors, including Amanda Plummer as Jo. Critics were unanimous in their agreement that the play was still as fresh and stimulating as it had been in 1960. The Manchester revival in 1989 also pleased the critics, although some of them disliked director Ian Hastings's decision to use contemporary costumes and references. The play was still timely, critics said. No artificial updating was needed.

The Lion in Love. Opened 5 September 1960, at the Belgrade Theatre, Coventry; 29 December 1960 at the Royal Court Theatre, London. Directed by Clive Barker. Opened 25 April 1963, at One Sheridan Square, New York, Ann Giudici director.

Based on one of Aesop's fables, *The Lion in Love* presents a middle-aged couple, Frank and Kit, as the lion and the woodchopper's daughter of the tale. Like the characters in *A Taste of Honey*, Frank, Kit, and their two grown children scrabble for existence, struggling valiantly against alcoholism, aging, and the harsh economic realities of life in a depressed town in the north of England. The play is marked by tough, witty, realistic dialogue and incidents.

This time, however, critics were less positive. The play was praised for its humor and honesty but was sharply criticized for its sprawling structure and lack of dramatic unity. *The Times* (''Lesser Impact of Miss Delaney's Second Play'') found the play intriguing but sketchy; marriage was a subject Delaney had only glanced at, not studied seriously, the review concluded. Tynan was more enthusiastic, especially on the subject of dialogue and characterization. ''Never . . . has the Northern working class had a stage chronicler as faithful as Miss Delaney,'' Tynan said. ''Her drinkers and dreamers, her banterers and reprovers, her smart young preeners and dowdy old moulters all have their counterparts in every [town] from Macclesfield to Moorecambe.'' This kind of praise was the exception, however, with most reviewers wondering if Delaney would ever fulfill the promise seen in her first play.

The run in Coventry closed after only a few performances, and the London run too was brief. New York critics received the play somewhat more kindly, finding its contrast between despair and laughter stimulating and its slice-of-life realism theatrically effective.

The House That Jack Built. Opened 3 October 1979, at The Cubiculo, a membership theatre-club in New York, Will MacAdam director.

In *The House That Jack Built* Delaney again presents a married couple struggling, with courage and humor, against a realistic assemblage of daily problems. More strongly perhaps than in her two previous plays she affirms the strength and value of the marital bond in the face of difficulty. Despite the brevity of its run the play was well reviewed in New York, winning praise for its realism and the quality of the acting. The *Village Voice* ("Theatre: The House That Jack Built") called it a "hard-won affirmation of married life," and Dace noted its incisive dialogue and lively characterization, finding it a continuation of Delaney's early promise.

ASSESSMENT OF DELANEY'S CAREER

Shelagh Delaney's impact on the modern theatrical scene is undeniable. More than thirty years after it was written, *A Taste of Honey* is still a title familiar to theater-goers and movie-goers alike, and Delaney's name is mentioned in many contemporary surveys of modern drama as well as those from the 1960s and 1970s. From the beginning, however, critics wondered whether her influence would extend much beyond her first play. As early as 1963 one commentator, Worsley, warned that praise that was too much and too soon might damage Delaney as it had other talented writers. Whether overpraise was the problem or not, Delaney's output for the stage has remained at one major contribution, *A Taste of Honey*, and two decidedly minor ones.

Yet hers is still a significant voice. From the first she was praised for adding a tough, realistic, colloquial note to dramatic discourse, and that note has stood the test of time. "I write as people talk," she told interviewers in the 1960s, and her characters sound as vital and convincing thirty years later as they did when they were created. She helped change the twentieth-century theatrical landscape, shaking up the genteel world of fashionable postwar drama with her losers and lowlifes, students and workers whose experiences were closer to everyday reality than were the witty subjects of popular drawing-room comedy. While her material might not seem startling now, her presentation of a sympathetic gay character and an interracial love theme was also ahead of its time in 1958. Although she was certainly not alone in these developments, *A Taste of Honey* was one of the first widely popular and influential plays to use such characters and themes.

Contemporary scholars can discover much in Delaney's work, small though her output is. Feminists especially should find her rebellious, sexually independent female characters intriguing. Tough, unsentimental, often unlucky but always resilient, their insistemce on aggressive self-definition came well before that stance became fashionable. Delaney has taken people whose lives had previously been marginalized or ignored and brought them to center stage.

ARCHIVAL SOURCES

Newspaper and magazine clippings relating to Delaney's career, including reviews of her plays, screenplays, and television productions, can be found in the Billy Rose collection at the Lincoln Center branch of the New York Public Library.

PRIMARY BIBLIOGRAPHY

Plays

The House That Jack Built. London: Duckworth, 1977.
The Lion in Love. New York: Grove Press, 1961. London: Methuen, 1961.
Sweetly Sings the Donkey. New York: Putnam, 1963. London: Methuen, 1964.
A Taste of Honey. New York: Grove Press, 1959. London: Methuen, 1959.

Newspaper and Magazine Articles

"Meeting Shelagh Delaney." *The Times* (2 Feb. 1959).
"How Imagination Retraced a Murder." *New York Times* (4 Aug. 1985): 15.
"My Clothes and I: Shelagh Delaney." *The Observer* (19 Apr. 1959).
"Never Underestimate 18-Year-Old Girls." *New York Times Magazine* (28 May 1961): 30+.

SECONDARY BIBLIOGRAPHY

Anderson, Lindsay. "A Taste of Honey." *Encore* (July-Aug. 1958): 42–43.
Anson, David. "Movies: An Escape from Escapism." *Newsweek* (5 Aug. 1985): 64.
Armstrong, W. A., ed. *Experimental Drama*. London: Bell, 1963: 186–203.
Aston, Frank [1]. "Miss Cuka Joins 'Honey.' " *New York World-Telegram & Sun* (17 May 1961).
———[2]. "Theater: British 'Taste of Honey' Flavors Lyceum Stage." *New York World-Telegram & Sun* (5 Oct. 1960).
Barnes, Clive. " 'Taste' of Boredom." *New York Post* (6 May 1981).
Beaufort, John. " 'Taste of Honey': A Winner Returns." *Christian Science Monitor* (6 May 1981).
Berney, K. A., ed. *Contemporary Dramatists*, 5th ed. London: St. James Press, 1993: 140–41.
Besas, Peter. "The Railway Station Man." *Variety* (20 Apr. 1992).
Bolton, Whitney. "Stage Review: 'A Taste of Honey' Candid, Affecting." *New York Morning Telegraph* (6 Oct. 1961).
Borak, Jeffrey. " 'A Taste of Honey' Still Has Things to Say." *Poughkeepsie Journal* (30 Aug. 1981): 30.
"A Born Dramatist." *The Times* (15 Feb. 1959).
Brien, Alan. "Critic's Choice: The London Season." *Theatre Arts* (May 1959): 9–10.
Buckley, Leonard. "St. Martin's Summer: London Weekend." *The Times* (8 July 1974).
Callery, Sean. "Memoir at Twenty-four." *Saturday Review* (24 Aug. 1963).
Calta, Louis. "Theatre: 3 Cast Changes Made in 'Taste of Honey.' " *New York Times* (17 May 1961).
Campbell, Patrick. "Slice of Life Not a Play." *Stage and Television Today* (11 July 1974).
Chapman, John. "Fine Performances in 'A Taste of Honey,' but It's a Taste of a Play." *New York Daily News* (5 Oct. 1960). In *New York Theatre Critics Reviews* 1960: 226.

Coleman, Robert. " 'Taste of Honey' Unpalatable." *New York Mirror* (5 Oct. 1960). In *New York Theatre Critics Reviews* 1960: 225.

Connors, Pat. "Who's Angry? Shelagh Delaney 'Babe in Arms.' " *New York World-Telegram & Sun* (16 Mar. 1966).

Cooke, Richard P. "The Theater: Hail Britannia!" *Wall Street Journal* (6 Oct. 1960).

Corliss, Richard. "Such Fun Singing the Blahs." *Time* (19 Aug. 1985): 71.

Corry, John. "Stage: Shelagh Delaney and Marital Tensions." *New York Times* (8 Oct. 1979).

Dace, Trish. "The House That Jack Built." *Soho Weekly News* (11 Oct. 1979).

Darlington, W. A. [1]. "About the Theatre: An Aftertaste of Honey." *Daily Telegraph* (19 Oct. 1959).

———[2]. "London Letter: Experimental Workshop and a Young Author in Theatrical Spotlight." *New York Times* (15 Mar. 1959): 3.

———[3]. "Plotless Plays." *Daily Telegraph* (13 Dec. 1959).

Dash, Thomas R. "Broadway Beehive Enlivened by Pungent 'Taste of Honey.' " *Women's Wear Daily* (5 Oct. 1960).

Denby, David. "Movies: Dance with a Stranger." *New York* (19 Aug. 1985): 81–82.

Esterow, Milton. "Shelagh Delaney Gets a Taste of U.S." *New York Times* (16 Mar. 1961): 42.

Field, Rowland. " 'Taste of Honey' Sweet." *Newark Evening News* (5 Oct. 1960).

Fields, Sidney. "The Apprenticeship of Shelagh Delaney." *New York Mirror* (23 Mar. 1961).

Gardner, Paul. "Shelagh Delaney's Third Play May Be Staged Off Broadway." *New York Times* (23 Apr. 1968).

Goring, Edward. "A Delaney Play Has Folded." *London Daily Mail* (15 Oct. 1960).

Gow, Gordon. "The White Bus." *Films and Filming* (Sept. 1968).

Griffiths, Trevor R., and Margaret Llewellyn-Jones, eds. *British and Irish Women Dramatists since 1958: A Critical Handbook.* Philadelphia: Open University Press, 1993: 18–20.

Haskell, Molly. "Lust Simple." *Vogue* (July 1985): 30.

Hatch, Robert. "Human Beings and Substitutes." *Horizon* (Mar. 1961): 102–3.

Helbing, Terry. "Another Taste." *New York Native* (7 Sept. 1981).

Herridge, Frances. "Across the Footlights: The 'Honey' Has a Different Taste." *New York Post* (17 May 1961).

Hope-Wallace, Phillip. "Shelagh Delaney's 'A Taste of Honey' at Wyndham's." *Manchester Guardian* (2 Feb. 1959).

Innes, Christopher. *Modern British Drama, 1890–1990.* Cambridge: Cambridge University Press, 1992: 448–51.

Kael, Pauline. "The Current Cinema." *New Yorker* (26 Aug. 1985): 63–65.

Kalem, T. E. "Theater: Game Loser." *Time* (7 June 1981).

Kauffmann, Stanley. "Cinema." *New Republic* (9 Sept. 1985): 22.

Kerr, Walter [1]. "Critic's Notebook: 'Taste of Honey' Author's Play, or Director's?" *New York Times* (26 Nov. 1981): C13.

———[2] "First Night Report: 'A Taste of Honey.' " *New York Herald Tribune* (5 Oct. 1960). In *New York Theatre Critics Reviews 1960*: 227.

Keyssar, Helene. *Feminist Theatre.* London: Macmillan, 1984: 38–43.

Kitchin, Laurence. *Mid-Century Drama.* London: Faber & Faber, 1960: 175–77.

Kopkind, Andrew. "Dance with a Stranger." *Nation* (30 Nov. 1985): 595–96.

Leonard, John. "Bad Luck of the Irish." *New York* (19 Oct. 1992): 92.

"Lesser Impact of Miss Delaney's Second Play." *The Times* (13 Sept. 1960): 13.

Little, Stuart [1]. "Theater News: Shelagh Delaney, 22, Here to See Her 'Taste of Honey.' " *New York Herald Tribune* (16 Mar. 1961).

———[2]. "Theater News—2d Delaney Play Heading Here." *New York Herald Tribune* (8 Feb. 1962).

MacInnes, Colin. "A Taste of Reality." *Encounter* (Apr. 1959): 70–71.

McClain, John. "Delaney Play Solid Success." *New York Journal American* (5 Oct. 1960).

Magid, Marion. "Miss Delaney's Bittersweet Adolescence." *Herald Tribune* (18 Aug. 1963): 8.

Mapplebeck, John. "Playwright on Probation." *Manchester Guardian* (20 Sept. 1960).

"Meeting Shelagh Delaney." *The Times* (2 Feb. 1959).

Mendelsohn, Edward. "Contrast in Modern Design: From Moscow Art to 'A Taste of Honey.' " *London Stage* (28 May 1959).

Middleton, Drew. "British Group Vows New Anti-Atom Protests; Bertrand Russell Released." *The Times* (19 Sept. 1964).

Novick, Julius. "Sweetly Sings the Donkey." *Village Voice* (12 Sept. 1963).

Oberg, Arthur K. "*A Taste of Honey* and the Popular Play." *Wisconsin Studies in Contemporary Literature* (summer 1966): 160–67.

Oliver, Edith [1]. "How Do You Say 'Love' in Hungarian?" *The New Yorker* (4 May 1963): 92–94.

———[2]. "Off Broadway: A Taste of Delaney." *The New Yorker* (11 May 1981): 72.

Oppenheimer, George. "On Stage: Moonlight in a Gutter." *Newsday* (12 Oct. 1960).

Painter-Downes, Mollie. "Cinema." *The New Yorker* (7 Feb. 1959): 97–98.

Pippit, Aileen. "A Taste for Life." *New York Times* (15 Sept. 1963).

Pope, W. Macqueen. "London Theatre: Delaney Play Talk of London." *New York Morning Telegraph* (18 Feb. 1959).

"Rex Reed." *New York Daily News* (8 July 1981): 5.

Rich, Frank. "Stage: 'A Taste of Honey' Revived at Roundabout." *New York Times* (29 April 1981): 3:1.

Sarris, Andrew. "Dance with a Stranger." *Village Voice* (13 Aug. 1985): 51.

Schickel, Richard. "Movie Review: Director Finney's Fine Debut." *Life* (8 Mar. 1968): 18.

Schmidt, Michael. "A Taste of Honey." *Daily Telegraph* (3 Aug. 1989).

"Screen: Rossellini, Brook, and Mostel." *New York Times* (21 Dec. 1970).

Sharp, Christopher. "A Taste of Honey." *Women's Wear Daily* (29 Apr. 1981).

Simon, John. "Paris When It Almost Sizzles." *New York Magazine* (11 May 1981): 60–61.

Stephens, Frances, comp. *Theatre World Annual*. No. 10, June 1958–May 1959. London: Barrie & Rockcliffe, 1959: 8, 9, 110–12.

Stone, Laurie. "Still Edible." *Village Voice* (20 May 1981).

" 'Stranger' Atypical British Film Fare." *Variety* (8 Aug. 1984).

"A Taste of Honey." *The Times* (28 May 1959).

"A Taste of Honey." *Variety* (12 Oct. 1960).

"A Taste of Theatre." *Village Voice* (5 Oct. 1960).

Taubman, Howard [1]. "A Fresh Talent: At 19 Shelagh Delaney Looks at Life Honestly in 'A Taste of Honey.' " *New York Times* (6 Nov. 1960): 2:1.

————[2]. "Theatre: Without Illusion." *New York Times* (5 Oct. 1960): 46.

Taylor, John Russell [1]. *Anger and After*. London: Methuen, 1969.

————[2]. "Way Down East: Joan Littlewood and the Theatre Workshop." In *The Angry Theatre: New British Drama*, ed. John Russell Taylor. Rev. ed. New York: Hill & Wang, 1969: 117–40.

"The Theatre: Lancashire Lass." *The New Yorker* (15 Oct. 1960): 73.

"Theater & Taste." *The Observer* (12 Feb. 1959).

"Theatre: *The House That Jack Built*." *Village Voice* (22 Oct. 1979): 67.

Tynan, Kenneth. "At the Theatre." *The Observer* (1 Jan. 1961).

Wainwright, Jonathan. "*A Taste of Honey*." *Independent* (3 Aug. 1989).

Wandor, Michelene [1]. *Carry on, Understudies: Theatre and Sexual Politics*. London: Routledge & Kegan Paul, 1986: 143–44, 147–48. First published as *Understudies*. London: Methuen, 1981.

————[2]. *Look Back in Gender*. London: Methuen, 1987.

Watt, Douglass. " 'A Taste of Honey' Could Use Some Spicing." *Daily News* (29 Apr. 1981): 55.

Watts, Richard, Jr. [1]. "The High Skill of Shelagh Delaney." *New York Post* (16 Oct. 1960).

————[2]. "Two on the Aisle: Another Striking English Drama." *New York Post* (5 Oct. 1960). In *New York Theatre Critics Reviews 1960*: 227.

Wellwarth, George. *The Theatre of Protest and Paradox*. London: McGibbon & Kee, 1962: 109–18.

Wheen, Francis. "Dance with a Stranger." *New Statesman* (1 Mar. 1985): 32.

Wilson, Angus. "At the Theatre: From Lancashire to the West End." *The Observer* (15 Feb. 1959).

Worsley, T. C. "Overpraise Crippler of Playwrights." *Herald Tribune* (11 Aug. 1963): 4:2.

David Edgar

(1948–)

ART BORRECA

Although he is best known for his historic nine-hour adaptation of Charles Dickens's *Nicholas Nickleby* for the Royal Shakespeare Company (RSC, 1980), David Edgar is one of Britain's leading political playwrights, as well as a prodigious journalist, social critic, and activist. Throughout Edgar's career these professions have been inseparable. All his plays have reflected a belief in the theatre as a necessary public forum, while his work outside the theatre has mirrored his drama's social concerns.

The seeds of Edgar's interests in theatre and politics were planted early. He was born into a theatrical family in Birmingham: his father, Barrie Edgar, was a television producer; his mother, Joan Burman Edgar, had been a radio announcer and actress; and three grandparents and an aunt were involved in theatre. As a child Edgar attended theatre regularly. He also absorbed what he has called a "fairly liberal political tradition" (Barker and Trussler).

Edgar pursued his interest in theatre throughout his school and university career. While attending Oundle public school from 1961 to 1965, he acted, designed productions, and wrote several plays. In 1965–1966 he taught at Oundle; in 1966 he entered Manchester University to become a director. At Manchester Edgar acted, directed, and wrote plays; he also edited the student newspaper and chaired the Socialist Society. After graduation Edgar worked as a political reporter for the *Bradford Telegraph and Argus* and wrote plays and theatre reviews in his spare time.

In 1970 Chris Parr, the head of the Bradford University Drama Department, asked Edgar to write a play for students. This one-act, *Two Kinds of Angel*, employed partly stereotyped characters to dramatize a social theme, and was later produced in London, Paris, Munich, and Lieges (France). In the early to mid-1970s Edgar wrote a series of one-act social dramas in this vein. As director at Bradford and later of Edinburgh's Pool Theatre, a lunchtime theatre, Parr staged several of them.

Parr's association with Edgar was the first among several that led Edgar to write plays full time. In 1972 Howard Brenton asked Edgar to contribute to *England's Ireland*, Portable Theatre's attack on the British presence in Northern Ireland. On this project Edgar collaborated with Brenton, David Hare, Snoo Wilson, and other young dramatists who, like himself had been deeply affected by the social upheavals of the late 1960s.

In 1971 Edgar began to work with The General Will, which was to become one of Britain's leading leftist theatre collectives. The Bradford University production of *The National Interest*, Edgar's attack on the Tory government, was the first of a series of collaborations between the playwright and the group. Edgar and The General Will created several agitprop works. All used popular forms and styles, such as gangster films, cartoons, Victorian melodrama, music hall, and game shows, to explore a wide range of social issues, from pornography to housing legislation to labor disputes. In 1974 Edgar and The General Will ended their collaboration over a disagreement about the group's purpose and methods.

From 1971 to 1976 Edgar wrote close to forty plays. All were produced by regional, fringe, and university theatres, including Manchester University, the Edinburgh Festival, and the Birmingham Rep, among many others. Although agitprop pieces are typical of Edgar's work in this period, he also experimented with more complex epic forms (e.g., *The End* [1972], *O Fair Jerusalem* [1975]) and with social realism (e.g., *Blood Sports* [1976]). During this period Edgar also adapted some of his plays for television and wrote original teleplays.

The Royal Shakespeare Company's 1976–1977 production of *Destiny* brought Edgar to the attention of a public wider than the regional and fringe audiences familiar with his work. The winner of the 1976 John Whiting Award, *Destiny* combined documentary sources, social realism, and epic techniques to dramatize the rise of British fascism in the wake of the British Empire's decline. The play was critically controversial and put Edgar in demand as a speaker on fascism in Britain. After 1976, Edgar continued to collaborate with such political theatres as 7:84, Pirate Jenny, and Monstrous Regiment. However, his better-known plays—including the adaptations *The Jail Diary of Albie Sachs* (1978) and *Mary Barnes* (1978)—were produced at major subsidized theatres such as the Royal Shakespeare Company and the Royal Court.

Edgar's adaptation work culminated in *Nicholas Nickleby*, which he adapted from Dickens in close collaboration with directors Trevor Nunn and John Caird, and with Royal Shakespeare Company actors, who improvised scenarios and characters for the work. *Nicholas Nickleby* won the Society of West End Theatres Award (1981) in London and the Antoinette Perry (Tony) Award (1982) in New York. The success of this work led the Royal Shakespeare Company to select *Maydays* (1983), Edgar's epic history of the British political left after

World War II, as the first new play to appear at the Barbican Theatre, the Royal Shakespeare Company's new London home.

Since *Maydays* Edgar has combined comedy of manners with social debate in *That Summer* (1987); adapted another classic Victorian novel, Robert Louis Stevenson's *The Strange Case of Dr. Jekyll and Mr. Hyde* (1991); and written the screenplay for Trevor Nunn's first film, *Lady Jane* (1986).

Edgar has also written two community plays, *Entertaining Strangers* (1985) and *Heartlanders* (1989); as well as two political parables examining the social upheaval in Eastern Europe following the collapse of the Soviet Union, *The Shape of the Table* (1990) and *Pentecost* (1994). Edgar wrote *Entertaining Strangers* at the invitation of Ann Jellicoe and the Colway Theatre Trust; the play was performed in the nave of St. Mary's Church, Fordington, by a cast of 188 amateurs ranging in age from three to eighty-five. The playwright revised the work for a smaller professional cast at the National Theatre, where it was restaged by Peter Hall in 1987. Working in collaboration with Stephen Bill and Anne Devlin, Edgar wrote *Heartlanders* for Birmingham's centenary celebrations.

Edgar's recent parable dramas, which he wrote for the Royal Shakespeare Company, have revitalized the concern with political processes seen in *Destiny* and *Maydays*. In the manner of a discussion drama, *The Shape of a Table* painstakingly depicted the negotiations between Communists and anti-Communists in the remaking of an Eastern European government after 1989. *Pentecost* combined a detective story with a hostage drama to explore the relationships among art, politics, and cultural identity; the play takes place entirely inside a church, where three art historians investigate the origins of a mysterious, historically significant fresco, only to find themselves held hostage by a group of Eastern European refugees seeking citizenship in the West.

Since the mid-1970s Edgar has received numerous honors, including a Bicentennial Fellowship (1978–1979). He has also been a resident dramatist at several universities and theatres. In 1989 he became an Honorary Artistic Associate of the Royal Shakespeare Company and was appointed chair of the University of Birmingham's M.A. course in playwrighting, the first of its kind in the United Kingdom.

Selected Biographical Sources: Barker and Trussler; Kalson; Page; Swain.

MAJOR PLAYS, PREMIERES, AND SIGNIFICANT REVIVALS: THEATRICAL RECEPTION

Destiny. 1976. Opened 22 September at the Other Place, Stratford-upon-Avon; moved 12 May 1977, to the Aldwych Theatre, London. Produced by the Royal Shakespeare Company. Directed by Ron Daniels. Revival: Half Moon Theatre, London, July 1985. Television production: Broadcast 31 January 1978, BBC1.

Critics praised *Destiny*'s depiction of political processes (see, in particular, Curtis), as well as its depiction of the psychology of fascism; but they also accused Edgar of leftist paranoia. Levin, Nightingale [1], Peter [5] and Wardle

[2] all lauded the play's social realism as forceful; yet Wardle called it "hate-filled" [2, 3], Peter thought it "scaremongering," and Levin and Nightingale found its politics "irritating" (Levin) or "paranoid" (Nightingale). Crick praised Edgar's empathy for his fascist characters but questioned the accuracy of his social analysis; Coleby found the play thought provoking but its plot overly complicated. One negative review (Turner) denounced the play's two characters as "sociological cardboard."

In 1986 there were contrasting opinions about how well the play had aged. Shorter argued that history had outrun the play, whereas Hay [2] thought the play had become more relevant: "[*Destiny* is] one of the most impressive political plays ever."

The Jail Diary of Albie Sachs. 1978. Opened 13 June at the Warehouse Theatre, London; moved to the Other Place, Stratford-upon-Avon, 11 April 1979. Produced by the Royal Shakespeare Company. Directed by Howard Davies. Revivals: Manhattan Theatre Club (NY), November 1979; Young Vic, London, June 1984. Television production: Broadcast 23 February 1981, BBC2.

A typical criticism of this adaptation of Albie Sachs's *Jail Diary*, which documents his political imprisonment for antiapartheid activism, was that the play was underdeveloped. Wardle [4] and Nightingale [5] thought it focused too much on Sachs's prison experience and not enough on his political background. Other critics thought Edgar's focus effective: Cushman [1], de Jongh, Jenkins [3], and Pixley said the play vividly dramatized Sachs's psychological survival. In contrast, Chaillet [2] found the depiction of solitary confinement unconvincing.

The American premiere of the play received polarized reviews. Whereas Gussow found the play didactic, Simon [2] called it "one of the most powerful stage works to come out of South Africa [sic]."

Mary Barnes. 1978. Opened 31 August at the Birmingham Repertory Theatre Studio; moved to Royal Court Theatre, London, 10 January 1979. Directed by Peter Farago. Revival: Long Wharf Theatre, New Haven (CT), March 1980.

Many critics (e.g., Aire, Chaillet [1], Cushman [2], Harsent, Peter [2]) found this adaptation of Joseph Burke and Mary Barnes's book, *Mary Barnes: Two Accounts of a Journey through Madness*, a compassionate account of her treatment for schizophrenia in a Laingian therapeutic community. However, as with Edgar's adaptation of *The Jail Diary of Albie Sachs*, some critics found the play excessively didactic (e.g., Aire, Peter [2], Harsent). Cushman [2] and King thought Edgar's attitude toward Laingian therapists was unclear. Keller lambasted the portrayals of patients and therapists alike as "infantile."

American critics also gave the play mixed reviews. Gussow [2] thought it compelling in its depiction of Barnes's psychological struggle but incomplete in its psychological and social analysis. Bly thought the play successful as a satire of 1960s psychotherapy but unsatisfying as a portrait of the Laingian movement.

The Life and Adventures of Nicholas Nickleby. 1980. Opened 6 June (Part One) and 12 June (Part Two) at the Aldwych Theatre, London. Produced by the Royal Shakespeare Company. Music and lyrics by Stephen Oliver. Directed by Trevor Nunn and John Caird. Revivals of the Royal Shakespeare Company production: Aldwych Theatre, London, November 1980 and January 1981; Plymouth Theatre (NY), October 1981. Additional revivals: Ohio Theatre, Cleveland, August 1982. Produced by Great Lakes Shakespeare Festival. Royal Shakespeare Theatre, Stratford-upon-Avon, December 1985, toured Newcastle, Manchester, Los Angeles, and New York. Produced by the Royal Shakespeare Company. Television production: Broadcast 7, 14, 21, and 28 November 1982, Channel 4 (U.K.).

Edgar's adaptation of Dickens sparked mixed judgments. In 1980 Fenton [1], Jenkins [1], and Keating and Wardle [5] thought Edgar captured the scope and tone of the novel. However, Nightingale [2] felt that the play was neither faithful to the novel nor a fully realized drama, and Cushman [3] thought it was neither horrific nor comic enough. In 1986 Billington [7] thought the adaptation unified by the motifs of London, money, and role playing, but Hoyle objected to its "obstructive modernisms."

In New York Rich felt the adaptation dramatized the breadth of the novel without creating a consistent theatrical point of view. Simon [1] complained about heart tugging in the portrayal of Smike and about the modernization of the novel's female characters; Asahina and Magnet criticized leftist polemical intrusions in the characterizations of Nicholas, Ralph, and Squeers. But most critics thought the production a triumph: "[*Nicholas Nickleby* is] a triumph of the stage rather than of dramatic art" (Brustein; also see Gilman).

Maydays. 1983. Opened 13 October at the Barbican Theatre, London. Produced by the Royal Shakespeare Company. Directed by Ron Daniels.

Like *Destiny*, Edgar's portrayal of the post–World War II British left sparked a debate about political theatre. Grant [1] saw *Maydays* as "a play by which all others on the theme of modern political history will come to be judged." Although they questioned the correctness of Edgar's historical analysis, as well as the play's caricatured characters and long monologues, Masters, Fenton [2], Billington [2], and Edwards [3] admired its fusion of social and individual experience and its epic-historical breadth and detail. Allen and Masters praised Edgar's portrayal of the Soviet defector Lermontov.

On the negative side, Hislop thought Edgar's epic form encouraged smugness on the part of the audience, while Jenkins [2] claimed the play dealt with a "politics of fantasy unrelated to the preoccupations of real people."

Entertaining Strangers. 1985. Opened 18 November at St. Mary's Church, Dorchester. Produced by Colway Theatre Trust. Music by Andrew Dickson. Directed by Ann Jellicoe. Revival: Cottesloe Theatre, London, October 1987. Produced by the National Theatre. Music by Dominic Muldowney. Directed by Peter Hall.

In its 1985 and 1987 productions this dramatization of the conflict between

Sarah Eldridge, the founder of the Eldridge Pope Brewery, and Henry Moule, a strict Victorian cleric, was praised as a triumph of community historical drama. Nightingale [6] called it "history graphically relived." Billington [1], Edwards [4], Porter, and Wardle [1] thought it successfully combined local history with analysis of the Victorian era.

One dissenting voice (Langton) called the work "an inconsistent admixture" of cartoonlike characters, period speech, and narrative red herrings.

That Summer. 1987. Opened 10 July at the Hampstead Theatre, London. Directed by Michael Attenborough.

Most critics praised selected aspects of this political comedy of manners, in which a left-leaning, bourgeois couple care for the daughters of a miner during the 1984 miners' strike. Edwards [1], Kingston, and Lloyd found the play successful as a comedy of bourgeois manners, and Radin praised Edgar's search for a "positive approach" to political theatre. However, all these critics, as well as Billington [5], Gordon, and Lyttle, criticized Edgar's play as politically schematic or didactic.

In uniformly positive reviews, others called *That Summer* an "elegant, human play" about "diverse lives [brushing] briefly against each other" (Kemp), and an "almost wholly successful marriage of the political drama with the domestic comedy" (Lawson).

The Shape of the Table. 1990. Opened 8 November at the Cottesloe Theatre (London). Produced by the Royal National Theatre. Directed by Jenny Killick.

Billington [5], Nightingale [3], and Peter [3] praised the authenticity of this discussion drama. Peter [3] claimed that "as a drama of pure politics in action, this is the best English play since Granville-Barker's *Waste*." Yet all these critics thought the play ambiguous or overwritten. Bergsman and Hennessey argued that Edgar didactically manipulated stereotyped characters.

Hilsky, an Eastern European, wrote from Prague: "I find two extraordinary qualities about [Edgar's] play. . . . He cleverly demonstrates the political drama of hair-splitting. . . . The other quality . . . is Edgar's feel for the ironies of the revolution in Eastern Europe."

The Strange Case of Dr. Jekyll and Mr. Hyde. 1991. Opened 27 November at the Barbican Theatre, London. Music by Robert Lockhart. Directed by Peter Wood.

Most critics felt that Edgar's *Jekyll and Hyde* suffered from its own identity crisis. Billington [4], Edwards [2], Lavender, and Nightingale [7] admired Edgar's reworking of Stevenson's story into a study of Victorian society and of Freudian psychology. But Billington [4] and Edwards [2] found Edgar's psychosocial exposition labored, and Billington [4], Lavender, and Nightingale [7] thought the play spoiled the melodrama and horror of the original. Duguid said that "[Edgar's] combination of entertainment and theorizing wholly engulfs Stevenson's austere and suggestive fable."

Only Peter [4] saw a unified work, "a thriller which holds you on the edge of your seat and makes you think."

Pentecost. 1994. Opened 12 October at The Other Place (Stratford-upon-Avon). Directed by Michael Attenborough. Produced by the Royal Shakespeare Company. Revival: The Young Vic, 31 May–5 Oct. 1995.

This political parable provoked typically divided reviews. Billington [3] admired the skill with which the first half of the play uses the mystery about the church fresco to explore "the illusion of the cohesive nation state," but he found that the hostage drama in the second half of the play "[widened] the territory so much as to burst open the dramatic form." Similarily, Nightingale [4] found the first half of the play a "neo-Shavian argy bargy" and the second half "implausible." However, he admired the way the hostage drama "transformed ideas into living, suffering people."

In contrast, although Peter [3] found the hostage situation "improbable," he praised the well-made manner in which Edgar turns it into a "a broad and gripping narrative in which everything is both metaphorical and real."

ASSESSMENT OF EDGAR'S CAREER

Because David Edgar's career embodies several social and theatrical developments in Britain since 1968, it is tempting to see him as a typical post-1968 dramatist. In the early 1970s Edgar's agitprop dramatized not only his own leftism but also the radical political consciousness of a generation deeply affected by the social transformations of the 1960s. In the mid-1970s Edgar began to write social realism; this shift of focus resembled comparable changes in the work of other political dramatists, most notably Howard Brenton and David Hare. Like Brenton and Hare, Edgar sought to move political theatre beyond the fringe to the larger subsidized theatres, and he has always denied any co-opting of his leftism by those theatres. Also like Brenton and Hare, Edgar has dramatized post–World War II British social history (e.g., *Destiny, Maydays*) and has published his political views widely outside the theatre.

But the view of Edgar as a typical post-1968 dramatist doesn't do justice to his work's complexity. Nor, for that matter, do most interpretations that acknowledge that complexity. Early criticism of Edgar discussed his mid-1970s social realism as a "development" from simple agitprop to complex social drama (see Itzin). Similarly, the only full-length study of Edgar places his early work into categories marking a development toward social realism (see Swain). Edgar's published comments in the mid-to-late-1970s encouraged this view, stressing the dramatic limitations of agitprop and discussing *Destiny* as an effort to dramatize the dynamic interplay between an individual's subjective perception and objective social reality (see Barker and Trussler; see also Edgar's "Address at Giessen Stadttheater, 30 September 1980," as well as his "Ten Years of Political Theatre," in *The Second Time as Farce*).

The stylistic and substantive variety of Edgar's plays since the mid-1970s casts doubt on a linear interpretation of his career (a doubt that Grant [2] expressed in early Edgar criticism). After *Destiny* Edgar continued to follow his earliest dramatic tendencies, most notably collective (or quasi-collective) theatrical creation. Throughout the 1980s Edgar continued to create work in collaboration with actors and directors, even though he had achieved the status of an important social dramatist. Following the success of *Destiny*, he created *Wreckers* (1977) with the 7:84 Theatre Company; *Our Own People* (1977) with Pirate Jenny; and *Teendreams* (1979) with Susan Todd and Monstrous Regiment. After *Maydays* he wrote *Entertaining Strangers* in collaboration with amateurs. Even on such mainstream projects as *Nicholas Nickleby* and *Dr. Jekyll and Mr. Hyde*, Edgar not only worked collaboratively with directors and actors but also fashioned himself a co-collaborator with Dickens and Stevenson (see Edgar's "Adapting Nickleby," in *The Second Time as Farce*).

Another recurrent tendency since Edgar's early career has been his use of epic forms to provoke political awareness. Along with his collaborations with The General Will, Edgar's agitprop work employed several stocks-in-trade of epic theatre as defined by Bertolt Brecht and developed by his emulators: documentary material, episodic structure, ironic juxtaposition, broad theatricality, and dramatic or historical analogy. In the tradition of British political theatre since the 1920s, Edgar combined these techniques with popular styles, sometimes alternating among several styles within the same play. *Tedderella* (1971), for example, employed the British pantomime to lampoon Ted Heath and the Common Market, and *The End* (1972) juxtaposed the history of the Committee for Nuclear Disarmament with an audience-participation "Cold War Game." Although they are less unidimensional in action and character than Edgar's agitprop, *Nicholas Nickleby*, *Entertaining Strangers*, and *The Strange Case of Dr. Jekyll and Mr. Hyde* all make comparable use of epic techniques and popular forms.

Rather than placing Edgar's plays within his so-called development —a job that Ansorge, Bull, Davis, Hay, Itzin, and Kalson have done fully for various plays—critics would do better to examine how the plays use theatre to dramatize social forces and provoke political consciousness. Such criticism would deal less with political agitation versus aesthetic complexity than with the cultural negotiation an Edgar play makes, the way it constructs a relation among politics, theatre, and audience perception and awareness. Such criticism would go beyond the interpretation of epic and popular forms to explore the impulses that drive Edgar to those forms in the first place.

These impulses would include Edgar's compulsion to "wright" his works, in the original meaning of the term "playwright" as a "maker of plays." Edgar constructs his work with a carpenterish eye for how theatrical materials and means can be made to dramatize social reality. This has been the source of many divided reviews, which have criticized plays as diverse as *Destiny*, *Entertaining Strangers*, *That Summer*, and *Pentecost* for being overly schematic theatrically and politically. However, the critical challenge doesn't end with pointing this out, as, for example, Cave does. The challenge is to examine how Edgar uses theatrical modes as diverse as social realism, promenade theatre, and comedy of manners to dramatize conflicting social perspectives; and to show where and how the playwright's perspective subsumes those.

The notion of Edgar as "wright" is especially relevant to his adaptations, where he dramatizes a dialectic between his present-day interpretation of a text and that text's historical time. *Mary Barnes*, for example, presents a critique of alternative psychiatry and communitarian living in the 1960s from the vantage point of the late 1970s. *Albie Sachs* questions the theatre's ability to grasp the weight of Sachs's experience. Both *Nickleby* and *Jekyll and Hyde* remake the novel into a highly theatricalized drama, on the one hand stressing the stage's ability to bring fictional characters and events to life, and on the other hand retaining some of the novel's third-person narration. These plays reinterpret the novels' plots and characters from modern political and psychological perspectives and make the audience aware of those perspectives. As Edgar noted of *Nickleby*, "The act of theatrical presentation in the theatre (an event quite specific in time) sought to 'frame' the original work . . . to perform the function of Picasso's plinth and signature" ("Adapting Nickleby," in *The Second Time as Farce*).

A related compulsion in much of Edgar's work is its theatricality, its self-consciousness of the theatre, and its capacity to dramatize social matters. In much of the agitprop work, as well as in *Albie Sachs*, *Nickleby*, *Entertaining Strangers*, and *Jekyll and Hyde*, Edgar employs either a metatheatrical approach or specific imagery to evoke a dialectic between the theatre and social reality, and between present and past. For example, *Nickleby*, *Entertaining Strangers*, and *Jekyll and Hyde*—what might be called Edgar's "Victorian Trilogy"—alternate between two or more narrative perspectives (e.g., third-person direct address and dialogue scenes) and contain highly theatricalized images (e.g., plays or performances within the play, the doubling of performers, the splitting of characters). Edgar's concern for theatricality extends to plays that are not overtly meta-theatrical: *Destiny*, *Maydays*, and *The Shape of the Table* all deal with the performative aspects of politics. The hostage "drama" of *Pentecost* is layered with additional levels of theatre and performance, as characters from diverse sociocultural backgrounds exchange mythic tales, which they variously narrate and act out for one another.

At the heart of Edgar's "wrighting" is an obsession with history and with the dialectic between the individual's private experience and the public, social world. Taking their cue from Edgar's comments on this subject (see second paragraph above), Bigsby, Peacock [1, 2], and Rabey [1, 2] have established how this dialectic drives Edgar's social realism (e.g., *Albie Sachs*, *Mary Barnes*, *Destiny*, and *Maydays*) and his view of post–World War II social history. Cohn and Innes have placed the dialectic within traditions of twentieth-century British drama and have also explored the dialectic as it is expressed in his more non-realistic works, such as *O Fair Jerusalem* and *Entertaining Strangers*.

What is needed now is greater understanding of this dialectic in relation to the dynamics of Edgar's theatricality as seen in his social realism and in his metatheatrical works. Our understanding of Edgar as a historical dramatist comes from extensive interpretation of *Destiny* and *Maydays*; little has been done to illuminate his construction of history in the Victorian plays and the relation between those plays and Edgar's social realism. This critical project needs to explore the Victorian plays in terms of the varieties of Edgar's theatricality since his early career. Edgar's historicism has always involved the effort to look backward and forward at once, to create theatre by drawing on vital forms from the theatrical past and employing them to stimulate an audience's thinking about past, present, and future. Outside the daily and weekly reviewers, criticism of Edgar has privileged his original plays over his adaptations and community plays, implicitly relegating them to second-class status and missing their fundamental place in Edgar's aesthetic and politics.

As a playwright concerned with society, history, and theatricality, Edgar has borne the anxiety of Brechtian influence that affected many dramatists of his generation, who in the 1960s and 1970s could not escape epic theatre as the predominant model of political theatre. But like Brenton and Hare, Edgar has adapted Brechtian techniques in terms of British theatrical traditions (see Edgar, "Ten Years of Political Theatre," in *The Second Time as Farce*). Critics have seen this in *Destiny* and *Maydays*, but less so in the adaptations and Victorian works. There is still much to be said about the British adaptation of epic theatre since the 1960s (see, for example, Borreca), and about Edgar's role in that adaptation. Moreover, *The Shape of the Table* and *Pentecost* have issued new challenges to the interpretation of his epic theatre. While these plays explore the kinds of broad social ideas dramatized in *Destiny* and *Maydays*, they do so in confined settings (a negotiating room, a small church), which intensify Edgar's scrutiny of the individual's relationship to society.

Edgar has been a crucial figure in the post–World War II development of epic theatre, metatheatre, and historical theatre in Britain. To encounter any Edgar play is to confront an effort to vitalize these elements of recent British theatre.

PRIMARY BIBLIOGRAPHY

Plays

Ball Boys. London: Pluto, 1978. (Also *The Best Short Plays 1982*. Ed. Ramon Delgado. Radnor, PA: Chilton, 1982).
Destiny. London: Methuen, 1976; revised 1978.
Dick Deterred. New York: Monthly Review Press, 1974.
Entertaining Strangers. London: Methuen, 1986.
Heartlanders (with Stephen Bill and Anne Devlin). London: Nick Hern, 1989.

The Jail Diary of Albie Sachs. London: Rex Collings, 1982.

Mary Barnes. London: Methuen, 1979; revised 1984.

Maydays. London: Methuen, 1983; revised 1984.

Nicholas Nickleby. 2 vols. New York: Dramatists Play Service 1982; Samuel French, 1983.

Our Own People (with *Teendreams*). London: Methuen, 1987.

Pentecost. London: Nick Hern, 1995.

The Shape of the Table. London: Nick Hern, 1990.

The Strange Case of Dr. Jekyll and Mr. Hyde. London: Nick Hern, 1992.

Teendreams (with Susan Todd). London: Methuen, 1979; revised, with *Our Own People*, 1987.

That Summer. London: Methuen, 1987.

Two Kinds of Angel and *The London Fringe Theatre.* Ed. V. E. Mitchell. London: Burnham House, 1975.

Vote for Them (with Neil Grant). London: BBC Books, 1989.

Wreckers. London: Methuen, 1977.

Anthologies

Plays, One. (*Destiny, Mary Barnes, The Jail Diary of Albie Sachs* [revised], *O Fair Jerusalem*). London: Methuen, 1987.

Plays: Two. (*Ecclesiastes, Nicholas Nickleby, Entertaining Strangers*). London: Methuen, 1990.

Plays: Three. (*Our Own People, Teendreams, Maydays, That Summer*). London: Methuen, 1992.

Shorts: Short Plays. (*Blood Sports, The National Theatre, The Midas Connection, Baby Love*). London: Nick Hern, 1989.

Essays and Articles on Drama and Theatre

"Address at Giessen Stadttheater, 30 September 1980." In *Angliestentag Giessen 1980*, ed. Herbert Grabes. Grossen-Linden: Hoffmann, 1981: 179–88.

"Faction Play." *The Listener* (1 June 1989): 13–14.

"Jingles, Jangles." *Marxism Today* (Jan. 1988): 44–45.

"The Lurking Threat to Radical Theatre." *The Guardian* (20 Mar. 1982): 10.

"On Drama-Documentary." In *Ah Mischief! The Writer and Television*, ed. Frank Pike. London: Faber & Faber, 1982: 14–29.

"Putting Politics on Stage." *New Socialist* 2 (1981): 38–41.

"Recrystallization of the Novel." *The Times* (26 Nov. 1980): 9.

"Respect for the Writer." *Theatre International* 1 (1981): 5–6.

The Second Time as Farce: Reflections on the Drama of Mean Times. London: Lawrence & Wishart, 1988.

"Socialist Theatre and the Bourgeois Author." In *Workers and Writers*, ed. Wilfred van der Will. Birmingham: Department of German, Birmingham University, 1975: 81–97.

SECONDARY BIBLIOGRAPHY

Aire, Sally. Rev. of *Mary Barnes. Plays and Players* 26.2 (1978): 19.

Allen, Paul. "Passing the Baton." *New Statesman* (28 Oct. 1983): 31–32.

Ansorge, Peter. *Disrupting the Spectacle: Five Years of Experimental and Fringe Theatre in Britain.* London: Pitman, 1975.

Asahina, Robert. Rev. of *Nicholas Nickleby. Hudson Review* 35.1 (1982): 92–98.

Barker, Clive, and Simon Trussler. "Towards a Theatre of Dynamic Ambiguities." *Theatre Quarterly* 9.33 (1979): 3–23.

Bergsman, Andrew. "Dignity in Defeat." *Times Literary Supplement* 23 (29 Nov. 1990): 1267.

Bigsby, C.W.E. "The Politics of Anxiety: Contemporary Socialist Theatre in Britain." *Modern Drama* 24.4 (Dec. 1981): 393–403. Rpt.in *Modern British Dramatists: New Perspectives*, ed. John Russell Brown. Englewood Cliffs, NJ: Prentice-Hall, 1984: 161–76.

Billington, Michael [1]. "In the Madding Crowd." *The Guardian* (17 Oct. 1987): 14.

———[2]. "New Maps of Revolution." *The Guardian Weekly* (23 Oct. 1983): 19.

———[3]."One Nation under a Grave." *The Guardian* (28 Oct. 1994): 2, 6–7.

———[4]. "Split Decision." *The Guardian* (29 Nov. 1991): 38.

———[5]. "Table That Straddles the Wall." *The Guardian* (10 Nov. 1990): 21.

———[6]. "Up the Bourgeois Value." *The Guardian* (13 July 1987): 10.

———[7]. "Victorians' Real Values." *The Guardian* (6 Jan. 1986): 9.

Bly, Mark. "Theatre in New Haven: The Strange Case of Mary Barnes." *Theater* 11.3 (1980): 104–7.

Borreca, Art. "The Making of the British History Play, 1956–1968." *Theater Three* 10–11 (1992): 11–36.

Brustein, Robert. "In the Constructive Element, Immerse." *New Republic* (28 Oct. 1981): 25–26.

Bull, John. *New British Political Dramatists: Howard Brenton, David Hare, Trevor Griffiths, and David Edgar.* London: Macmillan, 1984.

Cave, Richard Allen. *New British Drama in Performance on the London Stage, 1970–1985.* New York: St. Martin's Press, 1987.

Chaillet, Ned [1]. Review of *Mary Barnes. The Times* (7 Sept. 1978): 9.

———[2]. Review of *The Jail Diary of Albie Sachs* and *Treetops* by Nicholas Wright. *Plays and Players* (Aug. 1978): 18–19.

Cohn, Ruby. *Retreats from Realism in Recent British Drama.* Cambridge: Cambridge University Press, 1991.

Coleby, John. Review of *Destiny. Drama* 130 (1978): 79.

Crick, Bernard. "When Committed Theatre Moves from Agitprop to True Politics." *Times Higher Education Supplement* (20 May 1977): 11.

Curtis, Anthony. Review of *Destiny. Drama* 125 (1977): 58.

Cushman, Robert [1]. Review of *The Jail Diary of Albie Sachs. The Observer* (25 June 1978): 24.

———[2]. Review of *Mary Barnes. The Observer* (3 Sept. 1978): 23.

———[3]. "Novel Epic." *The Observer* (29 June 1980).

Davis, Jim. "Festive Irony: Aspects of the British Theatre in the 1980s." *Critical Survey* 3.3: 339–50.

de Jongh, Nicholas. Rev. of *The Jail Diary of Albie Sachs. The Guardian* (18 June 1978).

Duguid, Lindsay. "Examining the Beast Within." *Times Literary Supplement* (6 Dec. 1991): 18.

Edwards, Christopher [1]. "Culture Clash." *The Spectator* (25 July 1987): 37.

———[2]. "Hammered Horror." *The Spectator* (30 Nov. 1991): 58–59.

———[3]. Review of *Maydays. Drama* (1984): 25.

———[4]. "Victorian Values." *The Spectator* (24 Oct. 1987): 38–40.

Fenton, James [1]. "Face to Face with Dickens." *Sunday Times* (29 June 1980): 40.

———[2]. "The Long March to Conformity." *Sunday Times* (23 Oct. 1983): 39.

Gilman, Richard. Review of *Nicholas Nickleby. Nation* (7 Nov. 1981): 482–83.

Gordon, Giles. Review of *That Summer. Daily News* (13 July 1987).

Grant, Steve [1]. Review of *Maydays. Plays and Players* (Dec. 1983): 17–18.

———[2]. "Voicing the Protest: The New Writers."In *Dreams and Deconstructions: Alternative Theatre in Britain*, ed. Sandy Craig. Ambergate: Amber Lane Press, 1980: 116–44.

Gussow, Mel. Review of *The Jail Diary of Albie Sachs. New York Times* (19 Nov. 1979): C:15.

Harsent, David. "Open Nerves." *New Statesman* (19 Jan. 1979): 89.

Hay, Malcom [1]. "David Edgar: Public Playwright." *Drama* 151 (1984): 13–16.

———[2]. Review of *Destiny. Plays and Players* (Sept. 1985): 23.

Hennessey, Stewart. "Cardboard Cut-Outs." *New Statesman* (16 Nov. 1990): 31.

Hilsky, Martin. "The Prus and Cons." *Times Higher Education Supplement* (23 Nov. 1990): 16.

Hislop, Andrew. "Children of the Would-Be Revolution." *Times Literary Supplement* (28 Oct. 1983): 1187.

Hoyle, Martin. Review of *Nicholas Nickleby. Plays and Players* (Mar. 1986): 26–27.

Innes, Christopher. *Modern British Drama, 1890–1990*. Cambridge: Cambridge University Press, 1992.

Itzin, Catherine. *Stages in the Revolution: Political Theatre in Britain since 1968*. London: Methuen, 1980.

Jenkins, Peter [1]. "Challenging." *The Spectator* (28 June 1980): 25.

———[2]. "How to Play around with the Politics of Fantasy." *The Guardian* (26 Oct. 1983): 17.

———[3]. "With and without Walls." *The Spectator* (24 June 1978): 23.

Kalson, Albert. "From Agitprop to SRO: The Political Drama of David Edgar." In *Cultural Power/Cultural Literacy*, ed. Bonnie Braendlin. Tallahassee: Florida State University Press, 1991.

Keating, Peter. "Dramatizing Dickens." *Times Literary Supplement* (27 June 1980): 733.

Keller, Hans. "A Play Instead of a Play." *The Spectator* (20 Jan. 1979): 24.

Kemp, Peter. Review of *That Summer. The Independent* (13 July 1987).

King, Francis. "In Two Minds." *Sunday Telegraph* (14 Jan. 1979): 12.

Kingston, Jeremy. Review of *That Summer. The Times* (13 July 1987): B16.

Langton, Robert Gore. Review of *Entertaining Strangers. Plays and Players* (Dec. 1987): 22–23.

Lavender, Andy. "Snarling Beasties." *New Statesman* (6 Dec. 1991): 37–38.

Lawson, Mark. Review of *That Summer. Plays and Players* (Sept. 1987): 24.

Levin, Bernard. "A Lesson from the Greeks." *Sunday Times* (5 June 1977): 37.

Lloyd, John. "Class Reunion." *Times Literary Supplement* (24 July 1987): 796.

Lyttle, John. Review of *That Summer*. *City Limits* (16 July 1987).

Magnet, Myron. "Why *Nicholas Nickleby?*" *Commentary* 72.6 (1981): 75–78.

Masters, Anthony. "Flickering Flame." *The Times* (21 Oct. 1983): 7.

Nightingale, Benedict [1]. "Brum Boys." *New Statesman* (20 May 1977): 688.

———[2]. "Dickens in 3-D." *New Statesman* (27 June 1980): 979.

———[3]. "Eastern Tables Turned." *The Times* (10 Nov. 1990): 23.

———[4]. "History below the Surface."*The Times* (28 Oct. 1994): 33.

———[5]. "Lab-Rat." *New Statesman* (23 June 1978): 857–58.

———[6]. "Roll up, Roll Up." *New Statesman* (29 Nov. 1985): 43.

———[7]. "Skeleton in the Cupboard." *The Times* (28 Nov. 1991): 20.

Page, Malcolm, and Simon Trussler. *File on Edgar*. London: Methuen, 1991.

Peacock, Keith D. [1]. "Chronicles of Wasted Time." *Historical Drama*. Cambridge: Cambridge University Press, 1986: 195–212.

———[2]. *Radical Stages: Alternative History in Modern British Drama*. Westport, CT: Greenwood Press, 1991.

Peter, John [1]. "Politics in the Picture."*Sunday Times* (30 Oct. 1994): 17.

———[2]. "A Saga of the Split Mind." *Sunday Times* (3 Sept. 1978): 38.

———[3]. "A Spellbinding Swan Song." *Sunday Times* (11 Nov. 1990): 7:9.

———[4]. "Uneasy Head Beneath the Crown." *Sunday Times* (1 Dec. 1991): 6:6.

———[5]. "Unreal Worlds." *The Spectator* (21 May 1977): 28.

Pixley, Edward. Review of *The Jail Diary of Albie Sachs*. *Theatre Journal* 31.4 (Dec. 1979): 419–20.

Porter, Roy. "A Conversion to Charity." *Times Literary Supplement* 23 (29 Oct. 1987): 1169.

Rabey, David Ian [1]. "Audience Engagement and Reflexive History in the Plays of David Edgar." *Critical Quarterly* 25 (1983): 49–60.

———[2]. *British and Irish Political Drama in the Twentieth Century*. London: Macmillan, 1986.

Radin, Victoria. "The Pit and the Pendulum." *New Statesman* (24 July 1987): 19–20.

Rich, Frank. "Nicholas Nickleby arrives as a Two-Part 8 1/2 Hour Drama." *New York Times* (5 Oct. 1981): C13.

Shorter, Eric. Review of *Destiny*. *Daily Telegraph* (15 July 1985): 10.

Simon, John [1]. "A Gold-Plated "Nickleby." *New York* (19 Oct. 1981): 92–93, 95.

———[2]. "More than We Deserve." *New York* (3 Dec. 1979): 109–10.

Swain, Elizabeth. *David Edgar: Playwright and Politician*. New York: Peter Lang, 1986.

Turner, John. "Facing the Front." *Times Literary Supplement* (2 Aug. 1985): 852.

Wardle, Irving [1]. "Angels Step in Shadow of Strangers." *The Times* (16 Oct. 1987): 16.

———[2]. Review of *Destiny*. *The Times* (29 Sept. 1976): 12.

———[3]. "Hate-Filled with Merciless Clarity." *The Times* (13 May 1977): 15.

———[4]. Review of *The Jail Diary of Albie Sachs*. *The Times* (19 June 1978): 6.

———[5]. "A Joy We Don't Deserve." *The Times* (27 Nov. 1980): 11.

Bibliography

Trussler, Simon. *Theatre Checklist No. 20: David Edgar*. London: TQ Publications, 1979.

Michael Frayn
(1933–)

KAREN C. BLANSFIELD

Michael Frayn has enjoyed a multiple career as a journalist, novelist, screen-writer, and translator, as well as a playwright, earning him acclaim as a Renaissance man and England's "most versatile man of letters." He is, as one critic put it, "a prolific English literary polymath, a fluent professional who has bounded between genres with an insouciant neglect of the standard hierarchies." Frayn first became familiar to British readers through his humorous columns in the Manchester *Guardian* and *The Observer* in the 1950s and 1960s and then through his satirical novels. His theatre debut came in 1970 with a quartet of one-acts entitled *The Two of Us*, and his reputation as a playwright grew steadily through the next two decades, resting primarily on his hilarious farce *Noises Off* (1982) and his more serious *Benefactors* (1984).

Frayn was born 8 September 1933, in Mill Hill in northwest London, the only child of Thomas Allen Frayn, an asbestos salesman, and Violet Alice Lawson, a shop assistant, who was born in Chicago. When Frayn was eighteen months old, his family moved to Ewell in southwest London, where he attended the private Sutton High School for Boys and then Kingston Grammar School in Surrey. He earned a state scholarship to Emmanuel College in Cambridge, but before enrolling he served with the Royal Army from 1952 to 1954, eventually being commissioned an officer in the Intelligence Corps. During his national service Frayn trained as a Russian interpreter, acquiring a skill that would prove valuable in his later translations. He had already developed an interest in Russian culture, flirting briefly with communism as a youth and subsequently visiting Moscow often, while his admiration of the Russian dramatist Anton Chekhov is evident in his own carefully structured plays.

After his discharge Frayn studied philosophy at Emmanuel College, where he was deeply influenced by the ideas of Austrian expatriate Ludwig Wittgenstein, who had taught there until 1947. Frayn's work often reveals a Wittgensteinian concern with the relationship between reality and perception, with the manipulation that can occur in language, and with the disparity between what is said and what is meant. During his university years Frayn wrote prolifically, turning out humorous columns for the undergraduate newspaper as well as a weekly cartoon, writing for the premier humor magazine *Punch*, and, in his final year, collaborating with John Edwards on a musical comedy, *Zounds!*, for the annual May Week Footlights revue. Although that production was a flop, two of Frayn's sketches were included in a 1957 London production of Bamber Gascoigne's *Share My Lettuce*.

Following his graduation in 1957 Frayn spent five years with *The Guardian*, first as a reporter and then writing a column called "Miscellany" three times a week; in 1962 he moved to *The Observer*, where he produced a weekly column until 1968. Frayn's witty satire and his penchant for drama are evident in these early pieces, which are generally minifarces depicting the absurdities and banalities of domestic life. His sharp, humorous style is reminiscent of Woody Allen, James Thurber, and S. J. Perelman (whom Frayn admits he was trying to imitate), and his subjects often provided the seeds for later works. In 1960 Frayn married Gillian Palmer (from whom he was divorced in 1989); they have three daughters: Jenny, Susanna, and Rebecca. In June 1993 he married author Claire Tomalin, former literary editor of the London *Sunday Times*; the couple lives in London.

In the 1960s, increasingly dissatisfied with his satirical role as a journalist, Frayn began writing novels, hoping "to enter more fully and sympathetically into characters" (Nightingale [4]), although he continued to parody modern culture. His first novel, *The Tin Men* (1965), a futuristic satire on computers and automation, won the Somerset Maugham Award for fiction. Three more books followed in as many years: *The Russian Interpreter* (1966), a spy story that won the Hawthornden Prize; *Towards the End of the Morning* (1967), set in a newspaper office (published in the United States as *Against Entropy*), and *A Very Private Life* (1968), satirizing the upper-class desire for insulation from discomfort. Five years passed before the publication of his fifth novel, *Sweet Dreams* (1973), but during this time Frayn had begun writing television scripts, including *Second City Reports* (1964) and *One Pair of Eyes* (1968). His first dramatic works, *Jamie, On a Flying Visit* (1968)—which Frayn says came to him "virtually intact" during "one sleepless night"—and *Birthday* (1969) were produced for the BBC *Wednesday Play* series.

During the next two decades Frayn worked primarily as a playwright, although he also published a volume of philosophical musings, *Constructions* (1974), patterned after Wittgenstein's *Tractatus*. He continued doing occasional journalism, winning the National Press Club Award for distinguished reporting in 1970 for a series of articles on Cuba. After *The Two of Us* (1970) came *The Sandboy* (1971), *Alphabetical Order* (1975)—which won the *Evening Standard* Drama Award for best comedy of the year—*Clouds* (1976), *Donkeys' Years*

(1976)—named best comedy of the year by the Society of West End Theatre—and *Balmoral* (1978, also produced as *Liberty Hall*). The 1980s saw his two biggest hits, *Noises Off* and *Benefactors*—both of which won awards from the Society of West End Theatre and the *Evening Standard*—as well as *Make and Break* (1980), which ran for nearly a year in London. Frayn was also active in television during these years, contributing to the weekly BBC comedy series *Beyond a Joke* in the spring of 1972, to a Writers' Series with a piece on Laurence Sterne, in 1973, and to a six-part comedy series called *Making Faces* in the fall of 1975; in addition, he wrote a number of documentaries and travel pieces for the BBC, as well as the screenplay *Clockwise* (1986), starring John Cleese, and the television script for *First and Last* (1989), which won the 1990 International Emmy Award for outstanding achievement in drama programming. A film version of *Noises Off*, directed by Peter Bogdanovich, was also released in 1992, although Frayn did not write the screenplay (Marty Kaplan did), and the film fared poorly in both Britain and the United States.

Frayn seems to work in cycles as a novelist and playwright, producing primarily in one genre for extended periods. After his prolific theatrical period he returned to novels in the late 1980s, although his playwrighting continued to reveal itself in his use of first-person narrators. He produced three novels in rapid succession: *The Trick of It* (1989), *A Landing on the Sun* (1991), and *Now You Know* (1992), all of which were critically well received. While this success encouraged him to continue as a novelist, a major theatrical failure in 1990 with *Look, Look* probably contributed to his retreat from playwrighting; he returned to the stage in the summer of 1993 with a three-character play titled *Here*, which received mixed reviews.

Frayn's career as a translator began in the late 1970s when the National Theatre asked him to translate Leo Tolstoy's *The Fruits of Enlightenment* and Chekhov's *The Cherry Orchard*. He has since translated a number of Chekhov dramas, including *The Seagull*, *Uncle Vanya*, *Three Sisters*, and four vaudevilles, as well as an untitled early work known as *Platonov*, which Frayn adapted as *Wild Honey* in 1984. He also translated Jean Anouilh's *Number One* (1984) and Yuri Trifonov's *The Exchange* (1986), which the Russian author had adapted for the stage from his short novel. Frayn is continually praised for the accuracy, grace, and economy of his translations and has come to be considered the preeminent translator of Chekhov. One critic cited ''Frayn's contribution to a modern appreciation of Chekhov [as] enormous and distinguished'' (Edwards), and another noted his influence in dismantling the nostalgic sentimentalism surrounding Chekhov (Edwardes). Rissick said Frayn's rhythms in *Three Sisters* solved ''the perennial problem of English language Checkhov,'' while Morley [3] commented that Frayn's *Uncle Vanya* ''crowns his Chekhov quartet in glory.''

Remarkable as Frayn's diversity is, he has extended it even further by rewriting the libretto of an Offenbach opera, *La Belle Au Laine*. Creating a new story to fit the original music is, Frayn says, ''the hardest work I've ever done.''

The new version is to be produced by the English National Opera, whose director, Dennis Marks, commissioned the work.

Selected Biographical Sources: Page [1, 2]; Locke; Frayn, Preface, *Jamie on a Flying Visit*; Nightingale [4].

MAJOR PLAYS, PREMIERES, AND SIGNIFICANT REVIVALS: THEATRICAL RECEPTION

The Two of Us (Four one-act sketches: "Black and Silver," "The New Quixote," "Mr. Foot," and "Chinamen"). 1970. Opened 30 July at the Garrick Theatre, London for 210 performances, closing 30 January 1971. Produced by Michael Codron. Directed by Mark Cullingham. Revivals: American tour, 1975; "Chinamen" produced at the Harold Clurman Theatre (NY), 1986; Mexico, 1994; "Black & Silver" and "Mr. Foot" TV broadcast, 1995, Poland; "Chinamen" and "The New Quixote" TV broadcast, 1995, Czechoslovakia.

Despite a lukewarm reception, Frayn's first stage production ran for several months in the West End, and Marriott saw Frayn's potential for excellence. The play is actually a quartet of skits about domestic life, strung together in the manner of Neil Simon's *Plaza Suite*: three seriocomic pieces followed by a farce, "Chinamen," which was generally considered the strongest selection. Some reviewers, such as Barnes [3] and Bryden [2], found the whole production thin but mildly entertaining, whereas others, including Spurling, Hobson [2], and Wardle [1], considered the characters weak and the plots banal; a few noted the influence of the eighteenth-century Venetian dramatist Carlo Goldoni in "Chinamen," which was a forerunner of Frayn's biggest hit, *Noises Off*.

The Sandboy. 1971. Opened 16 September at the Greenwich Theatre, London, for twenty-five performances, closing 9 October. Directed by Robert Chetwyn. Produced by Greenwich Theatre.

Frayn's first full-length play, which features the omnipresent couple, concerns the making of a documentary about a successful city planner and was the precursor of his far superior *Benefactors*. Critics like Bryden [1] felt that the contrived structure, placing the audience in the role of the television crew, was awkward and unworkable, while Billington [4] was most bothered by the "surprising lack of theatrical invention." Lambert [2] found the play "badly overextended," and Wardle [3, 4], although acknowledging some effective passages, lamented "the sight of an intelligent writer defaming his own best equipment."

Alphabetical Order. 1975. Opened 11 March (previews 6–10 March) at the Hampstead Theatre Club, London, through 5 April; transferred 8 April to the Mayfair Theatre, London, closing in January 1976. Produced by Michael Codron. Directed by Michael Rudman. Opened at Long Wharf Theatre, New Haven (CT), 8 October 1976, for thirty-seven performances. Directed by Steven Robman. West Coast premiere at Matrix Theatre, Los Angeles, directed and produced by Richard Ross. Produced in Australia in October 1976. Adaptation produced by Granada Television, 1981. Performed on BBC Radio. U.K. tour 1988.

This play about the struggle between order and chaos was Frayn's first major theatrical success, although it fared better in England than in the United States. Set in the clippings library of a provincial newspaper, it drew on Frayn's own journalistic experience, like his earlier novel, *Towards the End of Morning*. As with *The Two of Us*, a number of critics found the play interesting and amusing but not very solid: Nightingale [1] felt that a third act would have strengthened it; Gilbert thought the play too literary for the stage; and Kerr, the severest critic, rebuked Frayn's failure to mesh the play's comic, serious, and symbolic aspects. But Cushman [3] rated it "the most likeable play" in London for months; Morley [2] dubbed it "a massively comic tribute to the futility of journalism," and Barnes [2] called it the best play about newspapers "since 'Front Page.'"

Donkeys' Years. 1976. Opened 15 July at the Globe Theatre, London, closing 18 February 1978. Produced by Michael Codron. Directed by Michael Rudman. U.K. tours 1978, 1993. Produced in Brussels, 1978; Poland, 1991. Repertory productions include Bristol Old Vic, Theatre Royal, 1979; New Theatre of Brooklyn, 1987 (NY premiere). Adaptation produced by ATV, 1978. Television production planned in Warsaw, Poland.

This farce about the twenty-year reunion of a group of college fellows was generally lauded as inventively entertaining. Many critics praised Frayn's skillful handling of farcical conventions and his puncturing of class pretensions. Wardle [2] and Ansorge classed it with other "university" plays, the latter noting "clumsy plotting" and a failure to comment on "the English educational scars." Some American critics felt the British humor didn't translate well in the United States, while others judged the play in light of *Noises Off* and *Benefactors*, since its belated New York premiere followed those successes.

Clouds. 1976. Opened 16 August at the Hampstead Theatre Club, London, closing 16 October. Directed by Michael Rudman. Produced by Hampstead Theatre. Transferred to Duke of York's Theatre, London, 1 November 1978; moved to Criterion Theatre, London, mid-May 1979, closing June 1979. Directed by Michael Rudman. Produced by Ray Cooney. Repertory productions include Perth, Liverpool, Edinburgh. Overseas productions include Australia, New Zealand, Holland, Brussels. U.S. debut in a Drama Guild production, Philadelphia, 1979. Performed on BBC Radio 1987.

Frayn drew from the ideas in his book *Constructions* for this play about three writers on a tour of postrevolutionary Cuba, which examines the differences in individual perceptions and challenges the notion of objective reporting. Its philosophical bent prompted comparisons to Shakespeare, although Robins dismissed Frayn as a philosophical "minnow." Critics noted a weak second half, a too-slick ending, and an overall lack of focus. But Billington [1] hoped it would be picked up in the United States; Radin enjoyed seeing "the war between the sexes explored so honestly and wittily," and Cushman [1] ranked it "a comedy in the classic line," comparing Frayn favorably with Tom Stoppard and Alan Ayckbourn.

Liberty Hall. 1978. Opened as *Balmoral* at Yvonne Arnaud Theatre, Guilford, 20 June. Produced by Michael Codron. Directed by Eric Thompson. Rewritten and produced as *Liberty Hall*, opening 24 January 1980 at the Greenwich Theatre, London. Produced by Michael Codron. Directed by Alan Dossor. Also produced in Pitlochry (Scotland), Manchester, and Leeds. Revival (as *Balmoral*): Bristol Old Vic, Theatre Royal, 6–30 May 1987. Directed by Leon Rubin. Also performed in Cambridge and Singapore.

Inspired by Frayn's frequent visits to Russia, *Liberty Hall* is an imaginative farce based on the premise that the 1917 revolution took place in Britain rather than Russia and is set at a State Writers Home. Turner applauded this creative boldness and praised the play's "hilarious moments, and engrossing originality." *The Observer* (Rev. of *Liberty Hall*), referring to it as a comedy of class-and-role reversal like *She Stoops to Conquer*, said the middle section was "golden" but the sequel "forced" and the preamble "protracted," while others judged it an enjoyable farce, even if somewhat mechanical and not particularly remarkable. The play has a rather tangled history, having undergone major rewrites during its stage life. Frayn himself called the initial production of *Balmoral* "terrible" but thought the revised version (*Liberty Hall*) at the Greenwich was "wonderful" (Frayn, Introduction, *Plays Two*).

Make and Break. 1980. Opened 18 March at the Lyric Theatre, Hammersmith, closing 19 April; moved to Haymarket, Theatre Royal, London, 24 April. Produced by Michael Codron. Directed by Michael Blakemore. U.K. tour, 1981. Opened in the United States 28 March–2 April 1983, at Wilmington (DE) Playhouse; moved to the Eisenhower Theatre, Kennedy Center for the Performing Arts, Washington, D.C., through 7 May. Closed out of town before its scheduled Broadway opening of 12 May. Staged in France by Jean Mercure as *Quoi Qu'on Fasse On Casse*, 1982. Also produced in Brussels. Produced in 1986 for BBC2 *Theatre Night* series, airing 7 June 1987; also performed on BBC Radio, 1994. Produced for radio by L.A. Theatreworks.

A critique of crass commercialism, this is one of Frayn's darker plays, although it received *Drama*'s award for best comedy. After its London success, the play failed in New York primarily because Peter Falk was miscast as the workaholic John Garrard. Set at a European trade fair, *Make and Break* concerns the competitive business world, the dangers of obsession, and the familiar Frayn confusion between what is real and what is simulated. Many critics were troubled by the subplots, weak characterization, or lack of originality, and Caldicott sensed an uneasy balance between humor and seriousness. But Ratcliffe judged it Frayn's "best play to date," and Wasserman considered it "probably the best play currently on the West End." Worth [2] applauded its complexity, and

Hobson [1] cited "a moment of mercy" that had not occurred in theatre since Odets's *Rocket to the Moon.*

Noises Off. 1982. Opened 23 February at the Lyric Theatre, Hammersmith, closing 27 March; moved 31 March to the Savoy Theatre, London, for over 1,400 performances, closing 1 November 1986. Produced by Michael Codron. Directed by Michael Blakemore. Opened in the United States 26 October 1983 (previews 22–25 October) at the Eisenhower Theatre, Kennedy Center for the Performing Arts, Washington, D.C. Moved 11 December 1983, to the Brooks Atkinson Theatre (NY) for 553 performances (twelve previews), closing (after cast changes) 6 April 1985. Original cast moved to Ahmanson Theatre, Los Angeles, 6 February–30 March 1985; Blackstone Theater, Chicago, 22 May 1985, for five weeks. Opened 5 September 1985, at Hershey (PA) Theatre for seventy-seven-city, thirty-two-week tour. Productions also staged in virtually every country (except Albania and China), including France, Australia, Israel, Iceland, Estonia, and Brazil. Major U.K. tour, 1987; PW Productions/Mobil Touring Theatre tour, February-May 1995 (directed by Peter Wilson), including Norwich, York, Richmond, Bath, Belfast, and other venues. The play continues to enjoy regular revivals worldwide, including 1993 productions in Paris (at the Palais Royal), Rhodes, and Russia. Released as film, 1992 (directed by Peter Bogdanovich). Major revivals scheduled for spring 1996 in Berlin, fall 1996 in Rome.

The three-act *Noises Off*, a slapstick farce about a second-rate troupe of actors performing a third-rate play called *Nothing On*, was an enormous hit in London and New York, establishing Frayn as a leading farceur in the tradition of Ben Travers and Georges Feydeau. Although a few reviewers, such as Brustein [1] and Roper, derided the play as little more than a mechanical laugh machine, most reviewers praised its ingenuousness, complexity, and humor, particularly in act 2, which Kroll called "masterly madness," Worell cited as "Frayn's most novel stroke," and Coveney described as "pure magic." On a broader scale, *Noises Off* was seen as an important contribution to the revival of farce. Rich [1] called the play "a forceful argument for farce's value as human comedy"; Simon said it made "a once thriving but lately moribund genre come alive again," designating Frayn "a superior Alan Ayckbourn"; and *Time* ["Pride of"] suggested that if "Pirandello had ever written a farce this would be it." Gill [2] dubbed *Noises Off* the " 'King Lear' of farces," ranking Frayn with Dante, Shakespeare, and Goethe; Billington [2] compared it to Peter Shaffer's *Black Comedy.*

Benefactors. 1984. Opened 4 April at the Vaudeville Theatre, London, for 600 performances, closing 7 September 1985. Produced by Michael Codron. Directed by Michael Blakemore. Opened in the United States 22 December 1985, at the Brooks Atkinson Theatre (NY), closing 29 June 1986, after cast changes, 217 performances (and twelve previews). U.K. tour, 1986, 1993. Revivals: Old Globe Theatre (San Diego), 1988; Athens, Greece, November 1993. Premiere productions in Germany, Greece (Athens), Scotland, New Zealand, Denmark, Austria, Canada, Hong Kong, Japan. Produced for BBC-TV 28 May 1989. Performed on BBC Radio 1987.

The somber sophistication of this play startled many theatre-goers after the hilarious antics of *Noises Off*, and Rich [2] found it "hard to fathom" that the two plays "were written by the same man." Still, it won a host of awards and attained rare financial success. Darker and more complex than Frayn's earlier works, *Benefactors* is also more topical, depicting an architect commissioned to convert a London slum to public housing, and its intricate structure prompted comparisons to Henrik Ibsen's *The Master Builder* and to Anton Chekhov. Some critics found themes of memory and human relationships: others viewed it within a social context. Simon, though troubled by its "insolubility," saw it as a play about change, and Gussow called it "a microcosm of colonialism." Barker considered it a decisive step in "Frayn's development as a major playwright," and Morley [1] classed Frayn with Harold Pinter and Tom Stoppard as "word-playing British dramatists of the late 1960s." But a few critics criticized *Benefactors*, including Brustein [2], who considered it manipulative, and Barnes, who [1] dismissed it as a "sincere" phony.

Look, Look. 1990. Premiered in Italy, January 1990. Opened 17 April at the Aldwych Theatre, London. (Previews from 30 March.) Closed in May after twenty-seven performances. Produced by Michael Codron. Directed by Mike Ockrent.

Produced after a six-year hiatus from playwrighting, *Look, Look* was a major flop that no doubt contributed to Frayn's subsequent withdrawal from the stage. A kind of mirror to *Noises Off*, the play focuses on the audience's reaction to an unseen play, evoking comparisons to Stoppard's *The Real Inspector Hound*. Holland attributed the play's failure to its poor structure, its clichéd characters, and the unrecognizability of the plays being mocked, while James said that a "protracted revue-sketch becomes an author's grouch, a good basic idea is overworked."

Here. 1993. Opened 29 July at the Donmar Warehouse, London, closing 11 September. Produced by Michael Codron. Directed by Michael Blakemore.

Critics were generally disappointed with Frayn's philosophical "chamber piece" about a young couple moving into a new flat, although Nightingale [3] was pleased by the return of one of theatre's "subtlest, most sophisticated minds." Whereas Gross considered the play "excellent" and Peter rated it "a touching, brilliant construction," others found it tedious, weighed down by its linguistic concerns. Its abstract, minimalist quality drew comparisons to Pinter and Samuel Beckett, although Frayn was judged less successful. Billington [3] rated the play "inherently undramatic," and Duguid thought Frayn successfully addressed many "ontological problems."

Now You Know. Opened 19 July 1995, Hampstead Theatre, London.

Stage adaptation by Frayn of his novel by the same name. Directed by Michael Blakemore.

ADDITIONAL PLAYS, ADAPTATIONS, AND TRANSLATIONS

Zounds!, Frayn's 1957 university production, was the only Footlights production that failed to earn a West End run. Two sketches from this revue were included in Bamber Gascoigne's *Share My Lettuce*, produced at the Lyric Hammersmith by Michael Codron in 1957. *Up*!, a 1970s precursor of *Benefactors*, was never produced. *Exits*, the one-act prototype for *Noises Off*, was written for Combined Theatrical Charities and performed 10 September 1977, at the Theatre Royal in Drury Lane. *Audience*, a one-act precursor of *Look, Look*, was presented on 4 October 1987, in *Colin Blakely, A Celebration*, at the Lyric Theatre in London. *The Cherry Orchard* (Chekhov) opened 14 February 1978, at the National's Olivier Theatre, London, produced by the National Theatre, and directed by Peter Hall. Numerous revivals followed. *The Fruits of Enlightenment* (Tolstoy) opened 14 March 1979, at the National's Olivier Theatre, London, closing in September, directed by Christopher Morahan. *Number One* (Anouilh) opened 24 April 1984, at the Queen's Theatre, London, closing 28 July. It was directed by Robert Chetwyn. *Wild Honey* (Chekhov) opened 19 July 1984, at the National's Lyttleton Theatre, London, closing 17 August 1985. It was directed by Christopher Morahan and received numerous worldwide revivals. *Three Sisters* (Chekhov) opened 11 April 1985, at the Royal Exchange Theatre, Manchester, closing 11 May, directed by Caspar Wrede. *The Seagull* (Chekhov) opened 7 November 1986 at the Palace Theatre, Watford, directed by Patrick Mason. *The Sneeze*, a translation and adaptation of eight Chekhov sketches and short stories, opened 23 August 1988 at Theatre Royal, Newcastle-upon-Tyne, transferring 21 September to the Aldwych Theatre, London, and closing 1 April, 1989. It was directed by Ronald Eyre. *Uncle Vanya* (Chekhov) opened 24 May 1988, at the Vaudeville Theatre, London, closing 12 November, directed by Michael Blakemore. *The Exchange* (Trifonov) opened 16 November 1989, at the Nuffield Theatre, Southampton, closing 9 December. It reopened on 19 February 1990, at the Vaudeville Theatre, London, closing 19 May, directed by Patrick Sandford.

ASSESSMENT OF FRAYN'S CAREER

As a journalist, novelist, and scriptwriter as well as a playwright, Michael Frayn has earned renown as a masterful and witty stylist who satirizes the shortcomings and absurdities of contemporary middle-class society, and he has been remarkably successful in all the media in which he has worked. His early columns for *The Observer* and *The Guardian*, primarily humorous spoofs on such mundane topics as cookbooks, refrigerators, cereal boxes, and advertisements, gained him a following among British readers and reflected the themes, style, and farcical bent of his later work. Frayn's fiction as well as his plays received critical attention from the outset, as have his translations and adaptations, and his status in all these fields has grown steadily through the years.

Reviewers saw in Frayn's early work a serious satirist with a trenchant view of modern society and an astute comic sensibility, even though some criticized his novels for weak characterization, contrived plotting, and repetitiveness. Trevor cited Frayn as "the only hatchet man of contemporary letters to combine a consistent attack with something that looks like a purpose"; and Taubman, writing of *The Russian Interpreter*, said that Frayn "doesn't invent absurdities so much as respond to real ambiguities in the [Cold War]." By 1970, when Frayn began writing plays, he had already published four novels and four collections of prose.

Frayn's theatre career got off to a slower start, taking a rather roundabout course. A disastrous acting stint in Nikolai Gogol's *The Inspector General* during his army service and the failure of his 1957 university production, *Zounds!*, deterred him from further stage aspirations, but he was eventually lured back through television. Frayn wrote his first two plays—*Jamie on a Flying Visit* and *Birthday*—for the BBC after unsuccessful attempts at both a television series and an adaptation of his novel *The Russian Interpreter*; in ensuing years he continued to write documentaries, travelogues, and comedy bits for this medium, as well a teleplay and adaptations of his plays. But having become "overimpressed," as Frayn put it, by the power of television's image and sound, he turned to the more narrow discipline of theatre. His professional stage debut came in 1970 with *The Two of Us*, a series of four revue sketches marked by the familiar Frayn features of domestic discontent, clever wordplay, and swift farcical comedy, and was followed the next year by *The Sandboy*, which also prefigured the later Frayn with its suburban couple. Most critics found these early works unremarkable, but his next two productions, *Alphabetical Order* and *Clouds*, were quite successful, marking Frayn as an accomplished and potentially strong playwright. Interestingly, these two plays were originally written for TV but rejected, and Frayn pared them down to suit theatrical constrictions.

The most prolific and significant period in Frayn's playwriting career came during the latter half of the 1970s and the early 1980s, during which he wrote six plays—including *Noises Off* and *Benefactors*—and established himself as one of Britain's leading contemporary playwrights. This fruitful era was followed by a fallow period, at least theatrically; his reemergence in 1990 with *Look, Look* was a disaster, prompting a retreat from the stage that ended in 1993 with *Here*, which opened to mixed reviews.

As a playwright Frayn's primary contributions have been in comedy and satire, and he is credited with helping to revive the genre of farce. He is a master of that form, and Gottlieb commented that Frayn illustrates "the theatrical *and* philosophical nature of the farce; a context of 'absurdism'; 'comic determinism' and an inability to 'play' the dynamics of 'tragi-comedy' ''. He is also one of the "second wave" playwrights who have focused on Britain's middle class. Along with Alan Ayckbourn, Peter Nichols, Tom Stoppard, Simon Gray, and other contemporaries, Frayn occupies a kind of middle ground between prewar aristocratic drama and the "angry theatre" of John Osborne and his followers. If the 1956 "revolution" can be said to have radically shifted the focus from the drawing room to the kitchen, writers like Frayn have shifted it to the living room. As veteran British critic Robert Cushman [2] said, Frayn is not a playwright of social upheaval but, rather, one of the "middle-class ironists," although he is neither didactic nor deliberately topical.

Frayn's plays are marked by underlying philosophical and social complexities, particularly the disparity between subjective and objective reality, the significance of human relationships, and the nature of language—ideas that reflect Wittgenstein's influence. Frayn has generally succeeded in incorporating these themes into the dramatic texture of his plays, and critics have generally praised the rich, multilayered quality of his work. But Frayn has also been criticized as being too intellectual, creating characters who are embodiments of ideas rather than real humans and, as Brustein [2] put it, "manipulating his people into one artificial contrivance or another, since they exist to illustrate a predetermined theme rather than to display a free and independent life of their own." But, voicing a sentiment common among critics, Nightingale [2] asserted that if Frayn is intellectual, he is "certainly one of the more entertaining British intellectuals." Frayn has also been faulted for weak endings—too slick or awkward—and Frayn himself has acknowledged this problem. It was most notable in *Noises Off*, for which he composed several different closings and finally came up with one he thought "quite workable" for the American premiere. According to Cushman [2], most British critics found the original ending unsatisfying but didn't really care because the rest of the play was so funny.

Unlike Pinter, James Saunders, and other contemporaries, Frayn is not particularly radical or experimental in his staging or text, tending instead toward realism and generally working within the traditional framework of time and space. Occasionally he deviates from this style, as in *The Sandboy*, where the audience becomes the imaginary film crew; *Clouds*, with its spare, antinaturalistic setting; *Make and Break*, with its protean partitioning unit; and *Benefactors*, which encompasses fifteen years in the characters' lives and uses flashbacks, reenactments, and direct address to the audience (a technique Peter Nichols uses as well). He sometimes builds on the structure of the well-made play, which like Chekhov's, is tight and economical. As Brown noted, "The confinement of the well-made play acts as a spur for Frayn's imagination so that, by writing compact comedies about people working together, he is able to explore large issues." Frayn's concern with the everyday matters and concerns of the middle class fits in with the slice-of-life realism that Worth [3] has observed as characteristic of postwar British drama. Work is a recurring framework for his plays, reflecting the influence of Chekhov as well as of Frayn's contemporary David

Storey, while domestic relationships, happiness, and change are some central concerns. But his dominant themes are the struggle between order and disorder and the issues of power and obsession, themes that reflect a need to structure and control life in an otherwise chaotic universe.

As with any living artist, assessments of Frayn's career are necessarily provisional, and areas for further study are subject to growth and change. It is clear, though, that Frayn has established himself as a major force in modern British theatre as well as in fiction, besides being a preeminent translator. Potential areas for Frayn studies include the relationships between Frayn's novels and his drama; his contributions to and innovations in farce; his use of the well-made play; a comparison of his reception and influence in Britain and in the United States; the influence of Wittgenstein and of Chekhov; Frayn as translator, and his concern with language as part of a trend in modern theatre.

PRIMARY BIBLIOGRAPHY

Plays

Alphabetical Order: A Play. London: Samuel French, 1976.
Alphabetical Order and *Donkeys' Years.* London: Eyre Methuen 1977.
Audience: A Play in One Act. London: Samuel French, 1991.
Balmoral. London: Methuen, 1987.
Benefactors. London: Methuen, 1984. London: Samuel French, 1984.
Birthday. London: Methuen, 1990.
Clouds. London: Methuen 1977. London: Samuel French, 1977.
Donkeys' Years: A Play. London: Samuel French 1977.
Here. London: Methuen 1993. New York: Samuel French, 1994.
Jamie on a Flying Visit and *Birthday.* Preface by Michael Frayn. London: Methuen, 1990.
Look, Look. London: Methuen, 1990.
Make and Break. London: Methuen, 1980. London: Samuel French, 1980.
Noises Off. London: Methuen, 1982. New York: Samuel French, 1982.
The Two of Us: Four One-Act Plays. New York: Samuel French, 1970. Glasgow: Fontana, 1970.

Anthologies

Plays: One. (*Alphabetical Order, Donkeys' Years, Clouds, Make and Break, Noises Off*). Intro. by Michael Frayn. London: Methuen, 1985.
Plays: Two. (*Benefactors, Balmoral, Wild Honey*). Intro. by Michael Frayn. London: Methuen, 1991.

Translations and Adaptations

Chekhov: Plays. (*The Seagull, Uncle Vanya, Three Sisters, The Cherry Orchard*, and four vaudevilles: "The Evils of Tobacco," "Swan Song," "The Bear," "The Proposal"). Trans. and intro. by Michael Frayn. London: Methuen, 1988.

The Cherry Orchard: A Comedy in Four Acts. Trans. and intro. by Michael Frayn. London: Methuen, 1978. London: Samuel French, 1978.

The Exchange. By Yuri Trifonov. Trans. and intro. by Michael Frayn. London: Methuen, 1986.

The Fruits of Enlightenment: A Comedy in Four Acts. By Leo Tolstoy. Trans. and intro. by Michael Frayn. London: Methuen, 1979.

Number One. By Jean Anouilh. Trans. by Michael Frayn. London: Samuel French, 1985.

The Seagull. By Anton Chekhov. Trans. and intro. by Michael Frayn. London: Methuen, 1986.

The Sneeze. By Anton Chekhov. Trans., adapted, and intro. by Michael Frayn. London: Methuen, 1989. Samuel French, 1989.

Three Sisters: A Drama in Four Acts. By Anton Chekhov. Trans. and intro. by Michael Frayn. London: Methuen, 1983.

Uncle Vanya. By Anton Chekhov. Trans. and intro. by Michael Frayn. London: Methuen, 1987.

Wild Honey. By Anton Chekhov. Trans., adapted and intro. by Michael Frayn. London: Methuen, 1984.

SECONDARY BIBLIOGRAPHY

Ansorge, Peter. "Donkey Years." *Plays and Players* (Sept. 1976): 31.

Barker, Felix. "*Benefactors*: Vaudeville." *Plays and Players* (June 1984): 24–25.

Barnes, Clive [1]. " 'Benefactors'—Noises On." *New York Post* (23 (Dec. 1985).

———[2]. "Drama: Touch of British Humor." *New York Times* (14 Oct. 1976): 46.

———[3]. "The Theater: Risky Atlantic Crossings." *New York Times* (11 Sept. 1970): 33.

Billington, Michael [1]. Review of *Clouds. New York Theatre Review* (Jan. 1979): 28.

———[2]. Review of *Noises Off. The Guardian* (24 Feb. 1982).

———[3]. "Room and Bored." *The Guardian* (6 Aug. 1993).

———[4]. "The Sandboy." *Plays and Players* (Nov. 1971): 47.

Brown, John Russell. *A Short Guide to Modern British Drama.* London: Heinemann Educational Books, 1982.

Brustein, Robert [1]. "Hard and Soft Machines." *New Republic* (9 July 1984): 26–27.

———[2]. "The Infidelity Play." *New Republic* (10 Feb. 1986): 25–26.

———[3]. "Snarls from the Bedclothes." *New Republic* (2 Feb. 1987): 27–29.

Bryden, Ronald [1]. Review of *The Sandboy. The Observer* (26 Sept. 1971): 35.

———[2]. Review of *The Two of Us. The Observer* (2 Aug. 1970): 25.

Caldicott, Leonie. Review of *Make and Break. Plays and Players* (Apr. 1980): 23–24.

Coveney, Michael. Review of *Noises Off. Financial Times* (24 Feb. 1982).

Cushman, Robert [1]. "Clouds over Cuba." *The Observer* (22 Aug. 1976): 20.

———[2]. "Frayn and Farce Go Hand in Hand." *New York Times* (11 Dec. 1983): B1, B4.

———[3]. "From Frayn to Beckett." *The Observer* (16 Mar. 1975).

Duguid, Lindsay. "Swells of Sadness." *Times Literary Supplement* (13 Aug. 1993).

Edwardes, Jane. Review of *Uncle Vanya. Time Out* (1 June 1988).

Edwards, Christopher. Review of *The Sneeze. The Spectator* (1 Oct. 1988).

Gilbert, W. Stephen. "Alphabetical Order." *Plays and Players* (May 1975): 22–23.

Gill, Brendan [1]. "Failed Frayn." *The New Yorker* (29 Dec. 1986): 76.

————[2]. Review of *Noises Off. The New Yorker* (19 Dec. 1983): 123.

Gottlieb, Vera. "Why This Farce? From Chekhov to Frayn—and Frayn's Chekhov." *New Theatre Quarterly* 7 (Aug. 1991): 217–28.

Gross, John. "Both Here and There." *Sunday Telegraph* (8 Aug. 1993).

Hobson, Harold [1]. Review of *Make and Break. Drama* 137 (July 1980): 35.

————[2]. Review of *The Two of Us. Sunday Times* (2 Aug. 1970): 19.

Holland, Peter. "Audience Participation." *Times Literary Supplement* (27 April 1990): 447.

James, John. "An Audience with Frayn." *Times Educational Supplement* (27 Apr.–3 May 1990): A44.

Kerr, Walter. "But What's It All About?" *New York Times* (17 Oct. 1976): D3, D17.

Kroll, Jack. "A Comedy of Utter Chaos." *Newsweek* (26 Dec. 1983): 68.

Lambert, J. W. [1]. "Castles in the Cuban Air." *Sunday Times* (22 Aug. 1976).

————[2]. Review of *The Sandboy. Sunday Times* (26 Sept. 1971).

Review of *Liberty Hall. The Observer* (27 Jan. 1980): 15.

Locke, Richard. "Oedipus Meets the Muse." *Wall Street Journal* (3 Apr. 1990): A22.

Marriott, R. B. "Redgrave and Briers." *Stage & Television Today* (6 Aug. 1970): 13.

Morley, Sheridan [1]. "Frayn's Refrain." *Playbill* (Jan. 1986): 8–13.

————[2]. Review of *Alphabetical Order. Punch* (2 Apr. 1975): 587.

————[3]. Review of *Uncle Vanya. Punch* (10 June 1988).

Nightingale, Benedict [1]. "Culture and Anarchy." *New Statesman* (14 Mar. 1975): 348.

————[2]. "The Entertaining Intellect." *New York Times Magazine* (8 Dec. 1985): 67, 125.

————[3]. "Home Truths Fall a Little Flat." *The Times* (5 Aug. 1993).

————[4]. "Michael Frayn: The Entertaining Intellect." *New York Times Magazine* (8 Dec. 1985): 67–68+.

Page, Malcolm [1]. "Michael Frayn." In *Dictionary of Literary Biography*, ed. Stanley Weintraub. Vol. 14. Detroit: Gale Research 1982: 336–41.

————[2]. In *Contemporary Novelists*, ed. D. L. Kirkpatrick. 4th ed. New York: St. Martin's Press, 1986: 309–10.

Peter, John, "Playing House." *Sunday Times* (8 Aug. 1993): 17.

Preston, John. "The Passions beneath the Propriety." *Sunday Telegraph* (22 Sept. 1991).

"Pride of the London Season." *Time* (12 July 1982): 66.

Radin, Victoria. Review of *Clouds. The Observer* (5 Nov. 1978): 28.

Ratcliffe, Michael. "Glenda's Marathon." *The Observer* (8 Apr. 1984): 19.

Rich, Frank [1]. " 'Noises Off,' A British Farce by Frayn." *New York Times* (12 Dec. 1983): C12.

————[2]. "Theatre: 'Benefactors,' A New Work by Frayn." *New York Times* (23 July 1984): C12.

Rissik, Andrew. Review of *Three Sisters. The Independent* (26 Mar. 1987).

Robins, Dave. Review of *Clouds. Plays and Players* (Oct. 1976): 27.

Roper, David. Review of *Noises Off. Event* (24 Feb. 1982).

Simon, John. "Houses Divided." *New York Magazine* (8 Jan. 1986): 50.

Spurling, Hilary. Review of *The Two of Us. Plays and Players* (Sept. 1970): 36.

Taubman, Robert. "Comedians of the Cold War." *New Statesman* (1 Apr. 1966): 477.

Trevor, William. Review of *The Tin Men. The Listener* (21 Jan. 1965): 115.

Turner, John Frayn. "Balmoral." *The Stage and Television Today* (29 June 1978): 13.

Wardle, Irving [1]. ''Frayn's First Play, Attempt at Comedy, Is Given in London.'' *New York Times* (1 Aug. 1970): 13.

———[2]. ''An Oxbridge Reunion Binge.'' *The Times* (6 July 1976).

———[3]. Review of *The Sandboy*. *The Times* (18 Sept. 1971): 8.

———[4]. '' 'The Sandboy,' a London Play, Has an Unworkable Structure.'' *New York Times* (18 Sept. 1971): 17.

Wasserman, Debbi. Review of *Make and Break*. *Other Stages* (26 Feb. 1981): 8.

Worell, Denise. ''Viewing a Farce from Behind.'' *Time* (30 Jan. 1984): 79.

Worth, Katharine [1]. ''Farce and Michael Frayn.'' *Modern Drama* 26.1 (Mar. 1983): 47–53.

———[2]. ''The Reality Business.'' *Times Literary Supplement* (18 Apr. 1980).

———[3]. *Revolutions in Modern English Drama*. London: G. Bell & Sons, 1972.

Pam Gems

(1925–)

SARAH J. RUDOLPH

Beginning in the early 1970s and continuing into the present, Pam Gems's career in the British theatre seems best described as an expansive one. Gems's drama features a wide range of subjects, employs a wide variety of stylistic devices, and has been produced by both the most established and the most experimental of theatres.

Gems was born Pam Price in Christchurch, Hampshire, in 1925. She grew up in poverty, and only a scholarship made it possible for her to attend grammar school. Leaving school at age fifteen, Gems worked at a variety of jobs until the outbreak of World War II. At that time she took a position as a machine gun accessor. This service entitled her to free college tuition. She studied psychology at Manchester University. There she met and married Ken Gems. The couple moved to London, and Gems took a job writing and doing audience research for the BBC.

In the years between 1952 and 1965 Gems had four children. She left the BBC to raise her children and became involved in the fringe theatre movement. Although she had been interested in playwrighting since childhood, Gems was not a produced playwright until she was forty-seven years old.

Gems's *Betty's Wonderful Christmas*, a children's play, was produced at the Cockpit Theatre in 1972. Shortly after this production Gems was asked to do some writing for Ed Berman's Almost Free Theatre. Offended by Berman's specific request for ''sexy pieces,'' Gems first demonstrated the penchant for controversy that surfaces throughout her career. She responded to his request with two monologues she describes as ''black pieces'' (qtd. in Wandor [3]). *My Warren* focuses on a young girl who flushes her baby down a toilet. *After Birthday* features an elderly, bedridden woman who is sent a vibrator by a practical joker and instead of taking offense—as was the joker's intent—responds with delight. These "black pieces" provided an early indication of both Gems's predilection for controversy and her interest in female characters.

Building upon this interest Gems became an active participant in the British theatre's growing women's movement. In 1973 her play *The Amiable Courtship of Mz. Venus and Wild Bill* was produced as part of the all-women's season at the Almost Free Theatre. In 1974 Gems wrote *Go West, Young Woman* (in a week's time) for production at London's Roundhouse Theatre.

With the 1976 production of *Dead Fish* at the Edinburgh Festival, Gems's career gained considerable momentum. The play focuses on four young women sharing a London flat and grappling with various lifestyle dilemmas. Retitled *Dusa, Fish, Stas and Vi*, the play transferred to London's Mayfair Theatre. There it met with critical acclaim and established Gems as a visible force in the London theatre.

Two other works produced in 1976 continued to establish Gems as a play-wright committed to writing good roles for women. These productions also reflected Gems's willingness to experiment with form. *Guinivere*, produced at the Edinburgh Festival, offers a terse, graphic, and defiantly contemporary di-alogue between Guinivere and Arthur. *The Project*, produced at Soho Poly, examines the changing relationships in the lives of two women and a man. In this play Gems put an interesting spin on the traditional love triangle plot by forming a partnership between the two female characters in the final scene. (*The Project* was retitled *Loving Women* for a 1984 production at the Arts Theatre.)

In 1977, with *Queen Christina*, a play about the seventeenth-century Swedish Queen who abdicated her throne to convert to Catholicism, Gems became the first woman playwright to be produced by the Royal Shakespeare Company. In 1978 Gems returned to the Royal Shakespeare Company's Other Place Theatre with *Piaf*. This play, based on the life of the French singer Edith Piaf, indicated Gems's ongoing interest in women's autobiography on stage. Jane Lapotaire's performance in the title role earned her a 1979 Olivier Award and a 1981 Tony Award after the production had transferred to Broadway's Plymouth Theatre.

The early 1980s were productive years for Gems. *The Treat* and *Aunt Mary*, two of Gems's most experimental, if least successful, plays were produced in 1982. In 1984 Gems returned to the Royal Shakespeare Company's Other Place with *Camille*, another strikingly modern version of a sentimental legend. The play was generally well received, with particular attention going to Frances Barber's performance as the title character. Gems's next play, *La Pasionara*, based on the life of Dolores Ibarruri, was given a 1985 production at the New-castle Playhouse. Whereas Gems took particular pride in this production, critics were largely unfavorable toward the script. During the 1986 season Gems con-tinued her relationship with the Royal Shakespeare Company, this time in Lon-don at the Barbican, with *The Danton Affair*. A sprawling epic translation and reworking of a 1930s work by Polish playwright Stanisława Przbyszewska, the play fared poorly with critics.

Whether or not the disappointing reaction to both *La Pasionara* and *The*

Danton Affair had anything to do with it is unclear, but Gems took a reprieve from production until 1991. During the spring and summer of that year, Gems's version of Anton Chekhov's *Uncle Vanya* toured the United Kingdom with the Renaissance Theatre Company. In early 1992 the Royal National Theatre produced the play in the Cottesloe. This highly praised production featured Ian McKellen and Anthony Scher. Gems has subsequently adapted her translation of *Uncle Vanya* for a film version to be directed by Sean Mathias and produced by Little Bird Productions.

In August 1991 Gems's *The Blue Angel* opened in a newly refurbished Other Place Theatre. Gems's version offers a stark contrast to the sentimentalized adaptation of the Thomas Mann novel offered by the famous 1929 film. Under the direction of Trevor Nunn and with Kelly Hunter as Lola, the play showed enough promise to be transferred to London's West End. There, however, it had a short life, meeting with mixed reviews and artistic inertia.

In fall 1993 Peter Hall directed a revival of *Piaf* starring Elaine Paige. Billed as "a musical play" with the lyrics of the Piaf songs newly translated by Gems from the French into English, the play has enjoyed a successful run at the Piccadilly Theatre, London.

Gems continues to work on new material as well as adaptations and translations. Simultaneous with the revival of *Piaf*, Gems's adaption of Henrik Ibsen's *Ghosts* ran at the Sherman Theatre, Cardiff, and on tour. Her play *Deborah's Daughter* is scheduled for an upcoming production in Manchester. She also has a new script, *Stanley*, based on the life of the artist Stanley Spencer, being considered for production with Anthony Scher in the title role.

In addition to her credits as a playwright, Gems has written two novels, *Mrs. Frampton* and *Bon Voyage, Mrs. Frampton*. The Spanish film company Expresso/Fortunata is currently adapting the first of these novels for a feature film.

Selected Biographical Sources: Betko and Koenig; Colvin; Gardner.

MAJOR PLAYS, PREMIERES, AND SIGNIFICANT REVIVALS: THEATRICAL RECEPTION

Dusa, Fish, Stas and Vi. 1976. Originally produced under the title *Dead Fish* at Kundry's Theatre for the August 1976 Edinburgh Festival, the play was re-titled for its December 1976 transfer to London's Hampstead Theatre Club. Directed by Nancy Meckler.

With its four colorful characters this play struck Billington and others as something of a landmark in women's theatre. Billington [1] expressed his relief that the play featured female characters "without being either shrill or freakish" and lauded Gems for being able to "tell it like it is." Other critics expressed similar sentiments. Wardle [1] proclaims that Gems's play is "by far the best written and most penetrating new feminist piece that has come my way," And Thinkell describes the writing as "crisp" with "no nonsense." Writing about the production, critics paid special attention to the juxtaposition of Gems' brief scenes and excerpts from pop records and radio call-in shows. Wandor [2], however, faulted the play for what she saw as an antifeminism apparent in the suicide of Fish. The play's most politically active character, Fish, kills herself over the breakup of her relationship with a man.

Queen Christina. 1977. Gems's play about the controversial seventeenth-century Swedish Queen, opened on 9 September at the Royal Shakespeare Company's Other Place Theatre, Stratford-upon-Avon. Directed by Ron Daniels.

The play uses an episodic structure to trace the infamous Queen's life from childhood through old age. Gems gives special attention to the conflicting messages Christina confronts in regard to her sexuality and gender identity.

Reviewers were more apt to be uniform in their praise of Sheila Allan's performance than in their regard for Gems's script. Some critics, including Barber and Peter, faulted the play for its sprawling episodic structure and diffuse focus. Carne argued that "too many subtleties are assumed," whereas "too many banalities are painfully explained." Gems was not, however, without her defenders. Billington [3] describes the play as a "dignified theatrical love letter." In addition to a number of revivals, the play had a 1992–1993 fringe production by the Absolute Theatre at the Man-in-the-Moon Theatre. The lead character's ambiguous sexual identity offered a vehicle particularly well suited to the current theatrical fascination with cross-dressing and gender bending.

Piaf. 1978. Opened at the Other Place, Stratford-upon-Avon. Directed by Howard Davies. Produced by the Royal Shakespeare Company. Moved to the Aldwych Theatre, London, the next season. Opened at the Plymouth Theatre (NY), 1981. Revived 1993 at the Picadilly Theatre, London.

Like many of Gems's play, *Piaf* has provided women performers with a star vehicle. Both Jane Lapotaire and Elaine Paige triumphed in portrayals of the colorful singer. Jane Lapotaire starred in the 1978 Royal Shakespeare Company's production at the Other Place before moving into the company's London headquarters, then at the Aldwych, and finally to Broadway.

Coveney [2] described Lapotaire as the embodiment of "bright-eyed effervescence and forthright sexuality," and Wardle [2] characterized her performance as one realizing "all the unstudied directness of the Piaf legend." McGarry contended that "Jane Lapotaire has taken the French legend by the throat and exposed her soul." Critics also agreed that Zoe Wanamaker playing Piaf's brazen sidekick, Toine, provided a fit match for Lapotaire. Wardle [2] described the Piaf-Toine relationship as a "a splendidly pugnacious double act." Their act made clear to him that the pair "never contemplate any other kind of life and get plenty of fun out of the job [prostitution]."

In addition to the attention given to the acting, critics made note of the production concept. Coveney [2] applauded Howard Davies for an effective "Brechtian production" taking place in an "ideal studio setting with ribbons of red neon light decorating a bare platform" and leaving "the audience to flesh out the bare but not so brittle bones." Critics of the Royal Shakespeare Company's premiere production also shared an admiration for Gems's script. McGarry credited Gems with giving Piaf "a kind of immortality." Wardle [2] lauded the play as "wonderfully adept at compression and cutting corners."

When the play opened in New York, Lapotaire and Wanamaker remained in the cast. Critics again generally praised the performances and had mixed reactions to the script. Rich wrote that Lapotaire's performance afforded her the "right to stand in for the 'Little Sparrow,' who died at age 47; one embraces her instantly and totally." He went on, however, to argue that the same could not be said for "Mrs. Gems's rather frail script." Watt had little complimentary to say for either the acting or writing. Kroll, on the other hand, described Lapotaire's performance as an electrifying one and Gems's work as having "power and velocity." Watt's review also contends that the cabaret style of the production—with its roots in the intimate stage of the Royal Shakespeare Company's Other Place—"loses some of its tension" in a Broadway Theatre.

The 1993 West End revival, under Peter Hall's direction and with Elaine Paige in the title role, met with critical response similar to that following the earlier productions of this script. Many critics, including Billington [2] and Doughty, suggested that Paige and Hall succeeded despite a flimsy script. When Doughty intimated that the production space seemed incompatible with the script and production concept, she picked up on a motif common to reviews of Gems's productions.

Camille. 1984. Opened October at the Other Place, Stratford-upon-Avon. Directed by Ron Daniels. After eighteen months transferred to Comedy Theatre, London.

The reviews of the Stratford production reveal patterns of reaction that persist in those of the comedy production. Gordon confesses that the Royal Shakespeare Company production brought him to tears in spite of Gems's attempts to strip the Camille legend of its sentimental distortions of prostitution. He writes that Marguerite (Frances Barber) and Armand's (Nicholas Farrell) bedroom scenes are "the most beautiful I've seen in a theatre." He realizes the relation of these scenes to the gist of the revisioning when he writes, "The stuff of Dumas fils' novel, of Verdi's opera seen through contemporary feminist eyes: how silly we men are, how absurd our pursuit of the orgasm, of security."

Many of the London reviews similarly identified tension between the lingering sentiment and the antisentimental impulse in the West End Comedy Theatre production. One of the most interesting observations about the London production came from Hirschhorn, who explained that the Gems play is one "hovering somewhere between the traditionally romantic approach and [Charles] Ludlam's blustering send up." Like many of his peers, Hirschhorn reserved his greatest accolades for Frances Barber in the lead role.

Whereas many critics commend the transfer from the small studio space to the more stately comedy, others argue—as Kroll did in writing about the New York production of *Piaf*—that the understated setting and production concept are at odds with the bigger theatre. Ratcliffe, for example, writes that the Royal Shakespeare Company production has "stayed exactly the same." There it may have been a "triumph," but on "a proscenium-arched stage as unlike as possible to the studio space for which it was devised," the production "isn't working."

The Blue Angel. 1991. Opening 29 August at the Royal Shakespeare Company's Other Place, Stratford-upon-Avon, *The Blue Angel* became part of the Royal Shakespeare Company's annual regional tour until February, when it transferred to London's Globe Theatre on 20 May 1992.

The Royal Shakespeare Company production of Gems's play, under the direction of Trevor Nunn and featuring Kelly Hunter as Lola, met with a warm reception. Many critics found the script somewhat uneven and tended to agree that Gems's work was at its strongest late in the play. Considerable attention went to the nature of Gems's adaptation. Comparisons to the 1930 film starring Marlena Dietrich typically suggested that Gems's bleaker and more haunting version had more similarity to the Heinrich Mann novel. Coveney [1], for example, wrote that in contrast to the film, Gems and Nunn reveal a much harsher story and extend the expressionist references right back to Frank Wedekind. Coveney was not alone in his reference to the expressionism of the production. Maria Bjornson's sets were largely considered the foundation for such a style. Nightingale described a set where the "floor is paved with cobblestones along which tram tracks run to a palatial arch and a zigzag staircase: here a giant mirror, there an askew streetlamp, above them a tiny, sloping bedroom." Worth noting here is that the same set was to be used in the Other Place's subsequent production of *Measure for Measure*.

Among the positive reactions to Trevor Nunn's direction was St. George's remark that "Nunn's direction is impeccable; the ensemble scenes seethe with energy, and the tense schoolroom is controlled to suite Madoc's stern, forbidding style. Nunn has never shied away from doing the obvious and making it work." However, while Hunter impressed some of her critics, others were less enthusiastic. Spencer noted that "sexual charisma is a highly personal and unanalyzable quality, but for me Miss Hunter just misses it."

When the play transferred to the West End, a familiar theme ran through a number of its reviews. St. George and Kellaway both noted that a good studio production doesn't necessarily transfer as a good West End production. Kellaway wrote that the transfer "was a lesson in the subjectivity of theatre going: what was magical in Norwich seemed frumpy in the West End." Overall, the critical reaction to the West End production was negative in tone. Morley offered one notable exception to the negativity. He proclaimed that "*The Blue Angel* is not only the best musical in town; in Pam Gems's script and Maria Bjornson's settings, it is also a brilliant summary of all the themes of 'Threepenny Opera' and 'Cabaret' and a reminder of the (principally) Friedrich Hollander songs to which Dietrich was to return at the end of the career they started."

ASSESSMENT OF GEMS'S CAREER

Given the scope of Gems's contribution to the British theatre, surprisingly little critical attention has been given to her work. Caryl Gardner predicted that Gems would "become the grand dame of the British theatre." Gardner asserts that where Caryl Churchill "may have conquered Broadway," it was Gems who "forced West End managers to reconsider the long held opinion that Agatha Christie is the only woman playwright of note the British theatre has produced" (12). Gems's prominence as the first woman playwright to be produced by the Royal Shakespeare Company as a playwright to have a series of premieres with the company as well as a number of West End productions, does establish her as a major force in the contemporary British theatre. Additionally, Gems's plays have been produced throughout the United States and Europe. Despite such visibility, however, no book-length treatment of the playwright exists. Gems is given attention in a handful of critical discussions, including Wandor [1] and Cave. However, much of what has been written about the playwright has been contained in the popular press.

Appraisals of Gems's work typically situate her within the context of feminist theatre and as a part of the growing visibility of women in the British theatre since the early 1970s. Gems herself has never seemed entirely comfortable with this association. Such resistance to feminist labels seems to have more to do with Gems's vision of artistic process than her politics. Throughout her career Gems has struggled to remain free from what she considers purely polemical writing. Nonetheless, in plays, essays, and interviews Gems consistently reveals a marked concern with the issues surrounding gender.

A consideration of Gems's career reveals how her concern with gender dynamics coexists with an empathy for the plight of the downtrodden, a fascination with revising historical images, and a deep suspicion of unchecked acceptance of traditional power structures.

Wandor [1] characterizes Gems as a playwright "gripped by the qualities of life at the bottom of the social heap" (162). The poverty Gems endured as a child made a lasting impression upon her, and her work reflects an acute sensitivity to the division between British socioeconomic classes. Some of Gems's most powerful scenes are those that expose the intersection of socioeconomic and gender oppression. *La Pasionara*, for example, offers a blunt understanding of its title character's exploitation not only by men but by wealthy women. And one of Gems's most striking revisions to the Camille legend is in her exposure of hard realities that make prostitution one of the very few viable options for women in poverty. Alexandre Dumas fils based his initial work—a novel—on the life of the French courtesan Marie DuPlessis. His novel and his play, as well as Guiseppi Verdi's *La Traviata*, which took up the same tale, treat prostitution with euphamism and sentimentality. Gems, on the other hand, follows more closely the hard realities of DuPlessis's life, which lead logically to prostitution. Gems's Marguerite reveals a life defined by poverty and early sexual abuse.

Gems frequently mingles such frank discussion with a decidedly sentimental streak. For some, however, the sentiment seems lost amid Gems's bolder strokes and, in turn, they find her characters lacking in subtlety. For example, Carne faults Gems for ''a superficial and recognizably 20th-century treatment of sexual politics appended to a rapid reading of the philosophical preoccupation of post-Reformation Europe.''

Despite the misgivings expressed in a handful of reviews, Gems must be given credit for her role in offering revisionist images of history that offer women challenging roles. These revisionings treat with sympathy characters such as Piaf and Queen Christina while revealing how they become not only victims but victimizers in societies characterized by uneven power distribution and rigid hierarchies of class and gender. Both Piaf and Queen Christina, for example, eventually emulate the very behavior that initially oppressed them. Queen Christina, bred to denigrate many of the characteristics ascribed to the feminine, scorns her mother. Only gradually does she realize how the attitudes she has internalized are the very ones that generated hostility toward her presence on the Swedish throne. Late in the play she becomes an isolated and lonely character mourning—if not for her mother—for motherhood. Early in *Piaf* the title character is prostituted and preyed upon; when she acquires wealth, however, she preys upon and prostitutes young men. Running counter to images of relationships based upon bartering and control, however, are more sentimental ones, particularly in Gems's treatment of Piaf's affair with boxer Marcel DuChamp.

To reinforce the tension between sentiment and antisentiment, Gems experiments with form and style. In the two plays discussed above Gems intermingles the conventions of realism with Brechtian techniques. In keeping with the goals of dramatic realism, the playwright does strive to incorporate the complex details of actual lives lead in her characterization of both Piaf and Queen Christina. Formally, however, both *Piaf* and *Queen Christina* adopt Brechtian models. Both are episodic and peopled with a number of characters who are given only cursory development. To some extent the Hall production of *Piaf* worked against the Brechtian form by integrating the songs more organically into the production—taking an approach more akin to that used in musical theatre than Brechtian style. Gems's acceptance of this change (not to mention her willingness to support it by translating the songs) typifies her flexibility and willingness to experiment.

Flexibility in terms of form and style has characterized Gems's career as a playwright. Whereas *Piaf* and *Queen Christina* strike something of a balance between Brechtian and realist techniques, *Camille* more closely resembles traditional realism. In this play Gems focuses on a more condensed time period and provides relatively extensive exposition to give her characters dimensionality and the semblance of unified personality. She also retains the general shape of the story she inherits. Her play moves from Marguerite and Armand's first acquaintance, through their passion, their separation and finally to the heroine's untimely death.

Consideration of the critical reaction to Gems's *Camille* contributes to the discussions surrounding form, style, and feminism. Because she does maintain grounding in traditional forms, some feminist critics have faulted her for failing to offer a more radical revisioning. Worth, for example, aligns Gems with her ''romantically minded predecessors glorifying the consumption of Marguerite.'' Gems herself has certain misgivings about approaching the Camille project and expresses continued dissatisfaction with the result—regretting particularly the decision to have Marguerite die late in the play.

At least one scholar, however, credits Gems with making formal choices that reinforce the feminist themes in *Camille*. Carlson [2] discusses the brief scenes that begin the play's acts. These scenes occur later on a chronological line than those that follow, giving something of a flashback effect to the bulk of the acts. Carlson argues that these scenes ''framing'' the play present Armand's—or the male's—perspective while the internal scenes present contrary perspectives, ''including Marguerite's'' situated in a ''female context.'' As Carlson implies, these scenes remind the reader and/or audience that a subjective lens filters the story, thereby dropping the guise of objectivity crucial to dramatic realism. Carlson also discusses Gems's use of the interlude to punctuate the narrative in Gems's revisioning.

As typified by the sultry interlude described above, Gems is capable of a rich theatricality. Given Gems's work with historical figures, her adaptations and revisions, it might be easy to lose sight of this theatricality and to characterize Gems as a playwright more preoccupied with the literary than the production aspects of theatre. However, one of Gems's strengths as a playwright is her flair for setting up striking stage imagery. Her best-known works, such as *Camille*, *Piaf*, and *Queen Christina*, do reveal this flair. However, some of Gems's most striking imagery can be found in the plays that have been less visible in her career. *The Treat* (1982) features some of the most haunting of images as it traces the physical and spiritual demise of Marie, a young prostitute.

The Treat's powerful last scene exemplifies Gems's skillful manipulation of visual imagery to offer concise stage metaphors. The play, with its almost expressionistic vignettes and Brechtian characters, also offers further insight into the innovation with form, style, and subject that characterize Gems's career. As with other playwrights, it is unfortunate that only the most commercially successful of Gems's plays have been studied. At this point there is still room and a need for more extensive consideration of her entire contribution to the theatre.

PRIMARY BIBLIOGRAPHY

Plays

Aunt Mary. In *Plays by Women*, ed. Michelene Wandor. Vol. 3. London: Methuen, 1984.
Dusa, Fish, Stas and Vi. In *Plays by Women*, ed. Michelene Wandor. Vol. 1. London: Methuen, 1982.

Piaf. London: Amber Lane Press, 1979.

Queen Christina. London: St. Luke's Press, 1982.

Queen Christina. In *Plays by Women,* ed. Mary Remnant. Vol. 5. London: Methuen, 1986.

Anthology

Three Plays: Piaf, Camille, and *Loving Women.* Harmondsworth: Penguin, 1985.

Essay on Drama and Theater

"Gender and Imagination." In *On Gender and Writing*, ed. Michelene Wandor. London: Pandora Press, 1983: 148–51.

SECONDARY BIBLIOGRAPHY

Barber, Michael. "Inquisitive View of a Scandalous Queen." *Daily Telegraph* (12 Sept. 1977): 53a.

Betko, Kathleen, and Rachel Koenig. "Pam Gems." *Interviews with Contemporary Women Playwrights.* New York: Beech Tree Books, 1987: 200–210.

Billington, Michael [1]. "First Night." *The Guardian* (11 Feb. 1977).

————[2]. Review of *Piaf. The Guardian* (5 Dec. 1993).

————[3]. Review of *Queen Christina. The Guardian* (May 1982).

Bray, Barbara. Introduction to *La Dame aux Camelias* by Alexandre Dumas fils. Trans. Barbara Bray. London: Folio Society, 1975.

Carlson, Susan [1]. "Process and Product: Contemporary British Theatre and its Communities of Women." *Theatre Research International* 13.3 (autumn 1988): 249–63.

————[2]. "Revisionary Endings: Pam Gem's *Aunt Mary* and *Camille.*" In *Making a Spectacle: Feminist Essays on Contemporary Theatre*, ed. Linda Hart. Ann Arbor: University of Michigan Press, 1989.

Carne, Rosalind. Review of *Queen Christina. Financial Times* (May 1992).

Cave, Richard Allen. *New British Drama in Performance on the London Stage: 1970–1985.* New York: St. Martin's Press, 1988.

Chevigny, Bell Gale. "Daughter's Writing: Toward a Theory of Women's Biography." In *Between Women: Biographers, Novelists, Critics, Teachers, and Artists Write about Their Work on Women*, ed. Carol Ascher, Louise DeSalvo, and Sara Ruddick. Boston: Beacon Press, 357–80.

Colvin, Claire. "Earth Mother from Christchurch." *Plays and Players* (Aug. 1982): 9–10.

Coveney, Michael [1]. "Blue Angel Delight." *The Observer* (1 Sept. 1991).

————[2]. Review of *Piaf. Financial Times* (13 Oct. 1978).

Doughty, Louise. Review of *Piaf. Mail on Sunday* (19 Dec. 1993).

Dumas fils, Alexandre. *La Dame aux Camelias.* Trans. Barbara Bray. London: Folio Society, 1975.

Gardner, Lyn. "Precious Gems." *Plays and Players* (Apr. 1985). 12–13.

Gordon, Giles. Review of *Camille. Punch* (6 Nov. 1985).

Hirschhorn, Clive. Review of *Camille. Sunday Express* (3 Mar. 1985).

Isaacs, David. ''The Calm Gentle Woman Pressing for Change.'' *Coventry Evening Telegraph* (9 Sept. 1977).

Kellaway, Kate. Review of *The Blue Angel*. *The Observer* (24 May 1992).

Kroll, Jack. ''Song of the Streets.'' *Newsweek* (16 Feb. 1981).

McGarry, Peter. ''Powerful Piaf.'' *Coventry Evening Telegraph* (12 Oct. 1978).

Morley, Sheridan. Review of *The Blue Angel*. *Herald Tribune* (27 May 1992).

Nightingale, Benedict. ''Seduced by Social Sleaze.'' *The Times* (31 Aug. 1991).

Peter, John. ''A Woman's Face.'' *Sunday Times* (15 Sept. 1982).

Ratcliffe, Michael. Review of *Camille*. *The Observer* (3 Nov. 1985).

Rich, Frank. ''Jane Lapotaire Scores in Piaf.'' *New York Times* (16 Feb. 1981.)

Spencer, Charles. Review of *The Blue Angel*. *Daily Telegraph* (22 May 1992).

St. George, Andrew. Review of *The Blue Angel*. *Financial Times* (23 May 1992).

Thinkell, Arthur. ''Girl Talk That Pulls No Punches.'' *Daily Mirror* (11 Feb. 1977).

Wandor, Michelene [1]. *Carry on, Understudies: Theatre and Sexual Politics*. London: Routledge & Kegan Paul, 1981.

———[2]. *Look Back in Gender: Sexuality and the Family in Post-War British Drama*. London: Methuen, 1987.

———[3]. ''Women Are Uncharted Territory.'' *Spare Rib* (Sept. 1977): 10–12.

Wardle, Irving [1]. ''Four Drop-outs from the Cat Race.'' *Financial Times* (11 Feb. 1977).

———[2]. Review of *Piaf*. *Financial Times* (12 Oct. 1978).

Watt, Douglas. '' 'Piaf' Strikes a False Note on Stage.'' *New York Daily News* (6 Feb. 1981).

Worth, Katharine. ''Images of Women in Modern English Theatre.'' In *Feminine Focus: The New Woman Playwrights*, ed. Enoch Brater. Oxford: Oxford University Press, 1989: 22.

Simon Gray

(1936–)

TONY J. STAFFORD

Simon Gray has not followed after theatrical fashions but has written for the theatre in his own unique way. Going against the trends in the British theatre in the 1960s when he began writing plays, and thereafter, he has usually written in a naturalistic stage style, in spite of the liberating influence of Brecht, and he has written about a social class that is neither deprived nor privileged.

Simon Gray was born 21 October 1936, in Hayling Island, Hampshire, England, to James Davidson Gray, a pathologist, and Barbara Celia Mary (Holliday) Gray. In 1940 Gray was evacuated to the safety of Montreal, Canada, to live with his paternal grandparents for the duration of World War II. It was there that he began his formal education. In 1945 he returned to England to continue his education at Portsmouth Grammar School and later at Westminster, a prestigious public school in London. Because of his background in the Canadian school system, he had a difficult time adjusting to Westminster's program. He confessed later that he felt at odds with the image of the "proper British schoolboy" that was held up for him to follow. After graduating from Westminster he moved with his family back to Canada, where he matriculated at Dalhousie University in Halifax, Nova Scotia. He graduated with honors from Dalhousie with a baccalaureate degree in English in 1957 and then traveled to France, where he took a lectureship in English at the Université de Clermont-Ferrand. In 1959 he enrolled in Trinity College of Cambridge University to do graduate work in English. Although he seemed not to be totally diligent about his studies, he nevertheless took an M.A. degree with honors in 1961 and received the Harperwood Travelling Studentship, which he used to spend six months in Spain. There he wrote his first novel, a satirical stab at life in the imaginary Canadian province of New Thumberland. The work was published in 1963.

He returned to Cambridge after his sojourn abroad and became a research student, first at St. John's College and later at Trinity, from which he received a second B.A. degree in English with honors in 1963. He became a supervisor in English at Trinity and during the academic year 1963–1964 he traveled to Canada to serve as a lecturer in English at the University of British Columbia in Vancouver, returning to Trinity in 1964 once more as a supervisor. In the midst of his academic peregrinations, on August 20, 1964, he married Beryl Mary Kevern, a picture researcher, and in 1965 he accepted a permanent faculty position in English at Queen Mary's College at the University of London and began to edit *Delta Magazine*. That same year his second novel, *Simple People*, based on his experience as an academician in England with a Canadian background, was published; a third novel, *Little Portia*, also appeared. By this time the literary critics had already noticed that in his novels ''the playwright is always trying to get out,'' and it was not long before he turned to the dramatic form when one of his short stories caught the attention of a television producer. Gray agreed to write the adaptation himself, and in 1966 the BBC broadcast it as *The Caramel Crisis*, the first of a dozen or so original television plays.

After seeing a production of Harold Pinter's *The Homecoming*, he decided to concentrate on playwrighting, and in 1967 *Wise Child*, based on an actual case of a man who murdered his mother for insurance money, was produced in London, where it enjoyed a respectable run, but it later drew the ire of the New York critics and closed after only four performances. That same year *Death of a Teddy Bear*, *Sleeping Dog*, and *A Way with the Ladies* were broadcast on BBC-TV, and the following year *A Comeback for Stark* was published under the pseudonym Hamish Reade.

Gray continued to struggle with a tepid reception from critics and the public. In 1969 *Dutch Uncle* was produced by the Royal Shakespeare Company, but negative reviews precluded any plans of moving it to a commercial West End theatre, and *Spoiled*, a stage adaptation of an earlier television play, closed after three weeks of playing to only partially filled houses.

Gray's fortunes changed drastically for the better in 1971 with the production of *Butley*, which enjoyed a highly successful run in London as well as in New York, where Alan Bates, in the lead role, won a Tony Award for best actor. This positive experience was followed by the success of *Otherwise Engaged* in 1975, which ran for two-and-a-half years in London before opening in New York in 1977.

Through the rest of the 1970s and through the 1980s, Gray continued to write and produce plays, such as *Dog Days* and *Molly* in 1976, *The Rear Column* in 1978, *Stage Struck* in 1979, *Quartermaine's Terms* in 1981, *The Common Pursuit* in 1984, *Hidden Laughter* in 1989, and *The Holy Terror* in 1991.

In spite of his success as a playwright and novelist, Gray continues to teach nineteenth-century English literature, commuting weekdays by subway to Queen Mary's College in the East End of London from his large Victorian terrace house in the Highgate section of north London. He is a great admirer of Charles Dickens, who is a major influence on his work, and of T. S. Eliot, of whom he says, "[My] life and work would have been very different if it hadn't been for him."

Selected Biographical Sources: Gale; Hamilton; Kerensky; Stephenson; Vinson.

MAJOR PLAYS, PREMIERES, AND SIGNIFICANT
REVIVALS: THEATRICAL RECEPTION

Wise Child. 1967. Opened 10 October at Wyndham's Theatre, London, under the direction of John Dexter. Sir Alec Guinness played the lead role of Mrs. Artminster, who is in fact a criminal on the run disguised as a woman. The play had a respectable run of close to 100 performances. It opened in New York on 27 January 1972, at the Helen Hayes Theatre, presented by Paul Alter and directed by James Hammerstein with Donald Pleasence in the lead role; but the critics were unmerciful and the play closed after only four performances.

In spite of repeated comparisons to the farces of Joe Orton, the general critical assessment was that Gray had not made up his mind whether to write a "full-blooded farce or a problem play" (Imhof, 228) and that the long set speeches counteract the play's farcical intent. John Russell Taylor [2] admits that "the play's situation is piquant and its elaboration quite adroit—almost adroit enough to hide its essential slimness and lack of real progression."

Dutch Uncle. 1969. Opened 17 March at the Aldwych Theatre, London, after a production in Brighton at the Theatre Royal that had opened on 3 March. Staged by the Royal Shakespeare Company in association with H. M. Tennent and Ernest Hecht and directed by Peter Hall.

Dutch Uncle starred Warren Mitchell, the actor from the extremely popular television comedy *Til Death Do Us Part.* This production was originally intended to be a tryout before transferring to the West End, but the first-night reviews were so devastating that the transfer never occurred. Taylor [2] observed that it was meant to be "a simple farce and nothing more. But as such, despite a few bright moments, it can be accounted only a fairly feeble example of the genre." Wardle labeled it "the saddest piece of butchery" he had ever seen at the Old Vic.

Spoiled. 1971. Opened 24 February at the Haymarket Theatre, London, for 135 performances. Directed by Stephen Hollis.

Spoiled is an expanded version of Gray's successful 1968 television play about the ambiguous relationship between an immature schoolmaster and his admiring, high-strung pupil and its effect on his troubled marriage. In New York it closed after three weeks of half-empty houses. Most critics perceived it as a departure from his earlier Ortonesque farces (Jones and Imhof). New felt that it demonstrates Gray's "relaxed command over the techniques of stage drama and the developing breadth of his social views." Taylor [2] saw it as a "sober and rather dull play" and felt that the climactic scene of the man seducing the boy and then being confronted by his wife "falls with a dull thud." Imhof said that "too many problems are touched upon without being fully accounted for," that the final outcome is "disappointing," and that the scene between the teacher and the pupil "strains our credulity."

Butley. 1971. Opened 14 July at the Criterion Theatre, London, directed by Harold Pinter with Alan Bates in the starring role. Won the *Evening Standard* Award as best play of the year.

Clive Barnes's [1] assessment was that Gray has written about his "half-baked academic" with "astonishing compassion" and that he has devised his comedy with "considerable adroitness"; Barnes also noted that "Butley is no major contribution to dramatic literature, but it is that sadly rare thing—a literate and literary comedy with a heart," and that it has done well in capturing a "specific mood and style." Taylor [3] observed that Gray has a "gift for depicting highly literate characters as though this is their normal habit of mind," that he shows "ingenuity in old-fashioned dramatic construction" and a "sensitivity to the unease of sexual borderlines as a motivating factor in life." In a later evaluation, Kerensky opined that "it is difficult to account for the great success of this play. It is both witty and psychologically interesting, but one might have expected that its appeal would be limited to middle-class intellectuals." In a scholarly treatise Blaydes notes that Gray has "effectively used allusions to literature to undermine the illusions of academe."

Otherwise Engaged. 1975. Opened 30 July at the Queen's Theatre, London, for a two-and-one-half-year run; presented by Michael Codron, directed by Harold Pinter, and starring Alan Bates. Won the *Evening Standard* Award for best play. An American production, featuring Tom Courtenay and, later, talk show host Dick Cavett, opened at the Plymouth Theatre (NY) in February 1977. Won the New York Drama Critics Circle Award for best play.

Most of the reviews were extremely positive, typified by Hobson's [2] labeling it "one of the best plays of our time . . . very delicate, very subdued, very subliminal." Alan Rich praised it for its "writing," its "elegant plotting," its "character-painting," and its "lovely compliments to the alert and intelligent among our theatregoers," and then he pronounced it a "wonderfully funny, incisively wise play, better even in impact and structure than his excellent *Butley.*" Novick declared it to reverberate "in the mind," to have the "smell about it of old boarding-school obsessions, erotic and otherwise"; he also declared that although it is "repetitive and predictable," it is "never boring." While Sainer quibbled about there being "a bit too much of poking around in the woodpile," he also proclaimed Simon Hench, the hero, to be a "treasure." Kerensky, in a later scholarly assessment, reduced the play to "a series of witty and sometimes outrageous revue sketches." But Hobson [2], in reviewing *Quartermaine's Terms*, made reference to *Otherwise Engaged* as evidence to pronounce all of Gray's plays as having a "power" that is "great and haunting."

A very perceptive and refreshing point of view came from Imhof in a scholarly evaluation of the play when, in disagreeing with the German critic of *Die*

Zeit, who said the play was about the "total indifference of an intellectual," he noted that the characters who barge into Simon's living room are to a "greater extent 'otherwise engaged' than Simon himself" and that none of them ever once consider "whether she or he is imposing upon Simon."

Dog Days. 1976. Opened 26 October at the Oxford Playhouse, Oxford, directed by Gordon McDougall for a brief run.

Dog Days received little critical attention, but Kerensky, in a scholarly assessment, called it "more moving" and "sharper in its psychological observations" than *Otherwise Engaged*.

Molly. 1977. Opened in November at the Watford Palace Theatre, London, directed by Stephen Hollis. Moved to New York, February 1978. It was first produced in Charleston, S.C. to open the New Spoleto Festival in May 1977.

Molly is a stage adaptation of Gray's television script *Death of a Teddy Bear* and loosely based on the Alma Rattenbury murder case of 1935. Imhof classifies it as "among Mr. Gray's least satisfactory dramatic exercises" and declares that "the character of Molly is a disaster." Oliver [2], admitting that it is "not a flawless work," nevertheless stated that "it adds up to a generally accomplished evening."

The Rear Column. 1978. Opened 22 February at the Globe Theatre, London, for forty-five performances, presented by Michael Codron and directed by Harold Pinter. Transferred to the Manhattan Theatre Club (NY) on 3 December.

The Rear Column is based on the historical event of Stanley's leaving behind a rear column while he traveled in other parts of Africa. The play was negatively reviewed by London critics. The main complaint seemed to be that Gray goes into Africa with modern eyes and practices historical revisionism. Fox labeled the play "a curious work" and complained that "there is no largeness of purpose possible in this play, and that, ultimately, is what belittles the script."

The American critics were more positive, generally praising it for its intelligent craftsmanship, for sympathetic characterizations, and for its insight and vision. While John Simon [3] qualified his praise by saying that it is not "exceptionally enlightening or original," he did say that it demonstrates a "shrewd command of dramatic strategy," "sharp but not unduly clever dialogue," and "firm control over character development and interaction." Oliver [4] called it "essentially a play of character, ironic and tragic" and that the characters are written with "admirable subtlety and clarity."

Close of Play. 1979. Opened 24 May in the Lyttleton Auditorium of the National Theatre, London, directed by Harold Pinter. Starred Sir Michael Redgrave and Dame Margaret Ashcroft. Transferred to the Manhattan Theatre Club (NY), 24 February 1981, directed by Lynne Meadow. *Close of Play* received acceptable reviews, which seemed fortunate at the time, considering that a strike at the National Theatre had interrupted rehearsals for six weeks after which Ashcroft broke her leg and had to be replaced by an understudy. The confusion over the reality of the father is focused on by Jenkins, who noted that "it is not quite clear whether he dies at the end, is dead throughout, or whether the whole play is intended to take place at his moment of dying."

Whereas London audiences and critics tended to think of the old man as having suffered a stroke, the American production tried to bring out the fact, according to Gray himself (see Blau), that he is already dead. Taylor [3] labeled it "solemn and slow and boring and obscurely symbolic." Hobson [1] said that "Gray takes a sour view of the world; and this sourness is . . . reflected in Henry's sexual stumble," but he did admit that Henry's confrontation with his father was "brilliant" and that Daisy's confession at the end, revealing happiness instead of misery, "gives to the play a truly magnificent ending."

Stage Struck. 1979. Opened 21 November at the Vaudeville Theatre, London, where it enjoyed commercial success and ran for almost two years.

The London critics were mainly disappointed, noting mostly its entertainment value and comparing it to Anthony Shaffer's *Sleuth* and Ira Levin's *Deathtrap*. Nightingale [3] roughed up the play and the playwright, threatening to scratch Gray's name "out of our professional address books." He called it "a distraction, an entertainment, . . . pretend[ing] to be nothing more" and "a not-very-remarkable example of the brand of thriller patented by Anthony Shaffer," but, he went on to say, it does display "some of that fascination with callousness, betrayal and general human perversity to be found at the puckered heart of Gray's best work." Nightingale also cuttingly suggested that Gray should write another play. Stephenson speculated that it "seems to have been hastily written and marks no real advance [for Gray] either dramaturgically or philosophically."

Hobson [4] praised the play for raising "questions that will furnish the audience with matter for long argument hours after they have left the theatre" and for its "sardonic and cynical wit."

Quartermaine's Terms. 1981. Opened 28 July at the Queen's Theatre, London, for 275 performances, presented by Michael Codron, directed by Harold Pinter, and featuring Edward Fox as St. John Quartermaine. New York opening at Playhouse 91, 24 February 1983, a Long Wharf Theatre production produced by John A. McQuiggan and Ethel Watt in association with Brent Peek Productions.

Most critics perceived the Chekhovian tradition behind the play's naturalism and sadness. By and large the American critics were impressed with Gray's efforts in this work. Hobson [3] felt it was "amusing and witty, its wit exceeded only by its delicate and infinite sadness, the infinite sadness of absolute and utter loneliness." Nightingale [4] called it a "refreshingly sensitive, observant piece; autumnal in mood," while Simon [1] praised it as being "a wonderfully restrained, irreverently humane, wryly tender play" and for keeping the audience suspended between "laughter and melancholy." This mixture was also noted by Frank Rich [2], who said it "is at once full of doom and gloom and bristling with wry, even uproarious comedy. The mixture is so artfully balanced that we really don't know where the laughter ends and the tears begin.''

The play tends to stand or fall on the way in which the title character, St. John Quartermaine, is perceived. Hobson [3] declared that ''his great loneliness . . . pierces the audience like a sword,'' whereas Rich analyzed Quartermaine as ''an anachronism carried through life by sheer inertia and by the cozy, quintessentially paternalistic institution that employs him.''

In assessing the play's meaning Frank Rich [2] said that ''the subject . . . is the decline of British life and institutions, and Nightingale [4] surmised that Gray ''isn't interested in moral blacks and whites.''

Not all the critical opinions, however, were positive. Taylor [3], for example, accused Gray of being ''actually boring,'' holding ''his characters at a distance . . . with great ingenuity but never actually persuading us to believe, much less to care.'' He suggested that Gray's plays need more ''heart'' because he is ''an accomplished entertainer who never cuts deep.'' Nelson conceded that the play is charming but that ''there are points at which charm loses its hold.'' Whereas some felt that Quartermaine's final words of ''Oh, lord'' were quite moving, Kerr said that the ''last few moments strike me as flattest of all. . . . The ambiguous 'Oh, lord' that he mutters before the last lights fade doesn't take us into the man's mind.'' Kerr also accused the play of being a ''highly schematic piece of work that . . . seems to have adopted the wrong scheme.''

The Common Pursuit: Scenes from the Literary Life. 1984. Opened 28 June at the Lyric Theatre, London, presented by the Lyric Theatre and directed by Harold Pinter. United States premiere at the Long Wharf Theatre, New Haven, (CT) on 11 January 1985. New York premiere 19 October 1986, Promenade Theatre.

The play was met with resistance in London and in the United States. Giles [2] wished Pinter had not directed it because of his efforts to ''shape this trivia into something of substance'' served only to bring out the play's ''intrinsic superficiality.'' Giles then called it a ''self-satisfied, verbally slack, intellectually vapid piece.'' Khan complained that ''we are expected to believe in the specialness of a group of people who seem to have nothing but a certain glib and mannered wit to recommend them.'' Only Kroll seemed to find something in the play to praise; he found ''Gray's tools sharp and polished as ever.'' He also called the characters a ''microcosm of the world of liberal culture that may be on the verge of extinction'' and praised Gray for contemplating ''this prospect with his seductive blend of melancholy and ironic wit.''

ADDITIONAL PLAYS, ADAPTATIONS, AND OTHER PRODUCTIONS

Gray did an adaptation of Fyodor Dostoyevski's *The Idiot*, which was produced in London in 1970, and an adaptation of Molière's *Tartuffe*, which was produced at the Kennedy Center in Washington, D.C., in 1982 and later in New York. Several plays were produced but had unsuccessful runs: *Dog Days*, in Oxford in 1976; *Melon* in London in 1987; *Hidden Laughter* in Brighton in 1989 and in London in 1990; and *Holy Terror* in Arizona in 1991. Gray has also had produced a number of teleplays for BBC-TV: *The Caramel Crisis* (1966), *Sleeping Dog* (1967), *Pig in a Poke* (1969), *Man in a Side-Car* (1971), *Plaintiffs and Defendants* (1975), *Two Sundays* (1975), *After Pilkington* (1986), *A Month in the Country* (1987), *The Holy Terror: Melon Revised* (1989), *Old Flames* (1990), and *They Never Slept* (1991).

ASSESSMENT OF GRAY'S CAREER

Simon Gray's evolution as a playwright must first be seen in the context of his other literary activities. He began as a novelist in 1963, writing three novels in succession, *Colmain*, *Simple People*, and *Little Portia*, and later adding a fourth, entitled *A Comeback for Stark* written under the pseudonym Hamish Reade. These novels gained respectability upon their publication but, more importantly, revealed a writer's natural talent for the dramatic form. In these narrative pieces, descriptions tend to become stage settings, action sounds like stage directions, and dialogue becomes the dynamics through which the story and conflicts are advanced. These works also contain in embryonic form some of the major ingredients of his plays: realistic style, a literary, often academic setting, and the struggle for selfhood.

Fiction also served as the basis for his transition to the dramatic form. Gray seems to have discovered his propensity for drama when in the process of writing a short story it came to him mostly in the form of dialogue. The story eventually evolved into the teleplay, *The Caramel Crisis*; this was followed by *Death of a Teddy Bear*, *A Way with the Ladies*, and *Sleeping Dog*. Thus began his second writing career, which served as a preparation for and a close link to playwrighting. In the course of his career he has written some twenty-odd teleplays and screen plays, in some cases adapting stage plays to television and cinema and in some cases converting teleplays to stage plays. This movement back and forth informs his work in both media, and certain motifs occur in both forms: ambiguous sexuality, games of dominance and submission, and a culture that contains shocking and brutal episodes. It must not be overlooked that Gray has been prolific in the field of script writing and that he has been quite successful at mass entertainment, producing television plays that are gripping and appealing to a wide audience.

According to Gray, he first turned to playwriting after seeing a production of Harold Pinter's *The Homecoming* in 1965.

Gray's uniqueness is best defined in the context of the theatrical milieu in which he arrived in the mid-1960s. A decade earlier the British theatre was shaken out of its drawing-room-comedy lethargy (the theatre of Somerset Maugham, Noël Coward, and Terence Rattigan) by the appearance of Samuel

Beckett's *Waiting for Godot*, the visitation of Bertolt Brecht's Berliner Ensemble repertory company, and the history-making production of John Osborne's *Look Back in Anger*. Beckett's play challenged audiences to come to the theatre to probe abstract ideas in dramatic form. Brecht's plays invited audiences to look at the stage as a stage and not as some pseudo-imitation of real life and to stand back and think about the undercurrent of ideas emerging in a dramatic context. Osborne's play, a watershed in British theatre history, compelled audiences to recognize that classes of society, other than the aristocracy, exist, feel, think, struggle, and are worthy of dramatic examination. These events helped to create a new British theatre by the end of the 1950s. The playwrights of the next decade—an extension of the so-called Angry Young Men of the 1950s—sought to write plays that dealt with ideas, that treated the stage as liberated from naturalism, and that wrote about the working class, from which they came.

During the 1960s British playwrights such as John Osborne, Arnold Wesker, Shelagh Delaney, and Edward Bond were writing about middle, lower, and impoverished classes; during this same period, playwrights such as John Arden, Brendan Behan, Tom Stoppard, and N. F. Simpson (followed later by playwrights such as Peter Nichols, Peter Barnes, Peter Shaffer, and Caryl Churchill) freed the stage from naturalistic clutter and treated the stage as a stage and a performance as a performance. Whether focusing on social class or experimenting with form, almost all sought to write plays that contained ideas, relevance, and significance.

In the midst of the trends of the 1960s in the British theatre, Simon Gray goes his own way. While others are attempting to push the stage to its abstract limits and away from naturalism, Gray embraces naturalism as his primary style. In *Butley* he goes so far as to center the action on one working day in the office of a teacher. Rarely in the course of his career has Gray strayed far from the path of mainstream realism. The exceptions are few: in *Close of Play*, for example, the dead father sits silently ignored throughout the play, speaking only at the end but the experiment seemed only to confuse critics and audiences. On the other hand, while the content of many British plays in the 1960s and thereafter deals with lower-class struggles, Gray depicts a world composed mostly of people who are intelligent, educated, verbal, and comfortable. And whereas many plays of that period deal overtly with social issues and ideas, Gray writes plays that have an un-self-conscious surface immediacy that belies their deeper significance and creates characters often unaware of polemics and issues.

In the aftermath of the appearance of his earliest plays, and occasionally thereafter as well, critics tried to identify the influences on him. After his first two farcical-like efforts, *Wise Child* and *Dutch Uncle*, critics identified the presence of Joe Orton (as well as Alan Bennett's *Habeas Corpus*), but Gray subsequently stated that at that time he was unfamiliar with Orton's plays. After the success of *Butley*, critics compared its verbal pyrotechnics to that of Tom Stoppard's *Jumpers*, while others saw the shaping hand of Pinter in its plotlessness. Later his *Spoiled* brought comparisons to Osborne's *West of Suez*; *The*

Rear Column suggested Joseph Conrad's *Heart of Darkness*, and Major Bartlett of the same play recalled Captain Queeg of *The Caine Mutiny*. After its West End appearance critics immediately categorized *Stage Struck* with Anthony Shaffer's *Sleuth* and Ira Levin's *Deathtrap*, and after *Quartermaine's Terms* they invoked the name of Anton Chekhov, especially since he is referred to in the play. The influences appear to be from everywhere when in fact they are from nowhere. Gray admits to a deep love for, and partial influence by, Charles Dickens, and he praises T. S. Eliot as his favorite poet, but what is ultimately clear is that Gray works independently of the literary and dramatic world around him and writes with his own voice.

Gray has gone his own way in the theatre, but that way has sometimes been costly to him, for he has suffered his share of failures and abuse for his risk taking. His works have been variously assessed, even as ''the saddest piece of butchery'' ever seen at the Old Vic, causing the audience to suffer from ''irritated restlessness.'' Once he was labeled ''the worst playwright in England,'' he has himself been brutally, but good-naturedly, frank about his failures. He called the opening night of *Dutch Uncle* ''the worst night in the British theatre,'' and he has noted his ''purple patch,'' a time during which he ''managed three flops in a row,'' himself classifying them as a ''flop total,'' a ''flop d'estime,'' and a ''flop merely.'' This happens to playwrights who take chances and go their own way. Everyone remembers *Hamlet* and *Long Day's Journey into Night*, but one needs to be reminded of *Titus Andronicus* and *Lazarus Laughed*. And while Gray has had his failures, he also has his share of successes. Among those that will be remembered favorably are *Butley*, *Otherwise Engaged*, and *Quartermaine's Terms*.

In Gray's most successful works, certain common elements appear. First, he writes about the world he knows best, the world of academicians, teachers, schools, and books (while Simon Hench in *Otherwise Engaged* is a publisher, his brother, a presence in the play, is a teacher). Second, the style of all three— *Butley*, *Otherwise Engaged*, and *Quartermaine's Terms*—is the style he is most at home with, a naturalistic, Chekhovian mood, sustained without straining from beginning to end. Third, the focus of each play is on an individual who is, at great sacrifice and without crusading for it, uncompromisingly himself and cannot be otherwise. It is this element, Gray's concern for the human being's struggle to be his or her unique self, that give Gray's plays their universal and enduring quality—and it comes from his own very personal experience of trying to be his own unique playwright.

PRIMARY BIBLIOGRAPHY

Plays

After Pilkington. London: Methuen, 1987.
Butley. London: Methuen, 1971.

Close of Play and *Pig in a Poke*. London: Eyre Methuen, 1980.

The Common Pursuit. London: Methuen, 1984.

Dog Days. London: Eyre Methuen, 1976.

Dutch Uncle. London: Faber & Faber, 1969.

Hidden Laughter. London: Faber & Faber, 1990.

Holy Terror. London: Faber & Faber, 1990.

The Idiot. Adapted from Fyodor Dostoyevski. London: Methuen, 1972.

Melon. London: Methuen, 1987.

Molly. London: Samuel French, 1979.

Old Flames and *A Month in the Country*. London: Faber & Faber, 1990.

Otherwise Engaged. London: Samuel French, 1976.

Otherwise Engaged and Other Plays. (*Plaintiffs and Defendants*, *Two Sundays*). London: Eyre Methuen, 1975; New York: Viking, 1976.

Quartermaine's Terms. London: Eyre Methuen, 1981; Revised, London: Methuen, 1983.

The Rear Column and Other Plays. (*Molly*, *Man in a Side-Car*). London: Eyre Methuen, 1978.

Sleeping Dog. London: Faber & Faber, 1968.

Spoiled. London: Methuen, 1972.

Stage Struck. London: Eyre Methuen, 1979.

The Holy Terror/Tartuffe: An Adaptation. London: Faber & Faber, 1990.

Wise Child. London: Faber & Faber, 1968.

Anthologies

The Definitive Simon Gray, I. (*Butley*, *Wise Child*, *Dutch Uncle*, *Spoiled*, *The Caramel Crisis*, *Sleeping Dog*). London: Faber & Faber, 1992.

The Definitive Simon Gray, II. (*Otherwise Engaged*, *Dog Days*, *Molly*, *Pig in a Poke*, *Man in a Side-Car*, *Plaintiffs and Defendants*, *Two Sundays*). London: Faber & Faber, 1992.

The Definitive Simon Gray, III. (*Quartermaine's Terms*, *The Real Column*, *Close of Play*, *Stage Struck*, *Tartuffe: An Adaptation*, *A Month in the Country*). London: Faber & Faber, 1992.

The Definitive Simon Gray, IV. (*Hidden Laughter*, *The Common Pursuit: Scenes from the Literary Life*, *The Holy Terror: Melon Revisited*, *After Pilkington*, *Old Flames*, *They Never Slept*). London: Faber & Faber, 1992.

Interviews

"Interview by Nan Robertson." *New York Times* (28 Feb. 1983): 3: 9.

"Interview by Sylvia Drake." *Los Angeles Times* (29 Jan. 1986): 6: 1.

"Interview" (with Peter Ansorge). *Plays and Players* (19 Aug. 1972): 33–34.

"Nightmare and Nicotine" (with Jeremy Kingston). *The Times* (7 June 1990): C18.

"Striking Up a Stage Partnership" (with John Higgins). *The Times* (14 Nov. 1979): B10.

"Teaching Is My Bloody Life" (with Mel Gussow). *New York Times* (9 Feb. 1977): C12.

SECONDARY BIBLIOGRAPHY

Barbera, Jack V. "A Key Allusion in *Otherwise Engaged.*" *Notes on Contemporary Literature* 9 (1979): 5–6.

Barnes, Clive [1]. "Butley." *New York Times* (1 Nov. 1972): 54.

———[2]. "The Idiot: Old Vic, London." *New York Times* (30 July 1970): 39.

Berkvist, Robert. "Simon Gray Explores the Roots of Atrocity: *Rear Column.*" *New York Times* (19 Nov. 1978): 5, 30.

Billington, Michael. "Quartermaine's Terms." *The Guardian* (31 July 1981): 11.

Blau, Eleanor. "Simon Gray Tries a 'Ghostly' Comedy: An Interview." *New York Times* (22 Feb. 1981): 2: 4.

Blaydes, Sophia B. "Literary Allusion as Satire in Simon Gray's '*Butley.*' " *Midwest Quarterly* 18 (July 1977): 374–91.

Burkman, Katherine. "The Fool as Hero: Simon Gray's *Butley* and *Otherwise Engaged.*" *Theatre Journal* 33 (1981): 163–72.

Clum, John M. "Eliot, 'Epipsychidion,' and the Post-modern Wasteland: Allusion in Simon Gray's *Butley* and Peter Gill's *Mean Tears.*" In *Text and Presentation: The University of Florida Department of Classics Comparative Drama Conference Papers*, ed. Karelisa Hartigan. Vol. 9. Lanham, MD: University Press of America, 1989.

Cornish, Roger, and Violet Ketels. Introduction to *Quartermaine's Terms. Landmarks of Modern British Drama*. Vol. 2. London: Methuen, 1985: 445–50.

Eder, Richard. "*Rear Column*, A Drama by Simon Gray." *New York Times* (20 Nov. 1978): C15.

Fields, Sidney. "*Wise Child.*" *Daily News* (27 Jan. 1972): 64.

Fox, Terry Curtis. "Heart of Grayness." *Village Voice* (4 Dec. 1978): 121–22.

Gale, Steven H. "Simon Gray." In *Critical Survey of Drama*, ed. Frank Magill. Vol. 2. Englewood Cliffs, NJ: Salem Press, 1985: 804–13.

Giles, Gordon [1]. "*Butley.*" *Plays and Players* (Oct. 1984): 32.

———[2]. "Person to Person." *The Spectator* 253 (14 July 1984): 33–34.

Grant, Steve. "*The Common Pursuit.*" *Plays and Players* (Aug. 1984): 26–27.

Hamilton, Ian. "Simon Gray." *New Review* 3 (Jan./Feb. 1977): 39–46.

Henrichs, B. "Ein Erfolgsstuck. Warum?" *Die Zeit* (4 Feb. 1977): 30.

Hobson, Harold [1]. "Hobson's Choice: '*Close of Play.*' " *Drama* (summer 1979): 41–42.

———[2]. "Hobson's Choice." *Drama* (winter 1981): 29–34.

———[3]. "*Quartermaine's Terms.*" *Drama* (winter 1981): 16–17.

———[4]. "Stage Struck." *Drama* (Jan. 1980): 36.

Imhof, Rudiger. "Simon Gray." In *Essays on Contemporary British Drama*, eds. Hedwig Bock and Albert Wertheim. Munich: Max Hueber Verlag, 1981: 223–52.

Jenkins, Peter. "Two for Tea." *The Spectator* (9 June 1979): 30.

Jones, John Bush. "The Wit and the Wardrobe: Simon Gray's Tragic (?) Comedies." *West Virginia University Philological Papers* 25 (1979): 78–85.

Kelly, Kevin. "Gray's Weightless *Hidden Laughter*: Vaudeville Theatre, London." *Boston Globe* (21 Aug. 1990): 55.

Kerensky, Oleg. *The New British Drama: Fourteen Playwrights since Osborne and Pinter*. New York: Taplinger, 1977.

Kerr, Walter. "How Can We Admire a Less than Human Hero?" *New York Times* (6 Mar. 1983): 2: 3, 7.

Khan, Nassem. "Modern Manners." *New Statesman* (13 July 1984): 34.

Kroll, Jack. "Six Refugees from a Lost World." *Newsweek* (11 Feb. 1985): 63.

Lambert, J. W. "Otherwise Engaged." *Drama* (winter 1975): 103–11.

Lawson, Mark. "Melon." *Plays and Players* (Aug. 1987): 20–21.

Mills, John. "Old Mr. Prickle-Pin: Simon Gray's Butley." *American Imago* 45 (1988): 411–29.

Nelson, Byron. "The Unhappy Mean in Simon Gray's *Otherwise Engaged.*" *Modern Drama* 224 (Dec. 1979): 365–74.

Nelson, Don. "*Quartermaine's Terms*: A Man's Betrayal." *Daily News* (25 Feb. 1983): 97. Reprinted in *New York Theatre Critics Reviews* 1983: 295.

New, William H. "Household Locks: The Plays of Simon Gray." *Dramatists in Canada: Selected Essays*. Vancouver: University of British Columbia Press, 1972: 163–72.

Nightingale, Benedict [1]. "Charting the Logic of Atrocity: *Rear Column.*" *New York Times* (5 Mar. 1978): 3: 24.

———[2]. "*Melon.*" *The Times* (3 July 1987): C720.

———[3]. "Play Off." *New Statesman* (30 Nov. 1979): 868–69.

———[4]. "A Spare Man." *New Statesman* (7 Aug. 1981): 23–24.

Nothof, Anne. "Simon Gray's Comedy of Bad Manners." *Essays in Theatre* (6 May 1988): 109–22.

Novick, Julius. "Looking down on the Plops." *Village Voice* (14 Feb. 1977): 81.

Oliver, Edith [1]. "The Theatre: *The Common Pursuit.*" *New Yorker* (3 Nov. 1986): 146.

———[2]. "The Theatre: 'Molly.' " *New Yorker* (6 Feb. 1978): 68.

———[3]. "Quartermaine's Terms." *New Yorker* (7 Mar. 1983): 110.

———[4]. "The Theatre: '*The Rear Column.*' " *New Yorker* (4 Dec. 1978): 84–85.

Raffetto, F. "*Butley* to End Season." *Biographical News* 1 (June 1974): 647.

Rich, Alan. "Otherwise Engaged." *New York Magazine* (14 Feb. 1977): 88–91.

Rich, Frank [1]. "*Melon.*" *New York Times* (25 June 1987): C19.

———[2]. "*Quartermaine's Terms.*" *New York Times* (25 Feb. 1983): C3.

Sainer, Arthur. "*Otherwise Engaged.*" *Village Voice* (28 Feb. 1977): 69.

Shafer, Yvonne. "Aristophanic and Chekhovian Structure in the Plays of Simon Gray." *Theatre Studies* 31/32 (1984–85/1985–86): 32–40.

Simon, John [1]. "Halting Hare, Galloping Gray." *New York Magazine* (24 Jan. 1983): 69–70.

———[2]. "Review of *Molly.*" *Hudson Review* (summer 1977): 88.

———[3]. "Oh, Dad, Poor Dad." *New York Magazine* (4 Dec. 1978): 146, 148.

Smith, Carolyn. "Simon Gray and the Grotesque." In *Within the Dramatic Spectrum*, ed. Karelisa Hartigan. New York: University of America Presses, 1986: 168–76.

Stephenson, Anthony. "Simon Gray." In *British Dramatists since World War II: Part I, A–L.* Vol. 13 of *Dictionary of Literary Biography*, ed. Stanley Weintraub. Detroit: Gale Research, 1982: 199–208.

Taylor, John Russell [1]. *Art and Commerce: The New Drama in the West End Marketplace*. London: Holmes & Meier, 1981: 176–88.

———[2]. " 'Three Farceurs': Alan Ayckbourn, David Cregan, Simon Gray." *The Sec-

laborated with six other writers in the experimental *Lay By* (he would also collaborate with three other writers on the play *Deeds* [1978]). *Sam, Sam* (written 1968–1969), Griffith's most overtly autobiographical play, opened in 1972.

In response to a request by Kenneth Tynan, Griffiths wrote *The Party* for the National Theater, and the play opened in 1973 with Laurence Olivier in one of the central roles. *The Party* was followed, two years later, by *Comedians*, Griffiths's best-known and most frequently produced play. *Comedians* opened in Nottingham in 1975, moved later that year to London and the following year to the West End. It played on Broadway in 1976 and has been regularly revived, most recently (Chicago, 1992) in a production with a black and Hispanic cast directed by Barney Simon of South Africa's Market Theater.

In 1972 and 1973 Granada Television broadcast eleven episodes of the *Adam Smith* series written by Griffiths (under the pseudonym Ben Rae). This was the first of a number of Griffiths's television plays to be produced: *The Silver Mask* (for the series *Between the Wars*, 1973), *All Good Men* (1974), *Absolute Beginners* (for the series *Fall of Eagles*, 1974), *Don't Make Waves* (for the series *Eleventh Hour*, 1975), *Through the Night* (1975), the eleven-episode series *Bill Brand* (1976), the seven-episode adaptation of *Sons and Lovers* (1981), *Country* (1981), *Oi for England* (1982), and the seven-episode series *The Last Place on Earth* (1985, based on the screenplay *Judgment over the Dead*). *Such Impossibilities*, written in 1972 for the series *The Edwardians*, was never produced. Griffiths has also adapted a number of his theater plays for television: *Occupations* (broadcast 1974), *Comedians* (1979), *The Cherry Orchard* (1981), and *The Party* (1988).

In 1977, Griffiths's adaptation of Anton Chekhov's *The Cherry Orchard* was produced in London, and in 1982 the stage version of *Oi for England* played in London and toured community venues in Greater London, Nottinghamshire, and South Yorkshire. Much of the time between these two productions was devoted to *Reds*, a screenplay (cowritten with Warren Beatty) on the life of the American socialist John Reed. This project, which would end in the film's release in 1981, provided Griffiths with the extensive and often frustrating experience of Hollywood's production methods. Since *Reds* Griffiths has completed a number of other screenplays; *Fatherland* (premiered 1986; released 1987) is the only one to have been produced. Griffiths won the British Academy of Film and Television Arts Award for screenplay in 1982.

The middle and late 1980s were a time of relatively little theatrical activity for Griffiths. In *Real Dreams* (1984), he adapted Jeremy Pikser's "Revolution in Cleveland"; the play premiered at the Williamstown (MA) Theatre Festival in a production directed by Griffiths, and it opened in London in 1986. After this play he wrote nothing for the stage for six years, returning to the theater in 1990 with the Chekhovian *Piano*, an adaptation of the Russian film *Unfinished Piece for Mechanical Piano* (based on Chekhov's *Platonov*). Griffiths seems to have discovered new possibilities for the theatre as a dramatic medium: in 1992 he directed his play *The Gulf between Us*, an impassioned response to the war in the Persian Gulf that represents—with its mixture of naturalism, fable, and dream play—a departure from the dialectical realism of his earlier plays. *Thatcher's Children*, Griffith's portrait of the generation that came of age in the 1980s, opened in May 1993.

Hope in the Year Two, a television play about Danton's final hours, was broadcast by the BBC in May 1994.

Selected Biographical Sources: Boireau; Croall; Hay; Itzin and Trussler; Kerensky; Klaus; Le Blond; Nightingale [7]; Poole and Wyver.

MAJOR PLAYS, PREMIERES, AND SIGNIFICANT REVIVALS: THEATRICAL RECEPTION

Occupations. 1970. Opened 28 October at the Stables Theatre Club, Manchester. Directed by Gordon McDougall. Opened 13 October at the Place Theatre, London. Directed by Buzz Goodbody. Revivals: Revised version, touring production by the 7:84 Theatre Company, May 1972; 28th Street Playhouse, March 1982.

Occupations, a play about the 1920 workers' uprising in Turin, was generally acclaimed. Whereas Young [1] considered the play dull, Wardle [4] found it "eloquent and bitterly well informed." Billington [4] praised the play as an unsentimental, particularized study of revolution and, like Thornber [2], admired its refusal to oversimplify its characters and issues. Although he regretted what he saw as a uniformity of tone, Nightingale [3] commended Griffiths's ability to sustain the play's action on both the political and human levels. Dawson called the play "a subtle political conflict." Rich, on the other hand, found the New York revival of *Occupations* "dreary," and he criticized the play for its length and its "pasteboard characters."

Sam, Sam. 1972. Opened 9 February at the Open Space Theatre, London. Directed by Charles Marowitz.

This story of working-class brothers, one of whom remains in poverty and squalor while the other rises to an upper-middle-class life, was received as a mixed success. Billington [7] shared the opinion of O'Connor and Wardle [8] when he suggested that the play's first half was "dazzlingly and specifically" written but that its second half was predictable in form and content. Nightingale [9] felt that it contained witty writing in places, but he considered the play less remarkable than *Occupations*.

The Party. 1973. Opened 20 December at the Old Vic Theatre, London. Produced by the National Theatre Company. Directed by John Dexter. Revised version taken on tour of universities; first performance 12 November 1974, at the University of Warwick, Coventry. Directed by David Hare. Revival: The Other Place, Stratford-upon-Avon, August 1984; moved to the Barbican Pit, London, April 1985.

Despite its prestigious production at the National, with Laurence Olivier as the Troskyite Tagg, *The Party* was on the whole poorly received. Calling the play "two-and-a-half hours of illustrated lecture," Nightingale [5] found the characterization minimal, the language dull, and the situation undramatic. Other critics agreed: Young [2] dismissively labeled the play "agitprop"; Wardle [6] suggested that Griffiths was more interested in argument than drama; and Hobson [2] felt that the play contained "intellectual tirades" without underlying emotion. Although Cushman [2] found its polemical speeches well written and superbly delivered, he criticized the play's "directionless, inconclusive ironies" and its gap between public argument and private lives. Billington [5], on the other hand, considered *The Party* one of the most "mind-stretching and politically sophisticated works" he had seen.

Comedians. 1975. Opened 20 February at the Nottingham Playhouse; moved 24 September to the Old Vic Theatre, London; moved 27 January 1976 to Wyndham's Theatre, London. Directed by Richard Eyre. Opened 28 November 1976, at the Music Box Theatre (NY). Directed by Mike Nichols. Revivals: Everyman Theatre, Liverpool, March 1987 (all-female cast); revised version, the Court Theatre, Chicago, April 1992 (black and Hispanic cast).

The London production of this best-known and most frequently revived of Griffiths's plays was greeted with widespread praise. Wardle [1] admired Griffiths's attention to characterization, while Billington [2] praised the play's combination of traditional structure and innovative content and its refusal to offer easy solutions for the issues it raises. Although Nightingale [1] found Griffiths's view of comedy occasionally humorless and inconsistent, he considered the play imaginative and provocative; Hobson [1] called it the most exciting play in London. The reviewers were unanimous in their praise of Jonathan Pryce's performance: his Gethin was called "miraculously supple" (Cushman [1]), "the most interesting [anti-hero] since Jimmy Porter" (Lambert). Response to the Broadway production of *Comedians* was more mixed. Watt called it "a strange, sad clown of a play," and Kalem judged it "scathingly funny, perceptively angry, and warmly humane," while Barnes praised its rich view of both comedy and humanity. Beaufort considered the play thought-provoking, animated by a "pulsing energy" and "articulately compelling conviction." Despite the tension he discerned between the play's comic level and theoretical level, Wilson called it "a novel and praiseworthy effort"; and although Novick considered its issues too simply drawn at times, he found it funny and stimulating. Feingold, on the other hand, criticized what he considered the rigidity of the play's structure and its "cheap laughs and simple doctrine," while Kerr criticized the second-act performances for their lack of humor.

Oi for England. 1982. Opened 9 June at the Royal Court Theatre Upstairs, London. Directed by Antonia Bird. Touring productions at nontheatrical community venues (Greater London, Nottinghamshire, South Yorkshire).

Although Radin found the basement world of this play (originally written for television) somewhat clichéd, Wardle [5] praised the authenticity of the characters' murderous anger. Both reviewers considered the character of Finn unconvincing in his political self-consciousness, while Nightingale [4] found the optimism represented by his final stance unpersuasive. De Jongh agreed, calling this optimistic ending "wish-fulfillment," but he praised the play's dramatic excitement and felt that this theatrical production sharpened its impact. Poole discussed the reaction of audiences to the play's touring production.

Real Dreams. 1984. Opened 8 August at the Williamstown (MA) Theatre Festival. Directed by Trevor Griffiths. Opened 30 April 1986, at the Barbican Pit, London. Directed by Ron Daniels.

Whereas Dunn considered *Real Dreams* tediously nostalgic ("This kind of play gives the Sixties a bad name"), other reviewers felt that Griffiths had achieved a complex portrait of the play's young radicals. According to Nightingale [8], Griffiths neither mocks nor romanticizes his idealistic characters; according to Wardle [7], he manages to marshall all the evidence against his characters without diminishing the power of their "real dream." Ratcliffe suggested that the characters' "earnest absurdities" were subject to nothing worse than affectionate teasing. Fender praised the play's combination of irony and sympathy, although like Peter [2] he criticized what he considered the simple affirmation of revolutionary faith at the play's end. Gussow called the play's Williamstown premiere "a heavy dose of reverse nostalgia"; Engstrom felt that while adroitly written, the play was marred by excessive shifting between seriousness and sendup.

Piano. 1990. Opened 8 August at the Cottesloe Theatre, London. Directed by Howard Davies.

Reviews of *Piano*, "a set of socialist ruminations on Chekhovian themes" (Nightingale [6]), tended to focus on the play's relationship to its Chekhovian sources. Peter [1] called the play "a harrowing comedy of doomed people . . . animated by black, clownish humor, and he suggested that *Piano* was more than a dramatic pastiche. Coveney characterized the play as "a diamond . . . bright, hard, unsentimental and funny," while Billington [6] suggested that the playwright's judgmental tendencies were invaded by Chekhov's comic detachment. Woddis took a more critical view of Griffiths's "third-hand Russian montage," claiming that the play succumbed to the stasis it described. Sherwood felt that the playwright's failure to integrate his peasants into the play rendered these characters one-dimensional and gave the play itself the feel of propaganda.

The Gulf between Us; or, The Truth and Other Fictions. 1992. Opened 16 January at the West Yorkshire Playhouse, Leeds. Directed by Trevor Griffiths.

This play, which occasioned denunciations in the Leads press and a demonstration by local British Legion members for its political stance toward the Gulf War (Lees and Furbisher), was criticized by its reviewers on more aesthetic grounds. Nightingale [2] disliked the pace of the first act, the departures from realism, and the motives of the play's central character, whereas Wardle [3], although finding moments of eloquence, questioned the play's reliance on sound and lighting effects and its use of "tirades." Taylor [1] and Morris criticized the play's mixture of styles and narrative material; to Armistead, *The Gulf between Us* was characterized by fuzziness, awkwardness, sentimentality, and oversimplification. Billington [3], by contrast, found the play bold, innovative, and courageous.

ASSESSMENT OF GRIFFITHS'S CAREER

Over the past twenty-five years Griffiths has established himself as a political dramatist of considerable range and sophistication; he has been called "as articulate and eloquent a thinker as the British stage possesses" (Nightingale [7]). Throughout his plays he has brought an acute sensitivity to the political dimensions of human action, and he has dramatized both the contexts and the conflicts of social and political interaction. Not surprisingly, given Griffiths's working-class background, his drama displays a particular sensitivity to issues of class within British society.

Although he was born earlier than David Hare, Howard Brenton, and many of the other dramatists of the left who emerged after 1968, Griffiths shares the commitment of these dramatists to socialist critique of capitalist society and to radical political change. His plays and films explore the historical landscape of socialism, its moments of crisis and opportunity: the 1903 London Second Party Conference, the Italian workers' uprisings of 1920, the 1945 Conservative defeat, the student movements of the 1960s, and the Labour governments of the 1920s and 1970s. At the same time Griffiths considers himself an "independent Marxist" (Hemming), and his plays have often been criticized by the radical press. Griffiths is interested in contradiction—"I've always thought about opposites, about the possibility of opposites for ideas" (Itzin and Trussler)—and his works address the contradictions that have animated and troubled twentieth-century socialism and its adherents: contradictions between social humanism and radicalism, theory and action, absolutism and compromise, political commitment and the demands of individuals, rejection of capitalist society and the necessary participation within its institutions. Although Griffiths never abandons his faith in political transformation, his plays analyze "the dilemmas which confront the radical imagination" (Ansorge [2]) with a mixture of compassion and critical penetration.

Griffiths's is a drama of ideas, and his early plays in particular are often structured to set the representatives of these ideas in dialectical relationship to one another: Kabak and Gramsci (*Occupations*), Ford and Tagg (*The Party*), Challenor and Waters (*Comedians*). But even those plays that most directly address political ideas are grounded in individual personality, the realm of the personal where social and political relationships are exposed in their complexity. Griffiths is interested, among other things, in the relationship between politics and sexuality: the deformation of sexuality by existing forms of social relationship, and the frequent conflict between sexuality and political commitment. This concern with the personal as a field of the political receives one of its most sophisticated explorations in *Comedians*, which addresses issues of class and social change by considering the psychology of laughter and the relationships of comedy to social and political awareness.

Griffiths differs from many of his contemporaries in political theater in his choice of naturalism as the principle stylistic vehicle of his plays. Calling himself a ''critical realist'' (Boireau), he has refused the devices of agitprop, Brechtianism, and other forms of nonrealistic dramaturgy popular in British political theatre since the 1960s. Naturalism has allowed Griffiths to investigate his characters and settings in their historical and individual particularity, and it has permitted him to address a more popular audience, a goal to which he has been committed throughout his career. Even while he has embraced the realist aesthetic, however, and defended it against his more radical critics, Griffiths has disrupted and modified it, importing such non-naturalistic elements as the music hall audience address in act 1 of *Sam, Sam* and the stylistic pastiche with which *The Party* opens. In part because of his work in television and film, Griffiths's plays since the 1980s reveal a deepening interest in what he has called ''postrealistic'' elements and in challenging the realist aesthetic from within (Wyver). Realism, in these recent plays, is increasingly bordered by other styles, other ways of seeing: Griffiths has characterized the second act of *Real Dreams* as ''almost filmic writing'' (Christy) and *The Gulf between Us* ''a strange dreamplay'' (Hemming).

Any assessment of Trevor Griffiths's career must underscore the importance of films and television drama—particularly the latter, which represents half of his dramatic output and includes much of his finest work. His earliest plays were written for television, and in contrast to those of his contemporaries who have scorned the medium, he has embraced it as a means of mass communication and social intervention (Wyver; Griffiths, Introduction to *Through the Night*). As part of the *Fall of Eagles* series, *Absolute Beginners* was seen in over sixty-five countries, and *Through the Night* (a play about the experience of a woman hospitalized for breast cancer) had more than 11 million viewers when it was first broadcast. Here, too, Griffiths writes against the medium he employs, challenging its conventions from within: *Country*, perhaps Griffiths's finest play for television, subverts the genre of the country-house play, while *The Last Place on Earth* (a dramatization of the race to the South Pole between Robert Falcon Scott and Roald Amundsen) challenges the myth making that often underlies the conventional drama of heroic exploration (see Poole and Wyver, Braun [1], and Tulloch).

ARCHIVAL SOURCES

Griffiths's manuscripts for *Reds* and the manuscripts and production scripts of his radio and television plays through 1982 are held in the Trevor Griffiths

Special Collection at the British Film Institute Library. All play manuscripts and film and television manuscripts since 1982 are held by the author.

PRIMARY BIBLIOGRAPHY

Plays

Apricots and *Thermidor*. London: Pluto, 1978.

The Cherry Orchard (Anton Chekhov's play, based on a translation by Helen Rappaport). London: Pluto Press, 1978; London: Faber & Faber, 1989.

Comedians. London: Faber & Faber, 1976; New York: Grove Press, 1976; New York: Samuel French, 1976; rev. ed., London: Faber & Faber, 1979.

Deeds (with Howard Brenton, Ken Campbell, and David Hare). *Plays and Players* 25 (May 1978): 41–50 [act 1]; *Plays and Players* 25 (June 1978): 43–50 [act 2].

The Gulf between Us: or, The Truth and Other Fictions. London: Faber & Faber, 1992.

Lay By (with Howard Brenton, Brian Clark, David Hare, Stephen Poliakoff, Hugh Stoddart, and Snoo Wilson). London: Calder & Boyars, 1972.

Occupations and *The Big House*. London: Calder & Boyars, 1972; rev., London: Faber & Faber, 1980.

Oi for England. London: Faber & Faber, 1982.

The Party. London: Faber & Faber, 1974.

Piano (based on the Russian film *Unfinished Piece for Mechanical Piano*). London: Faber & Faber, 1990.

Real Dreams (based on Jeremy Pikser's story ''Revolution in Cleveland''). London: Faber & Faber, 1987.

Sam, Sam. Plays and Players 19 (Apr. 1972): 65–78.

Thatcher's Children. In *Hope in the Year Two* and *Thatcher's Children*. London: Faber & Faber, 1994.

Thermidor. In *Apricots* and *Thermidor*. London: Pluto, 1978.

Essays and Articles on Drama and Theatre

Author's preface to *Piano*. London: Faber & Faber, 1990: v–vi.

Author's preface to *Through the Night and Such Impossibilities*. London: Faber & Faber, 1977: v–x.

''*The Cherry Orchard*.'' *The Cherry Orchard*. London: Faber & Faber, 1989: v–vi.

''In Defense of *Occupations*.'' *Occupations*. London: Faber & Faber, 1980: 7–11.

Introduction to *Sons and Lovers*. London: Spokesman, 1982: 7–12.

Letter to the editor. *Plays and Players* (Oct. 1974): 6.

Interviews

''Pat Silburn Talks to Trevor Griffiths'' (with Pat Silburn). *Gambit* 8:29 (1976): 30–36.

''Trevor Griffiths: Politics and Popular Culture'' (with Alison Summers). *Canadian Theatre Review* 27 (summer 1980): 22–29.

''Trevor Griffiths'' (with Nicole Boireau). *Coup de théâtre* 6 (Dec. 1986): 1–29.

SECONDARY BIBLIOGRAPHY

''After *Fanshen*: A Discussion.'' In *Performance and Politics in Popular Drama*, ed. David Bradby, Louis James, and Bernard Sharratt. Cambridge: Cambridge University Press, 1980: 297–314.

Andrews, Nigel. ''A Play Postscript.'' Interview with Trevor Griffiths. *Plays and Players* 19 (Apr. 1972): 82–83.

Ansorge, Peter [1]. ''Current Concerns.'' Interview with Trevor Griffiths and David Hare. *Plays and Players* (July 1974): 18–22.

———[2]. ''Trevor Griffiths.'' *Disrupting the Spectacle: Five Years of Experimental and Fringe Theatre in Britain*. London: Pitman, 1975: 63–67.

Armistead, Claire. Review of *The Gulf between Us*. *Financial Times* (24 Jan. 1992): 13.

Baker-White, Robert. ''Text and Stand-up Performance in Griffiths' *Comedians*: A Negotiated Dialectic of Stability and Subversion.'' *Essays in Theatre* 9 (May 1991): 159–68.

Barnes, Clive. Review of *Comedians*. *New York Times* (29 Nov. 1976): 34.

Bates, Merete. ''Love and Flannel.'' *The Guardian* (6 Nov. 1970): 8.

Beaufort, John. Review of *Comedians*. *Christian Science Monitor* (3 Dec. 1976): 35.

Bignell, Jonathan. ''Trevor Griffiths's Political Theatre: From *Oi for England* to *The Gulf between Us*.'' *New Theatre Quarterly* 37 (Feb. 1994): 49–56.

Billington, Michael [1]. ''Britain's New Political Dramatists.'' *New York Times* (18 Mar. 1979): B5.

———[2]. Review of *Comedians*. *The Guardian* (22 Feb. 1975): 10.

———[3]. Review of *The Gulf between Us*. *The Guardian* (23 Jan. 1992): 23.

———[4]. Review of *Occupations*. *The Guardian* (14 Oct. 1971): 10.

———[5]. Review of *The Party*. *The Guardian* (5 Jan. 1974): 8.

———[6]. Review of *Piano*. *The Guardian* (10 Aug. 1990): 31.

———[7]. Review of *Sam, Sam*. *The Guardian* (10 Feb. 1972): 10.

Braun, Edward [1]. Introduction to Trevor Griffiths, *Collected Plays for Television*. Londen: Faber & Faber, 1988: 1–33.

———[2]. ''Trevor Griffiths.'' In *British Television Drama*, ed. George W. Brandt. Cambridge: Cambridge University Press, 1981: 56–81.

Brownstein, Oscar Lee. ''The Structure of Dramatic Language and of Dramatic Form.'' *Assaph* 2 (1985): 1–14.

Bull, John. ''Trevor Griffiths: Strategic Dialectics.'' *New British Political Dramatists*. London: Macmillan, 1984: 118–50.

Carlson, Susan. ''Comic Collisions: Convention, Rage, and Order.'' *New Theatre Quarterly* 12 (Nov. 1987): 303–16.

Cave, Richard Allen. ''Trevor Griffiths.'' *New British Drama in Performance on the London Stage: 1970 to 1985*. Gerrards Cross: Colin Smythe, 1987: 213–48.

Chambers, Colin, and Mike Prior. *Playwrights' Progress: Patterns of Postwar British Drama*. Oxford: Amber Lane Press, 1987.

Christy, Desmond. ''Back to the Barricades.'' *The Guardian* (28 Apr. 1986): 11.

Cohn, Ruby. ''Modest Proposals of Modern Socialists.'' *Modern Drama* 25.4 (Dec. 1982): 457–68.

Coveney, Michael. Review of *Piano*. *The Observer* (12 Aug. 1990): 50.

Croall, Jonathan. "From Home to House." Interview with Trevor Griffiths. *Times Educational Supplement* (25 June 1976): 18–19.

Cushman, Robert [1]. Review of *Comedians. The Observer* (28 Sept. 1975): 22.

———[2]. Review of *The Party. The Observer* (30 Dec. 1973): 21.

Dawson, Helen. Review of *Occupations. The Observer* (17 Oct. 1971): 32.

de Jongh, Nicholas. Review of *Oi for England. The Guardian* (14 June 1982): 11.

Dixon, Stephen. "Joking Apart." *The Guardian* (19 Feb. 1975): 10.

Dunn, Tony. Review of *Real Dreams. Plays and Players* (July 1986): 27.

Eaton, Mick. "History to Hollywood." *Screen* 23 (July–Aug. 1982): 61–70.

Engstrom, John. Review of *Real Dreams. Boston Globe* (15 Aug. 1984): 67.

Featherstone-Thomas, Mark. "Goodbye, Mr. Chips." *Times Educational Supplement* (21 July 1978): 16.

Feingold, Michael. Review of *Comedians. Village Voice* (6 Dec. 1976): 97+.

Fender, Stephen. Review of *Real Dreams. Times Literary Supplement* (6 June 1986): 621.

Free, William J. "Class Values and Theatrical Space in Trevor Griffiths' *Sam, Sam*". In *Within the Dramatic Spectrum*, ed. Karelisa V. Hartigan. Lanham, Md.: University Press of America, 1986: 45–53.

Glenny, Misha. "Truth Is Otherwise: Trevor Griffiths in Conversation with Misha Glenny." *Judgment over the Dead*. London: Verso, 1986: ix–xlii.

Goldstein, Leonard. "Trevor Griffiths' *The Party* and the Left-Radical Critique of Bourgeois Society." *Political Developments on the British Stage in the Sixties and Seventies*. Rostock: Wilhelm-Pieck-Universität, 1976: 85–92.

Gottlieb, Vera. "Thatcher's Theatre—or, After *Equus*." *New Theatre Quarterly* 14 (May 1988): 99–104.

Grant, Steve. "Voicing the Protest: The New Writers." In *Dreams and Deconstructions: Alternative Theatre in Britain*, ed. Sandy Craig. Ambergate: Amber Lane Press, 1980: 116–44.

Gussow, Mel. Review of *Real Dreams. New York Times* (12 Aug. 1984): A49.

Hammond, Jonathan. "Trevor Griffiths." In *Contemporary Dramatists*, ed. James Vinson. 3rd ed. New York: St. Martin's Press, 1982: 327–29.

Hay, Malcolm. "Theatre Checklist No. 9: Trevor Griffiths." *Theatrefacts* 3.1 (1976): 2–8, 36.

Hayman, Ronald. "Trevor Griffiths: Attacking from the Inside." *The Times* (15 Dec. 1973): 9.

Hemming, Sarah. "Caught in the Crossfire." *Independent* (8 Jan. 1992): 17.

Hobson, Harold [1]. Review of *Comedians. Sunday Times* (5 Oct. 1975): 37.

———[2]. Review of *The Party. Sunday Times* (23 Dec. 1973): 27.

Hunt, Albert [1]. "Creation and Demolition." *New Statesman and Society* (17 Jan. 1992): 40.

———[2]. "A Theatre of Ideas." *New Society* (16 Jan. 1975): 138–40.

Innes, Christopher. *Modern British Drama, 1890–1990*. Cambridge: Cambridge University Press, 1992.

"Introduction: Trevor Griffiths Talks to the West Yorkshire Playhouse." *The Gulf between Us*. London: Faber & Faber, 1992: v–viii.

Itzin, Catherine. "Trevor Griffiths." *Stages of the Revolution: Political Theatre in Britain Since 1968*. London: Methuen, 1980: 165–75.

Itzin, Catherine, and Simon Trussler. "Transforming the Husk of Capitalism." Interview with Trevor Griffiths. *Theatre Quarterly* 6 (summer 1976): 25–46. Rpt. in *New Theatre Voices of the Seventies*, ed. Simon Trussler. London: Methuen, 1981: 121–33.

Kalem, T. E. Review of *Comedians*. *Time* (13 Dec. 1976): 88–90.

Kerensky, Oleg. "Trevor Griffiths." *The New British Drama*. London: Hamish Hamilton, 1977: 188–205.

Kerr, Walter. Review of *Comedians*. *New York Times* (5 Dec. 1976): B3.

Klaus, H. Gustav. "Trevor Griffiths." In *Contemporary Dramatists*, ed. D. L. Kirkpatrick. 4th ed. Chicago: St. James Press, 1988: 214–16.

Lambert, J. W. Review of *Comedians*. *Sunday Times* (23 Feb. 1975): 37.

Le Blond, Max. "Trevor Griffiths." *British Dramatists since World War II: Part I A–L*. In *Dictionary of Literary Biography*, ed. Stanley Weintraub. Vol. 13. Detroit: Gale Research, 1982: 218–25.

Lees, Caroline, and John Furbisher. "Gulf War Play Angers Veterans." *Sunday Times* (12 Jan. 1992): 6.

Marowitz, Charles. "New Playwrights Stir the British Stage." *New York Times* (20 June 1976): B7+.

Morris, Tom. Review of *The Gulf between Us*. *Times Literary Supplement* (7 Feb. 1992): 16.

Nightingale, Benedict [1]. Review of *Comedians*. *New Statesman* (3 Oct. 1975): 417–18.

———[2]. Review of *The Gulf between Us*. *The Times* (23 Jan. 1992): 20.

———[3]. Review of *Occupations*. *New Statesman* (29 Oct. 1971): 597–98.

———[4]. Review of *Oi for England*. *New Statesman* (25 June 1982): 26–27.

———[5]. Review of *The Party*. *New Statesman* (4 Jan. 1974): 25.

———[6]. Review of *Piano*. *The Times* (9 Aug. 1990): 20.

———[7]. "Trevor Griffiths Isn't Kidding in *Comedians*." *New York Times* (21 Nov. 1976): B5+.

———[8]. Review of *Real Dreams*. *New Statesman* (23 May 1980): 30–31.

———[9]. Review of *Sam, Sam*. *New Statesman* (18 Feb. 1972): 218.

Novick, Julius. Review of *Comedians*. *Village Voice* (6 Dec. 1976): 97+.

O'Connor, Garry. Review of *Sam, Sam*. *Financial Times* (10 Feb. 1972): 3.

Peter, John [1]. Review of *Piano*. *Sunday Times* (12 Aug. 1990): 5:3.

———[2]. Review of *Real Dreams*. *Sunday Times* (18 May 1986): 55.

Poole, Mike. "Trying to Get under the Skins." *The Guardian* (7 June 1982): 11.

Poole, Mike, and John Wyver. *Powerplays: Trevor Griffiths in Television*. London: BFI Publishing, 1984.

Quigley, Austin E. "Creativity and Commitment in Trevor Griffiths' *Comedians*." *Modern Drama* 24.4 (Dec. 1981): 404–23.

Rabey, David Ian. *British and Irish Political Drama in the Twentieth Century: Implicating the Audience*. London: Macmillan, 1986.

Radin, Victoria. Review of *Oi for England*. *The Observer* (20 June 1982): 33.

Ratcliffe, Michael. Review of *Real Dreams*. *The Observer* (18 May 1986): 21.

Rich, Frank. Review of *Occupations*. *New York Times* (26 Mar. 1982): C23.

Schechter, Joel. *Durov's Pig: Clowns, Politics, and Theatre*. New York: Theatre Communications Group, 1985.

Sherwood, Peter. Review of *Piano*. *Times Literary Supplement* (17 Aug. 1990): 874.

Sinfield, Alan. "Culture and Contest: *Oi for England* and the End of Consensus Politics." *Englisch Amerikanische Studien* 8 (1986): 418–26.

Smith, A.C.H. "The Politics of Coping." *The Guardian* (17 May 1993): 2: 2.

Taylor, Paul [1]. Review of *The Gulf between Us. Independent* (23 Jan. 1992): 13.

———[2]. Review of *Thatcher's Children. Independent* (26 May 1993): 17.

Thomas, Nigel. "Trevor and Bill: On Putting Politics before News at Ten." Interview with Trevor Griffiths. *The Leveller* (Nov. 1976): 12–13.

Thomsen, Christian W. "Three Socialist Playwrights: John McGrath, Caryl Churchill, Trevor Griffiths." In *Contemporary English Drama*, ed. C.W.E. Bigsby. New York: Holmes & Meier, 1981: 166–75.

Thornber, Robin [1]. "Balancing Act over the Gulf." *The Guardian* (16 Jan. 1992): 33.

———[2]. Review of *Occupations. The Guardian* (29 Oct. 1970): 10.

Trevor Griffiths et le théâtre engagé contemporain en Grande-Bretagne. Coup de théâtre no. 6 (Dec. 1986).

Tulloch, John. *Television Drama: Agency, Audience and Myth*. London: Routledge, 1990.

Tynan, Kathleen. "Party Piece." *Sunday Times Magazine* (9 Dec. 1973): 82–87.

Wandor, Michelene. *Look Back in Gender: Sexuality and the Family in Post-war British Drama*. London: Methuen, 1987.

Wardle, Irving [1]. Review of *Comedians. The Times* (25 Feb. 1975): 13.

———[2]. "Despised Theatrical Values on the Way Back." *The Times* (16 March 1983): 17.

———[3]. Review of *The Gulf between Us. Independent on Sunday* (26 Jan. 1992): 18.

———[4]. Review of *Occupations. The Times* (14 Oct. 1971): 13.

———[5]. Review of *Oi for England. The Times* (14 June 1982): 9.

———[6]. Review of *The Party. The Times* (21 Dec. 1973): 7.

———[7]. Review of *Real Dreams. The Times* (17 May 1986): 10.

———[8]. Review of *Sam, Sam. The Times* (10 Feb. 1972): 13.

Watt, Douglas. Review of *Comedians. New York Daily News* (29 Nov. 1976): 38.

Wertheim, Albert. "Trevor Griffiths: Playwriting and Politics." In *Essays on Contemporary British Drama*, ed. Hedwig Bock and Albert Wertheim. Munich: Max Hueber Verlag, 1981: 267–81.

Wilson, Edwin. Review of *Comedians. Wall Street Journal* (2 Dec. 1976): 22.

Woddis, Carole. Review of *Piano. Plays and Players* (Oct. 1990): 35.

Wolff, Janet, Steve Ryan, Jim McGuigan, and Derek McKiernan. "Problems of Radical Drama: The Plays and Productions of Trevor Griffiths." *Literature, Society, and the Sociology of Literature*. Colchester: University of Essex, 1977: 133–53.

Wyver, John. "Countering Consent." *Ah! Mischief: The Writer and Television*. London: Faber & Faber, 1982: 30–40.

Young, B. A. [1]. Review of *Occupations. Financial Times* (14 Oct. 1971): 3.

———[2]. Review of *The Party. Financial Times* (21 Dec. 1973): 3.

Christopher Hampton

(1946–)

WILLIAM J. FREE

Christopher Hampton was born in 1946 in the Azores, where his father was working as an engineer. He grew up in Aden and in Alexandria. He remembers a boyhood spent in expensive company houses provided with servants. His interest in drama began in Alexandria, where he saw his first play, Henrik Ibsen's *An Enemy of the People.* "I didn't really understand it," he says, "but it had a profound effect on me" ("Christopher Hampton's *Savages* at the Royal Court Theatre," 62). When he was eight, he wrote as a school exercise his first play, an adaptation of a Poe short story. The Suez crisis of 1956 ended Hampton's childhood in the colonies. He and his mother were forced to flee Egypt for England.

Back in England Hampton pursued his dual interests in language and drama. He attended preparatory school in Reigate and then spent the years 1959–1963 at Lancing College. The Lancing years produced two important events. First, he met another future playwright, David Hare, and began a close and mutually supportive friendship. Second, he extended his acquaintance with the theatre. He reports having read while at school the works of Arthur Miller and the plays of John Osborne. He also saw Peter Brook's production of *King Lear*, of which he later said, "That was what made me want to work in the theatre" (qtd. in Kerensky, 90).

The years between 1963 and 1968 were very eventful for Hampton. At seventeen he wrote an unpublished novel about his school days, he worked at odd jobs in London and in France while waiting to enter Oxford, and he wrote his first play, *When Did You Last See My Mother?* In the fall he entered New College, Oxford, to read French and German.

When Did You Last See My Mother? appeared as a Sunday night sans decor (without scenery or costumes but with a rehearsed cast) at the Royal Court

Theatre in 1966. Since 1956, the English Stage Company at the Royal Court had been England's premier showcase of new writing talent. The performance of *When Did You Last See My Mother?* received such a positive audience reaction that the Court, in association with producer Michael Codron, mounted a production at the Comedy Theatre in London's West End theatre district. Hampton had just turned twenty.

Rather than leaving school to become a full-time playwright, Hampton, after a short detour, returned to Oxford and his degree. He had neglected his studies during the production of *When Did You Last See My Mother?*, so he took a year off to brush up his German. The Hamburg Schauspielhaus theatre offered him a job translating and writing German précis of modern plays, but he was immediately let go in an administrative shift and was never paid. Left without money in Hamburg, he hitched a ride to Brussels and began research on the relationship of French symbolist poets Paul Verlaine and Arthur Rimbaud, who had lived together briefly in that city. His research took him to Paris, where he worked as a translator and began writing his second play, *Total Eclipse*, which he finished the following year. *Total Eclipse* became Hampton's second main-stage production at the Royal Court.

Hampton left Oxford with a first in languages in 1968. Just before his final exams he went to London to see John Osborne's *Time Present* at the Royal Court. While there he ran into the Court's artistic director William Gaskill, who offered him the job of literary manager, a new position created through an Arts Council grant. Hampton's principal job at the Royal Court was script reader, a task that involved reading the growing number of scripts submitted to the theatre, conferring with playwrights, attending staff meetings, writing reports, and attending rehearsals and performances both in London and in other parts of England. As he puts it: "In short, as resident dramatist, there was only one function I could find no time to perform: writing" (Findlater, 117). That problem was resolved when the Court hired David Hare to be Hampton's assistant, and within a year Hampton finished his third play, *The Philanthropist*. *The Philanthropist* became Hampton's first major critical and financial success, winning both the *Evening Standard* and the *Plays and Players* Award for best play of 1970.

The decade of the 1970s was a busy time for Hampton. His plays (*Savages* in 1973 and *Treats* in 1976) shared the Court stage with the early works of Athol Fugard, Sam Shepard, Edward Bond, David Hare, Caryl Churchill, Joe Orton, and Samuel Beckett. During that decade, Hampton worked on numerous adaptations and translations from writers as diverse as Ibsen, Chekhov, Molière, and the Austrian playwright Ödön von Horváth. These translations were performed internationally—in London's West End, at both the National and Royal Shakespearean Companies of London, in New York (including a translation of Ibsen's *A Doll's House* at the Vivian Beaumont Theatre in New York's Lincoln Center), and at the Shakespeare Festival in Stratford, Ontario. His adaptation of Chekhov's *Uncle Vanya* was greatly admired, and with Paul Scofield in the title role it played to forty-five full houses at the Royal Court. His translation of Molière's *Tartuffe* has become a standard acting edition.

In addition to translations and adaptations, Hampton wrote several television scripts based on his own plays as well as one original television play, *Able's Will* (1977). He continued his career as a television writer into the 1980s with adaptations of novels by Malcolm Bradbury (*The History Man* in 1981) and Graham Greene (*The Honorary Consul* in 1983). During these years he also wrote a number of screenplays, none of which, with the notable exception of *Dangerous Liaisons*, has been filmed and released.

In the 1980s Hampton also wrote three plays for the stage. Two of the plays met with only moderate success: an adaptation of George Critical recSteiner's novel *The Portage to San Cristobal of A. H.* and an original play titled *Tales from Hollywood*. But the third, *Les Liaisons Dangereuses*, achieved international fame both as a play and as a film. It won Hampton his third English best play award and his first American Academy of Motion Picture Arts and Sciences Oscar for best screenplay. He has followed that success with *White Chameleon*, a play about his boyhood in Egypt, and with the libretto for Andrew Lloyd Webber's *Sunset Boulevard*.

Selected Biographical Sources: Free; ''Christopher Hampton's *Savages* at the Royal Court Theatre''; Kerensky; Taylor.

MAJOR PLAYS, PREMIERES, AND SIGNIFICANT REVIVALS: THEATRICAL RECEPTION

When Did You Last See My Mother? 1966. Opened at the Royal Court Theatre, London, on 5 June. Directed by Robert Kidd. Production transferred to the Comedy Theatre, London, on 4 July. Produced in New York at the Young People's Repertory Theatre on 4 January 1967.

The London reviews were by and large favorable, seeing the eighteen-year-old Hampton as a promising young playwright. *The Times* (Review of *When Did You Last See My Mother?*) commented that Hampton avoided the usual pitfalls of the young writer and called the play ''a brilliant study.'' Jones called the play ''a bold study'' and compared Hampton's dialogue to that of John Osborne. Reviews of the New York production were mixed because of a weak production and awkward performances. Sullivan believed that the play might have been made compelling by a better production. Novick believed that Hampton, rather than being merely promising, had written ''a modest but successful work of art.''

Total Eclipse. 1968. Opened at the Royal Court, London, on 11 September. Directed by Robert Kidd. Revived at the Brooklyn Academy of Music (NY), in winter 1969; rewritten version at Lyric Hammersmith, London, 1981, directed by David Hare; this version at Westside Arts Theatre (NY), December 1984. Also revived at the Greenwich Theatre, London, in April 1993.

Wardle [5] praised Hampton's ability to create a compelling character in Rimbaud and asserted that the play demonstrated considerable dramatic skill. On the other hand, Trewin [2] found Hampton's writing to be excessive. David Hare said of the 1981 revival, "People were generally pleased to find that the play was much better than they had first thought." But Ragoff thought the 1984 New York production revealed a "drawing-room comedy in slightly embarrassed bedroom drag."

The Philanthropist. 1970. Opened at the Royal Court, London, on 3 August, for thirty-nine performances. Directed by Robert Kidd. Transferred to the Mayfair Theatre, London, in September 1970; revived in New York, 15 March 1971; at the Chichester Festival in 1985; at Wyndham's Theatre, London, in May 1991; at the Long Wharf (New Haven, CT) in January 1992.

Critics on both sides of the Atlantic were both enthusiastic and negative about the play. Wardle [2] called the play a "gently mocking comedy of academic manners." Barnes called Hampton "dazzlingly clever," declared the leading character "marvelously original," and described the play as "funny, literate, and literary." He compared Hampton's witty dialogue to that of Oscar Wilde— heady praise for any twenty-four-year old. On the other hand, Nightingale [1] found the play disappointing and particularly criticized Hampton's lack of political involvement, a characteristic he shared with his characters. Reviewing the Chichester Festival revival, Hurren admitted that he did not like the play as well as he had in 1970 and that it had "the too-visible earmarks of contrivance," but he concluded that the play was probably superior to the Chichester production.

Savages. 1973. Opened at the Royal Court, London on 12 April, for thirty-nine performances to near capacity houses. Directed by Robert Kidd. Transferred to the Comedy Theatre, London, in June. Produced in New York later in 1973; at the Mark Taper Forum, Los Angeles, in 1974. Shared the *Plays and Players* Award for best play of 1973 with Athol Fugard's *Sizwe Bansi Is Dead.*

Critics Wardle [4] and Esslin had difficulty reconciling the Indian legends that punctuate the play with the narrative action. Wardle [4] also felt that the main characters were insufficiently clarified, although he praised the play's many excellent lines. Nightingale [2] believed that Hampton's approach to a noble subject was flawed by his inability to choose between being an artist and being a propagandist.

Treats. 1976. Opened at the Royal Court, London, 19 February, for thirty-four performances. Directed by Robert Kidd. Revived at the Rose Theatre, London, September 1990.

Treats stimulated largely negative critical response. Hobson found the characters dull and puzzling, as did Wardle [6]. Wardle [6] contended that Hampton had created "attitudes," not characters. Nightingale [3] found the play implausible and its characters shallow. Sandy Wilson disliked the characters and considered the action to be "pasted together like a comic strip."

The Portage to San Cristobal of A. H. 1982. Opened at the Mermaid Theatre, London, 17 February. Directed by John Dexter. Adapted from the novel by George Steiner.

Radin wished Steiner's novel had never been made into this "shallow cleverly staged adaptation." But Trewin [1] found the play "absorbing," Wardle praised its relevance, and *The New Statesman* reviewer (Review of *The Portage to San Cristobal of A. H.*) compared Hampton's treatment of the theme of evil with that of Harold Pinter, John Whiting, and Edward Bond.

Tales from Hollywood. 1982. Opened at the Mark Taper Forum, Los Angeles, early in 1982. Directed by Gordon Davidson. Produced at the National Theatre, London, October 1983 until February 1984. National Theatre production directed by Peter Gill. Filmed by the BBC. Broadcast in the United States on PBS on 19 October 1992.

Critical reception in Los Angeles was generally negative. Hampton reported that one critic complained that the Forum should not pay a foreigner to insult the Los Angeles audience. London reviews were generally better than those in Los Angeles. Esslin [2] acknowledged the importance of Hampton's subject matter but believed that the play was weakened by its focus on gossipy anecdotes and the presence of a central character-narrator whom Esslin considered marginal. The reviewer of *the Illustrated London News* (Review of *Tales from Hollywood*) on the other hand, praised the play as "subtly layered." Aaron believed that Hampton had accurately captured "both the attractions and pitfalls of [Hollywood]."

Les Liaisons Dangereuses. 1985. Opened at the Royal Shakespeare Company's Other Place Theatre, Stratford-upon-Avon, 24 September. Directed by Howard Davies. Transferred to the Barbican Pit, London, and then to the Ambassadors Theatre, London. Produced in New York in 1987; in subsequent years produced in Dallas; Atlanta; Memphis; Louisville; Seattle; Belfast, Maine; Montgomery, Alabama; and Chicago. A frequent offering of university and community theatres since 1990. The London production won the 1986 *Plays and Players* Award for best play. The New York production was nominated for a Tony Award as best play of the season. Filmed under the title *Dangerous Liaisons*, in 1988; nominated for seven Academy Awards, including best picture; won three, including an Oscar for Hampton's screenplay.

At every point in its career the play has stimulated public and critical acclaim, making it perhaps the most successful new play of the 1980s. Wardle [1] praised the skill with which Hampton transformed Choderlos de Laclos's novel. Peter singled out for particular praise the "note of scathing irony" in the character of Valmont. Langton calls the play ''a scintillating drama that stands artistically independent of its literary forebear.''

White Chameleon. 1991. Opened at the Cottesloe Theatre, London, 14 February. Directed by Richard Eyre.

Kellaway wrote a glowing positive review, praising the balance with which Hampton handled both the narrative and the emotion of the play. Nightingale [4] contended that the play helped explain Hampton's impetus for becoming a playwright and illuminated the main theme of his career, ''not belonging.''

Sunset Boulevard (with Don Black) 1993. Music by Andrew Lloyd Webber. Opened at the Adelphi Theatre, London, on 17 February. Opened at the Minskoff Theatre in New York on 12 July. Both productions directed by Trevor Nunn. Shubert Theatre, Los Angeles, December 1993.

Rich generally disliked the play but did praise Hampton's and Black's libretto. Drake, however, condemned the changes the libretto made in Billy Wilder's sardonic view of Hollywood. Hewison thought the play a dilution of Billy Wilder's film and a far less telling criticism of Hollywood than was Hampton's play *Tales from Hollywood.*

ASSESSMENT OF HAMPTON'S CAREER

Evaluating the achievement of a living, contemporary author is made difficult by the current suspicion of standards. Deconstruction has condemned the traditional criteria of universal qualities and formal excellence for their inherent political and social bias, often leaving only personal prejudice as a basis of judgment. How, in such an atmosphere, can we evaluate Hampton's accomplishment?

Popular and financial success provides one measuring stick. Although often greeted with mixed critical response, the plays have attracted almost uniform support from audiences. Runs have ranged from four months for *The Portage to San Cristobal of A. H.* to several years for *Les Liaisons Dangereuses*. None of Hampton's plays has lost money for its investors. Four plays— *When Did You Last See My Mother?*, *The Philanthropist*, *Savages*, and *Les Liaisons Dangereuses*—have played in West End London theatres (the British equivalent of Broadway) and five— the last three named and also *Total Eclipse* and *Tales From Hollywood*—have received international productions. *The Philanthropist*, *Savages*, and *Les Liaisons Dangereuses* won a combination of four *Plays and Players* and *Evening Standard* Awards for best plays in their respective years. *Dangerous Liaisons* won Hampton an Oscar for best screenplay.

Hampton has also contributed to the art of translation, having produced and/ or published translations of thirteen European plays. In addition to works by Chekhov, Isaac Babel, Molière, and Georges Feydeau, he has translated four major plays of Ibsen: *Hedda Gabler* in 1970, *A Doll's House* translated in 1971 and filmed in 1973, *Ghosts* in 1978, and *The Wild Duck* in 1979.

Perhaps even more important is Hampton's bringing the plays of Ödön von Horváth to the English stage. In 1977, at the instigation of Maximilian Schell, Hampton translated Horváth's *Tales from the Vienna Woods*. The play was so popular that the National Theatre, for whom it was done, produced in 1978 Hampton's translation of Horváth's *Don Juan Comes Back from the War*. In 1989 Hampton did his third Horváth translation, *Faith, Hope, and Charity*, which appeared at the Lyric Theatre, London.

The postmodern rejection of the concept of universality, while closing the door to one kind of evaluation, has opened another. British playwrights are conscious of participating in what Max Stafford-Clark, the current artistic director of the Royal Court Theatre, calls ''the public debate that goes on in this country'' about how people should live. Hampton is sometimes accused of remaining aloof from that debate. Certainly, he does not write as directly about political issues as do his contemporaries Edward Bond, Howard Brenton, or Trevor Griffiths. With the exception of *Savages*, his plays refer to political issues through allusions rather than through direct action.

However, Hampton does deal, either directly or indirectly, with the tone of contemporary English life. One of the keys to Hampton's imagination, I believe, can be found in the introduction to his translation of Horváth's *Tales from the Vienna Woods*:

His [Horváth's] purpose was nothing less than to describe, in large-scale, but carefully constructed plays, the decay of a society haunted by inflation . . . and lurching towards Fascism. . . . The interplay between individual selfishness and the pressures of a society in crisis is impartially portrayed, and only the liveliness and compassion with which each individual character, even the most reprehensible, is drawn, show where Horváth's sympathies lay.

Materialism haunts Hampton's England more than does inflation, and it lurches more in the direction of Thatcherism than of fascism. But the statement quoted could be said to define Hampton's work as well as Horváth's. Hampton's plays may not challenge the validity of his audience's values as openly as do those of his more politically committed contemporaries. However, having engaged the audience on the level of its beliefs, he moves them to perceptions that are, if not quite disturbing, at least decentered. Individual selfishness and egocentrism abound among his characters. And like Horváth, Hampton portrays his characters with liveliness and comic compassion. Fools like Patrick in *Treats* or Philip in *The Philanthropist* engage our sympathy and laughter simultaneously. *Total Eclipse* and *Savages* contrast liberal and radical characters to reveal the dialectic tensions of their societies, whether of the hothouse world of nineteenth-century French poets or of the unresolved tensions between Anglo-American society and the Third World. The cold-blooded cruelty of characters in *Les Liaisons Dangereuses* is undercut both by their developing vulnerability to softer emotions and by our realization at the play's conclusion that they (to quote again Hampton's description of Hor-váth's characters) are "people who have been through bad times and have still worse to come." The play closes with an image that links the coming French Revolution of the 1790s to the upcoming decade of the 1990s, which certainly makes a political statement.

The ultimate estimate of any writer must concern the artistry of his work. Artistically, Hampton is a strong writer in three areas. First is his literate and witty use of dialogue. Hampton's wit has been compared to Wilde's and Shaw's. He has the rare gift of writing dialogue that is at once literate and be-lievable as conversation. In each of his plays Hampton creates a language suited to character, historical period, and situation. His finest achievement in language is *Les Liaisons Dangereuses*. The elegance of phrasing and sentence structure in that play produce a strong sense of historical distance without be-coming dated or stuffy.

A second artistic strength comes from Hampton's developing skill in creating powerful visual images. Beginning with *Total Eclipse* and continuing throughout his plays, the most memorable thing is often their imagery: the stabbing of Verlaine's hands, the Indian ritual in *Savages*, the *coup de théâtre* that begins *The Philanthropist*. This ability to mix powerful images and effective language places Hampton in the company of Tom Stoppard and Harold Pinter.

A third artistic strength comes from Hampton's structuring of scenes. Partic-ularly effective is his use of parallel scenes, scenes that repeat characters and actions, but with significant differences. In *Total Eclipse* the two images of Verlaine's hands, stabbed early in the play, kissed at the conclusion, provide a formal framework that helps the audience understand the action of the play. Beginning and ending *Savages* with fire, ritual, and the sound of the airplane bringing death to the Indians gives that play a powerful sense of closure, as does the scene of John's suicide in *The Philanthropist*, which is echoed in Philip's mock suicide at the end of the play.

Whether Hampton's work will continue to be produced in the future remains to be seen, but the value of what he has done as entertainment, and often as thoughtful entertainment, remains uncontested. At this writing Hampton is fifty years old. Given the average activity span of playwrights, he should have at least twelve more productive years ahead. Working at his characteristic pace, he should produce three or four more major plays, in addition to further trans-lations and screenplays. Should he continue to grow in writing skill and theat-rical maturity, he could someday be even more highly regarded by historians and critics than he is even today.

PRIMARY BIBLIOGRAPHY

Plays

Able's Will. London: Faber & Faber, 1979.
Dangerous Liaisons: The Film: A Screenplay. London: Faber & Faber, 1989.
Don Juan Comes Back from the War, by Ödön von Horváth. Trans. Christopher Hampton. London: Faber & Faber, 1978.
Faith, Hope, and Charity, by Ödön von Horváth. Trans. Christopher Hampton. London: Faber & Faber, 1989.
The Ginger Tree. London: Faber & Faber, 1989.
Hedda Gabler and *A Doll's House*, by Henrik Ibsen. Trans. Christopher Hampton. London: Faber & Faber, 1989,.
Les Liaisons Dangereuses. London: Faber & Faber, 1985.
Molière's *Tartuffe, or the Imposter*. Trans. Christopher Hampton. London: Faber & Faber, 1984.
The Philanthropist. London: Faber & Faber, 1970; rev. ed., 1985.
The Philanthropist: With Total Eclipse and Treats. London: Faber & Faber, 1991.
The Portage to San Cristobal of A. H. London: Faber & Faber, 1982.
Savages. London: Faber & Faber, 1974.
Sunset Boulevard (with Don Black). London: Faber & Faber, 1993.
Tales from Hollywood. London: Faber & Faber, 1983.
Tales from the Vienna Woods, by Ödön von Horváth. Trans. Christopher Hampton. London: Faber & Faber, 1978.
Total Eclipse. London: Faber & Faber, 1969.
Treats. London: Faber & Faber, 1976.
When Did You Last See My Mother? London: Faber & Faber, 1967.
White Chameleon. London: Faber & Faber, 1991.
The Wild Duck, by Henrik Ibsen. Trans. Christopher Hampton. London: Faber & Faber, 1982.

Articles and Interviews

"Christopher Hampton's *Savages* at the Royal Court Theatre" (with Robert Kidd and Paul Scofield). *Theatre Quarterly* 3 (Oct.–Dec. 1973): 60–78.
"Grasping the Strangeness of Reality." *Plays and Players* 23:11 (Aug. 1976): 42.
Introduction to *Tales from the Vienna Woods*, by Ödön von Horváth. Trans. by Christopher Hampton. London: Faber & Faber, 1978.
"Sloane Square Lessons." In *At the Royal Court*, ed. Richard Findlater. New York: Grove Press, 1981: 116–20.

SECONDARY BIBLIOGRAPHY

Aaron, Jules. "Exiles in Paradise: Christopher Hampton's *Tales from Hollywood*." *Theatre* 13.3 (Summer-Fall 1982): 70–73.
Barnes, Clive. Review of *The Philanthropist*. *New York Times* (16 Mar. 1971).

Bennett, Kenneth C. "*The Philanthropist* and *The Misanthrope*: A Study in Comic Mimesis." *Theatre Research International* 6 (1981): 85–92.

Black, Sebastian. "Makers of Real Shapes: Christopher Hampton and His Story-tellers." *Modern Drama* 25 (1982): 207–21.

Blaicher, Gunther. "Die Komodie im permissiven Zeitalter: zur Normenproblematic in Christopher Hampton's *The Philanthropist* (1970)." *Germanisch Romanische Monatsschrift* 35 (1985): 209–23.

Cameron, Ben. "*The Philanthropist*." In *Christopher Hampton: A Casebook*, ed. Robert Gross. New York: Garland, 1990: 39–52.

Carson, Katherine. "*Les Liaisons Dangereuses* on Stage and Film." *Literature/Film Quarterly* 19:1 (1991): 35–40.

Cohn, Ruby. "Christopher Hampton: In *Dangerous Liaisons*." In *Christopher Hampton: A Casebook*, ed. Robert Gross. New York: Garland, 1990: 3–15.

Colby, Douglas. " 'An Act of Suicide': *The Philanthropist* by Christopher Hampton." *As the Curtain Rises: On Contemporary British Drama, 1966–1976*. Madison, NJ: Fairleigh Dickinson University Press, 1978: 49–73.

Doty, Gresdna A., and Billy Harbin. *Inside the Royal Court Theatre, 1956–1981: Artists Talk*. Baton Rouge: Louisiana State University Press, 1990.

Drake, Sylvia, Review of *Sunset Boulevard*. *Los Angeles Times* (19 Dec. 1993).

Elsom, John. *Post-war British Theatre*. London: Routledge & Kegan Paul, 1976.

Esslin, Martin [1]. "In Search of *Savages*." *Theatre Quarterly* 3 (Oct.–Dec. 1973): 79–83.

———[2]. Review of *Tales from Hollywood*. *Plays and Players* (Nov. 1983).

Fiedler, Leonhard M. "*Geschichten aus Hollywood*." *Theatre Heute* 23 (9 Sept. 1982): 15–17.

Free, William J. *Christopher Hampton: An Introduction to His Plays*. San Bernadino, CA: Borgo Press, 1994.

Findlater, Richard. *At the Royal Court*. New York: Grove Press, 1981.

Glaap, Albert R. "Zeitgenössische Dramen als Beiträge zur Auseinandersetzung mit dem Nationalsozialismus." In *Literatur im Kontext*, ed. Renate Haas and Christine Klein-Braley. Sankt Augustin: Richarz: 209–20.

Gross, Robert. "Kane and Able: Welles's Film and Hampton's Screenplay." In *Christopher Hampton: A Casebook*, ed. Robert Gross. New York: Garland: 79–94.

Gussow, Mel. "A London Feast of Menace and Revenge." *New York Times* (31 July 1991): B1, C11.

Hall, Carol. "Valmont Redux: The Fortunes and Filmed Adaptation of *Les Liaisons Dangereuses*." *Literature/Film Quarterly* 19:1 (1991): 41–50.

Hammer, Stephanie-Barbe. "Romanticism and Reaction: Hampton's Transformation of *Les Liaisons Dangereuses*." In *Christopher Hampton: A Casebook*, ed. Robert Gross. New York: Garland, 1990: 109–31.

Hare, David. Review of *Total Eclipse*. *Plays and Players* (Oct. 1981): 49.

Hayman, Ronald. *British Theatre since 1955: A Reassessment*. Oxford: Oxford University Press, 1979.

Heinrich, Benjamin. "Krimi-Boulevard Kritik." *Theatre Heute* 12.2 (Feb. 1971): 40–41.

Hewison, Robert. Review of *Sunset Boulevard*. *Sunday Times* (18 July 1993).

Hilton, Julian. "The Court and Its Favours." In *Contemporary English Drama*, ed. C.W.E. Bigsby. New York: Holmes & Meier, 1981.

Hobson, Harold. Review of *Treats*. *Sunday Times* (8 Feb. 1976).

Holland, Peter. "The Director Intervenes: Christopher Hampton's *Savages*" *Comparative Darma* 13 (1979): 142–49.

Hurren, Kenneth. Review of the *Philanthropist. Plays and Players* (Sept. 1985).

Itzin, Catherine. *Stages in the Revolution: Political Theatre in Britain since 1968.* London: Eyre Methuen, 1980.

Jäger, Gerd. "Untätige Trauer." *Theatre Heute* 12.2 (Feb. 1971): 30–32.

Jones, D.A.N. Review of *When Did You Last See My Mother? New Statesman* (10 June 1966).

Kasarek, Hellmuth. "Revision." *Theatre Heute* 12.2 (Feb. 1971): 42–44.

Kellaway, Kate. Review of *White Chameleon. The Observer* (17 Feb. 1991).

Kerensky, Oleg. *The New British Drama.* London: Hamish Hamilton, 1977.

King, Kimball. "Treats: A Reassessment." In *Christopher Hampton: A Casebook*, ed. Robert Gross. New York: Garland, 1990: 71–77.

Knapp, Elise, and Robert Glen. " 'The Energy of Evil Has Diminished': Les Liaisons Dangereuse." *Eighteenth-Century Life* 14:2 (May 1990): 41–48.

Ladra, David. "De Choderlos de Laclos a Heiner Muller: *Les Liaisons Dangereuses.*" *Primer Acto: Cuadernos de Investigación Teatral* (Nov.–Dec. 1990): 82–87.

Langton, Robert Gore. Review of *Les Liaisons Dangereuses. Plays and Players* (Feb. 1986).

Maccubbin, Robert. "Christopher Hampton." *Eighteenth-Century Life* 14:2 (May 1990): 81–89.

Mews, Siegfried [1]. "The Exiles on Stage: Christopher Hampton's *Tales from Hollywood.* In *Christopher Hampton: A Casebook*, ed. Robert Gross. New York: Garland, 1990: 95–107.

———[2]. "Von der Ohnmacht der Intellektullen: Christopher Hampton's *Tales from Hollywood.*" *Exilforschung* 3 (1985): 270–85.

Müller, Christoph. "Lauter Zimmerschlachten." *Theatre Heute* 18.9 (Sept. 1977): 40–41.

Nightingale, Benedict [1]. Review of *The Philanthropist. New Statesman* (14 Aug. 1970).

———[2]. Review of *Savages. New Statesman* (20 April 1973).

———[3]. Review of *Treats. New Statesman* (13 Feb. 1976).

———[4]. Review of *The White Chameleon. The Times* (15 Feb. 1991).

Novick, Julius. Review of *When Did You Last See My Mother? Village Voice* (12 Jan. 1967).

Overton, Bill. "The Play of Letters: *Les Liaisons Dangereuses* on Stage." *Theatre Research International* 13.3 (autumn 1988): 263–74.

O'Grady, Jane. "Faithful in Their Fashion." *Times Literary Supplement* (17 Nov. 1989): 1268.

Peter, John. Review of *Les Liaisons Dangereuses. Sunday Times* (29 Sept. 1985).

Pietropoli, Cecilia. " 'Imagine the theatre as real': Christopher Hampton, Tom Stoppard e il dibattito sul teatro." *Quaderni di Filologia* 3 (1984): 203–16.

Review of *The Portage to San Cristobal of A. H. New Statesman* (26 Feb. 1982).

Rabey, David Ian. *British and Irish Political Drama in the Twentieth Century: Implicating the Audience.* New York: St. Martin's Press, 1986.

Radin, Victoric. Review of *The Portage to San Cristobal of A. H. The Observer* (21 Feb. 1982).

Ragoff, Gordon. Review of *Total Eclipse. Village Voice* (25 Dec. 1984).

Rich, Frank. Review of *Sunset Boulevard*. *New York Times* (14 July 1993).

Ripinskaia, L. V. "Nepolnoe otritsatel'noe predlozhenie v angliiskom dramaturgiches-kom tekste." In *Sistemnyi analiz khudozhestvennoga teksta*, ed. R. A. Kiseleva. Vologda: Vologodskii gosudarstvennyi pedagogicheskii inst., 1989.

Skloot, Robert [1]. "Theatrical Images of Genocide." *Human Rights Quarterly* 12:2 (May 1990): 185–201.

————[2].*"Savages*: 'We Have to Bring Them into Our World.' " In *Christopher Hampton: A Casebook*, ed. Robert Gross. New York: Garland, 1990: 53–69.

Schneider, Ruth M. "A Comedy of Manners in a World Gone Mad: Christopher Hampton's *The Philanthropist*." *Horizontes* 43 (1978): 59–67.

Servin, Micheline. "Ecrire disent-ils." *Le Temps Modernes* 4.74 (Jan. 1986): 174–78.

Stadelmaier, Gerhand. "Ödön aus dem Hollywald." *Theatre Heute* 24.5 (May 1983): 25–27.

Sullivan, Dan. Review of *When Did You Last See My Mother?* *New York Times* (5 Jan. 1967).

Tabori, George. "Statt des Urschreis das Unkichern." *Theatre Heute* 24.5 (May 1983): 30.

Review of *Tales from Hollywood*. *Illustrated London News* (Sept./Oct. 1983).

Taylor, John Russell. *The Second Wave*. London: Methuen, 1971.

Trewin, J. C. [1]. Review of *The Portage to San Cristobal of A. H. Illustrated London News* (Apr. 1982).

————[2]. Review of *Total Eclipse*. *Illustrated London News* (21 Dec. 1968).

Vaget, Hans-Rudolf. "Geschichten und Geschichte: Heinrich und Thomas Mann in Christopher Hampton's *Tales from Hollywood*." *Thomas Mann Jahrbuck* (1992): 97–114.

Wardle, Irving [1]. Review of *Les Liaisons Dangereuses*. *The Times* (26 Sept. 1985).

————[2]. Review of *The Philanthropist*. *The Times* (5 Aug. 1970).

————[3]. Review of *The Portage to San Cristobal of A. H. The Times* (18 Feb. 1982).

————[4]. Review of *Savages*. *The Times* (13 Apr. 1973).

————[5]. Review of *Total Eclipse*. *The Times* (12 Sept. 1968).

————[6]. Review of *Treats*. *The Times* (6 Feb. 1976).

Wehrli, Beatrice. "Horváth statt Brecht: ein Fallstudie." *Schweizer Monatshefte* 63 (1983): 505–18.

Review of *When Did You Last See My Mother? The Times* (5 July 1966).

Wilson, Ann. "Love under Censure: Homoeroticism in *When Did You Last See My Mother?*"In *Christopher Hampton: A Casebook*, ed. Robert Gross. New York: Garland, 1990: 17–38.

Wilson, Sandy. Review of *Treats*. *Plays and Players* (Apr. 1978).

BIBLIOGRAPHY

King, Kimball. "Christopher Hampton." *Twenty Modern British Playwrights: A Bibliography, 1956 to 1976*. New York: Garland, 1977: 59–64.

David Hare

(1947–)

JUDY LEE OLIVA

Since 1969, as one of the leaders of the fringe theatre movement in Great Britain, David Hare has continued to offer his unique critique of society and politics through theatre, television, and film as a playwright and director. The notion of identity and the search for identity in public and private lives unifies all his work. Hare portrays with eclectic theatricality and intelligent rhetoric British society's attempts and failures to come to terms with its own history.

Born 5 June 1947, at St. Leonards-on-Sea near Hastings in Sussex, Hare attended Lancing College and then spent three years at Cambridge, where he obtained a degree in English. Reared in the welfare state, too young to participate in World War II but old enough to understand and suffer its consequences, Hare became disillusioned with the state of public institutions. *Slag* (1971) and *The Great Exhibition* (1972) are early examples of Hare's ongoing invective against the effect of public institutions on private lives. He formed the Portable Theatre Company with Tony Bicat and wrote his first play, *How Brophy Made Good*, in 1969, launching his theatrical career. He was cofounder of the Joint Stock Company, which produced *Fanshen* in 1976. In both the Portable and Joint Stock, Hare often wrote in collective and collaborative situations. *Lay By* (1970), for example, was an effort for the Portable by Hare and six other writers, including Howard Brenton, with whom Hare was to collaborate later on two additional plays.

Slag (1971) marked Hare's initial move toward commercial West End theatre when it transferred to the Royal Court Theatre. It was conceived and written for the Hampstead Theatre Club, a more established group, although still experimental and less impoverished than the Portable.

Hare served as resident dramaturge for the Royal Court Theatre and helped to plan the season at Nottingham in 1978. His work from the mid-1970s to the end of that decade reflects a wider view of politics. These plays—including *Brassneck* (1973), with Howard Brenton; *Knuckle* (1974); *Fanshen* (1975), based on William Hinton's book; *Teeth 'n' Smiles* (1975); *Licking Hitler* (1978), a television play; *Plenty* (1978), probably his most recognized play; and *Deeds* (1978), in collaboration with several other writers—all explore the causes of postwar sociopolitical decline.

Hare's work in the 1980s, from *Dreams of Leaving* (1980), a play for television, to the film *Paris By Night* (1989) focus on either international political issues or universal private dilemmas. The plays, films, and television scripts written during this decade contain diverse subject matter and are difficult to categorize. However, whether the work has an overtly political bent, as in the play *A Map of the World* (1982) and the television play *Saigon: Year of the Cat* (1983), or more private political shadings, as in *Dreams of Leaving* (1980), the film *Wetherby* (1985), and the operetta *The Knife* (1987), at the center of each is the portrayal of how human behavior is affected by the sociopolitical system and how individuals struggle to bridge the gulf between them in human relationships.

The Secret Rapture, which premiered in London in 1988, marks a turning point in Hare's career and in his writing. The play followed the successful premiere of *Pravda* in London in 1985 and the well-received American premiere at the Guthrie Theatre in 1989. Although *The Secret Rapture* was a critical success in London, the American premiere was marred by controversy and the production closed in less than a month. In a vehemently written letter to the editor, Hare challenged *New York Times* critic Frank Rich regarding Rich's negative review, which Hare felt was responsible for the premature closing of the play. Hare's work has not been seen on the New York stage since the controversy. However, *The Secret Rapture*, along with *Racing Demon* (1990) and *Murmuring Judges* (1991), reveals a new subject matter in Hare's work, that of spirituality and issues of religion, faith, and justice. In addition, none of these plays were originally directed by Hare, who had previously directed most of the premiere productions of his plays in London and the United States. A fourth play, *Absence of War*, which opened at the National Theatre in London 2 October 1993, completes a trilogy along with *Racing Demon* and *Murmuring Judges* that deals specifically with the state of morality and ethics in British institutions. *The Secret Rapture* can be viewed as a transitional piece reflecting Hare's dramaturgy of the 1990s, which moves away from old concerns such as indictments of Thatcherism and capitalism, to new concerns that are more universal in nature, questioning the moral codes of society and the goodness, or lack of goodness, in humankind.

Selected Biographical Sources: Ansorge [2]; Bloom; Bull; Dunn [2]; Ford; Gussow; Hammond [2]; Oliva; Rabey.

MAJOR PLAYS, PREMIERES, AND SIGNIFICANT
REVIVALS: THEATRICAL RECEPTION

Slag. 1970. Premiered at the Hampstead Theatre Club, London, in April, transferred to Royal Court, London, and to New York in 1971. Directed by Roger Hendricks Simon for the Hampstead and by Max Stafford-Clark at the Royal Court.

The title refers to the leftover and wasted efforts of ideology of English institutions, seen in the form of Brackenhurst, a private girls school. The play deals with three female teachers who explore the outdated practices of traditional public school education alongside the new ethic of sexual anarchy and freedom. Kerensky called it "a zany farce" that "borders on slapstick." Waterhouse commented that "despite its depressing title, it is a finely tuned admirably effervescent romp." Taylor also noted the humor but recognized the underlying tension: "It is all very strange, very funny and quite violent in both word and action."

Brassneck. 1973. Written with Howard Brenton and first produced on 19 September at the Nottingham Playhouse, directed by Hare. Subsequently produced as a *Play for Today* on BBC television in 1975, directed by Mike Newell.

Ansorge [1] noted that *Brassneck* was the first major event from the fringe to take place before a mainstream audience. Wardle [1] called it a "pungent and ambitious task" attempting to "dissect society." The play portrays the iniquities of capitalism over a thirty-year period. The time span allows for an examination of three generations of the Bagley family, so that the decline of the family parallels the decline of the nation.

Knuckle. 1974. Produced at the Comedy Theatre, London, and directed by Michael Blakemore. Presented as a Theatre Night on BBC-TV in 1989. In 1987 it was revived at several regional theatres in England, including the Devonshire Park Theatre, Eastbourne. Chicago's Next Theatre produced it in 1989.

It was first seen in New York at the Hudson Theatre Guild in 1981, when reviewer Simon [2] characterized the play as a "piano piece for black keys; tricky but not unmusical." The play is a mystery in the style of Mickey Spillane. Although the play is a comedy, by parodying a familiar literary form, Hare subverts content and manipulates form in order to theatricalize aspects of morality. Billington [4] conceded that "in the end the form sags under the sheer weight for what it is asked to convey" but noted that it was "consistently entertaining."

Fanshen. 1975. Based on the book by William Hinton, produced by the Joint Stock Theatre Group, London, in April and directed by William Gaskill and Max Stafford-Clark. Presented in a television production on BBC2 in 1975. It was revived at the National Theatre, London, in 1988, directed by Les Waters. Milwaukee (WI) Repertory Theatre staged the first American production in its

1975–1976 season. It premiered in New York at the Soho Repertory Theatre in 1982.

Unlike many of Hare's plays, *Fanshen* is done regularly in regional theatre on both sides of the Atlantic. It presents the causes and effects of political change with specific focus on the individual and collective lives of the peasants in the Chinese village of Long Bow. Rabey concluded that the ''way that a relatively small nucleus of actors is required to play a multitude of characters aids the impression of collective effort and purpose.'' Itzin noted that ''the aesthetic clarity came as a consequence of getting the political lint.'' Coveney observed that ''where the play is specific, it is absolutely riveting. . . . Where the play is humanistic, the foibles and weaknesses of villagers struggling to make function a primarily moral system broaden the play's terms to embrace universal values.''

Teeth 'n' Smiles. 1975. Produced in September at the Royal Court Theatre, London, directed by David Hare. Revived the following year at Wyndham's Theatre, London. American productions include the premiere at the Folger Theatre, Washington, D.C. in the 1977–1978 season and in Chicago in 1981 by the St. Nicholas Theatre Company.

The play is a 1960s rock musical set at the Cambridge May Ball. Another example of Hare's invective against upper-class institutions, the content and form help to create the backstage story of a rock band as an allegory of society. It is a story of unrequitted love between Maggie and Arthur. Bryden noted that Hare portrays Maggie and Arthur's lost cause ''with a harsh tenderness which sometimes touches poetry'' but also contended that ''everyone in the play is a little too clever, too funny, too articulate to be true.''

Plenty. 1978. Premiered in April at the National Theatre, London, directed by David Hare. First produced in the United Sates at the Arena Stage, Washington, D.C. in 1980 directed by David Chambers. Subsequently produced at the Public Theater (NY) in October 1982 and then moved to the Plymouth Theatre (NY) in November, directed by Hare.

Plenty marked Hare's first major commercial success in the United States. Reviews were primarily positive, citing the passion, intelligence, and theatricality evident in the productions. In London, Wardle [4] noted that the drama ''makes the most sense as one that cuts across the political lines and divides the world between intelligent and stupid people.'' Of the American production Kerr observed that ''this woman and her country become dependent on that one fleeting embrace in France 'beneath a mackerel sky.' '' Ansorge [2] observed that ''running parallel to Susan's story is a powerful description of the economic and political decline of the English administrative class.'' Hare's structural technique is often criticized because he divides the play into twelve scenes that move back and forth in time, encompassing almost two decades. However, Bigsby's [1] observation regarding Hare's technique should be considered: ''The force of his images derives from the fact that they grow out of the sensibility of his individual characters but capture the mood of a culture.''

A Map of the World. 1982. First produced at the Adelaide Festival in Australia in March, directed by Hare. Subsequently transferred to the Opera House, Sydney. London premiere was at the National Theatre on 20 January 1983, directed by Hare. American premiere was at the Public Theatre in New York in October 1985. It has been revived periodically in regional theatre and recently in Canada at the Toronto Free Theatre in March 1989, and in Los Angeles, California, at the Odyssey Theatre in November 1992.

A Map of the World is Hare's most complex play in terms of content, form, and style. Rich [2] noted of the American production that it encompassed the ''perilous intersection of literary esthetics, global politics and private lives.'' Billington [5] appraised the play as a ''Wildean work about world politics,'' while Wardle [3] concluded that Hare had ''taken on Osborne's early role of the nation's moral conscience.'' Nightingale [4] described the play as a ''work of genuine search, struggle and discovery, and as rich as anything Hare has written to date.'' The most blatantly negative response was offered by Feingold with ''*A Map of the World* is the largest lump of bullshit and ineptitude I've ever come across in the professional theatre.'' The diversity of reaction to the play stems from the multiple dramaturgical levels that Hare employs. In simplest terms, *A Map of the World* is a play about a novel being filmed. The multiple themes express the idea of multiple misrepresentation in art, politics, and life. As Billington [5] noted, the play is ''built around a series of antitheses—the Third World and the West, fiction and reality, irony and commitment, reason and passion, the personal and political.''

Pravda. 1985. Written with Howard Brenton, produced at the National Theatre, London, in May, directed by Hare. Revived twice in 1986 with revised edition of text. First produced in the United States at the Guthrie Theatre, Minneapolis, in January 1989, directed by Robert Falls.

Some critics have called *Pravda* a companion piece to Hare and Brenton's *Brassneck*, similar in theatricality, but thematically actually more aligned with *A Map of the World*. The question of what is truth is a prevailing contextual notion. Ratcliffe [3] called it a ''play of symptoms, a diagnosis to sober up the spectators.'' Critics applauded the play as an indictment of power but criticized the portrayal of villain-hero Lambert Le Roux. Wardle [5] cited the problem as one of ''setting up a schematic collision between truth and lies and all your sympathy goes to the liar.'' The plot turns on Le Roux's rapacious consumption of British newspapers. The authors imply that the lack of opposition in all aspects of British life has created a weak and ineffective society, which stands helplessly vulnerable to capitalistic colonials like Lambert Le Roux.

The Secret Rapture. 1988. First performed at the Lyttleton Theatre, London, on 4 October, directed by Howard Davies. Subsequently revived in 1989 with change in cast. Produced at the Public Theatre (NY) in September 1989, directed by Hare. Subsequently transferred to the Barrymore Theatre (NY) in November.

Set in modern-day England, the play explores how two sisters cope with the death of their father and the subsequent repercussions of his absence. Coveney [6] pointed out that in the play "a sense of disappearing England is brilliantly conveyed through what people say rather than the events in themselves." Wardle [6] felt that the play added another dimension to Hare's political drama by "pushing social comedy to the boundary of spiritual inquiry." Kerensky viewed the play in terms of "the fragility of human relations in an age of social Darwinism." Billington [8] said that "as a portrait of our times, the play is lethal, accurate and witty" and that "it touches profounder chords than anything he has written before."

Racing Demon. 1990. Produced at the Cottesloe Theatre, London, on 1 February, directed by Richard Eyre. Subsequently moved to the larger Olivier Theatre, London, where it ran for over a year. Revived 1993.

The play explores how four clergymen struggle to make sense of their mission as charged by the hierarchy of the Church of England. Edwards [2] felt that the play lacked an historic and individual dimension, while Koenig [3] called it "all muffled anguish and thumping cliches." Christopher noted that "by distilling the arguments, Hare subtly caricatures the weaknesses of the Anglican Church: its comfy clubbiness, its banal inadequacy in dealing with social realities and the constant compromises . . . that constitute its unfashionable liberal flexibility." Billington [7] posed the pivotal question of the play in his review, which asked, "Can the church be taken serious(ly) if it divorces itself from sacrament and operates as a branch of the social services?" Hare's characters create what Hiley called a "cumulative tone" in which the dramatic action is pushed forward by what Christopher called "the value of doubt in every aspect of life."

ASSESSMENT OF HARE'S CAREER

Critics of Hare's work have both applauded and disapproved of it but have never dismissed his eclectic exploration of the social and political milieu in which he lives. Hare's work of more than two decades offers unique dramaturgical strategies employed to produce meaning rather than convey meaning, so that a pivotal element in Hare's dramaturgy lies with the audience. His politics onstage depends on the sociopolitical issues that foreground human behavior. Except for *Fanshen* every major character in Hare's plays, films, and collaborative works in some way exemplifies the notion of identity and how that identity is expressed, repressed, displaced, disguised, or achieved. He also employs other contextual notions in his work, including the indictment of governmental power structures and the depiction of the clash of values within society.

Notable differences in Hare's critique of the sociopolitical system begin to emerge after the fringe movement between 1974 and 1975. Before 1975 Hare's plays show a more overt concern for society's morals and for the inequities of class. These plays reflect a strong disenchantment with the Wilson government. Hare's characters in *Slag*, *Lay By*, *The Great Exhibition*, *Knuckle*, and to some extent *Brassneck* are all victims of the system. With *Teeth 'n' Smiles* the political critique changes focus; the culpability for the ineffectiveness and unhappiness of his characters is shared by the government and society. There is, however, a progression from *Brassneck* to *Pravda*, in which Hare's critique has evolved so that his sympathies are completely reversed. In *Brassneck* Hare continues to feel that England has a legacy of political ineptness and pretentiousness that creates a society full of victims. In *Pravda* Hare shows no real sympathy for a society that too readily accepts the role of victim.

Like many of the fringe plays, Hare's work of the early 1970s makes use of stark images, nudity, and burlesque. The ludicrous and often revolting action that accompanies such dramaturgical choices helps to reinforce the moral message. With the move to larger stages and larger audiences, Hare's critique, particularly from 1978 on, relies less on specific stark and repellent images and more on what Hare calls the "sensuality of objects" (Oliva, 179), small and often everyday objects that take on a heightened resonance and serve as images of isolation. These images often define the most profound moments in the play.

The moral critique which Hare addresses in his later plays is achieved by juxtaposing character and situation. Characters caught in a moral choice—like Jean in *Wetherby*, Sophia in *The Bay at Nice*, Mehta in *A Map of the World*, Isobel in *The Secret Rapture*, and Reverend Epsy in *Racing Demon*—subtly deliver Hare's moral stance, whether it be indicting sexual repression, the institution of marriage, political allegiance, family loyalty, or the goals of the Church of England.

Hare uses the structure of the text to reinforce content. He juxtaposes scenes so the contrast between one scene and the next helps to advance meaning. In *The Secret Rapture* he moves a step beyond juxtaposition by merging one scene with the next. He also does this in *Racing Demon* and to a lesser extent in *Murmuring Judges*. Juxtaposing scenes allows Hare the opportunity to force-frame events, situations, and characters, often to demonstrate an interpretation or an analysis of the effects of politics on society. Obviously Hare's work in film has contributed to this technique. His plays are often described as "cinematic." However, Hare feels that his work in film has enhanced his work on stage. Specifically, he says, "I've been trying to make the language of the theatre more supple, by my experience in film. . . . The form of plays has changed in the last ten years . . . because of a whole generation of playwrights brought up in the cinema, who bring to the theatre, who dream of fluent theatre, a theatre where you can go from place to place and dream, as you dream in the cinema" (Oliva, 180).

There is a cyclical nature in much of Hare's work. *Brassneck* opens with a teatime toast and concludes with a toast to capitalism. *Knuckle* shows Curly returning to his profession as an arms supplier, and *Licking Hitler* opens with

————[3]. *Disrupting the Spectacle: Five Years of Experimental and Fringe Theatre in Britain.* London: Pitman, 1975.

————[4]. "Humanity and Compassion Don't Count." *Plays and Players* (Feb. 1972): 18–20.

Barlas, Chris. Review of *Lay By. Plays and Players* (Nov. 1971): 47–48.

Barnes, Clive. Review of *Slag. New York Times* (22 Feb. 1971): 22.

Barnes, Julian. Review of *Dreams of Leaving. New Statesman* (25 Jan. 1980): 139.

Bigsby, C.W.E. [1]. "The Language of Crisis in British Theatre: The Drama of Cultural Pathology." In *Contemporary English Drama*, ed. Malcolm Bradbury and David Palmer. Stratford-upon-Avon Studies. London: Arnold, 1981: 11–52.

————[2]. "The Politics of Anxiety: Contemporary Socialist Theatre in England." *Modern Drama* 4.4 (Dec. 1981): 393–403.

Billington, Michael [1]. Review of *The Bay at Nice* and *Wrecked Eggs. The Guardian* (11 Sept. 1986): 12.

————[2]. Review of *Deeds. The Guardian* (10 Mar. 1978): 10.

————[3]. "Exit the Revolution." *The Guardian* (1 Nov. 1980): 10.

————[4]. Review of *Knuckle. The Guardian* (5 Mar. 1974): 10.

————[5]. Review of *A Map of the World. The Guardian* (28 Jan. 1983): 12.

————[6]. Review of *Pravda. The Guardian* (3 May 1985): 12.

————[7]. Review of *Racing Demon. The Guardian* (10 Feb. 1990).

————[8]. Review of *The Secret Rapture. The Guardian* (6 Oct. 1988): 25.

Bloom, Michael. "A Kindler, Gentler David Hare." *American Theatre* (Nov. 1989): 30–34.

Brown, John Russell, ed. *Modern British Drama: New Perspective.* Englewood Cliffs, NJ: Prentice-Hall, 1984.

Brustein, Robert. Review of *Murmuring Judges. New Republic* (17 Feb. 1992): 28.

Bryden, Ronald. Review of *Teeth 'n' Smiles. Plays and Players* (Nov. 1975): 21–23.

Buckley, Leonard. Review of *Brassneck. The Times* (23 May 1975): 9.

Bull, John. *New British Political Dramatists: Howard Brenton, David Hare, Trevor Griffiths, David Edgar.* London: Macmillan, 1983.

Cardullo, Bert. "Hare's *Plenty.*" *The Explicator* (winter 1985): 62–63.

Chaillet, Ned. Review of *Deeds. Plays and Players* (May 1978): 24–25.

Chernaik, Warren L. "Art and Politics: London Theatre since the Fifties." *London Journal* (winter 1982): 208–12.

Christiansen, Richard. Review of *The Secret Rapture. Chicago Tribune* (24 Sept. 1990): 14.

Christopher, James. Review of *Racing Demon. Time Out* (14 Feb. 1990).

Colvin, Clare. Review of *The Secret Rapture. Plays and Players* (Nov./Dec. 1988): 17–18.

Coveney, Michael [1]. Review of *The Bay at Nice* and *Wrecked Eggs. The Guardian* (1 Sept. 1986): 12.

————[2]. Review of *Fanshen. Plays and Players* (June 1975): 31.

————[3]. Review of *A Map of the World. Financial Times* (28 Jan. 1983): 15.

————[4]. Review of *Pravda. Financial Times* (3 May 1985): 21.

————[5]. "Turning over: The Background to *Fanshen.*" *Plays and Players* (June 1975): 10–13.

————[6]. Review of *The Secret Rapture. Financial Times* (5 Oct. 1988): 23.

Craig, Sandy, ed. *Dreams and Deconstruction: Alternative Theatre in Britain*. London: Pitman, 1988.

Curry, Jack. Review of *The Knife. USA Today* (11 Mar. 1987): 4.

Davie, Michael. Review of *Pravda. Times Literary Supplement* (17 May 1985): 551.

Denby, David. Review of *Damaged. New York* (14 Dec. 1992): 89.

Dunn, Tony [1]. "Joint Stock—The First Ten Years." *Plays and Players* (Jan. 1985): 15–18.

———[2]. "The Play of Politics." *Drama* 156 (1985): 13–15.

———[3]. "The Truth about *Pravda*." *Plays and Players* (June 1985): 18–20.

———[4]. "Writers of the Seventies." *Plays and Players* (May 1984): 12–13; (June 1984): 35–36.

Edwards, Christopher [1]. Review of *Murmuring Judges. The Spectator* (12 Oct. 1991): 44.

———[2]. Review of *Racing Demon. The Spectator* (17 Feb. 1990): 34.

Evans, Gareth, and Barbara Lloyd. *Plays in Review, 1956–1980: British Drama and the Critics*. New York: Methuen, 1985.

Feingold, Michael. Review of *A Map of the World. Village Voice* (8 Oct. 1985): 94.

Ford, John. "Getting the Carp out of the Mud." *Plays and Players* (Nov. 1971): 20.

Free, William J. "Mischief and Frustration in David Hare's *Knuckle*."In *Legacy of Thespis*, ed. Karelisa V. Hartigan. Lanham, MD: University Press of America, 1984: 23–30.

Gale, Steve H. "Sex and Politics: David Hare's *Plenty*." *Themes in Drama* 7 (1995): 213–20.

Gilbert, W. Stephen. Review of *Plenty. Plays and Players* (June 1978): 28–29.

Gold, Sylviane [1]. Review of *The Knife. Wall Street Journal* (31 Mar. 1987): 34.

———[2]. Review of *A Map of the World. Wall Street Journal* (15 Oct. 1985): 26.

Golomb, Liorah Anne. "Saint Isobel: David Hare's *The Secret Rapture* as Christian Allegory." *Modern Drama* 4.4 (Dec. 1990): 563–74.

Gordon, Giles [1]. Review of *A Map of the World. The Spectator* (5 Feb. 1983): 28.

———[2]. Review of *Pravda. Plays and Players* (Aug. 1985): 16–17.

Graffy, Julian. Review of *The Bay at Nice* and *Wrecked Eggs. Times Literary Supplement* (26 Sept. 1986): 1064.

Grantham, Bill. "Plays in Print: Political Drama." *Drama* 2.1 (Mar. 1986): 47–48.

Greer, Herb. Review of *Pravda. Encounter* (Sept./Oct. 1985): 36–38.

Grove, Valerie. "Sensitive Soul with a Demon of a Job." *Sunday Times* (11 Feb. 1990): E6.

Gussow, Mel. "What Pushes David Hare's Characters." *New York Times* (15 Mar. 1987): 5.

Hammond, Jonathan [1]. Review of *Knuckle. Plays and Players* (Apr. 1974): 40–41.

———[2]. "A Potted History of the Fringe." *Theatre Quarterly* 3 (1973): 37–46.

Harris, William. "Mapping the World of David Hare." *American Theatre* (Dec. 1985): 12–16.

Hassell, Graham. "Hare Racing." *Plays and Players* (Feb. 1990): 6–9.

Hebblethwaite, Peter. Review of *Racing Demon. Times Literary Supplement* (16 Feb. 1990): 172.

Henry, William [1]. Review of *A Map of the World. Time* (18 Oct. 1985): 113.

———[2]. Review of *Pravda. Time* (10 June 1985): 81.

Hiley, Jim. Review of *Racing Demon. The Listener* (22 Feb. 1990).

Holland, Mary. Review of *The Great Exhibition*. *Plays and Players* (Apr. 1972): 40–41.

Homden, Carol. "A Dramatist of Surprise." *Plays and Players* (Sept. 1988): 5–7.

Hurren, Kenneth. Review of *The Bay at Nice* and *Wrecked Eggs*. *Plays and Players* (Nov. 1986): 20–21.

Itzin, Catherine. *Stages in the Revolution: Political Theatre in Britain since 1968*. London: Methuen, 1968.

Kalem, T. E. Review of *Plenty*. *Time* (1 Nov. 1982): 78.

Kauffmann, Stanley [1]. Review of *Plenty*. *Saturday Review* (Mar./Apr. 1983): 41–42.

———[2]. Review of *Wetherby*. *New Republic* (12 Aug. 1985): 24–26.

Kennedy, Douglas. Review of *The Secret Rapture*. *New Statesman and Society* (14 Oct. 1988): 36–37.

Kerensky, Oleg. *The New British Drama: Fourteen Playwrights since Osborne and Pinter*. London: Hamish Hamilton, 1977.

Kerr, Walter. "Playwrights Are Growing Articulate Again." *New York Times* (31 Oct. 1982): 3.

Kingston, Jeremy. Review of *The Great Exhibition*. *Punch* (8 Mar. 1972): 328–29.

Koenig, Rhoda [1]. "Hare Apparent: On the Stage and on the Screen, David Hare Concentrates His Rage." *Vogue* (Feb. 1989): 202.

———[2]. Review of *Murmuring Judges*. *Punch* (23 Oct. 1991): 68–69.

———[3]. Review of *Racing Demon*. *Punch* (23 Feb. 1990): 34–35.

Larson, Jane Karsten. Review of *Plenty*. *Christian Century* 100 (1983): 277–78.

Leverett, James. Review of *The Secret Rapture*. *Village Voice* (7 Nov. 1989): 107.

Levin, Bernard [1]. Review of *Deeds*. *Sunday Times* (12 Mar. 1978): 37.

———[2]. Review of *Plenty*. *Sunday Times* (16 Apr. 1978): 37.

———[3]. Review of *Pravda*. *Sunday Times* (29 Oct. 1985): 16.

Lustig, Vera. Review of *Racing Demon*. *Plays and Players* (Apr. 1990): 35.

Morgan, Gwyn. Review of *Murmuring Judges*. *Plays and Players* (Dec.-Jan. 1991-92): 26.

Morley, Sheridan. "Hare's Breadth." *Punch* (19 Apr. 1978): 666.

Mortimer, John. "On the Left Side of the Law." *Sunday Times* (6 Oct. 1991): 10–11.

Nightingale, Benedict [1]. Review of *The Bay at Nice* and *Wrecked Eggs*. *New Statesman* (26 Sept. 1986): 30–31.

———[2]. Review of *Brassneck*. *New Statesman* (28 Sept. 1973): 443.

———[3]. "David Hare Captures His Muse on Stage." *New York Times* (22 Oct. 1989): 5+.

———[4]. Review of *A Map of the World*. *New Statesman* (4 Feb. 1983): 27–28.

———[5]. Review of *Murmuring Judges*. *London Times* (11 Oct. 1991): 20.

———[6]. Review of *Plenty*. *New Statesman* (21 Apr. 1978): 538.

———[7]. Review of *Pravda*. *New Statesman* (10 May 1985): 29–30.

Oliva, Judy Lee. *David Hare: Theatricalizing Politics*. Ann Arbor, MI: UMI Research Press, 1990.

Peter, John [1]. Review of *The Secret Rapture*. *Sunday Times* (9 Oct. 1988): 8.

———[2]. Review of *Murmuring Judges*. *Sunday Times* (13 Oct. 1991): 6/6a.

Rabey, David Ian. *British and Irish Political Drama in the Twentieth Century*. New York: St. Martin's Press, 1986.

Ratcliffe, Michael [1]. Review of *Dreams of Leaving*. *The Times* (18 Jan. 1980): 13.

———[2]. Review of *Pravda*. *The Observer* (5 May 1985): 23.

Rich, Frank [1]. Review of *The Knife*. *New York Times* (11 Mar. 1987): 22.

————[2]. Review of *A Map of the World*. *New York Times* (2 Oct. 1985): 23.

————[3]. Review of *The Secret Rapture*. *New York Times* (20 Dec. 1988): 19.

————[4]. Review of *The Secret Rapture*. *New York Times* (27 Oct. 1989): 13.

————[5]. "Theatre." *New York Times* (22 Oct. 1982): 3.

Rogoff, Gordon [1]. Review of *The Knife*. *Village Voice* (17 Mar. 1987): 91–92.

————[2]. *Theatre Is Not Safe, Theatre Criticism, 1962–1986*. Evanston, IL: Northwestern University Press, 1986.

Simon, John [1]. Review of *Fanshen*. *New York* (14 Feb. 1983): 76–77.

————[2]. Review of *Knuckle*. *New York* (30 Mar. 1981): 34–35.

————[3]. Review of *Plenty*. *New York* (24 Jan. 1983): 69–70.

Styan, J. L. *Modern Drama in Theory and Practice*. 3 vols. Cambridge: Cambridge University Press, 1981.

Taylor, John Russell [1]. Review of *A Map of the World*. *Plays and Players* (Mar. 1983): 30–31.

————[2]. *The Second Wave*. New York: Hill & Wang, 1971.

Wardle, Irving [1]. Review of *Brassneck*. *The Times* (20 Sept. 1973): 13.

————[2]. Review of *Deeds*. *The Times* (10 Mar. 1978): 10.

————[3]. Review of *A Map of the World*. *The Times* (28 Jan. 1983): 11.

————[4]. Review of *Plenty*. *The Times* (13 Apr. 1978): 7.

————[5]. Review of *Pravda*. *The Times* (3 May 1985): 12.

————[6]. Review of *The Secret Rapture*. *The Times* (5 Oct. 1988): 16.

Waterhouse, Robert. Review of *Slag*. *Plays and Players* (May 1970): 44–45.

Weiss, Hedy. "Steppenwolf Explores Hare's Elusive 'Rapture.' " *Chicago Sun-Times* (24 Sept. 1990): 25.

Wolf, Matthew. Review of *The Bay at Nice* and *Wrecked Eggs Chicago Tribune* (28 Sept. 1986): 12–13.

Yakir, Dan. "Hare Style." *Horizon* (Dec. 1985): 45–47.

Ann Jellicoe
(1927–)

JANICE OLIVER

Patricia Ann Jellicoe was born in Middlesborough, Yorkshire on 15 July 1927, the daughter of John Andrea Jellicoe and Frances Henderson. Her father was from a moderately well-to-do, southern English family, her mother from a lower-middle-class north country one. ''Between these two I oscillate,'' Jellicoe has said, speaking of what she sees as the sophisticated intellectual versus the more practical intuitive personality traits. Her parents separated when she was eighteen months old, and after a childhood spent mostly in a boarding school system whose conformist values she could not entirely accept, Jellicoe attended the Central School of Speech and Drama in London (1943–1947), training to be an actress; there she won many awards, among them the coveted Elsie Fogarty Prize.

Following a period of travel in Europe, where she sharpened the language skills she would use later in translating plays, Jellicoe began directing and solicited her friends in order to found the experimental Cockpit Theatre Club (1950–1953). There she directed eight plays in two years, one of which was hers, returning finally to the Central School to direct and teach (1953–1955). Jellicoe's 1950 marriage to C. E. Knight-Clark ended in divorce in 1961. During this period she wrote *The Sport of My Mad Mother* (1958) specifically for a playwrighting competition organized by *The Observer*. She won third prize, and the Royal Court Theatre, with which she would become affiliated for the next twenty years, promptly produced it, to little critical or commercial success: critics and audiences alike were baffled by the plotless, nonverbal nature of the piece, as well as by its overpowering rhythms and images that seem to represent the ascendence of violence in contemporary British society. Following *The Sport*'s success, Jellicoe was commissioned by the British Girl Guides Association to write a pageant to be performed by its members. For them she wrote

The Rising Generation, an absurdist fable that was rejected by the Guides, but which was successfully produced at the Royal Court in 1967 (see Wardle [1]). In 1962 Jellicoe married actor Roger Mayne, with whom she has had a daughter, Katkin Ann Mayne and a son, Thomas Jellicoe Mayne. In 1961 she wrote *The Knack*, a play warmly received when it was produced at the Royal Court in 1962. An exuberant comedy about three men whose varying degrees of skill at seducing women (the "knack") are tested when a young woman happens into their lives; the play was successfully adapted for Richard Lester's film *The Knack . . . and How to Get It* (1965). Jellicoe followed *The Knack* with a more conventionally written biographical piece called *Shelley; or, The Idealist* (1965), which found moderate success, and *The Giveaway* (1970), a domestic farce with absurdist elements that met with mixed, mainly lukewarm notices (see Wardle [2]).

From 1973 to 1975 Jellicoe worked as literary manager at the Royal Court; and in 1978, after she moved to Lyme Regis, Dorset, with her family, she became founding director of the Colway Theatre Trust, where she remained until 1985. In 1978 Jellicoe wrote and directed a community play, *The Reckoning*, a massive undertaking involving over seventy cast members and three stage spaces to tell the violent, dramatic story of the Monmouth rebellion in Lyme. Since then, Jellicoe has continued writing and producing for Community Theatre. After visiting Holbaek, Denmark, in 1987 to see a production of *The Knack*, she agreed to produce for this community, writing *Money and Land*, a play about events in 1789 that turned Denmark from a medieval country into a liberal democracy. In addition, she was instrumental in pairing Holbaek with Dorchester, where Danes took part in her play called *Under the God*, about the 789 A.D. Viking landing in Dorchester. Because of her efforts, strong bonds now exist between the people of the two towns. In 1992 Jellicoe wrote and directed *Changing Places* for Woking, Surrey, a play dealing with women's suffrage in relation to the history of the town.

Selected Biographical Sources: Doty; Goodman; Innes; Jellicoe, *Some Unconscious Influences in the Theatre*; Rusinko.

MAJOR PLAYS, PREMIERES, AND PRODUCTIONS: THEATRICAL RECEPTION

The Sport of My Mad Mother. 1958. Opened 25 February at the Royal Court Theatre, London, for fourteen performances. Produced by the English Stage Company; codirectors George Devine and Ann Jellicoe.

Its title taken from a hymn to the Hindu goddess of creation and destruction ("All creation is the sport of my mad mother Kali"), Jellicoe's stylistically experimental play involving a group of violent London teenagers provoked audiences, who felt confronted, and critics, who had difficulty in categorizing it because of its plotlessness. Smith saw the intent as being documentary, and Brien called it a "modern surrealist fantasy" that, while sometimes funny and symbolically powerful, failed to involve the audience in any human drama. *The Times* ("Court Theatre") reviewer acknowledged Jellicoe's skill with rhythmic language but faulted her for not providing a story or characters to involve the mind. Worsley says the play succeeds on the private level as image but not enough for it to become publicly relevant to the audience. Tynan and Granger found structural problems because the longer second act dispelled initial tension set up in act one. Despite much negative criticism, several critics, like Barber, used "effervescent" to describe the impact that Jellicoe's use of stage imagery had on them, and almost all were unqualified in their approval of her theatrical sense. Later critics (see Taylor) view this early play as a revolutionary example of a more intuitively based, director's theatre that makes strenuous demands upon an audience to experience the play directly, instead of processing it through the intellect first.

The Knack. 1961. Opened 9 October at the Arts Theatre, Cambridge. Opened 27 March 1962, at the Royal Court Theatre, London. Produced by the English Stage Company; codirectors Ann Jellicoe and Keith Johnstone. Opened 28 May 1964, in New York.

This comedy with ritualistic elements played out in a realistic setting proved a critical as well as commercial success. Gascoigne said Jellicoe wrote brilliantly about sexual manipulative games men and women play. Both reviews in *The Times* ("Drama beyond the Spoken Word" and "Naive Plot with Elusive Undercurrents") reported a Noël Coward–like influence in this play, first in her use of absurd moments and second, in the fact that talk has little to do with action. Less approving was the more traditionally minded Trewin, who thought the play had nothing to say, and said that badly. Later critics could see that *The Knack* falls within the realm of absurdist theatre, Clurman noting it "hovers" about it, and Simon observing that she practices the peculiarly English form of "domesticated" absurdism. Taylor hears in Jellicoe a formidable voice for an intuitive, theatrical drama independent of words. Some of the notoriety surrounding the play was generated by its successful adaptation for the screen. Richard Lester's Cannes Film Festival winning *The Knack . . . and How To Get It* increased interest in the play, which was still running in New York at the time (1965). Reviewing the film, Crowther thinks its slapstick force extends the arena from that of a bedroom in the play to all of London in the film.

ADDITIONAL PLAYS, ADAPTATIONS, AND PRODUCTIONS

Jellicoe wrote the stage adaptations of Henrik Ibsen's *Rosmersholm* (produced London, 1952; revised version produced London, 1959) and his *The Lady from the Sea* (produced London, 1961). She also adapted Friedrich Kind's libretto *Der Freischutz* (produced London, 1964), as well as Anton Chekhov's *The Seagull* (produced London, 1964). Her plays for children are collected in *3 Jelliplays* (London: Faber & Faber, 1975). When Jellicoe began her second career as a pioneer in community theatre, she wrote and directed the following: *Flora and the Bandits* (produced Dartington, Devon, 1976); *The Reckoning* (produced Lyme Regis, Dorset, 1978); *The Bargain* (produced Exeter, 1979); *The Tide* (produced Axminster, Devon, 1980); *The Western Women*, adapted from a Fay Weldon story (produced Lyme Regis, Dorset 1984); *Mark Og Mønt* (*Money and Land*) (produced Holbaek, Denmark, 1988); *Under the God* (produced Dorchester, 1989); *Changing Places* (produced Woking, Surrey, 1992).

ASSESSMENT OF JELLICOE'S CAREER

Jellicoe is primarily regarded today as one of the cadre of young writers whose work informed the early days of the Royal Court Theatre, itself a vital part of the postwar revolution British drama. As the lone woman in the Court's Writers Group that included playwrights like John Osborne, John Arden, Edward Bond, and Arnold Wesker, Jellicoe has spoken of the bias she sometimes felt against her, the only established woman in a group dominated by men (see Doty). She held her own, however, pushing for a chance not simply to collaborate with directors like George Devine, Michel Saint-Denis, Lindsay Anderson, and Tony Richardson, but to hone her own directing skills, getting the chance to direct being the reason she wrote plays in the first place. In current scholarship, however, she is considered less the director and more the writer, her reputation resting upon the stylistic innovations of her early plays (see Tschudin and Rusinko).

Jellicoe's experience as a director cannot be minimized and is vital to an assessment, since she views writing-to-directing as a continuum of experience derived from the same creative source and one that is inextricable with regard to her own work. She has said, and most agree, that the best productions of her plays have been directed by her (Jellicoe, ''Covering the Ground''). As evidence of her dedication to the craft, Jellicoe has continued for over four decades to direct scores of plays, covering an inclusive repertory from Aristophanes to Strindberg, Ibsen to Johnstone.

Being a director bore heavily on writing for Jellicoe because the process opened up into an improvisational interchange with others, thereby breaking down hierarchical divisions between writer, director, and actor to produce a communal script (see Innes). Even among the avant-garde group of early Royal Court writers, she broke ground in writing a nonliterary form that has subsequently influenced others. Jellicoe has said that her plays are about ''incoherent people . . . who have no power of expression,'' people whose sometimes violent frustration must be shown directly, in a drama of the senses emphasizing sound, image, and motion rather than words (Jellicoe, ''Interview''). Commentary about her work has subsequently centered upon the unique qualities of her experimental forms, especially on the nontextual nature of her plays.

As a precursor in the English theatre, Jellicoe is frequently included in feminist studies, mentioned as an early feminist who, like others in her time, rebelled against constrictive domestic roles for women (Goodman). Strong female characters abound in her plays, along with themes like female creativity and sexual prowess. In her capacity as literary manager at the Court, she was responsible for encouraging the work of several women writers, among them Mary O'Malley, Felicity Brown, and to a lesser extent Pam Gems (Jellicoe, ''Covering the Ground''). A fruitful area for study would involve examining Jellicoe's influence on subsequent women dramatists, concentrating especially on her contribution as one of the few women of her time in control of the entire theatre process.

With *The Knack* Jellicoe's reputation as a playwright peaked. Later plays, notably *Shelley; or The Idealist* and *The Giveaway*, have been largely ignored as experiments with conventional docudrama and absurdist farce that failed to win favor. Saying she ''seems to want to demonstrate that she is not limited to writing in just one way,'' Taylor, for one, faults her for not recreating the liveliness of her earlier work. In order to correct this misconception that Jellicoe failed in her later efforts because she did not replicate the earlier comedies, *Shelley*, especially, needs a reexamination, both in the light of its being a radical departure from her earlier work and in its feminist depiction of the women in Shelley's life.

In the 1970s Jellicoe wrote and directed several shorter plays, worked at the Royal Court as literary manager, made the choice to raise her children in Dorset, and found a niche in the developing community play movement, where she has flourished since. Community Theatre uses a core of professional theatre practitioners who work with amateur actors to produce a play exploring historical themes of a town. Realizing that she would be writing and directing a play in which her children, neighbors, and friends could take part, Jellicoe remarked, ''For the first time I didn't feel divided'' (Jellicoe ''Covering the Ground''). As has been the case for many women, private choices have affected public perceptions of Jellicoe's career. To many, working far from London in amateur productions might seem a less than wise career move, but Jellicoe herself sees it in more holistic terms, as a satisfying extension of her earlier career. And critics have found many of these plays examples of exciting experimental theatre (see Saddler). A many-faceted woman who began as an actress, wrote so that she could have an opportunity to direct, found phenomenal success in both London and New York, searched out other alternatives, and pursued a career as a groundbreaker on the community front, Ann Jellicoe proves a viable subject for biography.

PRIMARY BIBLIOGRAPHY

Plays

The Giveaway. London: Faber & Faber, 1970.
The Knack. London: Encore, 1962; New York: Samuel French, 1962.
The Rising Generation. In *Playbill 2*, ed. Alan Durband. London: Hutchinson, 1969.

Shelley; or, The Idealist. London: Faber & Faber, 1966; New York: Grove Press, 1966.
The Sport of My Mad Mother. London: Faber & Faber, 1958; revised 1964.

Books, Essays, Articles, and Interviews on Drama and Theatre

"Ann Jellicoe, Interviewed by Robert Rubens." *Transatlantic Review* 12 (spring 1963): 27–34.
"Covering the Ground." In *Women and Theatre: Calling the Shots*, ed. Susan Todd. London: Faber & Faber, 1984.
Community Plays: How to Put Them On. London: Methuen, 1987.
"Interview." *New Theatre Magazine* 1.4 (1960).
Some Unconscious Influences in the Theatre. Cambridge: Cambridge University Press, 1967.
"Theatre People Reply to Our Inquiry." *World Theatre* (Jan.–Feb. 1965): 44–53.
"The Writers' Group." In *At the Royal Court: 25 Years of the English Stage Company*, ed. Richard Findlater. New York: Grove Press, 1981.

SECONDARY BIBLIOGRAPHY

Barber, John. Rev. of *The Sport of My Mad Mother. Daily Express* (26 Feb. 1958).
Brien, Alan. "Tinkling Symbols." *The Spectator* (7 Mar. 1958): 296.
Clurman, Harold. *The Naked Image: Observations on the Modern Theatre.* New York: Macmillan, 1966.
"Court Theatre." *The Times* (26 Feb. 1958): 3.
Crowther, Bosley. "Screen: *The Knack* Opens at Plaza." *New York Times* (30 June 1965): 42.
"Documentary Melodrama of Poet's Life." *The Times* (19 Oct. 1965): 16.
Doty, Gresdna A., and Billy J. Harbin, eds. *Inside the Royal Court Theatre, 1956–1981: Artists Talk.* Baton Rouge: Louisiana State University Press: 1990.
"Drama beyond the Spoken Word." *The Times* (10 Oct. 1961): 16.
Gascoigne, Bamber. "With a Bare Bedstead." *The Spectator* (6 Apr. 1962): 445–46.
Goodman, Lizbeth. *Contemporary Feminist Theatres: To Each Her Own.* London: Routledge, 1993.
Granger, Derek. Review of *The Sport of My Mad Mother. Financial Times* (26 Feb. 1958).
Innes, C. D. "Present Tense—Feminist Theatre." *Modern British Drama, 1890–1990.* Cambridge: Cambridge University Press, 1992.
"Naive Plot with Elusive Undercurrents." *The Times* (28 Mar. 1962): 15.
Rusinko, Susan. *British Drama 1950 to the Present: A Critical History.* Boston: Twayne, 1989.
Saddler, Alan. Review of *The Reckoning. Plays and Players* (Feb. 1979): 29.
Simon, John. *Uneasy Stages: A Chronicle of the New York Theatre, 1963–1973.* New York: Random House, 1975.
Smith, Michael. Review of *The Sport of My Mad Mother. Village Voice* (8 June 1967): 20.
Taylor, John Russell. *Anger and After: A Guide to the New British Drama.* London: Methuen, 1962.

Trewin, J. C. "Making the Best of It." *Illustrated London News* (7 Apr. 1962): 554.

Tschudin, Marcus. *A Writer's Theatre: George Devine and the English Stage Company at the Royal Court Theatre, 1956–1965*. Bern: Herbert Lang & Co., 1972.

Tynan, Kenneth. Review of *The Sport of My Mad Mother*. *The Observer* (2 Mar. 1958).

Wardle, Irving [1]. "Effort to Extend Scope." *The Times* (9 Apr. 1969): 6.

———[2]. "Ghoul the Guides Missed." *The Times* (24 July 1967): 6.

Worsley, T. C. "Adolescents." *New Statesman* (8 Mar. 1958): 301.

Bernard Kops

(1926–)

WILLIAM BAKER

Bernard Kops was born in Stepney in the heart of the East End of London, a Jewish-immigrant area, in 1926, to a Jewish-Dutch immigrant cobbler who had come to London's East End in 1904 and to a mother born in London of Dutch-Jewish parents. He was the youngest of a family of four sisters and two brothers. The impoverished but intense, lively, and cosmopolitan environment, the anti-Jewish fascist demonstrations and counterdemonstrations of the immediate prewar period in the East End of London, wartime London, and his own Jewishness pervade Kops's work. His Jewishness is cultural and personal, yet Kops is not orthodox in a religious sense. Kops left school at thirteen to earn a living and worked in a variety of jobs, including a spell as a docker, chef, salesman, waiter, liftman, and barrow boy selling books in street markets. Since early childhood he read voraciously and wrote. Two early seminal literary influences upon him were Eugene O'Neill's *Mourning Becomes Electra* and the poetry and drama of T. S. Eliot. Evening drama classes at the Toynbee Hall in London's East End run by the legendary Marianne Watson formed the foundation for his dramatic methodology.

During World War II the Kops family moved around England in attempts to avoid the German blitz upon London, to which they frequently returned. After the war Kops acted in repertory theater, traveled through France, Spain, and Tangier, and lived in a caravan in Camden Town, North London. His mother died in 1951 and Kops was subsequently committed to a psychiatric hospital—experiences recorded in his lyric narrative poem *An Anemone for Antigone*. Kops has twice been institutionalized, and his concern with extreme mental states clearly has a personal genesis. *On Margate Sands* (1978), regarded by Toulson as Kops's "most mature novel," is a study of five former psychiatric hospital patients. His writing is inhabited by characters who live a frenetic existence plagued by extreme mood changes. One of Kops's central preoccupations is the fragile borderline between "sanity" and "insanity," "dreams" and "psychi-atric disturbances," "creativity" and "madness."

Stability came to Kops's life when he met Erica Gordon, a doctor's daughter, whom he married in 1956. They had four children, and since the 1950s Kops has earned his living as a professional writer, teacher or writer in residence at a theatre, cultural center, or college. Three books of poems—*Poems* (1955), *Poems and Songs* (1958), and *An Anemone for Antigone* (1959)— and a novel, *Awake for Mourning* (1958), appeared in the 1950s, as did his first play, *The Hamlet of Stepney Green* (1958), and *Goodbye World* (1959). In 1960 *Change for the Angel* and *The Dream of Peter Mann* were performed. *Stray Cats* and *Empty Bottles* (1961) and *Enter Solly Gold* (1964) coincide with a flurry of activities in other forms. The radio plays *Home Sweet Honeycomb* (1962) and *The Lemmings* (1963) were included in *Four Plays* (1964) with *The Hamlet of Stepney Green* and *Enter Solly Gold*. An autobiography, *The World Is a Wed-ding*, was published in 1963. The year before, a novel, *Motorbike* (1962), was published, and three years later came the novel *Yes from No-Man's Land*, fol-lowed by other novels: *The Dissent of Dominick Shapiro* (1966), *By the Waters of Whitechapel* (1969), and *The Passionate Past of Gloria Gaye* (1971). There followed the novels: *Settle down Simon Katz* (1973), *Partners* (1975) and *On Margate Sands* (1978). A host of radio and television plays were written during the 1970s, 1980s and early 1990s as were two collections of poetry, *For the Record* (1971) and the privately printed *Barricades in West Hampstead* (1988).

Kops never deserted the theatre. A play for children, *The Boy Who Wouldn't Play Jesus*, was produced in 1965. *David, It Is Getting Dark*, was produced in Rennes, France, in 1970. A television play written in collaboration with John Goldschmidt, *It's a Lovely Day Tomorrow*, was produced in 1976; there followed *More out Than In* in 1980 and the important *Ezra* in 1981. Also, a radio broadcast, *Simon at Midnight*, was produced in 1985, *Some of These Days* in 1990, and *So-phie (The Last of the Red Hot Mommas)* in 1991. Two other plays were performed in 1991: *Moss* and *Playing Sinatra*. Another play for young people, and one deal-ing with areas close to Kops's heart—the dream world of childhood and the ho-locaust—*Dreams of Anne Frank* opened at the Polka Theatre, London on 3 October 1992 and closed 28 November 1992. Writing has not brought Kops or his family riches. It is something he has just had to do. His fertile imagination is still producing thoughtful, moving masterpieces. The lean years and seeming neglect have not dimmed his muse or crushed his spirit.

Selected Biographical Sources: Kops, *The World Is a Wedding*; Hill; Night-ingale; Stanford; Willetts.

MAJOR PLAYS: THEATRICAL RECEPTION

The Hamlet of Stepney Green: A Sad Comedy with Some Songs. 1958. Opened 19 May at the Playhouse, Oxford, presented by the Meadow Players; moved 15 July to the Lyric Opera House, Hammersmith. In this production, directed by

Frank Hauser, the part of Bessie Levy was played by Thelma Ruby rather than Dorothea Phillips, who played the part in Oxford. The play also opened 13 November at the Cricket Theatre (NY), where it ran until 5 April 1959, for 166 performances.

Called "a fable with music," *The Hamlet of Stepney Green* uses music to evoke nostalgia and to provide a melancholic ironic commentary on the action, and re-create an East End of London (the equivalent of New York's Lower East Side) ambience. Reviewers criticized the length of the play, seen as a lack of dramatic discipline and control, especially, for instance, when Sam takes too long to die. Despite these criticisms reviews praised the play's sense of evanescence and rendering of ordinary London Jewish existence with its hopes, fears, music, and tears. Sicher sees *The Hamlet of Stepney Green* as continuing Shakespearian adaptations "in the early New York Yiddish theatre in terms of the rebellion of Jewish youth against their elders' adherence to bourgeois and religious values, and which is here coupled with the modern adolescent's difficulty in coming to terms with his own precocious sexuality and confused identity." MacInnes sees the play as "a lament for the bewailing past." The conclusion of act 2, scene 1—in which the mourners, with the ghost unseen to them joining in, recite the Kaddish, (the prayer for the dead)— is for MacInnes, "a most wonderful human, religious and theatrical triumph [for] these same characters," who immediately after "become once more the sagacious lunatics of wild, poetic force."

The Dream of Peter Mann. 1960. Opened 5 September at the Lyceum Theatre, Edinburgh, presented by Lynoq Productions as part of the Edinburgh Festival. Directed by Frank Dunlop, with decor by Richard Negri and music by Ricet-Barrier.

Half the first-night audience walked out of this attempt to portray a rebellion against a dominating Jewish mother. Peter's rebellion, according to Fisch, "functions as part of a Brechtian analysis of society and its imminent decay." Reviews were mixed, accusing Kops of attempting too much: of writing a play about life under the shadow of the hydrogen bomb; about Jewish oedipal rebellion; about the failure of love and adolescent relationships. Jones asserts that "despite its candid portrayal at the necessary moments of misery and terror, this is finally a joyous play and an affirmation of the love of life." Lumley sees the play as "not entirely successfully constructed." Taylor saw value in the dramatist's use of fantasy "but unfortunately the 'philosophy' weighs a little heavy on the piece and [Kops] does not seem to have quite the intellectual flexibility necessary to put over such a bold message about human values without making his drama naïve in the least acceptable sense."

Enter Solly Gold. 1962. Music by Stanley Myers, produced in Wellingborough, Northamptonshire and Los Angeles; revived briefly in London, 1970.

Written as part of the Centre 42 Trades Union Congress project of September 1960, the primary objective of which was to bring arts to the people, to everyday people who normally would not have the opportunity to go to the theater. *Enter Solly Gold* was chosen as the inaugural production for the Wellingborough Trades Union Festival and then performed throughout Britain in venues where live theatre was not usually seen. Consequently there were continual changes of cast and producers.

The theme of the conman escaping the ghetto to find himself in a materially wealthier but spiritually impoverished second ghetto in which he manages briefly to release a family of snobs from materialism to the enjoyment of life was commended. Nightingale writing in 1973 saw *Enter Solly Gold* as "perhaps [Kops's] best play to date." Taylor, however, saw it as "a very patchy play, but there are enough good patches to make it on the whole one of Kops's most fetching works." Wellwarth observes, "It seems hardly possible that the first two exercises in sophomoric philosophy were written by the same man who wrote the gay and witty *Enter Solly Gold*." Kops "seems to have committed the unforgivable crime in the eyes of the English critics by writing *Enter Solly Gold*. . . . He is guilty of not being serious."

David, la nuit tombe (*David, It Is Getting Dark*). 1970. Translated into French by Edith Zetline, and produced and performed in Rennes, France, by Laurant Jerzieff.

A political drama depicting the conflict between a right-wing English Jewish writer and a socialist English Jewish writer. According to Dace, "The successful right-wing writer . . . is driven so far as to plagiarize the work of a Jewish writer living in penury." It remains unperformed in English but ran briefly in France. *David* is important, as it can be viewed as a trial run for *Ezra*: it fuses Kops's obsession with failure and success, the need to love and be loved, loneliness and communication, Jewishness and anti-Semitism, the need for God, the way people exploit each other, and creativity.

Ezra. 1981. Opened at the New Half Moon Theatre, London, 5 April and ran until 12 May. Ian McDiarmid played the role of the poet Ezra Pound incarcerated by the Americans after World War II. Designed by Mick Bearwish and Martin Sutherland

The play, writes Sicher, is one that "ponder[s] the enigma of [a great poet] whose attitudes to the Jews define in one way the Jewishness, of the Jewish writer." For Grindea, "The uniquely sinister role of Pound's imprisonment and release is the core of *Ezra*," which "had a lamentably short run in the East End and a presentation on BBC Radio Three which was a memorable experience." Wardle [1] commented, "No other living playwright matches [Kops] in the virtuoso handling of dream logic." Of Ian McDiarmid's performance as the tormented Pound, Wardle [1] writes that he "ransacks the text to present a character who is both of heroic scale and in the grip of a diseased obsession." The production by Robert Walker "is set in the construction of rusted grids, scrap timber, and petrified rope which exists simultaneously in actuality and memory . . . allowing you to share Pound's perception of the surrounding characters."

Playing Sinatra. 1991. Opened at the Warehouse Theatre, Croydon, Surrey, 1 October. Directed by Ted Craig, designed by Michael Pavelka with Ian Gelder as Norman, Susan Brown as Sandra, and Stefan Bednarczyk as Phillip. Produced at the Greenwich Theatre, 25 March 1992, with the same cast and director.

Quinn calls *Playing Sinatra* "a corker of a play and a triumph for Kops, his best play in more than a decade—since *Ezra*." For Eyres, "Ted Craig's direction faithfully reflects the emotional profundity of the writing." Wright saw *Playing Sinatra* as "one of the most important new plays of the year, not because it does anything very novel technically or . . . stylistically, but because of the psychological depth and complexity that Kops achieves in his economical but oh-so-potent three-hander."

Dreams of Anne Frank. 1992. Opened 1 October at the Polka Theatre for Children, Wimbledon, and ran until 14 November. Kops at the time was the writer-in-residence at the theatre.

Helen Rose saw Kops's exploration of Anne Frank's dreams as "eloquent and compassionate" with the play blending "element of the daily, suffocating reality of life . . . with the flights of imaginary fantasy Anne escaped into." Hoyle focused on the surrealistic adult qualities of the play in which "Fran Cooper's evocative, faintly surreal design sets the tone beautifully for Leona Heimfeld's production." Klein sees "one of the central themes of the play as that of the bystander, the passive observer who chooses not to act." For O'Reilly, "Only the play's ending disappoints. What should be a moving last exit is followed by a speech by Anne's father in which he tells us that he would rather have his daughter alive than her diary . . . But the play has told us this already with more subtlety. The message doesn't need ramming home." Sonin observes that Kops "in the case of his heroine, reminded us all that though his words are a vital legacy, it was the life, no matter how short, that was infinitely more important!"

ADDITIONAL PLAYS, RADIO PLAYS, AND TELEVISION PLAYS

Three early playscripts, *Goodbye World* (produced briefly Guildford, Surrey, 1959), *Change for the Angel* (produced at the Arts Theatre, London, March 1960), and *Stray Cats and Empty Bottles* (Cambridge; 1961 brief revival, London, 1967), contain materials later used by Kops. The lengthy rambling dream sequences in *Goodbye World* were more suitable for the radio than the theatre. *Change for the Angel* is a lengthy-three act play, with the first of a long line of Kopsian characters just released from mental institutions, seemingly ill suited to adjust to the world they are thrust into. *Fear Fane* (1964), an unpublished play, was subsequently developed into Kops's novel juxtaposing fact and fantasy in the mind of an ex suburban housewife, Gloria Gaye, titled *The Passionate Past of Gloria Gaye* (1971).

The Boy Who Wouldn't Play Jesus, subtitled "A Modern Mystery Play for Children," with its completely empty stage set in the present was produced in London in 1965; it draws upon Kops's ethnic awareness of the pressure upon minority children to conform to often alien conventions in contemporary Britain.

More out Than In opened in Nottingham 5 October 1980, and was a touring production by the Midlands-based CVI Theatre Company. It opened at the Bush Theatre, London, on 8 November 1980, and ran until 3 December 1980. An adaptation from his novel *On Margate Sands*, the drama "is a tragicomic examination of psychiatric after-care: and of whether that term amounts to anything more than a pharmaceutical fraud." The production "marks the theatrical return of Bernard Kops after a gap of [more than] 10 years" (Wardle [2]). *Simon at Midnight* opened at the Young Vic, London, on 19 August 1985, and ran until 31 August 1985. The play mixes actuality and dream, and Wardle [2] writes, "There are passages where it works magically in this play. The key line is 'Some of our best friends are ghosts,' the point being that, as the past is as real to Simon as the present, dead and living can mix on equal terms."

Sophie (*The Last of the Red Hot Mommas*) opened at the New End Theatre, London, 20 November 1990, and ran until 14 January 1991. Using the character of the great Yiddish music hall singer Sophie Tucker, it juxtaposed song, dance, and memory to evoke atmosphere and continue Kops's explorations into the idea of memory, experience, and fantasy. Two other plays, *Moss* (originally a TV drama), which opened at the Etcetera Theatre, London, 19 February 1991, closing on 17 March 1991, and *Who Shall I Be Tomorrow*, which ran very briefly in 1992, explore similar areas.

Radio, with its pauses and silences, and as a vehicle for lyrical dream fantasy, seems a natural medium for Kops's *The Street Game: A Ballad of London*, an original radio play produced by Douglas Cleverdon and broadcast on the Third Programme on 21 July 1959. In it Kops drew on popular songs, street sounds, and cockney voices. *Home Sweet Honeycomb* (1962) and *The Lemmings* (1963) were written upon Kops's return from a visit to Eastern Europe, and both are "pessimistic plays." *Born in Israel*, broadcast in 1963, develops the Zionist side of the dramatist's dreams. *The Dark Ages*, broadcast the following year, returns to a bleak dystopian vision, whereas *Israel: The Immigrant* of 1964 is more balanced. *Bournemouth Nights* (1964, 1979) is set on the south coast, with a wealthy Jewish community. *I Grow Old, I Grow Old*, also broadcast in 1979, and *Over the Rainbow*, from the following year, concentrate on aging, its sadness and consolations. *Simon at Midnight* (1982) inhabits a fantasy world. *Trotsky Was My Father*, broadcast in 1984, powerfully uses a historic tragic figure as the vehicle for reflections on dreams and disillusionment. *Ezra* (1980) was originally a radio play and then converted into a theatrical play. *Some of These Days* (1986) is about Sophie Tucker; and *Kafé Kropotken* (1987), an anarchist collective.

Kops has written frequently for television, not perhaps his natural medium but more lucrative and reaching a wider audience than radio. He has adapted plays and written powerful documentaries based upon events such as the bombing of London and life during the German blitz of the early 1940s. *I Want to Go Home* (1963) focuses on social deprivation, *The Lost Years of Brian Hooper* (1967) and *Alexander the Greatest* (1971) on fantasies. *Just One Kid* (1974), set in London, focuses on a child growing up during the blitz. Kops adapted the Yiddish short story writer Isaac Bashevis Singer for *Why the Geese Shrieked* and *The Boy Philosopher* (1976). *It's a Lovely Day Tomorrow*, written with John Goldschmidt (1975), is a documentary set in wartime London. *Moss* (1975) returns to the world of dreams, of surviving failure. *Rocky Marciano Is Dead* (1976) uses the historical figure of popular culture, a boxer, to depict the independence of a failed entrepreneur, Harry. *Night Kids* (1983) deals with the contemporary reality of London, child runaways, drugs, and prostitution.

ASSESSMENT OF KOPS'S CAREER

The assessment of Kops in the first, second, third, and fourth editions (1973, 1977, 1982, 1988) of *Contemporary Dramatists* is instructive. The early assessments are by Nightingale, the later by Dace. The second edition's assessment remains the same as that of the first, apart from omitting a truncated last paragraph in which Nightingale's initial negative reaction to an unnamed stage play decries it as one of Kops's "weakest," one in which the playwright has deserted his traditional setting for "a non–East End, non-Jewish milieu . . . full of wooden, English upper-crust dialogue." Kops is contrasted with Arnold Wesker, and in other accounts with Harold Pinter. All three had a similar East End and/ or Jewish background and emerged as dramatists at about the same time. For Nightingale, Kops "has an exuberance, an instinctive sense of life, quite lacking in Wesker: he also has much less ability (and desire) to reflect, reason and philosophize. . . . The more 'intellectual' Kops becomes, the less successful he customarily is." Unlike Wesker, Kops has "no great political sophistication and no special ideological views to impose on his audience." For Nightingale, "The essential conflict at the center of all his work is between a life-wish and a death-wish." Nightingale notes the quality of "energy, fun and humor of much of his work, notably, perhaps, of *Enter Solly Gold*, his best play to date" and he sees a "weakness for emotional exaggeration and dramatic overstatement." He regrets that Kops "has largely deserted the theater for novels and TV," especially as his adherents "saw in his simplicity and natural intelligence, a corrective to the regenerate British Theatre's tendency to address itself too exclusively to the more educated and sophisticated."

Dace's later assessment is more comprehensive, taking into account Kops's poetry, fiction, and other work in various genres. There is the attempt to counter the allegations that Kops is a kitchen sink realist in the mode of John Osborne and the other Angry Young Men who emerged in the late 1950s. Dace observes that "Kops writes neither gritty nor cozy domestic drama. More often presentational than representational, offering parables upon human nature, his plays are theatrical poetry employing language—in its rhythms, rhymes, word play, and word choice—and conflicts not so much contemporary as timeless.'' The dilemma for Kops scholarship today is his neglect. If mentioned at all, he is referred to in the kitchen sink, Angry Young Men context. Kops's poetry, his novels, his television drama and documentary, his radio plays and his subsequent theatrical explorations are ignored, relegated to a marginal subtext. The neglect is curious but not surprising. Kops explores many of the major themes of our times and of all times: old age and mortality, yet the desire to live; dreams and hopes as psychological necessities in an increasingly bleak world. These are the central preoccupations of *Rocky Marciano Is Dead*, *The Lost Years of Brian Hooper*, and *Simon at Midnight*. Obsession with the past, past loves, and mortality are poignantly depicted through words, lyric, and music in *Playing Sinatra*. The Holocaust, cruelty, Jewish history, the attempt ''to reconcile . . . poetic genius with . . . fascism and anti-Semitism'' are the preoccupations of Kops's ''masterpiece'' (Dace) *Ezra*, which with *Dreams of Anne Frank* represents Kops's attempt to warn his audiences lest they forget recent traumatic events. *Ezra* inhabits the world of fantastic surrealist juxtaposition inherent in Kops's mature genius. Benito Mussolini and Antonio Vivaldare are as real for Pound, as are his mistress and the officials who put him into a cage.

Kops is still actively producing plays and poetry. His novels, ''an extension of his work as poet and playwright,'' written in ''rhythmic, almost ritualistic'' prose, with plots unfolding ''through dialogue'' (Toulson) seem a thing of the past. His last novel, *Margate Sands*, focusing upon psychiatric disturbance and the inadequacy of the British system to assist the ''disturbed,'' has given way to poetry, television serials using World War II motifs, such as the *The Survivor*, and drama centered around idols of popular culture such as Frank Sinatra and Sophie Tucker. Kops refuses to keep quiet, his creativity by no means burnt out. Almost like a character in one of his own works, he refuses to give up. Kops's depiction of frenetic states, of swings in mood and perception hasn't yet dried up. ''No other living English playwright matches Kops in the virtuoso handling of dream logic'' (Wardle [1]). His genius lives on: words pour out of him from his barricades in West Hampstead.

ARCHIVAL SOURCES

A few early Kops manuscripts may be found in the Harry Ransom Humanities Research Center at the University of Texas, Austin. By far the largest collection of his produced and unproduced, published and unpublished works are housed in the Lilly Library at Indiana University, Bloomington, or held privately by the present author, William Baker, who hopes to find a suitable home for them.

PRIMARY BIBLIOGRAPHY

Plays

The Boy Who Wouldn't Play Jesus. In *Eight Plays: Book I*, ed. Malcolm Stuart Fellows. London: Cassell, 1965.
David, It Is Getting Dark. Paris: Gallimard, 1970.
The Dream of Peter Mann. London: Penguin, 1969.
Dreams of Anne Frank. London: Samuel French, 1993.
Enter Solly Gold (music by Stanley Myers). In *Satan, Socialities, and Solly Gold: Three New Plays from England.* New York: Coward McCann, 1961.
The Hamlet of Stepney Green. London: Evans, 1959.
Playing Sinatra. London: Samuel French, 1992.

Anthology

Four Plays. (*The Hamlet of Stepney Green*, *Enter Solly Gold*, *Home Sweet Honeycomb*, *The Lemmings*). London: MacGibbon & Kee, 1964.

Other

Neither Your Honey nor Your Sting: An Offbeat History of the Jews. London: Robson, 1985.
The World Is a Wedding (autobiography). London: MacGibbon & Kee, 1963; New York, Coward McCann, 1964.

SECONDARY BIBLIOGRAPHY

Arditti, Michael. "Clinging to the Wreckage." *Financial Times Weekend* (10–11 Oct. 1992): 8.
Baker, William. "Bernard Kops."In *Critical Survey of Drama*, ed. F. N. Magill. Los Angeles: Salem Press, 1985: 1077–85.
Christopher, James. "Calling the Kops." *Time Out* (25 Mar.–Apr. 1, 1992): 14.
Cohn, Ruby. *Modern Shakespeare Offshoots.* Princeton NJ: Princeton University Press, 1976: 190–93, 217.
Dace, Tish. "Kops, Bernard." In *Contemporary Dramatists*, ed. D. L. Kirkpatrick. 4th ed. London: St. James Press, 1988: 303–4.
Eyres, Harry. Review of *Playing Sinatra. The Times* (3 Oct. 1991): 20.
Fisch, Harold. *The Dual Image.* New York: Ktav Publishing House, 1971: 128–29.
Grindea, Miron. "The Poet in the Cage." *Adam* 431–33 (1980): 2–5.
Hewison, Robert. Review of *Playing Sinatra. Sunday Times* (5 Apr. 1992): 9.
Hill, Douglas. "Kops, Bernard." In *Contemporary Poets*, ed. J. Vinson. 2nd, 3rd, 4th ed. New York: St. Martin's Press, 1975, 1980, 1985: 852–54; 855–57; 465–66.
Hoyle, Martin. Review of *Dreams of Anne Frank. The Times* (5 Oct. 1992): 20.
Jones, Mervyn. Introduction to *The Dream of Peter Mann.* Harmondsworth: Penguin, 1960: 9–11.

Klein, Reva. "Dreams to Interpret." *Times Educational Supplement* (2 Oct. 1992).

Knight, G. Wilson. "The Kitchen Sink." *Encounter* 31 (Dec. 1963): 48–54.

Kustow, Michael. "Note from the Road." *Plays and Players* (Dec. 1962): 26–27.

Limb, Sue. "The Modest Muse: Bernard Kops." *The Listener* (Apr. 1982): 32.

Lumley, Frederick. *New Trends in 20th Century Drama*. New York: Oxford University Press, 1972: 323–24.

MacInnes, Colin. "Bernard Kops." *Encounter* 14 (May 1960): 62–64.

Martin, Stoddard. Review of *Ezra*. *Times Literary Supplement* (29 May 1981): 603.

Nightingale, Benedict. "Kops, Bernard." In *Contemporary Dramatists*, ed. J. Vinson. 1st, 2nd, 3rd ed. New York: St. Martin's Press, 1973, 1977, 1982: 44–47; 454–56; 458–60.

O'Reilly, Sara. Review of *Dreams of Anne Frank*. *Time Out* (14–21 Oct. 1992): 15.

Quinn, Michael. Review of *Playing Sinatra*. *What's On* (9 Oct. 1991): 32.

Rose, Helen. Review of *Dreams of Anne Frank*. *Plays and Players* (Nov. 1992): 7.

Rusinko, Susan. *British Drama, 1950 to the Present: A Critical History*. Boston: Twayne, 1989: 158.

Sicher, Efraim. *Beyond Marginality: Anglo-Jewish Literature after the Holocaust*. Albany: SUNY Press, 1985: 45–54, 175–76, 190–92.

Sonin, David. Review of *Dreams of Anne Frank*. *Jewish Chronicle* (9 Oct. 1992): 20.

Stanford, Derek. "Kops, Bernard." In *Contemporary Novelists*, ed. J. Vinson. 2nd, 3rd ed. New York: St. Martin's Press, 1976, 1982: 771–73; 372–73.

Taylor, John Russell. *Anger and After: A Guide to the New British Drama*. Harmondsworth: Penguin, 1963: 152–61.

Toulson, Shirley. "Kops, Bernard." In *Contemporary Novelists*, ed. J. Vinson. 4th, 5th ed. New York: St. Martin's Press, 1986, 1991: 501–10; 537–39.

Wardle, Irving [1]. Review of *Ezra*. *The Times* (15 May 1981): 13.

———[2]. Review of *More out Than In*. *The Times* (18 Nov. 1980): 8.

Wellwarth, George. *The Theater of Protest and Paradox: Developments in the Avant-Garde Drama*. New York: New York University Press, 1971: 283–87.

Willetts, Sam. "Kops or Mobbers." *What's On* (25 Sept. 1991): 10.

Wright, Michael. Review of *Playing Sinatra*. *Time Out* (9–16 Oct. 1991): 10.

Liz Lochhead

(1947–)

ILONA KOREN-DEUTSCH

Liz Lochhead has earned an international reputation as a poet, but currently her playwrighting is best known within her native Scotland. Although her plays have generally been well received by both audiences and critics, Scottish playwrights have historically had difficulty attracting the attention of the rest of the world, largely due to English domination of the British theatre.

Liz Lochhead was born in 1947 in Motherwell, Lanarkshire, a steel town near Glasgow. She and her parents lived at first in a single room upstairs in her grandparents' house. Then they moved in with her other set of grandparents until eventually they got a new council house at Newarthill about four miles from Motherwell town centre. Her father, a miner's son, was a clerk in the local government. Her upbringing was traditional Scottish Presbyterian; there was much emphasis on church and Sunday school. Like fellow Glasgow writers Alasdair Gray and John Bryne after graduating from school, Lochhead attended the Glasgow School of Art, where she studied drawing and painting. It was also there that she began to write poetry, participating in a group that read and critiqued each other's poems. After graduating she taught art for eight years; she claims that she was a better teacher than an artist.

In 1978 she became the first recipient of the Scottish-Canadian Writers Exchange Fellowship. This event marked her transition to full-time writing. Her first efforts were poetry, which she performed herself. As she became increasingly well known on the British poetry-reading circuit for her dynamic presentation style, Lochhead became more interested in writing for the stage. Her first theatrical piece was the revue *Sugar and Spite*, which she wrote with playwright Marcella Evaristi in 1978. They toured with the piece and did a radio version as well. Then in 1980 she began work on a play about Mary Shelley and the creation of *Frankenstein*. After an unsuccessful first version, the script became *Blood and Ice*, Lochhead's first full-length play, which was produced successfully in 1982 at the Edinburgh Festival and in a slightly different form in 1984 by Pepper's Ghost Theatre Company in London.

Since then Lochhead has written a number of other plays and revues, mostly for Glasgow's Mayfest and the Edinburgh Festival Fringe; she has also written two series for the BBC and a film. She continues to write, perform, and publish her poetry. In addition, she has written two children's plays: *Shanghaied*, for Borderline Theatre, is about refugees, and *The Magic Island* is a version of Shakespeare's *The Tempest*. Seen through Miranda's eyes, *The Magic Island* is about letting go of power and adults learning from their children. The play also carries a strong environmental message.

Lochhead has held several Scottish Arts Council fellowships in creative writing—at Glendon College, Toronto; Duncan of Jordanstone College of Art, Dundee; and Edinburgh University. She has also held an Arts Council of Great Britain fellowship at the Tattenhall Centre, Cheshire. Lochhead has been a writer in residence at the Royal Shakespeare Company under a bursary from Thames Television. *Mary Queen of Scots Got Her Head Chopped Off*, written for the Communicado Theatre Company, won a Fringe First at the 1987 Edinburgh Festival and did much to increase Lochhead's international reputation as a playwright. In 1993 she ran as the Scottish Nationalist Association's candidate for rector of Glasgow University. She currently lives in Glasgow, where she is active in nationalist politics as well as in writing and performing.

Selected Biographical Sources: Koren-Deutsch [1, 3]; Lochhead, "Interview" (with Joyce McMillan), "Interview" (with Emily Todd).

MAJOR PLAYS, PREMIERES, AND SIGNIFICANT REVIVALS: THEATRICAL RECEPTION

Blood and Ice. 1984. Opened 27 February produced by Pepper's Ghost at New Merlin's Cave, London. Directed by Joanna Proctor. Designed by Stan Wolchover. Lighting by Wendy Davies.

Blood and Ice arose from Lochhead's desire to make connections between Mary Shelley's life and her rich imagination that created *Frankenstein*. It uses Shelley's life and art to question the value of liberal ideas about "free love" in the face of the imperative of childbearing. The play's first version, called *Mary and the Monster*, was produced at the studio of the Belgrade Theatre, Coventry, in March 1981. In 1982 a second version of the play, now called *Blood and Ice*, went on at the Traverse Theatre as part of the Edinburgh Festival. This version was critically well received, but Lochhead was still not satisfied. In the summer of 1983 Lochhead was contacted by the Royal Academy of Dramatic Arts, where Helena Kant-Howson had been hired to direct *Blood and Ice*, which some of the students had seen and loved. Lochhead was forced to withdraw the rights, however, when she found out they wanted to "workshop" the material and to "improvise" other scenes. A month later, with a very small budget Pepper's Ghost did *Blood and Ice* in a small North London pub theatre; and here the play worked to Lochhead's satisfaction.

Dracula. 1985. Opened 13 March at the Royal Lyceum Theatre, Edinburgh. Directed by Hugh Hodgart. Designed by Gregory Smith. Music by David Mc-Niven.

Lochhead's *Dracula* returns to Bram Stoker's story the tragedy that had been lost through years of horror movies and spoofs. It also shifts focus to the female characters, presenting them as complex and active, rather than as the one-dimensional victims they are in the Victorian novel and most of the movies based on it. Critics were enthusiastic about the play. *The Guardian* (Review of *Dracula*) wrote that "in this powerful and poetic version . . . Lochhead moves beyond Stoker. . . . The outpourings of a madman paradoxically reveal the sort of sanity Lear's Fool supplied and he becomes . . . an image of the chaotic un-acceptable truth within us all."

Tartuffe. 1986. Opened 24 January at the Royal Lyceum Theatre, Edinburgh. Directed by Colin MacNeil and Ian Wooldridge. Designed by Colin MacNeil.

Tartuffe was commissioned by the Lyceum as a new translation of Molière's play. Lochhead abandoned Molière's original Alexandrines, having decided that the original comic drive came from the rhyme, not the meter, of the play. Her translation, while rhyming throughout, is more notable for its original, invented, theatrical Scots, which Lochhead describes as "proverbial, slangy, couthy, cli-chéd, catch-phrasy, and vulgar . . . based on Byron, Burns, Stanley Holloway, Ogden Nash and George Formby, as well as the sharp tongue of my granny" (*Tartuffe*). Using the Scots language also led Lochhead to set her play in the 1920s, the era in which Hugh MacDiarmid's *A Drunk Man Looks at the Thistle* (1926) marked a rebirth of literature in Scots. It is also a time in which the upper classes of Scottish society mocked the English, allowing Lochhead a range of voices in which to write in order to keep the political satire Molière wrote, but which is lost on many English translations. The critics loved the play, al-though their reviews focused on the text rather than the production. McIntyre wrote that Lochhead "may well do for the Scots language on stage what Mac-Diarmid did on the page, creating a synthetic Scots that still echoes the old tongue." *The Guardian* (Review of *Tartuffe*) called the play "a complete the-atrical winner, a brilliant blend of traditional lowlands Scots, contemporary Glas-gow patter, and lethally sophisticated female wit." Likewise, *The Times* called it "a marvellously inventive and warmly funny verse translation."

Mary Queen of Scots Got Her Head Chopped Off. 1987. Opened 10 August at the Lyceum Studio Theatre, Edinburgh. Produced by Communicado Theatre Company. Directed by Gerard Mulgrew. Designed by Colin MacNeil. Produc-tion transferred to the Donmar Warehouse, London, opening 16 September 1987.

This play came about as the result of a phone call from Gerry Mulgrew, during which Lochhead mentioned that 1987 was the 400th anniversary of Mary Stuart's beheading. The play is important because it links Mary and Elizabeth together as women monarchs forced to rule their male-dominated societies. The play's somewhat Brechtian style is reminiscent of film or television; it is a visual, musical, and ritualistic theatre consisting of short scenes. As she did with *Tartuffe*, Lochhead paid special attention to the language of *Mary*, which is varied and poetic, with characters at times speaking sixteenth-century Scots or contemporary English, or a combination of the two, and Mary speaking an appropriately French-tinged Scots. While the Scottish critics were particularly approving of the Scottish nationalist slant of the play, all the critics were enthusiastic about the production, even supporting its feminism. *The Financial Times* particularly enjoying the play's music, dance, and processions, said the play's impact is "exhilarating, abrasive and hugely enjoyable." Wardle preferred the vigorous folklore of Lochhead's play to the formality of Schiller's *Mary Stuart*, which also played at the 1987 Edinburgh Festival.

The York Cycle of Mystery Plays. 1992. Opened 12 June at the Theatre Royal, York. Directed by Ian Forrest. Designed by Martin Johns. Choreography by Lorelei Lynn. Music by John Jannson.

This new translation is the first new version since the City of York revived the Mystery Cycle in 1951. Lochhead's translation retains some of the rhyme and alliteration of the original cycle, adding to the production's traditional sound. Relatively serious scenes in particular retain much of their medieval feel. On the other hand, the characters in the comic scenes speak in a language that is much more modern. Lochhead has also written parts of the script she felt were needed, such as a Cain and Abel play, which is missing from the original and for which Lochhead wrote a ballad called "The Sin Song." Lochhead has also pushed the script as far as possible toward feminism, allowing, of course, for its biblical subject matter. Critical reaction to the production was mixed. All the critics enjoyed the script, but toward the beginning of its run many objected to the play's five-hour length. By the end of the run the production had been cut down to about two and one-half hours, and the critics were much more positive. In addition, for the first time York moved the Mystery Cycle indoors in order to present the show every night, regardless of weather, and to allow for technical effects that could not be achieved outdoors. Some critics felt the technical benefits of the move outweighed the loss of tradition. Others, however, felt the change was unforgivable.

PERFORMANCE PIECES

Lochhead has published three books of poetry to date. Lochhead calls *True Confessions & New Clichés* "basically performance poems." However, she says, "I don't think other people see them as being written by two separate people the way I do" (qtd. in "Interview," with McMillan). *Bagpipe Muzak* contains both book and performance poetry. One-third of the book consists of performance pieces that Lochhead describes as "not even the best performance stuff I've written really, in some ways. You know it's very, very, almost . . . agit prop. Most of it was written for a purpose. So there are those. Some of them are parodies. I mean they are all right. I'm not knocking them" (qtd. in "Interview," with Todd, 86). The other two-thirds of the book are "voices, some of them in poetic form and some of them more lightly dramatic monologues" (Todd, 86).

Lochhead has always enjoyed performing her own poetry, but she understands that many people are afraid of performance.

I think that's actually one of the reasons why there are so few women poets. The idea of poetry as a public function in the old bardic tradition still lingers on, and that intimidates many women. But I always loved performing, and I liked the poets who read their work aloud. I think my poetry has always had an element of challenge in it, anyway— a kind of implicit 'well—where do you stand?' to the audience. So in a sense, I'm ready for a dialogue with an audience, and I'm not frightened of that. (McMillan)

Lochhead's best poetry does just that: it engages the audience in a dialogue rather than confronts them with polemic. That means allowing the audience their own responses to the poetry, rather than insisting upon one "correct" meaning.

Many of Lochhead's "book poems" are about love or sex or both. Lochhead writes her poems, whether intended for performance or not, in a consciously female voice, or more accurately, female voices. Most of these voices are from the west of Scotland. Lochhead's poetry satirizes and parodies male assumptions about reality. However, while being basically feminist the female speakers in Lochhead's poems are as distrustful of programmatic feminist response as they are of male presumption.

Another characteristic of Lochhead's poetry is a combination of narrative registers within the same poem. She gracefully combines colloquial speech with classical narrative. She is also fond of puns, as well as other ways to make conventional diction unconventional. Her presentation is frequently comic; its intent is usually serious. Her gift for written language serves her well in all her writing, as does her ear for how individual characters should speak.

ASSESSMENT OF LOCHHEAD'S CAREER

Lochhead is still writing, and so far her work has shown more stylistic variety than similarity. There are, however, four major thematic concerns that can be found throughout Lochhead's work: Scotland, history, "mythology," and women.

In several different interviews Lochhead has discussed what she considers to be a "split," or several splits, in the Scottish psyche. She has said that the really big split in Scotland is between the self and the other. This idea of the split has been a theme in Scottish literature in the past, such as in *Justified Sinner* and *Jekyll and Hyde*. For Lochhead, however, this concept means more than a split personality. If one is Scottish, because of English colonialism one internalizes not only Scottish culture but English culture as well. Lochhead has said that in some ways the Scots are in a position of being the feminine, in contrast with the English, who are the masculine, or the dominant. Within Scotland itself there are further splits: between male and female; and between Celt and Scot, the Celt being the female and the Scot being the male (Todd, 90). Lochhead's work reveals a longing for a way to unite these splits: "Sometimes you're so busy defining self that you are talking to other halves of yourself.... I think that there's a certain part of art which does aspire to androgyny" (Todd, 90).

Lochhead is a nationalist playwright. If she is critical of her country, it is because she cares deeply for it. This concern is demonstrated in part by her desire to stay in Scotland, rather than moving to London as other Scottish playwrights such as J. M. Barrie or C. P. Taylor have done in search of financial success. Her feeling for her country can also be seen in Lochhead's obvious delight in working with the Scots language. Two of her major plays are in Scots: *Tartuffe*, which is entirely in Scots, and *Mary Queen of Scots Got Her Head Chopped Off*, in which the Scottish characters speak Scots. There is a poem in *Dreaming Frankenstein* in Scots, and there are other poems written in different Scots "voices."

Most of Lochhead's major plays are historical drama. She enjoys writing in the genre because she finds it easier to release a play from realism when it is not set in the present; that is, Lochhead finds audiences to be more comfortable when not in the present. Historical drama is a useful means of critiquing the present without hitting too close to home.

History is also a good place to find the larger-than-life characters that Lochhead is drawn to. She likes to find "the human and the particular behind the archetype so that ordinary people become mythic" (Woddis). These mythic characters might be from actual ancient myths, as they are in some of the poems. *Mary Queen of Scots Got Her Head Chopped Off* contains major figures from chronological history, Mary Stuart and Elizabeth I, and the other characters involved with their lives. The York Mystery Cycle, to modern eyes a dramatization of the Bible, or to medieval eyes a representation of the history of the world from Creation to Judgment Day, contains the largest mythological figures in Lochhead's canon: God, the Devil, Mary, Jesus, and so on. Lochhead is also attracted to archetypal characters from literature such as Frankenstein and Dracula, and to their creators, Mary Shelley and Bram Stoker, who themselves have become major characters.

Although Lochhead's relationship to feminism is complex, her understanding of feminism is straightforward: "Feminism is about very simple issues.... I am a feminist.... All feminism means is equality for women" (personal interview). Her writing explores women's lives and women's emotions. To Lochhead that is political, but it is also entirely natural: "I can't not be a woman, the same way I can't not be Scottish" (personal interview). When asked about whether she feels a responsibility to Scottish literature, to contribute to it a female voice, Lochhead told Todd, "No. I don't feel that I have to do it. I feel it has to be done. . . . I don't actually have to worry about my writing filling in more of a female voice, because my writing is going to have a female voice. What am I going to do, sprout a penis?" (Todd, 92).

Although Lochhead's feminism is to a certain extent biological, she is not in favor of female separatism. Lochhead objects to a feminism that would dictate to women how they should or should not live. She has said, "I think that's the trouble with feminism. . . . I think it's whenever feminism becomes prescriptive" (Todd, 92). She is often as distrustful of feminist response as she is of male standards. This attitude is consistent with her desire to mend the splitting apart of Scottish society. She wants to find a common ground where women and men can unite: "What I would ideally like to do is give the male halves of themselves back to women, and the female halves of themselves back to men" (Nicholson, 204).

Lochhead's canon reveals linguistic virtuosity, wit, and imagination. She has shown herself to be a gifted playwright, poet, and performer from whom we can expect to see more. She is also delightfully open and accessible for discussing her work. The hope is that her future will include not only more productions of her plays outside of Scotland, but greater critical exposure.

ARCHIVAL SOURCES

Most of Lochhead's play manuscripts are located in the Scottish Theatre Archive, University of Glasgow. Her poetry manuscripts, as well as some of the plays, are located in the Mitchell Library, Glasgow, in the Scottish Writers Collection. The Mitchell Library also holds a scrapbook containing collected reviews and articles about Lochhead. Some copyrighted manuscripts are available in the National Library of Scotland, Edinburgh, and the British Library, Manuscripts Reading Room.

PRIMARY BIBLIOGRAPHY

Plays, Reviews, and Performance Pieces

Blood and Ice. In *Plays by Women*. Vol. 4. London: Methuen, 1985: 81–118.
A Bunch of Fives (with Tom Leonard, Sean Hardie, Dave Anderson, and Dave Mc-
    Lennan). Sections published in *True Confessions & New Clichés*. Edinburgh:
    Polygon Books, 1985.
Dracula. Harmondsworth: Penguin Books, 1988.
Mary Queen of Scots Got Her Head Chopped Off. 1987. Harmondsworth: Penguin
    Books, 1988.
The Pie of Damocles (with Tom Leonard, Alasdair Gray, and Jim Kelman). Sections
    published in *True Confessions & New Clichés*. Edinburgh: Polygon Books, 1985.

Quelques Fleurs. In *Bagpipe Muzak.* Harmondsworth: Penguin, 1991.
Red Hot Shoes. Sections published in *True Confessions & New Clichés.* Edinburgh: Polygon Books, 1985.
Same Difference. Sections published in *True Confessions & New Clichés.* Edinburgh: Polygon Books, 1985.
Sugar and Spite (with Marcella Evaristi). Sections published in *True Confessions & New Clichés.* Edinburgh: Polygon Books, 1985.
Tartuffe. Edinburgh: Polygon Books, 1986; Glasgow: Third Eye Centre, 1986.
Tickly Mince (with Tom Leonard, Alasdair Gray, and Jim Kelman). Sections published in *True Confessions & New Clichés.* Edinburgh: Polygon Books, 1985.
True Confessions. 1981. Published in *True Confessions & New Clichés.* Edinburgh: Polygon Books, 1985.
The York Cycle of Mystery Plays. 1992. Text available from Theatre Royal, York.

Interviews

"Interview" (with Joyce McMillan). *Scottish Theatre News* (1982).
"Interview" (with Emily Todd). *Verse* 8 (1991): 83–94.

SECONDARY BIBLIOGRAPHY

Barker, Rodney. of *Jock Tamson's Bairns. New Statesman and Society* (2 Feb. 1990): 35.
Blain, Virginia, Patricia Clemens, and Isobel Grundy. "Liz Lochhead." *The Feminist Companion to Literature in English.* New Haven CT: Yale University Press, 1990.
Review of *Dracula. The Guardian* (15 Mar. 1985).
Harvie, Jennifer. "Desire and Difference in Liz Lochhead's *Dracula.*" *Essays in Theatre* 11.2 (1993):133–43.
Klein, Riva. of *The Magic Island. Times Educational Supplement* (12 March 1993): 513.
Koren-Deutsch, Ilona [1]. "Feminist Nationalism in Scotland: *Mary Queen of Scots Got Her Head Chopped Off.*" *Modern Drama* 35.3 (Sept. 1992): 424–32.
———[2]. "A Mystery Cycle for the Modern World." *Western European Stages* 5 (1993): 21–24.
———[3]. "Pam Gems and Liz Lochhead: British Feminist Approaches to the History Play," M.A. thesis, Indiana University, 1990.
Review of *Mary Queen of Scots Got Her Head Chopped Off.* London: *The Financial Times* (12 Aug. 1987).
McIntyre. Review of *Tartuffe. Observer Scotland* (27 Jan. 1986).
Nicholson, Colin. "Knucklebones of Irony: Liz Lochhead." *Poem, Purpose and Place: Shaping Identity in Contemporary Scottish Verse.*" Edinburgh: Polygon, 1992. 202–23.
Stevenson, Randall. Rev. of *Jock Tamson's Bairns. Times Literary Supplement* (9 Feb. 1990): 45.

Review of *Tartuffe*. *The Guardian* (25 Jan. 1986).

Review of *Tartuffe*. *The Times* (27 Jan. 1986).

Wardle, Irving. Review of *Mary Queen of Scots Got Her Head Chopped Off*. *The Times* (12 Aug. 1987).

Woddis, Carole. Review of *The Magic Island*. *Glasgow Herald* (2 Feb. 1993).

John McGrath
(1935–)

MALCOLM PAGE

John McGrath's huge contribution to British theatre over more than thirty years has had little recognition because his plays have usually been performed only on tours and are frequently not published. He is also important as a theorist of left-wing popular theatre and for innovations in the early years of television drama.

He was born in Birkenhead on 1 June 1935, of Irish Catholic background, son of a teacher at a secondary modern school. Evacuated on the outbreak of war at the age of four to Buckley, North Wales, he remained there until he was sixteen. He won an Open Exhibition to St. John's College, Oxford, but had first to fill in a year (spent working on a farm and in a laundry) and to do two years National Service. He was in the Royal Artillery, first spending a miserable year as a gunner in Germany and then completing officer training, which led to time in Egypt, Jordan, Malta, Libya, and Italy.

McGrath read English at Oxford, staying on for a fourth year to take a Diploma in Education. As an army officer and at Oxford, he began "to discover what the class structure of Britain is about" and "the size of the gulf between my experience and life-style and the experience of the ruling class." His activities at Oxford included directing *Bloomsday* and Aristophane's *The Birds*, translating some French plays, writing theatre criticism in *Cherwell*, and completing *A Man Has Two Fathers*, put on by a student cast and favorably reviewed by Kenneth Tynan in *The Observer*.

Between 1959 and 1971 he worked in several areas. While a play-reader for the Royal Court Theatre he wrote *Why the Chicken?*, which toured provincially but never reached its destination in the West End. At this time he decided that "all the people I knew and cared about were watching television," so he intended "to use the popular medium in my own way, and contribute through that to people's lives." Starting as a script editor, he took a director's course, then—with Troy Kennedy Martin—created the celebrated *Z-Cars* series, using police work "to be a kind of documentary about people's lives," with the police as the means "of finding out about people's lives." After other writing and directing for television, he turned to film scripts, mostly for Ken Russell. *Billion Dollar Brain*, *The Virgin Soldiers* and *The Reckoning*, all adapted from novels, were made from 1967 through 1970; McGrath also values scripts that were not made, from André Malraux's *Man's Fate* to Patrick White's *Voss*. His own playwriting had resumed with the success of *Events While Guarding the Bofors Gun*, followed by *Bakke's Night of Fame*, *Comrade Jacob*, and *Random Happenings in the Hebrides*, and then by a number of plays for the Everyman Theatre in Liverpool. McGrath had married Elizabeth MacLennan, an actress, in 1962 (they have two sons and a daughter). His politicization, begun in the army, continued: he went to Paris during the uprising of May 1968 and wrote in *Black Dwarf* and *Seven Days*, weeklies that expressed the hopes of quick and radical change characteristic of the late 1960s.

In 1971 he founded the 7:84 Company—so-called because 7 percent of the population owns 84 percent of the wealth—a socialist group, primarily designed for touring to reach working-class audiences. In 1973 the company divided into two, English and Scottish, with McGrath as artistic director of both. The English company closed when the Arts Council subsidy was withdrawn in 1985, and in 1988 McGrath resigned as director of the Scottish company. In 1988 he stated, "During the last ten years I have written at least fourteen full-length plays for the stage, one opera libretto, seven television plays, one documentary and two feature films, as well as directing most of them and a few by other writers" (*The Bone Won't Break*).

Plays written for the companies divide into larger-scale plays for theatres and smaller-scale ones for arts centers, village halls, and working-men's clubs. Several are musicals, from folk to rock; several are semidocumentary, whether of the history of enclosures in England, 1760–1820 (*Big Square Fields*), of the rise of the multinationals and the implications for unions (*Lay Off*), or change in the Scottish Highlands since the 1745 rising in the ceilidh play *The Cheviot, the Stag, and the Black, Black Oil*. *Yobbo Nowt* was based on Maxim Gorki's *The Mother*, while *The Albannach* adapted a novel by Fionn MacColla, well known in Scotland. *Fish in the Sea*, *Little Red Hen*, and *Blood Red Roses* are identifiably family dramas, firmly rooted in place and—more important—in the politics of the time. McGrath's thinking about political and popular theatre, in the changing political climates of the 1970s and 1980s, was expressed in two books of lectures, *A Good Night Out* and *The Bone Won't Break*. Elizabeth MacLennan acted in many of the plays and wrote her own account of the companies in 1990 in *The Moon Belongs to Everyone*.

Since his involvement with 7:84 ended, McGrath has worked in film (*The Dressmaker*, from Beryl Bainbridge's novel), television (*The Long Roads*, 1993) and theatre—two epics of Scottish history, imaginatively staged by Wildcat in the Tramway in Glasgow. McGrath shows no sign of slowing down in the 1990s.

Selected Biographical Sources: McGrath, "Better a Bad Night in Boodle . . . "; Jager; Thomsen.

MAJOR PLAYS, PREMIERES, AND SIGNIFICANT REVIVALS: THEATRICAL RECEPTION

Events While Guarding the Bofors Gun. 1966. Opened 12 April at Hampstead Theatre Club, London. Directed by Ronald Eyre.

This all-male drama of the British army in Germany was highly praised. Critics found it accurate about army life, Rundall writing: "The smell is authentic: the army *is* like that." Hawkes focused on technique, admiring "tight structural construction, precise characterization and immediate dramatic strength." But reviewers knew the play was more than documentary. Gilliatt defined it as "a metaphor . . . about a man who sees his own life as ludicrous," and Hobson as tragedy: "The ending of absolute defeat is both shattering and sublime."

Fish in the Sea. 1972. Opened 26 December at Everyman Theatre, Liverpool. Directed by Alan Dossor. Revival: revised, 11 February 1975, Half Moon Theatre, London, and touring. 7:84 Company (England). Directed by Pam Brighton.

The 1975 production led Marcus [2] to declare, "McGrath is one of our major dramatists," for an "epic vision," "an ear for speech rhythms" and "a wonderful generosity of spirit, akin to O'Casey at his best." Some found it too long at three and one-quarter hours, and Griser complained that "there is nothing we don't already know." Typical were Elsom, liking "the detail and the emotional warmth," and Wardle, observing that the troupe combined "social authenticity with technical finesse." Hammond [1] judged that the personal level was treated more successfully than the political one, but Billington [1] believed McGrath was able "to put the political, social and emotional life of Liverpool onto the stage."

The Cheviot, the Stag, and the Black, Black Oil. 1973. Opened 24 April at Arts Centre, Aberdeen, toured 1973–1974. 7:84 Company (Scotland). Directed by McGrath. Revival: Clyde Theatre, Clydebank, 10 March 1991, toured July-October. Wildcat. Directed by John Bett.

The Cheviot opened unobtrusively but was a triumph with Scottish audiences, and the television showing made it famous. By 1991 it had, as McMillan [2] wrote, a reputation as "possibly the most successful piece of radical theatre Britain has seen." Taxidou found *The Cheviot* "entertaining and empowering," touching "the Scottish popular imagination." "Exhilarating" (Bruce), "vivid and vigorous" (Banks-Smith), "fluid and fast-moving" (Mathiesen), are typical comments. Many, like Banks-Smith, appreciated the differing moods: "good songs, old sorrows, new satire, bold jokes." McMillan [2] and Hennessey disliked the 1991 revival, but most found the message valid: "politically informed and aware rather than the more fashionable and painless 'politically correct' " for Taxidou.

Lay Off. 1975. Opened June at Lancaster University, and toured. 7:84 Company. Directed by McGrath.

This topical musical documentary about the rise of the multinationals and the implications angered Jones for its "cardboard cut-out caricatures" and "because I don't like being lectured to in the theatre." Otherwise, praise was general: by Lipman for a "warm, zestful and gay" cast, by Hammond [2] because *Lay Off* was "woven together with an immense flair and skill," and by McFerran for sketches ranging "from the outrageously funny to doomwatch 1984 type prophecies."

Little Red Hen. 1975. Opened 15 September at the Lyceum Theatre, Edinburgh, and toured. 7:84 Company. Directed by McGrath.

Little Red Hen was harshly criticized for one-sidedness, Robins finding it a "one-dimensional cartoon strip" with the company "mouthing the megalomaniac dreams of the left sects." Billington [3] noted that it didn't explore its enemies and rushed helter-skelter through the 1930s and 1940s. Reviewers by now knew what to expect of 7:84 and found the enthusiasm difficult to resist. For Lambert, it was "well contrived in terms of alternating domestic naturalism, song and dance, rhetoric"; for Nightingale, a work of "energy, verve" and "cutting wit"; and for Oliver, "typically full of vitality, humour, good songs and music, polemical overstatement and blistering home truths."

Out of Our Heads. 1976. Toured 1976–1977, including opening 12 April 1977, at the Royal Court Theatre, London. 7:84 Company. Directed by McGrath.

This drama divided the critics. Negative reviewers did not concede merit in the energy, songs, or ensemble playing, although Radin wrote "that even if one can't go to the end of McGrath's message, one applauds his means." Marcus [1] found it both "flabbily written" and treating its characters with contempt. Peter [2] was delighted with "an honest, perceptive and deeply human play, warm but tough," which was "first-rate theatre and a passionate plea for life."

The Baby and the Bathwater. 1984. Opened 19 October, Cumbernauld, and toured. 7:84 Company. Directed by McGrath.

This was a new direction, a series of linked monologues that showcased the versatility of Elizabeth MacLennan as, amongst others, a young and old George Orwell, a Glasgow schoolgirl, Rogoberta Menchu, and a monstrous U.S. Marine, Chuck Eagleburger. A Chilean guitarist sang between the monologues. Wilson found the show "entertaining and stimulating," whereas McMillan [1] found some parts "monotonous" and "unamusing," yet finally breaking through to a "a deeper and more serious level." For Hendry, the work was "very moving," a "fair and well-rounded analysis." Bartie concluded that "once again 7:84 question accepted values and received ideas and they do it in a way that is instructive but not patronising, serious and yet entertaining."

John Brown's Body. 1990. Opened 20 March at Tramway, Glasgow. Wildcat. Directed by McGrath.

This promenade production had action on two levels on all four sides of the hall and in the center, ambitiously telling the story of the Scottish working class over the last 200 years. Some comment was wholly negative: Coveney [1] saw "a sorry, incoherent jumble" and Wright found it "disappointingly shallow." More commonly, the content was faulted and the means praised: for Hoyle, "polemical theatre at its most partisan," with "exhilarating shafts of theatrical brilliance." Peter [3], who has always had difficulty in fairly assessing McGrath, hated the "drearily simplistic message" yet saw "all the best qualities of popular theatre: vigour, clarity, ensemble cohesion, and a robust sense of humour." Billington [2], ready to be more sympathetic to the message, left "intellectually hungry for a clearer definition of socialism's future," yet "as a theatrical spectacle, it is audacious and inventive." Moss found the TV version "highly effective political pantomime," and Stevenson [1] found that *John Brown's Body* revealed "Scottish radicalism" to be "a firm reality, clearly traceable over 200 years of the nation's history in response to misappropriation and oppression."

The Wicked Old Man. 1992. Opened 4 June at the West Yorkshire Playhouse, Leeds. Directed by Jude Kelly.

Reviewers were puzzled by this work, Coveney [2] finding it "a curious and moralistic satire." They could not agree on genre—Burke thought McGrath used "the Shavian method which allows social and political observations to bubble up above the frothy surface, in this case that of the TV sitcom," whereas Wainwright stated that the author "seeks to parody a popular dramatic form—here the whodunit—and transpose it for his own purposes." Kingston hated it: "A sense of how the people he writes about might actually live and speak and feel is fatally absent," In contrast the unpredictable Peter [1] admired the writing as "functional, tough, and occasionally mordantly funny," labeling it "a serious-frivolous thriller," "a black morality comedy and a grinning Grand Guignol."

ADDITIONAL PLAYS

Thirteen of McGrath's plays are published. The rest of his work includes at least twenty-three performed full-length plays, short plays, translations, adaptations, collaborations, an opera libretto, unperformed plays, film scripts, original plays for television, and various adaptations and documentaries for television.

ASSESSMENT OF MCGRATH'S CAREER

Assessment is unusually difficult. Bull groups McGrath with the left-wing playwrights Howard Brenton, David Edgar, Trevor Griffiths, and David Hare.

All four of these, however, have been staged by the National Theatre or Royal Shakespeare Company. Nearly all of McGrath's vast output has been "alternative," in the settings of political and touring theatre. For seventeen years he combined writing and directing with the learning-by-doing of operating a company, and for twelve of those years running two companies. Some of the experiences, and the lessons, are recorded in his two books.

As the British are so often pragmatists, *A Good Night Out* and *The Bone Won't Break* significantly provide a theoretical basis for McGrath's kinds of political theatre. (John Arden and Margaretta D'Arcy, Edward Bond, David Edgar, and Arnold Wesker are the other British contemporaries who have written at some length on their aesthetics and theories of theatre.) McGrath considers in broad terms what theatre can do and what it should be doing. Also, though, he writes with years of firsthand experience of reaching mass audiences with "a good night out" that is also a form of political education.

As Chambers and Prior observe: "Playwrights are usually judged on the texts they produce, but McGrath has dedicated himself to a type of theatre in which the text is not paramount." Much British criticism starts from the unexamined assumption that what Bull labels McGrath's "qualified form of agit-prop theatre" cannot also be aesthetically acceptable, hence such glib dismissals as Hayman's: "The fusion of personal and socio-political themes is perfunctory and unsuccessful." McGrath's admirers, such as Itzin and Van Erwen, lean to description of particular shows and of the variety of the plays. Even sympathizers appear to write with unease, aware that they are not the audience McGrath seeks.

One approach is to name the very small number of revivals by the 7:84 Company as including Joe Corrie's *In Time of Strife* (1928), Robert McLeish's *The Gorbals Story* (1946), and Ena Lamont Stewart's *Men Should Weep* (1947). Such McGrath texts as *Little Red Hen* and *Blood Red Roses* can be placed in this tradition of Scottish working-class drama. Similarly, *Soft on a Girl, Fish in the Sea* and *Yobbo Nowt* belong in the thin line of English working-class plays, following Walter Greenwood's *Love on the Dole* (1934) and Arnold Wesker's *Chicken Soup with Barley* (1958). That 7:84 also revived Ewan MacColl's *Johnny Noble* (1945), which MacColl called "an episodic play with singing," points to McGrath's favorite structure of short episodes and to his continued use of music (Brecht is also an influence: early in his career McGrath adapted *The Caucasian Chalk Circle* to a Liverpool building site). Music is used every where: in the documentaries, like *Lay Off*; in domestic pieces, like *Swings and Roundabouts*; and in histories, like *The Cheviot*.

The plays are written for particular audiences—the Scottish Highlands, the Scottish cities, the English urban working class. They are written for particular moments in time: *The Cheviot* at the time of the initial exploitation of North Sea oil; *Joe's Drum* when Scotland failed to achieve "devolution" of powers in 1979; *The Baby and the Bathwater* to counter what McGrath saw as George Orwell praised for the wrong reasons in 1984.

McGrath, an educator, challenges official history and mainstream views. He provides a people's look at the beginning of the Industrial Revolution in *Big Square Fields*; forces us to confront the facts of Central America in *The Baby and the Bathwater*; shows the rise of multinational companies and the consequent need for international union action in *Lay Off* and *Blood Red Roses*. He commemorates the Scots socialist hero John MacLean in *The Game's a Bogey*, and the Edinburgh tradition of popular protest in *Joe's Drum*.

McGrath is crucially a writer with a message. No one else would dare to be as explicit as he is at the end of the *The Cheviot*: "The people do not own the land. The people do not control the land. . . . We too must organize, and fight— not with stones, but politically, with the help of the working class in the towns, for a government that will control the oil development for the benefit of everybody." McGrath at best ranks with Maxim Gorki, Sean O'Casey, George Bernard Shaw, Clifford Odets, and the like, as a playwright who made people think and made a difference.

While his undoctrinal socialism determines all his writing, McGrath's greatest contribution may be in enhancing Scottish pride in a distinct identity and a radical tradition, as I have seen standing with 600 Glaswegians responding to *John Brown's Body* and sitting with an Edinburgh audience who all joined in singing "These are my mountains" in *The Cheviot*.

ARCHIVAL SOURCES

There are three collections. The archives of 7:84 (England) are at Cambridge University Library; the bulk of the archives of 7:84 (Scotland) are at the National Library of Scotland, Edinburgh, with some material in the Scottish Theatre Archive at Glasgow University Library. Some material is scattered among more than one collection; some McGrath material other than his 7:84 work is also in these collections. Cambridge, for instance, holds nine of the unpublished full-length plays listed below, as well as *The Adventures of Frank* (TV play based on *The Life and Times of Joe of England*), *Basement in Bangkok* as a film script, *Hover through the Fog* (performed as part of *Plugged-In*, but excluded from the published text), and the short plays *The Rat Trap* and *Sharpeville Crackers*. The scripts are variously accompanied by photos, posters, programs, clippings, budgets, tour logbooks, and correspondence. Nick Hern Books plans to publish a volume of six of McGrath's Scottish plays.

PRIMARY BIBLIOGRAPHY

Plays

Bakke's Night of Fame (based on the novel *A Danish Gambit*, by William Butler). London: Davis-Poynter, 1973.
Boom. New Edinburgh Review 30 (Aug. 1975): 11–30.
The Cheviot, the Stag, and the Black, Black Oil. London: Methuen, 1981.
Events While Guarding the Bofors Gun. London: Methuen, 1966.

Fish in the Sea. London: Pluto, 1977.
The Game's a Bogey. Edinburgh: EUSPB, 1975.
Joe's Drum. Aberdeen: Aberdeen People's Press, 1979.
Little Red Hen. London: Pluto, 1977.
Plugged-In (six one-act plays). *Plays and Players* (Nov. 1972).
Random Happenings in the Hebrides. London: Davis-Poynter, 1972.
Two Plays for the Eighties. (*Blood Red Roses* and *Swings and Roundabouts*) Aberdeen: Aberdeen People's Press, 1981.
Yobbo Nowt. London: Pluto, 1978.

Books and Articles on Drama and Theatre

The Bone Won't Break: On Theatre and Hope in Hard Times. London: Methuen, 1990.
"Clouding the Vision of the Possible." *The Scotsman* (27 Nov. 1976): Weekend Section: 1.
A Good Night Out: Popular Theatre: Audience, Class, and Form. London: Methuen, 1981.
"Living Dangerously." *The Guardian* (16 Oct. 1981): 11.
No Politics Please, We're British." *The Guardian* (5 Oct. 1984): 19.
" 'Pink Yuppie Takeover' of 7:84." *The Scotsman* (23 July 1988): 11.
"Radical Theatre in an Enterprise Culture." In *Glasnost in Britain?*, ed. Norman Buchan and Tricia Sumner. London: Macmillan, 1989: 173–78.
"Scotland: Up against It." *The Red Paper on Scotland.* Edinburgh: EUSPB, 1975: 134–40.
"Some Other Mechanism: 'Poetic' and 'Dramatic' Structure in Some Plays." *Encore* (26 July-Aug. 1960): 20–26.
"Songs of Experience." *The Scotsman* (17 Jan. 1987): Weekend Section: 1.
"The Theory and Practice of Political Theatre." *Theatre Quarterly* 35 (autumn 1979): 43–54.
"TV Drama; the Case against Naturalism." *Sight & Sound* 46 (spring 1977): 100–105.
"What Chance Popular Theatre?" *Marxism Today* (Feb. 1982): 35–36.

Interviews

"Are you Left or a Writer?" (with Merete Bates). *The Guardian* (Nov. 1971).
"Armed With the Truth"(with Aleks Sierz). *Red Pepper* (July 1994): 40–41.
"The Bark of a British Mongrel" (with Jennifer Selway). *The Observer* (31 Jan. 1993): 61.
"Better a Bad Night in Boodle . . . " In *New Theatre Voices of the Seventies*, ed. Simon Trussler. London: Methuen, 1981: 98–109.
"Behind the Fringe" (with Oscar Moore). *Plays and Players* (Apr. 1983): 11–13.
"Breaking Free of the Troubled English Giant" (with Catherine Itzin). *The Tribune* (30 Dec. 1977).
"Comedy with Chips" (with Stephen Gilbert). *Radio Times* (1–7 Nov. 1980): 9, 11.
"Have Story Need . . . Quantel" (with Sandy Craig). *Time Out* (31 Oct.–6 Nov. 1980): 18–19.
"New Directions" (with Ramona Gibbs). *Plays and Players* (Nov. 1972): xiii–xiv.
"Popular Theatre and the Changing Perspective of the Eighties" (with Tony Mitchell). *New Theatre Quarterly* 4 (Nov. 1985): 390–99.

"Power to the Imagination." *Scottish International* (Oct. 1971): 10–15.
"7:84 Six Years On" (with Ann McFerran). *Time Out* (8–14 Apr. 1977): 11, 13.
"Theatre for the People" (with Eugene Van Erwen). *Minnesota Review* 27 (fall 1986): 117–22.
"A Week in the Life of John McGrath" (with Sara Hemming). *The Independent* (20 Aug. 1994):28.

SECONDARY BIBLIOGRAPHY

Ansorge, Peter. *Disrupting the Spectacle*. London: Pitman, 1975: 59–63.
Banks-Smith, Nancy. "Play for Today." *The Guardian* (7 June 1974).
Bartie, Colin. "7:84 in 1984." *Wester Hailes Sentinel* (Nov.-Dec. 1984).
Beacham, Richard. "Political Theatre in Britain: The 7:84 Company." *Theatre* 10 (spring 1979): 49–53.
Bigsby, C.W.E. "The Politics of Anxiety: Contemporary Socialist Theatre in England." In *Modern British Dramatists: New Perspectives*, ed. John Russell Brown. Englewood Cliffs, NJ: Prentice-Hall, 1984: 161–76.
Billington, Michael [1]. Review of *Fish in the Sea*. *The Guardian* (13 Feb. 1975).
———[2]. Review of *John Brown's Body*. *The Guardian* (22 Mar. 1990).
———[3]. Review of *Little Red Hen*. *The Guardian* (1 June 1976).
Bruce, George. "Scotland." *Sunday Times* (25 Nov. 1973).
Bull, John. *New British Political Dramatists*. London: Macmillan, 1984: 18–24.
Burke, Jim. Review of *The Wicked Old Man*. *Plays and Players* (Aug. 1992): 91.
Caplan, Betty. "Exit Stage Left." *The Guardian* (30 Aug. 1990).
Chambers, Colin, and Mike Prior. *Playwrights' Progress*. Oxford: Amber Lane Press, 1987: 67–74.
Cherns, Penny, and Paddy Broughton. "John McGrath's *Trees in the Wind* at the North-cott Theatre, Exeter." *Theatre Quarterly* 19 (Sept.-Nov. 1975): 89–100.
Coveney, Michael [1]. Review of *John Brown's Body*. *The Observer* (1 Apr. 1990).
———[2]. Review of *The Wicked Old Man*. *The Observer* (21 June 1992).
Craig, Sandy. *Dreams and Deconstructions*. Ambergate: Amber Lane Press, 1980: 42–46.
Elsom, John. "Systems." *The Listener* (27 Feb. 1975): 280–81.
Gilliatt, Penelope. "Soldier's Revenge." *The Observer* (24 Apr. 1966): 25.
Gillman, P. "Enter Stage Left: The North Wind of Change." *Radio Times* (30 May 1974): 10, 13.
Griser, Mark. "Liverpool." *Plays and Players* (Mar. 1973): 55–56.
Hammond, Jonathan [1]. Review of *Fish in the Sea*. *Plays and Players* (Apr. 1975): 27–28.
———[2]. Review of *Lay Off*. *Plays and Players* (Sept. 1975): 35.
Hawkes, Catherine. Review of *Events While Guarding the Bofors Gun*. *Prompt* 8 (autumn 1966): 33.
Hayman, Ronald. *British Theatre since 1955*. Oxford: Oxford University Press, 1979: 88–92.
Hendry, Joy. Review of *The Baby and the Bathwater*. *The Scotsman* (Aug. 1985).
Hennessey, Stewart. "The Black, Black Lies." *New Statesman* (16 Aug. 1991): 34.
Hobson, Harold. Review of *Events While Guarding the Bofors Gun*. *Sunday Times* (17 Apr. 1966): 31.

Hohne, Horst. "Political Analysis, Theatrical Form, and Popular Language in the Plays of Charles Wood, Henry Livings, and John McGrath." *Zeitschrift fur Anglistik und Amerikanistik* 25, 1977: 332–50.

Hoyle, Martin. Review of *John Brown's Body*. *Financial Times* (26 Mar. 1990).

Itzin, Catherine. *Stages in the Revolution*. London: Methuen, 1980: 103–12, 119–28.

Jager, Andreas. *John McGrath und die 7:84 Company Scotland: Politik, Popularitat und Regionalismus im Theater der siebziger Jahre in Schottland*. Amsterdam: Verlag B. R. Gruner, 1986.

Jones, Graham. Review of *Lay Off*. *The Guardian* (16 June 1975).

Kershaw, Baz. *The Politics of Performance: Radical Theatre as Cultural Intervention*. London: Routledge, 1992: 132–67.

Kingston, Jeremy. "Wicked Waste of Time." *The Times* (12 June 1992): B2.

Kinnock, Glenys, and Fiona Millar, eds. "Elizabeth MacLennan." In *By Faith and Darius*. London: Virago, 1993: 177–81.

Klotz, Gunther. "Alternatives in Recent British Drama." *Zeitschrift fur Anglistik und Amerikanistik* 25 (1977): 152–61.

———. "Internationalism and Present British Drama." *Zeitschrift fur Anglistik und Amerikanistik* 27 (1979): 35–42.

Lambert, J. W. "Plays in Performance." *Drama* (autumn 1976): 38–39.

Lapenta, Daniel. "John McGrath's *Border Warfare*." *Theatre* 21 (winter-spring 1990): 113–15.

Lipman, Beata. "Cardiff." *Sunday Times* (15 June 1975).

Mackie, Lindsay. "Scot's Gist." *The Guardian* (15 Apr. 1974): 6.

MacLennan, Elizabeth. *The Moon Belongs to Everyone*. London: Methuen 1990.

Marcus, Frank [1]. "Lessons for Workers." *Sunday Telegraph* (17 Apr. 1977): 18.

———[2]. "Red Shadow." *Sunday Telegraph* (16 Feb. 1975): 14.

Mathiesen, Kenny. Review of *The Cheviot*. *The Scotsman Festival Supplement* (22 Aug. 1991):11.

McFerran, Ann. Review of *Lay Off*. *Time Out* (18 July 1975).

McMillan, Joyce [1]. Review of *The Baby and the Bathwater*. *The Guardian* (25 Oct. 1984).

———[2]. Review of *The Cheviot*. *The Guardian* (11 Mar. 1991).

Moss, Stephen. "Standing up to Two Centuries of Exploitation." *The Guardian* (20 Aug. 1990): 32.

Nightingale, Benedict. Review of *Little Red Hen*. *New Statesman* (11 June 1976).

Oliver, Cordelia [1]. Review of *Little Red Hen*. *The Guardian* (16 Sept. 1975).

———[2]. "Rape of a Nation." *The Guardian* (24 Nov. 1973): 10.

Peacock, D. Keith. *Radical Stages*. Westport, CT: Greenwood Press, 1991: 89–96.

Peter, John [1]. "Middle-Age Dread." *Sunday Times* (14 June 1992): 7:8.

———[2]. "An Opium for the People." *Sunday Times* (17 Apr. 1977): 37.

———[3]. "A Trot down the Dead End of Dogma." *Sunday Times* (25 Mar. 1990): E6.

Radin, Victoria. "Victims of the Bottle." *The Observer* (17 Apr. 1977): 26.

Robins, Dave. "Questions of History." *Plays and Players* (Aug. 1976): 24–25.

Rundall, Jeremy. Review of *Events While Guarding the Bofors Gun*. *Plays and Players* (June 1966): 48.

Spiers, David. "Interview with Jack Gold." *Screen* (July-Oct. 1969): 115–28.

Stevenson, Randall [1]. "Plugged into History." *Times Literary Supplement* (30 Mar. 1990).

————[2]. "Recent Scottish Theatre: Dramatic Developments?" *Scotland: Literature, Culture, Politics.* Heidelberg: Carl Winter, 1989: 187–213.

Taxidou, Olga. "Scotch Myths." *Times Literary Supplement* (9 Aug. 1991): 18.

Thomsen, Christian W. "Three Socialist Playwrights: John McGrath, Caryl Churchill, Trevor Griffiths." In *Contemporary British Drama.* ed. C.W.E. Bigsby. London: Arnold, 1981: 156–75.

Van Erwen, Eugene. *Radical People's Theatre.* Bloomington: Indiana University Press, 1988: 87–108.

Wainwright, Jeffrey. "Left for Dead." *The Independent* (16 June 1992).

Wardle, Irving. Review of *Fish in the Sea. The Times* (14 Feb. 1975).

Wilson, Brian. Review of *The Baby and the Bathwater. Glasgow Herald* (25 Oct. 1984).

Winkler, Elizabeth Hale. *The Function of Song in Contemporary British Drama.* London: Associated University Presses, 1990: 287–303.

Wright, Allen. Review of *John Brown's Body. The Scotsman* (22 Mar. 1990).

BIBLIOGRAPHY

Page, Malcolm. "John McGrath." *New Theatre Quarterly* 4 (Nov. 1985): 400–416.

Peter Nichols

(1927–)

KIM L. JONES-OWEN

Peter Nichols's long dramatic career has rewarded him with a number of coveted awards, but Nichols has, more than once, expressed frustration with playwriting and even vowed in 1983 that he was finished with the stage. That frustration, which was often vented through his plays, however, is one of his hallmarks as a contemporary writer. When he dramatically details personal crises or questions national institutions that typify twentieth-century British life, Nichols meta-theatrically reminds the audience that what they are seeing or reading is indeed, in every sense of the word, a *play*. His language is witty, his sets experimental, his comedy wry (or black), and his characters innovative: they directly address the audience, deftly slip into the past, or cleverly acknowledge their alter egos. Nichols believes that his stage plays betray "the implicit licence the audience" grants to a playwright: "to play the game of illusion by understood rules" (*Plays: One* 1987, xiii). Nichols's plays underscore the concept that contemporary theatre (and the life it mimics) is both illusionary and unpredictable.

Peter Richard Nichols was born 31 July 1927, in Bristol, England, to Richard George and Violet Annie Poole Nichols. He attended Bristol Grammar School (1936–1944), Bristol Old Vic Theatre School (1948–1950), and Trent Park Teachers Training College (1955–1957). Nichols served a three-year stint in the Royal Air Force (1945–1948), spent five years acting for repertory companies (1950–1955), taught two years of primary and secondary school (1957–1959), and for more than ten years wrote television scripts (1959–1975) prior to coming to the stage at the age of forty with over fifteen television productions to his credit. In 1959 he married Thelma Reed, and the couple had three daughters (one deceased) and one son.

Much of his television work provided early examples of Nichols's thematic and experimental interests, but ultimately the "box in the corner" limited the

scope of his writing (*Plays: One*, 1987, xii); the stage allowed for more innovative and sophisticated productions, something Nichols considered a realized
necessity for his first stage play *A Day in the Death of Joe Egg* (1967). Nichols
explained that from the outset he knew no British network would accept the
subject of *Joe Egg*, which "would be about an evening in the life of a couple
with a spastic child." He also knew that "no one, but no one, would counte-
nance this subject in terms of comedy" (Nichols qtd. in Brater, 357). Nichols
followed *Joe Egg* with two more critical and popular successes: *The National
Health, or Nurse Norton's Affair* in 1969 and *Forget-me-not Lane* in 1971.
These early plays all included autobiographical motifs: Nichols's daughter Abigail, a multiplegic, epileptic spastic with a damaged cerebral cortex, influenced
Joe Egg, and numerous hospital stays for a collapsed lung and his father's death
provided material for *The National Health* and *Forget-me-not Lane* respectively.
Chez Nous and *The Freeway*, both 1974 productions, were not resounding tri-
umphs, but Nichols garnered awards and attention in 1977 with his musical
Privates on Parade, grounded, once again, in an autobiographical context: his
Royal Air Force years in Malaysia. Prior to his 1981 achievement with *Passion
Play*, Nichols directed the opening of *Born in the Gardens* in 1979 to moderate
praise. The highly acclaimed *Passion Play* enjoyed numerous productions both
in England and the United States as well as a successful revival in 1984. In
1982 Nichols experimented with another musical comedy, *Poppy*, which was
not nearly as well received as *Privates* had been five years earlier. When the
play transferred to the Adelphi Theatre in 1983, Nichols announced that he was
finished with playwriting and would try his hand at novel writing. In 1984
Nichols published, instead, an autobiography, *Feeling You're Behind*, which
received mostly lukewarm reviews. Nichols's most recent play, 1987's *A Piece
of My Mind*, detailed the aesthetic, commercial, and, once again, autobiographical aspects of writing. Confessional in nature, the play allowed Nichols to offer
a piece of his mind on the nature of the contemporary British stage as he assessed his own artistic career and proved his consummate skill in innovative
characterizations and stage craft.

   Selected Biographical Sources: Nichols, *Feeling You're Behind*; Brater;
Jones; Miller.

MAJOR PLAYS, PREMIERES, AND SIGNIFICANT REVIVALS: THEATRICAL RECEPTION

A Day in the Death of Joe Egg. 1967. Opened at the Citizens Theatre, Glasgow,
on 9 May, directed by Michael Blakemore, nineteen performances; moved to
the Comedy Theatre, London, on 20 July, presented by Memorial Enterprises
(Albert Finney, Michael Medwin), 148 performances. Opened 1 February 1968,
at the Brooks Atkinson Theatre (NY), 154 performances; produced in Paris at
Gaite Montparnasse in 1968 as *Un Jour dans la Mort de Joe Egg* (trans. Claude
Roy); played at the Berlin Festival in Schlosspark by the Schiller Theater in

1968; filmed by Columbia Pictures in 1972. Revivals: Greenwich, 1972 (directed by Nichols) and Roundabout Theatre (NY), 1985; transferred to Longacre Theatre; also at Long Wharf, New Haven (CT) directed by Arvin Brown, transferred to New York.

The 1985 revival garnered Tony Awards for best revival and best actress, Stockard Channing. The first production won *Evening Standard* and *Plays and Players* Awards for best play and shared the John Whiting Award.

This black comedy, with touches of vaudeville and moments of domestic tragedy, was highly acclaimed in both London and New York. Barnes [1] classified Nichols's study of love, children, and marriage as "immensely moving, even profound," and Kerr [2], while he considered the play's ending flawed, accepted Nichols as a "new playwright of startling talent" (11). The early reviewers and interviewers were quick to identify the autobiographical context of the play, and Nichols was equally quick to call attention to the "fantastic" elements of the drama as well (Canby). Most critics still consider it one of Nichols's best efforts.

The National Health, or Nurse Norton's Affair. 1969. Opened at the National Theatre (Old Vic), London, on 16 October produced by Michael Blakemore; produced in Paris at Théâtre de la Ville in 1969 as *Sante Publique* (trans. Claude Roy); also at Theatre National, Brussels; Long Wharf Theatre, New Haven (CT) transferring to Circle in the Square (NY), on 10 October 1974. Produced at the Guthrie Theatre in Minneapolis in 1975, codirected by Nichols and Michael Laugham.

The first production won *Evening Standard* and *Play and Players* Awards for best play.

This drama was originally produced for television as *The End Beds* and revised at Kenneth Tynan's request for the National Theatre. Nichols added the soap opera parodies when he wrote the script for the stage. Bryden commented on Nichols's bad taste in dramatizing the deaths of terminally ill patients. Overall, however, the play received high praise for both its thematic content and theatrical innovation. Wardle [4] placed Nichols high in the category of talented British playwrights: "I know of none with Peter Nichols's power to put modern Britain on the stage and send the spectators away feeling more like members of the human race."

Forget-me-not Lane. 1971. Opened at the Greenwich Theatre, London, on 1 April, directed by Michael Blakemore; the same production opened at the Apollo Theatre, London, 28 April, produced by Memorial Enterprises; produced in Paris at Théâtre de la Renaissance, in June 1972 as *ne m'oubliez pas*. Also at Long Wharf, New Haven (CT), (1973) and later at the Mark Taper Forum, Los Angeles (later transmitted by WNET-TV). Revival: March 1990 at the Greenwich Theatre, directed by Nichols. Voted best British play of the season by *Variety*, March 1991, Greenwich Theatre.

This autobiographical memory play about fathers, sons, and family generations was warmly welcomed by most London critics. Wardle [2] compared it,
less favorably, to John Mortimer's *Voyage round My Father* but still praised
Nichols's fluid use of flashback and Blakemore's innovative set of "domesticity
and dream" created by a background of six doors. The reminiscence of "ex-
cruciatingly ordinary" adolescent events, however, did not please Kerr [1], as
he condemned the play as "pattern less, undisciplined." Not one to be bothered
by nostalgia, Barnes [2] called the play "lovely" and commented that all its
echoes of the past were "brilliantly recalled."

Chez Nous. 1974. Opened at the Globe Theatre, London, by Memorial Enterprises, on 6 February directed by Robert Chetwyn; also at the Manhattan Theatre
Club (NY) in 1977.

This domestic play addressed the issue of troubled marriages and received its
share of troubled reviews. Eder [1] complained that the characters were too self-
interested, the plot too contrived, and the comedy too brittle. Many questioned
the routine emptiness of this play compared to Nichols's earlier successes.

The Freeway. 1974. Opened at the National Theatre (Old Vic), London, on 2
October directed by Jonathan Miller.

This dystopian play, which featured an onstage traffic jam, was criticized for
offering characters as "static as the stranded cars" (Hobson [3]), and for not
depicting a more desperate, horrible situation. Nonetheless, Nichols used the
motor car stuck in a huge jam as a means to criticize the obsessive drive for
money and status as well as the docility of the masses when confronted with
authority. Nichols commented that his play was the first stage play to use the
idea of a traffic jam and "in view of its critical reception, may well be the last"
(*Plays: One*, 1991, 409).

Privates on Parade. 1977. Opened at the Aldwych Theatre, London, with the
Royal Shakespeare Company, on 17 February, directed by Michael Blakemore;
transferred to the Piccadilly Theatre on 2 February 1978, by Eddie Kulukundis
and Memorial Enterprises; opened 6 June 1979, at the Long Wharf Theatre,
New Haven (CT), directed by Arvin Brown. Also played in 1989 at the Roundabout Theatre (NY).

In London, it won *Evening Standard*, Society of West End Theatres, and Ivor
Novello Awards, and in New York a Critics Circle Award.

Nichols's first attempt at a musical brought largely rave reviews for his song,
dance, and music hall routines, although Nichols himself classified the play as
"neither fish nor fowl," noting that it had a "good deal of bitterness" for a
musical (qtd. in Demastes, 104). Critical commentators claimed Nichols had
found his voice again and was far more skilled in doubling as lyricist and
entertainer than most of his British playwright counterparts who tried to accom-
plish the same feat.

Born in the Gardens. 1979. Opened at the Theatre Royal, Bristol, on 29 August, directed by Nichols. It transferred to the Globe Theatre, London, on 23 January 1980, directed by Clifford Williams.

This most straightforward play in the Nichols's canon, depending on subtle characterization and the tradition of drawing room comedy, offered a successful study of the tensions between past and present, personal and public. Reviews were routine, citing adequate characterization in this, for Nichols, rather uneventful play (Chaillet). Wertheim classified it in the tradition of British homecoming plays, keeping company with T. S. Eliot's *The Family Reunion*, Harold Pinter's *The Homecoming*, and David Storey's *In Celebration*.

Passion Play. 1981. Opened at the Aldwych Theatre, London, with the Royal Shakespeare Company, on 8 January, directed by Mike Ockrent, fifty performances. Revived at the Haymarket Theatre, Leicester, on 8 March 1984, and transferred to Wyndham's Theatre, London, on 18 April 1984, directed by Mike Ockrent. As *Passion*, it opened at the Longacre Theatre (NY), on 15 May 1983, directed by Marshall W. Mason.

Received the *Evening Standard* Award for best play, 1981.

This innovative play addressed the popular, well-worn theme of adultery, but with enough technical finesse to raise it a level above its competition. Wardle [1] praised Nichols's theatrical skill, but questioned the necessity of the second act, which he saw as unnecessarily repetitive. Brustein accused Nichols of being unsure of what he wanted to write—"a sex comedy or a metaphysical drama" (24), but most critics acclaimed both Nichols's theme and his means of dramatizing it (Glendinning, Hobson [1]).

Poppy. 1982. Opened at the Barbican Theatre, London, by the Royal Shakespeare Company, on 5 October, directed by Terry Hands, music by Monty Norman. A new version transferred to the Adelphi Theatre, London, in 1983.

Received the Society of West End Theatre and Best British Musical Awards.

In the tradition of pantomime, this play received mixed reviews that were often overshadowed by Nichols's untimely announcement that he was finished with the theatre. This sprawling musical, complete with Gilbert and Sullivan patter songs and nautical dioramas, once again clarified Nichols's skill in writing very diverse kinds of plays, drawing on traditional theatrical forms and rendering them anew for the contemporary stage (Peter [2]).

A Piece of My Mind. 1987. Opened 1 April 1987, at the Apollo Theatre, London.

This confessional play, written in "blood, sweat, and vitriol," confirmed Nichols's return to the theatre after a self-declared hiatus from playwriting (Peter [1]). Many considered the drama of dyspeptic playwright Ted Forrest, who suffers through a writer's block, dazzling (Higgins), while also noting the ironic autobiographical context of the play. Kingston called its technical details "terrific" but lamented that the "brilliant parts do not fuse into a great whole."

ADDITIONAL PLAYS, ADAPTATIONS, AND PRODUCTIONS

Blue Murder (1995) has yet to recieve a full production, despite a successful fringe run in Bristol. In addition to his stage and television scripts, Nichols has also produced an adaptation of E. Nesbit's novel, *Harding's Luck*, 1974. Additionally, he has written six screenplays: *Catch Us If You Can (Having a Wild Weekend)*, 1965; *Georgy Girl*, 1966; *Joe Egg*, 1972; *The National Health*, 1973; *Privates on Parade*, 1983; and *Changing Places*, 1984.

ASSESSMENT OF NICHOLS'S CAREER

After years of personal and professional difficulties, Peter Nichols found his niche, at the age of forty, in writing for the stage—a venue where he could tell his own story, in his own voice. Viewing a first-act run-through of *A Day in the Death of Joe Egg* in 1967 brought Nichols to tears, the only time, he contends, he has wept about his daughter Abigail's disabilities. Nichols concluded that the tears were "atypical for what I had heard was not someone else's story but my own and, more important, not an echo of other writers or imitations of friends and family, but my own voice, a tone and rhythm that told me that at nearly forty, I'd cleared my throat at last and was saying what I meant" (*Feeling You're Behind*, 225–26).

Nichols's tone and rhythm in his ten stage plays is that of a comprehensive nature—the ability to realize a double perspective, a personal and national reality—in an ever-changing, innovative theatrical format. His dramatization of individual British lives frequently reveals the impact of national circumstances on those lives, as well as the sometimes universal implications. Nichols's dramas offer close scrutiny of contemporary sociopolitical concerns as he stages both the domestic and national stresses and strains of postwar England.

Nichols's plays with a domestic setting, *A Day in the Death of Joe Egg*, *Forget-me-not Lane*, *Chez Nous,* and *Passion Play*, detail the mutually destructive relationships between parent and child and husband and wife. Nichols creates characters who repeat patterns of behavior from generation to generation, suggesting that the familial institution ensures that children's lives will mimic those of their parents. As these grown children endure empty or restrictive marriages, they often contemplate or commit infidelities and secure what Enoch Brater calls the "lethal family trap" by making miserable the lives of their own children (360). In order to save these dramas from the maudlin or sentimental, Nichols employs highly theatrical forms and language. Such experimentation with the drawing room comedy and romantic farce results in a contemporary redefinition of the nature and function of these traditional styles. Nichols, additionally, abandons neat or happy endings in favor of open-ended questions about the nature of modern marriage, the impact of changing patriarchal and matriarchal roles, and the personal and national ramifications of dysfunctional postwar family units.

Nichols continues to use a group structure or a family metaphor in his national plays, *The National Health, or Nurse Norton's Affair, The Freeway, Privates on Parade, Born in the Gardens,* and *Poppy.* The family analogy is extended to non-nuclear family units such as soldiers in a military troop, patients in a hospital ward, and motorists in a traffic jam. The expansion of a group ideology into non-family units emphasizes that much of the conflict for Nichols's characters is based on the opposition between self and others. As he does in the domestic dramas, Nichols focuses on the plight of the individual within sanctioned, traditional groupings; yet in the national dramas, he goes further to emphasize the sociopolitical ways the community subsumes the life of the private citizen. Nichols is especially bothered by the docility of the masses when confronted with authority, establishing that, at least at one level, the aim of his political satires is to expose the degrading and damaging conventions of postwar governmental rule. Overall, Nichols condemns the contemporary British welfare state—with its complex bureaucracy that renders the individual powerless to determine his or her own course—but like his domestic plays, his national plays offer no absolute solutions to remedy the cultural conditions that plague his characters' lives.

Most of Nichols's characters recall or recreate a past based on more prescriptive or restrictive roles than those they play out in the present. They imagine a time when questions about the family (as institution), gender (as identification of the person), sexuality (as a basis for marriage), and colonialism (as extension of authority and Christianity) are not readily subject to debate. In contrast, Nichols's contemporary characters continually struggle with such issues. On a personal level, sexual politics—confusing or conflicting roles for both genders—and the ethics of passion—in a time when sexual identity and affairs of the heart are supposedly unrestrained—reduce many of Nichols's characters to uncertain, uncomfortable positions. On a social level Nichols offers definitive examinations of the state of the nation—institutions and ideologies—as he investigates contemporary British cultural practices and the decline of the empire into a second-rate international power. Nichols demands that his characters assess changes in traditional domestic and national conventions such as "the family" and imperialistic attitudes; yet his characters' comparative evaluation of the past and present is punctuated with both the possibility and the unlikelihood of their embracing cultural variation or change. Nichols, however, can be credited for undergoing a similar kind of assessment of self, though from an artistic perspective. His most recent staged play, *A Piece of My Mind,* tells the story of playwright Ted Forrest, who stumbles through a writer's block (prompted in part from his attempt to write a novel rather than a play), which has strong autobiographical ties to the years between 1983 and 1987, when Nichols tried to abandon playwriting in favor of novel writing.

The use of autobiographical motifs is not a rarity for Nichols; in fact, many of his plays have their basis in personal details. In the preface to his autobiography Nichols confesses to having "trotted out my life" in both his stage plays and television scripts and admits that "my friends and family had appeared in such thin disguise that sometimes only their names had been changed" (*Feeling You're Behind*, xi). Despite his at times wholesale use of personal experience, Nichols parlays autobiographical details into a contextual framework that supplies projections or evaluations of experience rather than an exact reproduction. The cumulative effect of incorporating autobiographical motifs into his plays is that the combination of personal experience and dramatic artistry produces a subjective yet also realistic reflection of the current state of domestic and political affairs in contemporary England.

Beyond the strength of his autobiographical and sociopolitical statements, Nichols's plays can be considered important commentaries on the form and function of other dramatic styles. He is highly skilled at fusing contemporary theatrical currents with a variety of traditional forms such as the problem play, drawing room comedy, pantomime, and music hall, while usually managing to forego contrivance of plot, theme, or character. Vague echoes of farce, comedy of manners, or drawing room comedy sound in Nichols's plays set within the family home (*Joe Egg*, *Chez Nous*, *Born in the Gardens*); and faint reverberations of the problem play ring in Nichols's national plays (*The National Health*, *The Freeway*, *Poppy*). Nichols follows the tradition and then expands the form; for example, he adapts the pantomime form in *Poppy*, uses music hall techniques in *Privates on Parade*, and contrasts the problems of the hospital patients with the soap-operatic love scenes between hospital staff in *The National Health*.

The direct audience address also can be seen, according to Cave, as an expansion and combination of the more typical devices of monologue, soliloquy, and aside (101). As a contemporary theatrical device the direct address enables Nichols to elicit simultaneous judgment and sympathy from the audience as they are invited to react to individual stage characters. In addition, Nichols occasionally follows or adapts the traditions or patterns used by other modern or contemporary playwrights. Nichols's stage plays include the Wilder-like use of a character as narrator, commentator, or stage manager, as seen in Barnet in *The National Health* and Frank in *Forget-me-not Lane*. Also, as did Eugene O'Neill and Brian Friel, Nichols uses dual-character representatives (the young and old versions of Frank and Ursula in *Forget-me-not Lane* and alter ego characters of Jim and Nell in *Passion Play*).

Nichols's theatrical innovations as well as his social, political, and aesthetic concerns situate him with many other new or second wave British dramatists, such as Harold Pinter, Tom Stoppard, Joe Orton, Peter Shaffer, and David Storey, who comprise a post-Osborne theatre movement. Nichols's contribution to the new wave is the sounding of his own voice, the clearing of his throat in innovative and diverse ways. No one theme or technique has become his singular hallmark; instead, Nichols has filled the stage with an ever-changing repertoire of black comedy, autobiographical tales, domestic tragedy, political satire, and lyrical song in a tone and rhythm of his own.

PRIMARY BIBLIOGRAPHY

Plays

Born in the Gardens. London: Faber & Faber, 1980.

Chez Nous. London: Faber & Faber, 1974.

A Day in the Death of Joe Egg. London: Faber & Faber, 1967; as *Joe Egg*, New York: Grove Press, 1967.

Forget-me-not Lane. London: Faber & Faber, 1971; New York: French, 1972.

The Freeway. London: Faber & Faber 1974.

The National Health, or Nurse Norton's Affair. London: Faber & Faber, 1970; New York: Grove Press, 1975.

Passion Play. London: Methuen, 1981, 1985; as *Passion*, New York: Methuen, 1983; also *The Plays of the Seventies.* New York: Methuen, 1986.

A Piece of My Mind. London: Methuen, 1987.

Privates on Parade. London: Faber & Faber 1977.

Poppy. London: Methuen, 1982.

Anthologies

Plays: One (Forget-me-not Lane, Hearts and Flowers, Neither Up nor Down, Chez Nous, The Common, Privates on Parade). London: Methuen, 1987.

Plays: One (A Day in the Death of Joe Egg, The National Health, Forget-me-not Lane, Hearts and Flowers, The Freeway). London: Methuen, 1991.

Plays: Two (Chez Nous, Privates on Parade, Born in the Gardens, Passion Play, Poppy). London: Methuen, 1991.

Autobiography

Feeling You're Behind: An Autobiography. London: Weidenfeld & Nicholson, 1984; Penguin, 1985.

Interview

"Peter Nichols on His Art, Politics, and Peers: An Interview" (with William Demastes). *Journal of Dramatic Theory and Criticism* 3.1 (1988): 101–11.

SECONDARY BIBLIOGRAPHY

Barnes, Clive [1]. Review of *A Day in the Death of Joe Egg. New York Times* (2 Feb. 1968): 28.

———[2]. Review of *Forget-me-not Lane. New York Times* (17 Aug. 1971): 27.

———[3]. Review of *The National Health. New York Times* (11 Oct. 1974): 28.

Billington, Michael. "Joe Egg's Dad." *The Guardian* (2 Dec. 1971): 10–11.

Brater, Enoch. "Peter Nichols." In *British Drama Since World War II: A Dictionary of Literary Biography*, ed. Stanley Weintraub. Vol. 13 Detroit: Gale Research, 1982: 354–64.

Brustein, Robert. "Love from Two Sides of the Ocean." *New Republic* (27 June 1983): 24–25.

Bryant, Richard. "Keeping the Heart and Soul Together." *America's Arena* (15 Nov. 1984): 6–8.

Bryden, Ronald. "Playwright Peter Nichols: The Comic Laureat of Bad Taste?" *New York Times* (10 Nov. 1974): 5.

Canby, Vincent. "Peter Nichols, 'Joe Egg' Author, Found Humor in Desperation." *New York Times* (3 Feb. 1968): 22.

Cave, Richard Allen. *New British Drama in Performance on the London Stage: 1970– 1985*. New York: St. Martin's Press, 1988.

Chaillet, Ned. Review of *Born in the Gardens*. *The Times* (24 Jan. 1980): 13.

Clayton, Thomas. "The Texts and Publishing Vicissitudes of Peter Nichols's *Passion Play*." *The Library: A Quarterly Journal of Bibliography* 9.4 (1987): 365–83.

Davison, Peter. *Contemporary Drama and the Popular Dramatic Tradition in England*. Totowa, NJ: Barnes, 1982.

Doust, Dudley. "Making Comedy out of a Family Tragedy." *Life* (24 Nov. 1967): 106– 109.

Eder, Richard [1]. Review of *Chez Nous*. *New York Times* 7 (Nov. 1977): 44.

———[2]. Review of *Privates on Parade*. *New York Times* 3 (May 1977): 49.

Foulkes, Richard. " 'The Cure is Removal of Guilt': Faith, Fidelity and Fertility in the Plays of Peter Nichols." *Modern Drama* 29.2 (1986): 207–15.

Glendinning, Victoria. "Only Four Can Play." *Times Literary Supplement* (23 Jan. 1981): 83.

Gow, Gordon. "Is George Cole Peter Nichols?" *Plays International* (Mar. 1987): 14– 15.

Gussow, Mel [1]. "Comically Carrying Culture to the Colonies." *New York Times* (23 Aug. 1989): 13.

———[2]. "When Writers Turn the Tables Rather than the Other Cheek." *New York Times* (16 July 1989): 5.

Hay, Malcolm. "Piece of Mind." *Plays and Players* (Jan. 1987): 4–5.

Hayman, Ronald [1]. "The Mimic Man." *The Times* (31 Mar. 1971): 11.

———[2]. *Playback*. 1973. New York: Horizon, 1974.

Hewes, Henry. "The British Bundle." *Saturday Review* (11 Sept. 1971): 20; 54.

Higgins, John. "Arthur Daley Going Straight." *The Times* (25 Mar. 1987): 21.

Hobson, Harold [1]. "Hobson's Choice." *Quarterly Theatre Review* 141 (1981): 18–21.

———[2]. "Household Words." *Sunday Times* (10 Feb. 1974): 29.

———[3]. "Under Steam." *Sunday Times* (6 Oct. 1974): 33.

Jones, Mervyn. "Peter Nichols, The Playwright Who Has Had Enough." *Quarterly Theatre Review* 148 (1983): 7–8.

Kerensky, Oleg. *The New British Drama*. New York: Taplinger, 1977.

Kerr, Walter [1]. "Down Memory Lane to a Dead End." *New York Times* (22 Apr. 1973): 10–11.

———[2]. Review of *A Day in the Death of Joe Egg*. *New York Times* (11 Feb. 1968): 1.

Kingston, Jeremy. "Brilliant Mixture Fails to Fuse." *The Times* (2 Apr. 1987): 19.

Lang, James M. "Staging an Image-System: Breaking down the Self in Peter Nichols' *Joe Egg*." *Essays in Theatre* 12.1 (1993): 63.

Miller, Brian. "Peter Nichols." In *British Television Drama,*. ed. George W. Brandt. Cambridge: Cambridge University Press, 1981: 110–36.

Nightingale, Benedict. Review of *Privates on Parade*. *New York Times* (6 Mar. 1977): 6.

Parkin, Andrew. "Casting the Audience: Theatricality in the Stage Plays of Peter Nichols." In *British and Irish Drama since 1950*, ed. James Acheson. Houndmills: Macmillan, 1993: 60–72.

Peter, John [1]. "Blood, Sweat, and Vitriol." *Sunday Times* (5 Apr. 1987): 52.

———[2]. "Opinion: No More Opium for the People?" *Quarterly Theatre Review* 147 (1983): 42.

Rosen, Carol. *Plays of Impasse: Contemporary Drama Set in Confining Institutions*. Princeton, NJ: Princeton University Press, 1983.

Rusinko, Susan. *British Drama 1950 to the Present: A Critical History*. Boston: Twayne, 1989.

Schlueter, June. "Adultery Is Next to Godlessness: Dramatic Juxtaposition in Peter Nichols's *Passion Play*." *Modern Drama* 24.4 (Dec. 1981): 540–45.

Scott, Catherine. "Plays in the Life of Joe Egg's Day." *The Guardian* (26 Jan. 1970): 8.

Simon, John. Review of *Passion*. *New York* (30 May 1983): 74–75.

Stiles, G. W. "Some Thoughts on Two Modern English Comedies." *Unisa English Studies* 9 (1971): 10–16.

Storm, William. "Adulteration as Clarity: Dramaturgical Strategy in Peter Nichols's *Passion Play*." *Modern Drama* 37.3 (Sept. 1994): 437.

Taylor, John Russell [1]. "British Dramatists: The New Arrivals: No. 1, Peter Nichols." *Plays and Players* 17 (1970): 48–51.

———[2]. *The Second Wave: British Drama for the Seventies*. New York: Hill & Wang, 1971.

Troxel, Patricia. "In the Name of Passion: A Comparison of Medieval Passion Plays and Peter Nichols's *Passion Play*." In *From the Bard to Broadway*, ed. Karelisa V. Hartigan. New York: University Press of America, 1987: 213–21.

Walker, J.K.L. "Wittier than Thou." *Times Literary Supplement* (17 Apr. 1987): 414.

Wardle, Irving [1]. "Doing Justice to the Theme of Adultery." *The Times* (14 Jan. 1981): 11.

———[2]. "Double Perspective." *The Times* (2 Apr. 1971): 10.

———[3]. "Old Passions, Modern Manners." *The Times* (7 Feb. 1974): 6.

———[4]. "Organization versus the Individual." *The Times* (17 Oct. 1969): 15.

Weightman, John. "Metaphysical Voids." *Encounter* 43 (1974): 64–66.

Wertheim, Albert. "The Modern British Homecoming Play." *Comparative Drama* 19.2 (summer 1985): 151–65.

BIBLIOGRAPHY

King, Kimball. "Peter Nichols." *Twenty Modern British Playwrights: A Bibliography, 1956 to 1976*. New York: Garland, 1977: 69–65.

Joe Orton
(1933–1967)

DON S. LAWSON

Joe Orton was born in Leicester 1 January 1933; his father was a gardener and his mother a machinist. Orton was a sickly child and indifferent student whose poor spelling would follow him throughout his brief literary career. In 1951, after a series of poor-paying jobs, Orton secured a Leicester Council grant to study in London at the Royal Academy of Dramatic Arts. There he met Kenneth Halliwell, his lifelong companion and lover, and eventual murderer. Halliwell, some seven years older, mentored Orton in a career in writing, both producing several failed novels. Antisocial in nature, the two tended to engage in petty acts of outrage, culminating in an extensive vandalizing of library books—including inserting obscene (and witty) marginalia and sexually suggestive photographs. They were both sentenced to six months in jail. While in jail Orton submitted his play *The Ruffian on the Stair* to the BBC in a prison envelope. It was accepted.

Accepting his role as social outcast—as both a "convict" and a homosexual—Orton enjoyed shocking proper society in his works. His plays eventually earned him such titles as "the Oscar Wilde of the Welfare State." When *Entertaining Mr. Sloane* made it to the West End in 1964, Orton's reputation as a playwright was made. Meanwhile Orton's lover and former mentor, Halliwell, remained unsuccessful and grew jealous of Orton's celebrity.

Two months after the opening of *The Ruffian on the Stair* and *The Erpingham Camp* (collectively titled *Crimes of Passion*), on 10 August 1967, Halliwell bludgeoned Orton to death in a jealous rage and then took his own life, thus tragically cutting short the life of a young talent.

Selected Biographical Sources: Lahr [5]; Trussler.

MAJOR PLAYS, PREMIERES, AND SIGNIFICANT
REVIVALS: THEATRICAL RECEPTION

Entertaining Mr. Sloane. 1964. New Arts Theatre Club, London, 6 May.

The play attracted attention sufficient to warrant its transfer to the West End. It received mostly positive reviews, particularly benefiting from a notice by Sir Terence Rattigan. After its move to the West End, a fierce newspaper discussion about the play's morality (or lack thereof) ensued, to which Orton himself contributed in the form of hilarious letters to the editor under the pseudonym of "Edna Welthorp (Mrs.)." The Broadway premiere of *Entertaining Mr. Sloane* took place on 12 October 1965, where the play ran a scant thirteen performances, perhaps as a result of mostly negative, even homophobic reviews. Taubman called the production "singularly unattractive" (13 October 1965). Revivals: Royal Court, 17 April 1975, the Lyric Hammersmith, 18 March 1981, and Cherry Lane Theatre (NY), 12 June 1981, for over 250 performances.

Loot. 1965. First produced in Cambridge, February; opened in London at the Neannetta Cochrane Theatre, 27 September 1966; transferred to the Criterion, London. At the Biltmore Theatre (NY), on 18 March 1968, for only twenty-two performances. Revivals: New York's CSC Repertory, 16 May 1973, the Royal Court, London, 2 July 1975, Ambassadors Theatre, London, 13 March 1984, Manhattan Theatre Club (NY), 4 February 1986, transferring to the Music Box Theatre (NY), for a combined total of 144 performances.

The Ruffian on the Stair. 1966. The Royal Court Theatre, London, 21 August.

This play was a dramatization of his and Kenneth Halliwell's unpublished novel *The Boy Hairdresser.*

What the Butler Saw. 1969. Opened at the Queen's Theatre, London, 5 March.

This was the first of Orton's plays not subject to the censorship of the Lord Chamberlain's Office. The production, despite an all-star cast, seems to have been a bit of a mixed bag. Not until the acclaimed revival at the Royal Court (July 1975), directed by Lindsay Anderson, did the play receive its due.

ASSESSMENT OF ORTON'S CAREER

At the time of his death Orton was thirty-four still near the beginning of what promised to be a brilliant career as a comic playwright. Since that promise never had the chance to be fulfilled, Orton's reputation rests on rather slender ground: three full-length plays (the last of which was still undergoing revision at the time of his death), four shorter plays, a brief dramatic sketch, three novels (two still unpublished), a diary, and an unproduced screenplay make up his entire literary ouevre. Despite this Orton is widely regarded as a major figure in post-war British drama, as perhaps the finest writer of English farce since Oscar Wilde.

During his lifetime Orton won the *Evening Standard* and *Plays and Players* Awards for the best play for *Loot*, his plays were receiving major West End productions, he had been commissioned to write a screenplay for a movie to star the Beatles, and he was very much the toast of the London theatre world for the last few years of his life. Since his death his plays have continued to be produced—West End revivals, Broadway productions, a season of Orton revivals at the Royal Court in 1975—and have been the focus of a great deal of literary study and analysis.

Taylor [2] writes of Orton, "There is no career more spectacular, and alas none briefer, than that of Joe Orton" (125). Elsom calls Orton "the best farce writer of our time" (92), a view echoed by Bigsby, who sees Orton as "the high priest of farce in the mid-sixties" (17). Lahr [2] calls Orton "the master farceur of his age" (7). Charney writes of Orton's farce, "Orton usually thought of farce as very close to tragedy" (129). Indeed, the theatrical sensibility that has come to be called Ortonesque is dependent upon an odd mixture of hilarity and seriousness, of wild violence or transgressive sexuality, all of which is discussed by the characters involved in very flat, ordinary, polite, and socially correct discourse. The continuing interest in Orton among scholars, students, theatre professionals, and audiences would indicate that Orton is a permanent feature of the theatrical and literary landscape of the second half of the twentieth century.

Orton has been exceptionally well served by John Lahr's superb biography, *Prick up Your Ears: The Biography of Joe Orton*. Alhough other sources (e.g., Charney, Frazer) provide biographical materials, none adds anything new to Lahr, which remains the essential source for information about the life of Orton. Some gay critics (de Jongh, Nakayama), however, have criticized Lahr's critical and biographical hegemony over Orton's work; for those who share these objections to Lahr or who want a different way of looking at Orton's life and times, Simon Shepherd's [1] dual biography of Orton and Halliwell provides another perspective on Orton's life and death. Orton's own diaries, obviously, are also full of autobiographical detail, although it would probably be a mistake to take them on face value; it is well to remember Orton's theatricalization of his life in interviews and other encounters with people, since the same kind of thing may be happening, at least in places, in the diaries.

Additionally, Orton's life and infamous death have served as the basis for three plays: Simon Moss's *Cock-Ups*, (1983) Lanie Robertson's *Nasty Little Secrets* (1983), and John Lahr's *Diary of a Somebody* (1987). There is also a film version of Lahr's biography, *Prick up Your Ears* (1987, director Stephen Frears). Alan Bennett's screenplay of the film has been published.

A number of critics cite Oscar Wilde as the primary precursor of Orton's unique theatrical sensibility; in a famous formulation, Ronald Bryden called Orton "the Oscar Wilde of Welfare State gentility" (qtd. in Hunt, 148). Perhaps Noël Coward, too, must be seen as a forerunner to Orton. In terms of structure, especially in the early plays, the presence of Harold Pinter cannot be ignored

(Charney, 14, 46; Lahr [2], *Complete Plays*, 17; Bull and Gray, 80–81). Both Hunt and Bigsby see traces of George Bernard Shaw in Orton's plays. Bigsby further notes the impact of Ronald Firbank and of Restoration comedy, but he never develops this material in any systematic way.

Orton's play *The Erpingham Camp* is consciously modeled on Euripides' play *The Bacchae* (Charney; Lahr [5]; Esslin; Walcot); Slater sees further Euripidean echoes in *What the Butler Saw*. Echoes of Jacobean tragedy can be found in Orton's work as well; Hutchings sees *What the Butler Saw* as a reworking of materials that can be traced to Cyril Tourneur, Thomas Middleton, and their contemporaries. Draudt finds similar debts to the drama of the later English Renaissance in *Loot*. Smith notes the influence of Ben Jonson's work on both *Loot* and *What the Butler Saw*, and Smith, too, cites Tourneur as a forerunner of Orton. Both Smith and Uthman posit important parallels between Orton's work and that of N. F. Simpson.

Bigsby's book-length treatment of Orton's work sees Orton as an important postmodernist, especially since he dispenses with old-fashioned concepts such as "plot, character, setting and theme, . . . verbal and psychological coherence" (17), a phenomenon Bigsby sums up as "the death of character" (13). Bigsby compares Orton to postmodern painters in that both Orton and several noted visual artists present "a world in which the surface is the reality, a post-moral world" (18). Bigsby proceeds to examine Orton's plays in chronological order, finally concluding with a chapter devoted to assessing Orton's place as a writer of comedy and to discussing Orton's relation to concepts such as camp and anarchy.

In the other full-length critical analysis of Orton, Charney identifies a series of thematic concerns shared by groups of the shorter plays and proceeds to show deeper and more developed thematic materials at the core of Orton's longer plays and his screenplay. For Charney the plays *The Ruffian on the Stair*, *Funeral Games*, and *Until She Screams* (revised from a 1960 salacious sketch entitled *The Patient Dowager*) represent Orton's experiments in style, his attempts to find his own voice and subject. Charney identifies Orton's pointed satire of authority figures (e.g., psychiatrists, police inspectors, fathers) as a central feature of his later plays. Charney's final chapter is a lengthy discussion of "the Ortonesque," which he defines as "a peculiar mixture of farce and viciousness, especially as it expresses itself in the greed, lust and aggression that lie just beneath the surface of British middle-class proprieties" (124), a more substantial definition than Lahr provides when he deems Ortonesque as "a shorthand adjective for scenes of macabre outrageousness" (*Prick up Your Ears*, 5).

By including a lengthy and detailed discussion of Orton, Taylor [2] virtually assured Orton's place in the contemporary dramatic canon. Taylor comments upon the dislocation in Orton's plays between violent, anarchic, and sexually transgressive materials and the commonplace everyday language used to discuss them: "The key to Orton's dramatic world is to be found in the strange relationship between the happenings of his plays and the manner in which the characters speak of them. The happenings may be as outrageous as you like in terms of morality, accepted convention or whatever, but the primness and propriety of what is said hardly ever breaks down'' (124). Taylor notes Orton's use of ''intricate and inventive euphemism'' (124) and calls him a ''master of verbal style'' (124). These comments set the stage for later Orton scholars who have adopted Taylor's ideas as critical commonplaces. Taylor proceeds to show Orton's increasing sophistication as a dramatist as it developed from the early, heavily Pinteresque plays, through Orton's mature work.

John Lahr [2] remains central in Orton criticism, even if his work has recently come under scrutiny, even attack, from gay critics. Lahr's work is the origin of a number of other critical commonplaces that the scholars who followed him have taken up: for example, his piece is heavy on the parallels between Orton's biography and his work, publishing sections of the then unavailable diaries.

An important early study of Orton by Shepherd [2] examines Orton's attempt to ''evaluate entertainment'' by showing the way in which ''the entertained become anarchic and violent, [while] the entertainers remain smiling and placid—because they are being paid. There is a separation between exploitative entertainers and [the exploited entertained], but both sides are nasty and unsympathetic'' (93). The Marxist underpinnings of Shepherd's argument and analysis are developed in discussion of *The Erpingham Camp*, *Entertaining Mr. Sloane*, and *What the Butler Saw*.

As Lahr had earlier done, Bull and Gray trace the impact of Orton's childhood and youth on his writing, essentially seeing the plays as being composed of transformed autobiographical materials (an idea Charney develops as well in the first chapter of his book): ''The connection between Orton's upbringing and his plays is important, more important than for any other English playwright'' (74). Bull and Gray's slant on the question of the relation between discourse and action in the Ortonesque is to argue that Orton's world is one ''in which activity is rigidly restricted and often incomprehensible to the participants because they lack a rational vocabulary in which to discuss their behaviour'' (85).

Of the major early assessments of Orton's work, Esslin's is the least complimentary. Esslin points out that the manuscript of *Ruffian* arrived at the BBC in an envelope mailed from prison, where Orton was serving a sentence for vandalizing library books. Esslin sees Orton's satire as revealing ''a violent desire to hurt . . . feelings, to revenge himself on society, to transgress its rules . . . merely for the elation of having got away with it'' (95). Esslin argues that even in Orton's best work, ''no insights are vouchsafed'' (106). Esslin sees nothing behind Orton's work but ''the rage of the socially and educationally underprivileged'' (107), finding that his plays exemplify ''the spiritual emptiness and—in spite of his obvious brilliance and intelligence—the thoughtlessness, the inability to reason and to analyze, of these deprived multitudes'' (107).

When more specialized studies of Orton began to appear in the early 1980s, a number of critics wrote on the subject of farce in Orton's work. Casmus traces

Orton's development as a writer of farce, arguing that "even as he progressed toward farce, Orton never strayed far from the accessible preserves of the well-made play" (462). Casmus's essentially generic study of Orton is the most detailed consideration of the form of Orton's plays, although she ultimately concludes that Orton "broke no new ground in dramatic form. . . . But he had begun to rediscover an old and honorable path too much in disuse" (467). Bermel's seemingly exhaustive and encyclopedic *Farce* treats Orton only cursorily, seeing his plays as having no more than a "cult foilowing" (321); thus he does not give Orton's work sustained examination or accord him the place in the history of farce he would appear to merit. On the question of Orton's form, Ronald Hayman asserts, "Joe Orton's importance as an innovator was proportional to his influence in reinstating farce as a vehicle for subject matter not normally accommodated by it" (38).

Dean follows this way of thinking, seeing Orton as radically redefining farce, as taking it out of the realm of the merely amusing and investing it with moral seriousness by forcing it to address controversial questions: "Orton realized the possibility for farce to convey a sense of the boundless, the unlimited, the Dionysiac" (492). Worth echoes this by claiming that Orton "is arrestingly original in his ability to push the dark elements so much to the fore" (76), thus underscoring the nature of Orton's theatrical sensibility as somewhat removed from the bare production of laughter.

Beehler deconstructs Orton's work by seeing it in the context of Orton's conviction for damaging library books by altering them so as to make them obscene by means of collage onto the books or by writing in or on them—what Beehler calls "Orton's theatricalization of the Library's closed and restricted space" (87). Beehler goes on to see Orton's writing as part of a dialectic of natural versus created and sees Orton's mutilation of books as providing a central metaphor for his works, many of which revolve around "a central mutilation, around a body whose wholeness is dismembered and disseminated" (94).

Walcot is the initial critic to examine in any systematic way the importance of homosexuality to Orton's work, taking Greek texts as both influences on Orton and as a paradigm for his writing. Although its early date (1984) is quite probably responsible for the lack of direct, sustained treatment of gay issues and for the absence of queer theory, this article is a starting place. Dollimore briefly discusses *What the Butler Saw* as "an angry repudiation of sexual repressiveness as enforced by the ideology of authentic, normal sexuality, now ratified by state law and the medical professions" (315), but it is Sinfield who gives the first true, detailed treatment of Orton as a "queer" writer, exploring the way "Orton's plays effected quite specific negotiations of [the] changing opportunities for theatre and male homosexuals" (259–60). Sinfield places Orton's work squarely in the midst of its historical context—the relaxation of censorship on the British stage, the beginning of the gay liberation movement, and the increasing appeal of camp sensibilities to mainstream audiences.

De Jongh claims, "Orton's importance in the history of the theatre's treatment of homosexual politics is vital'' (94), going on to see Orton as ''the theatre's first homosexual revolutionary'' (94). For Clum, Orton ''is not the great gay comic writer some heterosexual critics would make him but a transitional figure in gay drama'' (133). Lilly finds ''Orton's emphasis is on escape from drudgery, refusal of social orthodoxy, resistance to curbs on pleasure (in particular, sex) and rejection of all the lies necessary to build up a conformist society'' (179). Lilly makes an interesting argument for *The Good and Faithful Servant*, a television play, as Orton's most important work, his play most likely to endure.

Two recent articles have taken metacritical approaches to Orton's work. Nakayama examines the ways in which critical and scholarly reception of Orton's work has been profoundly shaped by Lahr's writing on Orton. Since Lahr has been called ''homophobic'' (de Jongh, 104), his centrality to Orton scholarship may indeed have directed scholars away from important aspects of the plays, particularly in terms of their expressions of sexuality; Nakayama sees Lahr as having ''domesticated'' Orton's plays by robbing them of their ''subversive content'' (185). Page's examination of Orton in the light of various literary theories and in response to earlier critics' approaches to the plays shows the richness of Orton's work and demonstrates that readers or audiences who bring different critical apparatuses to the plays come away with radically different responses to what they have seen or read. In particular, he remarks on the curious coincidence that Esslin finds Orton's chief weakness exactly where Bigsby sees a strength, in Orton's ''absence of any positive values'' (142).

Further Research Opportunities

The unpublished Orton juvenilia—most especially *Untitled Play*—need critical examination and publication so that scholars can have the complete works of Orton available for study and comment. Certainly editions of the two novels Orton wrote with Kenneth Halliwell should be issued. Orton's letters, housed at the Mugar Memorial Library of Boston University, should likewise be printed. The recent explosion of gay theory certainly has proved useful in analyzing Orton's plays, and much probably remains to be done in this area. Although Orton's complex borrowings from such playwrights as Harold Pinter and Euripides have been analyzed, there is still work to be done toward setting Joe Orton in his proper place in the history of English farce, most particularly in analyzing his relation with and possible debts to the dramatists of the English Restoration period.

PRIMARY BIBLIOGRAPHY

Plays

The Complete Plays. (*The Ruffian on the Stair, Entertaining Mr. Sloane, The Good and Faithful Servant, Loot, The Erpingham Camp, Funeral Games,* and *What the Butler Saw*). New York: Grove Press, 1976.

Crimes of Passion. (*The Ruffian on the Stair, The Erpingham Camp*). London: Eyre Methuen, 1967.

Entertaining Mr. Sloane. London: Hamish Hamilton, 1964; New York: Grove Press 1965.

Funeral Games and *The Good and Faithful Servant.* London: Eyre Methuen, 1970.

Loot. London: Eyre Methuen, 1967; New York: Grove Press, 1968.

The Ruffian on the Stair (original version). *New Radio Drama.* London: British Broadcasting Corporation, 1966: 196–233.

Until She Screams. In *Oh, Calcutta.* ed. Kenneth Tynan. New York: Grove Press, 1969.

What the Butler Saw. London: Eyre Methuen, 1969; New York: Samuel French, 1969.

Interviews

"Joe Orton Interviewed by Giles Gordon." *Transatlantic Review* 24 (spring 1962): 93–100. Rpt. in *Behind the Scenes*, ed. Joseph F. McCrindle. New York: Holt, 1971.

"Entertaining Mr. Loney: An Early Interview with Joe Orton." *New Theatre Quarterly* 4.16 (Nov. 1988): 300–305.

Published Letter

"Joe Orton to Frank Marcus." *London Magazine* (Apr. 1969): 56.

SECONDARY BIBLIOGRAPHY

Beehler, Michael. "Joe Orton and the Heterogeneity of the Book." *Sub-Stance* 33/34 (1982): 84–99.

Bermel, Albert. *Farce: A History from Aristophanes to Woody Allen.* Carbondale: Southern Illinois University Press, 1990.

Bigsby, C.W.E. *Joe Orton.* London: Methuen, 1982.

Bull, John, and Frances Gray. "Joe Orton." In *Essays on Contemporary British Drama*, ed. Hedwig Bock and Albert Wertheim. Munich: Hueber, 1981: 71–96.

Cardullo, Bert. "Orton's *Entertaining Mr. Sloane.*" *Explicator* 46.4 (summer 1988): 50–52.

Casmus, Mary I. "Farce and Verbal Style in the Plays of Joe Orton." *Journal of Popular Culture* 12 (spring 1980): 461–68.

Charney, Maurice. *Joe Orton.* New York: Grove Press, 1984.

Clum, John. *Acting Gay: Male Homosexuality in Modern Drama.* New York: Columbia University Press, 1992.

Curtis, David. "Those Awful Orton Diaries." *Sacred Heart University Review* 7.1–2 (fall-spring 1986–87): 40–51.

Dean, Joan F. "Joe Orton and the Redefinition of Farce." *Theatre Journal* 34.4 (Dec. 1982): 481–92.

de Jongh, Nicholas. *Not in Front of the Audience: Homosexuality on Stage.* London: Routledge, 1992.

Dollimore, Jonathan. *Sexual Dissidence*: *Augustine to Wilde, Freud to Foucault.* Oxford: Oxford University Press, 1991.

Draudt, Manfred. "Comic, Tragic, or Absurd? On Some Parallels between the Farces of Joe Orton and Seventeenth-Century Tragedy." *English Studies* 59.3 (June 1978): 202–17.

Durang, Christopher. "Loot Points: A Look at Joe Orton's Legacy." *Vanity Fair* (June 1986): 109–10.

Elsom, John. "The Man Who Said No and the Man Who Said Well." *London Magazine* (Apr. 1969): 91–96.

Esslin, Martin. "Joe Orton: The Comedy of (Ill) Manners." In *Contemporary English Drama*, ed. C.W.E. Bigsby. New York: Holmes & Meier, 1981: 95–107.

Fox, James. "The Life and Death of Joe Orton." *Sunday Times Magazine* (22 Nov. 1970): 44+.

Frazer, Keath. "Joe Orton: His Brief Career." *Modern Drama* 14.4 (Feb. 1972): 413–419.

Gallix, Andrew. *Joe Orton's Comedy of the Last Laugh.* New York: Garland, 1994.

Hayman, Ronald. *British Theatre since 1955: A Reassessment.* Oxford: Oxford University Press, 1979.

Hunt, Albert. "What Joe Orton Saw." *New Society* (17 Apr. 1975): 148–50.

Hutchings, William. "Joe Orton's Jacobean Assimilations in *What the Butler Saw.*" In *Themes in Drama 10: Farce*, ed. James Redmond. Cambridge: Cambridge University Press, 1988. 227–35.

Innes, Christopher. *Modern British Drama, 1890–1990.* Cambridge: Cambridge University Press, 1992.

Lahr, John [1]. "Artist of the Outrageous." *Evergreen Review* 14 (Feb. 1970): 30–34+.

———[2]. Introduction. *The Complete Plays.* By Joe Orton. New York: Grove Press, 1976: 7–28.

———[3]. Introduction and Editor's Note. *The Orton Diaries.* By Joe Orton. London: Methuen, 1986: 7–31.

———[4]. Introduction. *Up Against It.* By Joe Orton. New York: Grove Press, 1979. v–xvi.

———[5]. *Prick up Your Ears: The Biography of Joe Orton.* New York: Knopf, 1978.

Lawson, D. S. "Joe Orton." In *The Gay and Lesbian Literary Heritage*, ed. Claude Summers. Chester, CT: New England Publishing Associates, 1995: 327–29.

Lilly, Mark. *Gay Men's Literature in the Twentieth Century.* New York: New York University Press, 1993.

Loney, Glen [1]. "Giving Society a Goose: Joe Orton's Comedy of Revenge." *After Dark* (Dec. 1978): 44–55.

———[2]. "What Joe Orton Saw: Death and the Maiden." *After Dark* (Sept. 1970): 42–44.

Macintyre, Margaret, and David Buchbinder. "Having It Both Ways: Cross Dressing in Orton's *What the Butler Saw* and Churchill's *Cloud Nine.*" *Journal of Dramatic Theory and Criticism* 2.1 (1987): 23–39.

Marcus, Frank. "Comedy or Farce?" *London Magazine* (6 Feb. 1967): 73–77.

Marowitz, Charles. "Farewell, Joe Orton." *New York Times* (7 Apr. 1968): 2: 1.

McCray, Suzanne. "The Unrelenting Pessimism of Joe Orton." *Publications of the Arkansas Philological Association* 10.2 (1984): 37–47.

Nakayama, Randall S. "Domesticating Mr. Orton." *Theatre Journal* 45.2 (May 1993): 185–95.

Orr, John. *Tragicomedy and Contemporary Culture.* London: Macmillan, 1991.

Page, Adrian. "An Age of Surfaces: Joe Orton's Drama and Post-modernism." In *The Death of the Playwright? Modern British Drama and Literary Theory*, ed. Adrian Page. New York: St. Martin's Press 1992: 142–59.

Shepherd, Simon [1]. *Because We're Queers: The Life and Crimes of Kenneth Halliwell and Joe Orton*. London: Gay Men's Press, 1989.

———[2]. "Edna's Last Stand, or Joe Orton's Dialectic of Entertainment." *Renaissance and Modern Studies* 22 (1978): 87–110.

Sinfield, Alan. "Who Was Afraid of Joe Orton?" *Textual Practice* 4.2 (summer 1990): 259–77. Rpt. in *Sexual Sameness: Textual Differences in Lesbian and Gay Writing*, ed. Joseph Bristow. London: Routledge, 1992: 170–86.

Slater, Niall. "Tragic Farce: Orton and Euripides." *Classical and Modern Literature* 7.2 (winter 1987): 87–98.

Smith, Leslie. "Democratic Lunacy: The Comedies of Joe Orton." *Adam: International Review* 394–96 (1976): 73–92.

Strang, Ronald W. "*What the Butler Saw.*" In *Insight IV: Analyses of Modern British and American Drama*, ed. Herman Weiand. Frankfurt: Hirschgraben, 1975: 86–93.

Taubman, Howard. Review of *Entertaining Mr. Sloane. New York Times* (13 Oct. 1965).

Taylor, John Russell [1]. "British Dramatists—The New Arrivals—No. 7, The Late and Lamented Joe Orton." *Plays and Players* 18 (Oct. 1970): 14–17.

———[2]. *The Second Wave: British Drama for the Seventies*. New York: Hill & Wang, 1971.

Trussler, Simon. "Joe Orton." In *Contemporary Dramatists*, ed. James Vinson. Appendix. London: St. James Press, 1977: 984–86.

Uthman, Nuaiman A. "Joe Orton and N. F. Simpson: Farcical Absurdists?" *Journal of the College of Arts, King Saud University* 11.1 (1984): 41–47.

Walcot, Peter. "An Acquired Taste: Joe Orton and the Greeks." In *Legacy of Thespis: Drama Past and Present*, ed. Karelisa V. Hartigan. Vol. 4. Lanham, MD: University Press of America, 1984: 99–123.

Worth, Katharine J. "Form and Style in the Plays of Joe Orton." In *Modern British Dramatists*, ed. John Russell Brown. Englewood Cliffs, NJ: Prentice-Hall, 1984: 75–84.

BIBLIOGRAPHY

King, Kimball. "Joe Orton." *Twenty Modern British Playwrights: A Bibliography, 1956 to 1976*. New York: Garland, 1977: 77–83.

John Osborne
(1929–1994)

MALCOLM PAGE

John Osborne's fame arises largely from his first London play, staged at the Royal Court on 8 May 1956, by the recently formed English Stage Company. *Look Back in Anger* caught a new youthful mood, and Osborne was quickly given the fashionable label of Angry Young Man. Because of this success, a British dramatic renaissance began. Soon new plays by unknown writers were frequently staged; further, the ambitious young wannabee was likely to use the dramatic form instead of the novel. Some who followed in the next few years were political, as Osborne appeared to be: among these were John Arden and Arnold Wesker. Others of this first wave were as varied as Robert Bolt, Shelagh Delaney, Ann Jellicoe, and Harold Pinter. While attributing this all to *Look Back* of course oversimplifies (*Waiting for Godot* was admired in the previous year; Brendan Behan's *The Quare Fellow* was staged two weeks later), its impact was great. That Laurence Olivier took on the title role in Osborne's next play, *The Entertainer*, in the following year, consolidated Osborne's fame, and both plays were soon filmed.

Osborne has published two volumes of autobiography, taking his life to the mid-1960s, which are stylish and entertaining but not necessarily wholly reliable. The main facts of his life follow. He was born in London in 1929, the son of a commercial artist and a barmaid. He was able to attend a minor public school in Devon, from which he was apparently expelled for hitting a teacher. His class status is thus difficult to place, somewhere between the upper working class and the lowest fringe of the middle of the middle class. After working as a journalist on trade papers such as *Gas World*, he entered theatre by becoming an assistant stage manager for a tour, then acting in obscure small-town repertory companies such as Bridgewater and Kidderminster. This period included playing the title role in *Hamlet* in Hayling Island. Two plays, cowritten, were staged unnoticed in small Yorkshire repertory groups in 1950 and 1955; they remain unpublished.

He was engaged as an actor in London for the first time in the spring of 1956, by the English Stage Company. Coincidentally, the company accepted *Look Back*, then staged *The Entertainer* and in 1958 *Epitaph for George Dillon* (written earlier, with Anthony Creighton).

Meanwhile Osborne became a celebrity and he married—his second marriage—actress Mary Ure, who had created the part of Alison in *Look Back*. Their relationship attracted gossip columnists, who were among the targets of his next play, the musical *The World of Paul Slickey*. Critical response was bad and the run short; Osborne claims that the hostile first-night audience pursued him up Shaftesbury Avenue.

Osborne identified fervently with the Left in the essay ''They Call It Cricket'' in 1957, and in the Left-wing weekly *Tribune* he attacked the monarchy, the European Common Market and what he perceived as a drift to nuclear war in a notorious ''open letter'' entitled ''Damn you, England.'' In 1961 he was in Amsterdayamong the well-known names who founded the Committee of 100, to promote British unilateral nuclear disarmament, and was arrested and fined for taking part in a sit-down in Trafalgar Square. In the autobiography written thirty years later he scorns his earlier radicalism and activism.

For a while Osborne was prominent in the British film industry through the filming of *Look Back* and *The Entertainer* and with his only film script, his adaptation of Henry Fielding's *Tom Jones*, acclaimed in 1963.

Admired plays appeared between 1961 and 1971: *Luther*, a turn to history, starring Albert Finney; *Inadmissible Evidence*, starring Nicol Williamson; *A Patriot for Me*, *Time Present*, *The Hotel in Amsterdam*, and *West of Suez*. He adapted a drama by Lope de Vega as *A Bond Honoured* for the National Theatre and later Henrik Ibsen's *Hedda Gabler*, made a last stage appearance in 1964, acted occasionally in television and film, and began writing some television plays.

Osborne's private life continued to be in the public eye as in succeeding years he divorced Ure and married Penelope Gilliatt, a novelist and journalist; divorced Gilliatt and married Jill Bennett, an actress, of whom he writes with incredible viciousness in *Almost a Gentleman*; and divorced Bennett and in 1978 married Helen Dawson, a drama critic. During these years Osborne took on the lifestyle of a country gentleman, first on an estate in Edenbridge, Kent, and then at Craven Arms in Shropshire.

After *Watch It Come Down* was apathetically received at the National Theatre in 1976 comes a sixteen-year gap in stage plays till the appearance of *Déjàvu*, which intriguingly picks up the characters of *Look Back* a generation later. The autobiographies are the chief work of the 1980s. Between 1983 and 1993 four plays of his first decade—*Look Back*, *The Entertainer*, *Inadmissible Evidence*, and *A Patriot for Me*—were successfully revived in London.

Osborne's final work, which occupied the last two years of his life, was a

TV script for Channel 4, about Henry Purcell, an epic contrasting the richness of the art of the Restoration period with what Osborne saw as the mediocrity of his own time.

On 24 December 1994, Osborne died quietly of complications stemming from a diabetic condition.

Selected Biographical Sources: Athanason; Banham; Carter; Corliss; Hayman; Hinchliffe [1]; Trussler [2]; Osborne, *Almost a Gentleman*, *A Better Class of Person*.

MAJOR PLAYS, PREMIERES, AND SIGNIFICANT REVIVALS: THEATRICAL RECEPTION

Look Back in Anger. 1956. Opened 8 May with the English Stage Company at the Royal Court Theatre, London, in repertory. Directed by Tony Richardson. Revivals: Royal Court Theatre, October 1957; Royal Court Theatre, October 1968; Lyric Theatre, London, August 1989.

The myth is that the overnight reviews were damning. *The Times* critic (Review of *Look Back in Anger*) wrote that "its total gesture is altogether inadequate" and Shulman that "it aims at being a despairing cry but achieves only the stature of a self-pitying snivel." The other daily papers gave condescending approval to a faulty new piece, dutifully nodding to the efforts of a beginner. The performances by Kenneth Haigh and Mary Ure were admired. Tynan hailed it "the best young play of the decade." Nevertheless, box office figures suggest that the play was saved more by the showing of an excerpt on television some weeks later than by Tynan's review. Later critics argue that the play was "well-made," conventional, not revolutionary, for example, Thornber's "the last gasp of the old order." Peter [2] places *Look Back* as "the verdict of a young writer on an ageing civilisation." Gross [2] found at the 1989 revival that "it retains its power to grab hold of you and drag you into the lives of its characters."

The Entertainer. 1957. Opened 10 April at the Royal Court Theatre, London; reopened at the Palace Theatre, London, 10 September. Directed by Tony Richardson. Revivals: Greenwich Theatre, November 1974; Shaftesbury Theatre, May 1986.

Expectations aroused by *Look Back in Anger* and Laurence Olivier as the star meant much attention. Most of the praise was for Olivier, Hobson [2] exulting that "you will not see more magnificent acting than this anywhere in the world." Others (e.g., Worsley) faulted the construction and admired the language. Tynan identified the ambition, "putting the whole of contemporary England on to one and the same stage." By 1986, for Nightingale [4] it had "longwindedness"; for Edwards it was "exhaustingly painful," while King found it "still had the power to touch, chill and, in an odd way, even to cheer me." Billington [2] admired "Osborne's capacity to capture the texture of family life''; for Ratcliffe *The Entertainer* is ''a tragedy of twentieth-century English life.''

Luther. 1961. Opened 26 June with the English Stage Company at the Theatre Royal, Nottingham; transferred to Paris, the Royal Court Theatre; to Edinburgh Festival; finally, 5 September, to the Phoenix Theatre, London. Directed by Tony Richardson.

As with *The Entertainer*, Albert Finney taking the title role led to high expectations. Levin and others enjoyed a spectacular production and found in Finney ''a passion, a bursting, writhing conviction of holy righteousness.'' Gascoigne asserted that ''the seal on *Luther*'s excellence is Osborne's language.'' Hope-Wallace [3] complained that ''the theology and sociology seem to have been left out.'' Marcorelles identified ''only Tennessee Williams, with a dash of Brecht [*Galileo*]; or possibly . . . the birth of an English Anouilh.'' Later comment is tentative; Myer describes ''a traditional chronicle play with the faults and virtues of the form . . . worthy and often wordy.''

Inadmissible Evidence. 1964. Opened 9 September at the Royal Court Theatre, London; reopened 13 January 1965, at the Royal Court Theatre, transferred on 17 March to Wyndham's Theatre, London. Directed by Anthony Page. Revivals: Royal Court Theatre, August 1978; Lyttleton Theatre, June 1993.

Cushman explains of this drama that ''for some, it is the first work of his maturity, for others the last flaring of his youthful promise.'' As with most of the previous plays, reviewers especially praised Osborne's flair for language, even if this made his work close to monodrama, and the central performance, by Nicol Williamson. Hope-Wallace [2] complained that ''it makes very little use of dramatic surprise or curiosity,'' Richardson that it is ''a brilliant collection of notes for a play,'' and Seymour [1] that it ''diminishes into time-marking tedium.'' The 1978 revival was for Billington [3] an ''emotional drama of frightening, skull-battering power,'' and in 1993 Coveney found Maitland, the main character, ''one of the towering creations in post-war drama.'' Bryden [3] finds ultimately ''a modern version of *Everyman*.''

A Patriot for Me. 1965. Opened 30 June at the Royal Court Theatre, London. Directed by Anthony Page. Revivals: Palace Theatre, Watford, December 1973; Chichester Festival, May 1983; transferred to the Haymarket Theatre, London, August 1993.

Seymour [2] summed up the varied response: *A Patriot* ''has been highly praised and curtly dismissed. . . . It has that stamp of individuality which prompts clear-cut and decisive reactions.'' Gross [1] faulted ''the almost complete absence of genuine period flavour'' and Young judged its twenty-three scenes ''a very lazy and rather ineffectual way of writing a play.'' Simon, unsure what Osborne wanted to say about either homosexuality or the main character (Redl), found it ''as unnecessary a play as I have ever seen,'' and Kauffmann said that ''the character of Redl is followed, not explored.'' At the 1983 revival

Myers concluded, "As a piece of visual theatre it is stunning, as social comment, out of date." However, Alan Bates in the lead in 1983 impressed more than his predecessors had done, and Billington [3] was struck by him as an "isolated, self-discovering" hero. Findlater placed the essence as "the exploration of emotional ambivalence, social role playing and existential identity."

Time Present. 1968. Opened 23 May at the Royal Court Theatre, London; transferred to the Duke of York's Theatre, London, 11 July. Directed by Anthony Page.

Most comment was markedly and surprisingly negative, most savagely from Spurling: neither the "director, nor any member of his singularly unappealing cast seems to have managed to summon much enthusiasm for their admittedly hard task." Hope-Wallace [4] concluded that "as from so many of Mr. Osborne's plays one comes away with the memory only of a monologue." Bryden [1] thought the supporting characters were "too perfunctorily introduced to create any real conflict or plot," but Esslin praised "the three wickedly well observed show-business characters on the fringe." Esslin, though, saw a "moving and worthy melodramatic plot" resembling those of Noël Coward and Terence Rattigan, and French decided the piece was "a long, dyspeptic bellyache." Bryden [1], in contrast, believed this to be "Osborne's most mature, least self-indulgent play."

The Hotel in Amsterdam. 1968. Opened 3 July at the Royal Court Theatre, London; transferred to New Theatre, London, 6 September, and to the Duke of York's Theatre, London, 12 December. Directed by Anthony Page.

This play immediately followed *Time Present*, had the same director, was published with it, for a while both were advertised with the cryptic phrase "For the Mean Time," and Laurie, the lead, may be seen as a counterpart to Pamela of *Time Present*. Although Bowen criticized "plays of behavior instead of plays of event," Prideaux heard "a tired note of futility" and Hope-Wallace [1] noted that the jokes were "not everyone's cue for laughter," most reviewers enjoyed the drama. Weightman liked the way in which "the quality of a certain type of group friendship" was "delicately rendered." Bryden [2] found Paul Scofield as Laurie "a wonderfully complete tragicomic character, a kind of sold-out D. H. Lawrence of the McLuhan era," and he summed *The Hotel* up as "a powerful, mature moral indictment." Hobson [2] hailed "the best contemporary play in London, the richest in wit, the most arresting in mood . . . the most far-reaching and haunting in resonance."

West of Suez. 1971. Opened 17 August, at the Royal Court Theatre, London; transferred to the Cambridge Theatre, 6 October. Directed by Anthony Page.

Marcus defined the problem with *West of Suez*: "a conversation piece" that "defies classification in political, aesthetic or moral terms"; Wardle [2] and others found it "Chekhovian." Osborne's linguistic flair is again praised: "His uneven love affair with the language is unique on the modern English stage," wrote Dawson [2]. Once more Osborne supplied one dominant part, and the performance by Ralph Richardson was widely admired: Trussler [1] described his "craftily simulated air of absent-mindedness and benignity." Otherwise, the drama divided the critics. Dawson [1] enjoyed "a powerful and passionate work"; Hobson [1] judged "the wit and the theatrical effectiveness" undeniable; Morley [2] found it "potent, thoughtful and eminently entertaining." In contrast, Say defined it as "sprawling untidiness"; Trussler [1] found "it merely irritates"; Nightingale [3] described it as "self-satisfied"; Holland believed it "as sentimentally shallow as Coward."

Déjàvu. 1992. Opened 3 June, at the Comedy Theatre, London. Directed by Tony Palmer.

Coveney [1] enjoyed the play because Osborne "raises bilious invective to an art form and reminds us that good theatre is most powerful when it makes you want to shout back." Billington [1] was "moved by its inextinguishable sense of pain" and liked the "deeply self-referential" quality. Osborne was determinedly politically incorrect in Porter's attacks on feminists and "concern for AIDS sufferers, abused youngsters, the homeless and the handicapped" (Kemp). Such targets, wrote Edwardes, were "either way out of date or all too familiar to young fogeys or readers of *Private Eye*." As a sequel to *Look Back*, it sounded "both unintentionally ironic and intolerably smug" (Peter [1]); for Kemp, "Hark Back in Archness." Peter Egan was found too charming to convince in the central role, and Nightingale [2] expressed a common complaint: "What is missing is much in the way of event, let alone plot."

ADDITIONAL PLAYS AND ADAPTATIONS

Full-length plays: *The Devil Inside* and *Personal Enemy* (both coauthored and unavailable); *Epitaph for George Dillon* (with Anthony Creighton); *The World of Paul Slickey* (Osborne's only musical); *A Sense of Detachment*; *The End of Me Old Cigar*; *Watch It Come Down*.

One-act plays: *The Blood of the Bambergs* and *Under Plain Cover,* staged and published together as *Plays for England*.

Adaptations: *A Bond Honoured* (substantially adapted from Lope de Vega); *Hedda Gabler* (lightly adapted from Ibsen); *A Place Calling Itself Rome* (based on Shakespeare's *Coriolanus* and never performed); *The Picture of Dorian Gray* (from Oscar Wilde's novel); and *The Father* (from August Strindberg).

ASSESSMENT OF OSBORNE'S CAREER

The legendary status of *Look Back in Anger* not only obscures evaluating that drama but misleadingly suggests a falling-off, rather than varied achievements, over the next fifteen years. The plays since 1971, however, have been slight and disappointing.

Look Back in Anger presents Jimmy Porter, of working-class background, graduate of a university that is not even redbrick, but white tile, loving jazz and playing the trumpet, working at a candy stall, apparently an occupation chosen to convey his disillusion with middle-class life. Alison, his upper-middle-class wife, daughter of an Indian Army colonel, toils at the ironing board while Jimmy rages at what he reads in the Sunday newspapers. She eventually moves out and is replaced, at the ironing board and in Jimmy's bed, by an actress, Helena. A sadder, wiser Alison comes back at the end to a sentimental, whimsical reconciliation as a squirrel protected by a bear. The strengths of *Look Back* are its accuracy for a provincial way of life, rarely or never seen on the British stage at the time; an overt sexuality unusual on the British stage; Jimmy's eloquence; and Jimmy's ideas, expressing an unease markedly of the 1950s: "There aren't any good, brave causes left. If the big bang does come, and we all get killed off, it won't be in aid of the old-fashioned grand design. It'll just be for the Brave New-nothing-very-much-thank-you. About as pointless and inglorious as stepping in front of a bus."

Osborne returned to Jimmy Porter thirty-six years later in *Déjàvu*. The new Alison, still at the ironing board, is Jimmy's daughter by a failed second marriage, and the new Helena is a young friend of Alison's who abruptly falls for Jimmy at the act 2 curtain, as another Helena had once done. All the old topics— from Webster to the Bishop of Bromley, from church bells to the candy stall, from Jimmy's trumpet to the word "pusillanimous"—recur. *Déjàvu* is shapeless: Jimmy could orate forever, or at least till he passed out drunk. In a postmodern manner, *Déjàvu* comments on the original play, not merely shifting Jimmy to the 1990s.

Jimmy rants and rages about the state of Britain, exhausted by World War II, adjusting to the collapse of the British Empire, coping with the Cold War and the domination of the United States ("I must say it's pretty dreary living in the American Age—unless you're an American of course"). The condition of England becomes more centrally Osborne's subject in some later plays. *The World of Paul Slickey* takes a scattershot approach to targets from tax collectors to Tory dowagers. The one-acts, *Plays for England*, do not live up to the title: one is a strange study of the fetishism of a happy couple who are revealed to be brother and sister, the other a feeble mockery of the publicity around royal weddings. While *West of Suez* (alluding to Britain gradually abandoning the attempt to have a presence "east of Suez") obliquely reflects on changes in the nation, *The Entertainer* is his most successful and ambitious treatment. English decline is paralleled with the decline of the music hall—fine entertainment in the Edwardian era but in the 1950s seedy, third-rate, dependent on nudes (here, audaciously, a nude as Britannia), shortly to vanish. Old Billy Rice represents the past, his son Archie—putting on an act while dead behind the eyes—the present. The third generation may represent hope. The soldier son is killed in a colonial engagement and the daughter cries out, "Is it really just for the sake of a gloved hand waving at you from a golden coach?" She recovers, to assert at the end: "We've only got ourselves. Somehow, we've just got to make a go of it." Archie chooses England; he won't flee to Canada because "you can't get draught Bass in Toronto." Further, in presenting six members of a family across three generations, Osborne wrote, as Morley [1] put it, "the English *Long Day's Journey into Night*, a vast rambling family tragedy about death and failure and despair."

The theme of the end of the best of what used to be England is found too in the undervalued *Time Present*, in the death offstage of a Grand Old Man of the Theatre. In the foreground is the uneasy friendship of his daughter (an actress) and the woman Labour MP with whom she lives. Yet *Time Present* more accurately belongs with the domestic group among Osborne's work. The actress again has the one big role around whom the others revolve. This is even more true of *Inadmissible Evidence*, which provided a towering part for Nicol Williamson in London, in New York, and on film as a lawyer at the end of his tether. *The Hotel in Amsterdam*, in contrast, manages to be more of an ensemble piece, about six friends, around the movie business, who escape to the Netherlands for a weekend.

Both history plays are large-cast epics. Osborne must have chosen to write of Luther because of a curiosity about the historical roots of protest; he is also influenced by Erik Erikson's psychoanalytic study, *Young Man Luther*. *Luther*, as so often with Osborne, also provided a tremendous role in the title part, played in London and New York by Albert Finney. *A Patriot for Me* re-created life in Austria-Hungary before World War I, rousing interest in an army homosexual scandal.

Osborne's script contributed to the success of the movie *Tom Jones* in 1963; his several television plays appear as minor, ideas perhaps too slight for the stage.

Osborne has one of the gifts of a great playwright, creating distinctive and eloquent language. He has suffered because the huge impact of the first play, *Look Back in Anger*, means all later work has been compared with it. *The Entertainer* and *Luther* rank with the outstanding plays of his time; several others are middle-range achievements—among these are *Inadmissible Evidence* and *The Hotel in Amsterdam*. Others may have been staged and published only because of Osborne's reputation. Finally, critics must note the lower quality, followed by near silence, since the early 1970s.

ARCHIVAL SOURCES

Some material on the English Stage Company, and hence on most of Osborne's plays, is held by the Theatre Museum, Covent Garden, London.

PRIMARY BIBLIOGRAPHY

Plays

Déjàvu. London: Faber & Faber 1991.
The End of Me Old Cigar and *Jack and Jill*. London: Faber & Faber. 1975.
The Entertainer. London: Faber & Faber, 1957.
Epitaph for George Dillon (with Anthony Creighton). London: Faber & Faber, 1958.
Inadmissible Evidence. London: Faber & Faber, 1965.
Look Back in Anger. London: Faber & Faber, 1957.
Luther. London: Faber & Faber, 1961.
A Patriot for Me and *A Sense of Detachment*. London: Faber & Faber, 1983.
Plays for England. (*The Blood of the Bambergs*, *Under Plain Cover*). London: Faber & Faber, 1963.
Time Present and *The Hotel in Amsterdam*. London: Faber & Faber, 1968.
Watch It Come Down. London: Faber & Faber, 1975.
West of Suez. London: Faber & Faber, 1971.
The World of Paul Slickey. London: Faber & Faber, 1959.

Autobiography

Almost a Gentleman. London: Faber & Faber, 1991.
A Better Class of Person. London: Faber & Faber, 1981.

Book and Article on Drama and Theatre

Damn You, England: *Collected Prose*. London: Faber & Faber, 1994.
"They Call It Cricket." In *Declaration*, ed. Tom Machsler. London: MacGibbon & Kee, 1957: 61–84.

Interviews

"John Osborne." *The Playwrights Speak*. Ed. Walter Wager. New York: Dell, 1967: 90–109.
"John Osborne." (with Iain Johnstone). *The Listener* (3 July 1969): 17.
"John Osborne." (with Kenneth Tynan). *The Observer* (30 June 1968): 21; 7 July 1968: 21.
"John Osborne." (with Lewis Funke). *Playwrights Talk about Writing*. Chicago: Dramatic Publishing Co., 1975: 198–216.
"John Osborne." (with Polly Devlin). *Vogue* (June 1964): 98–99, 152, 168.
"John Osborne and the Boys at the Ball." (with A. Alvarez). *New York Times* (28 Sept. 1969): 2: 1, 6.
"Middle Age of the Angry Young Men." (with W. J. Weatherby). *Sunday Times* (1 Mar. 1981): 32–33.

SECONDARY BIBLIOGRAPHY

Anderson, Michael. *Anger and Detachment*. London: Pitman, 1976: 21–49.

Athanason, Arthur N. "John Osborne." In *British Dramatists since World War II*: *A Dictionary of Literary Biography*, ed. Stanley Weintraub. Vol. 13. Detroit: Gale Research, 1982: 371–92.

Banham, Martin. *Osborne*. Edinburgh: Oliver & Boyd, 1969.

Bannerjee, A. "A Modern Hamlet: Jimmy Porter In *Look Back in Anger*." *Hamlet Studies* (New Delhi) 15, 1–2 (summer-winter 1993): 81–92.

Billington, Michael [1]. "*Cri de Coeur* of an Eloquent Misfit." *Manchester Guardian Weekly* (21 June 1992): 23.

———[2]. "Keeping It in the Family." *Manchester Guardian Weekly* (22 June 1986).

———[3]. *One Night Stands*. London: Nick Hern, 1993: 126–27, 196–97.

Bowen, John. "Melancholy Jacques." *London Magazine* (8 Sept. 1968): 106.

Brown, John Russell. *Theatre Language*. London: Allen Lane, Penguin Press, 1972: 118–57.

Browne, Terry. *Playwrights' Theatre: The English Stage Company at the Royal Court*. London: Pitman, 1975.

Bryden, Ronald [1]. "Daughter in Revolt." *The Observer* (26 May 1968): 30.

———[2]. "Studies in Survival." *The Observer* (7 July 1968).

———[3]. *The Unfinished Hero*. London: Faber & Faber, 1969: 76–80.

Carter, Alan. *John Osborne*. Rev. ed. Edinburgh: Oliver & Boyd, 1973.

Corliss, Richard. "Obituary. The First Angry Man: John Osborne, 1929–1994." *Time* (9 Jan. 1995): 75.

Coveney, Michael [1]. "Something to Shout Back About." *The Observer* (14 June 1992): 65.

———[2]. "A Stiff Line in Vulgarity." *The Observer* (20 June 1993): 57.

Cushman, Robert. "Racing to Destruction." *The Observer* (17 Sept. 1978).

Dawson, Helen [1]. "Osborne's Island." *The Observer* (22 Aug. 1971): 24.

———[2]. Review of *West of Suez*. *The Observer* (10 Oct. 1971).

Denning, B. "John Osborne's War against the Philistines." *Hudson Review* 11 (1959): 411–19.

Dixon, Graham A. "Still Looking Back: The Deconstruction of the Angry Young Man in *Look Back in Anger* and *Déjàvu*." *Modern Drama* 37.3 (fall 1994): 521–29.

Edwardes, Jane. *Déjàvu*. *Time Out* (17 June 1992).

Edwards, Christopher. "Moments from History." *The Spectator* (21 June 1986): 33.

Elsom, John [1]. *Post-war British Theatre*. London: Routledge & Kegan Paul, 1976: 72–81.

———, ed. [2]. *Post-war British Theatre Criticism*. London: Routledge & Kegan Paul, 1981.

Esslin, Martin. "Anger, Twelve Years On." *Plays and Players* (July 1968): 25.

Evans, Gareth Lloyd. *The Language of Modern Drama*. London: Dent, 1977: 102–13.

Evans, Gareth, and Barbara Evans, eds. *Plays in Review, 1956–1980*. London: Batsford, 1985.

Ferrar, Harold. *John Osborne*. New York: Columbia University Press, 1973.

Findlater, Richard. "*A Patriot for Me*." *Plays and Players* (July 1983): 28–29.

French, Philip. *New Statesman* (31 May 1968): 737.

Gale, Steven H. "John Osborne: Look Forward in Fear." In *Essays on Contemporary British Drama*, ed. Hedwig Bock and Albert Wertheim. Munich: Max Hueber, 1981: 5–29.

Gascoigne, Bamber. "First Person Singular." *The Spectator* (4 Aug. 1961).

Gersh, Gabriel. "The Theatre of John Osborne." *Modern Drama* 10.3 (Sept. 1967): 137–43.

Goldstone, Herbert. *Coping with Vulnerability: The Achievement of John Osborne*. Lanham, MD: University Press of America, 1982.

Gross, John [1]. "Rebels and Renegades." *Encounter* (Oct. 1965): 42.

———[2]. "When Jimmy Raged and Alison Lay Down." *Sunday Telegraph* (13 Aug. 1989).

Hayman, Ronald. *John Osborne*. Rev. ed. London: Heinemann, 1972.

Hinchliffe, Arnold [1]. *John Osborne*. Boston: Twayne, 1984.

———[2]. "Whatever Happened to John Osborne?" In *Contemporary English Drama*, ed. C.W.E. Bigsby. London: Arnold, 1981: 52–63.

Hobson, Harold [1]. "Empire at Sunset." *Sunday Times* (10 Oct. 1971).

———[2]. Review of *The Entertainer*. *Sunday Times* (14 Apr. 1957).

———[3]. "Prisoners of Freedom." *Sunday Times* (7 July 1968): 49.

Holland, Mary. Review of *West of Suez*. *Plays and Players* (Oct. 1971): 38.

Hope-Wallace, Philip [1]. "Getting Away from It All." *Manchester Guardian Weekly* (11 July 1968).

———[2]. Review of *Inadmissible Evidence*. *The Guardian* (11 Sept. 1964).

———[3]. "A Masterpiece with Flaws." *The Guardian* (28 July 1961).

———[4]. Review of *Time Present*. *The Guardian* (24 May 1968).

Hunter, G. K. "The World of John Osborne." *Critical Quarterly* 3 (1961): 76–81.

Innes, Christopher. *Modern British Drama, 1890–1990*, Cambridge: Cambridge University Press, 1992: 98–113.

Karrfalt, David H. "The Social Theme in Osborne's Plays." *Modern Drama* 13.1 (Mar. 1970): 78–82.

Kauffmann, Stanley. *Persons of the Drama*. New York: Harper & Row, 1976: 181–83.

Kemp, Peter. "Tantrums and Teddy Bears." *Times Literary Supplement* (19 June 1992): 18.

Kennedy, Andrew. *Six Dramatists in Search of a Language*. Cambridge: Cambridge University Press, 1975: 192–212.

Kershaw, John. *The Present Stage*. London: Fontana, 1966: 21–42.

King, Francis. "Pearls before Swine." *Sunday Telegraph* (15 June 1986): 18.

Lahr, John. "Poor Johnny One-Note." *Up Against the Fourth Wall*. New York: Grove Press, 1970: 230–45.

Levin, Bernard. "I Salute the Golden Ageing of Albert Finney." *Daily Express* (6 Sept. 1961).

Review of *Look Back in Anger*. *The Times* (9 May 1956).

Marcorelles, Louis. "Luther as a Mixed-up Kid." *Encore* (Sept.–Oct. 1961): 32–36.

Marcus, Frank. "Conversation Piece." *Sunday Telegraph* (10 Oct. 1971): 18.

Marowitz, Charles [1]. *Confessions of a Counterfeit Critic*. London: Eyre Methuen, 1973.

———[2]. "Obituary: John Osborne." *Theatre Week* (9 Jan. 1995): 24.

Martin, Graham. "A Look Back at Osborne." *Universities & Left Review* 7 (autumn 1959): 37–40.

Morley, Sheridan [1]. *Our Theatre in the Eighties*. London: Hodder & Stoughton, 1990: 142–43.

———[2]. *Review Copies*. London: Robson, 1974: 87–88.

Myer, Michael Grosvenor. "*Luther*." *The Guardian* (15 Nov. 1985): 17.

Myers, Kathy. Review of *A Patriot for Me*. *City Limits* (20–26 May 1983).

Nightingale, Benedict [1]. "The Fatality of Hatred." *Encounter* 58 (May 1982): 63–70.

———[2]. "Is There Life beyond the Whinge?" *The Times* (12 June 1992).

———[3]. "Osborne's Old Times." *New Statesman* (27 Aug. 1971): 277.

———[4]. "Twat in the Sea." *New Statesman* (20 June 1986): 28.

Peter, John [1]. "Middle-Age Dread." *Sunday Times* (14 June 1992): 7: 8.

———[2]. "Young Man's Anger That Still Exposes an Age of Weakness." *Sunday Times* (13 Aug. 1989): C7.

Prater, Eugene Greeley. *An Existential View of John Osborne*. Freeman, SD: Pine Hill Press, 1993.

Prideaux, Tom. "Johnny's Dying One-Note." *Life* (2 Aug. 1968).

Rabey, David I. *British and Irish Political Drama in the Twentieth Century*. London: Macmillan, 1986: 78–84.

Ratcliffe, Michael. "Kate Ducks the Issues." *The Observer* (15 June 1986): 21.

Richardson, Jack. "The Best of Broadway." *Commentary* (Mar. 1966): 75.

Roberts, Mark. *The Tradition of Romantic Morality*. London: Macmillan, 1973: 1–26.

Rupp, Gordon. "Luther and Mr Osborne." *Cambridge Quarterly* 1 (winter 1965–66): 28–42.

Say, Rosemary. "One-Man Show." *Sunday Telegraph* (22 Aug. 1971): 12.

Seymour, Alan [1]. Review of *Inadmissible Evidence*. *The Observer* (21 Mar. 1965).

———[2]. "A Maturing Vision." *London Magazine* (Oct. 1965): 75–79.

Shulman, Milton. Review of *Look Back in Anger*. *Evening Standard* (9 May 1956).

Simon, John. *Uneasy Stages*. New York: Random House, 1975: 218–20.

Spurling, Hilary. "Ustiborne and Osnov." *The Spectator* (31 May 1968): 752.

Taylor, John Russell [1]. *Anger and After*. Rev. ed. London: Methuen, 1969: 39–66.

———, ed. [2]. *John Osborne: "Look Back in Anger": A Casebook*. London: Macmillan, 1968.

Thornber, Robin. "*Look Back in Anger*." *The Guardian* (12 Mar. 1992).

Trussler, Simon [1]. "Demonstration of Failure." *Tribune* (3 Sept. 1971).

———[2]. *John Osborne*. London: Longmans Green for British Council, 1969.

———[3]. *The Plays of John Osborne*. London: Gollancz, 1969.

Tynan, Kenneth. *A View of the English Stage*. London: Davis-Poynter, 1975: 176–78, 201–3.

Wandor, Michelene. *Look Back in Gender*. London: Methuen, 1987: 8–18.

Wardle, Irving [1]. "Looking Back on Osborne's Anger." *New Society* (16 June 1966): 22–23.

———[2]. Review of *West of Suez*. *The Times* (18 Aug. 1971).

Weiand, Hermann J., ed. "John Osborne." *Insight IV*. Frankfurt am Main: Hirschgraben Verlag, 1976: 93–102.

Weightman, John. "Grousers, Male and Female." *Encounter* (31 Sept. 1968): 45.

Worsley, T. C. "England, Our England." *New Statesman* (21 Sept. 1957): 343.

Worth, Katharine J. *Revolutions in Modern English Drama*. London: G. Bell, 1973: 67–85.

Young, B. A. *The Mirror up to Nature*. London: Kimber, 1982: 34–36.

BIBLIOGRAPHIES

King, Kimball. ''John Osborne.'' *Twenty Modern British Playwrights: A Bibliography, 1956 to 1976*. New York: Garland, 1977: 85–124.

Northouse, Cameron, and Thomas P. Walsh. *John Osborne: A Reference Guide*. Boston: G. K. Hall, 1974.

Page, Malcolm. *File on Osborne*. London: Methuen, 1988.

Louise Page

(1955–)

KURT EISEN

Since 1976, when her one-act *Want-Ad* was given a reading at the Royal Court—also the year she took her undergraduate degree—Louise Page has been writing plays that explore the often hidden aspects of women's lives and histories. Page's circumspect brand of feminism, as well as her closely observed portraits of frustration and compromise, have made her work the object of critical debate.

Born 7 March 1955 in London, Page lived subsequently in Liverpool and, from the age of five, in Sheffield. At five she also announced her ambition to become a writer; by age ten she was writing extravagant historical romances, with illustrations. In high school Page worked one hour each day on writing a novel she would eventually label, ''Please burn when I die.'' Meanwhile, friends to whom she read her fiction began to act out the narratives, which lead her to include more dialogue and ultimately to writing plays as such.

After reading in drama and theatre arts at the University of Birmingham, Page took a postgraduate diploma in theatre studies at the University of Wales, Cardiff, in 1977. The same year saw her play *Glasshouse* produced in Edinburgh and *Want-Ad* produced on tour. The following year *Tissue*, in which a case of breast cancer provokes questions about women's selves and sexuality, was produced in Birmingham, and a thirty-minute play about police justice, *Saturday, Late September*, was broadcast on BBC Radio.

From 1979 to 1981 Page was Yorkshire Television Fellow in Creative Writing at the University of Sheffield, while also finishing *Hearing* (1979), *Flaws* (1980), and *Housewives*, which was produced in 1981 for both radio and stage. Also broadcast on BBC Radio were *Angus Dei* (1980) and *Armistice* (1983). For television Page wrote the courtroom drama *Peanuts* (1982), the satirical *DIY in Venice* (1982), the series *Legs Eleven* (1984), and *Birds' Heads and Fishes'*

Tails (1986). In 1982 she won the George Devine Award and was appointed writer-in-residence at the Royal Court Theatre for 1982–1983.

Page scored her first major London production in 1982 with *Salonika*, her meditation on aging, love, and war; in 1985 the play had its New York premiere. After collaborating in 1983 as creative editor of the letters and interviews that comprise *Falkland Sound/Voces de Malvinas*, Page kept busy with London productions of *Real Estate* and *Golden Girls* (both in 1984) and a reworking of the fairy tale *Beauty and the Beast* (1985), commissioned by the Women's Playhouse Trust. The anti-Thatcherite *Hawks and Doves*, commissioned by the Royal Shakespeare Company in 1986, is still unproduced. Her most recently produced dramas include *Goat* (1986), the radio play *Working Out* (1988), *Diplomatic Wives* (1989), the children's play *Toby and Donna* (published in 1989), *Adam Was a Gardener* (1991), and *Like to Live* (1991), which imagines Hermione's sixteen-year exile in *A Winter's Tale*; in 1992 it was double-billed off-Broadway with *Tissue*. Page's *Royal Blood Bath 3*, adapted for children from Sophocles' *Antigone*, was funded by a 1992 educational grant to the Royal Shakespeare Company.

Selected Biographical Sources: ''Beauty and the Beast''; ''Emotion Is a Theatrical Weapon''; ''Louise Page.''

MAJOR PLAYS, PREMIERES, AND SIGNIFICANT REVIVALS: THEATRICAL RECEPTION

Hearing. 1979. Opened at the Birmingham Repertory Theatre. Directed by Ian Kellgren.

Treating the social, political, and psychological aspects of physical disability, this is the first of Page's two sweets-factory plays (the second was *Flaws* [1980]). Shorter [1] found most of the scenes too long and judged the play too slight to confirm the playwright's talent. Focusing more on the play's themes and plot, Aire stressed the relationship between the mother and her deaf adult daughter and commended Page for promoting greater awareness of neglected social problems.

Salonika. 1982. Opened 2 August at the Royal Court Theatre Upstairs, London. Directed by Danny Boyle. Opened 2 April 1985, at the Public/Anspacher Theater (NY).

Commissioned by the Royal Court to write on the theme of old age while herself only in her mid-twenties, Page also treats sex, war, and remembrance in this beach-resort idyll that baffled as many critics as it pleased. Enthusiastic reviews by Darvell and Mackenzie [2] affirmed the young playwright's maturity, and even largely negative reviews by Shorter [2] and King [3] conceded Page's future promise. Shulman [4] typified dissenting London critics in finding the ideas unclear. Franey, Shorter [2], and Morley [3] likewise discerned a rambling structure that imposed no clear pattern on individual details. Chaillet, Franey, and Mackenzie [2] noted the play's dreamlike quality; Shorter [2] and King [3] likened Page's sense of time past to J. M. Barrie's. Cushman [2] praised the handling of the ghost character, coining the term "retrospective beach-drama" for this and *Summer* by Edward Bond (a playwright whose influence Page has acknowledged). In 1985 New York critics had trouble discerning the play's meaning. Noting the parallels to Bond and Barrie, Rich [1] considered only the first act successful. Oliver [2] disliked the play's abstractions but found the general mood haunting, but Simon [2] dismissed the writing as "too clean, too remote, like a handshake with gloves on."

Falkland Sound/Voces de Malvinas. 1983. Opened 7 June at the Royal Court Theatre Upstairs, London. Directed by Max Stafford-Clark. Revival: Royal Court Theatre Upstairs, London, May 1990.

The posthumously published letters of Lt. David Tinker, killed on HMS *Glamorgan* during the Falklands war in 1982, form the basis of the first part of this work, with the second half compiled and edited by Page from taped interviews with others who directly or indirectly participated in the war. Most critics preferred the half based on Tinker's letters. Of the second half, Asquith [1] praised Page for her impressive editing of the interviews, but found some of it rambling, while de Jongh [1] called it anticlimactic. Billington [1] also noted the diminished force of the second half, but commended Page for constructing it as "less an anti-war diatribe than a feeling of the texture of ordinary lives." Reviewing the 1990 revival, Wardle [2] commended a lack of manipulation in Page's editing, while Hiley [1] praised her for avoiding "easy sentiment."

Real Estate. 1984. Opened 3 May at the Tricycle Theatre, London. Directed by Pip Broughton. Opened 4 March 1985, at the Arena Stage, Washington, D.C. Revival: December 1987, at the Theatre at St. Peter's Church (NY).

Written deliberately in response to *Salonika* at a time when Page carried the mixed-blessing label of "most promising," this "post-feminist kitchen sink" drama (Radin) explores both mother-daughter relations and traditional gender roles. Most reviewers of the London, Washington, and New York productions approved the ideas or situation as well as Page's thoughtful writing but deemed the resolution contrived or improbable. London critics, including Radin, Coveney, and Gordon also faulted the slow pacing of director Broughton, although Billington [2] stressed the playwright's own tedious exposition and the isolated "goldfish-bowl quality" of the action. Todd found the play's provocative insights undermined by a naturalistic form reminiscent of soap opera. Gordon praised the dignified and affectionate characterizations, but Gardner [3] found them emotionally shallow, "merely ciphers for topical attitudes and ideas." Among American critics Gussow [2] had strongest praise for Page's characterizations, but Rich [2] judged this play no better than *Salonika* at conveying emotion. Both Wittenberg and Simon [1] condemned the play as boring, hackneyed feminism, while Barnes declared the ending not so much contrived as unrevealing of the playwright's views, although he liked the formal tone of the dialogue. Noting her preference for *Salonika*, Oliver [1] found the characters too conspicuously manipulated by the playwright.

Golden Girls. 1984. Opened 20 June at the Other Place, Royal Shakespeare Company, Stratford-upon-Avon; moved to the Royal Shakespeare Company's Barbican Pit, London, in April 1985. Directed by Barry Kyle.

Commissioned by the Royal Shakespeare Company, this play takes up the theme of women's ambition evident in earlier works, this time complicated by conflicts of race and class and placed within the context of the ill-defined boundary between amateur and professional sports. The critics were mixed as usual on Page's writing but generally spoke well of Barry Kyle's direction and unanimously praised Josette Simon's performance as the senior member of the relay team. Wardle [1] and Tinker [2] likened Page's writing to that of a best-selling novelist, and Evans offered a dismissive, almost ranting critique of Page's writing, crediting the production's successes entirely to director Kyle. Hirschhorn, de Jongh [2], Gussow [3], and Morley [1] all praise Page's handling of multiple relationships and themes, whereas McFerran [2], Gardner [2], Hiley [2], and Asquith [2] complained of too many thematic or narrative strands. Hoyle [2] and McFerran [2] deemed its treatment of explicitly feminist issues unsatisfying. Many critics also faulted the use of cynical hack journalism as a plot device, but, they just as widely applauded was the strobe lighting in the climactic race scene.

Beauty and the Beast. 1985. Opened 26 November at the Liverpool Playhouse; moved 27 December to the Old Vic Theatre, London. Directed by Jules Wright.

The first play co-commissioned by the Women's Playhouse Trust and Methuen London, this refashioning of Mme. de Villeneuve's 1740 fairy tale incorporates an elaborate background with fairies in conflict with mortals. Critical response was divided on Page's expansion of the traditional tale. McFerran [1], Sutcliffe, and Shulman [1] found the plot cumbersome or convoluted, while Barber [1] and Gardner [1] registered a strong preference for Page's return to more familiar aspects of the tale in the play's second half. Grove praised Page's writing as "rich and complex," although Hoyle [1] and Shulman [1] found it stilted and formal. Gardner [1] and Barber [1] noted a lack of humor, although the fairy element reminded Barber [1] of *A Midsummer Night's Dream.* Hoyle [1], Ratcliffe, King [1], McFerran [1], and Gardner [1] all praised the production's visual effects, while Grove observed that children in the audience seemed captivated. More recently, Llewellyn-Jones has judged that the play pursues technical experimentation at the expense of its subversive ideological opportunities.

Goat. 1986. Opened 12 February at the Warwick Arts Centre. Directed by Pip Broughton.

First staged as a twenty-minute monologue at the Royal Shakespeare Company-W. H. Smith Stratford Youth Festival in 1984, this eighty-minute one-woman show was performed on tour in early 1986 by Paines Plough, also called the Writers Company. Especially resenting the device of directing the monologue at the audience as if it were the laboratory animal of the title, Cropper called the writing ''prolix, misconceived, confused, and confusing'' and acknowledged value only in the play's matrix of scientific, political, and ethical issues. Russell found the psychological exposition muddled but deemed the play worthwhile at least for its memorable verbal images. More recently, Llewellyn-Jones has called it ''gripping in performance,'' potent both emotionally and intellectually.

Diplomatic Wives. 1989. Opened 2 March at the Palace Theatre, Watford. Directed by Lou Stein.

Neither Wardle [2] nor Peter [1] found much to like in this story of a wife who relinquishes her own foreign-service career for the sake of her husband's less promising one. Wardle [2] called the writing ''limp and confusing,'' perhaps the result of what he called ''the author's determination never to judge anyone.'' Peter [1] acknowledged some promising dramatic issues but faulted the execution as ''almost didactic'' and ultimately unconvincing. Llewellyn-Jones, however, has cited this play as an example of Page's tendency to evade clear ideological positions, and of her ambiguous feminism.

Adam Was a Gardener. 1991. Opened 4 September at the Minerva Studio, Chichester. Directed by Caroline Sharman.

This ''evocative love affair between the past and the present'' (the play's subtitle) brings together an eighteenth-century man and a twentieth-century woman by means of a garden that he has designed and that she wishes to re-create from his notebooks. Critics unanimously praised Page's intelligence, but both Taylor and Nightingale [1] found the dialogue emotionally constrained. Macaulay praised the convincing eighteenth-century diction in the script and found the contrast of sensibilities absorbing. Spencer likewise endorsed the play's central idea, but deemed the characterizations vague and much of the writing less than vital.

ASSESSMENT OF PAGE'S CAREER

Page has attributed her success to coming along at a period ''when everyone wanted plays by women'' (''Beauty and the Beast''). The timing of Page's emergence does underscore two crucial aspects of her career. First, the exact nature of her feminist beliefs has certainly been the most persistent question raised by critics and interviewers, but equally important is the example of Page as a prolific and versatile artist in a medium notoriously unaccommodating to women writers. Likewise, the conflict between Wandor's account of Page's work as ''bourgeois feminist'' and Page's description of herself as ''socialist feminist'' (see ''Beauty and the Beast'') points to a key problem in assessing her career: that is, whether her sensitive dramatic treatments of several neglected aspects of women's lives in itself constitutes a subversive feminist agenda or if, as Wandor's phrase implies, her work ultimately fails to challenge the basic assumptions of middle-class culture.

Page's rejection of an agitprop or overtly confrontational style in favor of meditative, often ambiguous portraiture has bothered critics such as Wardle [2], who prefer more clearcut political stances. Page tries typically to cast light on facets of personal life that resonate with larger political import. Her earliest plays are built on specific themes that serve as critiques of British society in the 1970s. *Want-Ad*, for instance, examines the struggles of a young unwed mother but also condemns the brand of journalism that exploits personal tragedy; *Lucy* takes up the ethics of euthanasia, while *Tissue* confronts prevalent images of female sexuality and subjectivity by focusing on a young woman facing the prospect of a mastectomy. *Hearing* and *Flaws* both condemn the exploitation of factory workers and thus come closest to direct sociopolitical critique, but neither is primarily a "feminist" work.

In her breakthrough works of the 1980s, Page scrutinizes the choices women make in fashioning their lives, particularly the motives and costs of their ambitions. Indeed, the need for choice—whether this need is called "bourgeois" or "socialist"—may be called the crux of Page's drama and politics. Although she avoids official academic affiliations, Page sees her role as largely educative: to provoke thought rather than to offer a cathartic finale. The persistently mixed reviews of all her plays are themselves an indication of Page's relentless need to leave questions open.

Salonika established this pattern of critical response among London and New York reviewers while affirming Page's interest in technical experimentation. This play also established her as a writer of commissioned works, supported by patrons such as the Royal Court, the Royal Shakespeare Company, and the Women's Playhouse Trust, in addition to her many radio and television scripts. Her timing may have been lucky, but Page deserves credit for forging an exemplary career as a working playwright in Thatcherite Britain and afterward. Critics have acknowledged a particular strength in her work of these years, especially *Real Estate*: her sympathetic male characters. Page sees this as a way to avoid merely "preaching to the converted" and to show that men can also be agents of change ("Emotion Is a Theatrical Weapon").

With *Golden Girls* Page seems almost to be meditating on the cost of her own ambitions. Less experimental than *Salonika*, *Real Estate*, or even the expressionistic *Tissue*, *Golden Girls* is nonetheless dazzling for the excess of its thematic concerns, especially its willingness to tackle issues of race, class, and gender. Page's portrayal of the convergent demands of corporate and athletic success is shrewd, since in both the status of women may be quantified. Again the themes of choice and control are central: in exchange for corporate sponsorship and the chance of an Olympic gold medal, the athletes find themselves ceding control of their lives and bodies. Page's awareness that her own success in securing commissions is still the exception to a persistent bias against women playwrights may be discerned in the corporate or institutional pressures that descend on the "Golden Girls" of the women's relay team.

Llewellyn-Jones's judgment that "Page's plays tend more to experiment in technique than to develop ideological positions" overlooks the subversive, if subtle, effects of those innovations. For example, by recovering the older version of *Beauty and the Beast* with its fairy element and warrior queen motif, Page directs interest away from the beast-prince and his redemption through love. In the more conventional *Diplomatic Wives*, Page admits that her ending is "defeatist" since a talented woman rejects her career in favor of her marriage, but she also insists on its Brechtian captivity to "show" the pressures that too frequently force women to choose between an emotionally barren career and an intellectually stultifying marriage ("Emotion Is a Theatrical Weapon").

Clearly less boldly innovative than, for instance, Caryl Churchill and less overtly political than such feminist groups as the Monstrous Regiment or Women's Theatre Group, Page's preference for a quieter subversiveness that emphasizes education at least partly explains why she has turned recently to writing plays for younger audiences, including *Toby and Donna* (written in 1983, published in 1989), which treats the theme of date rape, and *Royal Blood Bath 3*, her 1992 adaptation of Sophocles' *Antigone*. In her introduction to *Plays: One* Page notes that for her writing is itself an educational process. At a point in her life that may fairly be termed "mid-career," Page continues to learn her craft. Perhaps her work belongs in spirit to the Thatcher era, of which it serves as both critique and chronicle; it remains to be seen if Page can return to the eminence that gained her productions on both sides of the Atlantic.

PRIMARY BIBLIOGRAPHY

Plays

Beauty and the Beast. London: Methuen, 1986.
Diplomatic Wives. London: Methuen, 1989.
Golden Girls. London: Methuen, 1985.
Real Estate. London: Methuen, 1985.
Salonika. London: Methuen, 1983.
Tissue. In *Plays by Women 1*, ed. Michelene Wandor. London: Methuen, 1982.
Toby and Donna. In *They Said You Were Too Young*, ed. Rony Robinson. London: Hodder & Stoughton, 1989.

Collection

Plays: One. (*Tissue, Salonika, Real Estate, The Guardian*.) London: Methuen, 1990.

Interviews

"Beauty among the 'Beasts' " (with Barney Bardsley). *Drama* 157 (185): 13–15.
"Beauty and the Beast" (with Claire Yandell). *Women's Review* 3 (1986): 30–31.

"Behind the Fringe" (with Oscar Moore). *Plays and Players* 360 (1983): 20–22.
"Cultivating the Land" (with Sabine Durrant). *Independent* (21 Aug. 1991): 22.
"Emotion Is a Theatrical Weapon" (with Elizabeth Sakellaridou). *New Theatre Quarterly* 6 (1990): 174–87.
"Interview with the Author" (with Rony Robinson). *They Said You Were Too Young.* London: Hodder & Stoughton, 1989: 157–59.
"Louise Page." *Interviews with Contemporary Women Playwrights.* Ed. Kathleen Betsko and Rachel Koenig. New York: Beech Tree, 1987: 353–64.

SECONDARY BIBLIOGRAPHY

Aire, Sally. Review of *Hearing. Plays and Players* (July 1979): 32–33.
Allen, Paul. Review of *Housewives. Drama* 140 (1981): 37–38.
Asquith, Ross [1]. Review of *Falkland Sound/Voces de Malvinas. City Limits* (June 1983).
———[2]. Review of *Golden Girls. The Observer* (2 May 1985).
Barber, John [1]. Review of *Beauty and the Beast. Daily Telegraph* (23 Dec. 1985).
———[2]. Review of *Falkland Sound/Voces de Malvinas. Daily Telegraph* (June 1983).
———[3]. Review of *Golden Girls. Daily Telegraph* (30 Apr. 1985).
Bardsley, Barney. Review of *Real Estate. Tribune* (1 June 1984).
Barnes, Clive. "Questionable Values in 'Real Estate.' " *New York Post* (2 Dec. 1987).
Beaufort, John. Review of *Real Estate. Christian Science Monitor* (9 Dec. 1987).
Billington, Michael [1]. Review of *Falkland Sound/Voces de Malvinas. The Guardian* (June 1983).
———[2]. Review of *Real Estate. The Guardian* (8 May 1984).
Caplan, Betty. "Quests for Truth." *New Statesman and Society* (27 Nov. 1992): 35–36.
Carne, Rosalind. Review of *Salonika. Financial Times* (Aug. 1982).
Chaillet, Ned. Review of *Salonika. The Times* (3 Aug. 1982): 7.
Cohen, Ron. Review of *Real Estate. Women's Wear Daily* (2 Dec. 1987).
Coveney, Michael. Review of *Real Estate. Financial Times* (9 May 1984).
Cropper, Martin. Review of *Goat. The Times* (18 Feb. 1986): 15.
Cushman, Robert [1]. Review of *Falkland Sound/Voces de Malvinas. The Observer* (June 1983).
———[2]. "Ghost of *Salonika." The Observer* (8 Aug. 1982): 27.
Darvell, Michael. Review of *Salonika. What's on in London* (Aug. 1982).
de Jongh, Nicholas [1]. Review of *Falkland Sound/Voces de Malvinas. Mail on Sunday* (June 1983).
———[2]. Review of *Golden Girls. The Guardian* (30 Apr. 1985).
Edwardes, Jane. Review of *Real Estate. Time Out* (10 May 1984).
Evans, Gareth Lloyd. "Midlands: Neither Good nor Evil." *Drama* 154 (1984): 41.
Franey, Ros. Review of *Salonika. City Limits* (Aug. 1982).
Gardner, Lyn [1]. Review of *Beauty and the Beast. City Limits* (3 Jan. 1986).
———[2]. Review of *Golden Girls. City Limits* (3 May 1985).
———[3]. Review of *Real Estate. City Limits* (18 May 1984).
Gold, Sylviane. Review of *Real Estate. Wall Street Journal* (9 Dec. 1987): 36.
Gordon, Giles. Review of *Real Estate. The Spectator* (19 May 1984).
Grove, Valerie. Review of *Beauty and the Beast. Londard Standard* (20 Dec. 1985).

Gussow, Mel [1]. "Her Dramas Ponder the Price of Liberation." *New York Times* (6 Dec. 1987): 2: 5.

——[2]. " 'Real Estate' Has Premiere in Capital." *New York Times* (6 Mar. 1985): C20.

——[3]. "Stratford Keeps Its Kingly Standards." *New York Times* (12 Aug. 1984): 2: 5.

Hiley, Jim [1]. Review of *Falkland Sound. The Listener* (24 May 1990).

——[2]. Review of *Golden Girls. The Listener* (9 May 1985).

Hirschhorn, Clive. Review of *Golden Girls. Sunday Express* (12 May 1985).

Holden, Stephen. Review of *Like to Live* and *Tissue. New York Times* (6 May 1992): C18.

Hoyle, Martin [1]. Review of *Beauty and the Beast. Financial Times* (20 Dec. 1985).

——[2]. Review of *Golden Girls. Financial Times* (30 Apr. 1985).

Khan, Naseem [1]. "Go-Getting." *New Statesman* (29 June 1984): 29.

——[2]. "London Fringe: Black Missionaries." *Drama* 153 (1984): 33–36.

King, Francis [1]. Review of *Beauty and the Beast. Sunday Telegraph* (29 Dec. 1985).

——[2]. Review of *Falkland Sound/Voces de Malvinas. Sunday Telegraph* (June 1983).

——[3]. Review of *Salonika. Sunday Telegraph* (Aug. 1982).

Kingston, Jeremy. Review of *Like to Live. The Times* (27 Dec. 1991): 10.

Kissel, Howard. "A Real 'Real Estate.' " *New York Daily News* (2 Dec. 1987).

Llewellyn-Jones, Margaret. "Claiming a Space." In *British and Irish Women Dramatists since 1958: A Critical Handbook*, ed. Trevor R. Griffiths and Margaret Llewellyn-Jones. Buckingham: Open University Press, 1993: 41–46.

Macaulay, Alastair. Review of *Adam Was a Gardener. Financial Times* (6 Sept. 1991).

Mackenzie, Suzie [1]. Review of *Falkland Sound/Voces de Malvinas. Time Out* (June 1983).

——[2]. Review of *Salonika. Time Out* (Aug. 1982).

McFerran, Ann [1]. Review of *Beauty and the Beast. Time Out* (2 Jan. 1986).

——[2]. Review of *Golden Girls. Time Out* (2 May 1985).

Morley, Sheridan [1]. Review of *Falkland Sound/Voces de Malvinas. Punch* (June 1983).

——[2]. Review of *Golden Girls. Punch* (15 May 1985).

——[3]. Review of *Salonika. Punch* (Aug. 1982).

Nightingale, Benedict [1]. Review of *Adam Was a Gardener. The Times* (5 Sept. 1991).

——[2]. Review of *Golden Girls. New Statesman* (3 May 1985).

Oliver, Edith [1]. Review of *Real Estate. The New Yorker* (14 Dec. 1987): 119.

——[2]. Review of *Salonika. The New Yorker* (15 Apr. 1985): 96.

Peter, John [1]. Review of *Diplomatic Wives. Sunday Times* (19 Mar. 1989): C11.

——[2]. Review of *Salonika. The New Yorker* (15 April 1985): 96.

Radin, Victoria. Review of *Real Estate. The Observer* (13 May 1984).

Ratcliffe, Michael. Review of *Beauty and the Beast. The Observer* (29 Dec. 1985).

Rich, Frank [1]. "On the Beach." *New York Times* (3 Apr. 1985): C17.

——[2]. " 'Real Estate,' By Author of 'Salonika' " *New York Times* (2 Dec. 1987): 28.

Russell, Barry. Review of *Goat. Drama* 160 (1986): 39.

Say, Rosemary. Review of *Golden Girls. Sunday Telegraph* (5 May 1985).

Shorter, Eric [1]. Review of *Hearing. Drama* 133 (1979): 66.

——[2]. Review of *Salonika. Daily Telegraph* (Aug. 1982).

Shulman, Milton [1]. Review of *Beauty and the Beast*. *Evening Standard* (23 Dec. 1985).

———[2]. Review of *Falkland Sound/Voces de Malvinas*. *Evening Standard* (June 1983).

———[3]. Review of *Golden Girls*. *Evening Standard* (30 Apr. 1985).

———[4]. Review of *Salonika*. *Evening Standard* (Aug. 1982).

Simon, John [1]. Review of *Real Estate*. *New York* (11 Jan. 1988): 58.

———[2]. Review of *Salonika*. *New York* (15 Apr. 1985): 95.

Spencer, Charles, Review of *Adam Was a Gardener*. *Daily Telegraph* (10 Sept. 1991).

Sutcliffe, Tom. Review of *Beauty and the Beast*. *The Guardian* (23 Dec. 1985).

Taylor, Paul. Review of *Adam Was a Gardener*. *Independent* (6 Sept. 1991).

Tinker, Jack [1]. Review of *Falkland Sound/Voces de Malvinas*. *Daily Mail* (June 1983).

———[2]. Review of *Golden Girls*. *Daily Mail* (15 May 1985).

Todd, Susan. "Territories." *New Statesman* (18 May 1984): 27.

Wallach, Allan. "One Family's 'Real Estate.' " *New York Newsday* (3 Dec. 1987).

Wandor, Michelene. *Carry on Understudies: Theatre and Sexual Politics*. Rev. ed. New York: Routledge, 1986: 180–81.

Wardle, Irving [1]. "All That Blisters." *The Times* (30 Apr. 1985): 10.

———[2]. Review of *Falkland Sound/Voces de Malvinas*. *Independent on Sunday* (13 May 1990).

———[3]. "Never the Judge." *The Times* (10 Mar. 1989): 20.

Williams, Ian. Review of *Beauty and the Beast*. *Tribune* (12 Dec. 1985).

Winterson, Jeanette. "Thoughtfully Ever After." *Times Literary Supplement* (10 Jan. 1986): 39.

Wittenberg, Clarissa K. Review of *Real Estate*. *Washington Review* 10 (1985): 21.

Harold Pinter

(1930–)

STEPHEN H. GALE

Harold Pinter is the most important and influential English-language dramatist of the second half of the twentieth century. Some critics claim that he is the most important and influential playwright of the entire century, an assessment based on the themes that Pinter explores in his plays and his style. His *The Birthday Party*, *The Caretaker*, *The Homecoming*, and *Old Times* have been accorded the status of modern classics.

Born on 10 October 1930, in Hackney, a working-class section of London, Pinter was the only child of a Jewish ladies' tailor, Hyman (Jack) Pinter, and his wife, Frances Mann Pinter. His earliest memories are of the family's brick house in a generally run-down area filled with railway yards, shops, and a smelly soap factory near the polluted River Lea.

Pinter was sent to Cornwall when World War II broke out. In 1944 he returned to London where he endured the German blitz—he saw the first flying bomb, and his garden was frequently in flames. The family had to evacuate their home several times, a traumatic experience that had a great impact on the young Pinter.

Pinter won a scholarship to the local all-boys grammar school, Hackney-Downes, where he studied until 1947. Under the direction of Joseph Brearley, his English master, he acted the part of Macbeth in 1946 and then Romeo. The only academic subject to interest him was English language and literature. He played football and cricket and ran the 100-yard dash in a school record time. At thirteen he had also had his first love affair and had begun writing poetry.

Pinter applied for a grant to study acting at the Royal Academy of Dramatic Art and he received a London County Council grant on the recommendation of producer R. D. (Reggie) Smith. After about two terms he found that he did not like the academy and faked a nervous breakdown in order to escape. Subsequently he enrolled at the Central School of Speech and Drama but was not a serious student there.

Following the war fascism began to be revived in London's East End. Pinter recalls encountering a considerable amount of violence there as gangs of toughs used to frequent the alleys that he walked through. The thugs carried broken milk bottles and threatened to "carve up" anybody whom they did not like, especially those who looked either Jewish (as did Pinter) or whom they took to be a Communist (again Pinter was a target because he carried school books). The dramatist-to-be learned how important language could be as he talked his way through these frightening situations on a regular basis. The encounters, plus tales of the treatment of Jews in Germany during Hitler's Third Reich, led Pinter to declare himself a conscientious objector when he turned eighteen. He refused to serve in the National Service and stood trial twice for this refusal though he escaped imprisonment.

In 1949 Pinter began writing "Kullus," a work that reappears in several forms in his later writing. In 1950 his first published writing appeared: the August issue of *Poetry London* contained his two poems "New Year in the Midlands" and "Chandeliers and Shadows." He wrote hundreds of poems at this time and started an autobiographical novel, *The Dwarfs*.

Most of his time, however, was involved with acting. The first threatre-going experience that Pinter had was seeing Sir Donald Wolfit in the role of King Lear. Later he was to act in a production with Wolfit. Reggie Smith helped Pinter find small parts on the radio; his first professional role was in the BBC home service broadcast "Focus on Football Pools" on September 19, 1950.

In 1951 Pinter began his acting career in earnest. He appeared in a role in the BBC's Third Programme production of Shakespeare's *Henry VIII*. Subsequently he answered Anew McMaster's advertisements for actors to participate in a Shakespearean tour of Ireland. During the following eighteen-month period of one-night stands, he became friends with Alun Owen, Patrick McGee, and Barry Foster. Pinter met Vivien Merchant while the two were acting at the King's Theatre in Hammersmith in 1953. In 1954 he assumed the stage name of David Baron and toured provincial England with a repertory company.

In 1954–1955 the prose version of "The Black and White" was written, and in 1955 he wrote the short story *The Examination*, which hearkens back to "Kullus." Pinter and Merchant met again in 1956 when they played leads opposite one another and the couple was married.

In 1957 Henry Woolfe, a repertory company friend of Pinter's, asked if he would write a play for production by the drama department at Bristol University. Four days later Pinter had finished his first play, *The Room*. Directed by Wolfe, *The Room* was entered in the *Sunday Times* student drama festival. One of the judges, critic Harold Hobson, was so impressed by the work that he wrote an admiring review of it. As a result, Michael Codron wrote to Pinter to find out if he had written a full-length play; Pinter had just completed *The Birthday Party*. In January 1958 Pinter's son Daniel was born. Three months later, on

April 28, 1958, *The Birthday Party* premiered at the Arts Theatre, Cambridge. Pinter helped in the directing. In May the production moved to the Lyric Theatre, Hammersmith, for its first London staging. It was a critical disaster.

Nevertheless, Pinter continued to write. *Something in Common*, an unperformed radio play, and *A Slight Ache* were both completed in 1958. The following year he created a group of revue sketches, "That's Your Trouble," "That's All," "Applicant," "Interview," "Dialogue for Three," and "Getting Acquainted." Also in 1959 *The Dumb Waiter* premiered at the Frankfurt (Germany) Municipal Theatre. Two of Pinter's sketches, "Trouble in the Works" and "The Black and the White," were included in Disley Jones's *One to Another*, a musical revue mounted at the Lyric Theatre in July. *A Slight Ache* was broadcast on the BBC Third Programme later that month, and in September another musical revue, *Pieces of Eight*, included Pinter's "Getting Acquainted," "Last to Go," "Request Stop," and "Special Offer."

The dramatist's fortunes began to change in 1960. *The Room*, which he directed, and *The Dumb Waiter* were produced at the Hampstead Theatre Club, and the BBC Third Programme broadcast *A Night Out*, with Pinter taking the role of Seeley. *The Birthday Party* was telecast by Associated Rediffusion Television and *A Night Out* was broadcast by ABC-TV. *Night School* was televised. Shortly afterward, *The Birthday Party* became Pinter's first play to be performed professionally in the United States when the Actors Workshop production in San Francisco opened on 27 July. The BBC broadcast *The Dwarfs* on its Third Programme. Also in 1960 the prose version of "The Black and the White" was published in the *The Spectator*.

The most important event for Pinter in 1960, however, was the premiere of *The Caretaker* at the Arts Theatre Club in London on 27 April. In May the production was moved to the Duchess Theatre in the West End. The play was critically acclaimed by Kenneth Tynan and other reviewers. It closed at the Duchess Theatre after 425 performances; in the meantime it had been judged by the *Evening Standard* as the best play of 1960, and when the drama moved to the United States, it was nominated for an Antoinette Perry (Tony) Award and the Newspaper Guild of New York cited *The Caretaker* as the best play of the year.

Nineteen sixty-one was a busy year: "Harold Pinter Replies," an essay, was published in *New Theatre* magazine; *A Slight Ache* was mounted at the Arts Theatre Club in London; "Afternoon Poem" appeared in *Twentieth Century*; an essay, "Writing for Myself," was published in *Twentieth Century*; *The Collection* was televised; and *A Night Out* was staged. In 1962 Pinter codirected *The Collection* with Peter Hall at London's Aldwych Theatre, "Between the Lines," an essay, was published in the *Sunday Times* (London), and the author read "The Examination" on the BBC Third Programme.

The next four years were impressive. *The Lover* was telecast in 1963 (and received the Guild of British Television Producers and Directors Award and the Prix Italia Television Drama at Naples Award for best script). Pinter subsequently directed the first stage presentation of the play when it opened at the Arts Theatre Club in London on the same bill with *The Dwarfs*. In 1963 the short story ''Tea Party'' was written, and Pinter won two Screenwriters Guild Awards, one for television play and one for screenplay.

Pinter's entrance into the world of the cinema, a subject in which he had shown an interest as a student, was a propitious one. His first screenplay, *The Caretaker*, based on his own drama, was released in 1963. Directed by Clive Donner and starring Alan Bates, Robert Shaw, and Donald Pleasence, the film received a Silver Bear Award at the Berlin Film Festival and a Certificate of Merit at the Edinburgh Festival. *The Servant*, Pinter's second screenplay, was also released in 1963, and in 1964 the quality of the author's screenwriting was further recognized by awards for *The Servant* from both the British Screenwriters Guild and the New York Film Critics. This film was the official British entry at the Venice Film Festival and the first New York Film Festival as well.

Five of Pinter's revue sketches (''Applicant,'' ''Dialogue for Three,'' ''Interview,'' ''That's All,'' and ''That's Your Trouble'') were broadcast on the BBC Third Programme in 1964, and Pinter read the prose version of *Tea Party* on the BBC Third Programme and directed a revival of *The Birthday Party* at the Aldwych in London too. ''Writing for the Theatre'' was published in *The Evergreen Review*; ''Applicant,'' ''Dialogue for Three,'' ''Interview,'' ''That's All,'' and ''That's Your Trouble'' were broadcast on the BBC Third Programme; and Pinter read *Tea Party* on the Third Programme. The prose version of *Tea Party* was published in *Playboy* in 1965, and subsequently the dramatic version was televised.

In 1965 Pinter won the British Film Academy Award for best screenplay for his 1964 scenario of Penelope Mortimer's *The Pumpkin Eater*. By now it was clear that his work in film carried over thematically and technically into his work for the theatre and vice versa, just as his radio and television writing had already had an impact on his dramaturgy. *Tea Party* was televised in England by BBC1 and throughout Europe as part of the European Broadcasting Union's 1965 *The Largest Theatre in the World* series. *The Homecoming* opened at the Aldwych under Peter Hall's direction. Pinter also acted in a BBC-TV presentation of Sartre's *No Exit* that year.

In 1966 Pinter's script for the film *Langrishe, Go Down* was published, a reflection of the author's increasing interest in writing for the cinema. That same year he was named Commander, Order of the British Empire in the Queen's Birthday List and *The Quiller Memorandum*, for which he wrote the screenplay, was released.

In 1967 two of Pinter's essays were published, ''Two People in a Room: Playwriting'' in *The New Yorker* and ''Beckett'' in the festschrift *Beckett at Sixty*. In 1967 *The Homecoming* moved to New York, where it won the Tony Award for best play on Broadway, the New York Drama Critics Circle Award for the best play on Broadway, and the Whitbread Anglo-American Award for the best British play on Broadway. Pinter acted in a BBC-TV telecast of *The Basement* and directed Robert Shaw's *The Man in the Glass Booth* in London as well and then took the play to New York, where he was nominated for a Tony for his directing. *Accident*, another Losey film from a Pinter screenplay, was released (Pinter played a small part in it). The film was named one of the year's best by the National Board of Review. At Joe Orton's funeral Pinter read a poem that he had written as a eulogy.

Nineteen sixty-eight proved to be a busy year. *Mac*, Pinter's fond memoir of his repertory experiences with Irish actor-manager McMaster, was published, the film version of *The Birthday Party* was screened in New York, *Landscape* was broadcast on the BBC Third Programme, *The Basement* began a run at the East Side Playhouse in New York, and the volume *Poems* was published. In 1968 much of Pinter's time was consumed in a battle with the Lord Chamberlain, who objected to several four-letter words in *Landscape*; the play was not given a license to be acted onstage. However, because radio was not subject to the Lord Chamberlain's censorship, the drama was performed on the BBC Third Programme.

In 1969 *Night* was produced and Pinter's screenplay adaptation of L. P. Hartley's *The Go-Between* was completed. Along with Donald Pleasence, the author appeared in the award-winning NBC Experiment in Television production of *Pinter People*. World premieres of Pinter's plays in 1969 include *Night*, which opened at the Comedy Theatre, and *Landscape* and *Silence*, at the Aldwych, mounted by the Royal Shakespeare Company.

Nineteen seventy was a relatively sparse year: "All of That," a poem, was published in the *Times Literary Supplement*, and Pinter was elected an honorary member by the Modern Language Association of America and awarded Hamburg University's Shakespeare Prize. He directed Simon Gray's *Butley* and James Joyce's *Exiles* in London. Unfortunately, from this point on, although more and more movies based on his fine filmscripts have been released, Pinter's other writing generally became increasingly sporadic and diminished both in quality and quantity for a period of seven or eight years.

In December 1971 "Speech: Hamburgh 1970" appeared in *Theatre Quarterly*. "Pinter on Beckett," an essay, was published in *New Theatre Magazine*, and "Poem" was published in the *New York Times* magazine. Peter Hall's production of *Old Times* opened at the Aldwych; six months later the play moved to New York. *Plays and Players* recognized *Old Times* with its award for best new play, and the drama was also nominated for a Tony. *The Go-Between* was released and won the Cannes Film Festival Golden Palm Award as best picture and Pinter received a British Academy of Film and Television Arts Award for his screenplay and a Writers Guild Award.

In 1972 Pinter wrote an adaptation of Marcel Proust's *À la recherche du temps perdu*, an interesting literary anomaly in that the screenplay has never been filmed, yet it has been published.

The essay "Pinter on Pinter" was included in *Cinebill* in 1973; *Monologue* was performed on British television; and the film version of *The Homecoming*, directed by Hall, was released. Pinter became an associate director at the National Theatre (an association that he maintained through 1983) and directed his first film, an adaptation of Gray's *Butley*. He also received the Austrian State Prize for European literature.

In 1974 Pinter directed John Hopkins's *Next of Kin* at the Old Vic, and ''An Unpublished Speech'' was published in *Theatre Quarterly*.

Hall's production of *No Man's Land*, starring John Gielgud and Ralph Richardson, opened at the Old Vic in 1975, and Pinter directed Gray's *Otherwise Engaged* in London. Vivien Merchant sued Pinter for divorce, naming noted biographer and novelist Lady Antonia Fraser as correspondent. After the divorce Pinter married Lady Antonia.

Pinter directed William Archibald's *The Innocents* at the Morosco Theatre in New York City that year and Noël Coward's *Blithe Spirit* at the National Theatre in London in 1977. A year later *Langrishe, Go Down* was televised, and *Betrayal* was staged at the National. The latter received the New York Critics Circle 1980 Award for best foreign play when it crossed the Atlantic Ocean. At this point Pinter seems to have lost his driving interest in writing for the theatre, although he continued to direct—Gray's *The Rear Column* at the Globe Theatre (1978) and *Close of Play* at the National (1979). Indeed, it was 1980 before anything else of professional significance occurred; *Family Voices* was broadcast on BBC3 Radio. This was followed by the first performance of *The Hothouse*, the original version of which had been completed in 1960, at the Hampstead Theatre Club in London, Pinter directing. Pinter was awarded the Pirandello Prize.

In 1981 *The French Lieutenant's Woman*, perhaps Pinter's finest film, was released and nominated for an Academy Award in the best screenplay adaptation category. The Bank of Delaware Common Wealth Award was presented to Pinter, and he directed Gray's *Quartermaine's Terms* at the Queen's Theatre. *Family Voices* was staged, *Victoria Station* and *A Kind of Alaska* premiered as part of a triple bill with *Family Voices* in 1982, and in 1983 *Players* was presented. The film version of *Betrayal* opened in London in 1982. Pinter continued directing, *Incident at Tulsa Hill* in 1982 and *The Trojan War Will Not Take Place* in 1983. Meanwhile, he continued to garner honors—the Donatello Prize in 1982 and another Academy Award nomination for best screenplay adaptation in 1983 (for *Betrayal*).

In 1984 *One for the Road* was published in the *New York Review of Books* and televised in 1985. Pinter directed Gray's *The Common Pursuit* in 1984 and Tennessee Williams's *Sweet Bird of Youth* in 1985. In 1985, too, the film *Turtle Diary* was released and the writer was honored with the Elmer Holmes Bobst Award for arts and letters. In 1986 Pinter directed Donald Freeze's *Circe and Bravo*. In 1987 *The Dumb Waiter*, directed by Robert Altman and starring John Travolta and Tom Conti, was telecast in the United States, as was *The Room*, also directed by Altman and featuring Linda Hunt, Annie Lennox, Julian Sands,

David Heublen, Abbott Anderson, and Donald Pleasence. Chapter 19 of *The Dwarfs*, the novel begun in 1950, was published in the inaugural issue of *The Pinter Review* that same year, and a second television version of *The Birthday Party*, this one directed by Kenneth Ives, was telecast on BBC2 with Pinter in the part of Goldberg (the play has also been filmed in French as *L'Anniversaire*, directed by Jean-Michael Ribes). The dramatist was given a Literary Lions Award by the New York Public Library. Chapter 10 from *The Dwarfs* was published in *The Pinter Review*, Vol. 2, in 1988, and Pinter directed the premiere of *Mountain Language*. Over the years the playwright has received numerous honorary degrees from American and British universities in recognition of his contributions to the arts.

Additional film and television credits include Pinter's television adaptations of Fred Uhlman's *Reunion*, released in 1989, and Elizabeth Bowen's *Heat of the Day*, directed by Christopher Morahan and televised by the BBC and by Granada Television in Great Britain in 1989 and in the United States in 1990; cinematic adaptations of Margaret Atwood's novel *The Handmaid's Tale*, directed by Volker Schlondorff, and Ian McEwan's *The Comfort of Strangers* were both released in 1990; Franz Kafka's *The Trial* was filmed in 1992. Pinter has also written a screenplay version of Joseph Conrad's *Victory*, which was published in 1990, although it has not yet been filmed.

In 1990 *The Dwarfs* was published and "It Is Here," a poem, appeared in the *Times Literary Supplement*. Pinter read Salman Rushdie's "Is Nothing Sacred?" as the Herbert Read Memorial Lecture, and "On Superman," a talk by Pinter, was broadcast on BBC4's *Opinion* series. He directed Jane Stanton Hitchcock's *Vanilla*. *Party Time* was read at the International Pinter Festival at Ohio State University in 1991 and premiered under Pinter's direction (cobilled with *Mountain Language*) at the Almeida Theatre in London. An audiotape of Pinter reciting "Focus on Football Pools" was presented at the Pinter Festival too. As part of the worldwide celebration of Pinter's sixtieth birtday, *Betrayal* (directed by David Leveaux) at the Almeida and *The Homecoming* (directed by Hall) and *The Caretaker* (directed by Pinter) at London's Comedy Theatre enjoyed major revivals in 1991. Also in 1991 *The New World Order* was published in the autumn issue of *Granta* and *The Pinter Review: Annual Essays* (Vol. 5), then performed, with Pinter as director, at the Royal Court Theatre. Several revivals were made in 1992: *No Man's Land* in London (Pinter playing Hirst); *The Birthday Party* in Glasgow, Scotland; *The Caretaker* in Nottingham; and *The Homecoming* in Columbus, Ohio. In 1993 Pinter directed David Mamet's *Oleanna*, and his full-length *Moonlight* premiered in London.

Selected Biographical Sources: Esslin [3]; Gale [3]; Hinchliffe [2]; Prentice; Pinter, "A Conversation (Pause) with Harold Pinter," "Harold Pinter: An Interview."

MAJOR PLAYS, PREMIERES, AND SIGNIFICANT
REVIVALS: THEATRICAL RECEPTION

The Room. (one-act). 1957. Opened at the old Drama Studio at Bristol University on 15 May, directed by Henry Woolf; first professional mounting at the Hampstead Theater Club 21 January 1960, directed by Harold Pinter; moved to the Royal Court Theatre, London, 8 March 1960 (double-billed with *The Dumb Waiter*), directed by Anthony Page; first American performance at the Encore Theatre, San Francisco, in 1960. Opened at Writers Stage (NY) on 9 December 1964.

The first of Pinter's plays to be produced, a comedy of menace, *The Room* sets the tone for all of Pinter's works that follow. Hobson [3] found the play a revelation in its excursion into the "nightmare world of insecurity and uncertainty" and praised the University's department of drama for having discovered Pinter's work in a review that attracted the attention of producer Michael Codron. Alvarez saw the violence and horror of the play growing out of Pinter's obsession with time and the indifference of society. Brien [2] found the play somewhere between Brecht and Paddy Chayefsky, with Pinter's drama of ritualism and manipulation remaining obstinately a-plicit. Dent found the play completely baffling.

The Birthday Party. 1958. Premiered at the Arts Theatre, Cambridge, under the direction of Peter Wood, on 28 April. Opened on 19 May at the Lyric Theatre, Hammersmith, closed on 24 May. Revival at Aldwych Theatre, London, 18 June 1964, directed by Pinter. Opened at the Actors Workshop, San Francisco, 27 July 1960, directed by Glynne Wickham. Revival: with *Mountain Language* by the Classic Stage Company Theatre (NY), directed by Carey Perloff, 17–22 April 1988.

Picking up where *The Room* left off, *The Birthday Party* continues Pinter's examination of the interrelated concepts of menace, verification, and communication. The early reviews were almost universally condemnatory: Shulman [1] found that the play was not funny but that it was opaque. Wardle [1], though, praised Pinter's theatrical ability and saw the play in terms of menacing intrusions. Hobson [3] called Pinter the "most original, disturbing, and arresting talent in theatrical London" and prophetically noted that the dramatist and the drama would be heard of again. Barber found the play boring. Barnes [1] found the play the newest good thing on Broadway and discussed the influence of Samuel Beckett, especially on the dialogue. Boothroyd called the play "a masterpiece of meaningless significance." Clurman [1] wrote positively about the New York production of *The Birthday Party*, which is "*not* obscure." On the other hand, Darlington found the play "most determinedly obscure." Gottfried found in the New York production proof that the play demonstrates Pinter's "status as an artist valid beyond time." The play was labeled "theatre of the absurd" by critics, who were angry because the drama did not conform to their traditional views of drama.

The Dumb Waiter. 1959. Premiered at the Frankfurt Municipal Theatre, Frankfurt-am-Main, 28 February. Opened at the Hampstead Theatre Club (co-billed with *The Room*), directed by James Roose-Evans, 21 January 1960; moved to the Royal Court Theatre, London, on 8 March, opened at the Cherry Lane Theatre (with *The Collection*) (NY) and the Provincetown Playhouse for 578 performances; opened at the Midway Theater (NY), on 31 March 1964, withdrawn on 12 April.

By the time *The Dumb Waiter* was mounted in London, British critics were beginning to be able to take Pinter on his own terms. In England and elsewhere, rather than simply dismissing him as obscure, critics were beginning to try to determine what Pinter's plays meant. Taylor noted that the two characters are menace personified, yet the menacers themselves can be menaced; Lambert [2] considered the "indefinable relevance to life as we live it" in the drama; Dash found the work ironic, vivid, and engrossing.

A Slight Ache. 1959. First performed as a radio play on the BBC Third Programme, 29 July, produced by Donald McWhinnie; opened at the Arts Theatre, London, 18 January 1961 (as part of a triple bill, *Three*—together with one-act plays by John Mortimer and N. F. Simpson); moved to the Criterion Theatre, London, with *The Room* at Writers Stage Theatre (NY), 1964. Revival at the Young Vic Theatre, London, June–July 1987 (on a bill with *The Lover*), directed by Kevin Billington. Revival at the Mark Taper Forum, Los Angeles, 31 March 1990, directed by Michael Arabian.

As Gale [3] pointed out, *A Slight Ache* was the first of several plays written for a radio or television medium and later adapted for the stage; the drama also served as a transition between the comedies of menace and the next phase in Pinter's writing. Hinchliffe [2] and Esslin [4] concluded that the matchseller does not exist but is, instead, a projection of the couple's anxieties; Gale argued that the character is physically present. Trewin found the play silly. Sheed found the play devoid of meaning. Muller called the play a "brilliantly sinister tour de force."

The Caretaker. 1960. Opened at the Arts Theatre, London, 27 April, presented by the Arts Theatre Club and directed by Donald McWhinnie; moved to the Duchess Theatre, London, on 30 May for 425 performances. Opened at the Schauspielhaus, Dusseldorf, 29 October as *der Hausmeister*. Opened at the Schubert Theatre, New Haven (CT), in 1961. Produced at the Lyceum Theatre (NY) 4 October 1961. Revival at the Mermaid Theatre, London, 2 March 1972; Greenwich Theatre (NY) in 1977, directed by Paul Joyce; revival at the National Theatre, London, in 1980, directed by Kenneth Ives; revival at the Circle in the Square Theatre (NY), by the Steppenwolf Theatre Company, directed by John Malkovich, 30 January 1986; revival at the Comedy Theatre, London, directed by Pinter, 20 June 1991.

The Birthday Party originally ran for only a week and total receipts were a mere 260 pounds eleven shillings eight pence (£260 11s. 8d.); barely two years later *The Caretaker* garnered the *Evening Standard* Award and the Page One Award of the Newspaper Guild of New York for best play of the year.

Noël Coward lauded Pinter for his "original and unmistakable sense of theatre"; Tynan found it a "play about people." Gale [3] concluded that the play, Pinter's first acclaimed masterpiece, is about how the relationship between two brothers is solidified when they combine to eject an intruder. Marowitz claimed that the drama is about love, which he equated with need; Kitchen considered *The Caretaker* to be at the peak of English compressionistic drama and "perfectly constructed." Hinchliffe [2] contended that the question asked by the characters is "What or who am I?" and the primary organizing factor is the dialogue. Boulton characterized the tramp Davies as the archetypal symbol of life as a journey. Keown was of the opinion that the play depended upon superb acting for its success, whereas Lambert [1] found that the strength of the play lay in Pinter's dealing with human relationships (1).

British dramatist Terence Rattigan once suggested to Pinter that *The Caretaker* was about "the Old Testament God and the New Testament God, with the caretaker as humanity," eliciting from Pinter the statement that "it's about two brothers and a caretaker."

The Collection. 1962. Opened at the Aldwych Theatre, London, 18, June, directed by Peter Hall and Harold Pinter. Produced (with *The Dumb Waiter*) at the Cherry Lane Theatre (NY), in 1962. Revival (on a double bill with *The Lover*) in Paris, October 1964, directed by Claude Regy.

This play is about two couples, one heterosexual and married and the other homosexual, who are placed in jeopardy because of an affair that may or may not have taken place between the wife and the younger homosexual. Hinchliffe [2] believes that the possibility that this affair took place causes "the two people in each [pairing] . . . to rethink the basis for their relationships." Based on the original stage production of *The Collection*, Ryan placed Pinter in the "theatre of the absurd." Shulman [2] enthusiastically called the play "a commentary on the inability of any of us to recognize the truth."

The Lover. 1963. Opened at the Arts Theatre Club, London (cobilled with *The Dwarfs*), directed by Harold Pinter. Produced at the Cherry Lane Theatre (NY), in 1964. Revival at the Young Vic Theatre, London, June–July 1987 (on a bill with *A Slight Ache*), directed by Kevin Billington. Revival (on a double bill with *The Collection*) in Paris, October 1964, directed by Claude Regy.

Kemp-Welch's 1963 television production of *The Lover* won the Prix Italia for television drama at Naples and Pinter won the Guild of British Television Producers and Directors Award for the script. Clearly in line with *A Slight Ache*, *The Caretaker*, and *The Collection*, this play is about the deteriorating relationship between a husband and wife. Gascoigne finds *The Lover* to be "an expressionistic drama about a young couple who can't reconcile their respectable idea of marriage with the violent ritual of their sexual passions."

The Homecoming. 1965. Produced at New Theatre, Cardiff, Wales. Opened at the Aldwych Theatre, London, 3 June, directed by Peter Hall. Opened as *Le Retour* at Théâtre de Paris, directed by Claude Regy; Music Box Theatre (NY), 3 January 1967; Revival at the Comedy Theatre, London, January 1991, directed by Peter Hall.

Considered one of Pinter's two best plays. Winner of the Antoinette Perry (Tony) Award and the New York Drama Critics Circle Award for the best play on Broadway and the Whitbread Anglo-American Award for the best British play on Broadway in 1967, *The Homecoming* is Pinter's most honored drama. A few critics such as Brien [1] were still unable to comprehend the depth of Pinter's dramas, and Brustein [3] found Pinter too "bizzare" and "vulgar," but most by this time had come to an understanding of both his themes and the dramatic devices through which he expressed those themes. Clurman [2] called the play "a powerful statement wrought by a master hand." Goldstone contended that *The Homecoming* contrasts male and female attitudes toward sexuality; Hall calls the play Teddy's, that is, a struggle between Teddy and his family for possession of Ruth; Hewes [2] praises the dramatist's achievements in this play and comments on the humor. Gilliatt saw the play as a territorial struggle. Gilman [2] commented on the movement toward a ritualistic and mythic confrontation between the characters' fantasies. Kerr found that *The Homecoming* functions according to existential principles, whereas Gale [3] determined that the play is about love and the lack of love—that is, the characters are so desperate to fulfill their emotional needs that they are willing to accept anything in order to do so.

Landscape. 1969. Produced by the Royal Shakespeare Company at the Aldwych Theatre, London, 2 July (on a double bill with *Silence*), directed by Peter Hall; Lincoln Center (NY), in April 1970.

Landscape represents a reversal in the author's normal creative process for although it was first presented on a BBC Third Programme broadcast, it was originally written for stage. When the play was submitted to the Lord Chamberlain for approval for production, the Lord Chamberlain refused to let it be acted without the removal of several offensive four-letter words. Pinter refused to alter the play, and it was broadcast intact. Subsequently the Lord Chamberlain's authority to censor plays was removed and the drama was presented on the stage. Barnes [3] discussed Pinter's greatness as being an "ability to see the world as it exists" in this drama. Brustein [1] noted Beckett's influence. Hobson's [2] laudatory review considered the theme of memory in *Landscape* and the continuing influence of the past on the present. Marcus [1] found the play a study in loneliness, a memory play illustrating man's isolation and later commented on Pinter's use of language and nonlanguage to convey meaning. Wardle [2] called *Landscape* "an elegaic mosaic" that is "a theatrical poem to which poetic rather than stage criteria apply"; Gale [3] noted that Pinter had moved from exploring the concepts of external and internal menace to a study of the mind, memory, and time, and that the dramatist's style had become considerably more lyrical and imagistic as he moved from concrete subjects to abstract subjects.

Old Times. 1971. Opened at the Aldwych Theatre, London, 1 June, directed by Peter Hall; the Billy Rose Theatre (NY), in November. Revived at the Roundabout Theatre (NY), December 1983, directed by Kenneth Frankel; revived at the American Theatre, St. Louis, October 1985, directed by David Jones.

Old Times, along with *The Homecoming*, is considered one of Pinter's two best plays. Aylwin claimed that the key to understanding *Old Times* is the concept of ambiguity; Braunmuller discussed links between the speaker and the narrated past, sexuality, and the function of filmic references, in particular *Odd Men Out*; Barnes [2] lauded *Old Times* as a memory play with similarities to James Joyce and Marcel Proust. Clurman [4] called the play Pinter's most poetic work, filled with masterly craftsmanship. Gill equated Pinter with William Faulkner and Beckett. According to Hewes [2], Anna and Kate shut Deeley out of their past. Weales found the work both effective and affective. Feldstein echoed this finding in her attempt to show the movement from victim or victimized to victim/victimized; Gillen [1] saw the characters as being fragmented and the play concerned with the metaphysical question of the nature of man, who is "doomed to desire completeness he can never possess and to make choices which constantly frustrate that desire"; Gale [3, 5] found the play to be about a contest between the husband and the former roommate for the wife, with a restructuring of the past used as a weapon to create a desired present.

No Man's Land. 1975. Opened at the National Theatre at the Old Vic, London, 23 April; presented at Wyndham's Theatre, London, 15 July, directed by Peter Hall; moved to Longacre Theatre (NY), 1976.

Clurman [3] liked the play but admitted that he was confused about its meaning. Cushman compares Spooner to Davies in *The Caretaker* and comments on the language of *No Man's Land*. Hughes called the play "archetypal Pinter." Kroll [2] discusses language, T. S. Eliot, symbolism, the nature of art, and the theme of identity seeking in the play. Lambert felt that the play exposes "the desperate shifts that human nature is sometimes put to at the behest of the will to live." Malkin found the play exhilarating theatre because of its humor as it explores the "dark inevitability of the future . . . of death in life."

Betrayal. 1978. Opened at the Lyttleton Theatre, London, 15 November, directed by Peter Hall; Trafalgar Theatre (NY), on 5 January 1980.

One of Pinter's most accessible and popular plays, about an affair between two married people, *Betrayal* moves backward from the results of an action to the initiating event. Jenkins called the play "a completely unromantic account of infidelity, including the adultery of truth" in which the chronology creates "a marvelous tension." Esslin [1] noted that the structure of *Betrayal* depends on a variation on one of Pinter's favorite motifs, the fallibility of memory, in a "horrifying portrait of a society, a way of life based on an infinite number of mutual betrayals."

ADDITIONAL PLAYS, ADAPTATIONS, AND PRODUCTIONS

In addition to his numerous short review sketches, a number of interesting albeit minor Pinter plays have been produced over the years. These include *A Night Out*, staged at the Gate Theatre, Dublin, 17 September. *The Basement* was staged on a double bill with *Tea Party* at the East Side Playhouse in New York City on 19 October 1968. *Night* was staged as a part of a collection of one-act plays, *Mixed Doubles*, at the Comedy Theatre, London, 9 April 1969, under the direction of Alexander Dore. *Silence*, directed by Peter Hall, was mounted with *Landscape* at the Aldwych Theatre, London, 2 July 1969. *Other Places*, a collection of three short plays—*Family Voices*, *Victoria Station*, and *A Kind of Alaska*—was first performed at the National Theatre, London, on 14 October 1982, under the direction of Peter Hall. *One for the Road* was first performed at the Lyric Theatre Studio, Hammersmith, 13 March 1984, directed by Pinter, with the first American production at the Manhattan Theatre Club in New York in April 1984. *Mountain Language*, directed by Pinter, was first performed at the National Theatre, London, on 20 October 1988. *The New World Order* was first performed by Pinter on an audiotape played at A Pinter Festival: An International Meeting at Ohio State University Thurber Theatre in Columbus, Ohio, on 20 April 1991; it was subsequently performed (again directed by Pinter) as part of a double bill with Ariel Dorfman's *Death and the Maiden* at the Royal Court Theatre Upstairs as part of the London International Festival of Theatre in July 1991. Its American premiere was directed by Richard V. Romajnoli at Georgetown University Hall of Nations, Washington, D.C., as part of the Potomac Theatre Project in August 1991. A staged reading of *Party Time*, directed by John Clum, was held at the Pinter Festival at Ohio State University in Columbus on 20 April 1991, by the Duke University Players and the New Cross Theatre from Goldsmith College, University of London. *Moonlight* premiered at the Almeida Theatre, London, directed by Peter Hall, in September 1993.

ASSESSMENT OF PINTER'S CAREER

When Pinter began writing dramas, he already had substantial experience as a repertory actor, an important element in his dramaturgy. This experience has been supplemented by his continued work as an actor throughout his career and by his work as a stage and film director. Truly a "man of the theatre," even in his first drama (*The Room*, in 1957), Pinter demonstrated that he understood stagecraft, and actors have always appreciated acting in the roles that he has written.

From the beginning of his career, however, Pinter's dramas have not been typical. Although they grew out of his experiences, the dramatizing of the images that remained in his mind, such as the picture of two men at a table at a party, were expressed in ways that led to his being called "obscure" and an absurdist. Pinter admits that his earliest works would never have been staged if Samuel Beckett's plays had not preceded them, but in truth his work is neither obscure nor absurd. Since it is not couched in traditional terms, critics and audiences alike had difficulty making his work conform to their preconceptions of what and how drama is. Still, over the years Pinter has been proven to be right—once audiences understood that his works were to be approached without any preconceptions, the power of the dramas were exerted in full force. As a result, Pinter is now considered the premiere English-language playwright in the second half of the twentieth century, and possibly the entire century's most influential and important dramatist.

Hobson [1] found great promise in *The Room*, the first of Pinter's plays to be produced. However, most early criticism, especially that by theatre reviewers, was extremely derogatory. Pinter's dramas were considered difficult and essentially meaningless. As might be expected, the early critical commentary on Pinter revolved around the elements in his plays that made them difficult for reviewers to understand. Even so, there was recognition that the room-womb imagery of *The Room*, the existence of menace tempered with humor, the theme of domination, and the intensity of confrontations with intruders were intriguing. Critics also noted the power of Pinter's language and his facility in reproducing ordinary speech, an ability that was likened to the accuracy of a tape recorder. Pinter had taken the pauses that appear in the dramas of Anton Chekhov and Samuel Beckett and refined them to the point that silence became an important tool in his dramaturgy. Barely ten years after the premiere of his first play, Pinter's works were the subject of two monographs. Hinchliffe [2], a typical introductory overview, included many valid insights and connections; Kerr looked at Pinter's work from an existential point of view. Within the next ten years five additional studies devoted to examining Pinter's work were published. Burkman [1] considered the ritualistic elements, Esslin [4] and Gabbard [1] expanded on Gordon's psychological approach, Quigley [3] approached the dramas from a linguistic point of view, and Gale [3] traced Pinter's thematic and stylistic development.

One key to understanding both Pinter's work and Pinter criticism is the realization that the content and style of his dramas have changed dramatically over the years. Naturally, the scholarship tends to focus on various aspects as they emerge in this writing. For instance, the term "absurdist" is still applied to Pinter occasionally, but since the premiere of *The Caretaker* in 1960 scholars have realized that it is not applicable. Gale [3] has shown that Pinter's thematic evolution has been organic. In the comedies of menace the dramatist was concerned with the omnipresence of menace and the individual's reaction to it—seeking sanctuary in *The Room*, running away in *The Birthday Party*, and finding that even the menacers are menaced in *The Dumb Waiter*. This is a logical progression. It is also logical, then, for Pinter to have moved on from the fact that the menace is internal and even the menacers are menaced to explore the ramifications of that concept in *The Caretaker* and subsequent plays. As he did this, interpersonal relationships, communications, and many of the themes that appeared in his earliest plays continue to appear, though transmogrified somewhat. This line of exploration culminates in *The Homecoming*.

At this point Pinter began delving into questions related to the workings of the human mind, the nature of time, and the interrelationships between memory and reality. The plays that followed (*Silence*, *Landscape*, and *Night*) lead up to *Old Times*. With the change in thematic direction, Pinter also altered his style drastically in order to better express these more abstract concepts; his writing became considerably more lyrical. And whereas earlier criticism had focused on the differences between appearance and reality, the new thematic explorations forced critics to consider that reality itself was mutable. In most of his later works Pinter has become consumed with political questions and the international violation of human rights. In the 1990s Knowles [1] and others have written about this new direction.

Because of the richness of Pinter's writing, the stylistic changes and magnificence of his use of language, especially in the plays of memory, and because of the depth and importance of his themes, critics continue to find much to write about in his plays. Still, there are areas that need attention. He has not written a major play since *Betrayal* in 1978, though he continues to write. His newer one-act plays, playlets, and revue sketches are interesting and offer reasonable subject matter for the critic and/or scholar. The whole new area of politics is but a major example of this. At the same time, there is currently a rereading of the earlier texts in light of Pinter's current political activities and interests. This is probably misguided, for the plays were written during a nonpolitical period in the author's life and should be considered within the context in which they were written. Dukore [3] and Diamond [2] have written studies of Pinter's use of comedy. Ben-Zvi and others have written about Pinter's female characters, essentially from a feminist perspective; this is another area where some corrective may be needed, for in some cases the critics have been incapable of looking beyond their own biases in an exercise of political correctness and as a result have not been able to examine the material in the plays except through that filter. Pinter's writing for the radio has been touched upon, but little has been written about his television work, especially as it is related to his stage dramas. This is true, too, in the area of his screenwriting. Pinter has been deeply involved in writing filmscripts since 1962. In the past twenty years his most significant artistic endeavors have been screenplays—*The Pumpkin Eater*, *Accident*, *The Go-Between*, *The French Lieutenant's Woman*, *The Handmaid's Tale*, and *The Comfort of Strangers*. Among one of the most important factors that needs to be assessed is the relationship between his writing for the theatre and his writing for the screen. Work in each area clearly influences his work in the other.

Without a doubt Harold Pinter is one of the most important writers of the twentieth century. For critics his appeal lies in his constant thematic evolution and in the parallel developments in his style. Unlike most dramatists Pinter is constantly in the process of becoming. As scholars continue to refine their examinations of his canon, they will find that his influence spreads far beyond the English-speaking theatre. This is both another subject for future scholarship and further evidence of the playwright's diversity, importance, and influence.

Critical as well as popular acceptance of Pinter's dramatic canon has undergone a dramatic turn-around over the years. The playwright's first three plays, *The Room*, *The Birthday Party*, and *The Dumb Waiter*, have been labeled "comedies of menace." Pinter's boyhood experiences obviously influenced the themes of these plays and the style with which he expressed those themes. Menace and dominance are his major concerns in these early dramas. The basic metaphor is that of a room or some other sanctuary about to be invaded. The person in the room understands that there is a menace outside the room, and in spite of loneliness and fear tries to communicate with the intruder in an attempt to verify whether it is friendly. Unfortunately, a vicious cycle develops. The room's inhabitant needs to communicate with the invader in order to determine whether he or she is friendly. However, because the inhabitant of the room, the protagonist, is afraid that some point of personal vulnerability will be revealed to the intruder, the character is so wary that communication is impossible. The result is that menace is increased, which in turn increases the need for verification and communication, which is not satisfied and thereby leads to additional menace, and so on.

Despite the ubiquitousness and omnipresence of menace, these plays contain a great deal of humor. Additionally, Pinter's method of presenting the material is not at all conventional (which led to his being considered an absurdist). While the dialogue is superrealistic, he presents no exposition and offers little or no explanation for what is going on onstage. Many critics and other theatre-goers were completely lost in their efforts to understand what the plays were about; they were considerably frustrated by the lack of conformity to what, according to their preconceptions, a drama ought to be. Critics such as Shulman [1] lambasted Pinter unmercifully.

In retrospect, it is much easier to see what Pinter was saying. Now that the audience realizes what Pinter is trying to do, there is more willingness to let him do it rather than trying to force him to do something that he never intended in the first place. In attempting to depict a world full of menace, Pinter involved his audience in the menacing situation.

What makes Pinter a great artist is the fact that he did not remain in the mode of the comedies of menace. While he was successful in expressing himself in those plays, his career has shown that he is a dramatic genius. Many authors write the same work over and over; not so with Pinter. Having established that menace is pervasive in the modern world, he turned his attention to the source of that menace. This led to a series of transitional plays, including *A Slight Ache*. By now audiences understood what Pinter was doing. It is obvious that his work in the revue sketches, radio, television, and film helped him hone his style and also introduced him to techniques from outside the sphere of traditional theatre that he effectively incorporated into his stagewriting.

The Caretaker was Pinter's first commercial success. In this play and those other stage, radio, and television scripts that follow, it is clear that menace does not derive from an external, physical source. It comes from within the individual and is psychological in nature. Interestingly, as Pinter considers a philosophical question in a series of plays, he brings together all the elements in one final play to sum up the series. *The Homecoming*, for example, Pinter's most honored work, sums up the second of his major thematic periods. In addition, he adjusts his style in order to more effectively reflect the themes that he is exploring as he moves from concept set to concept set.

Having determined the psychological nature of the source of menace and its location in the individual human mind, in *Night*, *Silence*, and *Landscape*, Pinter begins examining how the mind functions. Memory, time, and the nature of reality intermix to become the focal point of his interest. As his theme becomes more abstract, his style becomes more lyrical. The result is that someone unfamiliar with Pinter who sees *The Room* and *Landscape* would be hard-pressed to demonstrate that both plays were written by the same playwright. *Old Times*, Pinter's finest work to date, sums up the memory plays.

Although there have been several interesting short plays written since the staging of *Betrayal*, Pinter's recent creative efforts have largely been devoted to writing screenplays. He has written nothing of major significance for the theatre. Instead, he has turned his attention to politics. Early in his career Pinter answered a question about why he did not write about political and social matters by saying that these things were of only secondary importance. He felt that his examination of humanity's relationship to nature and especially individuals' relationships to one another was of far more consequence. Pinter's public political activities began when he went to Turkey with playwright Arthur Miller in March 1985 as a member of P.E.N. His friendship with other writers thrust him into the political arena as well—he is a close friend of Salman Rushdie, who was sentenced to death by the Ayatollah Khomeini of Iran for having written *Satanic Verses*, and of Václav Havel, president of Czechoslovakia. Although he eschewed politics in his early writing, during and since the 1980s he has been a visible and vocal protester for the cause of human rights, and his dramas have been almost exclusively political. Some critics have traced this apparent change in attitude to the influence of Lady Antonia Fraser, but as evidenced by his youthful espousal of a conscientious objector's stance, he has been politically involved for much of his life. The difference is that he tried to write apolitical plays throughout most of his career because he felt this was the best way to address the problems that concerned him; he now believes that the political concerns to which he has turned his attention are of such immediate and far-reaching importance that they must be made paramount in his work.

Following his marriage to Lady Antonia, Pinter has written no full-length dramas, and nearly everything that he has produced has been overtly political in nature. Ironically, nowadays most critics and the public willingly accept whatever he writes, including liberal and even leftist commentaries on current politics.

In summary, throughout Pinter's career there has been a steady thematic evolution with a concurrent and continual stylistic development. The thematic movement from exposure of menace naturally led him to an investigation into the source of menace, which in turn stimulated his interest in the interconnections of memory and time and the nature of reality. There are clear organic connections between the thematic periods in his writing. Simultaneously, he has changed his style to better express his new themes; form and content are intricately, efficiently, and effectively wedded.

Harold Pinter's major contributions to modern drama lie in the areas of language (realistic dialogue) and exposition (the presentation of characters and their motivations as they would be exhibited in real life). The significance of his themes, the insights into human nature that he provides, and the combination of emotional impact and intellectual depth in his works have made Pinter one of the most influential and important playwrights in the history of English drama.

ARCHIVAL SOURCES

No major archival sources for Pinter's works exist, although in 1990 the Harold Pinter Society established the Harold Pinter Archives. These are still very much in the initial stage, but information on the holdings is available from the Harold Pinter Society, President and Archivist Steven H. Gale, Kentucky State University, Frankfort, Kentucky 40601.

PRIMARY BIBLIOGRAPHY

Plays

The Birthday Party. London: Encore, 1959; New York: Grove Press, 1967.

The Birthday Party: A Play in Three Acts. London: Methuen, 1960.

The Birthday Party and Other Plays. (Includes *The Room* and *The Dumb Waiter*). London: Methuen, 1960.

The Birthday Party and *The Room*. New York: Grove Press, 1961.

The Caretaker. London: Methuen, 1969; New York: Grove Press, 1964.

The Caretaker and *The Dumb Waiter: Two Plays*. New York: Grove Press, 1961.

The Collection and *The Lover*. London: Methuen, 1963.

The Homecoming. London: Methuen, 1965; 2nd edition, London: Methuen, 1966; New York: Grove Press, 1966.

Landscape. London: Emanuel Wax for Pendragon, 1968.

Landscape and *Silence*. (Also includes *Night*). London: Methuen, 1969.

The Lover and Other Plays. (Includes *Tea Party* and *The Basement*). New York: Grove Press, 1967.

The Lover, Tea Party, and *The Basement*. New York: Grove Press, 1967.

Monologue. London: Covent Garden Press, 1973.

Mountain Language. London: Faber & Faber, 1988; New York: Grove Press, 1988.

A Night Out, Night School, and *Revue Sketches: Early Plays by Harold Pinter*. New York: Grove Press, 1968.

No Man's Land. London: Methuen, 1975; New York: Grove Press, 1975.

Old Times. London: Methuen, 1971; New York: Grove Press (Black Cat), 1971.

Other Places: Three Plays. (*A Kind of Alaska, Victoria Station, Family Voices*). London: Methuen, 1982; New York: Grove Press, 1983.

A Slight Ache and Other Plays. (Includes *A Night Out* and *The Dwarfs*). London: Methuen, 1961.

Anthologies

Complete Works: One. New York: Grove Press, 1977; rpt. 1981.

Complete Works: Two. New York: Grove Press, 1977; rpt. 1981.

Complete Works: Three. New York: Grove Press, 1978; rpt. 1981.

Complete Works: Four. New York: Grove Press, 1978; rpt. 1981.

Plays: One. London: Eyre Methuen, 1976.

Essays and Articles on Drama and Theatre

"Beckett." In *Beckett at Sixty: A Festschrift*, ed. John Calder. London: Calder & Boyars, 1967: R86.

"Harold Pinter Replies." *New Theatre Magazine* 11.2 (Jan. 1961): 8–10.

"The Knight Has Been Unruly: Memories of Sir Donald Wolfit." *The Listener* 79 (18 Apr. 1968): 501.

Mac. London: Emanuel Wax for Pendragon, 1968. Rpt. *Harper's Bazaar* 102 (Nov. 1968): 234–35; in *Good Talk 2: An Anthology from BBC Radio.*, ed. Derwent. New York: Grove Press, 1977; rpt. in *Complete Works: Three*. New York: Grove Press, 1978: 9–18.

"Pinter on Beckett." *New Theatre Magazine* 11.3 (May–June 1971): 3.

"Pinter on Pinter." *Cinebill* 1.2 (Oct. 1973): 7.

"Two People in a Room: Playwriting." *The New Yorker* 43 (25 Feb. 1967): 34–36.

"Writing for Myself." *Twentieth Century* 168 (Feb. 1961): 172–75.

"Writing for the Theatre." *Evergreen Review* 8 (Aug.–Sept. 1964): 80–82; rpt. in *Complete Works: One*. New York: Grove Press, 1977: 9–16.

Interviews

"A Conversation (Pause) with Harold Pinter" (with Mel Gussow). *New York Times Magazine* (5 Dec. 1971): 42–43+.

"Harold Pinter: An Interview" (with Lawrence M. Bensky). *Paris Review*, 10. no. 20 (fall 1966): 12–37.

SECONDARY BIBLIOGRAPHY

Adler, Thomas [1]. "From Flux to Fixity: Art and Death in Pinter's *No Man's Land*." In *Critical Essays on Harold Pinter*, ed. Steven H. Gale. Boston: G. K. Hall, 1990: 136–42.

———[2]. "Pinter/Proust/Pinter." In *Harold Pinter: Critical Approaches*, ed. Steven H. Gale. Madison, NJ: Fairleigh Dickinson University Press, 1986: 128–39.

Alvarez, A. "Wanted: A Language." *New Statesman* (10 Jan. 1960): 150.

Aylwin, Tony. "The Memory of All That: Pinter's *Old Times*." *English* 22 (autumn 1973): 99–102.

Baker, William, and Stephen E. Tabachnick. *Harold Pinter*. Writers and Critics Series. Edinburgh: Oliver & Boyd, 1973; New York: Barnes & Noble, 1973.

Barber, John. "A Warning Perhaps, but a Bore!" *Daily Express* (20 May 1958): 12.

Barnes, Clive [1]. "The Theatre: Pinter's Birthday Party." *New York Times* (4 Oct. 1967): 40.

———[2]. "Stage: Caught in the Sway of a Sea-Changed Pinter" *New York Times* (18 Oct. 1971): C8.

———[3]. "Stage: Pinter's Small Talk of Reality." *New York Times* (3 Aug. 1971): 43.

Ben-Zvi, Linda. "*Monologue*: The Play of Words." In *Critical Essays on Harold Pinter*, ed. Steven H. Gale. Boston: G. K. Hall, 1990: 128–36.

Bold, Alan, ed. and intro. *Harold Pinter: You Never Heard Such Silence*. London: Vision Press, 1984; Totowa, NJ: Barnes, 1985.

Boothroyd, Basil. "At the Play." *Punch* (28 May 1958): 721.

Boulton, James T. "Harold Pinter: *The Caretaker* and Other Plays." *Modern Drama* 6.2 (Sept. 1963): 131–40.

Brater, Enoch. "*The French Lieutenant's Woman*: Screenplay and Adaptation." In *Harold Pinter: Critical Approaches*, ed. Steven H. Gale. Madison, NJ: Fairleigh Dickinson University Press, 1986: 139–53.

Braunmuller, A. R. "Pinter's *Silence*: Experience without Character." In *Harold Pinter: Critical Approaches*, ed. Steven H. Gale. Madison, NJ: Fairleigh Dickinson University Press, 1986: 118–28.

Brien, Alan [1]. "In London: *The Homecoming*, 'An Unnerving Horror-Comic Skill.' " *Vogue* (15 Sept. 1965): 75.

———[2]. "The Guilty Seam." *The Spectator* (29 Jan. 1960): 137–38.

Brown, John Russell [1]. *Theatre Language: A Study of Arden, Osborne, Pinter and Wesker*. London: Penguin, 1971; rpt., New York: Taplinger, 1972.

———[2]. "Mr. Pinter's Shakespeare." *Critical Quarterly* 5.3 (autumn 1963): 251–65.

Brustein, Robert [1]. "The English Stage." *New Statesman* (6 Aug. 1965): 193–94.

———[2]. "Pared to Privacy, Melting into Silence." *The Observer* (6 July 1969): 22.

———[3]. "Saturn Eats His Children." *New Republic* (28 Jan. 1967): 34–36.

Burkman, Katherine H. [1]. *The Dramatic World of Harold Pinter: Its Basis in Ritual*. Columbus: Ohio State University Press, 1971.

———[2]. "*Family Voices* and the Voice of the Family in Pinter's Plays." In *Harold*

Pinter: Critical Approaches, ed. Steven H. Gale. Madison, NJ: Fairleigh Dickinson University Press, 1986: 164–75.

———[3]. "Harold Pinter's *Betrayal*: Life before Death—and After." In *Critical Essays on Harold Pinter*, ed. Steven H. Gale. Boston: G. K. Hall, 1990: 142–56.

———, ed. [4]. *Pinter at Sixty*. Bloomington: Indiana University Press, 1993.

Cima, Gay Gibson. "Acting on the Cutting Edge: Pinter and the Syntax of Cinema." In *Critical Essays on Harold Pinter*, ed. Steven H. Gale. Boston: G. K. Hall, 1990: 244–58.

Clurman, Harold [1]. Review of *The Birthday Party*. *Nation* (23 Oct. 1967): 412–14.

———[2]. Review of *The Homecoming*. *Nation* (7 June 1971): 732–33.

———[3]. Review of *No Man's Land*. *Nation* (27 Nov. 1976): 572–73.

———[4]. Review of *Old Times*. *Nation* (6 Dec. 1971): 603.

Coward, Noël. "These Old-Fashioned Revolutionaries." *Sunday Times Magazine* (15 Jan. 1961): 23.

Cushman, Robert. "Mr. Pinter's Spoonerisms." *Observer Review* (27 Apr. 1975): 32.

Darlington, W. A. "Mad Meg and Lodger. Play Revels in Obscurity." *Daily Telegraph* (20 May 1958): 10.

Dash, Thomas R. "Two Ironic Pinter Plays Are Vivid and Engrossing." *Women's Wear Daily* (27 Nov. 1962): 28.

Dent, Alan. "He Gets His Effect by Silence." *News Chronicle* (9 Mar. 1960): 5.

Diamond, Elin [1]. "The Parody Plays [*The Dumb Waiter*]." In *Critical Essays on Harold Pinter*. ed. Steven H. Gale. Boston: G. K. Hall, 1990: 47–65.

———[2]. *Pinter's Comic Play*. Lewisburg, PA: Bucknell University Press, 1985.

Dohmen, William F. "Time after Time: Pinter Plays with Disjunctive Chronologies." In *Harold Pinter: Critical Approaches*, ed. Steven H. Gale. Madison, NJ: Fairleigh Dickinson University Press, 1986: 187–202.

Dukore, Bernard F. [1]. *Harold Pinter*. New York: Grove Press 1982.

———[2]. "My, How We've Changed." In *Harold Pinter: Critical Approaches*, ed. Steven H. Gale. Madison, NJ: Fairleigh Dickinson University Press, 1986: 25–30.

———[3]. *Where Laughter Stops: Pinter's Tragicomedy*. Columbia: University of Missouri Press, 1976.

Esslin, Martin [1]. "Betrayal." *Plays and Players* (Jan. 1979).

———[2]. "Evaluation." In *Critical Essays on Harold Pinter*, ed. Steven H. Gale. Boston: G. K. Hall, 1990: 298–304.

———[3]. "Harold Pinter's Work for Radio." In *Harold Pinter: Critical Approaches*, ed. Steven H. Gale. Madison, NJ: Fairleigh Dickinson University Press, 1986: 47–64.

———[4]. *The Peopled Wound: The Work of Harold Pinter*. New York: Doubleday/Anchor, 1970; rev. as *Pinter: A Study of His Plays*. London: Eyre Methuen, 1973; *Pinter: The Playwright*. Portsmouth, NH: Heinemann, 1984.

———[5]. *The Theatre of the Absurd*. New York: Doubleday/Anchor, 1961.

Feldstein, Elayne Phyliss. "From Novel to Film: The Impact of Harold Pinter on Robert Maugham's *The Servant*." In *Critical Essays on Harold Pinter*, ed. Steven H. Gale. Boston: G. K. Hall, 1990: 175–83.

Fuegi, John. "The Uncertainty Principle and Pinter's Modern Drama." In *Harold Pinter: Critical Approaches*, ed. Steven H. Gale. Madison: NJ: Fairleigh Dickinson University Press, 1986: 202–9.

Gabbard, Lucina Paquet [1]. *The Dream Structure of Pinter's Plays: A Psychoanalytic Approach*. Rutherford, NJ: Fairleigh Dickinson University Press, 1976.

———[2]. "The Pinter Surprise." In *Harold Pinter: Critical Approaches*, ed. Steven H. Gale. Madison: NJ: Fairleigh Dickinson University Press, 1986: 175–87.

Gale, Steven H. [1]. "Art Objects as Metaphors in Harold Pinter's Screenplays." In *Pinter at Sixty*, ed. Katherine H. Burkman. Bloomington: Indiana University Press, 1993.

———[2]. "Breakers of Illusion: George in Edward Albee's *Who's Afraid of Virginia Woolf?* and Richard in Harold Pinter's *The Lover*." *Vision* 1.1 (fall 1979): 70–77.

———[3]. *Butter's Going Up: A Critical Analysis of Harold Pinter's Work*. Durham, NC: Duke University Press, 1977.

———[4]. "Character and Motivation in Harold Pinter's *The Homecoming*." *Journal of Evolutionary Psychology* 8.3–4 (Aug. 1987): 278–88.

———[5]. "Deadly Mind Games: Harold Pinter's *Old Times*." In *Critical Essays on Harold Pinter*, ed. Steven H. Gale. Boston: G. K. Hall, 1990: 211–28.

———[6]. "Harold Pinter." *Encyclopedia of World Literature in the Twentieth Century*. Vol. 3. 2nd ed. New York: Frederick Ungar, 1983: 533–38.

———[7]. "Harold Pinter's *Family Voices* and the Concept of Family." In *Harold Pinter: You Never Heard Such Silence*, ed. Alan Bold. London and New York: Vision/Barnes & Noble, 1984: 146–65.

———[8]. "Harold Pinter's *No Man's Land*: Life at a Standstill." *Jewish Quarterly* 24.4 (winter 1976/77): 13–18, 20.

———[9]. "Nature Half Created, Half Perceived: Time and Reality in Harold Pinter's Later Plays." *Journal of Evolutionary Psychology* 5.3–4 (Aug. 1984): 196–204.

———[10]. "Observations on Two Productions of Harold Pinter's *Old Times*." *Pinter Review* 1.1 (1987): 40–43.

———[11]. "The Variable Nature of Reality: Harold Pinter's Plays in the 1970's." *Kansas Quarterly* 12.4 (fall 1980): 17–24.

———[12]. "The Writing of Harold Pinter: An Overview." *Literary Half-Yearly* 22.2 (July 1979): 79–89.

Garner, Stanton B., Jr. "Correcting the Space: Scenic Negotiations in *No Man's Land*." In *The Pinter Review: Annual Essays, 1989*, ed. Francis Gillen and Steven H. Gale. Tampa: University of Tampa, 1989: 1–8.

Gascoigne, Bamber. "Love in the Afternoon." *The Observer* (22 Sept. 1963): 26.

Giantvalley, Scott. "Toying with *The Dwarfs*: The Textual Problems with Pinter's 'Corrections.' " In *Harold Pinter: Critical Approaches*, ed. Steven H. Gale. Madison, NJ: Fairleigh Dickinson University Press, 1986: 72–82.

Gibbs, Patrick. "People Shut in Private Worlds: Symbolic Plays." *Daily Telegraph* (9 Mar. 1970): 14.

Gill, Brendan. "The Cry." *The New Yorker* (27 Nov. 1971): 89.

Gillen, Francis [1]. " 'All These Bits and Pieces': Fragmentation and Choice in Pinter's Plays." *Modern Drama* 17.4 (Dec. 1974): 477–87.

———[2]. "Harold Pinter's *The Birthday Party*: Menace Reconsidered." In *Harold Pinter: Critical Approaches*, ed. Steven H. Gale. Madison, NJ: Fairleigh Dickinson University Press, 1986: 38–47.

———[3]. "Nowhere to Go': Society and the Individual in Harold Pinter's *The Hot-*

house." In *Critical Essays on Harold Pinter*, ed. Steven H. Gale. Boston: G. K. Hall, 1990: 164–75.

Gilliatt, Penelope. "Achievement from a Tight-Rope." *The Observer* (6 June 1965): 25.

Gilman, Richard [1]. *Common and Uncommon Masks*. New York: Random House, 1971.

———[2]. "Mortal Combat." *Newsweek* (16 Jan. 1967): 93.

Goldstone, Herbert. "Not So Puzzling Pinter: *The Homecoming." Theatre Annual* 25 (1969): 20–27.

Gordon, Lois. *Stratagems to Uncover Nakedness: The Dramas of Harold Pinter*. Columbia: University of Missouri Press, 1968.

Gottfried, Martin. *"The Birthday Party." Women's Wear Daily* (4 Oct. 1967): 44.

Hall, Stuart. "Home Sweet Home." *Encore* (July–Aug. 1965): 30–34.

Hewes, Henry [1]. "Odd Husband Out." *Saturday Review* (4 Dec. 1971): 20, 22.

———[2]. "Pinter's Hilarious Depth Charge." *Saturday Review* (21 Jan. 1967): 61.

Hinchliffe, Arnold P. [1]. "After *No Man's Land*: A Progress Report." In *Harold Pinter: Critical Approaches*, ed. Steven H. Gale. Madison: NJ: Fairleigh Dickinson University Press, 1986: 153–64.

———[2]. *Harold Pinter*. New York: Twayne, 1967; rev., New York: G. K. Hall, 1981.

Hirsch, Foster. *"The Go-Between."* In *Critical Essays on Harold Pinter*, ed. Steven H. Gale. Boston: G. K. Hall, 1990: 183–91.

Hobson, Harold [1]. "Larger than Life at the Festival." *Sunday Times* (6 July 1969): 52.

———[2]. "Paradise Lost." *Sunday Times* (6 July 1969): 52.

———[3]. "The Screw Turns Again." *The Sunday Times* (25 May 1958): 11.

Hollis, James R. *Harold Pinter: The Poetics of Silence*. Crosscurrents/Modern Critiques Series. Carbondale: Southern Illinois University Press, 1970.

Houston, Beverle, and Marsha Kinder. "The Losey-Pinter Collaboration." In *Critical Essays on Harold Pinter*, ed. Steven H. Gale. Boston: G. K. Hall, 1990: 191–209.

Hudgins, Christopher [1]. *"The Basement*: Harold Pinter on BBC-TV." In *Critical Essays on Harold Pinter*, ed. Steven H. Gale. Boston: G. K. Hall, 1990: 89–101.

———[2]. "Intended Audience Response, *The Homecoming*, and the 'Ironic Mode of Identification.' " In *Harold Pinter: Critical Approaches*, ed. Steven H. Gale. Madison: NJ: Fairleigh Dickinson University Press, 1986: 102–18.

Hughes, Catherine. "Pinter and 'Pinteresque.' " *America* (11 Dec. 1976): 424.

Jenkins, Peter. Review of *Betrayal*. *The Spectator* (25 Nov. 1978): 24.

Jiji, Vera M. "Pinter's Four Dimensional House: *The Homecoming*." In *Critical Essays on Harold Pinter*, ed. Steven H. Gale. Boston: G. K. Hall, 1990: 101–11.

Keown, Eric. "At the Play." *Punch* (11 May 1960): 665.

Kerr, Walter. *Harold Pinter*. New York: Columbia University Press, 1967.

Knowles, Ronald [1]. "Harold Pinter, Citizen." In *The Pinter Review: Annual Essays, 1989*, eds. Francis Gillen and Steven H. Gale. Tampa: University of Tampa, 1989: 24–34.

———[2]. "The Primacy of Performance in Pinter's Plays." In *Critical Essays on Harold Pinter*, ed. Steven H. Gale. Boston: G. K. Hall, 1990: 219–20.

Kroll, Jack. "The Puzzle of Pinter." *Newsweek* (29 Nov. 1976): 74–78, 81.

Lambert, J. W. [1]. *"The Caretaker." Sunday Times* (1 May 1960): 25.

———[2]. "Plays in Performance." *Drama* 117 (summer 1975): 37–55.

Malkin, Lawrence. "Pinter's New World." *Time* (19 May 1975): 80.

Marcus, Frank [1]. "A Couple of Half-Pinters." *Sunday Telegraph* (6 July 1969): 14.

———[2]. "Pinter: The Pause That Refreshes." *New York Times* (12 July 1969): D8.

Marowitz, Charles. "Theatre Abroad." *Village Voice* (1 Sept. 1960).

Muller, Robert. "Hate Yourself Though You May, You'll Enjoy These Plays." *Daily Mail* (19 Jan. 1961): 3.

Powlick, Leonard. " 'What the Hell Is *That* All About?': A Peek at Pinter's Dramaturgy." In *Harold Pinter: Critical Approaches*, ed. Steven H. Gale. Madison, NJ: Fairleigh Dickinson University Press, 1986: 30–38.

Prentice, Penelope A. *Harold Pinter: Life, Work, and Criticism*. Fredericton: York Press, 1991.

Quigley, Austin [1]. "Design and Discovery in Pinter's *The Lover*." In *Harold Pinter: Critical Approaches*, ed. Steven H. Gale. Madison, NJ: Fairleigh Dickinson University Press, 1986: 82–102.

———[2]. "The Language Problem." In *Critical Essays on Harold Pinter*, ed. Steven H. Gale. Boston: G. K. Hall, 1990: 270–98.

———[3]. *The Pinter Problem*. Princeton, NJ: Princeton University Press, 1975.

Ryan, Stephen P. "The London Stage." *America* (27 Oct. 1962): 956–58.

Sahai, Surendra. *Harold Pinter: A Critical Evaluation*. New York: Longwood, 1981.

Sheed, Wilfrid. "Absurdity Revisited." *Commonweal* (30 Apr. 1965): 193–94.

Shulman, Milton [1]. "Sorry, Mr. Pinter, You're Just Not Funny Enough." *Evening Standard* (20 May 1958): 6.

———[2]. "Pinter in His Best Hypnotic Mood." *Evening Standard* (19 June 1962): 10.

Smith, Leslie. "Pinter the Player." In *Critical Essays on Harold Pinter*. ed. Steven H. Gale. Boston: G. K. Hall, 1990: 230–44.

Sykes, Alrene. *Harold Pinter*. New York: Humanities Press, 1970.

Taylor, John Russell. *Anger and After: A Guide to New British Drama*. London: Methuen, 1962.

Thompson, David T. *Pinter: The Player's Playwright*. New York: Schocken Books, 1985.

Trewin, J. C. "Cutting It Short." *Illustrated London News* (4 Feb. 1961): 192.

Trussler, Simon. *The Plays of Harold Pinter: An Assessment*. London: Gollancz, 1973.

Tucker, Stephanie. "Cinematic Proust Manifested by Pinter." In *Critical Essays on Harold Pinter*, ed. Steven H. Gale. Boston: G. K. Hall, 1990: 209–19.

Tynan, Kenneth. "A Verbal Wizard in the Suburbs." *The Observer* (5 June 1960): 16.

Wardle, Irving [1]. "The Birthday Party." *Encore* 5 (July–Aug. 1958), 39–40.

———[2]. "Pinter Theatrical Twins in Pools of Solitude." *The Times* (4 July 1969): 7.

Weales, Gerald. "The Stage: Odd Man Out." *Commonweal* (17 Dec. 1971): 278.

Wertheim, Albert. "Tearing of Souls: Harold Pinter's *A Slight Ache* on Radio and Stage." In *Harold Pinter: Critical Approaches*, ed. Steven H. Gale. Madison: NJ: Fairleigh Dickinson University Press, 1986: 64–72.

Worth, Katharine. "Pinter's Scenic Imagery." In *Critical Essays on Harold Pinter*, ed. Steven H. Gale. Boston: G. K. Hall, 1990: 258–69.

Zeifman, Hersh. "Ghost Trio: Pinter's *Family Voices*." In *Critical Essays on Harold Pinter*, ed. Steven H. Gale. Boston: G. K. Hall, 1990: 156–64.

BIBLIOGRAPHIES

Gale, Steven H. *Harold Pinter: An Annotated Bibliography*. Boston: G. K. Hall, 1978.
Imhoff, Rudiger. *Pinter: A Bibliography*. London: TQ Publications, 1975.
King, Kimball. "Harold Pinter." *Twenty Modern British Playwrights: A Bibliography, 1956 to 1976*. New York: Garland, 1977: 125–92.

Stephen Poliakoff
(1952–)

WILLIAM W. DEMASTES

Stephen Poliakoff was born in London 14 December 1952, the son of a Russian Jewish immigrant who moved with his family to England in 1924 and an English mother who was for a brief time an actress. He was educated at Westminster School and for two years at King's College, Cambridge, but he left Cambridge without taking a degree. Determined to be a writer, at fourteen he wrote a novel and at sixteen mounted a performance in London of his first play, *Granny* (1969), which actually received minor notice by a few established critics. *Bambi Ramm* followed the next year. A successful collaborative work entitled *Lay By* (1971), with several rising stars—Howard Brenton, Brian Clark, David Hare, Hugh Stoddart, and Snoo Wilson—was produced at Edinburgh's Traverse Theatre, gaining even more recognition for Poliakoff. In association with the English Stage Company at the Royal Court Theatre, *Pretty Boy* was given a Sunday evening tryout in 1972, when Poliakoff was just twenty. *The Carnation Gang* (1974) followed. Both plays reveal what will be Poliakoff's continued interest in a generally adolescent cast of characters cut off from hope and opportunity by an uncaring, manipulative modern Britain, in the 1960s holding so much promise, but now reverting to a new conservatism.

Poliakoff was a prolific writer, and numerous plays and major productions quickly followed: *Clever Soldiers* (1974); *Hitting Town* (1975); *Heroes* (1975); *City Sugar* (1976); *Strawberry Fields* (1977); *Shout across the River* (1978). In 1975 Poliakoff received the Most Promising Playwright Award from the London *Evening Standard*. From 1976 to 1977 he was writer-in-residence at the British National Theatre.

Much of Poliakoff's recent energy has been focused in television and cinema, including the filmscripts *She's Been Away* (1989) and *Close My Eyes* (1992).

Selected Biographical Sources: Kerensky; Salmon.

MAJOR PLAYS, PREMIERES, AND SIGNIFICANT
REVIVALS: THEATRICAL RECEPTION

Lay By (with Howard Brenton, Brian Clark, Trevor Griffiths, David Hare, Hugh Stoddart, and Snoo Wilson). 1971. Opened at the Traverse Theatre, Edinburgh, 24 August; moved to the Royal Court Theatre, London, 26 September.

A dramatization of a newspaper account of a woman raped by a lorry driver while his girlfriend looked on, the play, according to de Jongh, "conveys an image of [human] flesh as so much exploitable poundage." Nightingale [10] commends the seamlessness of the collaboration, but was emotionally drained by the message and stark presentation of the play, described as society's brutal inhumanity toward its less successful members. Nightingale [10] adds that his fellow viewers were likewise visibly disturbed by the play. A vivid corpse scene seems to have captured everyone's memory. Wardle [1] reports being impressed by the honest sense of desolation presented in the play, seeing the piece as an excellent demonstration of good writing and economical staging.

Clever Soldiers. 1974. Hampstead Theatre Club, London, 25 November, for twenty-eight performances.

Nightingale [4] observes that the play reveals a young playwright "of great promise and some spleen." Set in the World War I period, the play indicts Oxford snobbery and brutality.

Hitting Town. 1975. Bush Theatre Club, Shepherd's Bush, London, 15 April, for eighteen performances. Directed by Tim Fywell. Opened in New York at the South Street Theater, January 1979, directed by Richard Hamburger.

Nightingale [6] observes that Poliakoff "has only just evolved from peascod into apple," but he is already demonstrating talent and promise. Like *Clever Soldiers*, the play has "nervy, edgy dialogue" threatening every moment to explode. It is an "unhackneyed" depiction of the results of a loveless, friendless, urban environment. Reviewing the New York revival, Eder [2] called it much slighter than the other two imports (*City Sugar* and *Strawberry Fields*), despite its "sharp and focused dialogue." There was indeed a focused "energy of outrage," but not much for it to work upon. It was ultimately an "unsatisfactory sketch."

Heroes. 1975. Royal Court Theatre Upstairs, London, 1 July, for nineteen performances.

About contemporary fascism and poverty, this third Poliakoff play that Nightingale [5] has seen confirms for him the playwright's distinctive voice. The world Poliakoff dramatizes is a "peculiar world, maybe a perverse one; but it is out of peculiarity and perversity that interesting playwrights emerge."

City Sugar. 1975. Bush Theatre, Shepherd's Bush London, 9 October; revised and opened at the Comedy Theatre, London, 4 March 1976, for seventy-four performances; presented by Michael White. Directed by Hugh Thomas. Revived

5 June 1978, Phoenix Marymount Theatre (NY); and August 1980, Westside Mainstage (NY), directed by Robert Greenwood.

Nightingale [2] notes that Poliakoff has moved from incest (*Hitting Town*) to sadism (*City Sugar*) and shows that human dignity can survive "even in Leicester." Trewin found the play the "most consistently enjoyable" of West End works this season. Hurren, however, suggests that Poliakoff has been hauled from the fringe to the West End "perhaps prematurely." He "doesn't have a lot to say as yet." Nightingale [3] only in part agrees, seeing the play as "eloquent, intelligent," though the intimacy of the Shepherd's Bush Theatre was more suitable for the play than was the Comedy Theatre. Wardle [3] saw the Comedy Theatre production as a "scathingly brilliant play," favorably commenting on the theme that drugs are a social tool used "to dull the victim to carrying out mindless tasks." Reviewing the New York productions of both *Strawberry Fields* and *City Sugar*, Oliver saw *City Sugar* as the better play, but she found that obvious comparison (given "low-class" subject matter) to Harold Pinter, Joe Orton, and David Mamet do Poliakoff "no good." Eder [1] likewise comments on both plays, seeing them as two aspects of Poliakoff's "central vision of the unbearableness of life in contemporary Britain." Eder adds that Poliakoff is not part of the last generation's Angry Young Men but part of this generation's "Desperate Young Men." The play, he notes, unites realism and absurdism and demonstrates a witty command of his vision, ultimately highlighting Poliakoff's strengths as *Strawberry Fields* does not; *Strawberry Fields* went "unconvincingly too far," whereas *City Sugar* more appropriately remained "mired in the futility of its protagonist." Reviewing the 1980 revival, Corry noted that both the earlier and current productions were "admirable." But although the play accurately depicts the tawdriness of contemporary life, it doesn't offer alternatives. Poliakoff, like the play's disc jockey, despairs pretty much because the 1960s are no more; this is a too vague, perhaps even "too elitist" point of concern. The despair over the "decline of popular taste; emptiness of success; vacancy of the public mind" signals an elitism that leaves Corry uncomfortable. But the play is still "wonderfully theatrical."

Strawberry Fields. 1977. Cottesloe Theatre of the National Theatre, London, 31 March. Directed by Michael Apted. Revived 4 June 1978, Manhattan Theatre Club (NY); directed by Stephen Pascal.

Nightingale [7] calls this fable "implausible," which makes it difficult to take seriously. Something of a play about the National Front, the play presents a 1960s-generation disillusionment resulting from the conservatism of the 1970s. After Poliakoff's previous two successes, Nightingale [7] says, "This can't be reckoned much more than a talented disappointment." Whitehead supposes that this is the kind of play to produce in the minimalist, radical Cottesloe Theatre. He sees Poliakoff presenting more disgust than sympathy for his central characters, whose choices have moved them to right-wing extremism. Perhaps better as a film, the play, Whitehead concludes, "just doesn't work." Of the New

York revival, Kauffmann calls Poliakoff's writing "diffuse" and a "dilution of a better young English playwright," Heathcote Williams. The production, however, confirmed Kauffmann's belief that better theatre can be found beyond Broadway. Eder [3] reports that "the intensity . . . keeps getting ahead of its credibility," adding, it "begins solidly and spins off into tenuousness," falling dangerously into "abstract shadows."

Shout across the River. 1978. By the Royal Shakespeare Company at the Warehouse Theatre, London, 21 September. Directed by Bill Alexander. Revived 2 January 1980, Phoenix Theatre (NY), directed by Robert Woodruff. Revived Old Red Lion Theatre, London, January 1991. Directed by Andrew Groves.

Nightingale [9] insists that despite being at times an implausible tale about a delinquent girl and agoraphobic mother, the play "has received less respect than it merits." Again Nightingale [9] argues that Poliakoff "has a quirkier and perhaps more original talent than his fellow-prophets." Jenkins sees Poliakoff's ear for detail as both his strength and his weakness. Jenkins says Poliakoff is what David Hare calls a "social secretary." Of the New York revival (starring Ellen Barkin), Gill calls *Shout across the River* "an incoherent little play." Gill reports that he hears Poliakoff is "an exceptionally prolific young man, and I am sorry to hear it." Gussow sees the play not as slice-of-life realism but as decided theatricalization, though he worries that some is not intentional. Although "a step removed from naturalism, the tone wavers," and we often wonder which scenes to take literally. Gussow concludes also that the play doesn't shock—as intended—and its discursiveness at times becomes quite impassive. Wright, however, observes that in the 1991 revival the text shows its staying power.

The Summer Party. 1980. Crucible Theatre, Sheffield, 12 March, for twenty-eight performances. Directed by Peter James.

Set in an open air concert where the crowd is cheated out of what it pays for and thereby turns ugly, *The Summer Party*, Allen reports, once again contains several implausible elements. Allen does insist, however, that, "technically, the show is terrific." Chaillet, in exasperation, complains that Poliakoff has apparently run out of things to say and is repeating things just to hear himself on stage.

Favourite Nights. 1981. Lyric Theater, Hammersmith, 2 November, twenty-four performances. Directed by Peter James.

Nightingale [8] observes that Poliakoff once again demonstrates that evolution means adapting to environment, and from Poliakoff's perspective adapting "means erosion or worse." Wardle [2] calls it a "feeble piece," adding, "[Terence] Rattigan could have got a good play" out of this material, about a proper girl by day turned "escort" by night; Poliakoff, however, does not.

Breaking the Silence. 1984. The Barbican Pit, London, 6 November. Staged by the Royal Shakespeare Company, London; closed 21 March 1985. Opened 28 May 1985, the Mermaid Theatre, London; closed 16 June. Directed by Ron Daniels.

King [1] observes that the play's primary appeal lies in "the quirky originality of its setting and theme." *Breaking the Silence* is set in 1920s Russia, where a poverty-stricken family makes a home of a railway car, a perfect symbol "of lives confined to predeterminate grooves." Bardsley agrees that Poliakoff has a "quirky eye for a bizarre story," although this one is not as good as *City Sugar*. Nightingale [1] completely dismisses this play, saying, "Maybe some things are just too factual to be true." Billington [1], however, observes, "The play may not, like the very best Poliakoff, shock you into new recognition; but it has a strong narrative and the authentic stamp of a personal story that had to be told." Of the revised Mermaid production, Barber observes, "I minded none of the implausibilities," and he notes that Alan Howard's presence in the play, after three years' absence from the stage, is a blessing. Garner provides an interesting analysis of the play by comparing it to David Mamet's *American Buffalo* and Beckett's *Not I*.

Coming in to Land. 1986. Lyttleton Theatre of the National Theatre, London, 18 December; closed 20 April. Directed by Peter Hall.

Edwards observes "an oddly disconnected quality" about the play, a study of a Polish design student, newly settled in England, whose "quirky passionate nature" throws an English youth, Neville, "into a state of emotional confusion." What is disconnected, says Edwards, is that he never quite emerges from his confusion. King [2] notes that the scene of interrogation in the second act alone makes the play worth seeing, and Maggie Smith's performance is likewise worthwhile: "Here is a case of a good dramatist below his usual form being redeemed by a great actress above even hers." Ray observes that the play is more like four plays, with Poliakoff "embarking on a variety of inconsistent and contradictory dramatic styles."

Playing with Trains. 1989. The Pit of the Royal Shakespeare Company, London, 29 November; closed 17 March 1990. Directed by Ron Daniels.

The production starred Michael Pennington as Bill, an inventor and entrepreneur who tries to slow British discoveries from leaving the country. Anderson summarizes the theme: "We're good at inventing but bad at exploiting the commercial potential of our inventions." Anderson concludes that the idea is overstated and that Poliakoff in fact dealt "with the theme of obsessive genius far better" in *Breaking the Silence*. Kellaway observes, "The overriding tone of Poliakoff's writing is bitter." She concludes: "Poliakoff's arguments are agile, the emotions are slacker, less interesting. Ron Daniels' trenchant production offers us an excellent machine looking needlessly for a heart."

ADDITIONAL PLAYS AND PRODUCTIONS

Granny, 1969, London; *Bambi Ramm*, 1970, Abbey Community Centre, London, 7 September; *Day with My Sister*, 1971, Traverse Theatre, Edinburgh, 21 October; *Pretty Boy*, 1972, Royal Court Theatre, London, for one performance,

24 September; *Berlin Days*, 1973, Little Theatre, London; *The Carnation Gang*, 1974, Bush Theatre Club, London, 23 September; *American Days*, 1979, I.C.A. Theatre, London, 12 June, for thirty-six performances, directed by John Chapman and Tim Fywell.

ASSESSMENT OF POLIAKOFF'S CAREER

Nightingale [8] observed in 1981 that Poliakoff's "career to date has consisted of making field trips into the urban rain-forest and sending back reports on the customs and artifacts he has incredulously observed." Since 1981 Poliakoff has gotten slightly more upscale in his choice of subject matter, but his reports still include stinging indictments of Britain's callousness toward its underrepresented masses and general ineptitude. Stylistically noted for his language of assault, reminiscent of Pinter, his dialogues throughout his career have remained idiomatically accurate and biting. Martin sees Poliakoff expanding beyond a Brechtian agenda, arguing less for an agenda of change and presenting instead a commentary on the decay and ruin brought on by our immediate past.

His earlier career was marked with a promise of things to come, although it should be noted that he has yet fully to replace his earlier accepted and understandable aggressive antagonism with a later, expected vision of an alternative to those activities, customs, and events he earlier lambasted. One could observe that this limitation, if not overcome, will relegate Poliakoff to the ranks of a minor contributor to recent British drama, though one should be reminded of two key points: writers many years his senior have likewise floundered when attempting to derive alternative social constructs, and Poliakoff is still only in his forties, despite many years on the theatre scene—the anger still present even today may eventually be replaced by a mature vision that through his considerable theatrical talent may ultimately find its way to the stage.

Predicting or hoping for future growth, however, should not be considered justification for downplaying Poliakoff's considerable accomplishments to date. In 1979 Billington [2] grouped Poliakoff with David Hare, Trevor Griffiths, David Edgar, and Howard Brenton—calling them "Britain's New Political Playwrights"—and observed that although he could not guess where British drama would go from that point, "it is worth stressing that it has reached a mass audience . . . and that it has begun to occupy the theater's commanding heights." Indeed, Poliakoff and his generation have succeeded at moving from the fringe to center stage, bringing with them voices and material previously not permitted on the stage. Billington [2] also notes that Poliakoff and others are perhaps rightly less optimistic about the possibilities of radical change—as, say, an American Clifford Odets or the British Angry Young Men of the 1950s and 1960s were—and although Marxists still take the stage, "the more interesting writers are not so fervently optimistic: they realize that waiting for Lefty can be as exhausting as waiting for Godot." Waiting for someone or something is, essentially, what Poliakoff refuses to do. Perhaps for him a political transformation is less to be desired than an understanding of the human spirit, which may be the first step to an existential change in that spirit.

In fact reviewers like Eder [1] have noted that Poliakoff's theatre is a fusion of absurdism and realism, an observation made years earlier of Pinter's theatre. However, Poliakoff is decidedly more socially engaged than Pinter. Perhaps seeing Poliakoff activating that abstract philosophy of absurdism in his politically charged plays is precisely what other reviewers and critics have missed. Perhaps Poliakoff is in fact advocating a change of spirit rather than legislative, political, and/or social change. That this possibility escapes many critics is obvious. Primarily realistic, Poliakoff's plays almost exclusively invite social commentary. When moments of the fantastic and absurd occur, critics have written his works off as "implausible." It may, however, be that Poliakoff is inviting us to move beyond the linearity of plausible narrative to probe other regions of human activity, which intersect our material reality and even affect that reality but which all too often are ignored in favor of other, external, fixes. Rabey is right to include Poliakoff in his discussion of British political drama, but such an approach to Poliakoff's work may be incomplete. Cave discusses Poliakoff in his section on the Marxism of Edward Bond, but materialist transformation of society, again, seems not to be Poliakoff's ultimate goal. It is reasonable to assume that establishing an equitable distribution of wealth, say, between the North and the South, would be welcomed, but Poliakoff's plays include characters rising to financial success only to report the hollowness of their accomplishments. Chandhuri's discussion is particularly insightful in this regard.

In 1977 Kerensky reserved one of his fourteen chapters for Poliakoff, noting that Poliakoff is the youngest to be included. Kerensky observes in his conclusion, "Stephen Poliakoff wonders how long he will last as a playwright; most of the playwrights wonder how long Britain will last; and in the present economic climate we must all wonder how long, and in what form, the theatre can last." Poliakoff has recently turned more fully to television and film, but he has successfully written for the stage since 1977. And although economic crises persist in both Britain and the British theatre, both have nonetheless survived. Lacking the political agenda many seem to believe will save the world, Poliakoff's theatre may in fact provide the actual direction for substantial change: a fresher look at what the theatre can do (advise the critics) and what society must do (advise fellow citizens).

PRIMARY BIBLIOGRAPHY

Plays

American Days. London: Eyre Methuen, 1979.
Breaking the Silence. London: Methuen, 1984.
City Sugar. London: Samuel French, 1976.
Clever Soldiers. London: Samuel French, 1976.
Coming in to Land. London: Methuen, 1984.

Favourite Nights and *Caught on a Train*. London: Methuen, 1982.
Hitting Town and *Sugar City*. London: Eyre Methuen, 1976.
Lay By (with Howard Brenton, Brian Clark, Trevor Griffiths, David Hare, Hugh Stoddart, and Snoo Wilson). London: Calder & Boyers, 1972.
Playing with Trains. London: Methuen, 1989.
Runner and *Soft Targets*. London: Methuen, 1984.
Shout across the River. London: Eyre Methuen, 1979.
Sienna Red. London: Methuen, 1992.
Strawberry Fields. London: Eyre Methuen, 1977.
The Summer Party. London: Eyre Methuen, 1980.

Anthology

Plays: One. (Clever Soldiers, Hitting Town, City Sugar, Shout across the River, American Days, Strawberry Fields). London: Methuen, 1989.

Essays and Articles on Theatre and Drama

Introduction to *Plays: One*. London: Methuen, 1989: ix–xv.

Interview

"Coming of Age" (with Lyn Gardner). *Drama* 163 (1987):19–20.

SECONDARY BIBLIOGRAPHY

Allen, Paul. "Constabular Campery." *New Statesman* (21 Mar. 1980): 448–49.
Anderson, Paul. Review of *Playing with Trains*. *The Tribune* (8 Dec. 1989).
Barber, John. Review of *Breaking the Silence*. *Daily Telegraph* (29 May 1985).
Bardsley, Barney. Review of *Breaking the Silence*. *The Tribune* (16 Nov. 1984).
Billington, Michael [1]. Review of *Breaking the Silence*. *The Guardian* (7 Nov. 1984).
———[2]. "Britain's New Political Playwrights." *New York Times* (18 Mar. 1979): D5.
Cave, Richard Allen. *New British Drama in Performance on the London Stage: 1970–1985*. Gerrards Cross: Colin Smythe, 1987.
Chaillet, Ned. Review of *The Summer Party*. *The Times* (17 Mar. 1980).
Chandhuri, Una. *Staging Places: The Geography of Modern Drama*. Ann Arbor: University of Michigan Press, 1995.
Corry, John. Review of *City Sugar*. *New York Times* (4 Aug. 1980): C13.
Coveney, Michael. "Strange and Listless Journeys." *Drama* 156 (1985): 9–12.
Craig, Randall. Review of *Clever Soldiers*. *Drama* 116 (1975): 69–71.
de Jongh, Nicholas. Review of *Lay-by* [sic]. *The Spectator* (4 Sept. 1971): 346.
Eder, Richard [1]. Review of *City Sugar*. *New York Times* (6 June 1978): C3.
———[2]. Review of *Hitting Town*. *New York Times* (9 Jan. 1979): C9.
———[3]. " 'Strawberry Fields' Staged." *New York Times* (5 June 1978): C15.
Edwards, Christopher. Review of *Coming in to Land*. *The Spectator* (17 Jan. 1987).

Garner, Stanton B., Jr. *Bodied Spaces: Phenomenology and Performance in Contemporary Drama*. Ithaca: Cornell University Press, 1994.

Gill, Brendan. Review of *Shout across the River*. *The New Yorker* (14 Jan. 1980): 56.

Gussow, Mel. Review of *Shout across the River*. *New York Times* (3 Jan. 1980): C12.

Hurren, Kenneth. Review of *City Sugar*. *Illustrated London News* (May 1976): 72.

Jenkins, Peter. Review of *Shout across the River*. *The Spectator* (30 Sept. 1978): 24.

Kauffmann, Stanley. Review of *Strawberry Fields*. *New Republic* (8 and 15 July 1978): 28–29.

Kellaway, Kate. Review of *Playing with Trains*. *The Observer* (3 Dec. 1989).

Kerensky, Oleg. *The New British Drama: Fourteen Playwrights since Osborne and Pinter*. New York: Taplinger, 1977.

King, Francis [1]. Review of *Breaking the Silence*. *Sunday Telegraph* (11 Nov. 1984).

———[2]. Review of *Coming in to Land*. *Sunday Telegraph* (11 Jan. 1987).

Martin, Matthew. "Stephen Poliakoff's Drama for the Post-Scientific Age." *Theatre Journal* 45.2 (May 1993): 197–211.

Nightingale, Benedict [1]. Review of *Breaking the Silence*. *New Statesman* (16 Nov. 1984).

———[2]. Review of *City Sugar*. *New Statesman* (17 Oct. 1975): 481–82.

———[3]. Review of *City Sugar*. *New Statesman* (12 Mar. 1976): 338.

———[4]. Review of *Clever Soldiers*. *New Statesman* (29 Nov. 1974): 798.

———[5]. Review of *Heroes*. *New Statesman* (11 July 1975): 62–63.

———[6]. Review of *Hitting Town*. *New Statesman* (11 Apr. 1975): 492–93.

———[7]. "Holocaustic." *New Statesman* (15 Apr. 1977): 505–6.

———[8]. "In Alphaville." *New Statesman* (6 Nov. 1981): 448–49.

———[9]. "That England." *New Statesman* (29 Sept. 1978): 418.

———[10]. "Treated like Meat." *New Statesman* (3 Sept. 1971): 310.

Oliver, Edith. Reviews of *Strawberry Fields* and *City Sugar*. *The New Yorker* (19 June 1978): 54.

Rabey, David Ian. *British and Irish Political Drama in the Twentieth Century: Implicating the Audience*. Houndsmill: Macmillan, 1986.

Ray, Robin. Review of *Coming in to Land*. *Punch* (21 Jan. 1987).

Salmon, Eric. "Stephen Poliakoff." In *British Dramatists since World War II: Part II, M–Z: A Dictionary of Literary Biography*. Vol. 13, ed. Stanley Weintraub. Detroit, MI: Gale Research, 1982: 413–19.

Trewin, J. C. Review of *City Sugar*. *Illustrated London News* (May 1976): 72.

Wardle, Irving [1]. "Descending into the Grassmarket." *The Times* (26 Aug. 1971): 6.

———[2]. Review of *Favourite Nights*. *The Times* (3 Nov. 1981): 10.

———[3]. "Technological Nightmare in a Supermarket." *The Times* (5 Mar. 1976): 10.

Whitehead, Ted. "On the Road." *The Spectator* (16 Apr. 1977): 32.

Wright, Michael. Review of *Shout across the River*. *The Times* (7 Jan. 1991): 14.

Willy Russell
(1947–)

CHRIS JONES

Despite training as a hairdresser instead of a playwright, Willy Russell has become one of the most popular and commercially successful British authors of the last two decades. He has enjoyed a string of West End hits, especially *Educating Rita*, *Blood Brothers*, and *Shirley Valentine*, as well as considerable success in the United States through several film adaptations of his works. Writing primarily about working-class characters from the north of England trapped in deprived economic circumstances, Russell has generally eschewed political polemics in favor of fables of working-class self-empowerment told in a lightly comedic and highly accessible style. Steyn and others have sometimes found his work to be trite and bathetic, but commercial theatre audiences have usually responded favorably to his plays' gentle warmth and to the stoic, self-deprecating humor long associated with Russell's native Liverpool.

The son of a fish-and-chips shop owner, Willy Russell was born in Whiston near Liverpool in 1947. An unsuccessful student, he left school with minimal formal qualifications and became a hairdresser before taking a warehouse job. His spare time in the late 1960s was spent playing folk music in the many Liverpool clubs, where he met his wife, Annie (the woman who took Russell to the theatre for the first time). Returning to study through evening classes, the young man ultimately trained to be a teacher. After seeing an Everyman Theatre, Liverpool, production of John McGrath's *Unruly Elements*, Russell decided, at the age of twenty, to become a playwright. In June 1972 his one-act plays *Keep Your Eyes Down* and *Sam O'Shanker* were produced at St. Katherine's College, Liverpool, under the collective title *Blind Scouse* and later taken to that year's Edinburgh Festival Fringe. McGrath happened to attend this fringe production and persuaded Alan Dossor, then artistic director of the Everyman, to see Russell's work. This led to Russell's writing his first play for the Liverpool theatre,

When The Reds . . . (1972), an adaptation of Alan Plater's play *The Tigers Are Coming OK*.

Russell's big national breakthrough came in 1974. *John, Paul, George, Ringo . . . and Bert*, a musical play about the Beatles, was commissioned by Dossor at the Everyman and given a tiny budget of £1,000. Later in the year it transferred to the Lyric, Shaftesbury Avenue, just before Russell reached the age of twenty-seven. Two major national tours and several European productions followed the West End run. According to Russell, a Broadway production was planned and a film version commissioned, but due to litigation by Paul McCartney neither was ever produced, although Russell did write an unpublished screenplay commissioned by McCartney entitled *Band on the Run*. Despite his growing success, Russell was still making his living by working as a teacher.

Breezeblock Park, a working-class comedy of manners, was commissioned in 1975 and directed by Dossor in both Liverpool and London. The following year Russell wrote a radio play entitled *I Read the News Today* and the BBC Birmingham television play *Our Day Out*, which was transmitted nationally three times to huge audiences and subsequently in 1983, made, into a musical play for the stage, produced both at the Everyman and at London's Young Vic. That year, 1976, also saw the first production of the play *One for the Road*, under the title *Painted Veg and Parkinson*, at the Manchester Contact Theatre. Under its final title the play was to tour nationally, be performed at the Liverpool Playhouse in 1980, and finally reach the West End in 1987 in a new updated version as a vehicle for popular comedian Russ Abbott.

Russell's next television play for schools, written after the Manchester premiere of *One for the Road*, entitled *Lies*, was transmitted by the BBC in November 1977.

In 1978 Russell wrote a play for Yorkshire Television entitled *Daughters of Albion*; he also wrote *Stags and Hens*. The play was originally produced by students at Manchester Polytechnic, where Russell was now a fellow in creative writing, and it was subsequently revised as a stage play. The Liverpool Everyman produced the work, under the direction of Chris Bond, in October 1978.

Commissioned by the Royal Shakespeare Company and directed by Mike Ockrent, *Educating Rita* was first performed at London's Warehouse Theatre during June 1980, before transferring to the much larger Piccadilly Theatre in September of the same year. A major national tour followed the two-and-a-half-year West End run, and Russell wrote the Academy Award–nominated screenplay for the 1983 Lewis Gilbert film version. Russell also collaborated with American playwright Ntozake Shange to produce a racially charged version of *Educating Rita*, which has been produced in at least thirty countries, including Turkey, Mexico, Denmark, and Germany.

Blood Brothers originated in 1981 as a nonmusical play commissioned by Paul Herman's Merseyside Young People's Theatre Company for secondary-school children. The musical version opened 8 January 1983, at the Liverpool Playhouse (where Russell was reluctantly serving as an associate artistic director), from where it transferred to the Lyric Theatre, London. After a hesitant start the production proved reasonably popular and ran for over six months, eventually closing on October 22 of that year. A further touring production was prepared, like the original directed by Chris Bond and Danny Hillier, and it went out on the road in 1984.

A stage version of *Our Day Out* was presented at the Everyman during April 1983, and it was also produced at London's Young Vic, opening on 29 August of the same year.

Russell then spent a period of time writing music. His next major play, *Shirley Valentine*, was commissioned by Glen Walford, by now the artistic director of the Liverpool Everyman Theatre, where it opened in 1986. This production is well known because Noreen Kershaw, the original Shirley Valentine, became ill with appendicitis and Russell himself took over the role and performed the play for the final weeks of its sold-out limited run.

In January 1988, *Shirley Valentine* opened at London's Vaudeville Theatre for a limited season, and the production closed on 30 April of the same year. Pauline Collins and the entire creative team recreated the London success, virtually intact, on Broadway on 16 February 1989. That production, which starred Ellen Burstyn in its latter stages, closed on 25 November 1989, after over 300 performances.

Remarkably, *Shirley Valentine* was revived in the West End just over one year after its initial closing—one of the fastest revivals in contemporary theatre history. This new production, which featured a different location (Liverpool became Glasgow, Scotland), director, and performer opened at the Duke of York's Theatre on 28 June 1989. The film version of *Shirley Valentine*, starring Pauline Collins, was released in September 1989.

Russell adapted his own script as the screenplay for Mike Ockrent's poorly received 1990 film of *Stags and Hens*, newly entitled *Dancin' thru the Dark*. Russell's wife served as producer.

When *Shirley Valentine* opened initially in the West End, a London revival of *One for the Road* was already playing at the Lyric Theatre (it had opened 21 October 1987, and had a successful run, finally closing on 23 April 1988). Another production of *Blood Brothers* at the Albery Theatre, which opened on 28 July 1988, completed Russell's trio of simultaneous West End successes. Several cast changes and six years after this *Blood Brothers* revival opened, the production is still playing.

After several years of speculation as to whether *Blood Brothers* would ever appear on Broadway, the musical finally opened at the Music Box Theatre on 25 April 1993, where it met with mixed reviews but strong box office results. During 1994 a road company version of the Broadway production starred Petula Clark and David Cassidy.

Selected Biographical Sources: Gill; Glaap [1]; Jones.

MAJOR PLAYS, PREMIERES, AND SIGNIFICANT
REVIVALS: THEATRICAL RECEPTION

John, Paul, George, Ringo . . . and Bert. 1974. Opened 21 May at the Every-man Theatre, Liverpool, for six performances. Moved to the Lyric Theatre, London, 15 August for 416 performances. Produced by Robert Stigwood and Michael Codron. Directed by Alan Dossor. Revivals: London Old Vic, 1988.

Winner of the London Theatre Critics and *Evening Standard* Award for the best musical of the year, this review-format show told the story of the rise and fall of the Beatles through the eyes of a fictional character (and narrator) named Bert, who recounts his tales to a character called "the Kid." An onstage band punctuated the show with Beatles music, and Russell himself wrote two original songs. Some critics found the work flippant; Billington [5] called the play a "frivolous show about a fascinating subject." But the majority of reviews were favorable. O'Keiff found the play to be full of "hilarious" Liverpudlian humor, and Wardle [3] observed that here (for the first time he could remember) "was a showbiz musical that does not subscribe to showbiz values."

Breezeblock Park. 1975. Opened 8 May at the Everyman Theatre, Liverpool. Opened 12 September 1977, at the Mermaid Theatre, London; moved to the Whitehall Theatre, London, 3 November 1977. Produced by Michael Codron. Directed by Alan Dossor.

This working-class comedy of manners is set in a living room on a large public housing estate on Christmas Eve. It follows the attempts of a young woman to escape her impoverished environment while being forced to deal with the pretentious stupidity of her parents and relatives. Several critics found the form somewhat hackneyed, but the director defended the work in print as a play that is "strong and raw and makes absolutely no obeisance to middle class liberal standards" (Coveney [2]).

One for the Road. 1976–1987. Opened at the Manchester Contact Theatre in November for fourteen performances under the title *Painted Veg and Parkinson*. Directed by Caroline Smith. Revivals: Nottingham Playhouse, March 1979; Liverpool Playhouse, July 1980; Ashcroft Theatre, Croyden, February, 1985 (revised version). Opened at the Lyric Theatre, London, 21 October 1987. Directed by William Gaunt. Produced by Bob Swash.

Another comic exposé of domestic strife, this play follows a first-generation, middle-class couple. Husband Dennis, tired of his wife's and pretentious neighbor's complaints, tries to find the courage to lose his material trappings and hitchhike away to pursue his dreams. After waiting eleven years for a London production, the play opened to poor reviews: critics were inclined to consider the play inferior to Russell's later plays. Thorncroft described the 1987 London revival as "insubstantial, off-the-peg Russell." Billington [6] complained that comedian Russ Abbott dominated that revival, while others like Hirschhorn considered him to be a "versatile, entertainment machine." Attracted by the marquee name, audiences responded to the production in large numbers.

Stags and Hens. 1978. Opened 11 October at the Liverpool Everyman Theatre for forty-eight performances. Directed by Chris Bond. Revivals: Duke's Playhouse, Lancaster, 1982; Old Vic, London, 1980; London Young Vic, 1987.

Emanating from an exercise for students of television studies at Manchester Polytechnic, *Stags and Hens* is set in the men's and women's bathrooms of a Liverpool nightclub. On the eve of her marriage to a hometown boy, the central character is deciding whether or not to leave her home town (and dull fiancé) for the bright lights of London. This piece was very successful in its initial production in Liverpool but was not performed again for four years. London critics admitted that audiences seemingly enjoyed the play, but the scribes tended to see its appeal as parochial—Lubbock, for example, acknowledged that the piece would play well on Merseyside, but he argued that its location overwhelmed the London production.

Educating Rita. 1979. Opened 10 June at the Warehouse Theatre, London; moved 19 August 1980, to the Piccadilly Theatre, London, for 800 performances. Directed by Mike Ockrent. Produced by the Royal Shakespeare Company. Revivals: Liverpool Playhouse, 1981, codirected by Russell; British national tour, 1982–1983. Opened at the Westside Arts Theatre (NY), 7 May, 1987. Directed by Jeff Perry. Produced by Steppenwolf Theatre Company.

The story of the educational and personal relationship between a drunken Open University professor and his nontraditional student, *Educating Rita* brought Russell international fame, banishing any perception of a rather parochial northern dramatist. In all of its productions the play was greeted with highly favorable critical comment, with Howard and Billington [2] especially enthusiastic. Already familiar with the movie version, American reviewers (such as Henry) of the 1987 off-Broadway Steppenwolf production were pleased to see *Educating Rita* finally in New York—Barnes, for example, argued that the piece was a deft exploration of the power and hunger of the working class and the ability of its members to usurp the position of their mentors.

Blood Brothers. 1983. Opened at the Everyman Theatre, Liverpool, 8 January 1983. Opened at the Lyric Theatre, London, 11 April 1983. Directed by Chris Bond. Produced by Bob Swash. Revivals: Albery Theatre, London, 1988 (still running). Opened at the Music Box Theatre (NY), 11 April 1993. Directed by Chris Bond. Produced by Bill Kenwright.

Despite its great box office success, this musical fable of twins separated at birth has met with mixed critical comments—reviewers tended to either love or hate this folk-pop musical. Some commentators praised its simplicity, regionalism, class consciousness, gentle didacticism, and earthy determination to give as much weight to the spoken word as to the sung concept number. Coveney [1], though, described the work as a "rather strange hybrid of operatic melodrama, sentimental romance and ebullient social comment," while Gardner simply argued that the show was "a bloody mess." Steyn was particularly vitriolic, calling Russell's lyrics "trite" and "old-hat." Billington [1] summed up many critics' ambiguity by declaring the show to be "brilliant melodrama." Regardless of these complaints, the show has had great success at the box office on both sides of the Atlantic.

Shirley Valentine. 1986. Opened at the Everyman Theatre, Liverpool, 13 March 1986. Directed by Glen Walford. Opened 22 January 1988, Vaudeville Theatre, London. Directed by Simon Callow; moved 16 February 1989, to the Booth Theatre (NY) for 300 performances. Revivals: Duke of York's Theatre, London, June 1989.

A two-act monologue about the self-emancipation of a Liverpool housewife, all of the many productions of *Shirley Valentine* have been generally well received, even though Armistead observed after the London opening that "any male playwright who sits down to write a full-length play on the innermost emotional life of a woman must, one might think, be presumptuous, or reckless, or both." (Armistead went on to pen a largely favorable review.) All the major male critics in the West End and on Broadway praised the work's spirit and humor. After the New York opening Kissell reported that the audience "had fallen in love with Shirley."

ADDITIONAL PLAYS, ADAPTATIONS, AND PRODUCTIONS

Two one-acts, *Keep Your Eyes Down* and *Sam O'Shanker*, were produced in 1971 under the collective title *Blind Scouse*. Russell's first play for the Liverpool Everyman (also written in 1973), entitled *When the Reds . . . ,* was produced in 1976 at Liverpool's Everyman and London's Young Vic. Written for schools, the television play *Lies* was transmitted by the BBC in November 1977.

ASSESSMENT OF RUSSELL'S CAREER

Despite beginning his career in a manner firmly grounded in alternative theatre styles and venues, Russell has subsequently worked almost entirely within the mainstream, for-profit theatre and has remained apparently unconcerned about artistic legitimacy—at least, if such legitimacy must come at the expense of the entertainment of his audience. Unlike the work of many of the other "alternative" British writers of his generation—such as Steve Gooch, Howard Brenton, or Caryl Churchill—Russell's work has been largely ignored by academic critics. This could be because of this author's disdain for high-art themes and terminology (a point of view he articulates explicitly in *Educating Rita*), a steadfast refusal to discuss or produce his work in the subsidized citadels of the university stage and lecture hall, and his determination to write from a working-class perspective in a manner that is relevant to and can easily be understood by a working-class audience.

The lack of academic analyses does not reflect a paucity of audiences or productions; Russell's numerous works have reached an extraordinarily large number of people. In fact, more of Russell's plays were produced in Britain during 1984 than those of any other playwright except William Shakespeare. In 1988 three Russell plays—*Shirley Valentine, One for the Road*, and *Blood Brothers*—ran simultaneously as major commercial productions in large West End theatres, an achievement for a contemporary playwright that is without any recent parallel. As well as many of his plays becoming staples of the British repertory movement, Russell's first play, *John, Paul, George, Ringo . . . and Bert*, played in the West End for over twelve months. *Educating Rita* ran for over two and a half years. Two productions of *Blood Brothers* have enjoyed a combined, still open West End run of some six years, and *Shirley Valentine* not only enjoyed a successful Broadway run throughout most of 1989 but was revived in the West End just months after its original limited-run production closed in preparation for its move to Broadway.

Certainly, all of Russell's plays are open to a variety of formal criticisms. With their naturalistic structures and reliance on broad, highly visual humor and one-line jokes, his early plays are conventional in structure and at times superficially mannered in theme. *Blood Brothers* manipulates its audience through an awkwardly poetic mixture of sentiment, catharsis, and class consciousness. The characters in *Breezeblock Park* and *One for the Road* often appear artificial and polemical. There are no subtleties of character in the avowedly melodramatic *John, Paul, George, Ringo . . . and Bert*, nor is there any great new psychological or other insight on the real-life figures that Russell includes in the play— the Beatles are treated as the semimythic icons they are within the popular consciousness. And *Shirley Valentine* invites the complaint from feminist writers that the central character's apparent salvation from the problems caused by a man comes merely from the love of another man.

This lack of interest in direct political themes notwithstanding, it must be noted that all of Russell's dramas are primarily about working-class characters— a focus that is, in itself, unusual for the commercial theatre. Few other playwrights in the twentieth century have achieved commercial success in the live theatre by writing realistically about the working classes. Moreover, Russell's authentic working-class background means that he has never encountered some of the problems of dislocation faced by the educated middle-class playwrights. Unlike such authors as John Osborne or Arnold Wesker in the 1950s, as well as David Hare, Howard Brenton, or David Edgar in more recent years, Russell did not go away to university and never became divorced—intellectually or geographically—from his working-class roots. One result of that lack of upheaval is that his plays consistently reflect a feeling that they were written from within, and not from the point of view of someone now cast on the outside and feeling dislocated from his or her roots. Russell, though a playwright who largely avoids self-conscious theorizing, does not have a doubtful relationship with the cultural form he writes about, and even perpetuates. His plays rarely attack middle-class values; they focus on, instead of lamenting, the division between the British classes.

Russell has argued that there has long been a tacit agreement in the English theatre—the working class could only be discussed if they were seen sitting in the kitchens of England plotting revolution. Russell found reality to be very different. After acknowledging the discomfort the play causes to middle-class liberals, *Breezeblock Park*'s director, Alan Dossor, said that the play is "strong and raw and makes absolutely no obeisance to middle class liberal standards" (Coveney [2]). The same could be said about all of Russell's work.

Russell's unabashed sense of truth mercilessly attacks such foibles of working-class life as an obsession with material possessions (especially being the first one to own something), an inability to speak directly about sex or illness, inverted snobbery, ignorance, drunkenness, tyranny, lack of artistic taste and tenderness, and a variety of other peccadilloes and serious flaws. His methodology employs one-liners and contrived but accessible comedy that attempts to duplicate working-class life as exactly as possible without trying to sanitize any aspect of it. Like the traditional comedy of manners, such early plays as *Breezeblock Park*, *Stags and Hens*, and *One for the Road* are essentially about how people behave rather than what they do or why they do it, and the plays' characters see pseudorefined artifice as being essential to a civilized existence. Just as in the historical model of the comedy of manners, which stresses the particular amenities of style and sophistication, Russell's working-class characters play games based on the edicts of fashion and live in fear of being ridiculed for lack of expert knowledge, wit, or taste. These plays are more interested in the quality of social behavior than in the conditions that produce it, which accounts for their lack of overt didacticism.

There are some fascinating differences from the traditional comedy of manners model, however. Russell is concerned with *working-class* manners: the women are dominant and play the manners game much more expertly than their less-sophisticated husbands. Taste and fashion is largely expressed through crass materialism, wit through half-remembered jokes, and knowledge through misunderstood clichés. The plays' interest in the need to be charming and witty and display other affectations of behavior is firmly rooted in working-class traditions. In other words, just as the comedy of manners traditionally parodies middle-class behavior, its impact relying on the vicarious pleasure of seeing one's own society's mores affectionately satirized, plays like *Breezeblock Park* carry precisely those same themes into the purview of the working classes, giving them access to what is generally regarded as a sophisticated, traditional form of drama. Russell, then, adroitly took over a middle-class form and uses it to express the dreams and frustrations of the working class.

One of Russell's most useful achievements has been his ability to show that the commercial theatre can accommodate plays with progressive agendas, contrary to the traditional academic view that most progressive social commentary is found far from Leicester Square. *Educating Rita* seems to contradict that point. Few contemporary plays from the fringe or alternative sectors have explored canonical issues, the class-bound nature or art, and the boundaries of what constitutes literature in such an extended fashion.

Yet this play is accessible to a wide-ranging audience (Russell steadfastly refuses to write comedy that jokes at the expense of ignorance), and it does not shrink from the sociopolitical position that education is a valid tool for working-class emancipation. The play was clearly written to galvanize others from Rita's background into following her course—Henry noted that the character of Rita is ''no winsome waif, but an embodiment of sheer will-power.'' Russell suggests that Rita is merely a representative of an entire lost class whose achievements could be equal to those on the other side of the barrier. The play is a noteworthy combination of the didactic and the popular.

Shirley Valentine similarly demonstrates the shallowness of the assumption that Broadway can have nothing to do with art or entertainment anymore. The piece is a one-woman monologue that consists of the musings of a forty-two-year-old, uneducated housewife from Liverpool who addresses the wall of her sanitized kitchen during the first act, and a rock off the coast of a Greek Island during the second. Her lack of education and avowed anti-intellectualism means that she would appear to lack the language of feminist discourse, and she is hardly in a position to intellectually debate the role of women in society (or, indeed, her own role), in the manner of a heroine of a play by Caryl Churchill or Megan Terry. With *Shirley Valentine* Russell charts the territory of sexual fulfillment, misogynistic oppression, wasted female lives, and the importance of self-fulfillment and feminist emancipation. In short, this is a remarkable play that follows a course that many have argued to be impossible in a commercial arena.

For all Russell's fascination with the depiction of working-class life, the most constant theme of his work is the importance of class mobility—his sympathetic, intelligent central characters variably want to escape their limited world, despite being faced by clannish, churlish peers, themselves complicit in denying class mobility, and tyrannically preventing the escape of those who try to leave. Throughout Russell's work, this image of a character longing for a better life reappears time after time.

Most of these characters have a very ill defined sense of what they want—and they often discover that their dreams are artificial. But they usually retain their optimistic sense of yearning and provide Russell with his overriding dramatic theme—the abiding truism that for most ordinary people, life could always be better.

ARCHIVAL SOURCES

Manuscripts of the unpublished Russell plays can be found in the Unity Theatre Archive, Merseyside Museum of Labor History, Liverpool; the British Theatre Association Play Library, London; and in the playwright's personal collection.

PRIMARY BIBLIOGRAPHY

Plays

Blood Brothers. London: Samuel French, 1985; Hutchinson, 1986.
Breezeblock Park. London: Samuel French, 1978.
Educating Rita. London: Samuel French, 1981; Longman, 1984.
I Read the News Today. London: Samuel French, 1987.
One for the Road. London: Samuel French, 1980; rev. and rewritten, 1985.
Our Day Out. London: Methuen, 1984; Samuel French, 1984.
Shirley Valentine. London: Samuel French, 1988.
Terraces. London: Hutchinson, 1973.

Anthologies

Educating Rita; Stags and Hens; and Blood Brothers: Two Plays and a Musical. London: Methuen, 1986.
Shirley Valentine and *One for the Road.* London: Methuen, 1988.
Studio Scripts: Our Day Out and Other Plays. (*Our Day Out, The Boy with the Transistor Radio, Terraces, I Read the News Today*). London: Hutchinson Educational, 1977.

SECONDARY BIBLIOGRAPHY

Armistead, Claire. Review of *Shirley Valentine. Plays and Players* (Mar. 1988): 26.
Barnes, Clive. Review of *Educating Rita. New York Post* (8 May 1987): 10.
Billington, Michael [1]. Review of *Blood Brothers. The Guardian* (9 Jan. 1983): 12.
———[2]. Review of *Educating Rita. The Guardian* (17 June 1986): 20.
———[3]. "Getting the Abbott Habit." *The Guardian* (23 Oct. 1987): 20.
———[4]. "A Housewife's Charter." *The Guardian* (23 Jan. 1988): 12.
———[5]. Review of *John, Paul, George, Ringo . . . and Bert. The Guardian* (16 Aug. 1974): 8.
———[6]. *One for the Road. The Guardian* (23 Oct. 1987): 20.
Coveney, Michael [1]. Review of *Blood Brothers. Financial Times* (9 Jan. 1983): 10.
———[2]. "Everyman in Good Humor." *Plays and Players* (Aug. 1975): 15.
———[3]. Review of *John, Paul, George, Ringo . . . and Bert. Financial Times* (24 May 1974): 10.
———[4]. Review of *Shirley Valentine. Financial Times* (29 June 1989): 10.
———[5]. "Working the System." *Plays and Players* (Dec. 1973): 16–19.
Gardner, Lyn. Review *Blood Brothers. City Limits* (28 Jan. 1988).
Gill, John. *Willy Russell and His Plays.* Wirral, Merseyside: Countyvise Limited, 1992.
Glaap, Albert-Reiner [1]. *Educating Rita: Comments and Study Aids.* Frankfurt am Main: Verlag Mortiz Diesterweg, 1984.
———[2]. "Perspectives on Language in Performance." *Studies in Linguistics, Literary Criticism, and Language Teaching and Learning.* Tubingen: Guner Nerr Verlag, 1987.

Henri, Adrian. Review of *John, Paul, George, Ringo . . . and Bert. Plays and Players* (Sept. 1974): 36–37.

Henry, William. Review of *Educating Rita. Time* (25 May 1977): 38.

Hirschhorn, Clive. Review of *One for the Road. Sunday Express* (25 Oct. 1987).

Howard, Simon. Review of *Educating Rita. Plays and Players* (June 1980): 19–20.

Hughes, Dusty. "Band on the Run." *Time Out* (2–8 Aug., 1974): 14–15.

Jones, Christopher. *Populism, the Mainstream Theatre, and the Plays of Willy Russell.* Unpublished diss. Ann Arbor, MI: University Microfilms, 1989.

Kissell, Howard. Review of *Shirley Valentine. New York Daily News* (16 Feb. 1989).

Lubbock, Tom. Review of *Stags and Hens. Plays and Players* (Aug. 1984): 32.

Maddox Brenda. "Shirley Decides She's Had Enough." *New York Times* (12 Feb. 1989): 14.

McGrath, John. *A Good Night Out.* London: Methuen, 1981.

Neustatter, Angela. "Interview with Willy Russell." *The Guardian* (14 Aug. 1974): 10.

Nightingale, Benedict. "They May Be Blood Brothers but Class Will Tell." *New York Times* (18 Apr. 1993): 6.

O'Keiff, Richard. Review of *John, Paul, George, Ringo . . . and Bert. Plays and Players* (July 1974): 57.

Rich, Frank. Review of *Shirley Valentine. New York Times* (16 Feb. 1989).

Steyn, Mark. Review of *Blood Brothers. The Independent* (1 Aug. 1988): 20.

Thornber, Robin [1]. Review of *Blood Brothers. The Guardian* (5 June 1985): 15.

———[2]. Review of *John, Paul, George, Ringo . . . and Bert. The Guardian* (22 May 1974): 12.

———[3]. "The School in the Pool." *The Guardian* (6 Mar. 1979): 12.

Thorncroft, Anthony. Review of *One for the Road. Plays and Players* (Jan. 1988): 35.

Wardle, Irving [1]. "Demolition Derby." *The Times* (23 Oct. 1987).

———[2]. Review of *Our Day Out. The Times* (31 Aug. 1983): 8.

———[3]. Review of *John, Paul, George, Ringo . . . and Bert. The Times* (16 Aug. 1974).

———[4]. "Scouse Mouse Breaks out in the Aegean." *The Times* (23 Jan. 1988): 20.

———[5]. "Twins Caught in a Fatal Trap." *The Times* (12 Jan. 1983): 9.

Williams, Ian. "Russell's Road." *Plays and Players* (Nov. 1987).

Peter Shaffer
(1926–)

C. J. GIANAKARIS

Few dramatists during the last half of the twentieth century equal British author Peter Shaffer in providing intellectual plays that also entertain through exciting story-telling techniques.

Using articulate, even elegant language, and often featuring innovative dramatic constructs, Shaffer presents rich possibilities for engaging theatre. Nor has he remained rooted in a single dramatic style. Shaffer has proven a master with social realism (as in *Five Finger Exercise*), but also with technical acrobatics that create layers of narrative (as in *Amadeus*, *Royal Hunt of the Sun*, *Equus*, and *Yonadab*). Moreover, he exhibits exceptional ability with a variety of comic modes. His farce *Black Comedy* remains a foremost example today of that demanding genre. At the same time he excels in sophisticated drawing room repartée with impressive one-act plays (*White Liars, The Public Eye, The Private Ear*) and the 1987 comic hit *Lettice & Lovage*. Such theatrical strengths have helped Shaffer earn two Tonys (for *Equus* and *Amadeus*), an Oscar (for the film *Amadeus*), and numerous other major awards such as the *Evening Standard* Drama Award, the *Plays and Players* Award, and the London Theatre Critics Award.

His parents Jack and Reka Shaffer came from the world of commerce in Liverpool, England, where Peter was born into a Jewish household. By scant minutes Peter Levin Shaffer was preceded in birth (15 May 1926) by an identical twin, Anthony, who also became a Tony-winning playwright in 1971 for his mystery drama *Sleuth*.

In 1936 the Shaffer family moved to London. The twins attended St. Paul's School, where training was rigorous and challenging. During this early period of education, Peter undertook serious instruction in piano. Music remains very important for him, as evidenced in several of his dramas, most notably *Amadeus*.

Bad eyes precluded an armed forces stint for Shaffer during World War II. He instead was conscripted as a ''Bevin Boy'' for home-front service from 1944 until 1947. The twins then went to Cambridge, where Peter read history. After graduation Shaffer unsuccessfully sought work in London's publishing houses. New York City first became his home in 1951 until 1954, when he returned to London, where he worked for the music publisher Boosey & Hawkes. Since the 1960s, he has maintained homes in both London and New York.

Curiously, Shaffer's first writing ventures were in fiction, specifically, three murder mysteries. *The Woman in the Wardrobe* (1951) was published under the pseudonym Peter Antony—the name also used when coauthoring *How Doth the Little Crocodile?* (1952) with his brother Anthony. Another detective story, *Withered Murder*, followed in 1955.

During the mid-1950s Peter Shaffer wrote some carefully plotted drama for television and radio. He thus has experimented with drama in several formats. Peter Shaffer continues to write, with premieres of his plays typically occurring every two or three years. In recent years, he has relented in his candid distaste for the academy and has taken a nonpermanent professorship at Oxford on two occasions.

His most recent work was *The Gift of the Gorgon* (1992), a mystery of high drama set on a Greek island, concerning a brilliant but eccentric British dramatist. Like his 1985 London hit *Yonadab*, *Gorgon* was first directed by Sir Peter Hall and has not yet been staged in the United States. And as with all his works, Shaffer continues to revise his scripts, seeking to sharpen their edge for more theatrical effectiveness. A film of *Lettice & Lovage* is in the works with a screenplay by Shaffer.

Selected Biographical Sources: Gianakaris [4]; Klein [2].

MAJOR PLAYS, PREMIERES, AND SIGNIFICANT REVIVALS: THEATRICAL RECEPTION

Five Finger Exercise. 1958. Opened 16 July 1958, at the Comedy Theatre, London, for 610 performances. Directed by John Gielgud.

In an exceptionally long run for a serious drama, *Five Finger Exercise* earned glowing reviews and irrevocably launched Shaffer's career. Brien praised Shaffer as a keen observer, while Dallas declared the future of British theater lay in part with Shaffer. Walsh considered Shaffer an overnight sensation in British theater. A young Kenneth Tynan, however, found the play's desperate tonality difficult to believe.

In the United States, reaction to *Five Finger Exercise* was even more laudatory. *Time* magazine (Review of *Five Finger Exercise*) praised the keen dialogue and well-crafted tense atmosphere. Atkinson thought the play a ''gem of civilized theatre.'' Bolton [1] stated it was ''engrossing theatre.'' A discordant note was sounded by Chapman [1], though, who thought the play intelligent but without a central significance.

Five Finger Exercise won Shaffer the London *Evening Standard* Award as the most promising British playwright of 1958, initiating him to the public as an up-and-coming writer to watch. Revivals of the work have not been profuse since, but a fascinating, if wrong-headed movie version was shot in 1962, directed by Daniel Mann.

The Public Eye/The Private Ear. 1962. Opened 10 May as a double bill at the Globe Theatre, London. Directed by Peter Wood. Featured Maggie Smith.

Critical response was divided, some reviewers preferring one play over the other, others just the opposite. An enthusiastic review was written by Darlington [2], calling both plays clever and very funny; Shulman expressed reservations but acknowledged their sharp wit; and Trewin described Shaffer as an understanding playwright. American critics expressed even greater pleasure in the works. *Time* ("Love Antic and Frantic") believed *The Public Eye* excels in "freshness and invention." Bolton [2] exclaimed that Shaffer wrote in a "heavenly, smooth and persuasive way." The headline for Chapman's [3] views declared both plays "Irresistible English Comedies."

When played together in bookend fashion, they provide a humorous look at courtship rituals and young love. A well-cast movie of *The Public Eye* (entitled *Follow Me!*) was released in 1972.

The Royal Hunt of the Sun. 1964. Premiered as part of the Chichester Festival on 7 July. Directed by John Dexter. Moved to the London Old Vic. New York opening at the ANTA Theatre, 26 October 1965.

Of the several major landmarks in Peter Shaffer's career, *The Royal Hunt of the Sun* deserves special notice. The achievement of *Royal Hunt* encompasses many factors, both thematic and structural. No small-scale domestic issues dominate here. Shaffer aims to argue the biggest issues known to humankind; most specifically, is there truly a god, and if so what are his ground rules for mortal beings? *Royal Hunt* combines the abstract intellectualism of absurdism with earthly concerns of Brechtian theater.

The premiere cast included actors who were eventually to become mainstays on the British stage. Colin Blakely and Robert Stephens (as Pizarro and Atahuallpa, respectively) earned high praise, as did Derek Jacobi, Edward Petherbridge, and Michael Byrne. Critical reaction was very positive, Levin declaring that "no greater play has been written and produced . . . in my lifetime." Barker states that this ambitious work is exceptional spectacle touched by the historical imagination.

As is typical with Peter Shaffer, he was not wholly satisfied with the script for *Hunt*, and he revised the play considerably before its New York opening. Now playing Pizarro was Christopher Plummer, while David Carradine took on the physically demanding role of Atahuallpa. Theater critics of the American production responded even more enthusiastically than for the earlier British staging. Chapman [4] wrote that *Hunt* reflected "theatrical writing at its beautified best." Esslin points out the play's "first-rate text," while Hewes [1] thought

Hunt "that season's thrilling and imaginative event." McCarten describes it as a wholly enthralling play. Taubman praised the author's fine intelligence and bold imagination.

Late in the 1960s a Canadian-produced film version was made of *Royal Hunt of the Sun,* directed by Irving Lerner; it received very poor reviews even from Shaffer.

Black Comedy. 1965. Opened 27 July at the Chichester Festival. New York premiere at the Ethel Barrymore Theatre, on 12 February 1967.

Serious drama has not been Shaffer's sole strength. Even as he was writing a monumental spectacle such as *Royal Hunt,* he also could conceive a riotous farce like *Black Comedy.* The National Theatre organization opened Shaffer's frantic comedy *Black Comedy* at the Chichester Festival, starring Derek Jacobi, Albert Finney, and Maggie Smith, helping to make this one of the finest farces of modern times.

Black Comedy won many admirers from the outset. Darlington [1] considers the piece surefire funny, while Hobson [1] thought that *Black Comedy* was side-splitting farce. Nearly two years later *Black Comedy* enjoyed a Broadway opening, and again the piece benefited from an all-star cast that included Michael Crawford, Lynn Redgrave, Peter Bull, Donald Madden, and Geraldine Page. *Time* (Review of *Black Comedy* and *White Lies*) declared it an unflaggingly funny farce. Although not as ecstatic as the *Time* reviewer, Barnes [2] appreciated the play's brilliant comic base. Hewes [2] thought it one of that season's premium theatrical romps. The occasional negative verdict usually singled out excessive length of *Black Comedy* as a fault, while a very few objected to the one-joke premise of the work. Specifically, the dark-light schema dominated everything on the stage. Revivals of this Shafferian gem are frequent, and it has assumed the status of a minor comic masterpiece of our day.

White Lies/The White Liars/White Liars. 1967. Opened 12 February at the Ethel Barrymore Theatre (NY). Directed by John Dexter. Reworked as *The White Liars,* it opened at the Lyric Theatre, London in 1968, directed by Peter Wood.

In a reversal of the pattern typifying Shaffer's career, the one-acter *White Lies* opened first on Broadway rather than in London. Shaffer wrote it especially to perform with *Black Comedy* in a single evening's entertainment. Thus, it opened with its better-known companion piece at the Ethel Barrymore Theatre. The three-person play featured Michael Crawford, Donald Madden, and Geraldine Page. *White Lies* was uniformly panned. Repeatedly, critics stated that having *Black Comedy* on the same bill saved the evening. Among those making this observation were Barnes [2], Clurman [1], Gottfried [1], and Hewes [2].

Shaffer himself recognized that something was akilter with the psychological drama, and he revised it substantially to produce a second version. That reworking, entitled *The White Liars,* opened in 1968, featuring Ian McKellen. Still not satisfied, the dramatist revised the play again. It is that second revision, called *White Liars*, that Shaffer has chosen to be published as his definitive (for now, at least) text. From the pen of any ordinary playwright, *White Liars* might be able to make a case for itself. For Shaffer, however, the work remains interesting in premise but not especially satisfying.

Shrivings. 1970. Premiered on 5 February at the Lyric Theatre, London, directed by Peter Hall. Reopened on 26 November 1975, at the Theatre Royal, York.

A more serious detour in Peter Shaffer's headlong rush toward stage fame came with *The Battle of Shrivings*, which included cast members John Gielgud, Patrick Magee, and Wendy Hiller. *Battle* was Shaffer's first and only complete failure in the theatre. He revised the text substantially for another opening, this time at York, with Donald Palmer and Peter Schofield in lead parts. Nor did the revised work gain approval. No printed text of *The Battle of Shrivings* was published; the revised version, called *Shrivings*, has been published, although no major production of it has yet been attempted in the United States.

Critics were particularly harsh in assessing *Battle*. *Time* (Review of *The Battle of Shrivings*) declared the work to be ''a Shaw play without Shaw.'' *Variety* reviewer ''Bail'' sees the play's energy falter, and Nightingale [3] calls it a very bad play. Most criticisms focused on the drama's excessive length (it does run longer than even *The Royal Hunt of the Sun*) and its bombastic language and effects. The few reviewers who offer some compensations for the acknowledged excesses of *Battle* point out the play's cleverness and wit (Marcus) and its honorable seriousness that gives an audience much to ponder (Hope-Wallace). Shaffer remains sensitive to the disappointment caused by the failure of *Battle*; he still believes the revised piece *Shrivings* will eventually find an audience to appreciate it.

Equus. 1973. Opened 26 July at the Old Vic Theatre, London, as part of the National Theatre's season. Directed by John Dexter. Opened in New York on 24 October 1974, at the Plymouth Theatre.

Equus now stands as one of Peter Shaffer's most successful and popular works. That acceptance did not come all at once, though; nor has it been uniform among critics. A chance remark by a friend regarding a country boy who blinded some horses led Shaffer to write *Equus*. As performed by Alec McCowen and Peter Firth, under the brilliant guidance of director John Dexter, *Equus* gradually went on to earn a secure spot in the contemporary theater repertoire.

A set of negative reviews appeared early on, claiming *Equus* to be pretentious, shallow, and facile. Such sentiments were heard from Christie, Davies, and Dawson. But their negative verdicts were soon swamped by a tidal wave of very enthusiastic reviews. Billington [1] thought *Equus* to be a bold and brilliant drama. Hobson [2] described it as ''a moving and deeply profound play.'' Kerr reversed his previous sharp criticism of Shaffer, praising him now as a playwright long sought by the theater public.

By the time of the New York opening of *Equus* took place, critical consensus overwhelmingly favored the play. The role of the psychiatrist Martin Dysart became much coveted among actors. Joining Peter Firth, who reprised his part as the boy Alan, were such strong performers as Anthony Hopkins, Richard Burton, and Anthony Perkins. Critics began to perceive not shallow ideas but profound concepts in the script. Barnes [4] points out deep mind-probing in the play. Beauford calls it a remarkable work, and Clurman [2], though dubious of the play's psychological underpinnings, nonetheless raves about its brilliant theatricality. Gill [2], meantime, discusses how ingenious Shaffer is with *Equus*. A persistent residue of criticism does remain, however, concerning Freudian elements in *Equus*, as remarked on by Gottfried [2].

Equus is one of Shaffer's most anthologized plays, and revivals of it can be found around the world with some regularity. Its issue of generational conflict has made it especially popular on college campuses. A controversial movie adaptation was made in 1976, using a screenplay written by Shaffer. Starring were Richard Burton and Peter Firth (the original Alan Strang), and celebrated Hollywood director Sidney Lumet guided the endeavor. Much of their work stands up very well according to film values, and both Burton and Firth received Oscar nominations; so too did Shaffer for the movie script.

Amadeus. 1979. Opened on 2 November at the National Theatre (London). Directed by Peter Hall. Opened in New York on 17 December 1980, at the Broadhurst Theatre.

Shaffer's star rose decisively and permanently following the acclaim for *Equus*. Yet his next work, *Amadeus*, dwarfed even the impressive achievement of *Equus*. Award-winning performances by Paul Scofield, Simon Callow, and Felicity Kendal took full advantage of Shaffer's articulate script and provocative central premise. Fueling the play's enormous celebrity, too, was the contretemps created by a small but vocal band of detractors. They took Shaffer to task for allegedly depicting Wolfgang Amadeus Mozart in an unfair way in the play. Even today the play is rarely staged in or around Vienna, where Mozart spent much of his career.

Not surprisingly, then, the initial reports regarding *Amadeus* gravitated toward the Mozart matter that so obsessed—and catalyzed—London's cultural scene. Leading the newspapers' attack on Shaffer was Fenton [2], who wrote a blurb that lambasted Shaffer, calling the new play "appalling" and Paul Scofield's Salieri performance "mediocre." Not long afterward Fenton [1] continued his attack on Shaffer, asserting that *Amadeus* was "perfectly nauseating" because its author was a dreadful writer. Nightingale [1] questions whether Shaffer deserved such outstanding talent as director Peter Hall and actor Paul Scofield. Nightingale [2] previously stated that *Amadeus* did little to increase Shaffer's stature as a playwright. Equally unimpressed by *Amadeus* was Young, who called the work "hollow as a strip-cartoon."

But gradually, after *Amadeus* had been named best play of 1979 by the London *Evening Standard*, the critical view changed decisively, once and for all. Even more important was the substantial revision Shaffer made on the play in preparation for its American production later in 1980. A successful preview period of the revised script in Washington, D.C.'s National Theatre tightened and tuned up the show, so that its Broadway opening proved a unanimous triumph. With Ian McKellen and Tim Curry in the Salieri and Mozart roles, respectively, the American version took off. Numerous Tony Awards went to the play and Shaffer, among others, and *Amadeus* enjoyed a very long run in New York before road companies began taking it around the country.

Barnes wrote highly laudatory coverage for *Amadeus*. Based on its opening night, Barnes [1] termed *Amadeus* "a total, iridescent triumph." Later Barnes [3] underscores the play's "sublime subtlety." Gill [1] acknowledges the intellectual cleverness of both playwright and his Salieri protagonist. Leighton calls it "Shaffer's marvelous play." Kroll [2] praises the play's brilliant theatricality while continuing to question any profundity in the work.

Just as successful as the stage play was the 1984 movie of *Amadeus*. Nine Academy Awards went to the movie, including best picture, best director (Milos Forman), best actor (F. Murray Abraham), and best screenplay (Shaffer himself, with much encouragement from Forman).

Amadeus is performed repeatedly and often on world stages. Reasons are self-evident: Shaffer focused on a universally accepted genius for the play's ostensible subject, he delineated a wiley antagonist worthy to be Mozart's nemesis, and he utilized imaginative scenic modes to gain needed flexibility of chronology and space.

Yonadab. 1985. Opened 4 December at the National Theatre (London), directed by Peter Hall.

Writing the film script for *Amadeus* consumed several years in Shaffer's life in the 1980s. Shaffer still found time to complete another ambitious play entitled *Yonadab*. After the huge success of *Amadeus*, the National was ready to go all out on Shaffer's next work, and the cast and director chosen for *Yonadab* was exceptional. In lead roles were Alan Bates, Richard Warner, Patrick Stewart, Leigh Lawson, Anthony Head, and Wendy Morgan.

Shaffer drew part of the inspiration for the sordid tale making up *Yonadab* from a popular novel called *The Rape of Tamar*, by South African novelist Dan Jacobson. The biblical narrative concerned was the book of Samuel in the Old Testament, where the story told involved rape, incest, fratricide, and a variety of other moral sins. Some reviewers coped readily with the play's sensitive topics. Tinker, for instance, was uneasy at the absence of answers to the play's questions, but thought that the resulting search for answers surely "is the mark of a fine and fulfilling play." Even when not totally comfortable with the violent, provocative nature of the play, certain critics recognize the special strengths of *Yonadab*. Billington [3] wrote that "Shaffer has ... always been a powerful image-maker and Peter Hall's production makes the most of the play's visual possibilities." Peter, however, did not get past the strong sexual element in the play when he wrote, "Theatre as voyeurism. . . . Shaffer ends up with a slack and prurient literary melodrama of sexual revenge."

Partly because of its topics and the discomfort they effect, *Yonadab* has not been eagerly sought out for an American staging and so still has not been produced in the United States. Once scheduled for a New York opening, it has been postponed several times as wary producers wait for Peter Hall to become available to direct—as he did in London. Meantime, Shaffer continues to revise the script until the right opportunity arises to mount a production in New York. But those who saw *Yonadab* in London (as did this observer) recognize it to be a genuine thriller, featuring spectacular scenic effects and a provocative central theme.

Lettice & Lovage. 1987. Opened 6 October at the Theatre Royal in Bath, England. Opened 27 October at the Globe Theatre, London. Opened at the Ethel Barrymore Theatre (NY) in March 1990, directed by Michael Blakemore.

Peter Shaffer surprised the theater world with an exceptionally clever and likable comedy entitled *Lettice & Lovage*. Instead of taking place in the shadowy corridors of an ancient regime, *Lettice & Lovage* is set in contemporary London. The play's two major leads are women, and the operative situation concerns how history—and historical structures—should be respected in our own times.

Shaffer wrote the lead role of Lettice Douffet (Lettice, short for Laetitia) for Maggie Smith— and the role fit Ms. Smith's particular stage persona perfectly. At the play's London opening, the second lead role—that of Lotte—was performed with equal brilliance by Margaret Tyzack. Both repeated their London successes in the New York production, and both actresses won Tony Awards for their work. Michael Blakemore's direction and Shaffer's play also received Tony nominations.

Critics, like audiences, acclaimed *Lettice & Lovage* from the start. Wardle [1] pointed out that "it is an original and often hilarious treatment of an important and theatrically neglected subject." Charles Osborne praises the play directly: "Peter Shaffer has written an original, highly entertaining and intelligent comedy." A minority of observers found *Lettice & Lovage* wanting. Ratcliffe thought that "whimsy" led the plot "into the land beyond belief." Billington [2] termed the work a "whimsically enjoyable, if slightly overweight, conservationist comedy."

American reviewers found more to laud in the Broadway production, evidently, than their English counterparts. Oliver termed the play "a source of continuous delight," while Kroll [3] thought it a "pure draft of high-styled Wildean comedy." Most enthusiastic was Popkin's review, calling the play and Maggie Smith "surely the most effective laugh-machine that Broadway has seen in many years."

During the early 1990s *Lettice & Lovage* has been seen by thousands outside New York thanks to a successful road company production starring Julie Harris. In early 1995 Shaffer was preparing a screen script for *Lettice & Lovage* to star Maggie Smith, allowing millions more viewers to share its zany yet provocative qualities.

The Gift of the Gorgon. 1992. Opened 5 December at the Barbican Pit Theatre in London. Directed by Peter Hall. Moved March 3, 1993, to Wyndham's Theatre, London.

Produced under the auspices of the Royal Shakespeare Company, *Gorgon* showcased top-flight performers Judi Dench, Michael Pennington, and Jeremy Northam. *Gorgon* sold out regularly in the small Pit Theatre, so the entire production was shifted to Wyndham's Theatre. Some revisions were undertaken to better fit the larger theatre during the remainder of its run. Since then Shaffer has continued to tinker with the text, rearranging some of the sections and simplifying certain confusing scenes.

On the whole, critical response was good, if not ecstatic. Somewhat akin to *Shrivings* and to *Yonadab*, *Gorgon* contains scenes of physical and psychological violence, sometimes tempering an otherwise strongly positive reaction. The London *Sunday Times* (Review of *The Gift of the Gorgon*) reviewer called it "a hard, terrible and brilliant new play. . . . Its elaborate intellectual construction contains a vivid and all too topical message that grabs you by the throat." *Time Out* (Review of *The Gift of the Gorgon*) reported that "Shaffer is one of those writers who can really hit you in the guts while simultaneously finding a dramatic structure to contain and propel his anger." Like *Yonadab*, a tentative production had been scheduled for an American staging, but none has been forthcoming as of early 1996. Again, Peter Hall has proven an elusive director to tack down for sufficient time to mount a show he originally directed in London. Shaffer remains stoical about such delays, however.

ASSESSMENT OF PETER SHAFFER'S CAREER

Foremost among the dominant characteristics of Peter Shaffer's plays are the inventiveness of their style and the significance of their themes—a combination that has earned the playwright an impressive theater following. Shaffer's two Tony Awards (for *Equus* and *Amadeus*), an Oscar for his film script of *Amadeus*, and numerous other nominations reflect a writer of exceptional talent *and* popularity. Looking back over the dozen or so important dramas Shaffer has written, one cannot miss seeing the variety of their structures. For Shaffer, that diversity in form has proven a mixed blessing. For one group of critics, his multiplicity of theatrical models complicates attempts to label him according to a neat taxonomy (Klein [2], xi). While early critics may have felt justified to pigeon-hole his plays within naturalism based on *Five Finger Exercise*, Shaffer then produced a multi-layered historical epic, *The Royal Hunt of the Sun*—a surprise magnified by his claim that *Royal Hunt* existed in manuscript form before *Five Finger Exercise*.

Not that Shaffer totally removed himself from realism, the style into which he was born and raised. Even his most radical formats in *Royal Hunt, Equus, Amadeus, Yonadab,* and *Gift of the Gorgon* upon closer analysis reveal scenes and dialogue rooted in realism. Further, his one-act plays, as well as *Shrivings* and *Lettice & Lovage*, depend in some measure on social realism. Yet his writings rarely remain ''realistic'' in a pure sense but, rather, are alloyed with fresh devices. Peter Shaffer's eagerness to experiment with unconventional narrative frameworks thus emerges as a key to his playwrighting. Narrative—means for telling a story—has always been of central concern, and his shifting narrative paradigms baffle commentators expecting a textbook consistency of style.

For some, Shaffer's works smack too much of the ''theatrical,'' a coded expression indicating they are to be held suspect (Plunka, 13). Shaffer's own question for these critics—how can a piece for the theater *not* be theatrical?—should put such complaints to rest but of course does not. Audiences isolate no single ''Shaffer'' but an evolving artist ever seeking effective shapes for his ideas. *Royal Hunt*, for all its unique imaginative techniques, resonates with Artaudian ''total theater'' and Brechtian devices. Most obvious is an ''epic'' framework combining grand historical events with highly personalized actions (reviews by John Chapman, and others). To lead spectators through the shifting and telescoping time zones, Shaffer chose to employ a specific ''narrator''—Pizarro's aide Martin. But Shaffer was not wholly effective in adapting Martin for different time periods. Ultimately he created two ''Martins'' for the task: Old Martin, connoting the play's ''present time,'' comments for us (choruslike) about the events; Young Martin, the same character but when a youth, comments about ongoing events to the audience during their actual enactment. Fifteen years later in *Amadeus* Shaffer chose not to cast two actors as narrator. Using a simple, quick change of outer garb and wig, the same actor playing Salieri serves both in the past when young and in the action's ''present.'' By the time he came to write *Amadeus*, Shaffer recognized pitfalls in shifting plot coordinates with respect to time, space, and narrator perspective. *Amadeus* contains episodes telescoping both space and time, thanks to Salieri's narrating mobility.

Yonadab similarly displays a smooth mastery of chronological shifting, again operating on two time levels. *Gift of the Gorgon*, his most recent drama, shows Shaffer working on three different time planes simultaneously. Moreover, the tiered time levels seem fused seamlessly. In any overview of Shaffer's writings, the growth in his narrative ingenuity needs to be acknowledged, as does his debt to no single earlier author.

The second crucial factor in Shaffer's dramas is the important nature of their themes, with the comic one-actors being the chief exceptions. Most other dramatists working today operate within the realms of personal psychology or domestic conflict (as in power struggles within the family or social structures, political or ''cause'' agendas, and the like). But with few exceptions (*Five Finger Exercise* and the one-act comedies), Shaffer's stories are constructed on large-scale metaphysical, moral, or aesthetic issues. Even *Five Finger Exercise* transcends typical domestic drama touching on simple homey problems. A network of intertwined relationships exists there between the individual and his family, his society, and his true inner identity. *Five Finger Exercise* offers an early portrayal of a protagonist confronting his gay nature. Enriching the plot is another fundamental social issue: art and culture *versus* crass business and wealth. Paradoxically, *Exercise* works despite sometimes heavy-handed language that borders on bathos.

Shaffer largely resolved the problem of overheated rhetoric over the course of his career, but not instantaneously. During the early years of his writing, critics often called Shaffer to task for excessive rhetoric, sometimes bordering on bombast (Gottfried [3]; Marowitz). Moreover, because of the more serious matters probed in his dramas, Shaffer invited the criticism of some who think his subjects shallow, mere window dressing to advance simplistic notions about difficult problems (Dawson on *Equus*, Gottfried [3] on *Royal Hunt*, Simon on *Amadeus*). Significantly, however, audiences typically grasp Shaffer's intentions from the start, and recalcitrant critics often revise earlier judgments.

What Peter Shaffer does, after all, is to fasten on humankind's most basic questions for consideration in his dramas. God, issues of his existence, and, if so, the place of death in the human experience all drive the story of *Royal Hunt*. The limits of Good and of Evil are played out in *Shrivings*. The uneasy relationship between society's strictures and an individual's self-actualization constitutes the core argument debated throughout *Equus*. *Amadeus* considers the nature of genius while also introducing the unanswered question concerning God's possible existence in the world. *Yonadab*, too, poses the question of moral limits on humans, tied to debate on God's existence. *Lettice & Lovage*, though a comedy, nonetheless returns to the individual *versus* society's demands as its nexus. Peter Shaffer, in short, leaves his audiences with much to ponder after the curtain has fallen, critics to the contrary be damned.

As for the immediate future, Peter Shaffer—now in his sixties—has not slowed down with his writing. In recent conversations he speaks of rethinking the form of *Yonadab*, to project it with a Racinean barrenness. *Lettice & Lovage* is currently being rewritten by its author as a movie script requiring a shift of its subject onto a larger canvas. *Gorgon* will eventually come to the States when the original director, Peter Hall, finds time to head the production. Shaffer has hinted, too, that another new work may be waiting in the wings. Peter Shaffer is by no means ready to set down his pen, and audiences should await his future work with open arms and minds.

PRIMARY BIBLIOGRAPHY

Plays

Amadeus. London: André Deutsch, 1980; rev. version, New York: Harper & Row, 1981; Harmondsworth: Penguin, 1981.

Black Comedy (with *White Lies*). New York: Stein & Day, 1967; (with *White Liars*) London: Samuel French, 1967; rev. version, New York: Samuel French, 1968.

Equus. London: André Deutsch, 1973; London: Samuel French, 1974; New York: Avon Books, 1975.

Five Finger Exercise. London: Hamish Hamilton, 1958; New York: Harcourt Brace, 1959.

The Gift of the Gorgon. Harmondsworth: Viking/Penguin, 1993.
Lettice & Lovage. London: André Deutsch, 1988; rev. version, London: André Deutsch, 1988; (with *Yonadab*) London: Penguin, 1989; retitled *Lettice & Lovage*, New York: Harper & Row, 1990.
The Private Ear (with *The Public Eye*). London: Hamish Hamilton, 1962; New York: Stein & Day, 1964; London: Samuel French, 1964; New York: Stein & Day, 1964.
The Public Eye (with *The Private Ear*). London: Hamish Hamilton, 1962; London: Samuel French, 1962; New York: Stein & Day, 1964.
The Royal Hunt of the Sun. London: Hamish Hamilton, 1964; New York: Stein & Day, 1965; New York: Ballantine, 1966; London: Samuel French, 1968.
Shrivings. London: André Deutsch, 1974; (with *Equus*) New York: Atheneum, 1974.
White Lies (with *Black Comedy*). New York: Stein & Day, 1967.
White Liars (with *Black Comedy*). London: Samuel French, 1967; London: Hamish Hamilton, 1968; rev. version, London: Samuel French, 1976.
Yonadab. Rev. version, Harmondsworth: Penguin, 1989; (with *Lettice & Lovage*) Harmondsworth: Penguin, 1989.

Anthologies

The Collected Plays of Peter Shaffer. (From *Five Finger Exercise* through *Amadeus*). New York: Harmony Books, 1982.
Peter Shaffer: Four Plays. (*Black Comedy, White Liars, The Private Ear, The Public Eye*). Harmondsworth: Penguin, 1981.
Peter Shaffer: Three Plays. (*Equus, Five Finger Exercise, Shrivings*). Harmondsworth: Penguin, 1976.

Essays and Articles on Drama and Theatre

"The Cannibal Theater." *Atlantic Monthly* (Oct. 1960): 48–50.
"*Equus*: Playwright Peter Shaffer Interprets Its Ritual." *Vogue* (Feb. 1975): 136, 192.
"Figure of Death." *The Observer* (4 Nov. 1979): 37.
"In Search of a God." *Plays and Players* (Oct. 1964): 22.
"Labels Aren't for Playwrights." *Theatre Arts* (Feb. 1960): 20–21.
"Making the Screen Speak." *Film Comment* (Sept./Oct. 1984): 51ff.
"Paying Homage to Mozart." *New York Times Magazine* (2 Sept. 1984): 22ff.
"Salieri Really Was the Only Choice." *New York Times* (14 Oct. 1984): 2:8.
"Scripts in Trans-Atlantic Crossings May Suffer Two Kinds of Changes." *Dramatists Guild Quarterly* (spring 1980): 29–33.
" 'To See the Soul of a Man.' " *New York Times* (24 Oct. 1965): 2:3.
"What We Owe Britten." *Sunday Times* (18 Nov. 1973): 35.

Interviews

"Mostly *Amadeus*" (with Roland Gelatt). *Horizon* (Sept. 1984): 49–52.
"Playwright's Moral Exercise" (with Joseph A. Loftus). *New York Times* (29 Nov. 1959): 2: 1ff.

"The Royal Hunt of the Playwright" (with Michael Reidell). *Theatre Week* (2 Apr. 1990): 30–34.
"Shaffer Details a Mind's Journey in *Equus*" (with Mel Gussow). *New York Times* (24 Oct. 1974): 2: 50.
"The Two Sides of Theatre's Agonized Perfectionist" (with Brian Connell). *The Times* (28 Apr. 1980): 7.
"Why Are There Two U's in *Equus*?" (with Tom Buckley). *New York Times Magazine* (13 Apr. 1975): 20ff.

SECONDARY BIBLIOGRAPHY

Atkinson, Brooks. "Family Affairs: Peter Shaffer's *Five Finger Exercise* Has Been Staged by John Gielgud." *New York Times* (13 Dec. 1959): 2:3.
"Bail." Review of *The Battle of Shrivings*. *Variety* (11 Feb. 1970): 61.
Barber, John. Review of *Yonadab*. *Daily Telegraph* (6 Dec. 1985): 18.
Barker, Felix. "A Young Man's Dazzling Success." *Evening Standard* (12 Sept. 1964): 37.
Barnes, Clive [1]. "*Amadeus*: A Total Triumph." *New York Post* (18 Dec. 1980): 39.
———[2]. "Amiable *Black Comedy* Succeeds in Its Aim of Providing Simple Entertainment." *New York Times* (19 Oct. 1967): 58.
———[3]. "Change Aids *Amadeus*." *New York Post* (31 Dec. 1980): 17.
———[4]. "*Equus* a New Success on Broadway." *New York Times* (25 Oct. 1974): 26.
Review of *The Battle of Shrivings*. *Time* (30 Mar. 1970): 77.
Beauford, John. "Brilliant British Import: Shaffer's Inventive *Equus* Hits Broadway." *Christian Science Monitor* (4 Nov. 1974): 29.
Billington, Michael [1]. Review of *Equus*. *Manchester Guardian* (27 July 1973): 12.
———[2]. Review of *Lettice & Lovage*. *The Guardian* (28 Oct. 1987): 9.
———[3]. Review of *Yonadab*. *Manchester Guardian* (6 Dec. 1985): 10.
Review of *Black Comedy* and *White Lies*. *Time* (17 Feb. 1967): 70.
Bolton, Whitney [1]. "Engrossing, Adult British Import." *New York Morning Telegraph* (4 Dec. 1959): 2.
———[2]. "London-versus-N.Y. Comparisons of Shaffer Plays Are Invidious." *New York Morning Telegraph* (14 Oct. 1963): 2.
Brien, Alan. Review of *Five Finger Exercise*. *The Spectator* (25 July 1958): 133–34.
"British Plays Modified for Broadway." *The Times* (31 Dec. 1965): 13.
Buckley, Tom. " 'Write Me,' Said the Play to Peter Shaffer." *New York Times Magazine* (13 Apr. 1975): 20ff.
Chapman, John [1]. "*Five Finger Exercise* a Doodle." *New York Daily News* (3 Dec. 1959).
———[2]. "Peter Shaffer's Surprises." *New York Sunday News* (19 Feb. 1967): S3.
———[3]. "*Private Ear* and *Public Eye* Are Irresistible English Comedies." *New York Daily News* (10 Oct. 1963): 37.
———[4]. "*Royal Hunt of the Sun* a Lovely Play." *New York Sunday Times* (7 Nov. 1965): 2:3.
Christie, Ian. Review of *Equus*. *London Daily Express* (27 July 1973): 10.
Clurman, Harold [1]. Review of *Black Comedy* and *White Lies*. *Nation* (27 Feb. 1967): 285–86.

————[2]. Review of *Equus*. *Nation* (16 Nov. 1974): 506–7.

Dallas, Ian. "The Naturalists." *Encore* (10 Sept. 1958): 24–28.

Darlington, W. A. [1]. Review of *Black Comedy*. *London Daily Telegraph* (28 July 1965): 16.

————[2]. Review of *The Private Ear* and *The Public Eye*. *London Daily Telegraph* (11 May 1962): 16.

Davies, Russell. Review of *Equus*. *New Statesman* (3 Aug. 1973): 165–66.

Dawson, Helen. Review of *Equus*. *Plays and Players* (Sept. 1973): 43–45.

Ebner, Dean. "The Double Crisis of Sexuality and Literature." *Christianity and Literature* 30 (1982): 29–47.

Esslin, Martin. "All in the Text." *Plays and Players* (Feb. 1965): 34.

Fenton, James [1]. "Can We Worship This Mozart?" *Sunday Times* (23 Dec. 1979): 43.

————[2]. Squib on *Amadeus*. *Sunday Times* (18 Nov. 1979): 38.

Review of *Five Finger Exercise*. *Time* (14 Dec. 1959): 77.

Gelatt, Roland. "Peter Shaffer's *Amadeus*: A Controversial Hit." *Saturday Review* (Nov. 1980): 11–14.

Gianakaris, C. J. [1]. "A Playwright Looks at Mozart: Peter Shaffer's *Amadeus*." *Comparative Drama* 15.1 (spring, 1981): 37–53.

————[2]. "Drama into Film: The Shaffer Situation." *Modern Drama* 28.1 (1985): 83–98.

————[3]. "*Lettice & Lovage*: Fountainhead of Delight." *Theatre Week* (2 Apr. 1990): 22–25.

————[4]. *Peter Shaffer*. Macmillan Modern Dramatists Series. London: Macmillan, 1992; New York: St. Martin's Press, 1992.

————[5], ed. *Peter Shaffer: A Casebook*. New York: Garland, 1991.

————[6]. "Shaffer's Revisions in *Amadeus*." *Theatre Journal* 25.1 (1983): 88–101.

Review of *The Gift of the Gorgon*. *Time Out* (2–9 Jan. 1993): 33.

Review of *The Gift of the Gorgon*. *The Times* (7 Dec. 1992): 15.

Gill, Brendan [1]. "Bargaining with God." *The New Yorker* (29 Dec. 1980): 54.

————[2]. "Unhorsed." *The New Yorker* (4 Nov. 1974): 123–24.

Glenn, Jules [1]. "Alan Strang as an Adolescent: A Discussion of Peter Shaffer's *Equus*." *International Journal of Psychoanalytic Psychotherapy* (1976): 473–87.

————[2]. "Twins in Disguise: A Psychoanalytic Essay on *Sleuth* and *The Royal Hunt of the Sun*." *Psychoanalytic Quarterly* 29 (1974): 288–302.

Gottfried, Martin [1]. Review of *Black Comedy*. *Women's Wear Daily* (13 Feb. 1967): 9.

————[2]. "*Equus* in London." *Women's Wear Daily* (16 Jan. 1974): 22.

————[3]. Review of *The Royal Hunt of the Sun*. *Women's Wear Daily* (27 Oct. 1965): 55.

Hewes, Henry [1]. "Inca Doings." *Sunday Review* (13 Nov. 1965): 71.

————[2]. "When You're Having More than One." *Saturday Review* (25 Feb. 1967): 59.

Hobson, Harold [1]. "Riot of Laughter." *Christian Science Monitor* (4 Aug. 1965): 4.

————[2]. "A Triumph at London's National Theater." *Christian Science Monitor* (10 Aug. 1973): 14.

Hope-Wallace, Philip. Review of "The Battle of Shrivings." *Manchester Guardian* (6 Feb. 1970): 8.

Huber, Werner, and Hubert Zapf. "On the Structure of Peter Shaffer's *Amadeus*." *Modern Drama* 27 (1984): 299–313.

Kerr, Walter. "A Psychiatric Detective Story of Infinite Skill." *New York Times* (2 Sept. 1973): 2: 1ff.

Klein, Dennis A. [1]. "*Amadeus*: The Third Part of Peter Shaffer's Dramatic Trilogy." *Modern Language Studies* 13 (1983): 31–34.

———[2]. *Peter Shaffer*. Rev. ed. Twayne's English Authors Series. New York: Twayne, 1993.

Kroll, Jack [1]. "Four from the London Stage." *Newsweek* (13 Jan. 1986): 64–65.

———[2]. "Mozart and His Nemesis." *Newsweek* (29 Dec. 1980): 58.

———[3]. Review of *Lettice & Lovage*. *Newsweek* (2 Apr. 1990): 61.

Leighton, Kerner. Review of *Amadeus*. *Village Voice* (24 Mar. 1981): 29.

Levin, Bernard. "Thank You Mr S for the Greatest Play in My Lifetime." *London Daily Mail* (9 Dec. 1964): 12.

Lounsberry, Barbara. "God-Hunting: The Chaos of Worship in Peter Shaffer's *Equus* and *The Royal Hunt of the Sun*." *Modern Drama* 21.1 (1978): 13–28.

"Love Antic and Frantic." *Time* (18 Oct. 1963): 76 ff.

Marcus, Frank. "Poet v. Philosopher." *London Sunday Telegraph* (8 Feb. 1970).

Marowitz, Charles. Review of *The Royal Hunt of the Sun*. *Encore* 12 (Mar.–Apr. 1965): 44–45.

McCarten, John. "Gods against God." *The New Yorker* (6 Nov. 1965): 115–16.

Nightingale, Benedict [1]. "In London, the Talk Is of *Amadeus*." *New York Times* (23 Dec. 1979): 2: 5ff.

———[2]. "Obscene Child." *New Statesman* (9 Nov. 1979): 735.

———[3]. "Some Immortal Business." *New Statesman* (13 Feb. 1970): 227.

Oliver, Edith. Review of *Lettice & Lovage*. *The New Yorker* (9 Apr. 1990): 67.

Osborne, Charles. Review of *Lettice & Lovage*. *London Daily Telegraph* (28 Oct. 1987): 17.

Peter, John. Review of *Yonadab*. *Sunday Times* (8 Dec. 1985): 25.

Plunka, Gene A. *Peter Shaffer: Roles, Rites, and Rituals in the Theatre*. Rutherford, NJ: Fairleigh Dickinson University Press, 1988.

Popkin, Henry. Review of *Lettice & Lovage*. *Theater Week* (16 Apr. 1990): 38.

Ratcliffe, Michael. Review of *Lettice & Lovage*. *The Independent* (30 Oct. 1987): 14.

Shulman, Milton. Review of *The Private Ear* and *The Public Eye*. *London Evening Standard* (11 May 1962): 21.

Simon, John. "Amadequus, or Shaffer Rides Again." *New York* (29 Dec. 1980–5 Jan. 1981): 62–63.

Taubman, Howard. "About a *Royal Hunt . . .*" *New York Times* (14 Nov. 1965): 2: 1.

Taylor, John Russell. *Peter Shaffer*. Writers and Their Works Series. London: Longmans, 1974.

Tinker, Jack. Review of *Yonadab*. *London Daily Mail* (5 Dec. 1985): 23.

Trewin, J. C. Review of *The Private Ear* and *The Public Eye*. *Illustrated London News* (26 May 1962): 86.

Tynan, Kenneth. Review of *Five Finger Exercise*. *The Observer* (20 July 1958): 13.

Walls, Doyle W. "*Equus*: Shaffer, Nietzsche, and the Neuroses of Health." *Modern Drama* 27 (1984): 314–23.

Walsh, Michael. Review of *Five Finger Exercise*. *London Daily Express* (17 July 1958):
  5.
Wardle, Irving [1]. Review of *Lettice & Lovage*. *The Times* (28 Oct. 1987): 21.
———[2]. "Spy of History." *Sunday Times* (6 Dec. 1985): 13.
Young, B. A. Review of *Amadeus*. *London Financial Times* (5 Nov. 1979): 15.

BIBLIOGRAPHIES

Cook, Virginia, and Malcolm Page, eds. *File on Shaffer*. London: Methuen, 1987.
Eberle, Thomas. *Peter Shaffer: An Annotated Bibliography*. New York: Garland, 1991.
Klein, Dennis A. *Peter and Anthony Shaffer: A Reference Guide*. Boston: G. K. Hall,
  1982.

Tom Stoppard
(1937–)

RICHARD CORBALLIS

Although there has been no shortage of scholarly comment on Tom Stoppard's work, his life remains thinly documented. Since he became a celebrity in the 1970s details of his domestic life have been reported in the press, but his reticence on private matters has ensured that we know only the bare outlines of his earlier career.

He was born Tomas Straussler in 1937 in Zlin, Czechoslovakia, where his father (Eugene) was a doctor with the Bata shoe company. In 1939—before Tomas could develop any competence in the Czech language—Bata transferred the Strausslers to Singapore. There appear to be Jewish connections on at least one side of the family, but these have never been documented. Subsequent events in Stoppard's life, including his work on behalf of Soviet Jews in the 1980s and his second marriage (in 1972) to Miriam Moore-Robinson, have maintained the Jewish connection.

When the Japanese invaded Singapore in 1942, Tomas, his mother (Martha), and his elder brother (who seems never to have been identified by name) were evacuated to Darjeeling, India. His father remained in Singapore, and—in Stoppard's typically reticent words, which are all we have to go on—he "didn't survive the war" ("An Interview with Tom Stoppard").

In India the two boys attended English-speaking schools. In 1946 their mother married a major in the British army, Kenneth Stoppard, whose surname was adopted by her sons. The family settled in the United Kingdom, where Tom was educated at Dolphin Preparatory School, Nottinghamshire (1946–1948), and Pocklington School, Yorkshire (1948–1954).

The Stoppard family moved to Bristol in 1950, and when Tom left school in 1954 he got a job there as a journalist. His work on a series of newspapers and journals—increasingly as a drama critic—from 1954 until 1963 sharpened his writing skills and his theatrical instincts.

In 1962 he moved to London, and while still freelancing as a journalist, he wrote *A Walk on the Water*—a play about a man who (a little like Stoppard himself) has given up a steady job to pursue his ideas. It was designed for the stage, but was first produced on television, then on radio (BBC, 1965) before becoming his second full-length play to be staged in England (under the title, *Enter a Free Man*) in 1968.

Although Stoppard has remained an occasional journalist throughout his career, playwriting became his primary source of income in 1964. In that year the BBC broadcast two short radio plays (*The Dissolution of Dominic Boot* and *"M" Is for Moon among Other Things*); Faber & Faber published three of his short stories in an anthology of works by new writers called *Introduction 2*; and he contributed five episodes to the popular radio serial, *The Dales*. A ninety-minute television script called "This Way Out with Samuel Boot," also written in 1964, was rejected; it has never been performed. Tynan notes that "it is the last Stoppard play with a message (i.e., property is theft) that could be described as leftist."

On the strength of his work to date Stoppard won a Ford Foundation grant that enabled him to write full-time in Berlin over the summer of 1964. One of the three other recipients of the grant was James Saunders. Saunders's 1962 play *Next Time I'll Sing to You* clearly had a profound effect on Stoppard, who reviewed it for *Scene* on 9 February 1963. As late as *Arcadia* Stoppard seems to have remembered the hermit in Saunders's play. Much more substantial is the influence of Saunders on the work that grew out of Stoppard's sojourn in Berlin, *Rosencrantz and Guildenstern Are Dead* (see Sammells).

Stoppard's 1964 draft of *Rosencrantz* took the form of a one-act comedy in verse. It was performed under the title "Rosencrantz and Guildenstern Meet King Lear" by English amateurs in Berlin. Whether it was this play or an ur-text of the later *Rosencrantz and Guildenstern Are Dead* that was performed by the Questors Theatre, Ealing, later in 1964 remains uncertain (see Brassell). Neither text has been published.

While in Berlin Stoppard made a rare appearance as an actor—in a low-budget film with a Dutch director, based on a story by Jorge Luis Borges. (He had earlier appeared in a documentary filmed in Bristol by John Boorman, and he planned at one point to play the part of the narrator in *Squaring the Circle*.) More important, on 30 June 1964, he attended—in Hamburg—the first stage production of one of his plays: *Old Riley geht über'n Ozean*—a German version of *A Walk on the Water*. Fifteen years later Stoppard renewed his association with Hamburg when he won the prestigious Shakespeare Prize.

In 1965, back in England, he pursued his career as a creative writer "for hire," producing for the BBC World Service seventy episodes of *A Student's Diary*, a series broadcast in Arabic about an Arab student living in London. A one-act play written in 1960, *The Gamblers*, had its first—and, it would appear, last—production at Bristol University at that time. In the same year he married his first wife, a nurse named Jose Ingle. The marriage lasted six years and produced two sons (Oliver and Barnaby), who were put in their father's custody after the divorce.

In retrospect 1966 can be seen as a watershed year for Stoppard. His only novel, *Lord Malquist and Mr Moon*, commissioned by Anthony Blond in 1963, finally appeared. Two short plays were broadcast—one for radio, one for television. In May he made his debut with the Royal Shakespeare Company (who had taken an option on *Rosencrantz and Guildenstern Are Dead* in 1965, but let it expire) as the cotranslator of Slawomir Mrozek's *Tango*. But the most important event of the year was the staging of *Rosencrantz and Guildenstern Are Dead* (heavily revised since 1964) at the Edinburgh Festival. Ronald Bryden's rave review caught the attention of Kenneth Tynan, at that stage a literary adviser to the National Theatre, and the play was quickly scheduled for production at the Old Vic Theatre.

This production won Stoppard the John Whiting Award and the first of his five *Evening Standard* Awards to date. (The others have been for *Jumpers*, *Travesties*, *Night and Day*, and *The Real Thing*.) The Broadway version picked up a Tony Award and the Drama Critics Circle Award. Subsequently *Travesties* and *The Real Thing* have repeated this New York double. Two television plays were also broadcast in 1967, and his radio play *Albert's Bridge* won the Prix Italia.

He again produced new work for television and the stage in 1968, and in 1970 he repeated the feat of 1967: a stage play (*After Magritte*), a radio play (*Where Are They Now?* for the BBC Schools program), and a television play (*The Engagement*, screened by NBC in the United States and, briefly, in some U.K. cinemas).

Dogg's Our Pet, written in 1971 for the opening of Ed Berman's Almost Free Theatre, demonstrated that Stoppard had extended the interest in philosophy that was already evident in *Rosencrantz and Guildenstern Are Dead*. In *Jumpers*—the play that began Stoppard's on-going association with director Peter Wood—he extended it still further; two of the principal characters in the play (Sir Archibald Jumper and George Moore, who even bears a famous philosopher's name) are academic philosophers, and a third (Crouch) is an enthusiastic amateur. The fourth principal (Dotty) is, as her name suggests, a woman undergoing a nervous breakdown. Whether there is any connection between her predicament and that of Jose Stoppard, who is reputed to have suffered a breakdown at the time of her divorce the year before, is another biographical issue that has never been explored.

Stoppard also produced an important radio play in 1972: *Artist Descending a Staircase*—a script Stoppard believed impervious to stage adaptation until Islington's King's Head Theatre followed by New York's Helen Hayes Theatre proved him wrong in 1988 and 1989 respectively.

A brief association with the Greenwich Theatre in 1973 saw him back in the role of translator (of Federico García Lorca's *The House of Bernarda Alba*— an unlikely choice for such a cerebral man) and making his debut as a director in Garson Kanin's *Born Yesterday*. This remains his only recorded direction of a play by another author.

Stoppard has often commented skeptically on the activities of academic critics (''Playwrights and Professors''), but several of his own plays fall into a category that has been labeled ''theatre of criticism'' (see Berlin). *Rosencrantz and Guildenstern Are Dead* and *Arcadia* are obvious examples. His huge success of 1974, *Travesties*—arguably his masterpiece to date—is another, focusing as it does on James Joyce and Tristan Tzara, with Oscar Wilde prominent in the background. There may well be a veiled allusion to Joyce in *Jumpers* too, since the ''eternal triangle'' at its center in many respects resembles the Bloom-Molly-Boylan triangle in *Ulysses*.

As usual the year following a major play was devoted to less ambitious projects. There were two works for BBC-TV: *The Boundary*, a short collaboration with Clive Exton, written, rehearsed, and performed within a week; and an adaptation of Jerome K. Jerome's *Three Men in a Boat*. A little earlier he had completed a thorough-going screen adaptation of Thomas Wiseman's novel *The Romantic Englishwoman*—the first of his eight filmscripts to date.

Stoppard ''came out'' as a spokesperson on public events in 1976. Two light-weight pieces produced to order for Ed Berman's Inter-Action Company (a fifteen-minute rescension of *Hamlet*—actually written in 1972, but mislaid for four years—and a highly commercial diptych, *Dirty Linen* and *New-Found-Land*) gave little hint of the transformation to come, although the latter ostensibly alludes to political issues. Of much more significance, however, was the meeting (in April) with Victor Fainberg, an exile from the Soviet Union who raised Stoppard's consciousness regarding the abuse of psychiatric treatment in that country. Stoppard addressed a Trafalgar Square rally on the subject in August, and then marched to the Soviet embassy to deliver a petition on dissidents' rights.

These events led to a visit to Moscow and Leningrad early in 1977 (designated International Prisoner of Conscience Year by Amnesty International), and Stoppard went on to write the first of his political dramas, *Every Good Boy Deserves Favour: A Play for Actors and Orchestra*, which premiered in July 1977, with André Previn conducting his own score for the production. The play is closely based on an article by Fainberg.

In the previous month Stoppard had visited Prague, where he met Václav Havel, the playwright and dissident, currently in the news as one of the signatories of Charter '77. Out of this experience, colored by his past experience in journalism and his love of sport, came one of his finest works, the television play *Professional Foul*. On the last day of 1977 came the announcement of the award of a C.B.E.

Stoppard's campaign against communism and for Western democracy continued through the rest of the 1970s and the 1980s—in newspaper articles, in plays like the diptych *Dogg's Hamlet, Cahoot's Macbeth,* and *Squaring the Circle,* and in his ongoing relationship with Václav Havel, including an adaptation of Havel's *Largo Desolato.* The obverse of this campaign was his public support for Margaret Thatcher's Conservative party in the election of 1983.

Stoppard seems to have found it difficult to exploit his new political awareness in his mainstream West End plays, perhaps because he chose this moment to eschew the subsidized theatres (the National and the Royal Shakespeare Company) for which his previous full-length plays had been written and to work instead with a commercial entrepreneur, Michael Codron. *Night and Day* and *The Real Thing* are both conservatively realistic in style, and both touch on politics only obliquely, the former focusing on Stoppard's old metier of journalism, the latter on love and art. Since Henry, the man at the center of *The Real Thing,* is a highly articulate playwright, the play was quickly read autobiographically, the relationship between Henry and Annie being interpreted as a belated celebration of Stoppard's second marriage. In fact the 1980s brought an ironical twist, when Felicity Kendal, who played Annie (and Christopher) in *On the Razzle,* and all Stoppard's female leads since, was identified as Stoppard's new partner in 1988. He and Miriam Moore-Robinson divorced on 11 February 1992.

Stoppard has produced adaptations frequently and original plays rather rarely from the late 1970s. A series of filmscripts includes a version of his own *Rosencrantz and Guildenstern Are Dead,* directed by himself, which was voted best film at the 1990 Venice Film Festival. He translated the libretto of Prokofiev's *The Love of Three Oranges* in 1983. Most important, he produced four versions of European classics, most of them evidently chosen by Peter Wood (Colvin): *On the Razzle, Undiscovered Country, Dalliance,* and *Rough Crossing*—listed here in what is generally regarded as their order of merit. All were performed at the National Theatre, to whose board he was appointed in 1989.

Since *The Real Thing,* his only original stage plays have been the underrated *Hapgood* and *Arcadia. Hapgood*—like the much earlier *Neutral Ground*—is a spy thriller in the John le Carré mold. This same genre was delightfully spoofed in *The Dog It Was That Died,* written for radio in 1982. In a more earnest mood Stoppard returned to India, the land of his early childhood, in another radio play, *In the Native State* (1991).

Selected Biographical Sources: ''Ambushes for the Audience''; Amory [1]; Billington [6]; Brassell; Hunter; Kelly; Page; Ryan; Tynan.

MAJOR STAGE PLAYS, PREMIERES, AND SIGNIFICANT REVIVALS: THEATRICAL RECEPTION

Tango. (English version of Slawomir Mrozek's play). 1966. Opened 25 May at the Aldwych Theatre, London. Produced by the Royal Shakespeare Company. Directed by Trevor Nunn.

The play was not popular with the critics, the anonymous *Times* review (''Polish Writer's Target in Doubt'') noting that "it is not funny enough." Other versions of Mrozek's original have since been preferred.

Rosencrantz and Guildenstern Are Dead. 1966. Opened 24 August at the Cranston Street Hall, Edinburgh. Produced by the Oxford Theatre Group. Directed by Brian Daubney. Opened 11 April 1967, at the Old Vic Theatre, London. Produced by the National Theatre. Directed by Derek Goldby. Revivals: Alvin Theatre (NY), 16 October 1967; Criterion Theatre, London, 8 July 1974; Lyceum Theatre, Edinburgh, 13 April 1978; Young Vic, London, October 1979; Roundabout Theatre (NY), 17 May 1987; Piccadilly Theatre, London, 16 June 1987.

"It's the most brilliant debut by a young playwright since John Arden's," wrote Bryden [3] of the 1966 Edinburgh production. Hobson felt much the same about the London production, calling it "the best first London-produced play written by a British author since Harold Pinter's *The Birthday Party*." The play was often designated "absurdist," although Berlin found the allusions to Samuel Beckett, Luigi Pirandello, and others so self-conscious that he suggested the label "theatre of criticism." Brustein reacted negatively to this self-consciousness, complaining in Leavisite terms that "Stoppard does not fight hard enough for his insights." Weightman [2] and Marcus were similarly negative, but Bryden [3] found "tragedy . . . in this comic looking-glass," and Wardle [4] responded to "powerful feeling" as well as "technical brilliance." Barnes [2] found the play "very chilling" as well as "very funny, very brilliant"; Kerr [1] complained of "crushing overlength" and felt that the characterization suffered from the fact that "Mr Stoppard himself is watching too closely," but he conceded that "the evening's compensations grow upon one steadily."

Enter a Free Man. 1968. Opened 28 March at the St. Martin's Theatre, London. Directed by Frith Banbury. Revivals: St. Clement's Church (NY), 17 December 1974; Perry Street Theatre (NY), September 1984.

Stoppard himself has disparaged the characterization in this play, which is "about some people I had seen in other people's plays" (Amory [1])—in particular Arthur Miller's *Death of a Salesman* and Robert Bolt's *Flowering Cherry* (hence Stoppard's habit of referring to it as "Flowering Death of a Cherry Salesman"). The critical reception was generally lukewarm, although Bryden [2] felt the play "confirms most of the things one hoped that Stoppard's second play would confirm," notably "that his flair for language and turning ideas on their heads is genuine and original."

The Real Inspector Hound (one act). 1968. Opened 17 June, at the Criterion Theatre, London. Produced by Michael Codron. Directed by Robert Chetwyn. Revivals: Theatre Four (NY), 23 April 1972; Shaw Theatre, London, 6 November 1972; Young Vic, London, 23 November 1976; Lyttleton Theatre, London, 9 September 1985.

Morley [2] claims that this play is "only challenged by Peter Shaffer's *Black*

Comedy in the post-war realm of minor theatrical classics." It has certainly been enormously popular with amateurs and professionals alike. Bryden [1] was one of a few early critics who felt "you could argue that the play, behind its frivolity, juggled with ideas as serious as [*Rosencrantz*]."

After Magritte (one act). 1970. Opened 9 April at the Green Banana Restaurant, London. Produced by the Ambiance Theatre Club. Directed by Geoffrey Reeves. Revivals: Theatre Four (NY), 23 April 1972; Shaw Theatre, London, 6 November 1972.

Craig spoke for many critics when he reported that Stoppard had here "gone wholeheartedly for absurdist theatre." Others, swayed by the allusion to Magritte (teased out by Harris), saw the play as surreal. But Goldstein (followed by Zeifman) drew attention to the title's pun on "after," which turns the play into something neither absurd nor surreal: "a teasing problem in logic, a conundrum to be unravelled" (Bigsby).

Jumpers. (1972). Opened 2 February at the Old Vic Theatre, London. Produced by the National Theatre. Directed by Peter Wood. Revivals: Eisenhower Theatre, Kennedy Center, Washington, D.C., 19 February 1974; moved 22 April to the Billy Rose Theatre (NY); Lyttleton Theatre, London, 21 September 1976; Aldwych Theatre, London, 1 April 1985.

Michael Hordern and Diana Rigg—"a stunning central duet" (Wardle [5])—and the rest of the original cast set a standard that subsequent interpreters have struggled to emulate. Wardle [4] noted that "given the abstraction of their origin, they do achieve as much personal reality as the action requires." Nightingale [3] also noted "a nice sense of individual character." The New York cast was less successful, prompting Kauffmann to complain of "the triteness of the characters,"among other things and Simon [1] to castigate Stoppard for "fatally neglecting the safety network of solid character, plot, and structure." This production also suffered from "a distracting set" (Wilson), and from a troupe of jumpers who were slicker than they should have been. There was a threat of closure after thirty-two performances, but the play then settled down to a respectable run, its "verbal acrobatics and intellectual cartwheels" impressing Gussow [3] and others. The 1976 London revival was likewise something of a disappointment, despite the resources of the newlybuilt Lyttleton Theatre and the reappearance of Hordern; Nightingale [4] found "the general tone . . . too manic, too frantic." Cushman added that both Graham Crowden (1972) and Julian Glover (1976) "came out wooden" in the role of Archie.

Travesties. 1974. Opened 10 June, at the Aldwych Theatre, London; moved 30 October 1975, to the Ethel Barrymore Theatre (NY). Produced by the Royal Shakespeare Company. Directed by Peter Wood. Revivals: Oxford Playhouse, January 1986; Cocteau Repertory Theatre (NY), November 1989; Barbican Theatre, London, 16 September 1993.

Rather than risk a repeat of the difficulties that almost sank *Jumpers* in New York, the Royal Shakespeare Company transported the original production there after a season in London. It was a resounding success in both places, Billington [7] finding it "a dazzling pyrotechnical feat that combines Wildean pastiche, political history, artistic debate, spoof reminiscence, and song-and-dance in marvellously judicious proportions," Kalem describing it as a "tinderbox of a play blazing with wit, paradox, parody, and, yes, ideas," and Rich looking deeper to find in John Wood's Carr "a touching centre . . . under the sheen of [the play's] immense daring." There were a few dissenting voices, Tynan, for example, likening it to "a triple-decker bus that isn't going anywhere," Weightman [1] complaining that "the character of Joyce is a failure, a kind of blank," and Wardle [6] noting the play's "complete failure to absorb Lenin." James, too, felt that Lenin was "a small but troublesome spanner in the play's glistening works." He noted that in the London production's "first run Lenin was too sympathetic, and in the second he was too diffident." *Travesties* has worn better than *Jumpers*; Whitford recently opined that it could "lay claim to being the most astonishing [play] in the modern English repertoire."

Dirty Linen and New-Found-Land. 1976. Opened 6 April at the Almost Free Theatre, London; moved 16 June to the Arts Theatre, London. Produced by Inter-Action. Directed by Ed Berman. Revivals: West End Theatre, Washington, D.C., followed by the Eisenhower Theatre, the Kennedy Center, in Washington, D.C., 1976; moved 11 January 1977 to the John Golden Theatre (NY); Shaw Theatre, London, 27 April 1981.

This clever but unpretentious "knickers farce" (Leonard) with its inset celebration of Ed Berman's naturalization as a British subject was described by Simon [2] as "just good, clean—or not-so-good and not-so-clean—fun." Gussow [6] called it "a tidal basin of laughter . . . a word spree," although he complained that the two monologues in *New-Found-Land* were "a bit too long." Barnes [1] felt that the New York production (also directed by Berman) was better than the London one because the acting was "a shade more forceful."

Every Good Boy Deserves Favour: A Play for Actors and Orchestra. 1977. Opened 1 July at the Royal Festival Hall, London, as part of the John Player Centenary Festival. Directed by Trevor Nunn. Revivals: Mermaid Theatre, London, 14 June 1978; Kennedy Center, Washington, D.C., July 1978; Metropolitan Opera House (NY), 30 July 1979; the Barbican, London, 25 June 1982; Queen Elizabeth Hall, London 26 June 1987.

Lauded by Levin [2] as an enhancement of "civilization itself" and by Wardle [1] for "gloriously" proving that "to be serious . . . you do not have to be dull," this idiosyncratic music drama (whose author is notoriously unmusical) was not universally popular, several critics agreeing with Cairns that "Stoppard has allowed himself to be carried away by his own comic invention," so that "with all its sincere and deeply serious intentions, it only toys with its subject." Gussow [5] found the New York season (directed by Stoppard himself) "more comic" than the Mermaid one which used a smaller orchestra, but like some later critics (Corballis, Kelly) he disputed aspects of the symbolic use of the music. A problematic detail in the depiction of the colonel is discussed in Kuurmann ("An Interview with Tom Stoppard").

Night and Day. 1978. Opened 8 November at the Phoenix Theatre, London. Produced by Michael Codron. Directed by Peter Wood. Revivals: Kennedy Center, Washington, D.C., October 1979; moved 27 November 1979, to the ANTA Theatre (NY).

Claiming he was "sick of flashy mind-projections," Stoppard had long talked of writing "a quiet play" (Hayman). The result troubled several critics, including Levin [1], who regretted the play's "horribly clumsy preaching, stiff with caked earnestness," Kerr [2], who found its "Shavian . . . debate . . . a good bit less than enthralling," and Nightingale [2], who felt that Stoppard's powers of characterization were not always adequate to his new naturalistic mode and that he sided "too wholeheartedly with dread and paranoia" in his depiction of trade union issues. A trade unionist writing under the name of "Marc" pulled no punches on the latter issue, attacking not only Stoppard but the play's dedicatee, Paul Johnson, "the man who saw through Socialism to become, in Michael Foot's words, Mrs Thatcher's swooning disciple." The critics of London's conservative *Telegraph* newspaper, however, liked the play, King [2] admiring its "Shavian intelligence, vivacity and wit," and Barber [1] hailing it as a "savagely serious drama." The London production was more successful than the New York one, which closed after ninety-five performances—despite the appearance of Maggie Smith in the role of Ruth ("a class act," according to Kerr [2]).

Dogg's Hamlet, Cahoot's Macbeth. 1979. Opened 21 May at the Arts Centre, University of Warwick; toured the United Kingdom, including London (Collegiate Theatre, Bloomsbury, beginning on 30 July 1979); toured the United States, including Washington, Boston, San Francisco, and New York (22 Steps Theatre, beginning 3 October 1979). Produced by the British-American Repertory Company. Directed by Ed Berman.

The play was caviare to the general, Watt complaining of "mere conceits," Sharp dismissing it as "smart-ass," and Gussow [2] as "marginal." However, it won something of a cult following on British and American campuses and was praised by Kroll ("the incorrigibly playful Stoppard has never been more serious than in this most playful of his works") and by Billington [3] ("an ingenious attempt to combine Shakespeare, linguistic jokes, political coment and zany farce").

On the Razzle (English version of Johann Nestroy's *Einen Jux will er sich machen*). 1981. Opened 18 September at the Lyttleton Theatre, London, after a brief run at the Edinburgh Festival, 1–5 September. Produced by the National Theatre. Directed by Peter Wood. Revival: Arena Stage, Washington, D.C., November 1982.

Why this play has had no New York production remains a mystery, unless

The Matchmaker or *Hello Dolly*—both of which stem from the same Nestroy play—preempted it. Most of the London critics agreed that it represented ''verbally Stoppard's best sustained fireworks to date'' (Barber [2]). A few, however, complained that the ''verbally hyperactive script'' was wasted on the lightweight plot, and in any case inhibited proper appreciation of ''raw comic event'' (Nightingale [5]), while Fenton felt that Stoppard's version, which was about ''nothing at all,'' betrayed the social comment of Nestroy's original.

The Real Thing. 1982. Opened 16 November at the Strand Theatre, London. Produced by Michael Codron. Directed by Peter Wood. Revivals: Plymouth Theatre (NY), 5 January 1984.

In London and especially in New York, where both the text and the design were streamlined, *The Real Thing* was a great critical success. Morley [3] called it ''the warmest and the most touching play [Stoppard] has ever written''; Grant praised its ''genuine passion''; Barber [3], noting that Stoppard had here ''succeeded in his ambition to write a quiet play,'' praised the dialogue of Henry and Annie—''bare-nerved and pulled taut by the stresses of self-conscious people who strain always to tell the truth about themselves''; Billington [5] called it ''that rare thing in the West End ... an intelligent play about love.'' There was some criticism from Billington [5], Asquith [2], and others of the character of Brodie, the politically committed would-be playwright, who was seen as too easy a target for Henry's wit, so that the play contains ''an unspoken assumption that impassioned political drama is irreconcilable with irony and finesse'' (Billington [5]). Amory [2] went further, arguing that ''only Henry comes to life, ... the others exist so that he can think and feel about them.'' King [3] went further still, dismissing the play as ''both theatrical and literary in the pejorative senses of those epithets.''

Rough Crossing (English version of Ferenc Molnar's *Játèk a Kastélyban*). 1984. Opened 30 October at the Lyttleton Theatre, London. Produced by the National Theatre. Directed by Peter Wood. Revivals: New Theatre of Brooklyn (NY), February 1990.

The play was almost universally panned by the London critics and was withdrawn early from the National Theatre's repertoire. Ratcliffe called it ''the worst play ever written by a good writer about bad writing, and the most laboured comedy ever constructed around the subject.'' Its only saving grace was felt to be the character of Dvornichek, ''a landlubber waiter who grows in stature until he becomes a sort of one-man deus ex machina'' (Edwards [2]). André Previn's incidental music was dismissed by Edwards [2] as ''rather unmemorable spoof period numbers,'' but praised by Barber [4] as ''delicious.'' The play worked better in the ''scaled down chorus-less touring version'' performed in Brooklyn (Gussow [1]).

Dalliance (English version of Arthur Schnitzler's *Liebelei*). 1986. Opened 27 May at the Lyttleton Theatre, London. Produced by the National Theatre. Directed by Peter Wood. Revival: Long Wharf Theatre, New Haven (CT), April 1987.

Dismissed by several critics as "slight" (Coveney, Christie) and inferior to Schnitzler's original (Billington [2]), *Dalliance* was not without its champions— for example, King [1], who found it "one of the most enjoyable plays in London." The decision—Peter Wood's rather than Stoppard's, it would seem—to change the setting of the final scene (a graveyard in Schnitzler; the wings of a theatre in Stoppard) was praised by Morley [1], who felt that Stoppard had managed "to invoke the shades of Pirandello and [Sir Arthur Wing] Pinero as well as those of Schnitzler himself."

Largo Desolato (English version of Václav Havel's play). 1986. Opened October at the Theatre Royal, Bristol. Produced by the Bristol Old Vic. Directed by Claude Whatham. Revivals: Yale Repertory Theatre, New Haven (CT), 26 October 1990.

Woddis described the play as "a cross between *The Real Thing* and the darker hues of Kafkaesque surrealism." Wardle [3] felt that "in Tom Stoppard's version it emerges as a wonderfully comic and unselfpitying piece."

Hapgood. 1988. Opened 8 March at the Aldwych Theatre, London. Produced by Michael Codron. Directed by Peter Wood. Revivals: Doolittle Theatre, Los Angeles, April 1989; Mitzi Newhouse Theatre, (NY), 4 December 1994.

As Edwards [1] observed, "For some reason Stoppard seems not to have carried the critics with him on this occasion." While Edwards [1] himself felt that Stoppard was here "at the top of his ingenious form," most critics deprecated the play's "passionless permutations" (Kemp), its "tricks for tricks' sake" (Radin). Billington [4], however, reckoned that "Stoppard's hint that there are, in the end, values worth preserving" prevented "the play [from] becoming a theatrical Mensa-test," while Asquith [1] noted that the title role "is by far the best role Stoppard has written for a woman," starring Felicity Kendal in London and Stockard Channing in New York (see Simonson).

Arcadia. 1993. Opened 4 April at the Lyttleton Theatre, London. Produced by the National Theatre. Directed by Trevor Nunn. Opened 30 March at the Vivian Beaumont Theatre, Lincoln Center (NY). Directed by Trevor Nunn.

Wardle [2] welcomed "a return to the Stoppard of *Jumpers* and *Travesties* . . . after the sterile ingenuity of *Hapgood*." Spencer agreed that this play represented "a terrific return to form," and Billington [1], one of the few critics who liked *Hapgood*, remarked that Stoppard's "ideas and his sympathies work in total harness and give the play a strong pulse of feeling." Many critics failed to feel this "pulse," however. The more charitable among them praised instead "the perfect marriage of ideas and high comedy" (Nightingale [1]), whereas others complained of a "fatal lack of living contact between ideas and people" (Peter [1]), of "simple concepts . . . pretentiously arrayed" (de Jongh [1]). Later assessments by Clinton and Demastes have suggested *Arcadia* is Stoppard's stongest work so far. Similarly, Leithauser and Greene were impressed with the New York production.

Indian Ink. 1995. Opened 27 February 1995 at the Aldwych Theatre, London. Directed by Peter Wood.

This stage adaptation of Stoppard's radio play *In the Native State* was seen by Paton as an elegant chamber piece on a topic (the relationship between Britain and India) used by others to compose epics. Peter [2] described it as a haunting and elegaic companion to *Arcadia*, but de Jongh [2] complained that it went into too many ''discursive directions'' to be satisfying.

ADDITIONAL PLAYS AND PRODUCTIONS

The House of Bernarda Alba, Stoppard's translation, opened 22 March 1973, at the Greenwich Theatre, London. Another translation, of Arthur Schnitzler's *Undiscovered Country*, was produced at the Olivier Theatre, London, in 1979. In 1983 Stoppard wrote the libretto to Prokofiev's opera *The Love of Three Oranges*.

Minor stage plays (all one-act) include *The Gamblers* (unperformed since 1965), *Rosencrantz and Guildenstern Meet King Lear* (1964), *Dogg's Our Pet* (1971) and *The Fifteen Minute ''Hamlet''* (1976), the latter two of which were stitched together to form the first part of the 1979 diptych *Dogg's Hamlet, Cahoot's Macbeth*. Several of the radio and television plays (including *''M'' Is for Moon among Other Things, If You're Glad I'll Be Frank, Albert's Bridge, A Separate Peace*, and *Artist Descending a Staircase*) have also been success-fully staged. A play begun for *The Observer*'s 1958 drama competition ''petered out after a dozen pages that were not unlike *Look Back in Anger*'' (''The Definite Maybe'') and seems now to have sunk without a trace.

ASSESSMENT OF STOPPARD'S CAREER

When Stoppard began writing, English theatre was dominated by what Tynan called ''the hairy men—heated, embattled, socially committed playwrights, like John Osborne, John Arden, and Arnold Wesker.'' By contrast, Stoppard's plays, like those of a few others, were ''smooth . . . apolitical.'' This lack of social commitment immediately made him unpopular with a handful of radical critics (e.g., Roberts) and at least one radical playwright (Edward Bond). Those who were not offended were often hard pressed to categorize his work. Initially many of them resorted to the term ''absurdism,'' since this seemed to be the prevailing alternative to the ''kitchen sink'' realism initiated by Osborne. ''Existentialism'' was also frequently invoked, usually rather more casually (e.g., Brassell, Corballis). But titles like ''Absurdism Altered'' (Gianakaris), ''Postabsurdism'' (Zeifman [2]), and even ''Godot Comes'' (Duncan) indicated an awareness that these labels fitted rather imperfectly—mainly because Stoppard's absurdism

Anthologies

Albert's Bridge and Other Plays. (*Albert's Bridge, If You're Glad I'll Be Frank, Artist Descending a Staircase, Where Are They Now?, A Separate Peace*). New York: Grove Press, 1977.

The Dog It Was That Died and Other Plays. (*The Dog It Was That Died, The Dissolution of Dominic Boot, "M" Is for Moon among Other Things, Teeth, Another Moon Called Earth, Neutral Ground, A Separate Peace*). London: Faber & Faber, 1983.

The Real Inspector Hound and Other Entertainments. (*The Real Inspector Hound; Dirty Linen; Dogg's Hamlet, Cahoot's Macbeth; After Magritte*). London: Faber & Faber, 1993.

Squaring the Circle. (*Squaring the Circle, Every Good Boy Deserves Favour, Professional Foul*). London: Faber & Faber, 1984.

Stoppard: The Plays for Radio, 1964–1991. (*The Dissolution of Dominic Boot, "M" is for Moon among Other Things, If You're Glad I'll Be Frank, Albert's Bridge, Where Are They Now?, Artist Descending a Staircase, The Dog It Was That Died, In the Native State*). London: Faber & Faber, 1994.

Stoppard: The Television Plays, 1965–1984. (*Teeth, A Separate Peace, Another Moon Called Earth, Neutral Ground, Professional Foul, Squaring the Circle*). London: Faber & Faber, 1994.

Translations/Adaptations

Largo Desolato, by Václav Havel. London: Faber & Faber, 1987; New York: Grove Press, 1987; Havel, Václav. *Selected Plays*. London: Faber & Faber, 1994.

Tango, by Slawomir Mrozek. Trans. Nicholas Bethell, adapted by Tom Stoppard. London: Cape, 1968; *Three East European Plays*. Harmondsworth: Penguin, 1970.

Undiscovered Country, by Arthur Schnitzler: "*Das Weite Land*" . . . *in an English Version by Tom Stoppard*. London: Faber & Faber, 1980.

Essays and Articles on Drama and Theatre

"The Definite Maybe." *Author* 77 (1967): 18–20.

"I'm Not Keen on Experiments." *New York Times* (8 Mar. 1970): 2:17.

Is It True What They Say about Shakespeare? Oxford: Oxford University Press, 1982.

"Orghast." *Times Literary Supplement* (1 Oct. 1971): 1174.

"Playwrights and Professors." *Times Literary Supplement* (13 Oct. 1972): 1219.

"Something to Declare." *Sunday Times* (25 Feb. 1968): 47.

"Tom Stoppard on a New Writer." *Scene* (9 Feb. 1963): 46–47.

"A Very Satirical Thing Happened to Me on the Way to the Theatre Tonight." *Encore* 10 (1963): 33–36.

"Yes, We Have No Banana." *The Guardian* (10 Dec. 1971): 10.

Interviews

"An Interview with Tom Stoppard" (with Joost Kuurmann). *Dutch Quarterly Review of Anglo-American Letters* 10. (1980): 41–57.

'The Playwright and the Professors: An Interview with Tom Stoppard'' (with Katherine
E. Kelly and William W. Demastes). *South Central Review* 11.4 (winter 1994):
1–14.

SECONDARY BIBLIOGRAPHY

"Ambushes for the Audience: Towards a High Comedy of Ideas." *Theatre Quarterly*
4.14 (1974): 3–17.
Amory, Mark [1]. "The Joke's the Thing." *Sunday Times Magazine* (9 June 1974): 68–
74.
———[2]. Review of *The Real Thing. The Spectator* (27 Nov. 1982): 32–33.
Archer, Mark. "Is There a Place for the Play of Ideas?" *Drama* 174 (1989): 10.
Asquith, Ross [1]. Review of *Hapgood. City Limits* (17 Mar. 1988).
———[2]. Review of *The Real Thing. City Limits* (18 Nov. 1982).
Ayer, A. J. "Love among the Logical Positivists." *Sunday Times* (9 Apr. 1972): 16.
Barber, John [1]. Review of *Night and Day. Daily Telegraph* (9 Nov. 1978): 15.
———[2]. Review of *On the Razzle. Daily Telegraph* (23 Sept. 1981).
———[3]. Review of *The Real Thing. Daily Telegraph* (17 Nov. 1982).
———[4]. Review of *Rough Crossing. Daily Telegraph* (31 Nov. 1984).
———[5]. "Tragi-Comical Study of a Philanderer." *Daily Telegraph* (21 June 1979):
15.
Barnes, Clive [1]. " '*Dirty Linen*' Sparkles in Wind of Laughter." *New York Times* (12
Jan 1977): 3:18.
———[2]. "Theater: *Rosencrantz and Guildenstern Are Dead.*" *New York Times* (17
Oct. 1967): 53.
Bennett, Jonathan. "Philosophy and Mr Stoppard." *Philosophy* 50 (1975): 5–18.
Berlin, Normand. "*Rosencrantz and Guildenstern Are Dead*: Theatre of Criticism."
Modern Drama 16.3 (Sept. 1973): 269–77.
Bigsby, C.W.E. *Tom Stoppard.* 2nd ed. Harlow: Longman, 1979.
Billington, Michael [1]. Review of *Arcadia. The Guardian* (14 Apr. 1993).
———[2]. Review of *Dalliance. The Guardian* (29 May 1986).
———[3]. Review of *Dogg's Hamlet, Cahoot's Macbeth. The Guardian* (31 July 1979).
———[4]. Review of *Hapgood. The Guardian* (10 Mar. 1988).
———[5]. Review of *The Real Thing. The Guardian* (17 Nov. 1982).
———[6]. *Stoppard: The Playwright.* London: Methuen, 1987.
———[7]. Review of *Travesties. The Guardian* (11 June 1974).
Brassell, Tim. *Tom Stoppard: An Assessment.* London: Macmillan, 1985.
Brater, Enoch. "Parody, Travesty and Politics in the Plays of Tom Stoppard." In *Essays
on Contemporary British Drama*, eds. Hedwig Bock and Albert Wertheim. Munich: Max Hueber, 1981: 357–82.
Brustein, Robert. "Waiting for Hamlet." *New Republic* (4 Nov. 1967): 25–26.
Bryden, Ronald [1]. "A Critics' Nightmare." *The Observer* (23 June 1968): 26.
———[2]. "Follow-up Debut." *The Observer* (31 Mar. 1968): 31.
———[3]. Review of *Rosencrantz and Guildenstern Are Dead* (Edinburgh production).
The Observer (28 Aug. 1966): 15.
Cairns, David. Review of *Every Good Boy Deserves Favour. Sunday Times* (27 June
1982): 39.

Cave, Richard Allen. *New British Drama in Performance on the London Stage*. Gerrards Cross: Colin Smythe, 1987.

Christie, Ian. Review of *Dalliance*. *Daily Express* (28 May 1986).

Clinton, Craig. Review of *Arcadia*. *Theatre Journal* 46.2 (May 1994): 270–72.

Colvin, Clare. "The Real Tom Stoppard." *Drama* 161 (1986): 9.

Corballis, Richard. *Stoppard: The Mystery and the Clockwork*. Oxford: Amber Lane Press, 1984; New York: Methuen, 1984.

Coveney, Michael. Review of *Dalliance*. *Financial Times* (28 May 1986).

Craig, Randall. "Plays in Performance." *Drama* 100 (summer 1970): 36–37.

Cushman, Robert. "Moral Gymnastics." *The Observer* (26 Sept. 1976): 24.

de Jongh, Nicholas [1]. Review of *Arcadia*. *Evening Standard* (14 Apr. 1993).

———[2]. Review of *Indian Ink*. *Evening Standard* (28 Feb. 1995).

Delaney, Paul. *Tom Stoppard: The Moral Vision of the Major Plays*. London: Macmillan, 1990.

Demastes, William W. "Re-Inspecting the Crack in the Chimney: Chaos Theory from Ibsen to Stoppard." *New Theatre Quarterly* 10 (Aug. 1994): 242–54.

Duncan, Joseph E. "Godot Comes: *Rosencrantz and Guildenstern Are Dead*." *Ariel* 12 (1981): 57–70.

Edwards, Adam, and Leonardo Castillejo. Review of *Hapgood*. *Mail on Sunday* (20 Mar. 1988).

Edwards, Christopher [1]. Review of *Hapgood*. *The Spectator* (19 Mar. 1988).

———[2]. Review of *Rough Crossing*. *The Spectator* (10 Nov. 1984).

Ellmann, Richard. "The Zealots of Zurich." *Times Literary Supplement* (12 July 1974): 744.

Fainberg, Victor. "My Five Years in Mental Hospitals." *Index on Censorship* 4.2 (1975): 67–71.

Fenton, James. "Mr Stoppard Goes to Town." *Sunday Times* (14 Oct. 1981): 43.

Gianakaris, C. J. "Absurdism Altered: *Rosencrantz and Guildenstern Are Dead*." *Drama Survey* 7 (1968–69): 52–58.

Gilbert, Stephen W. Review of 'The House of Bernarda Alba.' " *Plays and Players* (May 1973): 42–43.

Goldstein, Leonard. "A Note on Stoppard's *After Magritte*." *Zeitschrift fur Anglistik und Amerikanistik* 23 (1975): 16–21.

Gollob, David, and David Roper. "Trad Tom Pops In." *Gambit* 37 (1980): 5–17.

Goodwin, Noel. "The Love of Three Oranges." *Times* (10 Oct. 1983): 12.

Grant, Steve. Review of *The Real Thing*. *Time Out* (26 Nov. 1982).

Greene, Alexis. Review of *Arcadia*. *Theatre Week* (17 Apr. 1995): 23–24, 33.

Gussow, Mel [1]. "A Breezy Voyage on a Stoppardian Sea." *New York Times* (23 Feb. 1990): C3.

———[2]. Review of *Dogg's Hamlet, Cahoot's Macbeth*. *New York Times* (4 Oct. 1979).

———[3]. " '*Jumpers*' Author Is Verbal Gymnast." *New York Times* (23 Apr. 1974): 36.

———[4]. "Play: With Stoppard in Schnitzlerland." *New York Times* (27 Feb. 1981): C4.

———[5]. "Theater: Tom Stoppard's 'Every Good Boy Deserves Favour.' " *New York Times* (31 July 1979): 3: 8.

———[6]. "Tom Stoppard's Sex Scandals of '76." *New York Times* (27 June 1976): 2: 5.

Harris, Wendell V. "Stoppard's *After Magritte*." *The Explicator* 24 (1976): item 40.

Hayman, Ronald. *Tom Stoppard*. 4th ed. London: Heinemann, 1982.

Highfield, Roger. Review of *Arcadia. Daily Telegraph* (15 Apr. 1993).

Hobson, Harold. Review of *Rosencrantz and Guildenstern Are Dead. Sunday Times* (16 Apr. 1967): 49.

Hunter, Jim. *Tom Stoppard's Plays*. London: Faber & Faber, 1982.

Innes, Christopher. "*Hapgood*: A Question of Gamesmanship." *Modern Drama* 32.2 (June 1988): 315–17.

James, Clive. "Count Zero Splits the Infinite." *Encounter* 45 (1975): 68–76.

Jenkins, Anthony. *The Theatre of Tom Stoppard*. Cambridge: Cambridge University Press, 1987.

Jensen, Henning. "Jonathan Bennett and Mr Stoppard." *Philosophy* 52 (1977): 214–17.

Kalem, T. E. "Dance of Words." *Time* (10 Nov. 1975).

Kauffmann, Stanley. *Persons of Drama: Theater Criticism and Comment*. New York: Harper, 1976.

Kelly, Katherine E. *Tom Stoppard and the Craft of Comedy: Medium and Genre at Play*. Ann Arbor: University of Michigan Press, 1991.

Kemp, Peter. Review of *Hapgood. Independent* (10 Mar. 1988).

Kennedy, Andrew. "Tom Stoppard's Dissident Comedies." *Modern Drama* 25 (Dec. 1982): 469–76.

Kerr, Walter [1]. "Taking Revenge on Life." *New York Times* (29 Oct. 1967): 2: 1,3.

———[2]. "Theater: Tom Stoppard's 'Night and Day.' " *New York Times* (28 Nov. 1979): 3: 21.

King, Francis [1]. Review of *Dalliance. Sunday Telegraph* (1 June 1986).

———[2]. Review of *Night and Day. Sunday Telegraph* (12 Nov. 1978).

———[3]. Review of *The Real Thing. Sunday Telegraph* (21 Nov. 1982).

Kroll, Jack. Review of *Dogg's Hamlet, Cahoot's Macbeth. Newsweek* (24 Sept. 1979).

Leithauser, Brad. "A House of Games." *Time* (10 Apr. 1995): 78.

Leonard, John. "Tom Stoppard Tries on a Knickers Farce." *New York Times* (9 Jan. 1977): 2:1.

Levenson, Jill. "Views from a Revolving Door: Tom Stoppard's Canon to Date." *Queen's Quarterly* 78 (1971): 431–42.

Levin, Bernard [1]. Review of *Night and Day. Sunday Times* (12 Nov. 1978): 37.

———[2]. "Stoppard's Political Asylum." *Sunday Times* (3 July 1977): 37.

"Marc." "A Play for Paul." *Sunday Times* (29 Oct. 1978): 32.

Marcus, Frank. "Theatre: Ancient and Modern." *London Magazine* (1967 July): 76.

Morley, Sheridan [1]. Review of *Dalliance. Punch* (4 June 1986).

———[2]. "Happy Returns." *Punch* (1 Dec. 1976): 1043.

———[3]. Review of *The Real Thing. Punch* (24 Nov. 1982).

Nightingale, Benedict [1]. Review of *Arcadia. Times* (14 Apr. 1993).

———[2]. "Have Pinter and Stoppard Turned to Naturalism?" *New York Times* (3 Dec. 1978): 2: 4.

———[3]. *An Introduction to Fifty Modern British Plays: A Reader's Guide*. London: Heinemann, 1982.

———[4]. "Not So Farce." *New Statesman* (1 Oct. 1976): 457.

———[5]. "Theatre." *New Statesman* (2 Oct. 1981): 27.

Page, Malcolm. *File on Stoppard*. London: Methuen, 1986.

Paton, Maureen. Review of *Indian Ink. Daily Express* (28 Feb. 1995).

Perrett, Roy W. "Philosophy as Farce, or Farce as Philosophy." *Philosophy* 59 (1984): 373–81.

Peter, John [1]. Review of *Arcadia*. *Sunday Times* (18 Apr. 1993).

———[2]. Review of *Indian Ink*. *Sunday Times* (5 Mar. 1995).

"Polish Writer's Target in Doubt." *The Times* (26 May 1966): 19.

Radin, Victoria. Review of *Hapgood*. *New Statesman* (18 Mar. 1988).

Ratcliffe, Michael. Review of *Rough Crossing*. *The Observer* (4 Nov. 1984).

Rich, Alan. "Memorabilia." *New York* (17 Nov. 1975): 103.

Roberts, Philip. "Tom Stoppard: Serious Artist or Siren?" *Critical Quarterly* 20 (1978): 84–92.

Robinson, Gabriele Scott. "Nothing Left but Parody: Friedrich Durrenmatt and Tom Stoppard." *Theatre Journal* 32.1 (Mar. 1980): 85–94.

Sammells, Neil. *Tom Stoppard: The Artist as Critic*. Basingstoke: Macmillan, 1988.

Shulman, Milton. "The Politicizing of Tom Stoppard." *New York Times* (23 Apr. 1978): 2:3.

Simon, John [1]. "Flying Philosophers, Poetic Pederasts." *New York* (11 Mar. 1974): 84.

———[2]. "Theatre Chronicle." *Hudson Review* 30 (1977): 260.

Simonson, Robert. "The Heart of 'Hapgood.' " *Theatre Week* (2 Jan. 1995): 13–16.

Spencer, Charles. Review of *Arcadia*. *Daily Telegraph* (14 Apr. 1993).

Tynan, Kenneth. *Show People: Profiles in Entertainment*. New York: Simon & Schuster, 1979.

Wardle, Irving [1]. "Abundance of Bright Ideas." *The Times* (2 July 1977): 7.

———[2]. Review of *Arcadia*. *Independent on Sunday* (18 Apr. 1993).

———[3]. "A Comic Left Alone." *The Times* (14 Oct. 1986): 11.

———[4]. "Drama Unearthed from Elsinore's Depths." *The Times* (12 Apr. 1967): 8.

———[5]. "Jumpers." *The Times* (3 Feb. 1972): 13.

———[6]. "A Web to Snare Three Giants." *The Times* (11 June 1974): 7.

Watt, Douglas. Review of *Dogg's Hamlet, Cahoot's Macbeth*. *New York Daily News* (4 Oct. 1979).

Weightman, John [1]. "Art Versus Life." *Encounter* 43 (Sept. 1974): 57–59.

———[2]. "Mini-Hamlets in Limbo." *Encounter* 29 (July 1967): 38–40.

Whitaker, Thomas R. *Tom Stoppard*. London: Macmillan, 1983.

Whitford, Frank. "Tour de Farce." *Times Literary Supplement* (1 Oct. 1993): 19.

Wilkie, Tom. Review of *Hapgood*. *The Independent* (23 Mar. 1988).

Wilson, Edwin. "Stoppard's Gem in a Distracting Set." *Wall Street Journal* (11 Mar. 1974).

Woddis, Carole. Review of *Largo Desolato*. *City Limits* (12 Feb. 1987).

Zeifman, Hersh [1]. "Tomfoolery: Stoppard's Theatrical Puns." *Yearbook of English Studies* 9 (1979): 204–20.

———[2]. "A Trick of the Lights: Tom Stoppard's *Hapgood* and Postabsurdist Theater." In *Around the Absurd*, ed. Enoch Brater and Ruby Cohn. Ann Arbor: University of Michigan Press, 1990: 175–202.

BIBLIOGRAPHIES

Bratt, David. *Tom Stoppard: A Reference Guide*. Boston: G. K. Hall, 1982.

Carpenter, Charles A. ''Bond, Shaffer, Stoppard, Storey: An International Checklist of Commentary.'' *Modern Drama* 24 (1981): 546–56.

King, Kimball. ''Tom Stoppard.'' *Twenty Modern British Playwrights: A Bibliography, 1956 to 1976*. New York: Garland, 1977: 217–30.

Ryan, Randolph. ''Theatre Checklist No. 2: Tom Stoppard.'' *Theatrefacts* 2 (May–July 1974): 3–9.

David Storey

(1933–)

WILLIAM HUTCHINGS

David Storey was born on 13 July 1933, in Wakefield, Yorkshire; he is the third son of Frank Richmond Storey, a coal miner, and Lily Cartwright Storey. He was educated at the Queen Elizabeth Grammar School (1943–1951) and the Wakefield School of Art (1951–1953). From 1952 through 1956 he played professional rugby-league football for the Leeds Rugby League Club—an experience that formed the basis of his first novel, *This Sporting Life* (1960), as well as his third play, *The Changing Room* (1971). In 1953, while continuing to play rugby for Leeds, he moved to London to attend the Slade School of Art, where he became a prize-winning student. He thus led a "dual" life that he has described in detail in his essay "Journey through a Tunnel": as he commuted weekly from London to the north to play rugby-league football, his existence seemed acutely divided into binary oppositions of artist and athlete, mind and body, London and Leeds. This sense of a "divided self," which appears repeatedly in his plays and novels, was discussed at greatest length in his novel *Radcliffe* (1963).

In 1956 Storey married Barbara Rudd Hamilton and received his diploma from the Slade School of Art. During the next four years he worked at a variety of jobs, including as a postman, a bus conductor, a workman on a crew erecting showground tents, a farm worker, and a teacher in a secondary school in the East End of London.

Storey's first novel, *This Sporting Life*, won the Macmillan Fiction Award in 1960. His first play, *The Restoration of Arnold Middleton*, was produced in 1966 in Edinburgh and at the Royal Court Theatre in London in 1967 before transferring to the Criterion Theatre in London's West End and winning its author the *Evening Standard* Award for most promising playwright of the year. During the next five years four more of Storey's plays were produced to widespread critical acclaim and popular success in both London and New York, where he has received the New York Drama Critics Circle Award for best play in 1971, 1972, and 1974—becoming the only playwright to have been so frequently honored in so little time. Nevertheless, Storey continued to regard himself primarily as a novelist; the plays were written remarkably quickly, often in a matter of two or three days, as a ''holiday'' from writing fiction.

From 1972 through 1974 Storey served as associate artistic director of the Royal Court Theatre. In 1973 his verse drama *Cromwell* (in which the title character never appears), starring Albert Finney, was produced there, though it closed after a short run. *The Farm*, a domestic drama about misunderstandings between a father and his daughters, opened at the Royal Court in 1973 and transferred to the Mayfair Theatre in London. *Life Class*, which opened at the Royal Court in 1974 and starred Alan Bates as a beleaguered art teacher, was notable for the presence of a nude model on stage and the simulated rape that two of the art students perpetrate as a hoax. It is the most thematically complex and controversial of Storey's plays, raising issues of art and life, illusion and reality, and the nature of ''invisible events'' both in the theatre and outside it. The same year, Storey became a fellow at University College, London.

In 1975 the film version of *In Celebration* was released by the American Film Theatre series, directed by Lindsay Anderson from Storey's script. *Night*, a play about actors in rehearsal, was planned for production at the Edinburgh Festival that year but was withdrawn by Storey, who was dissatisfied with the script. Instead, he offered *Mother's Day*, a farce that some have compared to works by Joe Orton because of its deliberate outrageousness and its humor based on the characters' violation of various sexual and social taboos. The play was declined by Edinburgh authorities but in 1976 was produced at the Royal Court, where it received exceptionally hostile reviews and closed shortly thereafter. The same week, Storey's novel *Saville* was published to critical acclaim; it later won the Booker Prize, Britain's foremost award for fiction.

Due to changes in the management at the Royal Court Theatre, Storey found himself out of favor there—and uninterested in the more overtly political plays being produced there, which he considered a form of philistinism. He was then convinced that his career as a playwright had come to an end. In 1978, however, *Sisters* opened at the Royal Exchange Theatre in Manchester but did not transfer to London. His next play was *Early Days*, which was produced at the National Theatre (Cottesloe) in 1980 and starred Ralph Richardson, for whom it was explicitly written. A television adaptation, directed, like the stage version, by Lindsay Anderson, was shown on London Weekend Television in 1981 and in the United States on PBS.

In 1985 a play entitled *Phoenix* was produced by the amateur group Ealing Questors and subsequently staged by Century Theatre in Huddersfield and Rotterham, although it has never been published. *The March on Russia* was produced at the National Theatre (Lyttleton) in 1989, directed by Lindsay

Anderson; its subject is the Pasmore family that was depicted in his novel *Pasmore* (1972).

In 1972 the publication of *Storey's Lives: Poems, 1951–1991* revealed a heretofore little-known aspect of Storey's career; few of his poems had previously been published, apart from a few appearing in theatre programs or within the texts of the plays themselves. *Stages*, produced at the National Theatre in 1992, was in many ways as minimalist as *Home* and *Early Days*, although it returned to a number of familiar themes of psychological breakdown, art and reality, and familial disintegration. When published in 1992, it was accompanied by an unproduced two-character play, *Caring*.

Selected Biographical Sources: Duffy; Gindin; Gussow [5]; Hutchings [4]; Sage, "David Storey in Conversation."

MAJOR PLAYS, PREMIERES, AND SIGNIFICANT REVIVALS: THEATRICAL RECEPTION

The Restoration of Arnold Middleton. 1966. Opened 22 November at the Traverse Theatre Club, Edinburgh. Directed by Gordon McDougall. Opened at the Royal Court Theatre, London, on 4 July 1967, for twenty-two performances. Produced by the English Stage Company. Directed by Robert Kidd. Transferred to the Criterion Theatre, London, on 31 August 1967 for eighty-five performances. Produced by Donald Albery for Calabash Productions. Directed by Robert Kidd.

Storey's first play concerns the psychological breakdown and "restoration" of a beleaguered schoolteacher who, after a night of drinking with his wife and her mother, spends the night with his mother-in-law. Taylor [1] praised the play's treatment of madness, "not allowing us to realize for sure that Arnold is going mad until he is on the point of being restored," whereas Darlington [1] contended the "hero talked on till he had a fit." Billington [3] stressed the play's humor, while Wardle [5] found the play "partly brilliant and partly incoherent." Storey's recollection of the way the "restoration" was performed and his reasons for adding it in rewriting the play from its original version (entitled *To Die with the Philistines*) are discussed in Hutchings [4].

In Celebration. 1969. Opened 22 April at the Royal Court Theatre, London, for sixty-seven performances. Produced by the English Stage Company. Produced by the Arena Stage Company, Washington, D.C., June 1974. Directed by John Dillon. Revival: Manhattan Theatre Club (NY), November 1984.

This, the most successful of Storey's "family" plays, concerns the return of three now-adult sons to their working-class parents' home in order to celebrate their parents' wedding anniversary. Long-suppressed resentments simmer amid poignant memories of sons who, though educated out of their working-class roots, find little or no satisfaction in their ostensibly successful middle-class lives. Nightingale [2] succinctly summarized the major themes of this "unusually stimulating play,'' relating them to the theories of R. D. Laing, while Holmstrom deftly characterized the sons as ''the Revenger, the Crippled, [and] the Crucified.'' Shorter [1] found it ''classically laid out as if to Aristotle's rules and simmering with Freudian implication.''

The Contractor. 1969. Opened 20 October at the Royal Court Theatre, London, for thirty-three performances. Produced by the English Stage Company. Directed by Lindsay Anderson. Transferred to the Fortune Theatre, London, on 6 April 1970. Produced by Michael Codron. Directed by Lindsay Anderson. Produced at the Long Wharf Theatre, New Haven (CT), December 1971. Directed by Barry Davis. Opened at the Chelsea Theatre, Manhattan (NY), on 9 October 1973, for seventy-two performances.

The first of Storey's ostensibly ''plotless'' plays to have been produced, *The Contractor* consists of the onstage construction of a wedding marquee (tent) and its demolition on the morning after the wedding; the allegedly ''central'' event—the wedding itself—takes place between the acts and offstage. The relationships among three generations of the Ewbanks family and among the workmen constructing the tent are subtly juxtaposed, with myriad implications about the nature of family bonds, the meaning of work, and the effects of class. Storey himself remarks on the multiple possible meanings of the tent as a symbol in Taylor [1] and remarks to Hastings that he sees the play ''much as a piece of music with 12 instruments for the characters and the tent as the temporary thing they create.'' Kalem [5] considers it ''the symbol of the rise and fall of national greatness.''

Home. 1970. Opened 17 June at the Royal Court Theatre, London, for forty performances. Produced by the English Stage Company. Directed by Lindsay Anderson. Transferred to the Apollo Theatre, London, on 29 July for forty performances. Directed by Lindsay Anderson. First presented in New York on 17 November 1970, at the Morosco Theatre for 110 performances. Produced by Alexander H. Cohen. Directed by Lindsay Anderson.

Much of the initial critical attention given to *Home* focused on the casting of Sir Ralph Richardson and Sir John Gielgud, which Kalem [2] termed a ''Duet of Dynasts''; that they were several decades older than the script specified was overlooked, although the casting tended to make the play more about the problems of aging than Storey had initially intended (see Hutchings [4], 120). He also remarked to Hayman [2] that reviewers ''did a disservice to the play'' in disclosing that the characters are in fact confined in a mental ''home''—a fact whose disclosure is deferred for some time in the theatre. Wardle [3] considered the play a ''muted . . . social tragedy'' whose characters create ''a pitiful replica of life outside,'' and thought ''the weak link in the play [to be] its excessive economy of dialogue.'' The most detailed critical analysis of it is by Ecker (in German).

The Changing Room. 1971. Opened 9 November at the Royal Court Theatre, London, for thirty-nine performances. Produced by the English Stage Company.

Directed by Lindsay Anderson. Transferred to the Globe Theatre, London, on 15 December for 108 performances. Opened at the Long Wharf Theatre, New Haven, (CT) December 1972. Directed by Michael Rudman. Opened in New York on 6 March 1973, at the Morosco Theatre for 191 performances. Directed by Michael Rudman.

Like *The Contractor*, *The Changing Room* is essentially a "plotless" play, depicting seemingly mundane events in a locker room before, during, and after a rugby match. Kalem [8] maintained that "with deceptive quietude" Storey developed his "central concern" (here as in previous plays) that "life is war on the installment plan," with the rugby match the characters' "catchpenny Armageddon." Kauffmann [1] considered it "a quiet, daring poetic act" of "naturalism in contemporary perspective," although its "character revelations are banal and unenlightening."

Life Class. 1974. Opened at the Royal Court Theatre, London, on 9 April for fifty-four performances. Produced by the English Stage Company. Directed by Lindsay Anderson. Transferred to the Duke of York's Theatre, London, on 4 June for forty-eight performances. Opened at the Manhattan Theatre Club (NY), December 1975.

Gilbert discussed its "dialectic on life and art, enduring and creating, proceeding and observing" and considered the play as Storey's "valediction" to the theatre or at least "to the careful portrayal of 'that incredible miasma we call life' which has made Storey's name and about which he has surely said all he's got to say," although he expressed hope for a new direction in his writing. Kalem [4] found some of the play's "talk gassily inflated, [although] some of it is nutcracker tough, and some of it is like a muted dirge for a dying civilization." Lambert [3] considered it a "lament for lost opportunities" in an educational system "in which the aimlessness of the students is matched only by the disappointed incompetence of their teachers."

Mother's Day. 1976. Opened 22 September at the Royal Court Theatre, London, for thirty-nine performances. Produced by the English Stage Company. Directed by Robert Kidd.

Storey's farce, intended to depict a family in which all "normal" values were reversed, was almost unanimously denounced by the critics. Lambert [1] contended that the play "would have been better consigned to the wastepaper basket" and that Storey "is soon out of his range when he deserts the tough and tender naturalism in which he excels." Wardle [8] declared Storey "wholly deficient in farcical talent," while Billington [6] described the play as a "calculated exercise in bad taste comedy" and "a stinker." For defenses of the play, see Kerensky and Randall [1]; both were published well after the play had closed. For Storey's account of the critical reaction and defense of the play, see Hutchings [4].

Early Days. 1980. Opened 20 April at the Cottesloe Theatre of the National Theatre, London. Directed by Lindsay Anderson. Produced at the Eisenhower Theatre of the Kennedy Center, Washington, D.C., June 1981.

Noting that the play's action "goes virtually nowhere," Kalem [1] claimed that "through Kitchen's lips, Storey has his spare, harsh, tender say about love, life, time, memory, and death." Kroll [1] considered Storey's work "not so much a play as it is a concert for this ineffable instrument," Richardson, who "plays the music of mortality." Chaillet [1] contended that "the old man's speech is purposefully disordered as if Mr. Storey wanted to allow Sir Ralph ample opportunity for improvisational amnesia" and found him "ruthlessly entertaining," although "the play is a pale shade of the robust writing Mr. Storey offered when he originally wrote for the Royal Court."

The March on Russia. 1989. Opened 6 April in the Lyttleton Auditorium of the National Theatre, London. Presented by the National Theatre Company. Directed by Lindsay Anderson. American premiere at the Cleveland (OH) Play House in April 1990. Opened in New York at the Chelsea Stage at the Hudson Guild, 7 November through 2 December 1990. Directed by Josephine R. Abady.

Wilders remarked that the play is "so like" *In Celebration* "as to seem like a revised version of that original work," although Anderson's "perfect production of a moving [play]" reflected "some of the changes which have occurred in Britain during the past two decades" since *In Celebration* was first staged. The most detailed critical analyses of the play are by Pittock [2] and King.

ADDITIONAL PLAYS, ADAPTATIONS, AND PRODUCTIONS

Storey's other stage plays include *Cromwell* (1973), a history play in which the title character never appears; it was written in blank verse. *The Farm* (1973) and *Sisters* (1978) are domestic dramas. *Phoenix* (1985), which has not been published, received limited exposure through regional and amateur productions in England. For a detailed description and analysis of this play, based on the unpublished script, see Pittock [1]. Another unpublished work, *Night* (1976), was withdrawn from the Edinburgh Festival before production; it was set on a bare stage and concerned the thoughts of a number of actors in rehearsal. *Stages* (1992), presented at the Royal National Theatre, is a retrospective examination of its central character's mental breakdown and continues Storey's exploration of dramatic minimalism. An unproduced two-character play entitled *Caring* has been published with *Stages*; *Caring* is described in Storey's introduction as "very much written as a play within a play."

Storey's first writing for performance was the screenplay of his novel *This Sporting Life*, directed by Lindsay Anderson and released in 1963; he also wrote the screenplay for *In Celebration* (1974), also directed by Anderson, as part of the American Film Theatre series. The television adaptations of *Home* (1973) and *Early Days* (1981) were also from Storey's scripts, and he wrote a television adaptation of James Joyce's short story "Grace" in 1974.

ASSESSMENT OF STOREY'S CAREER

Among the works of the "second generation" of dramatists associated with the English Stage Company at the Royal Court Theatre, the plays of David Storey are remarkable for the diversity of their form, their understated eloquence, and the recurrence of a number of themes that have become uniquely his own. In contrast to the strident anger and agitprop often associated with the late 1960s and 1970s, Storey's plays are subtle rather than strident, relying on Chekhovian principles of dramaturgy while advancing his forebear's techniques. Storey's plays are unpolitical, unpolemical, and determinedly understated; their "central events" typically occur offstage and between acts, focusing the audience's attention on "interior action" as his characters cope—or fail to cope—with domestic crises, personal and familial breakdowns, and their place in an increasingly perplexing world whose former certainties and erstwhile values seem no longer to suffice in their lives. Although he is best known for such ostensibly plotless works as *The Changing Room*, *The Contractor*, and *Home*—plays whose style he has characterized as "poetic naturalism"—he has also written a number of more traditionally structured domestic dramas (*The Restoration of Arnold Middleton*, *In Celebration*, *The Farm*, *Sisters*, *Early Days*, and *The March on Russia*), as well as a blank verse history play whose title character never appears (*Cromwell*) and a farce (*Mother's Day*) whose controversial inversion of "normal" family values, blunt language, and blithe violation of sexual taboos outraged the reviewers of its day. Yet throughout them all, a number of Storey's characteristic concerns persist: the nature of the modern family, the effects of social class (not only for those who remain in the class into which they were born but also for those who escape from it), the devaluation of traditional ritual, the tenuousness of "sanity," the dignity of work, and the perennial need to establish oneself (if only temporarily) as a participating member of a group that transcends and subsumes the self.

Storey's plays have been widely acclaimed as meticulously detailed "slices of life" in which traditional action and conflict have been muted in scenes from everyday life, revealing character and theme with subtle elaborations of tone and mood. However, *The Changing Room*, *The Contractor*, and *Home* are also surprisingly innovative works whose subtly contrapuntal dramaturgy achieves and sustains a unique and delicate balance between seen and unseen events. In these, as in almost all his plays, Storey's often minimal dialogue skillfully blends naturalistic speech and poetic nuance. The plays are deliberately uneventful: that is, their major "events"—the wedding and reception in *The Contractor*, the rugby match in *The Changing Room*, the anniversary party in *In Celebration*, the military battles in *Cromwell*—occur offstage and between the acts. In several of the plays, anticipated events—a parental visit in *The Restoration of Arnold*

Middleton, an engagement announcement in *The Farm*—simply never come to pass. Storey's deliberate "dislocation" or "removal" of his plays' central "dramatic" events—and the resulting, often-alleged "plotlessness" of his plays— is unique in contemporary theatre.

Throughout his career, Storey has consistently been deeply concerned with the nature of the modern family, the types of rituals that families honor, and the importance of such rituals in a world that has, since the Industrial Revolution, undergone a process of radical desacralization that has accelerated throughout the twentieth century, for reasons that scholar Mircea Eliade has detailed in such books as *The Sacred and the Profane*. Among the families in Storey's plays (the Ewbanks in *The Contractor*, the Shaws of *In Celebration*, the Pasmores of *March on Russia*, the Slatterys of *The Farm*), the changing mores and values of twentieth-century Britain become readily apparent: the working-class parents of the now-adult "professional" offspring in Storey's plays find themselves unable to understand their grown children's anxieties, their discontentedness with life, their unstable marriages, and their inability to enjoy the benefits of the education and "advantages" that the parents labored so hard for so many years to provide. Members of the younger generation, though acknowledging the loving sacrifices that made possible their social "advancements," often find themselves cut off from their class origins (having been "educated out of" the working class at universities) and equally ill at ease among the "professional" classes. The mutual incomprehension that divides the generations is at best only temporarily and strainedly overcome during the family rituals for which they convene as the plays begin.

In contrast to such devalued traditional rituals, which fail to unite their participants in any meaningful or sustaining way, an alternative means of overcoming such alienation through the shared endeavor and common goals of a nonfamily unit is revealed through the *onstage* actions of Storey's plays. The workmen constructing the tent in *The Contractor* and the rugby players in *The Changing Room* take part in activities that are, in effect, major but nontraditional rituals in their lives, affording them a temporary but significant unity that the more traditional patterns of behavior fail to provide to the families involved. By examining the effects of such commonplace events rather than exceptional ones, Storey's plays portray truly ordinary—even mundane—life and find there a significance and expressiveness that is uniquely his own. His dialogue is spare and functional, punctuated with meaningful pauses, always appropriate for the characters, seldom deliberately "profound." His workmen, athletes, and "ordinary people" rarely explain their feelings at great length (a tendency to which his teachers, Arnold Middleton and Allott in *Life Class* are more prone); in Storey's self-styled "plays of undertatement," as in Anton Chekhov's drama, subtext is all-important. Although few of his characters understand or could articulate such matters as the devaluation of ritual and the effects of ever-increasing secularity and commercialism on mid-twentieth-century lives, they intuit the impact of such forces on their personal lives. Accordingly, one of the foremost themes of Storey's plays is the way in which men and women attempt to cope (not always successfully) with the complexity, the uncertainty, and the rapid, often bewildering changes that characterize modern life. After demonstrating the consequences of modern existence without meaningful ritual in such works as *The Restoration of Arnold Middleton*, *In Celebration*, and *Home*, Storey presents the seemingly ordinary, wholly un-self-conscious rituals of *The Changing Room* and *The Contractor*. Unadorned with the contrivances of a traditionally dramatic "plot," these plays suggest the hitherto unrecognized means through which, via nontraditional rituals based in work and play, individuals may, at least temporarily, find the vital orientation and security that are perennial human needs.

By focusing the audience's attention on these autonomous images of non-traditional rituals, rather than on traditional machinations of a plot, Storey's plays demand new standards in assessing the "action" that takes place on stage. Considerations of the effectiveness and eloquence of the theatrical image supercede traditional concerns with plot, action, contrivance, and character development. Storey's own dramatic and aesthetic theory of so-called invisible events is set forth in *Life Class*, which is not only his most complex play but one of the most original and unusual works of metatheatre in contemporary drama. The play is set in an art classroom where before an onstage "audience" of mostly uncomprehending students, Allott, Storey's artist-protagonist, expounds his theories of life, art, and "invisible events"; using the visual arts as a trope for the theatre, *Life Class* offers a detailed discussion (and justification) of Storey's unique dramatic theory, as embodied in *The Contractor* and *The Changing Room* in particular. The play's startling central event—which, uncharacteristically, occurs *onstage*—is the rape of the nude model by one of the students; it is soon revealed to have been a hoax, a convincingly realistic deception, an "imitation" of "life," an "act of theatre," in effect a play-within-a-play—as well a brutal assertion of "life" over "art," an ultimate assertion of crude and sordid physical reality over the supposedly transcendent and spiritual realm of art. The convening of the class for such a lofty purpose is itself a form of nontraditional ritual in an all-too-desacralized world; the act of violation is thus a profanation of Allott's wholly secularized temple. The action of this play, like that of its supposedly plotless predecessors, is *not* merely a random slice of life realistically portrayed, and the remarks of Allott and one of his students, Sanders, set forth more about *how* work is to be understood (a technique applicable to his other plays as well) rather than specifically *what* the action of the play means. *Life Class* is thus best regarded as the culmination of a series of particularly innovative if seemingly "uneventful" plays that are unique in modern theatre, wherein a new dramatic form—the theatrical "invisible event"—was developed, refined, and ultimately defended in a uniquely provocative way.

With the exception of his controversial attempt at black farce in *Mother's Day*, Storey's subsequent plays are noteworthy primarily as stylistic innovations and refinements of his earlier dramatic technique rather than as innovations in content. Thus, *The March on Russia* and *Sisters* are extensions of the "domestic realism" of *In Celebration* and *The Farm*, while *Early Days*, written for Ralph Richardson, is a minimalist portrait of old age with clear precedents in *Home*. *Stages* is more complex, however, as it constitutes the third play in two separate groupings that can be considered trilogies in Storey's works: as a play whose central character is recovering from a nervous breakdown, its content is closely akin to *The Restoration of Arnold Middleton* and *Life Class*; however, its minimalist stage form (with only minimal stage directions and no specified set) and its spare dialogue relate it clearly to *Home* and *Early Days*.

ARCHIVAL SOURCES

Storey's papers are collected at Boston University. The screenplay of *This Sporting Life* is held at the Theatre Arts Library at University of California, Los Angeles.

PRIMARY BIBLIOGRAPHY

Plays

The Changing Room. London: Cape, 1972; New York: Random House, 1973.

The Contractor. London: Cape, 1970; New York: Random House, 1970; *Plays and Players* (Dec. 1969): 63–86.

Cromwell. London: Cape, 1973.

The Farm. London: Cape, 1973.

Home. London: Cape, 1970; New York: Random House, 1971; *Plays and Players* (Aug. 1970): 61–77; *Plays of the Year* [1971]. Vol. 41. London: Elek Books, 1972.

In Celebration. London: Cape, 1969; New York: Grove Press, 1969; *Plays and Players* (June 1969): 35–55; *Plays of the Year* [1969]. Vol. 38. London: Elek Books, 1970.

Life Class. London: Cape, 1975.

The March on Russia. London: Samuel French, 1989.

The Restoration of Arnold Middleton. London: Cape, 1967; *Plays of the Year* [1967]. Vol. 35. London: Elek Books, 1968; Also in *New English Dramatists*. Vol. 14. Harmondsworth: Penguin, 1970.

Anthologies

The Changing Room, Home, and The Contractor: Three Plays by David Storey. New York: Bard-Avon, 1975.

In Celebration and *The Contractor.* Harmondsworth: Penguin, 1977.

Home, The Changing Room, and *Mother's Day.* Harmondsworth: Penguin, 1978.

Early Days/Sisters/Life Class. Harmondsworth: Penguin, 1980.

In Celebration, The Contractor, The Restoration of Arnold Middleton, and *The Farm.* Harmondsworth: Penguin, 1982.

Storey: Plays: One. (The Contractor, Home, Stages, Caring). London: Methuen, 1992.

Essays and Articles on Drama and Theatre

Introduction to *Storey: Plays: One. (The Contractor, Home, Stages, Caring)*. London: Methuen, 1992.

"Journey through a Tunnel." *The Listener* (1 Aug. 1963): 159–61.

"On Lindsay Anderson." *Cinebill: The American Film Theatre—The Second Season.*" New York: AFT Distributing Corp., 1975.

"Working with Lindsay." In *At the Royal Court: 25 Years of the English Stage Company*, ed. Richard Findlater. New York: Grove Press, 1981: 110–15.

Interviews

"Conversation with David Storey" (with Ronald Hayman). *Drama* 99 (winter 1970): 47–53; rpt. in Ronald Hayman, *Playback*. New York: Horizon, 1974: 7–20.

"David Storey in Conversation" (with Victor Sage). *New Review* (Oct. 1976): 63–65.

"David Storey Interviewed by Brendan Hennessy." *Transatlantic Review* 33–34 (1969): 5–11.

"Shop Talk with a British Playwright: David Storey Discusses *Home* and Other Scripts" (with Glenn Loney). *Dramatists Guild Quarterly* 8 (spring 1971): 27–30.

SECONDARY BIBLIOGRAPHY

Ansorge, Peter [1]. "*The Contractor.*" *Plays and Players* (May 1970): 46.

————[2]. "The Theatre of Life: David Storey in Interview." *Plays and Players* (Sept. 1973): 32–36.

Barber, John [1]. " 'Changing Room' One of Year's Best." *Daily Telegraph* (10 Nov. 1971): 10.

————[2]. "Defeated Anti-hero of 'Life Class.' " *Daily Telegraph* (11 Apr. 1974): 13.

————[3]. "Laboured Bad Taste in Orton-Type Farce." *Daily Telegraph* (23 Sept. 1976): 13.

————[4]. "Rich Contrast of Idealist and Two Wastrels." *Daily Telegraph* (16 Aug. 1973): 13.

————[5]. "Tart Comedy of Men with the Marquee." *Daily Telegraph* (7 Apr. 1970): 16.

————[6]. "Verbal Torments of Marquee Men." *Daily Telegraph* (21 Oct. 1969): 15.

Barnes, Clive [1]. " 'Home' and 'Contractor' Shine in London Season." *New York Times* (17 Aug. 1970): 32.

————[2]. "On the Stage, King Comedy Reigns." *New York Times* (26 Sept. 1976): 54.

————[3]. "Stage: 'Changing Room.' " *New York Times* (19 Nov. 1972): 79.

————[4]. "Stage: 'The Contractor." *New York Times* (9 Dec. 1971): 63.

————[5]. "Stage: Two Plays by Storey in London." *New York Times* (11 Sept. 1973): 55.

————[6]. "Stage: 'Changing Room' Opens at Morosco." *New York Times* (7 Mar. 1973): 37.

————[7]. "Storey's 'In Celebration.' " *New York Times* (31 May 1974): 22.

————[8]. ''Theatre: David Storey's 'Contractor.' '' *New York Times* (18 Oct. 1973): 66.

————[9]. ''Theatre: 'Home' Arrives.'' *New York Times* (18 Nov. 1970): 41.

Billington, Michael [1]. ''A Play Worth Having.'' *The Times* (23 Apr. 1969): 16.

————[2]. ''Dramatising Work.'' *The Times* (7 Apr. 1970): 8.

————[3]. ''First Nights: *The Restoration of Arnold Middleton.*'' *Plays and Players* (Sept. 1967): 30.

————[4]. ''Guys Hold More than Guy-Ropes.'' *The Times* (21 Oct. 1969): 14.

————[5]. ''Making Life Work on Two Levels.'' *The Times* (4 Apr. 1970): 21.

————[6]. ''*Mother's Day.*'' *The Guardian* (23 Sept. 1976): 8.

Brooks, Jeremy, and J. A. Lambert. ''David Storey Week: Triumph and Disaster.'' *Sunday Times* (26 Sept. 1976): 35.

Brown, Geoff. ''*Mother's Day.*'' *Plays and Players* (Dec. 1976): 35–36.

Browne, Terry W. *Playwrights' Theatre: The English Stage Company at the Royal Court Theatre.* London: Pitman Co., 1975.

Brustein, Robert. '' . . . Or Just 'Conscientious Naturalism'?'' *New York Times* (18 Mar. 1973): 2: 1.

Bryden, Ronald. ''Cromwell.'' *Plays and Players* (Oct. 1973): 47–49.

Bygrave, Mike. ''David Storey: Novelist or Playwright?'' *Theatre Quarterly* 1.2 (Apr.–June 1971): 31–36.

Cahn, Victor L. ''The Joy of Being Part of a Team.'' *New York Times* (10 June 1973): 2: 11.

Chaillet, Ned [1]. ''Pale Shadows of Old Court Days.'' *The Times* (23 Apr. 1980): 13.

————[2]. ''Sisters.'' *The Times* (14 Sept. 1978): 12.

Cohn, Ruby. ''Artists in Play.'' In *David Storey: A Casebook*, ed. William Hutchings. New York: Garland, 1992: 73–88.

Coveney, Michael [1]. ''*The Farm.*'' *Financial Times* (27 Sept. 1973).

————[2]. ''*Sisters.*'' *Financial Times* (13 Sept. 1978).

Darlington, W. A. [1]. ''Hero Talked on Till He Had a Fit.'' *Daily Telegraph* (6 July 1967).

————[2]. ''Is This a Plot or Isn't It?'' *Daily Telegraph* (3 Nov. 1969): 11.

————[3]. ''Where Do They Go From Here?'' *Daily Telegraph* (20 July 1970): 7.

Dawson, Helen. ''*The Farm.*'' *Plays and Players* (Nov. 1973): 42–43.

DiGaetani, John L. ''David Storey.'' *A Search for a Postmodern Theater: Interviews with Contemporary Playwrights.* New York: Greenwood Press, 1991: 259–64.

Duffy, Martha. ''An Ethic of Work and Play.'' *Sports Illustrated* (5 Mar. 1973): 66–69.

Dutton, Richard. ''*Home* by David Storey.'' *Modern Tragicomedy and the British Tradition: Beckett, Pinter, Stoppard, Albee, and Storey.* Norman: University of Oklahoma Press, 1986: 151–61.

Ecker, Gisela. ''David Storey: Home—'schones Wetler heute'oder Strukturen des 'small talk.' ''*Englisches Drama von Beckett bis Bond.* Munich: Fink, 1982: 250–71.

Flatley, Guy. '' 'I Never Saw a Pinter Play.' '' *New York Times* (29 Nov. 1970): 2: 1, 5.

Frankel, Haskel [1]. ''All the World's a Locker Room in Superlative New David Storey Play.'' *National Observer* (9 Dec. 1972): 24.

————[2]. ''Mr. Storey's Cosmic 'Contractor': Nothing Less than a Masterpiece.'' *National Observer* (11 Dec. 1971): 24.

Free, William J. [1]. "The Ironic Anger of David Storey." *Modern Drama* 16.3–4 (Dec. 1973): 306–17.

———[2]. "Space, Language and Action in *The Contractor*." In *David Storey: A Casebook*, ed. William Hutchings. New York: Garland, 1992: 199–211.

Free, William J., and Lynn Page Whittaker. "The Intrusion Plot in David Storey's Plays." *Papers on Language and Literature* 17 (spring 1982): 151–65.

Gilbert, W. Stephen. "*Life Class*." *Plays and Players* (May 1974): 26–27.

Gill, Brendan. "Goal to Go." *The New Yorker* (19 Mar. 1973): 92.

Gindin, James. "David Storey." In *British Dramatists since World War II: Part II: M–Z. A Dictionary of Literary Biography*, vol. 13, ed. Stanley Weintraub. Detroit: Gale Research. 1982: 501–13.

Gussow, Mel [1]. "David Storey's 'The Farm' Is Family Play about Forces That Hold People Together." *New York Times* (12 Oct. 1976): 45.

———[2]. "New Drama Goes off off Broadway." *New York Times* (12 Nov. 1976): C3.

———[3]. "Stage: 'Life Class' at the Theatre Club." *New York Times* (15 Dec. 1975): 43.

———[4]. "Strength of Yorkshire Unfurls with Truth." *New York Times* (15 Oct. 1974): 44.

———[5]. "To David Storey, a Play Is a 'Holiday.' " *New York Times* (20 Apr. 1973): 14.

Hayman, Ronald [1]. *British Theatre since 1955: A Reassessment*. Oxford: Oxford University Press, 1979. 55–58.

———[2]. "*Early Days*." *Plays and Players* (May 1980): 28.

Hewes, Henry [1]. "Knights at a Round Table." *Saturday Review* (12 Dec. 1970): 63.

———[2]. "Storey Theatre." *Saturday Review of the Arts* (Apr. 1973): 77.

———[3]. "Theatre in England." *Saturday Review* (25 July 1970): 20.

———[4]. "True Storey." *Saturday Review/World* (18 Dec. 1973): 47.

Higgins, John. "David Storey: Night and Day." *The Times* (16 Sept. 1976): 13.

Hobson, Harold [1]. "The Quality of 'Life Class.' " *Sunday Times* (23 June 1974): 28.

———[2]. "Rural Rites." *Sunday Times* (30 Sept. 1973): 29.

Holland, Mary. "*The Changing Room*." *Plays and Players* (Jan. 1972): 44–47.

Holmstrom, John. "Keep It Mum." *Plays and Players* (June 1969): 26–29.

Hughes, Catherine [1]. "Broadway Hails Britannia." *America* (16 Jan. 1971): 47.

———[2]. " 'The Farm'; 'Poor Murderer.' " *America* (8 Apr. 1972): 304.

———[3]. "Tenting Tonight." *America* (3 Nov. 1973): 334.

Hutchings, William [1]. "David Storey's Aesthetic of 'Invisible Events.' " In *David Storey: A Casebook*, ed. William Hutchings. New York: Garland, 1992: 105–22.

———[2]. " 'Invisible Events' and the Experience of Sports in David Storey's *The Changing Room*." *Proteus: A Journal of Ideas* 3.1 (spring 1986): 1–7.

———[3]. " 'Much Ado about Almost Nothing' or, The Pleasures of Plotless Plays." In *Within the Dramatic Spectrum*, ed. Karelisa V. Hartigan. Lanham, MD: University Press of America, 1986: 107–14.

———[4]. *The Plays of David Storey: A Thematic Study*. Carbondale: Southern Illinois University Press, 1988.

———[5]. " 'Poetic Naturalism' and Chekhovian Form in the Plays of David Storey." In *The Many Forms of Drama*, ed. Karelisa V. Hartigan. Lanham, MD: University Press of America, 1985. 79–85.

————[6]. "The Work of Play: Anger and the Expropriated Athletes of Alan Sillitoe and David Storey." *Modern Fiction Studies* 33.1 (spring 1987): 35–47.

Joyce, Steven. "A Study in Dramatic Dialogue: A Structural Approach to David Storey's *Home*." *Theatre Annual* 38 (1983): 65–81.

Kalem, T. E. [1]. "Caustic Imp." *Time* (8 June 1981): 56.

————[2]. "Duet of Dynasts." *Time* (30 Nov. 1970): 48.

————[3]. "Family Communion." *Time* (10 June 1974): 106.

————[4]. "In a Mood for Rape." *Time* (5 Jan. 1976): 77.

————[5]. "Laureate of Loss." *Time* (27 Dec. 1971): 55.

————[6]. "On to the Triple Crown." *Time* (5 Nov. 1973): 84.

————[7]. "Rock of Ages." *Time* (15 Oct. 1976): 87.

————[8]. "Sisyphus Agonistes." *Time* (18 Dec. 1973): 84–85.

Kalson, Albert E. "Insanity and the Rational Man in the Plays of David Storey." *Modern Drama* 19.2 (June 1976): 111–28.

————. Rev. of *Mother's Day* and *The Farm*. *Educational Theatre Journal* 29.2 (May 1977): 260–62.

Kauffmann, Stanley [1]. Review of *The Changing Room*. *New Republic* (14 Apr. 1973): 22, 33.

————[2]. "Notes on Naturalism: Truth Is Stranger as Fiction." *Performance* 1 (1974): 33–39.

Kerensky, Oleg. "David Storey." *The New British Drama: Fourteen Playwrights since Osborne and Pinter*. London: Hamish Hamilton, 1977: 3–17.

Kerr, Walter [1]. "British Writers." *New York Times* (9 Sept. 1973): 2: 1.

————[2]. " 'The Changing Room': Something like Magic . . . " *New York Times* (18 Mar. 1973): 2: 1.

————[3]. "Like Pinter, Except . . . " *New York Times* (29 Nov. 1970): 2: 1.

————[4]. "Too Many Questions." *New York Times* (24 Oct. 1976): 2: 1.

King, Kimball. "The March on Russia." In *David Storey: A Casebook*, ed. William Hutchings. New York: Garland, 1992: 213–20.

Knapp, Bettina L. "David Storey's *In Celebration* and Gabriel Cousin's *Journey to the Mountain Beyond*: From 'Maw' to Mater Gloriosa." *Theatre Annual* 33 (1977): 39–55.

Kroll, Jack [1]. "The Playing's the Thing." *Newsweek* (16 June 1980): 82–83.

————[2]. "Raising the Roof." *Newsweek* (13 Jan. 1971): 114.

————[3]. "Sporting Life." *Newsweek* (19 Mar. 1973): 86.

————[4]. "Team of Destiny." *Newsweek* (11 Dec. 1972): 71.

Lambert, J. W. [1]. "David Storey Week: Triumph and Disaster." *Sunday Times* (26 Sept. 1976): 35.

————[2]. "Globetrotting Theatre." *Drama* 133 (summer 1979): 15.

————[3]. "Lost Horizons." *The Times* (14 Apr. 1974): 34.

Lawson, D. S. " 'Insuring People against Disaster': The Uses of Comedy in the Plays of David Storey." In *David Storey: A Casebook*, ed. William Hutchings. New York: Garland, 1992: 173–86.

Lewson, Charles. " 'The Changing Room.' " *The Times* (16 Dec. 1971): 18.

Mayer, David. "*Sisters*." *Plays and Players* (Nov. 1978): 21.

Nightingale, Benedict [1]. "Everyman on His Uppers." *New Statesman* (19 Apr. 1974): 558–59.

————[2]. "Three Sons." *New Statesman* (2 May 1969): 631–32.

Novick, Julian [1]. "Can 'the Facts' Alone Make a Play?" *New York Times* (3 Dec. 1972): 2: 13.

———[2]. "Two Plays at Washington's Arena Stage about the Work Ethic." *New York Times* (3 Dec. 1972): 2: 3.

Oliver, Edith [1]. "Off Broadway: Change and Decay in All around I See." *The New Yorker* (25 Oct. 1976): 61–62.

———[2]. "Off Broadway: David Storey's Tent Show." *The New Yorker* (29 Oct. 1973): 107–9.

Overbeck, Lois More. " 'What It Is to Be a Woman' in the Plays of David Storey." In *David Storey: A Casebook*, ed. William Hutchings. New York: Garland, 1992: 141–72.

Pearce, Howard D. "A Phenomenological Approach to the *Theatrum Mundi* Metaphor." *PMLA* 95.1 (Jan. 1980): 42–57.

Pittock, Malcolm [1]. "David Storey's *Phoenix*: A Dream of Leaving."*English Studies* 71.5 (Oct. 1990): 410-25.

——— [2]. "Storey's Portrayal of Old Age: *The March on Russia*." *Neophilologus* 78 (1994): 329-341.

Porter, James E. "*The Contractor*: David Storey's Static Drama." *University of Windsor Review* 15.1–2 (1979–80): 66–75.

Quigley, Austin E. "The Emblematic Structure and Setting of David Storey's Plays." *Modern Drama* 22.3 (Sept. 1979): 259–76; rpt. in *Contemporary British Drama, 1970–1990*, ed. Hersh Zeifman and Cynthia Zimmerman. Toronto: University of Toronto Press, 1993: 163–83.

Randall, Phyllis R. [1] "Another Storey: A Reappraisal of *Mother's Day*." In *David Storey: A Casebook*, ed. William Hutchings. New York: Garland, 1992: 187–98.

———[2]. "Division and Unity in David Storey." In *Essays on Contemporary British Drama*, ed. Hedwig Bock and Albert Wertheim. Munich: Hueber, 1981: 253–65.

Reinelt, Janelle [1]. "The Central Event in David Storey's Plays." *Theatre Journal* 31 (1979): 210–20.

———[2]. "Storey's Novels and Plays: Fragile Fictions." In *David Storey: A Casebook*, ed. William Hutchings. New York: Garland, 1992: 53–72.

Roberts, Philip. "David Storey's *The Changing Room*." *The Royal Court Theatre, 1965– 1972*. London: Routledge & Kegan Paul, 1986: 107–20.

Rosen, Carol [1]. "*Home*." *Plays of Impasse: Contemporary Drama Set in Confining Institutions*. Princeton, NJ: Princeton University Press, 1983: 128–46.

———[2]. "Symbolic Naturalism in David Storey's *Home*." *Modern Drama* 22.3 (Sept. 1979): 277–89.

Rusinko, Susan. "A Portrait of the Artist as Character in the Plays of David Storey." In *David Storey: A Casebook*, ed. William Hutchings. New York: Garland, 1992: 89–104.

Shorter, Eric [1]. "Family Home Truths Grippingly Studied." *Daily Telegraph* (23 Apr. 1969): 21.

———[2]. "*Phoenix*." *Daily Telegraph* (13 Mar. 1985).

———[3]. "Regions." *Drama* 133 (summer 1979): 70–72.

———[4]. "Strained Plot Leads to Anticlimax." *Daily Telegraph* (27 Sept. 1973): 14.

Simon, John [1]. "Theatre Chronicle." *Hudson Review* 27 (1974): 82–83.

———[2]. "*Life Class*." *New York* (23 Sept. 1974): 67.

Stinson, John J. "Dualism and Paradox in the 'Puritan' Plays of David Storey." *Modern Drama* 20.2 (June 1977): 131–43.

Taylor, John Russell [1]. "British Dramatists: The New Arrivals, III—David Storey, Novelist into Dramatist." *Plays and Players* (June 1970): 22–24.

———[2]. "David Storey." *The Second Wave: British Drama of the Sixties*. London: Eyre Methuen, 1971; rev. 1978: 141–54.

———[3]. "First Nights: *The Restoration of Arnold Middleton*." *Plays and Players* (Sept. 1967): 42.

———[4]. "*Home*." *Plays and Players* (Aug. 1970): 30–34.

Thorber, Robin. "*Phoenix*." *The Guardian* (13 Mar. 1985).

Troxel, Patricia M. " 'We Have No Turning Back': Authority, Culture, and Environment in the Dramas of David Storey." In *David Storey: A Casebook*, ed. William Hutchings. New York: Garland, 1992: 25–52.

Wall, Stephen. "Kitchen Agonistes." *Times Literary Supplement* (2 May 1980): 495.

Wardle, Irving [1]. "David Storey's Needless Chronicle on War." *The Times* (11 Aug. 1973): 9.

———[2]. "*The Changing Room*." *The Times* (10 Nov. 1971): 12.

———[3]. "Flawless Tone." *The Times* (18 June 1970): 8.

———[4]. "*Life Class*." *The Times* (10 Apr. 1974): 13.

———[5]. "Mr. Storey Brilliant When in Focus." *The Times* (6 July 1967): 8.

———[6]. "New Play by Storey Stars Two Knights at the Royal Court." *New York Times* (20 June 1970): 23.

———[7]. "Storey Returns Home to Yorkshire." *The Times* (29 Sept. 1973): 9.

———[8]. "Unanswered Questions after Coming to the Finest Family in the Land." *The Times* (23 Sept. 1976): 13.

Waterhouse, Robert. "*The Contractor*." *Plays and Players* (Nov. 1969): 26–27.

Weales, Gerald. "A Change for the Best." *Commonweal* (6 Apr. 1973): 114.

Weaver, Laura H. [1]. "The City as Escape into Freedom: The Failure of a Dream in David Storey's Works." *West Virginia University Philological Papers* 28 (1983): 146–53.

———[2]. "Madness and the Family in David Storey's Plays." In *David Storey: A Casebook*, ed. William Hutchings. New York: Garland, 1992.

———[3]. "Rugby and the Arts: The Divided Self in David Storey's Novels and Plays." In *Fearful Symmetry: Doubles and Doubling in Literature and Film*, ed. Eugene J. Crook. Tallahasse: University Presses of Florida, 1981: 149–62.

Weightman, John [1]. "Art versus Life." *Encounter* (Sept. 1974): 57–59.

———[2]. "The Outsider in the Home." *Encounter* (Sept. 1967): 40–44.

Weintraub, Bernard. "The Rugby Field on the Stage." *New York Times* (13 Dec. 1971): 52.

Wilders, John. "Compassionate Commonplaces." *Times Literary Supplement* (14–20 Apr. 1989): 396.

Worth, Katharine J. *Revolutions in Modern English Drama*. London: Bell, 1973: 26–30, 38–40.

Young, B. A. [1]. "*Cromwell*." *Financial Times* (17 Aug. 1973): 3.

———[2]. "*Early Days*." *Financial Times* (23 Apr. 1980): 21.

———[3]. "*Life Class*." *Financial Times* (10 Apr. 1974): 3.

———[4]. "*Mother's Day*." *Financial Times* (24 Sept. 1976): 3.

BIBLIOGRAPHIES

Carpenter, Charles A. ''Bond, Shaffer, Stoppard, Storey: An International Checklist of Commentary.'' *Modern Drama* 24 (1981): 546–56.

Hutchings, William, ed. ''Bibliography'' [annotated]. *David Storey: A Casebook.* New York: Garland, 1992.

King, Kimball. *Twenty Modern British Playwrights: A Bibliography, 1956 to 1976.* New York: Garland, 1977: 231–39.

C. P. Taylor
(1929–1981)

WILLIAM W. DEMASTES

C. P. Taylor was born Cecil Philip Taylor on 6 November 1929, in Glasgow, Scotland, to Max George Taylor, a watchmaker, and Fay Leventhal Taylor. His Jewish roots and upbringing during World War II left him with an early fear that Britain would be invaded and he would follow the continental Jews to death camps. Later came his concerns with the pervading intolerance and anti-Semitism within his home country.

Taylor's formal educational was nominal, extending to only two years at Queen's Park Secondary School. He took numerous odd jobs, generally related to electrical work, and engaged in occasional charity work. In 1955 he married Irene Diamon, whom he later divorced, marrying Elizabeth Screen in 1967. He had four children: Avram, Clair, David, and Catherine.

Taylor's playwriting career began with the production of the musical *Aa Went te Blaydon Races*, produced in 1962 at the Newcastle Playhouse, followed by *Happy Days Are Here Again*, his first play to see the London stage, in 1964 at the Arts Theatre. His work is distinguished by a determined theatricality, usually including music of the music hall variety. His first decided success occurred in 1966. After working primarily in Scotland and mostly for the Edinburgh Traverse Theatre, Taylor moved his Traverse production *Bread and Butter* (1966) to Traverse's new London venue, the Jeannetta Cochrane Theatre, where it was well received by the critics. In 1968, Taylor became literary adviser to the Northumberland Youth Theatre Association, devoting much of his time to writing scripts for young people. In 1971 he also committed to television, becoming script editor for the ''burns'' series of television plays and writing for BBC Educational Television.

Most of his work beyond youth theatre and television continued to premiere at the Traverse in Edinburgh, a venue in which Taylor felt very comfortable.

Many of Taylor's works illustrate a direct debt to vaudevillian performance. *The Black and White Minstrels* (1972), *Schippel* (1974), and *Walter* (1977) are clear examples of this influence. But, with the production of *Good* by the Royal Shakespeare Company in 1981, Taylor blended his theatrical and musical sensibilities with his social concerns—best earlier demonstrated in *Bread and Butter*—to create a play that is clearly his best work.

Tragically, however, months after the September premiere of *Good*, Taylor passed away, on 9 December 1981. One can only wonder, had Taylor lived, would *Good* have been the culmination of his work or the beginning of a mature phase in his career?

Selected Biographical Sources: Dukore; Friesner.

MAJOR PLAYS, PREMIERES, AND SIGNIFICANT REVIVALS: THEATRICAL RECEPTION

Bread and Butter. 1966. Traverse Theatre, Edinburgh. Moved to the Jeannetta Cochrane Theatre, London, July 1966. Directed by Michael Geliot.

Depicting a thirty-year-long dialogue between two Jewish couples in Glasgow, *Bread and Butter* is one of the first plays produced by London Traverse in its new home. Jones reports that the dialogue technique actually involves the audience "with the low-class passions of the characters." Spurling sees Taylor's language as subtle as Bertolt Brecht's but sees Shakespeare, not Brecht, as Taylor's overall guide, working from "inside out." Trewin [1] compares the play to Nöel Coward's *Cavalcade*, preferring it to Taylor's as he would a banquet to a frugal picnic: "The butter is scraped too thinly over the bread." *The Times* ("Touching Comedy with a World Backcloth") reported that the play's two central characters are a splitting of Taylor's main character from his recent one-act play *Allergy*. Torn between "socialist conviction and personal peace," two characters provide "a running dialogue between acquiescence and political activism" from the 1930s to the present. It is a "touching comedy" sure to "please those with a taste for Jewish dialogue."

Schippel (adapted from a work by Carl Sternheim). 1974. Traverse Theatre, Edinburgh. Revived: Open Space Theatre, London, 1975. Retitled *The Plumber's Progress* and opened at the Prince of Wales's Theatre, London, 1975.

Trewin [2] observes that the very funny play owes more to the play's star, Harry Secombe, whose "moon-faced benignity, and occasional flinty resolve," captivates the audience. Nightingale [2] sees Taylor as a playwright who is benign and humane, "more inclined to tease his enemies with sly irony than trounce them with curt contempt."

Walter. 1977. Traverse Theatre, Edinburgh, opened August.

Chaillet calls it an excellent commemoration of Scottish music hall performer Walter Jackson. In part a "meditation on popular art and politics," *Walter* is in fact two plays—*Getting By* and *Going Home*—although Chaillet suggests a fine three-act play could be made of the two: it drags on occasion.

Bandits. 1977. Staged by the Royal Shakespeare Company at the Royal Shakespeare Company Warehouse, London, August.

Conrad suggests that the work is a good play that wants to become a B-movie. The play explores petty gangsterism in Newcastle, cinematic in its fluidity and dependent on a general style that is "American at heart," and finally not successfully transferable to the back streets of Newcastle. The play does not achieve its terse intentions, says Conrad, becoming instead "luridly glamorous."

Good. 1981. Staged by the Royal Shakespeare Company, 2 September at the Warehouse, London, directed by Howard Davies. Transferred to the Aldwych Theatre, London, 22 April–29 May 1982. Opened 13 October 1982, at the Booth Theatre (NY).

Wardle calls it a "fine play" about betrayals accumulated through minor compromises rising to major atrocities. The play's "great technical achievement is to combine a fluid interplay of past and present." Wardle adds, "The control of stage time is masterly." Of the West End transfer, Shulman suggests that the play loses some of its intimacy in the bigger, Aldwych, theatre, but the play still manages to remind us "that the road to Hell is not merely paved with good intentions but crowded with well-meaning people." Cushman [2] observe that the play "is a believable and theatrically ingenious, picture of a man stumbling into genocide." Watt called the New York production, "very clever, if unduly attenuated," and fully credited Alan Howard as Professor Halder for the success of the play. Barnes observes: "This is a play for the mind and heart, an incandescent evening in the theater that lights up the conscience." Rich says Taylor has written a play with an "intelligent, light touch in a most imaginative form"; however, one is likely to leave the theatre "stimulated but unsatisfied." Wilson, however, calls it "both exhilarating and deeply disturbing." Beaufort observes that although "[t]his production examines and exposes the evils inherent in the sacrifice of moral and intellectual integrity to the demands of a brutal dictatorship," he agrees with many other critics that, "there seems to be something missing in the Halder equation": "Why should he display a consistently overriding lack of integrity and moral courage?"

Bring Me Sunshine, Bring Me Smiles (originally, *The Saints Go Marching In*). 1982. Newcastle Playhouse, 14 January; Shaw Theatre, London, 15 April–1 May; directed by John Blackmore.

Taylor's last completed play is generally considered "overtly sentimental" (Woddis) and too talky (Cushman [1]). Cushman [1] observes, "Some lines are funny, most seem truthful, but the total is (a) too much and (b) not enough." Nightingale [2] says the play lacks the tough-mindedness of *Good*, primarily because its theme lacks an SS menace, but Taylor does report the lives of unemployed Newcastle shipwrights with telling accuracy. Nightingale [1] also reports that Taylor told the director he wanted to show "working people exploring their own feelings . . . with the same concern and sensitivity that had usually been the province of plays of middle-class origin." Nightingale [1] also observes of Taylor that his "much-missed generosity of spirit and wry, forgiving humour, that tolerance of human failing . . . could (be it admitted) sometimes go too far."

ADDITIONAL PLAYS, ADAPTATIONS, AND PRODUCTIONS

Aa Went te Blaydon Races (1962. Newcastle Playhouse); *Mister David* (1962. Revival: Jewish State Theatre, Warsaw, Poland, 1967); *Happy Days Are Here Again* (1964. Arts Theatre, London. Revival: Manhattan Theatre Club [NY], October 1972); *Of Hope and Glory* (1965. Traverse Theatre, Edinburgh); *Fable* (1965. Close Theatre, Glasgow); *Allergy* (1966. Traverse Theatre, Edinburgh); *The Ballachulish Beat: A Play with Songs* (1967); *Who's Pinkus? Where's Chelm?* (1966. Revival: Cochrane Theatre, London, 1967); *What Can a Man Do?* (1968. Newcastle Theatre); *Thank You Very Much* (1969. Northumberland Experimental Youth Theatre); *Truths about Sarajevo/Lies about Vietnam* (1969. Traverse Theatre, Edinburgh); *Brave* (1970. Northumberland Experimental Youth Theatre); *The Black and White Minstrels* (1972. Traverse Theatre, Edinburgh); *Some Enchanted Evening* (1977. Traverse Theatre, Edinburgh); *And a Nightingale Sang . . .* (1977. Live Theatre Company, Newcastle. Revived: Queen's Theatre, London, 1979); *Operation Elvis* (1978. Newcastle); *The Magic Island* (1979. Newcastle); *The Rainbow Coloured Disco Dancer* (1980. South Tyneside); *Happy Lies* (1981. New Town Junior School, Hebburn); *The Piggy Bank* (1989. Adapted from Eugene Labiche; Greenwich Theatre, London, August 7–September 16); *C. P. Taylor Festival* (November, 1989. Newcastle).

ASSESSMENT OF TAYLOR'S CAREER

Friesner summarizes Taylor's work as follows: "Taylor's is a distinctive dramatic style: lively, inventive, full of humour but always sharply aware of the ironies of life and the complexities of human experience." During a career sadly abbreviated by an early death, Taylor wrote nearly eighty plays, demonstrating an admirable diversity given that they were written variously for the Edinburgh Traverse Theatre, regional and community theatres in and around Newcastle—especially for the Live Theatre—numerous London fringe venues, and the Royal Shakespeare Company.

Interested in reaching audiences other than those typically attending traditional theatre venues, Taylor worked hard to engage youths and working class citizens in the theatre, especially in his work with the Live Theatre. Decidedly "middle-brow" in inclination, Taylor incorporated the kinds of material comfortably familiar to such groups, including music hall and dance hall routines and working-class settings. *Schippel* and *Walter* are two very specific works utilizing vaudevillian strategies and locales to create working-class entertainments but with a clear social vision of interrelated responsibility in mind.

While he saw conditions among the working class as brutally harsh, Taylor's spirit of generosity particularly sympathized with the youth thrust into such an environment. His extensive involvement in youth theatre and his numerous extant youth dramas attest to his sympathy and to a determination to help those caught in an apparently hopeless social trap. The example of Taylor's using his talent as he did would surely be an admirable one for others to follow.

Taylor's reputation today rests primarily with his 1981 play, *Good*. His personal concern about a continued anti-Semitism—evidenced in earlier works such as *Bread and Butter* as well—is here presented in a highly theatrical manner tempered, as always, in a way not usually presented by his more angry theatre colleagues. To be able to voice such anger, one must clearly take sides and see the opponent as clearly evil or corrupt. Taylor chose, instead, to reveal the daily betrayals that lead to the creation of such enemies, suggesting that the enemy forever lies within all of us. This far more complicated and complex understanding of human behavior is what distinguishes Taylor from many of his second wave peers, as John Russell Taylor identifies him, and from his Angry Young Men predecessors.

In fact, John Russell Taylor sees Taylor best at work when he focuses on his ''Glasgow-Jewish-Marxist'' roots, implying that Taylor is best when he writes from within rather than from observing without. Although *Good* is set not in Glasgow but in Germany it does not detract from this point in that Taylor has merely changed the landscape, only to more frighteningly convey a sense that what happened in Germany can happen in our own neighborhood. Given that Taylor is warning his own neighborhood, and not merely charging it against some abstract ''other,'' his temperate zone is perfectly appropriate. Dukore's comparative analysis of *Good* and Peter Barnes's *Laughter!* makes an excellent point: ''[W]hereas Barnes creates sympathy for the Auschwitz administrators but then demonstrates how misplaced such sympathy is, Taylor stops after the first step.'' Although Barnes creates a world where we could possibly exile fascists and proto-fascists, Taylor suggests that we need to understand them so that we can prevent them from becoming monsters. After all, they are us, our friends and neighbors, and our responsibility is to preserve the community, not to expunge it of its undesirables.

Dukore's comparative study suggests a direction in which further to study Taylor. Rabey, for example, observes that Stoppards's use of music in *Every Good Boy Deserves Favour* occurs in *Good* as well. From this one theatrical similarity one may be able to move to other points of convergence between Tom Stoppard and Taylor. Cave's brief discussion of Taylor is placed in his chapters discussing the Marxism of Edward Bond; Taylor certainly deserves greater consideration in discussions or studies of Marxism on the British stage, as well as in studies of working-class themes in general, studies that should include far more than Taylor's, *Good*. There are also other themes and traditions to which Taylor's contributions should be noted. His concerns about British anti-Semitism place him in the same tradition as Arnold Wesker, for example. His involvement in such theatre activities as the Traverse Theatre and the London fringe also warrant further note.

If *Good* calls our attention to Taylor, it should also call attention to the fact that *Bread and Butter* is worth revisiting and that his legacy of theatre scripts for youth and meeting halls should not be abandoned to an archives shelf.

ARCHIVAL SOURCES

A manuscript collection of Taylor's works can be found in the National Library, Edinburgh, Scotland.

PRIMARY BIBLIOGRAPHY

Plays

Allergy. Harmondsworth: Penguin, 1966.
And a Nightingale Sang . . . London: Methuen, 1979.
Apples. London: Hutchinson, 1976.
The Ballachulish Beat. London: Rapp & Carroll, 1967.
Bandits. Tyne & Wear: Iron Press, 1977.
Bloch's Play. Edinburgh: Scottish Theatre Editions, 1971.
Bread and Butter. Harmondsworth: Penguin, 1967.
Cromwell. In *Making a Television Play: A Complete Guide from Conception to B.B.C.*
    Production. Newcastle upon Tyne: Oriel Press, 1970.
Good. London: Methuen, 1982.
Good and *And a Nightingale Sang*. London: Methuen, 1990.
Happy Days Are Here Again. Harmondsworth: Penguin, 1968.
The Killingworth Play. Tyne & Wear: Iron Press, 1976.
North. London: Methuen, 1988.
Some Enchanted Evening. London: Hutchinson, 1979.
Thank You Very Much. London: Methuen, 1970.
Truth about Sarajevo/Lies about Vietnam. Edinburgh: Scottish Theatre Editions, 1970.
Walter. Huddersfield: Woodhouse Books, 1980.
Words. London: Hutchinson, 1973.

Anthology

Live Theatre: Four Plays for Young People (Operation Elvis, The Magic Island, The
    Rainbow Coloured Disco Dancer, Happy Lies). London: Methuen, 1983.

Related Work

Making a Television Play: A Complete Guide from Conception to B.B.C. Production.
    Newcastle upon Tyne: Oriel Press, 1970.

SECONDARY BIBLIOGRAPHY

Barnes, Clive. " 'Good' Couldn't Be Better Showing Man at His Worst." *New York Post* (14 Oct. 1982).

Beaufort, John. "Royal Shakespeareans Offer an Unsettling Play Set in Nazi Germany." *Christian Science Monitor* (21 Oct. 1982).

Cave, Richard Allen. *New British Drama in Performance on the London Stage: 1970 to 1985*. Gerrards Cross: Colin Smythe, 1987.

Chaillet, Ned. "The Personalities of Pete Kelly." *The Times* (30 Aug. 1977): 13.

Conrad, Peter. Review of *Bandits*. *New Statesman* (12 Aug. 1977): 222–23.

Cushman, Robert [1]. Review of *Bring Me Sunshine, Bring Me Smiles*. *The Observer* (17 Apr. 1982).

———[2]. Review of *Good*. *The Observer* (22 Apr. 1982).

Dukore, Bernard F. "People like You and Me: The Auschwitz Plays of Peter Barnes and C. P. Taylor." *Essays in Theatre* 3.2 (May 1985): 108–24.

Friesner, Susan. "The Plays of C. P. Taylor." *Contemporary Review* 255 (1989): 309–11.

Jones, D.A.N. Review of *Bread and Butter*. *New Statesman* (15 July 1966): 104.

Nightingale, Benedict [1]. Review of *Bring Me Sunshine, Bring Me Smiles*. *New Statesman* (17 Apr. 1982).

———[2]. Review of *Schippel, the Plumber's Progress*. *New Statesman* (17 Oct. 1975): 481.

Rabey, David Ian. *British and Irish Political Drama in the Twentieth Century: Implicating an Audience*. Houndsmill: Macmillan, 1986.

Rich, Frank. "Theater: 'Good,' on Becoming a Nazi." *New York Times* (14 Oct. 1982).

Shulman, Milton. Review of *Good*. *The Standard* (22 Apr. 1982).

Spurling, Hilary. Review of *Bread and Butter*. *The Spectator* (15 July 1966): 81, 84.

Taylor, John Russell. *The Second Wave: British Drama for the Seventies*. New York: Hill & Wang, 1971.

"Touching Comedy with a World Backcloth." *The Times* (8 July 1966): 18.

Trewin, J. C. [1]. "Across the Years." *Illustrated London News* (23 July 1966): 29.

———[2]. "A Sense of Humour." *Illustrated London News* (Dec. 1975): 105.

Wardle, Irving. "Good." *The Times* (10 Sept. 1981): 12.

Watt, Douglas. " 'Good' Has Glow, but Its Star Is Brilliant." *New York Daily News* (14 Oct. 1982).

Wilson, Edwin. "On Becoming a Nazi." *Wall Street Journal* (20 Oct. 1982).

Woddis, Carole. Review of *Bring Me Sunshine, Bring Me Smiles*. *City Limits* (17 Apr. 1982).

Timberlake Wertenbaker

(1944?–)

CARLA J. McDONOUGH

Timberlake Wertenbaker gained wide recognition in 1988 with *Our Country's Good*. This play examines issues of colonialism and of the theatre's power to transform our lives in its story of the 1789 convict performance of George Farquhar's *The Recruiting Officer* on the shores of the newly founded Australian colony. Its historical setting reflects Wertenbaker's tendency to draw upon history, legend, and myth throughout her career. The play's themes of role playing and of the battle to establish self-worth appear in some form in all her works.

Biographical information about Wertenbaker is limited because of the author's aversion to confusing her personal life with her work. As she told one reporter, ''I resent the idea that you have to look into a writer's life in order to explain the work, because that assumes there is no transformation, no creative process involved'' (Morley [1]). However, the outline of her life implies a cosmopolitan experience that is certainly reflected in her drama. Born in New York and raised in the Basque region of France, Wertenbaker returned to the United States to attend St. John's College in Annapolis, Maryland, from which she graduated in 1966. After college she worked for a while as a writer for Time-Life Books in New York before moving to Greece as a teacher of French and English. In Greece she wrote and produced children's plays, confirming her interest in theatre.

Moving to England in the 1970s, Wertenbaker sent some of her plays to various theatres. *Case to Answer* was picked up by the Soho Poly. Soon she was involved in the Women's Theatre Group and the Shared Experience Company (created by Mike Alfreds), among other fringe theatres in and around London. Her early plays, still unpublished, were performed in this venue, including *This Is No Place for Tallulah Bankhead* (1978), *Second Sentence* (1980), *Case to Answer* (1980), and *Breaking Through* (1980). *New Anatomies* was performed at the Edinburgh Theatre Festival in 1981 by the Women's Theatre Group. Two more plays were produced outside London, *Inside Out* (1982) and *Home Leave* (1982). *The Third* won Wertenbaker the All London Playwrights Award in 1983.

Wertenbaker's translations of Pierre Marivaux's *False Admissions* and *Successful Strategies* premiered in 1983 at the Lyric Studio Theatre in London, starting her secondary career as a highly adept translator of other playwrights' works. She has commented that working so closely inside another playwright's work has been quite educational in regard to her own plays (Wolf). Her success with the Marivaux translations prompted the Royal Shakespeare Company to engage her to translate Ariane Mnouchkine's *Mephisto*, which opened in April 1986 at the Barbican. However, Wertenbaker's most ambitious translation came with *The Thebans*, an adaptation and translation of Sophocles' Theban plays for the Royal Shakespeare Company. The seven-hour spectacle, directed by Adrian Noble, premiered in Stratford-upon-Avon in October 1991. Wertenbaker's other translations include Federico García Lorca's *The House of Bernarda Alba* (1980), a radio play of Jean Anouilh's *Leocadia* (1985), and Maurice Maeterlinck's *Pelleas and Melisande* (1988).

During the 1984–1985 season Wertenbaker served as writer-in-residence at the Royal Court Theatre, with whom she has done her most well known work. *Abel's Sister* (1984) and *The Grace of Mary Traverse* (1985) were produced as part of this association. The Royal Court also connected her with its artistic director Max Stafford-Clark, who suggested that she write a play based on Thomas Keneally's novel *The Playmaker* about the first theatrical production to take place on the shores of the convict colony of Australia. As Stafford-Clark had done with other writers for the Royal Court, such as Caryl Churchill, he scheduled workshops that put together the actors, himself, and the writer to sketch out the basic approach to the play, then sent Wertenbaker off to write it. This experience led to her best-known and most well received play, *Our Country's Good*, which opened in September 1988 in repertory with the eighteenth-century play that the convicts performed, *The Recruiting Officer*. *The Love of the Nightingale* (1989) was staged the following season at the Royal Court but failed to garner the attention that has been bestowed upon her latest work, *Three Birds Alighting on a Field* (1991), about the art world and its politics in London. *Three Birds*, like *Our Country's Good*, treats the ability of art to transform life.

Timberlake Wertenbaker's being in midcareer makes a definitive assessment of her work and its importance difficult to determine. However, she has already established herself as a powerful voice in British theatre.

Selected Biographical Sources: McMurray; Chaillet; Cantacuzino; Devries; Morley[1]; and Wolf.

MAJOR PLAYS, PREMIERES, AND SIGNIFICANT
REVIVALS: THEATRICAL RECEPTION

New Anatomies. 1981. Edinburgh Theatre Workshop, Edinburgh Festival. Produced by the Women's Theatre Group. Reopened 30 September at ICA by Women's Theatre Group. Directed by Nancy Diuguid. Revivals: Man in the Moon, London, March 1990; Home for Contemporary Theater and Art (NY), February 1990.

Writing for the Women's Theatre Group, Wertenbaker intended that five women play both the male and the female roles in *New Anatomies*, a fitting method of presenting the play's central message about the masquerade of gender. The story details the adventurous life of Isabelle Eberhardt, a European woman who impersonated an Arab man and spent much of her short life traveling through the deserts of Algeria in her quest for sexual identity and freedom. Most commentary regarding the play appears in response to the revivals that followed the success of *Our Country's Good*, a success most of the critics note as they approach *New Anatomies*. Peter [3] commented of the 1990 London revival that the playwright's work here is "poignant, dispassionate and witty." However, Wright noted that the play "occasionally lacks focus and unity," relying too heavily on "witticisms." The New York production prompted Gussow [2] to remark that Wertenbaker's approach to her fascinating subject was "bold but erratic." Carlson's analysis spends more time examining the complexities of sexuality, desire, and gender, and the mutability of all three within Wertenbaker's portrait of Isabelle.

Abel's Sister. 1984. Opened 7 August at the Royal Court's Theatre Upstairs. Directed by Les Waters.

Wertenbaker wrote this play in conjunction with Yolande Bourcier, whose poems and stories inspired the play. The play's main character, Sandra, is a spastic, the result she believes, of her twin brother's movements while both were still in their mother's womb. Sandra arrives at her brother's house for a visit intending to revenge herself on her brother and to rail against her fate, but hers is not the only bad luck in the play. The brother and his wife have a troubled marriage, and their next-door neighbor is a veteran of America's war in Vietnam. Billington [1] remarks that the play is about "our inescapable solitude," as we witness each of the characters needing something from the others but being unable to truly connect. Gardner notes that the play explores "aspects of disablement but also of loneliness, feminism, suffocating relationships, brothers and sisters and trendy leftist stances," rating it as one of the best plays of the year and attesting to Wertenbaker's tendency toward covering several issues in any one play.

The Grace of Mary Traverse. 1985. Opened 17 October at the Royal Court Theatre, London. Directed by Danny Boyle.

This eighteenth-century tale of a young woman's "Rake's Progress" from gentility to gaming and whoring picks up the recurring themes in Wertenbaker's work of the confining nature of gender roles and the importance of language in shaping personality and reality. The play is generally interpreted as a feminist piece partly because it examines the destructiveness of male behavior by having a woman enact it. Radin describes Wertenbaker's language as "taut and driving," whereas Peter [4] complains that the quality of this play is "strained," an idea in search of a form. Rabey, in one of the few critical articles addressing Wertenbaker's work, points out that it is Wertenbaker's desire to master language, not to fit the woman's patriarchal role of "mak[ing] the other person say interesting things," that gives the play its key theme and its resonance. Chaillet, writing before *Our Country's Good*, calls *Grace* a "dramatic fantasia" that is Wertenbaker's most important work. The play won Wertenbaker the *Plays and Players* Award for most promising playwright.

Our Country's Good. 1988. Opened in early September at the Royal Court Theatre, London. Transferred to the West End in December 1989 after tours to Toronto (October 1989 at the Bluma Appel Theatre) and Sydney (June 1989). Directed by Max Stafford-Clark. American productions: Opened 13 September 1989, at the Mark Taper Forum, Los Angeles; directed by Max Stafford-Clark and Les Waters; 1990 Hartford Stage Company, Hartford, Connecticut; directed by Mark Lamos. Moved to the Nederlander Theatre, New York, on 29 April 1991.

The prompt tours of the original Royal Court's production to Canada and Australia as well as the rapidly staged U.S. productions of *Our Country's Good* attest to the general acclaim with which the play was received. This story of the first theatrical production on the shores of Britain's new colony of Australia in 1789 was written to be performed in repertory with *The Recruiting Officer*, which Stafford-Clark had planned for his 1988–1989 season. The convicts' performance of Farquhar's play provides *Our Country's Good* with its captivating theme regarding the transforming power of the theatre as the convicts find their humanity by acting it out. The play's melding of the historical event with this theme was generally praised by critics, even prompting Baker, editorialist for the *New York Times*, to muse upon America's similar tendency of brutalizing its criminals instead of humanizing them. Similarly philosophical remarks came from more traditional reviewers of the theatre. Wardle [3] defines the play's theme as human reclamation and the birth of self-respect. Many reviewers light upon two scenes, that of Liz Morden finally speaking to her captors to avoid hanging and that of the rehearsal that takes place to the sound of a convict's whipping, as being the most poignant in portraying the message that language and art can give us our humanity even in the face of brutalizing treatment. In both scenes convicts find a voice to assert their humanity in the presence of their captors by using the style of speaking they have learned through the words of Farquhar. Sullivan points out that the play's popularity may rest on its ultimately conservative turn. Although the play begins by exposing the abuse of the poor in the project of empire, it ends by ''espous[ing] the greatness of canonical texts, . . . and it shows a benevolent ruler who eventually brings his flock into line.'' The rebellious convicts are conquered by being made to act like, and therefore comply with, their ''betters.'' *Our Country's Good* earned the playwright several awards, including the Olivier Award for best play (1988), the *Evening Standard* Award for best play of the year (1988), and the New York Drama Critics Circle Award for best foreign play (1991).

The Love of the Nightingale. 1988. Opened 28 October at the Other Place in Stratford-upon-Avon. Transferred to the Pit in London in August 1989. Produced by the Royal Shakespeare Company. Directed by Garry Hynes.

Wertenbaker's retelling of the Philomele and Procne myth portrays the brutality of patriarchy in its attempts to possess and silence women. Case notes that Wertenbaker's portrait of Philomele is distinctive because of her unusually assertive nature, indicated by her ability to engage in philosophical discourse and her attempted seduction of the sea captain, which stand in contrast to Procne's submission to her role as property passed from father to husband. Here, as in *The Grace of Mary Traverse* and somewhat in *New Anatomies*, issues concerning the space allowed or denied female discourse within the patriarchy are explored. Rabey argues that this play is the culmination of Wertenbaker's exploration of language and is therefore her most profound play.

Three Birds Alighting on a Field. 1992. Opened 5 September at the Royal Court Theatre. Directed by Max Stafford-Clark.

Wertenbaker's portrait of Biddy, an unsure English wife of a wealthy Greek who grows into a knowledge of her own self-worth as she learns about the value of art, was generally praised for its careful weaving of the themes of value in art and life. This satire of the art world in contemporary England drew some comparisons to Caryl Churchill's *Serious Money* by Wolf, Morley [2], Wardle [5], and Spencer [2]. The reviews were generally favorable with some reservations to the effect that Wertenbaker at times has tried to do too much. The insertion of the Philoctetes myth was generally seen as a mistake by critics (see Spencer [2], Peter [2], Billington [2], and Edwardes for examples). Like *Our Country's Good*, this play confronts the question of the purposes and meaning of art in our lives. It also expands upon the role-playing aspect of human life that has fascinated Wertenbaker throughout her career—that we are either the roles we are forced to play or those we choose to play. Sullivan notes a similarity with *The Grace of Mary Traverse* in that both Biddy and Mary Traverse are wealthy women who venture into the public arena in order to learn more about themselves and their world. The examination of the wealthy in both plays leads Sullivan to conclude that Wertenbaker actually ''looks at wealth *not* poverty as a condition to be remedied before all can be well.'' *Three Birds* garnered another Olivier Award nomination and won the author the Susan Smith Blackburn Prize for playwriting (1992).

ADDITIONAL PLAYS, TRANSLATIONS, AND PRODUCTIONS

Very little information or critical response exists for Wertenbaker's early plays. *Home Leave* (1982) and *Inside Out* (1982) grew out of either historical events or legends. *Home Leave* is set at the end of World War II and is about women factory workers. *Inside Out* reworks a Japanese legend of the courtesan Ono No Komachi, whose lover Shosho kills himself in an attempt to prove his love by undertaking a difficult journey every night in order to be with her 100 nights in a row. Chaillet briefly discusses both of these plays, describing them as examples of Wertenbaker's tendency toward ambiguity in her presentation of character. *Case to Answer*, produced by the Soho Poly in 1980, explores the oppression within a male-female relationship that finally leads the woman, Sylvia, to place a gun to the head of her husband Niko as a final way to express herself, in both the vocal and metaphysical sense. Rabey's discussion of Wertenbaker's work briefly treats this play's implications regarding language as a tool to affirm or to deny identity. Little or no critical work has been devoted to *The Third*, *Second Sentence*, and *Breaking Through*, all produced in or around London in 1980.

In contrast to her early plays, Wertenbaker's translations have received more notice. Her most well received translations have been the two Marivaux plays, *Successful Strategies* and *False Admissions*. Master's rather sexist comment regarding *Successful Strategies* describes her translation as "disprov[ing] the old saying that translations, like women, can never be both beautiful and faithful." Her work with Marivaux has received the most praise, perhaps because as Chaillet notes, his themes are close to her own. Both *Mephisto* and *The Thebans* received more mixed reviews. With *Mephisto* it becomes difficult to distinguish whether reviewers' generally negative opinions of Mnouchkine's play were worsened or eased by Wertenbaker's translation. Like *Mephisto*, *The Thebans* drew a skeptical response from most reviewers who disliked Adrian Noble's lengthy spectacle of a production, but Wertenbaker was praised by Wardle [4] for streamlining the three plays and by Cartledge for providing "eminently speakable" language. However, the recurring complaint from reviewers in regard to the translation was that the language was uneven, unacceptably mixing contemporary English idioms with a more classical-biblical language that tends toward bothos (Taylor [1], St. George, Spencer [1]). Despite these possible shortcomings Wertenbaker's translations as a whole remain an impressive body of work, attesting to her commitment to theatre and its many voices in addition to further emphasizing her fascination with language, a theme that recurs in many of her own plays.

ASSESSMENT OF WERTENBAKER'S CAREER

The most notable characteristic of Wertenbaker's career is its variety. She demonstrates her ability to work equally well with historical sources, or historical periods, and with contemporary settings. Indeed, it would seem that for her, one leads quite naturally into the other. Her translations further attest to her interest in the intertextuality of her work and that of other writers. She learns her craft better, as she herself states, by getting inside another writer's work (Wolf). Wertenbaker's body of work shares many of the same themes or concerns, most of them stemming from feminist issues that can and do apply to experiences other than those of women alone. Language and silence are often played off against each other as her characters search for their identities through the use of language or are denied their identity by being silenced in one way or another. Another theme that appears recurrently is the theatrical aspects of humans' lives, the roles people play, and the dangerous assumptions people make about others regarding such issues as gender and class. *Our Country's Good* certainly speaks to these themes and remains critically the most well received of her plays thus far. In this play she focuses her message, refusing to fall into the trap of trying to say too much, a problem some critics have mentioned in regard to *Abel's Sister* (Hewison) and *Three Birds Alighting on a Field* (Edwardes, Hurren). However, other reviewers have welcomed Wertenbaker's wealth of ideas as examples of the rich, provocative nature of theatre (Patrick, Armistead). As critics such as Rabey, Chaillet, Wilson, and Case note, Wertenbaker's themes place her comfortably within a feminist canon, but they do not isolate her there. Her questioning of the implications of identity and its related themes of self-worth and value as they are reflected in the roles we play and the words we speak are as international as her own upbringing.

PRIMARY BIBLIOGRAPHY

Plays

The Grace of Mary Traverse and *Love of the Nightingale*. London: Faber & Faber, 1989.
New Anatomies. London: Faber & Faber, 1984.
Our Country's Good. London: Methuen, 1988.
Three Birds Alighting on a Field. London: Faber & Faber, 1992.

Translations of Plays

False Admission, Successful Strategies, La Dispute: Three Plays by Marivaux. Bath: Absolute Classics, 1989.
Leocadia. In *Five Plays* by Jean Anouilh. London, Methuen, 1987.
The Thebans: Oedipus Tyrannos, Oedipus at Colonus, and Antigone. London: Faber & Faber, 1992.

SECONDARY BIBLIOGRAPHY

Armistead, Claire. Review of *Three Birds Alighting on a Field. Financial Times* (12 Sept. 1991).

Baker, Russell. "Makes You Think." *New York Times* (18 May 1991): 1: 23.

Billington, Michael [1]. Review of *Abel's Sister. The Guardian* (8 Aug. 1994).

———[2]. Review of *Three Birds Alighting on a Field. The Guardian* (12 Sept. 1991).

Brustein, Robert. "Robert Brustein on Theater: Dress-up Plays." *New Republic* (10 June 1991): 27, 29–30.

Cantacuzino, Marina. "Why Writing Came Second." *Sunday Times* (6 Apr. 1986): C49.

Carlson, Susan. "Self and Sexuality: Contemporary British Women Playwrights and the Problem of Sexual Identity." *Journal of Dramatic Theory and Criticism* 3.2 (1989): 157–78.

Cartledge, Paul. "Colonus in Colour." *Times Literary Supplement* (22 Nov. 1991): 18.

Case, Sue-Ellen. "The Power of Sex: English Plays by Women, 1958–1988." *New Theatre Quarterly* 7 (1991): 238–45.

Chaillet, Ned. "Timberlake Wertenbaker." In *Contemporary Dramatists*, ed. D. L. Kirkpatrick. 4th ed. Chicago: St. James Press, 1988: 553–55.

Collings, Matthew. Review of *Three Birds Alighting on a Field. City Limits* (19 Sept. 1991).

Cropper, Martin. "London Theatre: Open and Closet." *The Times* (24 Oct. 1985): 17.

Davis, Jim. "Festive Irony: Aspects of British Theatre in the 1980's." *Critical Survey* 3.3 (1991): 339–50.

Devries, Hilary. "Of Convicts, Brutality and the Power of Theater." *New York Times* (30 Sept. 1990): H10, 34.

Edwardes, Jane. Review of *Three Birds Alighting on a Field. Time Out* (18 Sept. 1991).

Fenton, James. "Marriage by Design." *Sunday Times* (13 Nov. 1983): 38.

Gardner, Lyn. Review of *Abel's Sister. City Limits* (17 Aug. 1984).

Gussow, Mel [1]. "Of Convicts, the Stage and Australia's Beginnings." *New York Times* (21 Oct. 1990): 1: 59.

——— [2]. "A Sexual Cover-up in 'New Anatomies.' " *New York Times* (22 Feb. 1990): C19.

Hewison, Robert. "An Affair of the Heart." *Sunday Times* (12 Aug. 1984): G37.

Hurren, Kenneth. Review of *Three Birds Alighting on a Field. Mail on Sunday* (15 Sept. 1991).

Irwin, Robert. "The Game of Camels." *Times Literary Supplement* (16 Mar. 1990): 284.

James, John. "Laughing through Tears." *Times Educational Supplement* (16 Sept. 1988): 36.

Kennedy, Douglas. "Hey, Big Spender." *New Statesman and Society* (8 Dec. 1989): 44–45.

Kingston, Jeremy [1]. "Masterpiece Alight with Truth." *The Times* (12 Sept. 1991): 20.

———[2]. "Tedious and Trivial Pursuit." *The Times* (10 June 1992): Life and Times Section: 3.

Kramer, Mimi. "Our Culture's Good." *The New Yorker* (20 May 1991): 94–95.

LaRue, Michele. "*Our Country's Good*: Three Approaches to a Play about Theatre and Australian History." *Theatre Crafts* 25.3 (1991): 40–43, 61, 63, 65–70.

MacCarthy, Fiona. "Looking for the Inner Life." *Times Literary Supplement* (20 Sept. 1991): 18.

Mason, John Hope. "Formality and Abandon." *Times Literary Supplement* (25 Nov. 1983): 1323.

Masters, Anthony. "Theatre: *Successful Strategies.*" *The Times* (16 Nov. 1983): D10.

McMurray, Emily J., ed. "Timberlake Wertenbaker." *Contemporary Theatre, Film, and Television.* Vol. 10. Detroit: Gale Research, 1983: 435–36.

Morley, Sheridan [1]. "Gender Is Not the Case." *The Times* (7 Nov. 1988): 20.

———[2]. Review of *Three Birds Alighting on a Field. Herald Tribune* (18 Sept. 1991).

Neill, Heather. "Theban Marathon Enters Stratford." *Sunday Times* (27 Oct. 1991): 6: 9.

Nokes, David. "Stage Struck on the Fatal Shore." *Times Literary Supplement* (23 Sept. 1988): 1049.

Patrick, Tony. "Mysterious, Beautiful Silence." *The Times* (24 Aug. 1989): 16.

Peter, John [1]. "The Art: *Three Birds Alighting on a Field.*" *Sunday Times* (15 Sept. 1991): 5: 14.

———[2]. "The Moving Lessons That History Can Teach Us." *Sunday Times* (18 Sept. 1988): C11.

———[3]. "Political Realism Crushed by Paranoia." *Sunday Times* (11 Mar. 1990): E4.

———[4]. "The Shock of the New." *Sunday Times* (27 Oct. 1985): D43.

Rabey, David Ian. "Defining Differences: Timberlake Wertenbaker's Drama of Language, Dispossession, and Discovery." *Modern Drama* 33.4 (Dec. 1990): 518–28.

Radin, Victoria. "Sex for Sale." *New Statesman* (8 Nov. 1985): 32.

Richards, David. "In the Language of Lockjaw, Subtext Is All." *New York Times* (19 May 1991): 25.

Rose, Helen. "Reviews: *Three Birds Alighting on a Field.*" *Plays and Players* (Nov. 1991): 24.

Seibert, Gary. "Theater: Under the London Sun." *America* (16 Sept. 1989): 145.

Shulman, Milton. Review of *Three Birds Alighting on a Field. Evening Standard* (11 Sept. 1991).

Simon, John. "Shows within Shows." *New York* (13 May 1991): 88, 90.

Spencer, Charles [1]. Review of *The Thebans. Daily Telegraph* (4 Nov. 1991).

———[2]. Review of *Three Birds Alighting on a Field. Daily Telegraph* (12 Sept. 1991).

St. George, Andrew. Review of *The Thebans. Financial Times* (4 Nov. 1991).

Stafford-Clark, Max. *Letters to George: The Account of a Rehearsal.* London: Nick Hern Books, 1989.

Sullivan, Esther Beth. "Hailing Ideology, Acting in the Horizon, and Reading between Plays by Timberlake Wertenbaker." *Theatre Journal* 45.1 (Mar. 1993): 139–54.

Taylor, Paul [1]. Review of *The Thebans. The Independent* (5 Nov. 1991).

———[2]. Review of *Three Birds Alighting on a Field. The Independent* (12 Sept. 1991).

Taylor, Val. "Mothers of Invention: Female Characters in *Our Country's Good* and *The Playmaker.*" *Critical Survey* 3.3 (1991): 331–38.

Wardle, Irving [1]. Review of *Abel's Sister. The Times* (8 Aug. 1984): Arts, 7.

———[2]. "*False Admissions.*" *The Times* (9 Nov. 1983): F11.

———[3]. Review of *Our Country's Good. The Times* (10 Sept. 1988): 38.

———[4]. "*The Thebans.*" *Sunday Independent* (10 Nov. 1991).

————[5]. Review of *Three Birds Alighting on a Field*. *The Independent on Sunday* (15 Sept. 1991).

Wilson, Ann [1]. "*Our Country's Good*: Theatre, Colony, and Nation in Wertenbaker's Adaptation of *The Playmaker*." *Modern Drama* 34.1 (Mar. 1991): 23–34.

————[2]. "The English Stage Company Visits the Canadian Stage Company." *Queen's Quarterly* 97 (spring 1990): 140–53.

Wolf, Matt. "Love Returns to the Court." *The Times* (9 Sept. 1991): Arts Section: 11.

Wright, Michael. "New Anatomies." *The Times* (9 Mar. 1990): 16.

Arnold Wesker
(1932–)

ROBERT WILCHER

Arnold Wesker first came to prominence as one of the new generation of British dramatists fostered by the English Stage Company, which had its first major success with John Osborne's *Look Back in Anger* at the Royal Court Theatre in May 1956. Since the critical acclaim that greeted *Chicken Soup with Barley* (1958), *Roots* (1959), and *I'm Talking about Jerusalem* (1960), Wesker has gone on to write more than thirty plays in a variety of styles, but he is still best known as the author of this early trilogy.

Arnold Wesker was born of Jewish parents on 24 May 1932, in Stepney in the East End of London. His father, Joseph Wesker, who worked as a garment maker, and his mother, Leah Perlmutter Wesker, had migrated from Russia and Hungary and his early years were spent in the close community of an extended family. He attended local elementary schools, was evacuated from London at the beginning of the war in 1939, and completed his formal education at Upton House Central School in Hackney. After leaving school at the age of sixteen, he followed a number of trades before being drafted into the Royal Air Force for two years of National Service in 1950. It was while working in Norfolk between 1952 and 1954 as a seed-sorter, farm laborer, and kitchen porter that he met Dusty (Doreen) Bicker, whom he was to marry in 1958. In 1954 he decided to train as a pastry cook and was later employed in this capacity in a Paris restaurant, where he saved enough money to enroll at the London School of Film Technique in 1956. While there he was prompted by a competition sponsored by *The Observer* newspaper to attempt a stage play, *The Kitchen*, and under the impact of *Look Back in Anger* he wrote *Chicken Soup with Barley*. A chance meeting with theatre and film director Lindsay Anderson brought Wesker to the attention of George Devine, the artistic director of the English Stage Company. On Devine's recommendation, *Chicken Soup with Barley* was directed by John Dexter at the Belgrade Theatre in Coventry before transferring to the Royal Court Theatre in July 1958. *Roots*, also directed like all the early works by Dexter, had a brief run in a West End theatre following another transfer from the Belgrade to the Royal Court. Its success earned Wesker the *Evening Standard* Award for most promising playwright of 1959. In the same year, *The Kitchen* was given a Sunday night production at the Royal Court and Wesker's son, Lindsay Joe, was born. *I'm Talking about Jerusalem* was completed in 1960, and during June and July the entire Wesker *Trilogy* was performed at the Royal Court.

For Wesker 1961 was an eventful year. His daughter Tanya Jo was born, *Roots* was produced off-Broadway, and *The Kitchen* was released as a film and given a full production in an extended stage version. Wesker also spent one month in prison for demonstrating against nuclear weapons and was appointed artistic director of Centre 42, a project named after Resolution 42 at the 1960 Trades Union Congress, which had accepted a proposal initiated by Wesker himself that the Labour movement had a responsibility to promote the cultural enrichment as well as the material prosperity of working people. A second son, Daniel, was born, and Wesker's own career as a dramatist continued with a successful transfer from the Royal Court to the West End of *Chips with Everything*, which was voted best play of 1962 and in 1963 became the first of his works to be produced on Broadway. During the 1960s, however, he was increasingly preoccupied with the activities of Centre 42. Early on, six arts festivals were mounted in different parts of the country; later a Victorian engine shed in the Chalk Farm district of London was acquired and developed into a performance space known as the Roundhouse; but as idealism evaporated in the face of financial crisis, Wesker lost heart and the project was wound up in 1970. The three plays that he wrote during this period, *Their Very Own and Golden City* (first performed in Belgium and awarded the Italian Marzotto Prize for Drama in 1964), *The Four Seasons* (1965), and *The Friends* (1970), were poorly received in Britain, and in 1972 Wesker fell out with both the National Theatre and the Royal Shakespeare Company over abortive productions of *The Old Ones* (which Dexter took to the Royal Court Theatre) and *The Journalists* (which was eventually given its professional premiere in Germany in 1981).

Apart from *Caritas*, which premiered at the National Theatre in 1981, most of Wesker's plays from the 1970s and 1980s have received their first performances overseas. In Britain his later work has been confined mainly to repertory theatres in the provinces or fringe theatres in the capital. A new development in Wesker's art came in 1989 with the commissioning of *Beorhtel's Hill*, a community play performed by a cast of local people to celebrate the fortieth anniversary of Basildon, one of the new towns created as part of the postwar building program. In the same year, *The Merchant*, now renamed *Shylock*, was given a rehearsed reading at the Riverside Studios, Hammersmith, in the hope of stimulating financial support for a full-scale production in London.

Selected Biographical Sources: Coppieters; Hayman; Itzin [1, 2]; Leeming

[1, 3]; Wesker, "Art and Action," *As Much as I Dare*, "Discovery;" "How We Met," "An Interview with Arnold Wesker: Centre 42," "Playwright to Watch."

MAJOR PLAYS, PREMIERES, AND SIGNIFICANT
REVIVALS: THEATRICAL RECEPTION

The Kitchen. 1959 (written 1956). Sunday night "production without decor," 13 September at the Royal Court Theatre, London; revised, longer version opened 19 June 1961, at the Belgrade Theatre, Coventry; moved 27 June to the Royal Court Theatre, London. Directed by John Dexter. Revivals: New Theatre Workshop (NY), May 1966; moved to New 81st Street Theatre (NY), June 1966; Royal Court Theatre, London, February 1994.

This play puts on stage the daily routine in the kitchen of a large restaurant. Alvarez, who saw the first Sunday night production, declared it "the best play of the decade." Roberts [3] commented on its authenticity and admired its "warmth and humanity." *The Times* reviewer ("Symbolism Too Vague") also saw it as "the work of a natural realist" but lamented the absence of a strong narrative interest. Tynan [3] was struck by the originality of a piece that dramatizes both the processes and the human consequences of "repetitive toil," and suggested that it was reminiscent of early Eugene O'Neill. The revival in 1994 was given an enthusiastic reception by Coveney [3], who felt that it worked "perfectly in both the physical and metaphorical spheres," and by Nightingale [4], who considered it to be "as striking a blend of objective observation and moral fervour as the modern theatre can offer."

Chicken Soup with Barley. 1958. Opened 7 July at the Belgrade Theatre, Coventry; moved 14 July to the Royal Court Theatre, London. Directed by John Dexter. Revivals: Royal Court Theatre, London, June 1960, as part of the trilogy; Shaw Theatre, London, April 1978, as part of the trilogy.

Centered on portraits of Wesker's own parents, this play spans two decades of public and private history, from the idealism of 1936 to the disillusionment of 1956. Early reviews were generally favorable. Both Tynan [1] and Worsley [1] responded positively to the combination of political problems and human values embodied in the family saga; and Jackson [1], who found the play "strong in dialogue, throbbing with purpose," saw great potential in this new dramatist. Fay [1], however, was less impressed by the political dimension, and *The Times* ("Guest Play at Royal Court") thought it had "some difficulty in concentrating its meaning." Wardle [4] was surprised to find that in the 1978 revival this "extraordinary document of the 1950s" still came over as a "moving and illuminating work"; and Levin [3] felt that the quality of the entire trilogy was "undiminished by the passing years."

Roots. 1959. Opened 25 May at the Belgrade Theatre, London; moved 30 July to the Duke of York's Theatre, London. Directed by John Dexter. Revivals:

Royal Court Theatre, London, June 1960, as part of the trilogy; Mayfair Theatre (NY), March 1961; Shaw Theatre, London, May 1978, as part of the trilogy; National Theatre, London, February 1989 (after touring from October 1989).

More narrowly focused on a domestic and personal situation than the other two components of the trilogy, this play was admired as much for the realism of its presentation of the lives and language of agricultural laborers (Jackson [2], Tynan [5]) as for the theatrical excitement of its heroine's dance at the climax of the second act (Hobson [1], Roberts [4]). In 1959 *The Times* (''Play with New and Good Idea'') had reservations about Wesker's ability to select and focus his material but in 1960 (''Best of the Trilogy'') acknowledged that this was ''unquestionably the best'' of the plays in the trilogy. Reactions to the 1978 revival were positive: Wardle [2] found that ''the miraculous final speech'' still made its impact, and Billington [4] was ''as moved as ever by Wesker's hard-won, unsentimental optimism.'' For Kellaway the 1988 touring production brought out ''the complexity of trying to change people'' and was ''at once fresh and dated''; and Peter [3] considered that it leapt off the stage of the National Theatre with ''confidence and conviction'' and that its message was ''still worth listening to.''

I'm Talking about Jerusalem. 1960. Opened 28 March at the Belgrade Theatre, Coventry; moved to Royal Court Theatre, London, 27 July, as part of the trilogy. Directed by John Dexter. Revival: Shaw Theatre, London, June 1978, as part of the trilogy.

Less well received than the other two parts of the trilogy, this play charts the failure of an experiment in socialist living. The reviewer in *The Times* (''The Trilogy Completed'') disliked the ''long and rather arid exchange of slogans,'' and Tynan [4], while admiring the depiction of political idealism in the first two acts, felt that the ending was blurred by ''sentimentality and intellectual flabbiness.'' What for Fay [2] was a ''loosely constructed script'' with ''little dramatic shape'' was more favorably regarded by Roberts [2] as ''more ambitiously lyrical'' and ''looser in style'' than its companion pieces. Unlike Nightingale [2], who was surprised that the 1978 revival made ''a solider impact than its rather flimsy reputation promised,'' de Jongh [1] regarded the play with hindsight as ''ominous of the playwright's general falling off.''

Chips with Everything. 1962. Opened 27 April at the Royal Court Theatre, London; moved 12 June to the Vaudeville Theatre, London. Directed by John Dexter. Simultaneous productions 30 April at Citizens Theatre, Glasgow, directed by Callum Mill, and 30 April at the Playhouse, Sheffield, directed by Geoffrey Ost. Revivals: Plymouth Theatre (NY), October 1963; Birmingham Repertory Theatre, April 1981.

Set during the eight weeks of basic training, this play was praised by Hope-Wallace [1] for the documentary accuracy of its portrayal of air force life, but Brien [1] dismissed this realism as merely the ''surface gloss'' for the ''ponderous machinery of allegory.'' Many reviewers emphasized Wesker's break with naturalism and the political force of his attack on the class system ("Mateship against Authority," Worsley [2], Hobson [2], Tynan [2], Roberts [1]). For Wardle [6], the Royal Court's naturalistic style muffled the "loathing for the class tyranny of service life," which came over more clearly at Sheffield. In a review of the Glasgow production, Hamilton hailed *Chips with Everything* as "without question the work of a major writer," but he regretted the way the political pamphleteer undermined the work of the dramatist. Dexter [2] called it "the most stimulating play" he had ever directed. McKee found the 1981 revival "a powerful piece of theatre," which was still "exciting after nearly 20 years."

The Four Seasons. 1965. Opened 24 August, Belgrade Theatre, Coventry; moved 9 September to Golders Green Hippodrome, London; moved 21 September to Saville Theatre, London. Directed for Coventry by Henrik Hirsch and for London by Arnold Wesker. Revival: Theatre Four (NY), March 1968.

Few reviewers responded favorably to Wesker's open abandonment of naturalism for a more lyrical and abstract approach in this depiction of the burgeoning and fading of love between a man and woman. Esslin [1] felt that the framework of the seasons led to "the boredom of predictability," and Gilliatt objected to the overt symbolism of set and costumes. The language was disliked by Brien [2], who found it "pseudo-poetry," and by Hope-Wallace [2], who dismissed the play as "utterly ineffective as a piece of drama." Hobson [3] agreed that it failed as drama but admired it as "a poem," which "sings, often beautifully." *The Times* ("Love without the Social Pressures") saw the exclusion of economic and social pressures from the world outside the lovers' relationship as its main flaw.

Their Very Own and Golden City. 1966. Opened 19 May at the Royal Court Theatre, London. Directed by William Gaskill. First production in French, November 1965, at the Belgian National Theatre, Brussels. Revival: Municipal Theatre, Aarhus, Denmark, May 1974.

Many reviewers remarked on the similarities between the Centre 42 project and the plot of this play, which dramatizes an architect's lifelong and doomed crusade to realize a utopian dream. *The Times* ("Split between Vision and Reality") review of the Royal Court production noted the skill with which "the freely episodic construction" was handled, but both Esslin [2] and the special correspondent who reported for *The Times* from Brussels ("Belgians Present New Play") had their doubts about Wesker's use of flashback. It was Esslin [2], however, who passed the most favorable verdict on the "intellectually stimulating" story, the vividly realized characters, and the important subject matter in a play that "throbs with real anguish, real love, real feeling." Among those who were less impressed, Brien [3] saw it as a courageous but failed attempt at "a sociological epic," Bryden [1] dismissed it as "an old-fashioned chronicle of compromised ideals," and both D.A.N. Jones and Hope-Wallace [3] felt it needed trimming. Wesker himself was more satisfied with the result when he was given the opportunity to direct a revised version of the play in Denmark.

The Friends. 1970. Opened 24 January at the Lilla Teatern, Stadsteater, Stockholm. Directed by Arnold Wesker. Opened 19 May at the Roundhouse, London. Directed by Arnold Wesker.

Centered on the reactions of a group of middle-aged friends to the illness and death of the most optimistic spirit among them, this exploration of lost idealism provoked some hostile reviews. Wesker had failed ''to transform inchoate emotion into drama'' (Taylor [2]); his play was nothing but ''a requiem for seven voices, all of them Wesker's'' (Marcus); there was ''little objective, individual life'' in the characters (Nightingale [5]); there was ''an orgy of recrimination and self-searching'' combined with ''an almost total lack of action'' (Bryden [2]). Even Barber [3], who responded to the ''quiet chamber music'' of this ''delicate mood-piece,'' felt that as drama it was ''static, little more than a series of monologues.'' Wesker was stung into replying to his critics in ''Casual Condemnations.''

The Old Ones. 1972. Opened 8 August at the Royal Court Theatre, London. Directed by John Dexter. Revival: The Kammerspiele, Munich, February 1973; the Lambs (NY), December 1974.

For Billington [3], this ''moving, compassionate'' study of old age came to a climax with ''a traditionally Weskerian assertion of the joy of life'' and in dramatic method it was an extension of Wesker's ''quest for non-narrative theatre.'' Say also related this ''beautifully attuned survey of near senility'' to the abandonment of ''strictly narrative format.'' Less favorably disposed to this aspect of the play, Wardle [1] thought it was ''lacking in forward drive,'' Hurren dismissed the ''series of brief vignettes'' as ''entirely aimless,'' and Barber [2] wished that Wesker ''had provided a story'' instead of ''an album of snapshots.'' In spite of its ''flaws,'' Seymour felt that ''its almost musical structure'' was ''studded with telling and beautiful observation.''

The Journalists. 1977. Scheduled for production in 1972 by the Royal Shakespeare Company at the Aldwych Theatre, London, but abandoned in the face of opposition from the actors. Opened in an amateur production 27 March, at the Criterion Theatre, Coventry. Directed by Geoff Bennett. Opened in first professional production 10 October 1981, in Landesbuhne (Wilhelmshaven). Directed by Klaus Hoser.

Set in the offices of a national Sunday newspaper and orchestrating a large cast of characters and a number of stories, this play was praised by Billington [5] for its ''originality of form'' and ''richness of content.'' The same reviewer expressed some doubts about the play's analysis of the role of the press in contemporary society but applauded the documentary realism with which it captured the routines of a newspaper office and the ''slowly accelerating rhythm'' of the Criterion production.

The Wedding Feast. 1974. Opened 8 May at the Stadtsteater, Stockholm. Directed by Gun Arvidsson. Opened 20 January 1977, at the Leeds Playhouse. Directed by John Harrison and Michael Attenborough. Revival: Birmingham Repertory Theatre, June 1980.

Based on a short story by Dostoevsky and relocated in Norfolk, this disturbing comic parable about the unbridgeable social gulf between boss and workers elicited the best crop of reviews since *Chips with Everything*. Wardle [5] saw evidence of Wesker's talent "getting into its stride again," Levin [4] thought it "a penetrating, valuable and compassionate study, in Mr Wesker's earlier mode," Nightingale [1] welcomed the return to his work of "mental rigour, wit, humour, contemporary point, dramatic tension," and Coult praised his "wry skill in the dramatising of class relations." Many reviewers, however, shared Wardle's reservations about the use of a narrator in the prologue. The Birmingham revival had a mixed reception, with Peter [4] finding a potentially "excellent" play damaged by "much that is clumsy and superfluous," Hart condemning the prologue as "pedantically discursive" but enjoying the buildup to "a moving and politically resonant showdown," and Matheson praising "the integrity and authenticity" of the portrayal of working-class domestic culture.

The Merchant (now named *Shylock*). 1976. Opened 8 October at the Royal Dramaten Theater, Stockholm. Directed by Staphan Roos. Opened 16 November 1977, at the Plymouth Theatre (NY). Director John Dexter. Opened 12 October 1978, at the Birmingham Repertory Theatre. Director Peter Farago. Revival: a reading-workshop production as *Shylock* at the Riverside Studios, London, October 1989.

The Broadway production, which closed after a handful of performances, was damned by Eder as "weak" in structure and "fitful and uncertain" in dramatic impact. It received more positive reviews in Britain. Clive Barnes, who praised the trial scene as "a gem of staging," argued that Wesker's rewriting of *The Merchant of Venice* to expose the obscenity and pain of anti-semitism was perhaps his "finest play." Aire admired the "richness and diversity" of what she saw as "Wesker's exploration of his own Jewish inheritance." For Chaillet [2], the Birmingham production was both "compelling" as a play and "passionate" as a document. Levin [2], however, dismissed it as "grimly literary," and Everitt was bewildered by its mixture of "theatrical magic and pedestrian blundering." The workshop production in 1989 convinced Lemmon that it would be a travesty if this "challenging" work, which "engages us intellectually and emotionally," were not seen on the West End stage.

Love Letters on Blue Paper (one act). 1977. Opened 14 October at the Syracuse Stage (NY). Directed by Arthur Storch. Opened 15 February 1978, at the Cottesloe auditorium, London. Directed by Arnold Wesker.

Adapted from a short story by Arnold Wesker, this celebration of married love in a series of letters written by a woman to her dying husband was felt by Nightingale [3] to have "a strange and haunting authenticity," which carefully avoids sentimentality. Other reviewers, less charitably disposed, found it "elegiacally self-admiring" (Wardle [3]), "strident, limp and awash with clichés" (Levin [1]), and "very old-fashioned, romantic, patriarchal" (Whitehead).

Caritas. 1981. Opened 7 October at the Cottesloe Auditorium, London. Directed by John Madden.

Several reviewers commented adversely on Wesker's tampering with historical facts in this play about a fourteenth-century anchoress: Fenton [2] thought that it resulted in "an anachronistic philosophy of liberation," Chaillet [1] that there was a failure to "dramatize" the parallels between private and public worlds, and Roper that the play's concept of history was "crude." There was some praise from Cushman, Coveney [2], and Barber [1] for the intensity of the second half, in which the anchoress was seen immured in her cell, but most agreed with Shrimpton that the first half was "frigid costume drama."

Annie Wobbler. 1983. Opened 5 July at the Birmingham Repertory Theatre Studio; moved 26 July to the New End Theatre, London. Directed by Arnold Wesker. Revivals: Fortune Theatre, London, November 1984; Westbeth Theatre (NY), October 1986.

These three monologues written for a single actress received mixed reviews, with many praising the performance more than the writing, although Peter [1] found the text "bristling with humour and observation" and Fenton [1] commended it for being "idiomatically written." The "three rich, ripe, varied character-studies" appealed to Billington [1], but for Asquith they were no more than "a series of auditions." The first monologue by Annie was widely admired, but many reviewers shared Colvin's opinion that the other two were merely "vehicles for Wesker." Wandor [1] spoke up for the portrait of Annabella, the successful novelist, as "Wesker at his most sharp and satirical."

Yardsale (one act). 1985. Opened 12 August at the Edinburgh Festival. Directed by Eric Standige. Revival: Lyric Theatre Studio, Hammersmith, London, February 1987, in a double bill with *Whatever Happened to Betty Lemon?*

Whatever Happened to Betty Lemon? (one act). 1986. Opened 12 November at the Théâtre du Rond-Point, Paris. Directed by Jean-Michel Ribes. First British production opened 17 February 1987, at the Lyric Theatre Studio, Hammersmith, London, in double bill with *Yardsale*. Directed by Arnold Wesker.

Kingston's verdict was that in neither of these two monologues for a single actress "do the emotions shape themselves into a satisfying form," and Rissik found the attempt at poetic monologue merely "sentimental" and "dull." In de Jongh's [2] view, the monologue form was an evasion of "full theatrical life." Armistead, while expressing reservations about *Yardsale*, considered *Betty Lemon* "an altogether funnier and tarter play" and Walker welcomed the return of a "vigorously sardonic East End voice" in Wesker's writing.

Beorhtel's Hill. 1989. Opened 5 June at the Towngate Theatre, Basildon. Directed by Jon Oram and Steve Woodward.

This community play, commissioned by the Colway Theatre Trust to mark the fortieth anniversary of the New Town of Basildon, was criticized for a lack of narrative focus by Peter [2] and by Coveney [1], who thought it "something of a patchwork, colourful but spineless." Billington [2] applauded Wesker's "gritty professionalism" and reported that after a "rather thin-textured" beginning, the play took off in the second half when "genuine moral conflicts" emerged. Several reviewers were surprised by what Billington called the "blend of criticism . . . and celebration." Kemp, for example, concluded that this "civic cavalcade," with its "sour commentary" on "betrayed ideals and municipal shoddinesses," was the "most uncompromisingly individual of community plays."

ADDITIONAL PLAYS AND PRODUCTIONS

The Nittingham Captain, a documentary play for narrator, voices, and orchestra, was first performed 11 September 1962, in Wellingborough as part of the earliest of the festivals mounted by Centre 42. *Four Portraits—Of Mothers* was first performed on 2 July 1982, at the Mitzukoshi Royal Theatre as part of the Tokyo Festival of One-Act Plays, given its United Kingdom premiere on 20 August 1984, at the Netherbow Theatre as part of the Edinburgh Festival, and first performed in London on 20 October 1987, at the Half-Moon Theatre. *One More Ride on the Merry-Go-Round* was premiered at the Phoenix Theatre, Leicester, on 25 April 1985. *When God Wanted a Son* was performed as a reading on 19 February 1989, to raise funds for the Jackson's Lane Community Theatre. *Caritas* was reworked as a libretto for an opera with music by Robert Saxton in 1988. Several plays have not yet been staged: *The New Play* (1969), *Sullied Hands* (1981), *Cinders* (1983), *Toys* (1985), *Badenheim 1939*, adapted from a novel by Aharon Appelfeld (1987), *Lady Othello* (1987), *The Mistress* (1988), *Three Women Talking* (1990), *Letter to a Daughter* (1990), *Blood Libel* (1991), and *Wild Spring* (1992).

ASSESSMENT OF WESKER'S CAREER

The critical stir caused by the early productions of the trilogy and *The Kitchen* fixed in the public consciousness an image of Wesker that has been difficult to dislodge, in spite of later developments in the dramatic style and thematic focus of his work. He is still best known to the British theatre-going public as the author of *Roots* and *Chips with Everything*. It is indicative of the subsequent cooling of enthusiasm that the only major revivals in London have been of the complete trilogy in 1978, of *Roots* by the National Theatre Company in 1988, and of *The Kitchen* in 1994; and it remains an anomaly that his two best plays of the 1970s, *The Wedding Feast* and *The Merchant*, have never been given full productions in London.

Reviewers and academic critics have been too ready to judge later works with reference to the stereotype established by the first five plays, which categorizes Wesker as a social realist with a warm heart, an ear for working-class language, and a burning mission to improve the cultural lot of those deadened by drab surroundings and the routines of repetitive manual labor. Among those who first undertook to assess the achievement of the trilogy, Goodman invoked the example of Clifford Odets and suggested that Wesker was using the stage as a platform for the New Left; Findlater noted the significant step of presenting working-class characters on the stage as human beings with their own rights and problems; and A. R. Jones emphasized the urgency and compassion that Wesker brought to the task of regenerating people and society. A more recent survey of Wesker's career by Chambers and Prior concentrates almost exclusively on the trilogy, dismissing *Their Very Own and Golden City* as much more dated than other mid-1960s plays like John Osborne's *Inadmissible Evidence* and Edward Bond's *Saved*, and giving short shrift to the later work.

Although some early commentators, like Mander, emphasized the socialism of the trilogy and some, like Hobson [2] and Kitchin [1], regarded *Chips with Everything* as powerfully subversive of the English class system, it was also recognized, by Tynan [1] and Findlater among others, that Wesker was stronger on moral imperatives and compassionate concern for the individual than on economic or political analysis. As his work has evolved, it has become clearer that what drives him as an artist is not a commitment to any party or program but a passionate belief in the value of human beings and their potential for a better life (Anderson). Itzin [2] sees a distinct shift from socialist to humanist issues by the end of the 1960s, and the process of transition has been traced from *The Four Seasons* to *The Old Ones* by Bowering; whereas Leeming [4] identifies the early 1970s as the watershed in Wesker's development.

From the beginning Wesker has chosen to dramatize the failure rather than the achievement of those dedicated to an idealistic vision of the future, whether it takes the form of international communism in *Chicken Soup with Barley*, an architect's dream of building an urban environment in which the human spirit could flourish in *Their Very Own and Golden City*, the attempt to breach the social barriers that divide capitalist from workers in *The Wedding Feast*, or the friendship between Jewish loan-banker and Christian merchant that challenges racial intolerance in *The Merchant/Shylock*. Many critics have remarked on this pattern of idealism fading into disillusionment, but what should also be emphasized is the resilience with which some of Wesker's most striking characters confront disappointment and defeat. Furthermore, as Zimmermann has pointed out, the dialectic between recalcitrant reality and utopian hope that lies at the heart of Wesker's dramas of disillusionment is a means of protecting the necessary dream of a better future from the twin dangers of facile optimism and nihilistic despair.

Two commonplaces of criticism, established in relation to the trilogy by such commentators as Taylor [1], are that Wesker's characters are often merely mouthpieces for his ideas and that his control over the structure of his plays is at best casual. The first of these recurring charges, which was still being leveled at *Annie Wobbler* and *Beorhtel's Hill* in the 1980s, has been countered by Leeming and Trussler's argument that Wesker allows for the impact of environment upon personality and takes full account of the social as well as the psychological dimension of behavior, and by Anderson's insight into his refusal to separate ideas from their human context, so that political argument becomes part of the texture of his characters' lives.

The other repeated complaint of the reviewers, that Wesker cannot select and shape his material effectively, is often provoked by the absence of conventional narrative plots. More considered analyses of the dramatic structure of plays like *The Friends* (by Kustow, Mannheimer [1], and Leeming [4]) and *The Old Ones* (by Bowering and Morgan) have called upon such musical terms as counterpoint and harmony, polyphony and rhythmic coherence to describe the ways in which voices and events are juxtaposed and interwoven. Other attempts to disengage the later work from the stereotype of the formless slice of life have invoked the theatrical model of the Chekhovian ensemble play (Leeming and Trussler, Morgan) or have highlighted the extent to which Wesker's naturalism, even in such early plays as *The Kitchen* and *Roots*, is enriched and complicated by symbolism (Latham, Costello) and expressionistic techniques (Leeming and Trussler, Worth).

Wesker's mastery of Jewish rhythms and idioms has frequently been highlighted by reviewers, and Tynan [1] early on discerned the marks of a Jewish sensibility in *Chicken Soup with Barley*. In 1965 Wellwarth compared the trilogy with Odet's *Awake and Sing!* and denigrated *I'm Talking about Jerusalem* as a recycling of Yiddish theatre clichés. The year before Wesker had rejected Wager's suggestion that he was a Jewish playwright rather than a playwright who happened to be a Jew. By 1970, however, he admitted to Hayman that he was beginning to feel protective about his inheritance, which became a thematic issue in *The Old Ones* and dominated *The Merchant*, a play written deliberately to counteract the anti-Semitism he perceived in *The Merchant of Venice*. (For Wesker's views on Shakespeare's play, see "Why I Fleshed out Shylock" and "A Nasty Piece of Work.")

Another feature present in his work from the start but more obvious with the monologue plays of the 1980s is the prominence given to female characters. From Sarah Kahn and Beatie Bryant in the trilogy to Christine in *Caritas*, Annie Wobbler, and Betty Lemon, Wesker has provided some of the richest roles for women in contemporary theatre.

There has been a tendency to write Wesker off as a historical phenomenon associated with the early years of the English Stage Company, but recent revivals of *Roots*, *Shylock*, and *The Kitchen* have demonstrated that he can still be a vital presence in the British theatre and his characteristically honest response to the commission for a community play with a cast of over a hundred is welcome evidence of his continuing ability to sustain something more substantial than the monologue form. Whatever the future may hold in the way of new work, both the range and the quality of Wesker's output so far should secure him an important place in the history of postwar drama.

PRIMARY BIBLIOGRAPHY

Plays

Annie Wobbler. In *Words International* (December 1987 and January 1988).

Beorhtel's Hill. Basildon: Colway Theatre Trust, 1989.

Bluey. In *Words International* (August 1985).

Caritas. London: Cape, 1981.

Chicken Soup with Barley. In *New English Dramatists*. Vol. 1. Harmondsworth: Penguin, 1959.

Chips with Everything. London: Cape, 1962; New York: Random House, 1963; in *New English Dramatists*. Vol. 7. Harmondsworth: Penguin, 1963.

Four Portraits—Of Mothers. *Stand* 29 (winter 1987–88).

The Four Seasons. London: Cape, 1966; in *New English Dramatists*. Vol. 9. Harmondsworth: Penguin, 1966.

The Friends. London: Cape, 1970.

I'm Talking about Jerusalem. Harmondsworth: Penguin, 1960.

The Journalists. London: Writers and Readers Publishing Cooperative, 1975; in *The Journalists: A Tryptich*. London: Cape, 1979.

The Kitchen. London: Cape, 1961; New York: Random House, 1962; in *New English Dramatists*. Vol. 2. Harmondsworth: Penguin, 1960.

Little Old Lady. In *New Plays 1*, ed. Peter Terson. Oxford: Oxford University Press, 1988.

Love Letters on Blue Paper. London: TQ Publications, 1978.

Menace. *Jewish Quarterly* 10 (spring 1963). In *Six Sundays in January*. London: Cape, 1971.

The Merchant. East Germany: Henschel Verlag, 1977; London: Methuen, 1983; *Adam International Review* Nos. 401–3 (1977–78).

The Nottingham Captain. In *Six Sundays in January*. London: Cape, 1971.

The Old Ones. London: Cape, 1973; London: Blackie, 1974; *Plays and Players* (Oct. 1972).

Roots. Harmondsworth: Penguin, 1959.

Shoe Shine. In *New Plays 3*, ed. Peter Terson. Oxford: Oxford University Press, 1989.

Their Very Own and Golden City. London: Cape, 1966; in *New English Dramatists*. Vol. 10. Harmondsworth: Penguin, 1967.

The Wedding Feast. *Plays and Players* (Apr.–May 1977).

Whatever Happened to Betty Lemon? In *Plays International* (Apr. 1987).

Yardsale. In *Plays International* (Apr. 1987).

Anthologies

Arnold Wesker: Volume 1. (*Chicken Soup with Barley, Roots, I'm Talking about Jerusalem*). Harmondsworth: Penguin, 1979.

Arnold Wesker: Volume 2. (*The Kitchen, The Four Seasons, Their Very Own and Golden City*). Harmondsworth: Penguin, 1990.

Arnold Wesker: Volume 3. (*Chips with Everything, The Friends, The Old Ones, Love Letters on Blue Paper*). Harmondsworth: Penguin, 1990.

Arnold Wesker: Volume 4. (*The Journalists, The Wedding Feast, Shylock*). Harmondsworth Penguin, 1990.

Arnold Wesker: Volume 5. (*Yardsale, Whatever Happened to Betty Lemon?, Four Portraits—Of Mothers, The Mistress, Annie Wobbler*). Harmondsworth: Penguin, 1990.

Arnold Wesker: Volume 6. One More Ride on the Merry-Go-Round, Caritas, When God Wanted a Son, Lady Othello, Bluey). Harmondsworth: Penguin, 1990.

The Plays of Arnold Wesker: Volume 1. (*The Kitchen, Chicken Soup with Barley, Roots, I'm Talking about Jerusalem, Chips with Everything*). New York: Harper & Row, 1976.

The Plays of Arnold Wesker: Volume 2. (*Their Very Own and Golden City, The Friends, The Old Ones*). New York: Harper & Row, 1977.

The Wesker Trilogy. (*Chicken Soup with Barley, Roots, I'm Talking about Jerusalem*). London: Cape, 1960; New York: Random House, 1961.

Essays and Articles on Drama and Theatre

''Art and Action.'' *The Listener* (10 May 1962): 806–8.

''Art Is Not Enough.'' *Twentieth Century* 169 (1961): 190–94.

As Much as I Dare: An Autobiography (1932–1959). London: Century, 1994.

''Butterflies with Everything.'' *The Guardian* (9 Aug. 1972): 8.

''Casual Condemnations: A Brief Study of the Critic as Censor.'' *Theatre Quarterly* 2 (1971): 16–30.

''A Cretinue of Critics.'' *Drama* (winter 1972).

''Discovery.'' *Transatlantic Review* 5 (1960): 16–18.

''Debts to the Court.'' In *At the Royal Court: 25 Years of the English Stage Company*, ed. Richard Findlater. Oxford: Amber Lane Press, 1981.

''Extracts from a New York Journal Kept during Rehearsals of 'The Merchant.' ''In *A Night at the Theatre*. Ed. Ronald Harwood. London: Methuen, 1982.

''From a Writer's Notebook.'' *Theatre Quarterly* 6 (1972): 8–13.

''How to Cope with Criticism.'' *Plays and Players* (Dec. 1972): 18–19.

''Interpretation: to Impose or Explain.'' *Performing Arts Journal* 32 (1988): 62–76.

''An Interview with Arnold Wesker'' (with Walter Wager). *Playbill* (1964); rpt. in *The Playwrights Speak*, ed. Walter Wager. London: Longmans, 1969.

''A Journal of 'The Journalists.' '' *Theatre Quarterly* 26 (1977): 3–17.

''Let Battle Commence!'' *Encore* 5 (Sept.–Oct. 1958); rpt. in *The Encore Reader*, ed. Charles Marowitz, Tom Milne, and Owen Hale. London: Methuen, 1965.

''A Nasty Piece of Work.'' *Sunday Times* (6 June 1993): 9.2–3.

''The Nature of Theatre Dialogue.'' *New Theatre Quarterly* 8 (1986): 364–68.

''The Playwright as Director.'' *Plays and Players* (Feb. 1974): 10–12.

''So You Want to Write Plays.'' *The Observer* (18 Nov. 1984): 53.

''The Strange Affair of the Actors' Revolt.'' *Sunday Times* (30 Aug. 1981): 25–27.

''Wesker versus Taylor.'' *Plays and Players* (Nov. 1972): 22–25.

''Why I Fleshed out Shylock.'' *The Guardian* (29 Aug. 1981): 9.

Interviews

"Arnold Wesker: An Interview" (with Giles Gordon). *Transatlantic Review* 21 (1966): 15–25.

"Arnold Wesker and John Dexter" (with Ronald Hayman). *Transatlantic Review* 48 (1973–74): 89–99.

"From Merchant to Shylock" (with Mat Wolf). *City Limits* (12–19 Oct. 1989): 68.

"His Very Own and Golden City" (with Simon Trussler). *Tulane Drama Review* 11 (1966–67): 192–202; rpt. in *Theatre at Work*, ed. Charles Marowitz and Simon Trussler. New York: Hill & Wang, 1967.

"How We Met: Arnold Wesker and Dusty Wesker" (with Sue Fox). *Independent Sunday* (23 Oct. 1994): 72.

"If It Weren't for the Foreigners, I Should Be in Despair" (with Maureen Cleave). *Observer Magazine* (4 Oct. 1981): 35–39.

"An Interview with Arnold Wesker: Centre 42." *Encore* 9 (May–June 1962): 39–44.

"Interviews with Edward Bond and Arnold Wesker" (With Karl-Heinz Stoll). *Twentieth-Century Literature* 22 (1976): 422–32.

"On Playwriting: Interview with Arnold Wesker" (with Robert Skloot). *Performing Arts Journal* 2 (1978): 38–47.

"Play Rights" (with Nigel Lewis). *The Guardian* (18 June 1974): 12.

"Playwright to Watch" (with Laurence Kitchin). *Times* (21 Sept. 1959): 5; rpt. in Kitchin [2].

"A Sense of What Should Follow" (with Simon Trussler, Catherine Itzin, and Glenda Leeming). *Theatre Quarterly* 28 (1977): 5–24.

"The System and the Writer: Wesker Interviewed." *New Theatre Magazine* 11 (1971): 8–11.

SECONDARY BIBLIOGRAPHY

Adler, Thomas P. "*The Wesker Trilogy* Revisited: Games to Compensate for the Inadequacy of Words." *Quarterly Journal of Speech* 65 (1979): 429–38.

Aire, Sally. Review of *The Merchant*. *Plays and Players* (Dec. 1978): 28.

Alter, Iska. " 'Barbaric Laws, Barbaric Bonds': Arnold Wesker's *The Merchant*." *Modern Drama* 31.4 (Dec. 1988): 536–47.

Alvarez, A. "As We Like It." *New Statesman* (12 Sept. 1959): 304.

Andereth, Max. "Sartre and Wesker: Committee Playwrights." *Comment* 5 (July–Aug. 1964): 18–28.

Anderson, Michael. "Arnold Wesker: The Last Humanist?" *New Theatre Magazine* 8 (1968): 10–27.

Armistead, Claire. Review of *Yardsale/Whatever Happened to Betty Lemon? Plays and Players* (April 1987): 21.

Asquith, Ross. Review of *Annie Wobbler*. *The Observer* (18 Nov. 1984): 27.

Barber, John [1]. "Far-fetched Wesker." *Daily Telegraph* (8 Oct. 1981): 15.

———[2]. "Max Wall Bestrides Wesker's 'Old Ones.' " *Daily Telegraph* (9 Aug. 1972): 13.

———[3]. "Not the Best of Friends from Wesker." *Daily Telegraph* (20 May 1970): 16.

Barnes, Clive. "Shylock Revisited." *The Times* (3 Dec. 1977): 13.

Barnes, Philip. *A Companion to Post-war British Theatre.* London: Croom Helm, 1986.

"Belgians Present New Play by Arnold Wesker." *The Times* (10 Nov. 1965): 15.

"Best of the Trilogy: Mr Wesker's 'Roots.' " *The Times* (29 June 1960): 4.

Billington, Michael [1]. Review of *Annie Wobbler. The Guardian* (27 July 1983): 9.

————[2]. "Battle of the Refugees." *The Guardian* (9 June 1989).

————[3]. "The Old Ones at the Royal Court." *The Guardian* (9 Aug. 1972): 8.

————[4]. Review of *Roots. The Guardian* (9 May 1978): 8.

————[5]. "Wesker's Journalists." *The Guardian* (28 Mar. 1977): 8.

Bowering, Peter. "Wesker's Quest for Values." *Adam: International Review* 401–3 (1977–78): 69–85.

Brien, Alan [1]. "Chips off a New Block." *Sunday Telegraph* (6 May 1962): 10.

————[2]. Review of *The Four Seasons. Sunday Telegraph* (26 Sept. 1965): 12.

————[3]. "Own Golden Centre 42." *Sunday Telegraph* (22 May 1966): 12.

Brown, John Russell. *Theatre Language: A Study of Arden, Osborne, Pinter, and Wesker.* London: Allen Lane, 1972.

Bryden, Ronald [1]. "A Breeze of Inspiration." *The Observer* (22 May 1966): 24.

————[2]. "Wesker's Ritual of Atonement." *The Observer* (24 May 1970): 28.

Burrows, Jill. "Wesker's Angels." *Times Educational Supplement* (26 May 1989): B5.

Cave, Richard Allen. *New British Drama in Performance on the London Stage, 1970–1985.* Gerrards Cross: Colin Smythe, 1987.

Chaillet, Ned [1]. Review of *Caritas. The Times* (8 Oct. 1981): 12.

————[2]. Review of *The Merchant. The Times* (17 Oct. 1978): 10.

Chambers, Colin, and Mike Prior. *Playwright's Progress: Patterns of Postwar British Drama.* Oxford: Amber Lane Press, 1987.

Colvin, Clare. Review of *Annie Wobbler. Plays and Players* (Jan. 1985): 38.

Coppieters, Frank. "Arnold Wesker's Centre Forty-two: A Cultural Revolution Betrayed." *Theatre Quarterly* 18 (1975): 37–54.

Costello, Tom. "The Defeat of Naturalism in Arnold Wesker's *Roots.*" *Modern Drama* 21.1 (Mar. 1978): 39–46.

Coult, Tony. Review of *The Wedding Feast. Plays and Players* (Mar. 1977): 30–31.

Coveney, Michael [1]. Review of *Beorhtel's Hill. Financial Times* (9 June 1989): 21.

————[2]. Review of *Caritas. Financial Times* (8 Oct. 1981): 21.

————[3]. "Hot Pots of Desire." *The Observer* (27 Feb. 1994): 10–11.

Cushman, Robert. Review of *Caritas. The Observer* (11 Oct. 1981): 29.

de Jongh, Nicholas [1]. Review of *I'm Talking about Jerusalem. The Guardian* (13 June 1978): 8.

————[2]. "In the Wake of Love." *The Guardian* (19 Feb. 1987): 10.

Dexter, John [1]. "Working with Arnold." *Plays and Players* (Apr. 1962): 11.

————[2]. "Chips and Devotion." *Plays and Players* (Dec. 1962): 32.

Eder, Richard. Review of *The Merchant. New York Times* (17 Nov. 1977).

Esslin, Martin [1]. Review of *The Four Seasons. Plays and Players* (Nov. 1965): 40–41.

————[2]. "Wesker's Visionary." *Plays and Players* (July 1966): 12, 57.

Everitt, Anthony. Review of *The Merchant. Birmingham Post* (13 Oct. 1978): 6.

Fay, Gerard [1]. "A Taste of Wesker." *The Guardian* (9 June 1960): 7.

————[2]. "Words Fail Wesker." *The Guardian* (29 July 1960): 7.

Fenton, James [1]. Review of *Annie Wobbler. Sunday Times* (10 July 1983): 41.

————[2]. "Arnold's History Lesson." *Sunday Times* (11 Oct. 1981): 40.

Findlater, Richard. "Plays and Politics." *The Twentieth Century* 168 (1960): 235–42.

Gilliatt, Penelope. "Wesker's Whoppers." *The Observer* (26 Sept. 1965): 24.

Goodman, Henry. "The New Dramatists: 2. Arnold Wesker." *Drama Survey* 1 (1961): 215–22.

"Guest Play at Royal Court: Study of Family Weakness." *The Times* (15 July 1958): 5.

Hamilton, Peter. Review of *Chips with Everything*. *Plays and Players* (July 1962): 23, 50.

Hart, D. J. Review of *The Wedding Feast*. *Birmingham Post* (6 June 1980): 4.

Hayman, Ronald. *Arnold Wesker*. 3rd. ed. London: Heinemann, 1979.

Hobson, Harold [1]. "Author and Actress." *Sunday Times* (5 July 1959): 12.

————[2]. Review of *Chips with Everything*. *Sunday Times* (29 Apr. 1962): 41.

————[3]. Review of *The Four Seasons*. *Sunday Times* (26 Sept. 1965): 45.

Hope-Wallace, Philip [1]. Review of *Chips with Everything*. *The Guardian* (28 Apr. 1962): 5.

————[2]. Review of *The Four Seasons*. *The Guardian* (22 Sept. 1965): 9.

————[3]. "New Wesker Play." *The Guardian* (20 May 1966): 9.

Hurren, Kenneth. Review of *The Old Ones*. *The Spectator* (19 Aug. 1972): 291–92.

Innes, Christopher. *Modern British Drama, 1890–1990*. Cambridge: Cambridge University Press, 1992.

Itzin, Catherine [1]. "A Sense of Dread and Isolation." *Tribune* (13 Oct. 1978): 8–9.

————[2]. *Stages in the Revolution: Political Theatre in Britain since 1968*. London: Eyre Methuen, 1980.

Jackson, Peter [1]. Review of *Chicken Soup with Barley*. *Plays and Players* (Sept. 1958): 11.

————[2]. Review of *Roots*. *Plays and Players* (Aug. 1959): 15.

Jones, A. R. "The Theatre of Arnold Wesker." *Critical Quarterly* 2 (1960): 366–70.

Jones, D.A.N. "Arnold and the Unions." *New Statesman* (27 May 1966): 785.

Kellaway, Kate. "Travelling Players." *The Observer* (30 Oct. 1988): 43.

Kemp, Peter. "Basildon Bondage." *The Independent* (9 June 1989): 18.

Kenshaw, John. *The Present Stage: New Directions in the Theatre Today*. London: Collins, 1966.

Kingston, Jeremy. "Wesker Double Bill." *The Times* (19 Feb. 1987): 17.

Kitchin, Lawrence [1]. "Drama with a Message: Arnold Wesker." In *Experimental Drama*. ed. William A. Armstrong. London: Bell, 1963.

————[2]. *Mid-Century Drama*. 2nd. ed. London: Faber & Faber, 1962.

Kleinberg, Robert. "Seriocomedy in *The Wesker Trilogy*." *Educational Theatre Journal* 21.1 (Mar. 1969): 36–40.

Kustow, Michael. "Wesker at the Half-way House." *Plays and Players* (Oct. 1973): 32–35.

Latham, Jacqueline. "*Roots*: A Reassessment." *Modern Drama* 8.1 (Mar. 1965): 192–97.

Lee, Jennie. "Wesker's 'Centre 42.' " *Encounter* 19 (1962): 95–96.

Leech, Clifford. "Two Romantics: Arnold Wesker and Harold Pinter." *Contemporary Theatre*. Ed. John Russell Brown and Bernard Harris. Stratford-upon-Avon Studies 4. London: Arnold, 1962.

Leeming, Glenda [1]. *Arnold Wesker*. Writers and Their Work Series. London: Longmans, 1972.

————[2]. ''Articulacy and Awareness: The Modulations of Familiar Themes in Wesker's Plays of the 70s.'' In *Contemporary English Drama*, ed. C.W.E. Bigsby. Stratford-upon-Avon Studies 19. London: Arnold, 1981.

————[3]. ed. *Wesker on File*. London: Methuen, 1985.

————[4]. *Wesker the Playwright*. London: Methuen, 1983.

Leeming, Glenda, and Simon Trussler. *The Plays of Arnold Wesker: An Assessment*. London: Gollancz, 1971.

Lemmon, David. ''Reading between the Lines.'' *The Guardian* (18 Oct. 1989): 41.

Levin, Bernard [1]. Review of *Love Letters on Blue Paper*. *Sunday Times* (19 Feb. 1978): 37.

————[2]. Review of *The Merchant*. *Sunday Times* (15 Oct. 1978): 35.

————[3]. Review of *The Trilogy*. *Sunday Times* (18 June 1978): 38.

————[4]. Review of *The Wedding Feast*. *Sunday Times* (23 Jan. 1977): 39.

Lloyd Evans, Gareth [1]. *The Language of Modern Drama*. London: Dent, 1977.

————[2]. ''A Step towards the Sink.'' *The Guardian* (20 June 1961): 9.

''Love without the Social Pressures.'' *The Times* (11 Sept. 1965): 10.

Mander, John. *The Writer and Commitment*. London: Secker & Warburg, 1961.

Mannheimer, Monica [1]. ''Major Themes in Arnold Wesker's Play *The Friends*.'' *Moderna Sprak* 66 (1972): 109–16.

————[2]. ''Ordering Chaos: ''The Genesis of Arnold Wesker's *The Friends*.'' *English Studies* 56 (1975): 34–44.

Marcus, Frank. Review of *The Friends*. *Sunday Times* (28 Apr. 1962): 4.

Matheson, T. P. Review of *The Wedding Feast*. *Times Literary Supplement* (20 June 1980): 704.

McKee, Victoria. Review of *Chips with Everything*. *Birmingham Post* (3 Apr. 1981): 6.

Morgan, Marjory M. ''Arnold Wesker: The Celebratory Instinct.'' In *Essays on Contemporary British Drama*, ed. Hedwig Bock and Albert Wertheim. Munchen: Max Hueber Verlag, 1981.

Nightingale, Benedict [1]. ''Liftoff.'' *New Statesman* (28 Jan. 1977): 131.

————[2]. ''Those Were the Days.'' *New Statesman* (16 June 1978): 827.

————[3]. ''Wartlessness.'' *New Statesman* (24 Feb. 1978): 266.

————[4]. ''Wesker in the West End.'' *The Times* (24 Feb. 1994): 35.

————[5]. ''Wesker in the Wilderness.'' *New Statesman* (29 May 1970): 780.

O'Connor, Gary. ''Production Casebook No. 2: Arnold Wesker's 'The Friends.' '' *Theatre Quarterly* 2 (1971): 78–92.

Page, Malcolm. ''Whatever Happened to Arnold Wesker? His Recent Plays.'' *Modern Drama* 11 (1968): 317–25.

Peter, John [1]. Review *Annie Wobbler*. *Sunday Times* (25 Nov. 1984): 40.

————[2]. Review *Beorhtel's Hill*. *Sunday Times* (11 June 1989): C8.

————[3]. ''Nurturing the Natural Fruits of Comic Roots.'' *Sunday Times* (12 Feb. 1989): C9.

————[4]. Review *The Wedding Feast*. *Sunday Times* (15 June 1980): 41.

''Play with New and Good Idea: The Virtue of Mr. Wesker's 'Roots.' '' *The Times* (1 July 1959): 15.

Rabey, David Ian. *British and Irish Political Drama in the Twentieth Century*. Basingstoke: Macmillan, 1986.

Ribalow, Harold U. *Arnold Wesker*. New York: Twayne, 1965.

Rissik, Andrew. "Very Shallow Roots: Wesker Double Bill." *The Independent* (19 Feb. 1987): 12.

Roberts, Peter [1]. Review of *Chips with Everything*. *Plays and Players* (July 1962): 20–21.

———[2]. Review of *I'm Talking about Jerusalem*. *Plays and Players* (Sept. 1960): 11.

———[3]. Review of *The Kitchen*. *Plays and Players* (Aug. 1961): 13.

———[4]. Review of *Roots*. *Plays and Players* (Aug. 1960): 15.

Roper, David. Review of *Caritas*. *Plays and Players* (Jan. 1982): 32–33.

Rothberg, Abraham. "East End, West End: Arnold Wesker." *Southwest Review* 52 (1967): 368–78.

Say, Rosemary. Review of *The Old Ones*. *Sunday Telegraph* (13 Aug. 1972): 14.

Scott, Michael. *Shakespeare and the Modern Dramatist*. 2nd. ed. Basingstoke: Macmillan, 1994.

Seymour, Alan. "Wesker Undefeated." *The Observer* (13 Aug. 1972): 25.

Shrimpton, Nicholas. Review of *Caritas*. *Times Literary Supplement* (16 Oct. 1981): 1203.

"Split between Vision and Reality." *The Times* (20 May 1966): 8.

Stevens, Mary. "Wesker's The Wesker Trilogy." *The Explicator* 43.3 (1985): 45–48.

Taylor, John Russell [1]. *Anger and After: A Guide to the New British Drama*. 2nd. ed. London: Methuen, 1969.

———[2]. Review of *The Friends*. *Plays and Players* (July 1970): 46.

"The Trilogy Completed." *The Times* (28 July 1960): 5.

Tynan, Kenneth [1]. Review of *Chicken Soup with Barley*. *The Observer* (12 June 1960): 24.

———[2]. "The Chip on the Shoulder." *The Observer* (6 May 1962): 27.

———[3]. "The Genealogy of Arnold Wesker." *The Observer* (2 July 1961): 22.

———[4]. Review of *I'm Talking about Jerusalem*. *The Observer* (31 July 1960): 19.

———[5]. "The Under-Belly of Laughter." *The Observer* (3 July 1960): 25.

———[6]. *A View of the English Stage*. St. Albans: Paladin, 1976.

Walker, J.K.L. Review of *Yardsale/Whatever Happened to Betty Lemon?* *Times Literary Supplement* (27 Feb. 1987): 214.

Wandor, Michelene [1]. Review of *Annie Wobbler*. *Plays and Players* (Oct. 1983): 38–39.

———[2]. *Look Back in Gender: Sexuality and the Family in Post-war British Drama*. London: Methuen, 1987.

Wardle, Irving [1]. "Battling on into Senility." *The Times* (9 Aug. 1972): 10.

———[2]. "Just What Wesker Wanted: Roots." *The Times* (9 May 1978): 16.

———[3]. Review of *Love Letters on Blue Paper*. *The Times* (16 Feb. 1978): 9.

———[4]. "Muzzling the Cynic: *Chicken Soup with Barley*." *The Times* (4 Apr. 1978): 13.

———[5]. Review of *The Wedding Feast*. *The Times* (21 Jan. 1977): 13.

———[6]. "Wesker in Sheffield." *The Observer* (6 May 1962): 27.

Wellwarth, George E. *The Theatre of Protest and Paradox: Developments in the Avant-Garde Drama*. London: MacGibbon & Kee, 1965.

Whitehead, Ted. "Missus' Art." *The Spectator* (25 Feb. 1978): 25.

Wilcher, Robert. *Understanding Arnold Wesker*. Columbia: University of South Carolina Press, 1991.

Worsley, T. C. [1]. Review of *Chicken Soup with Barley*. *New Statesman* (19 July 1958): 82.

———[2]. Review of *Chips with Everything*. *Financial Times* (30 Apr. 1962): 5.

Worth, Katharine J. *Revolutions in Modern English Drama*. London: Bell, 1972.

Zimmermann, Heinz. ''Wesker and Utopia in the Sixties.'' *Modern Drama* 29 (1986): 185–206.

BIBLIOGRAPHY

King, Kimball. ''Arnold Wesker.'' *Twenty Modern British Playwrights: A Bibliography, 1956 to 1976*. New York: Garland, 1977: 241–68.

Hugh Whitemore

(1936–)

WALTER H. PLACZEK

Hugh Whitemore was born 16 June 1936 in Tunbridge Wells, England. In his youth he was educated at the Judd School in Tunbridge Wells and the King Edward VI School in Southhampton. He graduated from the Royal Academy of Dramatic Art in 1958 with initial ambitions to become an actor.

Although Whitemore has written five successful works for the stage since 1977, television and film work grounds his reputation as a writer. Author and adaptor of over thirty-five works for television, he has won numerous awards throughout his career. Television credits include British Writers Guild Awards for best television dramatization for *Cider with Rosie* (1971), based upon Laurie Lee's novel about rural life in the Cotswold valley during the 1920s, and *Breeze Antsey* (1972), part of the *Country Matters* series. He has won Emmy awards for best foreign television series for *Horrible Conspiracies* (1971) and *Concealed Enemies* (1984). The former focused upon the political intrigue surrounding the execution of Mary, Queen of Scots, while the latter, part of the PBS *American Playhouse* series, depicts events surrounding the trials of Alger Hiss and the actions of the House Un-American Activities Committee during the late 1940s. Film credits include the 1982 film *Return of the Soldier*, based on the Rebecca West novel that deals with a soldier's amnesia caused by traumatic experiences during World War I, and the 1987 adaptation of Helen Hanff's novel *84 Charing Cross Road*, which examines the long-distance friendship of a lonely American woman writer and a British seller of rare literary works.

Hugh Whitemore's stage career consists of five plays, all of which have been produced in London's West End and four of which have had subsequent New York productions. *Stevie, Pack of Lies, Breaking the Code,* and *The Best of*

Friends were performed on both sides of the Atlantic. His most recent play, *It's Ralph*, did not receive a New York production.

   Selected Biographical Sources: Bull; Huebl; Whitemore, "Interview."

MAJOR PLAYS AND PREMIERES:
THEATRICAL RECEPTION

Stevie. 1977. Opened in London at the Vaudeville Theatre, 23 March, closed 25 October. Opened in New York at Manhattan Theatre Club, 18 February 1979, for twenty performances.

   Set in a North London home, this work illustrates the life of the poetess Stevie Smith (1902–1971). Smith, who never married, lived with an elderly aunt (known as the "Lion Aunt") for most of her adult life. While these two characters form the focal point of the play, a male actor binds the work together through narration and portrayal of a number of male figures (such as a newspaper reporter and fiancé) who came in and out of Smith's life. The play incorporates much of Smith's poetry, which has been described as idiosyncratic and shifting in tone; as Anthony Smith writes in *The Oxford Companion to 20th-Century Poetry in English*, Smith's work was characterized by "quick changes of tone, abrupt veerings between comic and tragic, absurd and solemn, and a range of lyrical, satirical, discursive, and flippant modes."

   For the play, Whitemore did extensive interviews with colleagues of Smith and utilized many real-life incidents that had been related to him. Critics found the play engaging. Itzin deemed the play "remarkable," while Curtis found it "hard to explain why the piece is so moving"—and thought perhaps it lies in the fascination of seeing a woman of exceptional gifts encased in a mask of ordinariness." Gussow [1] commented that the play is "modest, low-key . . . and one that is not without its rewards." London critics also deemed exceptional praise upon Glenda Jackson in the title role, while Roberta Maxwell also garnered praise for Jackson's portrayal in the New York production.

Pack of Lies. 1983. Originally presented at the Theatre Royal, Brighton, 11 October. Opened in London at the Lyric Theatre, 26 October. Closed 15 September 1984, after 367 performances. Opened in New York at the Royale Theatre, 11 February 1985. Closed 25 May 1985, after 120 performances.

   Whitemore originally dramatized these historical events in a less-fictionalized, more documentary fashion in the 1971 television script *Act of Betrayal*. The play, which occurs in the London suburb of Ruislip in late 1960 and early 1961, is based upon the true story of Helen and Peter Kroger, a seemingly ordinary suburban couple who were, in fact, spies for the Soviet Union. The play depicts, in a series of realistic scenes connected by direct monologues to the audience, how British intelligence monitors the activities of the Krogers from the home of the Jacksons, their next-door neighbors and best friends. The script focuses on the Jacksons as they attempt to deal with the emotional challenges represented by the conflict between loyalty to their friends and the demands of the state. Critics received the work in a basically positive manner. Wardle suggested that ''the very banality of the story gives it a moral force beyond the scope of the most sensational plot,'' while Barnes [1] found the play ''absolutely engrossing.'' However, critics also suggested that the play was generally slow in starting (most of the early scenes are of domestic life prior to the arrival of British intelligence and establish relationships rather than advance the storyline) and had mixed reactions to the intermittent monologues. Some found the monologues to be intrusive and distracting from the realistic style of the piece; while others suggested they served a vital function through illuminating character and setting the dramatic rhythm.

Breaking the Code. 1986. Originally presented at the Yvonne Arnaud Theatre in Guildford, 15 September. Opened in London at the Theatre Royal, Haymarket, 21 October. Subsequently moved to the Comedy, London, 17 June 1987. Closed 4 September 1987. Opened in New York at the Neil Simon Theatre, 15 November 1987. Closed 10 April 1988, after 161 performances.

The play is based upon the book *Alan Turing, The Enigma* by Andrew Hodges. In a series of interconnected short scenes that flow back and forth in time, the play reveals the life of Alan Turing, the mathematical genius who deciphered a key German code during World War II but was later arrested and forced to undergo medical treatment for his homosexual tendencies; he subsequently committed suicide in 1954 at the age of forty-two. Reviews of both the London and New York productions were mixed. Critics tended to find the play flawed, suggesting the work was talky and lacked a cohesive dramatic line. Rich [2] commented that the ''play's talkiness, glibness, and stubborn resistance to the grand dramatic gesture are readily apparent.'' All, however, went out of their way to give high praise to the performance of Derek Jacobi, who played Turing on both sides of the Atlantic. Hirschhorn wrote that ''were it not for Jacobi's own particular genius for making the most out of the least, the evening would barely have justified its existence as drama.'' Wilson [2] suggested, ''Many of the play's shortcomings . . . are successfully camouflaged by the performances of Mr. Jacobi and his colleagues.''

The Best of Friends. 1988. Opened in London at the Apollo Theatre, 10 February. Closed 23 April 1988. Opened in New York at the Westside Theatre, 7 March 1993. Closed 11 April 1993, after sixty-one performances.

The work is based upon the letters passed back and forth over a twenty-five-year span between the playwright George Bernard Shaw, Sir Sydney Cockerell, who was director of the Fitzwilliam Museum in Cambridge, and Dame Laurentia McLachlan, a nun who eventually became abbess at Stanbrook Abbey in Worcestershire. Reviews of the London production tended to focus less upon the work itself, which was drawn, in most cases, word for word from the numerous correspondence that passed between the three parties, and more upon the acting, particularly of Sir John Gielgud as Cockerell, who, at age eighty-three at the time of the production, had already entered the legends of British acting. As Ratcliffe [1] states, the play's "main purpose is to bring Sir John Gielgud back to the London stage after nearly an absence of 10 years, and for this it is warmly welcome." The other actors—Rosemary Harris and Ray McNally—also received high praise. The majority of critics found the script to be static, claiming that the work lacked a definitive and cohesive story line; the production received praise, however, for the fact that the evening permitted rich characterizations of vibrant historical figures to emerge from three outstanding performers.

It's Ralph. 1991. Originally presented at Theatre Royal, Brighton, 11 October. Opened in London at the Comedy Theatre, 28 October. Closed 28 December.

This play represents the only Whitemore stage work not based on historical characters or incidents. Andrew, an egotistical journalist, and Claire, his younger second wife, are startled at their weekend country estate by the arrival of Ralph, a friend from Andrew's past. Past secrets and intrigues slowly unravel until the unexpected death of Ralph. Critics highlighted the shift from an initial light and comic tone to one of personal despair and desperation. Spencer wrote, "It's a curious play, because the stock situations of stage comedy . . . are mixed with more serious themes." Most critics found this change distracting and the play unfocused in theme and concept. Morley wrote, Whitemore's "writing is often savagely funny but it is also oddly ill-focused, so entire scenes drift around in search of a purpose or a punch line." Timothy West received high praise for his portrayal of Andrew.

ASSESSMENT OF WHITEMORE'S CAREER

No formal critical work has been done to evaluate Whitemore as a playwright. The two productions that have received the majority of public attention stem from the actors involved: Derek Jacobi, who played Alan Turing in both the London and New York productions of *Breaking the Code*, and Sir John Gielgud as Sir Sydney Cockerell in *The Best of Friends*.

Several areas for formal exploration are possible. Since four of Whitemore's five stage works are based upon actual figures and incidents, an evaluation would be in order of how Whitemore adapts and utilizes historical material on the stage. This critical assessment would be insightful, since Whitemore integrates actual documents—the poetry of Smith, the speeches of Turing, the letters between Shaw, Cockerell, and McLachlan—into his plays. An analysis of Whitemore's dramatic methods would be valuable, since his plays do not represent strict linear realism but rather, incorporate a diversity of techniques such as the insertion of poetry into *Stevie*, the direct audience address in *Pack of Lies*, and the temporal shifting of *Breaking the Code*. This analysis could serve to explicate the overall impression of the production reviews that suggest that Whitemore's plays often emphasize character development rather than a singular, forward movement of action. As a unit Whitemore's plays often engage social questions; an investigation of the broader themes that run along the totality of his work (such as the function of genius within the social order, or the conflict between the state and individual conscience) would prove useful. Since he began writing for British and American television long before writing for the stage, one might explore his television career to compare thematic and structural approaches between his work in the different genres particularly since, like his plays, much of his television work is based upon historical events.

PRIMARY BIBLIOGRAPHY

Plays

The Best of Friends. Oxford: Amber Lane Press, 1988.
Breaking the Code. Oxford: Amber Lane Press, 1987; New York: Samuel French, 1988.
It's Ralph. Oxford: Amber Lane Press, 1991.
Pack of Lies. Oxford: Amber Lane Press, 1983; New York: Samuel French, 1985.
Stevie. London: Samuel French, 1977; Oxford: Amber Lane Press, 1984.

Essays on Drama and Theatre

Foreword. *Pack of Lies*. By Whitemore. New York: Samuel French, 1983: 7–8.
Foreword. *Stevie*. By Whitemore. Oxford: Amber Lane Press, 1983: 7–12.
Introduction. *The Best of Friends*. By Whitemore. Oxford: Amber Lane Press, 1987: 7–9.

Interview

Contemporary Authors. Vol. 132. Detroit: Gale Research, 1991: 459–61.

SECONDARY BIBLIOGRAPHY

Barnes, Clive [1]. "Pack of Lies' Revives Broadway." *New York Post* (12 Feb. 1985).
———[2]. "What He Didn't Compute." *New York Post* (16 Nov. 1987).
Berman, Paul. Review of *Pack of Lies*. *Nation* (23 Mar. 1985): 343–45.
Bull, John. "Hugh Whitemore." In *Contemporary Dramatists,* ed. D. L. Kirkpatrick. 4th ed. London: St. James Press, 1988: 563–64.
Curtis, Anthony. Review of *Stevie*. *Drama* (summer 1977): 57.
Edwards, Christopher. Review of *Pack of Lies*. *Drama* (1984): 36.
Gordon, Giles. Review of *The Best of Friends*. *Drama* (1988): 32.
Göranzon, Bo. "Eigmakoden." *Entré* 18 (1991): 29–32.
Gussow, Mel [1]. "Childlike Poet." *New York Times* (19 Feb. 1979): C16.
———[2]. "A Drama Undramatized, or Keeping 'Code' Secret." *New York Times* (3 Dec. 1987).
Hirschhorn, Clive. Review of *Breaking the Code*. *Sunday Express* (26 Oct. 1986).

Huebl, Katherine. "Hugh Whitemore." In *Contemporary Authors*. Vol. 132. Detroit: Gale Research, 1991: 458–59.

Itzin, Catherine. "Stevie." *Plays and Players* (May 1977): 26–27.

Kissel, Howard. "A Tale of Hearts and Minds." *New York Daily News* (16 Nov. 1987).

Morley, Sheridan. Review of *It's Ralph. Herald Tribune* (30 Oct. 1991).

Nightingale, Benedict. Review of *It's Ralph. The Times* (30 Oct. 1991): 20.

Oliver, Edith. "Miss Smith and Miss Maxwell." *New Yorker* (26 Feb. 1979): 78, 80.

Ratcliffe, Michael [1]. Review of *The Best of Friends. The Observer* (14 Feb. 1988).

———[2]. Review of *Breaking the Code. Drama* (1988): 32.

Rich, Frank [1]. " 'Pack of Lies' at the Royale." *New York Times* (12 Feb. 1985): C13.

———[2]. "Stage: 'Breaking the Code.' " *New York Times* (16 Nov. 1987).

———[3]. "Stage: John Gielgud Stars in London Play." *New York Times* (12 Feb. 1988): C3.

Spencer, Charles. Review of *It's Ralph. Daily Telegraph* (30 Oct. 1991).

Suavage, Leo. "Pick of the Pack." *New Leader* (14–28 Jan. 1985): 18–19.

Simon, John. "Stevie's Little Wonders." *New York Magazine* (12 Mar. 1979): 74–75.

Trewin, J. C. "Gielgud's Great Career." *Drama* (1988): 9–11.

Wardle, Irving. "Torment of Spies Best Friends." *The Times* (27 Oct. 1983): 13.

Wilson, Edwin [1]. "Drama: Lies and Spies." *Wall Street Journal* (14 Feb. 1985).

———[2]. "The Tragedy of Alan Turing." *Wall Street Journal* (20 Nov. 1987).

Zoglin, Richard. "A Bizarre Political Mystery." *Time* (7 May 1984): 108.

John Whiting
(1917–1963)

THOMAS T. APPLE

Today when John Whiting's work is recalled by nonspecialists, *The Devils* (1961), his dramatization of Aldous Huxley's *The Devils of Loudon*, seems to be the reason. Ken Russell's film of the play partly accounts for that, since productions of the play itself have been few and far between. Whiting's other, better plays—*The Conditions of Agreement* and *Saint's Day* (1984), *A Penny for a Song* (1950), and *Marching Song* (1952)—met with serious disapproval at their first performances and have seldom been enacted since. Nonetheless, Whiting secured real support, both practical and sympathetic, from people very important in the English theatre, people who viewed and still view him as a first-rate writer. He makes too obscure a part of the current English-speaking theatre largely because of his initial reception on the commercial stages. Some recent scholarship has successfully attempted to explain this anomaly in Whiting's reputation and in so doing claim him as a compelling but mostly unrecognized voice that deserves to be re-produced.

The son of an army officer, Whiting was born in Salisbury on 15 November 1917, as World War I reached its most inhuman stage. He entered the Royal Academy of Dramatic Art in 1934, graduating three years later and then joining various repertory companies; his break into the theatre came through acting, something that may partially heighten the theatricality of his dramas. He then served in the anti-aircraft artillery during World War II, despite his initial pacifism, and was discharged in 1944 due to ''nervous debility'' (Salmon [1], 17). In 1940, while in the army, he married Asthore Lloyd Mawson; they would have two sons and two daughters. Whiting's death of cancer on 16 June 1963, ironically took place during the last phase of Britain's postwar decline in cultural and political prestige and power, caused largely in part by the events of both wars. His life as a practicing playwright, roughly 1946–1961, was an embattled one, constituted of at least three powerful texts powerfully denied their proper stature by both producer and public. If we assume that a writer necessarily responds to social as well as personal conditions, then Whiting's lifetime offered an unusually disturbed pattern of human thought and action, general and specific.

Selected Biographical Sources: Hayman [1]; Lucas; "John Whiting: An Interview"; Salmon [1]; Slater; Trussler [2].

MAJOR PLAYS, PREMIERES, AND SIGNIFICANT REVIVALS: THEATRICAL RECEPTION

Saint's Day. 1948. Winner of the play competition in the Arts Theatre Festival of Britain, 1948. Produced by Arts Theatre, London, directed by Stephen Murray. Revived by Stratford East in 1965, directed by David Jones.

Barber found the play incomprehensible. Hobson thought the world of the play a "universe of grotesques, and for that reason uninteresting." Only theatre people like Peter Brook, Tyrone Guthrie, and John Gielgud believed that *Saint's Day* was, in Gielgud's words, "moving, beautiful and fascinating." Its initial naturalistic tone shifts into surrealism, the characters undergo jarring development, and the play requires of the audience an imaginative effort of an untimely kind. Innes sees the play as a precursor of *Waiting for Godot.*

A Penny for a Song. 1949. Produced by Tennent Productions at the Haymarket Theatre, London, directed by Peter Brook. Thirty-six performances. Revived in a rewritten version in 1962 at the Aldwych, London, directed by Colin Graham.

Baxter found *Penny* "not a play, a comedy or even a farce . . . [but] a superbly mounted . . . rag—fifth form without the excuse of adolescence." Worsley [2] discovered "no play here . . . [but rather] a series of charades." This historical drama imagines the unheroic acts of persons outside heroic circumstances who nonetheless wish to be heroes, whether large- or small-scale. Love and war meet eccentricity, and the English gentry meet the coming of Napoleon's reputation, not the Emperor himself.

Marching Song. 1952. Opened at St. Martin's Theatre, London, directed by Frith Branbury. Forty-three performances.

Unlike most, *The Times* critic (Review of *Marching Song*) found the play "refreshingly sincere . . . an evening of genuine tension . . . more intellectual than dramatic. . . . Mr Whiting appears more interested in ideas than in people." Typically, *Marching Song* impressed itself as "the author's failure to work out his position in adequately human or adequately philosophical terms." Whiting here tries to represent the internal contradictions of personality, the conflict between self and duty, and the necessary incompatibility of affairs of the heart and affairs of the state. All these characters are caught at the point where idea and action cannot be reconciled, where a species of inhuman action must be taken—or refused—by a human being in order to remain human. Whiting believed this play to be antitheatrical insofar as it addresses the relatively static and unresolvable dilemma of circumstantial personal freedom.

The Devils. 1961. Produced at the Aldwych Theatre, London, 20 February, commissioned for the National Theatre by Peter Hall and directed by Peter Wood. Premiered in New York, 1965, Broadway Theatre, directed by Michael Cacoyannis.

Tynan [2] held the play to be a treatment of ''a squalid footnote to the history of superstition . . . dignified beyond its deserts by an extremely gifted dramatist.'' Craig endorsed the stature of the playwright: ''Mr Whiting makes the best of our playwrights since the war seem mere byways in the drama.'' Of the New York production Kerr wrote that *''The Devils* is a play of massive height and width and no depth at all.'' Yet again, Whiting subjects his audience to extreme emotional and intellectual ambiguity, although the drama uncharacteristically ends in moments of clear moralizing. Father Grandier's tortured life ends in torture and ends because of it; the resemblance between self-inflicted wounds and socially imposed ones finally breaks down, leaving us to wonder how many kinds of devils there are. The play unfolds episodically, cinematically, with many minor characters and fast-paced shifts in setting (Hayman [1]).

The Conditions of Agreement. 1965 (written 1948). Opened at the Bristol Old Vic Little Theatre, directed by Christopher Denys.

In response to this production, Wardle wrote: ''If any play of [Whiting's] pre-figures the comedy of menace . . . it is this unknown early piece. . . . The affinity with Pinter is . . . close.'' The gratuitous urges of self-delusion and its tendency to make others suffer are dramatized here, with every character limited by false drives and incomplete self-knowledge. The disquieting plot is left unresolved, insofar as the characters' motivations remain finally mysterious and the play seems without point.

ADDITIONAL PLAYS, ADAPTATIONS, AND PRODUCTIONS

No More A-Roving (1946); *The Gates of Summer* (1953, produced at Oxford University in 1956, directed by Peter Hall); *No Why* (1957, commissioned by Peter Hall, produced in 1964, directed by John Schlesinger); *A Walk in the Desert* (1959, produced by the BBC in 1960, directed by Naomi Capon); *No Man* (1958–1961), rewritten in part as *The Nomads* but never produced in either version.

ASSESSMENT OF WHITING'S CAREER

Whiting's career is apparently not a typical one. He enjoyed little conventional success in the theatre, even withdrawing from it for some years—roughly, 1953–1960—to earn a living writing screenplays for mostly second-rate films. His last play, *The Devils*, secured a certain high regard, but by then his life, let alone his career, was nearly finished. And since the mid-1960s Whiting's plays have been, as suggested above, rarely produced, despite the enhancement of his reputation through the work, principally, of Ronald Hayman.

Yet the intrinsic theatricality of Whiting's plays motivated directors of the stature of Peter Hall, Peter Brook, Stephen Murray, Peter Wood, and John Schlesinger to undertake their original production; that is the qualities of the scripts won the deep attention of some of the persons directly involved in sustaining English theatre during the 1950s and 1960s. On the ground that the divergence of opinion between the money-making theatre and theatre per se means something, four plays, especially, deserve to be reread and judged anew: *The Conditions of Agreement, Saint's Day, A Penny for a Song,* and *The Devils*.

As Dickey observes, and Whiting himself claimed, it is not the artist's work to explain his art post facto, but merely to present it in the first place. This is an unaccommodating view and typifies a distinctly postwar, if not postmodern, attitude to playwriting. Paradoxically, although Whiting refused to concern himself with prewar values—the past, as theatre-goers would have it—he nonetheless embedded his dramatic actions in a fictional past. We are more in the presence of human beings per se than some aggregation of sentimentalized types; behavior is thought to stem directly from personal and social experience rather than from any set of innate qualities of character. Whiting serves, therefore, as a transitional figure in more than one sense: not only do his plays bridge the stylistic development from the poeticism of Fry and Eliot to the militantly prosaic social drama of Harold Pinter and Arnold Wesker, but they mark the passage from drawing-room comedy, romance, and melodrama to a kind of existentialism. Salmon [1] even suggests the Whiting's dramatic vision "sees the spirit of life as divided against itself, permanently and irrecoverably."

Moreover, despite his attempts to give voice to common human concerns, Whiting's patrician values were in conflict with the increasingly dominant "leveling" tendency of the 1950s and 1960s. He wished also to counter what he saw as the habitual and uncritical emotionalism of the new drama, the unthoughtful inarticulations, the too ambiguous silences, the calculatedly inexplicable menace.

One would expect a playwright's first well-finished play to exhibit most of the hallmarks of the work as a whole and to deal with ongoing themes according to a pattern that becomes more or less established. *The Conditions of Agreement* fulfills the expectations. Behind the facade lies not truth but a counterfacade, and beneath every surface motive an ulterior motive can be found. We make ourselves believe that something is the case, or that someone is a certain kind of being, and whether or not the reality supports our belief, we believe it anyway. People are crippled by the past—some physically, some emotionally, some spiritually, some intellectually. Of these, the closest bond seems to be, if the world of *Conditions* is taken as representative, between emotional and intellectual incapacity.

Whiting offers no adequate reason for any character's action, and when the torture ends in general indifference, no cause is given for that either. The play works against our expectations of setting, character, and motive, providing little in the way of conventional cause and effect and suspending us between the ultimate inconsequentiality of the events in the Doon home and its ominous atmosphere. Since that atmosphere partakes of the rationalizing of the irrational by way of personal history and private desire, *Conditions* is disquieting. The unfolding of the quite modest plot proceeds against the grain of the quite im-modest character development, and the kind of resolution implied by events never comes. By the time of *The Devils*, Whiting will again seize on an instance of torture to represent human interaction, and so square the circle of his dramatic concerns. But the latter-day torture proceeds from a clear process of plot and character alike, a symmetry untypical of Whiting that may account for the play's comparative popularity.

Saint's Day takes place, like most of Whiting's work, in a dwelling apart from its neighborhood. It considers the artist's relation to society and the con-sequent dynamic of image and self-image. As Trussler [2] argues, the play represents the power of "dissociated reality" (50) to expunge all other kinds. Robinson [3] rightly sees the nihilism of the characters as enabling them to enact their destruction.

A Penny for a Song is superficially distinct in psychology and dramaturgy, but Whiting's interest in the interactions of violence, love, individuality, and domesticity work here very strongly beneath the surface. Although Salmon [1] finds it a "small play . . . but genuine" (162), he believes it nevertheless asks some of Whiting's "perennial questions: of the relationship between the artist and the man of action, and . . . the possibility that the artist has no function" (151). The partially rewritten version of 1962 presents the "dark romanticism" (160) Salmon finds definitive of a Whiting drama more clearly than the earlier version, making explicit, therefore, Whiting's philosophical intention.

The playwright seems to privilege whimsicality as the means of realizing the self. In *Penny* if the world comes to you—or seems to—then in order to preserve the self a person must encounter it, encompass it, and so possess it insofar as possible; but going out into the world seems to entail loss of self and world alike; witness the disillusioning and disillusioned experiences of the other characters. Whiting first resolves his play according to a species of comic vision, treating the dilemmas and problems of *Saint's Day* more brightly and jovially. But the later treatment (1962) makes everything that had been light and opti-mistic, heavy and pessimistic. The carryover undertones of nihilism and despair, only detectable in 1949, become in the revision almost didactic overtones. Surely Whiting's response to a now decade-old negative critical reception and a knowl-edge of his deteriorating health made the angle of this revision more acute.

Finally, *The Devils* is the culmination of Whiting's career, and the play's significance matches its meaning. The protagonist wishes to be moral and self-centered at the same time. The authorities wish him to be one or the other, not both. The conflict proves fatal to Urbain Grandier and subversive of all the authorities, causing even his accuser, Sister Jeanne, to suffer self-doubt and despair. Whiting's own attempt to be moral, in the sense that he envisioned certain subjects to need *his* dramatizing, his way, encountered the wish that the attempt be modified, either away from such morality or toward self-centeredness. Such far more successful and respected playwrights as Samuel Beckett and Harold Pinter are careful neither to point morals nor to write self-centeredly. The trend in then-contemporary drama found expression in characters without traditional selves, without traditional morality, in most unusual circumstances. And although *The Devils* more obviously operates from within that psychic territory than Whiting's other major plays, those other plays are concentric to and formative of its essential ethos. Whiting's work is a substantial whole and should be so considered—and so reconsidered.

PRIMARY BIBLIOGRAPHY

Plays

The Devils. London: Heinemann, 1961; New York: Hill & Wang, 1961; in *New English Dramatists*. Vol. 6. London: Penguin, 1963.

The Gates of Summer (*Die Tore des Sommers*). Frankfurt am Main: S. Fischer Verlag, 1960.

Marching Song. London: Samuel French, 1954; London: Heinemann, 1962; *New English Dramatists* Vol. 5. London: Penguin Plays, 1962.

No More A-Roving. London: Heinemann, 1975.

No Why. London: French's Acting Edition; *London Magazine* (May 1961): 52–62.

A Penny for a Song. London: Heinemann Educational Books, 1964.

Saint's Day. London: Heinemann, 1963; *Plays of the Year*, edited by J. C. Trewin. Vol. 6, 1951. London: Plays of the Year Co. and Elek Books, 1952.

Collected Editions

The Collected Plays of John Whiting. Ed. Ronald Hayman. 2 vols. London: Heinemann, 1969.

The Plays of John Whiting. London: Heinemann, 1957.

Interview

"John Whiting: An Interview"(with Tom Milne and Clive Goodwin). *Encore* (Jan./Feb. 1961).

SECONDARY BIBLIOGRAPHY

Adler, Henry. "Wanamaker and Whiting." *Encore* (Nov.–Dec. 1957).

Armstrong, William A. "Tradition and Innovation in the London Theatre, 1960–61." *Modern Drama* 4 (1961): 184–95.

Ashcroft, Peggy, and John Gielgud. Letter to *The Times* on *Saint's Day*. *The Times* (26 Sept. 1951).

"An Author and His Producer." *The Stage* (8 Mar. 1951).

Banham, Martha, ed. "John Whiting." *The Cambridge Guide to World Theatre*. Cambridge: Cambridge University Press, 1988.

Barber, John. Review of *Saint's Day*. *Daily Express* (6 Sept. 1951).

Baxter, Beverley. Review of *A Penny for a Song*. *Evening Standard* (2 Mar. 1951).

"Bright Young Men of the Theatre–II: John Whiting." *Sketch* (30 June 1954): 613.

Brustein, Robert. "Missed Masterpieces." *Plays and Players* (Feb. 1966): 60–61, 67.

Bryden, Ronald. "Whiting's Way." *New Statesman* (14 May 1965): 773–74.

Buckle, Richard. "Making Us Cry." *Plays and Players* (June 1954): 6–7.

Craig, H.A.L. "John Whiting." *New Statesman* (24 Feb. 1961): 317–18.

Dickey, Johanna. *Strategies of Menace in the Plays of John Whiting, Harold Pinter and Sam Shepard*. Stanford, CA: Stanford University Press, 1988.

Dubois, Theodore. *Existence and Self-Transcendence in the Plays of John Whiting*. Unpublished M.A. thesis, Brown University. 1971.

Ferman, James. "The Theatre of John Whiting." *Granta* (24 Apr. 1954): 23–27.

Ferman, James, and Peter Hall. "John Whiting, un nouvel auteur dramatique anglais." *La Revue des Lettres Modernes* (Aug.–Sept. 1954): 145–53.

Firth, Peter, and Athea Tregoer. "*Saint's Day*: A Critical Discussion." *Varsity* (15 Nov. 1952).

Fischer, Peter. "Versuch über das scheinbar absurde Theater." *Merkur* (Feb. 1965): 151–63.

Fry, Christopher [1]. "John Whiting's World." *The Listener* 72 (1964): 837–40.

———[2]. "The Plays of John Whiting." *Essays by Divers Hands* 34 (1966).

Gielgud, John. Review of *Saint's Day*. *The Times* (12 Sept. 1951).

Graham, Diana Devlin. *An Analysis of John Whiting's Position in Modern British Drama*. Unpublished M.A. thesis, University of Minnesota. 1969.

Guthrie, Tyrone, and Peter Brook. Letter to *The Times* on *Saint's Day*. *The Times* (12 Sept. 1951).

Guy, Vincent. "The Black World of John Whiting." *Isis* (15 Feb. 1964).

Hall, Peter [1]. "A Man Born to Be Unlucky?" *New York Times* (14 Nov. 1965).

———[2]. "*Saint's Day*." *The Cambridge Review* (9 Nov. 1952).

Hamilton, Iain. "*Saint's Day*." *The Speculator* (14 Sept. 1951): 328.

Hamilton, Peter. "Edinburgh 1962." *Plays and Players* (Oct. 1962): 18–21.

Hayman, Ronald [1]. *John Whiting*. London: Heinemann, 1969.

———[2]. "John Whiting and *Marching Song*." *Nimbus* (autumn 1954): 50–58.

———[3]. "Tragedy in the Holiday Camp: the Plays of John Whiting." *London Magazine* (Sept. 1969): 83–92.

Hobson, Harold [1]. "Glitter." *Sunday Times* (28 Sept. 1952).

———[2]. "The Involved Theatre." *The Theatre Now*. London: Longmans, 1953: 99–109.

———[3]. Review of *Saint's Day*. *Sunday Times* (9 Sept. 1951).

Hoefer, Jacqueline. "Pinter and Whiting: Two Attitudes toward the Alienated Artist." *Modern Drama* (Feb. 1962): 402–8.

Hope-Wallace, Philip. Review of *Saint's Day*. *Manchester Guardian* (7 Sept. 1951).

Hurrell, John Dennis. "John Whiting and the Theme of Self-Destruction." *Modern Drama* (Sept. 1965): 134–41.

Innes, Christopher. *Modern British Drama*. Cambridge: Cambridge University Press, 1992.

Kerr, Walter, Review of *The Devils*. *New York Herald Tribune* (17 Nov. 1965).

Lucas, Walter. "Obituary: John Whiting." *Drama* (autumn 1963): 38–39.

Lyons, Charles. "The Futile Encounter in the Plays of John Whiting." *Modern Drama* (Dec. 1968): 283–98.

Macowan, Michael. "This Age of Discovery." *Plays and Players* (Oct. 1953): 10.

Mangham, Ian Leslie. "Plays of a Private Man." *New Theatre Magazine* 4.2 (1965): 21–25.

Review of *Marching Song*. *The Times* (9 Apr. 1954).

Milne, Tom [1]. "The Hidden Face of Violence." *Encore* (Jan.–Feb. 1960): 14–20.

———[2]. "John Whiting." *Plays and Players* (Aug. 1964): 7.

"Mr. John Whiting: An Inventive Dramatist." *The Times* (17 June 1963).

O'Connor, Garry. "The Obsessions of John Whiting." *Encore* (July–Aug. 1964): 26–36.

Robinson, Gabrielle [1]. "Beyond the Waste Land: An Interpretation of John Whiting's *Saint's Day*." *Modern Drama* 14 (Feb. 1972): 463–77.

———[2]. "A Private Mythology: The Manuscripts and Plays of John Whiting." *Modern Drama* 14 (May 1971): 23–26.

———[3]. *A Private Mythology: The Manuscripts and Plays of John Whiting*. Lewisburg, PA: Bucknell University Press, 1988.

———[4]. "The Shavian Affinities of John Whiting." *The Shaw Review* 17 (May 1974): 86–98.

Salmon, Eric [1]. *The Dark Journey: John Whiting as Dramatist*. London: Barrie & Jenkins. 1979.

———[2]. "John Whiting, the Neglected British Dramatist," *Nagyvilág* (Hungary) (June 1974).

———[3]. "John Whiting's New-Found Play." *The Spectator* (31 Mar. 1973).

———[4]. "John Whiting's Unpublished Novel." *London Magazine* (Feb./Mar. 1973).

Slater, Charles, F. *John Whiting: The Man and His Plays*. M. A. thesis, University of California, 1963.

Taylor, John Russell, "Prologue: The Early Fifties." In *Anger and After*. 2nd edition, London: Methuen, 1969: 23–26.

Toynbee, Philip. "The Laziness of Readers." *The Observer* (30 Sept. 1951).

Trewin, J. C. [1]. "The New Plays." *Lady* (20 Sept. 1951).

———[2]. "Questions about a Prizewinner." *John O'London's Weekly* (28 Sept. 1951).

———[3]. "Two Morality Playwrights: Robert Bolt and John Whiting." In *Experimental Drama*, ed. William A. Armstrong. London: Bell, 1963: 103–27.

Trussler, Simon [1]. "The Plays of John Whiting." *Tulane Drama Review* (winter 1966).

———[2]. *The Plays of John Whiting*. London: Victor Gollancz, 1972.

Tynan, Kenneth [1]. *Curtains: A Critic's View of Plays, Players, and Theatrical Events, 1950–1960*. London: Longmans, Green, 1961.

———[2]. Review of *The Devils*. *The Observer* (26 Feb. 1961).

———[3]. "Out of Touch." *The Observer* (6 Oct. 1957).

Williams, Raymond. "*Marching Song*: John Whiting." *Drama from Ibsen to Brecht*. London: Chatto & Windus, 1968: 316–18.

Wardle, Irving. Review of *The Condition of Agreement*. *The Times* (15 Oct. 1965).

Worsley, T. C. [1]. "Critics of the Critics." *New Statesman and Nation* (13 Oct. 1951): 404.

———[2]. Review of *A Penny for a Song. New Statesman and Nation* (10 Mar. 1951).

Young, Gregory James. *"The Devils": A Critical Analysis of a Play by John Whiting.* Unpublished M.A. thesis, San Francisco State University. 1983.

Snoo Wilson

(1948–)

DAWN DIETRICH

Having attained minor cult status in Great Britain, Snoo Wilson is perhaps more recognized for his absurdist contributions to the fringe theatre than for the interventionist strategies he attempted to inject into mainstream theatrical practices. Given the comparison that is usually made with Portable Theatre playwrights Howard Brenton and David Hare, Wilson is certainly less high profile but also more unorthodox and creative.

Born Andrew Wilson on 2 August 1948, in Reading, Berkshire, Snoo Wilson grew up in an academic household, the child of Pamela Mary Boyle Wilson and Leslie Wilson, both teachers. As a young man Wilson attended Bradfield College, Berkshire, from 1962–1966, and then enrolled at the University of East Anglia, Norwich, from 1966 to 1969, where he graduated with upper-second-class honors in English and American studies.

During his college days Wilson began writing experimental plays and revues for student productions such as *Girl Mad as Pigs* (1967), *EllaDaybellefesse's Machine* (1967), and *Charles the Martyr* (1970). He also adapted existing texts for the stage, including a dramatic script of Virginia Woolf's novel *Between the Acts* (1969), which was performed in Colchester and Canterbury. These early dramatic experiences proved valuable to Wilson in that they prepared him for his role in organizing the Portable Theatre, an itinerant, noncommercial organization designed to promote experimental and political plays. Here Wilson worked as a writer and director, beginning in 1969, when socialist fervor was running high and there was hope that radical theatre practices could inaugurate real political changes.

Although Wilson himself was less influenced by the socialist politics of the Portable Theatre and more interested in surrealist and symbolist stage experiments, he was every bit the upstart, often surprising audiences by undermining the "naturalist" assumptions governing theatrical production. Yet Wilson also worked collaboratively with fellow Portable playwrights David Edgar, Howard Brenton, and David Hare on productions such as *Lay By* and *England's Ireland*. Many critics, including Grant, acknowledge the Portable experience as one that fostered in its playwrights a penchant for social-political commentary, formal invention, verbal eloquence, and spare stage sets.

Soon after an initial period of collaboration at the Portable, however, Wilson began authoring plays on his own. Beginning with *Pignight* and *Blowjob*, the young playwright demonstrated a predilection for nonliterary, highly visual theatre; and his experiments manipulating space and time in lieu of narrative thread either delighted or dismayed audiences of the time.

Not surprisingly Wilson also found himself drawn toward the prospects for television drama, and he worked for a while as the script editor for the BBC's *Play for Today* (1972–1973), in addition to writing his own television scripts. After a few trial runs Wilson realized the artistic constraints of a medium supported largely by commercial enterprise and turned again toward his stage works, which had begun receiving more widespread recognition in larger London venues. At this time *The Pleasure Principle* (1973) opened at the Theatre Upstairs, along with *Vampire* (1973) at the Oval House, and *The Beast* (1974) at the Place. Within a short time Wilson had caught the attention of mainstream critics and was billed as one of the talented young playwrights to emerge from the Portable Theatre. Yet the next few years would mark the high point of Wilson's collaboration with mainstream theatres, and he would produce most of his later work in smaller, fringe theatres such as The Bush in London.

During the mid-to-late 1970s Wilson worked as the director of the Scarab Theatre, producing several of his own plays, including *The Everest Hotel*. He also gained experience working as dramaturge for the Royal Shakespeare Company's Script Department during 1976, the same year *The Soul of the White Ant* opened to critical acclaim. And in 1978, while acting as the Henfield Fellow at the University of East Anglia, Snoo Wilson received the John Whiting Award for his play *The Glad Hand*, which was performed at the Royal Court Theatre. This flush of events reached a pinnacle a few years later when Wilson was named the 1980 U.S. Bicentennial Fellow in Playwriting.

Most recently Wilson has written *Flaming Bodies* (1979), *The Grass Widow* (1983), *More Light* (1987), and *Callas* (1990), all of which have met with mixed reviews. In addition to these more popular productions, he has written a host of television and stage works that have been produced but remain unpublished. These include *After Lysistrata* (1979), *Salvation Now* (1981), and *Loving Reno* (1983). Interestingly, Wilson's ability to adapt to different genres has not been limited to television plays. The playwright has also experimented with the novel, the screenplay, and the libretto, often creating new texts from preexisting playscripts, as in the case of *A Greenish Man*, originally written as a television piece in 1975, then produced as a play in 1978; or *Space Ache*, originally scored as a musical (1980) and later turned into a novel (1984). Wilson demonstrates his versatility in these various media, but also his interest in erasing or confusing preestablished boundaries. Perhaps this is why his greatest work of late has taken place in the opera, where his visual panache combines skillfully with his script writing. In David Pountney's production of Offenbach's *Orpheus in the Underworld* (1985), Wilson successfully melds word and image in an adaptation of the libretto by Hector C. Crémieux and Ludovic H. Halévy. This opera opened at the English National Opera and played to widespread acclaim, perhaps accomplishing for Snoo Wilson the perfect balance between the visual and the literary. Since the late 1980s, Snoo Wilson has occasionally taught college, including a lectureship at the University of California at San Diego, and he continues to write plays and prose fiction. He resides in London with his wife, Ann McFerran, and their two sons and daughter.

Selected Biographical Sources: Bierman; Hammond [2]; James; Wilson, "Interview with Snoo Wilson."

MAJOR PLAYS, PREMIERES, AND SIGNIFICANT REVIVALS: THEATRICAL RECEPTION

Pignight (one act). 1971. Performed on tour by Portable Theatre, with showings at the Traverse Theatre, Edinburgh, the Young Vic Studio, and the Kings Head, Islington. Directed by Snoo Wilson.

Set on a Lincolnshire pig farm, *Pignight* depicts the mechanized destruction and processing of the farm animals as a metaphor for capitalist greed and violence. Billington [2] criticized the play for its lack of sequential plot development, arguing that the "shuffling" of the characters and scenes simply bewildered theatre-goers. But Coe praised the work for its multiple levels of reality and fantasy and their fusion into a psychedelic whole. She also cited the play as evidence of Wilson's interest in political drama.

Blowjob. 1971. Performed by the Portable Theatre at the Edinburgh Festival. Directed by David Hare. Toured at the Kings Head, Islington, November 10.

A violent play about urban terrorism and anarchy, *Blowjob* was praised by Wardle [1] for resisting "phony logic with everything tied up into neat linear sequence." Yet this same critic also noted Wilson's propensity for spectacle and sensationalism. Grant [4] saw the production as a "violent exercise in alienation," an example of the kind of "political" theatre Wilson does best; and Bierman argued that *Blowjob* was an excellent example of Wilson's style of creating characters who are involved in complex chains of events.

The Pleasure Principle. 1973. Opened 26 November at the Royal Court Theatre Upstairs, London. Directed by David Hare.

Revealing Wilson's interest in Freudian analysis, this play teases out two characters' responses to Freud's "pleasure principle." Ansorge [2] praised the play, although he didn't feel that the production lived up to the promise of its first act. Coe, on the other hand, found worthy elements throughout the production, noting especially Wilson's use of surreal aspects to develop meaning in the play. Bierman, likewise, complimented Wilson as a "master of magic" who amazed audiences with his stunning "coups de théâtre."

Vampire. 1973. Performed on tour with the Paradise Foundry, 28 April at the Oval House, London. Directed by Malcolm Griffiths. Revised version opened at the Bush Theatre, London, 15 March 1977. Published version performed by New York Theatre Studio, 1978.

Set in three different time periods, this play depicts the "vampiric" nature of white, patriarchal culture by featuring different women in each of the three acts struggling with society's definitions of their cultural roles. Coveney stated that "[time] has not diminished [the] power and originality [of *Vampire*]," noting that structurally the play is all middle, with each moment sustaining itself in a strong and independent way. He applauded Wilson's resistance to "narrative plot progression" and "moral purpose." Likewise, James Bierman appreciated the way events came together with comic unity, and Ansorge [1] praised Wilson for his "intriguing use of a traditional three-act play format."

The Everest Hotel (one act). 1975. Opened by the Scarab Theatre at the Bush Theatre, London, 31 December. Directed by Snoo Wilson.

This play merges fantasy with reality as three young women stuck in a hotel on Mt. Everest simultaneously "perform" and "act out" a religious coup in communist-block countries. Although Hammond [1] termed the play a "divertissement" compared to the likes of *Vampire*, *The Pleasure Principle*, and *The Beast*, he nonetheless found the play to be "chock-full of ideas, conceits, and images." Praising Wilson's innovative set design, Bierman noted the use of a "mutable stage" that served as various locations throughout the drama.

The Soul of the White Ant. 1976. Opened in February at the Soho Poly, London. Directed by Dusty Hughes and designed by Di Seymour, with music by Tim Thomas. Revised version performed 30 March 1976, at the Bush Theatre, London.

Wilson was greatly praised for this drama, which depicts injustices under South African apartheid. Using a stage metaphor of a queenless termite colony, Wilson was able to create a powerful play around a central Afrikaans character, Eugène Marais: writer, drug addict, visionary. Grant [3] deemed the hallmark of *The Soul of the White Ant* its "intelligence," describing the play as "Athol Fugard seen from the other end of the telescope." But Craig went further, declaring it Wilson's best play to date. Bierman argued that although the drama is centered in political events, it does not address those issues directly, but Coe cited the play as an *example* of Wilson's personal commitment to contemporary political situations.

The Glad Hand. 1978. Opened 11 May at the Royal Court Theatre. Directed by Max Stafford-Clark and designed by Peter Hartwell. Received the John Whiting Award.

Inspired by the etchings of Piranesi, Wilson created an oil tanker for the stage set of this bizarre play involving political intrigue and the manipulation of synchronous events. Grant [4] praised *The Glad Hand* as one of Wilson's best plays ever, and Treglown [2] compared the style of the play to the fiction of Kurt Vonnegut and Richard Brautigan. He stated in his review, "It's . . . an absurdist drama which cares about the world we live in, a surreal work of social realism." Coe similarly praised the original nature of the work but emphasized issues of human emancipation, while Bierman saw the locus of the work in the tension between the environment and its inhabitants.

A Greenish Man (one act). 1978. Opened 20 November at the Bush Theatre, London. Directed by Dusty Hughes.

Intended to "read" like a B-movie, this play about Northern Ireland was created by Wilson to feed off its own violence and destruction. Grant [4] felt the play failed because Wilson didn't tie up the many strands of ideas comprising the performance, but Coe praised this technique, seeing it as a way to resist easy solutions to complex problems. Bierman, on the other hand, recognized in *A Greenish Man* the versatility of Wilson's staging effects, such that the settings transform themselves as part of the action.

Flaming Bodies. 1979. Opened 11 December at the Institute of Contemporary Arts Theatre, London. Directed by John Ashford.

Set in a Los Angeles film producer's office, this play features the adventures of Mercedes, an obsessive script editor who has just been fired from her job. In the play bizarre images combine to create a surreal mixture of Freudian and Judeo-Christian motifs. Bierman saw *Flaming Bodies* as similar to *Space Ache*, for both feature characters who face despair and continue to struggle with "faith." Nightingale [4] appreciated the play's farcical moments, "many of them couched in the gaudy-gothic style which has made Snoo Wilson something of a cult." But Taylor found the play "sophomoric," falling quite short of "deliciously campy."

Space Ache. 1980. Music by Nick Bicât. Produced by Tricycle Theatre at Cheltenham and London.

Wilson creates a campy sci-fi version of a future world run amok by totalitarianism. Nightingale [3] praised the play for its satirical sci-fi but argued that the production could be "tougher, more concentrated and pointed." Goldman contended that although the play began with an interesting premise, it "degenerate[d] into a flabby mixture of 'Close Encounters of the Cryogenic Kind' and 'Biggles Flies Undone.' " Yet Browning and Thwaite praised its "high-spiritedness" and humor. Browning asserted, "Snoo Wilson's *Space Ache* succeeds in bemusing and disturbing its audience." Bierman noted the enormous technical demands the play requires of a producing company.

More Light: A Play about the Heretic Giordano Bruno. 1987. Opened 17 February at the Bush Theatre, London. Directed by Snoo Wilson and Simon Stokes.

This play, which takes place in heaven, features Giordano Bruno's battle with the pope, who is obsessed with conspiracy theories. Although Hiley criticized the play for "proliferating improvisations" and described Wilson as a "sort of magic realist without, in theatrical terms, much of the realism," Ratcliffe saw the play as a "clever, cheerful, oblique and fairly chaotic piece which best comes alive when Wilson leaps clear of his homework and hammers his fantastical inventions home."

ADDITIONAL PLAYS, ADAPTATIONS, AND PRODUCTIONS

Snoo Wilson has written musicals, screenplays, and libretti in addition to stage and television plays. *England, England*, a rock musical, written in collaboration with Kevin Coyne, was produced in 1977. *Son of Freud*, a musical about Freud in the underworld, was written in 1983, and most recently Wilson has completed the text for his musical *80 Days* (1988). The author's screenplays include *Sunday for Seven Days* (1971), *Pignight* (1978), and *Shadey* (1985), but he has gained more recognition for his opera translations: *La Colombe* (Gounod), 1983, and *Orpheus in the Underworld* (Offenbach), 1985.

ASSESSMENT OF WILSON'S CAREER

Wilson's drama is mostly categorized in terms of what it is not or what it resists. When compared with conventional literary drama, his plays appear quirky, nonlinear, disjunctive, and often confusing in terms of spatial and temporal orientation—what Nightingale [3] loosely describes as "predictably unpredictable." Scholars are quick to point out that many of Wilson's strategies are "antinaturalistic" or "nontraditional," and he is often described as a "surrealist" playwright (see Gussow). Such descriptions may be helpful in terms of placing Wilson within a literary framework, but they rarely do justice to his plays, which in themselves are unconventional and outside the mainstream canon. A more fruitful way to analyze Wilson's work is through the context of performance, with an emphasis on the visual aspects of his work, for many of the "coups de théâtre" that critics find "distracting" or "sensationalist" (see Wardle [1] and Bierman) or that theatre-goers find so "spectacular" beg a different interpretation in light of recent performance art and cross disciplinary excursions into opera, musicals, film, and television drama. Placed in a context where visual analogues can "legitimately" comment on linguistic and narrative structures, Wilson's work takes on a new dimension—one that underscores the vitality of his stage productions. For instance, it might prove fruitful to look at Wilson's dramatic work in the context of British film director Peter Greenaway's work. The two are interested similarly in language constructs, synchronization, and the use of visual analogues to represent the unconscious or internal states of mind. Critics have connected Wilson's work to visual artists Paul Klee, Max Ernst, and René Magritte, but no one has performed a substantial study relating

Wilson's stage work to modern visual art (see Coe). This seems lacking, since Wilson (*The Glad Hand*) himself makes references to his work in terms of perception and visual technique, even attributing his inspiration for *The Glad Hand* to Piranesi's etchings. Wilson's own ease in moving among genres and translating texts for different media suggests an interest in the conventional boundaries that separate and legitimize the arts.

In a similar way, Wilson's association with the experimental and politically vested Portable Theatre has boxed him in another dramatic straight jacket. In the early days, compared with playwrights Brenton and Hare, Wilson was less overtly political and even distrustful of plays with didactic motives (see Bierman). In his view, the surrealist notion of surrendering to language and symbols of the unconscious is the only ''political'' response one can make in the face of the complexities of everyday life. Wilson displays classical formalist perspective when he describes his artistic conscience as ''aesthetic.'' But perhaps Wilson is ''political'' in the broader sense that his ultimate goal is to transform the relationship of the audience to the play. One could say that he is more interested in the ''politics of drama'': what forms and/or venues the theatre needs to develop in order to address new issues, how the actor-audience relationship can be redefined, how new stage languages can be created and expanded to include scenic and spatial elements.

Since the Portable days Wilson has remained close to the fringe scene, whereas the other playwrights have become increasingly popular with the larger established theatres. What all this has meant is that Snoo Wilson doesn't really ''fit'' in the established theatre scene and has yet to be recognized on his own terms. To date very little exists in the way of serious critical work on Wilson. There are a handful of articles from various theatre journals, several interviews in these same journals, short reviews, the inclusion of Wilson in the Portable Theatre history (represented by several books), and Wilson's own (unsatisfactory) treatises on his stage work. Essentially Wilson's low profile and association with the fringe have relegated him to minor status as a playwright, but not one without remarkable interest.

In terms of style Wilson is drawn to characters on the edge—mad individuals, Satanists, magicians, vampires, drug addicts, schizophrenics—in campy situations that often involve the irrational, whether in the guise of dreams, sex, psychic healings, or astrological predictions. Bierman claims that Wilson writes about subjects that can not be known and that his plays, particularly *The Beast*, *Vampire*, *The Glad Hand*, and *Flaming Bodies*, center their drama on exploring such mysteries.

Wilson's interest in psychology, and in particular the work of Sigmund Freud and Carl Jung, surfaces in the way in which he uses the proscenium frame to represent the outer limits of the rational mind, while using the stage itself as the playground for the irrational or the unconscious mind. In *The Pleasure Principle*, for instance, gorillas first surface in a character's dream and then appear for real on the stage. Wilson talks about his plays as being given free reign for unrestrained impulses; he sees the theatre as the place to test ideas, to parade the shocking and the absurd, to stir audiences from their complacency. Often this means deemphasizing plot and using spatial and temporal techniques to blur the distinctions between the world of the mind and the "external" world of reality. For Wilson this means imagining new ways to exploit stage media and space. The playwright often uses synchronous events, simultaneous stage settings, and jarring discontinuities to establish such surreal effects. Wilson's theatrical metaphors can serve to heighten or intensify the action, as Bierman points out, but when his scenic techniques become too dissociated from the dialogue of the play, the production can seem confusing or self-indulgent, as critics Ansorge [2], Ford, and Grant [4] have noted.

When questioned about his "anarchic imagination," Wilson sees himself as influenced most by the "absurdists" such as Eugène Ionesco and Samuel Beckett and surrealists such as Alfred Jarry and August Strindberg, but his drama might be said to have as much in common with fiction writers Richard Brautigan and Kurt Vonnegut for its fantasist qualities (see Treglown [2]). In many instances, Wilson undermines naturalist assumptions by subverting narrative practices. Rather than tell a story with stage pictures, Wilson creates a series of dramatic associations that make wild leaps in space and time but hold together through a kind of internal logic all their own (see Bierman). For the most part, Wilson has been criticized for such bold theatrics, but some critics such as Coveney have praised his formal experimentation on the stage. In Wilson's theatrical universe, frozen sperm dumped into a river can impregnate two women, socially outcast individuals can be cryogenically frozen and sent to orbit in space, and cars can come crashing through stage walls; but not without a "Wilsonian" reason for such action. The power of Wilson's stage world is that it creates its own context, which takes on meaning precisely through its hyperreal images, circuitous cross-references, and ironic juxtapositions.

PRIMARY BIBLIOGRAPHY

Plays

The Beast. Plays and Players 22 (Dec. 1974 and Jan. 1975).
The Everest Hotel. Plays and Players 23 (Mar. 1976): 41–50.
Flaming Bodies. London: Calder, 1982.
The Glad Hand. London: Pluto Press, 1979.
The Grass Widow. London: Methuen, 1983.
A Greenish Man. London: Pluto Press, 1979.
More Light: A Play about the Heretic Giordano Bruno. Oxford: Mandrake, 1990.
The Number of the Beast. London: Calder, 1982.
Pignight and *Blowjob*. London: Calder & Boyars, 1975.
The Pleasure Principle: The Politics of Love, *The Capital Emotion*. London: Eyre Methuen, 1974.
Reason. Gambit 29 (1976): 79–89.

The Soul of the White Ant. New York: Samuel French, 1983.
Space Ache. London: Chatto & Windus, 1984.
Vampire. London: Amber Lane Press, 1977.

Collaborative Plays

Lay By. London: Calder & Boyars, 1973.
England's Ireland. London: Pluto Press, 1972.

Essays and Articles on Drama and Theatre

"Magic Rose." In *The Warehouse: A Writer's Theatre*, ed. Walter Donohue. Dartington: Dartington College of Arts, 1979: 33.
"Man Almost Bites Dog." *Plays and Players* 23 (Mar. 1976): 10.
"The Means of Production." *Gambit* 26–27 (fall 1975): 29–33.
"The Sense of the Sublime." *Plays and Players* 27 (Nov. 1979): 10, 12.
"Snoo Wilson Comments." In *Contemporary Dramatists*, ed. James Vinson. London: St. James, 1977: 877–78.
"Two Approaches to the 'Other.' " *Theatre Quarterly* 6:24 (winter 1976–77): 74–76.
"The Wickedest Man in the World." *Plays and Players* 22 (Dec. 1974): 36–38.

Interviews

"Beastly! The Devil's Disciple" (with Dusty Hughes). *Time Out* (15–21 Nov. 1974): 22–23.
"Interview with Snoo Wilson" (with Michael Coveney). *Time Out* (30 Nov. 1979): 18.
"New Gothic Realists, Phantasists." *Gambit* 29 (1976): 5–29.
"A Theatre of Light, Space, and Time"(with Clive Barker, Malcolm Hay, and Simon Trussler). *Theatre Quarterly* 10:37 (1980): 3–18.
"Theatre on the Wrong Side of the Law" (with Joel Schechter). *Theatre* (spring 1981): 56–60.
"Vamped by History" (with Peter Ansorge). *Time Out* (18–24 Mar. 1977): 8–9.
"Vampire" (with John Ford). *Plays and Players* 20 (July 1973): i, iii.

SECONDARY BIBLIOGRAPHY

Ansorge, Peter [1]. *Disrupting the Spectacle*. London: Pitman, 1975: 13–18, 51–53.
———[2]. Review of *The Pleasure Principle*. *Plays and Players* (Jan. 1974): 55.
Bierman, James. "Enfant Terrible of the English Stage." *Modern Drama* 24.4 (Dec. 1981): 424–35.
Billington, Michael [1]. Review of *The Pleasure Principle*. *The Guardian* (27 Nov. 1973).
———[2]. Review of *Pignight*. *The Times* (5 Mar. 1971).
———[3]. Review of *The Soul of the White Ant*. *The Guardian* (31 Mar. 1976).
———[4]. Review of *Vampire*. *The Guardian* (16 Mar. 1977).

Browning, John. Review of *Space Ache. Books and Bookmen* (Apr. 1984): 35.

Buckroyd, Peter. "British Drama, 1975–1985." *Rocky Mountain Review of Language and Literature* 40 (1986): 49–66.

Chaillet, Ned [1]. Review of *Flaming Bodies. The Times* (12 Dec. 1979).

———[2]. "Marais Resurrected." *The Times* (4 Feb. 1976): G9.

———[3]. "The Unpredictable Snoo Wilson." *The Times* (10 May 1978).

Coe, Ada. "From Surrealism to Snoorealism: The Theatre of Snoo Wilson." *New Theatre Quarterly* 17 (1989): 73–85.

Coveney, Michael. Review of *Vampire. Plays and Players* 24 (May 1977): 29.

Craig, Randall. Review of *The Soul of the White Ant. Drama* 21 (summer 1976): 79.

Cushman, Robert [1]. "Aboard the Good Ship Snoo." *The Observer* (21 May 1978).

———[2]. "Con Tricks." *The Observer* (24 Nov. 1974): 32.

———[3]. Review of *Vampire. The Observer* (5 Aug. 1973).

Davies, Andrew. *Other Theatres: The Development of Alternative and Experimental Theatre in Britain.* London: Macmillan, 1987.

de Jongh, Nicholas. "Edinburgh: *Lay By.*" *The Guardian* (26 Aug. 1971).

Donohue, Walter, ed. "The Warehouse: A Writer's Theatre." *Theatre Papers* 3 (1979–80): 1–40.

Elsom, John. "Hands from the Grave." *The Listener* (7 Apr. 1977): 453–54.

Ford, John. Review of *The Beast. Plays and Players* (Jan. 1975): 33.

Goldman, Rowena [1]. Review of *Space Ache. Drama* 139 (1981): 48.

Grant, Steve [1]. "Magical Moments." *The Observer* (9 Dec. 1979): 19.

———[2]. "The New Writers." In *Dreams and Deconstructions: Alternative Theatre in Britain*, ed. Sandy Craig. London: Amber Lane Press, 1981.

———[3]. Review of *The Soul of the White Ant. Plays and Players* (Apr. 1976): 36–37.

———[4]. "Snoo Wilson." In *Contemporary Dramatists*, ed. James Vinson. London: St. James, 1977: 871–73.

Gussow, Mel. "Surrealistic *Soul of the White Ant.*" *New York Times* (28 Jan. 1982).

Hammond, Jonathan [1]. Review of *The Everest Hotel. Plays and Players* (Mar. 1976): 34–35.

———[2]. "Snoo Wilson." In *Contemporary Dramatists*, ed. James Vinson. London: St. James, 1977: 878–79.

———[3]. Review of *Vampire. Plays and Players* (June 1973): 54–55.

Hiley, Jim. Review of *More Light. The Listener* (26 Feb. 1987).

Hobson, Harold [1]. Review of *The Pleasure Principle. Sunday Times* (2 Dec. 1973): 37.

———[2]. "That Old Black Magic." *Sunday Times* (24 Nov. 1974).

———[3]. "Tiger, Tiger, Burning Bright." *Sunday Times* (8 Feb. 1976): 37.

Holt, Hazel. "Green for Confusion." *The Stage* (17 May 1979): 27.

Hughes, Dusty. "Snoo Wilson." *Time Out* (12–18 Nov. 1971).

Itzin, Catherine. *Stages in the Revolution: Political Theatre in Britain since 1955.* London: Eyre Methuen, 1980.

James, Alby. "Snoo Wilson: The Eclectic Dramatist." *Gambit* 36 (1980): 11–19.

Marriott, R. B. Review of *A Greenish Man. The Stage* (23 Nov. 1978): 11.

Nightingale, Benedict [1]. "Bourgeois and the Beast." *New Statesman* (22 Nov. 1974): 750.

———[2]. "Conundrums." *New Statesman* (7 Dec. 1973).

———[3]. "Green Tongues." *New Statesman* (28 Nov. 1980): 32–33.

———[4]. "Lurid Hubbub." *New Statesman* (14 Dec. 1979): 952.

———[5]. "Make-Believe." *New Statesman* (16 Jan. 1976): 79.

———[6]. Review of *The Number of the Beast. New Statesman* (19 Feb. 1982).

Peter, John. Review of *England, England. Sunday Times* (28 Aug. 1977).

Randall, Craig. "Experimental." *Drama* 104 (spring 1972): 44.

Ratcliffe, Michael. Review of *More Light. The Observer* (22 Feb. 1987).

Shorter, Eric. Review of *More Light. Daily Telegraph* (18 Feb. 1987).

Taylor, John Russell. Review of *Flaming Bodies. Plays and Players* 27 (Jan. 1980): 24.

Thwaite, Anthony. "Dickensian Underworld." *The Observer* (19 Feb. 1984).

Treglown, Jeremy [1]. Review of *England, England. Plays and Players* (Oct. 1977): 27.

———[2]. Review of *The Glad Hand. Plays and Players* (July 1978): 18–19.

Wardle, Irving [1]. Review of *Blowjob. The Times* (11 Nov. 1971).

———[2]. Review of *The Glad Hand. The Times* (13 May 1978).

———[3]. Review of *The Pleasure Principle. The Times* (28 Nov. 1973).

BIBLIOGRAPHY

Trussler, Simon, Malcolm Page, and Elaine Turner. "Snoo Wilson: Checklist No. 4."
    New Theatre Quarterly 17 (Feb. 1989): 86–104.

Selected Bibliography

The following is a selected general bibliography of book-length studies devoted in whole or in part to British drama and theatre during the years 1956–present.

Anderson, Michael. *Anger and Detachment: A Study of Arden, Osborne, and Pinter*. London: Pitman, 1976.

Barnes, Philip. *A Companion to Post-war British Theatre*. Totowa, NJ: Barnes & Noble, 1986.

Brater, Enoch, and Ruby Cohn, eds. *Around the Absurd. Essays on Modern and Postmodern Drama*. Ann Arbor: University of Michigan Press, 1990.

Brook, Peter. *The Shifting Point, 1946–1987*. New York: Harper & Row, 1987.

Brown, John Russell. *Theatre Language: A Study of Arden, Osborne, Pinter, and Wesker*. London: Allen Lane, 1972.

Bull, John. *New British Political Dramatists: Howard Brenton, David Hare, Trevor Griffiths, and David Edgar*. London: Macmillan, 1984.

Carlson, Susan. *Women and Comedy: Rewriting the British Theatrical Tradition*. Ann Arbor: University of Michigan Press, 1991.

Cave, Richard Allan. *New British Drama in Performance on the London Stage, 1970–1985*. Gerrards Cross: Colin Smythe, 1987.

Chambers, Colin. *Other Spaces: New Theatre and the RSC*. London: Methuen, 1980.

———, and Mike Prior. *Playwright's Progress: Patterns of Postwar British Drama*. Oxford: Amber Lane Press, 1987.

Cohn, Ruby. *Retreats from Realism in Recent English Drama*. Cambridge: Cambridge University Press, 1991.

Craig, Sandy. *Dreams and Deconstructions: Alternative Theatre in Britain*. London: Amber Lane Press, 1980.

Davies, Andrew. *Other Theatres: The Development of Alternative and Experimental Theatre in Britain*. London: Macmillan, 1987.

Doty, Gresdna, and Billy J. Harbin, eds. *Inside the Royal Court Theatre, 1956–1981: Artists Talk*. Baton Rouge: Louisiana State University, 1990.

Dutton, Richard. *Modern Tragicomedy and the British Tradition: Beckett, Pinter, Stoppard, Albee, and Storey*. Brighton: Harvester, 1986.

Elsom, John. *Post-war British Theatre Criticism*. London: Routledge & Kegan Paul, 1981.

Esslin, Martin. *The Theatre of the Absurd*. Garden City, NY: Anchor, 1962.

Findlater, Richard, ed. *At the Royal Court: 25 Years of the English Stage Company*. Ambergate: Amber Lane Press, 1981.

Griffiths, Trevor R., and Margaret Lewellyn-Jones, eds. *British and Irish Women Dramatists since 1958: A Critical Handbook*. Buckingham: Open University Press, 1993.

Hayman, Ronald. *The Set-up: An Anatomy of the English Theatre Today*. London: Methuen, 1973.

———. *The British Theatre since 1955: A Reassessment*. Oxford: Oxford University Press, 1979.

Haynes, John. *Taking the Stage*. London: Thames & Hudson, 1986.

Hobson, Harold. *Theatre in Britain: A Personal View*. Oxford: Phaidon, 1984.

Innes, Christopher. *Modern British Drama, 1890–1990*. Cambridge: Cambridge University Press, 1992.

Itzin, Catherine. *Stages in the Revolution: Political Theatre in Britain since 1968*. London: Methuen, 1980.

Kennedy, Andrew. *Six Dramatists in Search of a Language*. Cambridge: Cambridge University Press, 1975.

Kerensky, Oleg. *The New British Drama: Fourteen Playwrights since Osborne and Pinter*. New York: Taplinger, 1977.

Keyssar, Helene. *Feminist Theatre: An Introduction to Plays of Contemporary British and American Women*. London: Macmillan, 1984.

McGrath, John. *A Good Night Out: Popular Theatre: Audience, Class, and Form*. London: Methuen, 1981.

McMillan, Joyce. *The Traverse Theatre Story, 1963–1988*. London: Methuen, 1988.

Morley, Sheridan. *Our Theatres in the Eighties*. London: Hodder & Stoughton, 1990.

Nightingale, Benedict. *A Reader's Guide to 50 Modern British Plays*. London: Heinemann, 1982.

Page, Adrian. *The Death of the Playwright? Modern British Drama and Literary Theory*. Basingstoke: Macmillan, 1992.

Peacock, D. Keith. *Radical Stages: Alternative History in Modern British Drama*. Westport, CT: Greenwood Press, 1991.

Rabey, David Ian. *British and Irish Political Drama in the Twentieth Century: Implicating the Audience*. Houndsmill: Macmillan, 1986.

Roberts, Philip. *The Royal Court Theatre, 1965–1972*. London: Routledge & Kegan Paul, 1986.

Rodger, Ian. *Radio Drama*. London: Macmillan, 1982.

Rowell, George, and Anthony Jackson. *The Repertory Movement: A History of Regional Theatre in Britain*. Cambridge: Cambridge University Press, 1984.

Rusinko, Susan. *British Drama 1950 to the Present: A Critical History*. Boston: Twayne, 1989.

Salmon, Eric. *Is the Theatre Still Dying?* Westport, CT: Greenwood Press, 1985.

Smith, Leslie. *Modern British Farce: A Selective Study of British Farce from Pinero to the Present Day*. Totowa, NJ: Barnes & Noble, 1989.

Taylor, John Russell. *Anger and After*. London: Methuen, 1969.

———. *The Second Wave: British Drama for the Seventies*. New York: Hill & Wang, 1971.

Trewin, Wendy, and J. C. Trewin. *The Arts Theatre, London, 1927–1981*. London: Society for Theatre Research, 1986.

Tynan, Kenneth. *Show People: Profiles in Entertainment*. London: Weidenfeld & Nicolson, 1980.

van Berchem, Sam. "*England's Ireland*." *Time Out* (29 Sept.–5 Oct. 1972): 33.

Wandor, Michelene. *Carry on, Understudies: Theatre and Sexual Politics*: London: Routledge & Kegan Paul, 1986.

———. *Drama Today: A Critical Guide to British Drama, 1970–1990*. London: Longmans, 1993.

———. *Look Back in Gender: Sexuality and the Family in Post-war British Drama*. London: Methuen, 1987.

Weintraub, Stanley, ed. *British Drama since World War II, parts I and II: A Dictionary of Literary Biography*, Vol. 13. Detroit: Gale Research 1982.

Wilmut, George. *From Fringe to Flying Circus: Celebrating a Unique Generation of Comedy, 1960–1980*. London: Eyre Methuen, 1980.

Winkler, Elizabeth H. *The Function of Song in Contemporary British Drama*. Newark, NJ: Delaware University Press, 1990.

Worth, Katharine J. *Revolutions in Modern English Drama*. London: Bell, 1973.

Worthen, William B. *Modern Drama and the Rhetoric of Theater*. Berkeley, University of California Press, 1992.

Young, B. A. *The Mirror Up to Nature: A Review of the Theatre, 1964–1982*. London: Kimber, 1982.

Index of Names

Page numbers in **boldface type** indicate location of main entries.

Index of Titles

About the Editor and Contributors

THOMAS T. APPLE is assistant professor of English and Director of Theatre at Widener University, Chester, Pennsylvania.

WILLIAM BAKER is professor of English at Northern Illinois University at DeKalb. He has coauthored *Harold Pinter* (1973) and is the author of six monographs and the editor of George Eliot's Pate holograph notebooks. He edits *George Eliot–George Henry Lewes Studies*. Author of numerous articles on Anglo-Jewish writers, he is currently at work on a descriptive bibliography of Harold Pinter's works and a monograph on Bernard Kops.

KAREN C. BLANSFIELD is a doctoral candidate in English at the University of North Carolina at Chapel Hill, where she has taught in the Department of English, in the School of Journalism and Mass Communication, and with the UNC Principals' Executive Program. She is the author of *Cheap Rooms and Restless Hearts: A Study of Formula in the Stories of O. Henry* (1988) as well as essays in *World Literature Criticism* (1992), *Twentieth Century Science Fiction Writers* (1986, 1991), *The Best of O. Henry*, and the catalog raisonné *Rosemary Feit Covey: The Prints 1970–1990*. She has published articles and reviews in *Journal of American Drama and Theatre*, *Studies in American Humor*, *The Threepenny Review*, *San Francisco Review of Books*, *New England Theatre Journal*, *Mid-American Review*, and other journals and is currently working on a book about Michael Frayn and Peter Nichols. She has also written numerous features and reviews for magazines and newspapers, including *The San Francisco Chronicle*, *Atlanta Journal-Constitution*, *Chicago Tribune Magazine*, *American Way*, Raleigh *News & Observer*, and *Northeast Magazine*.

ART BORRECA is assistant professor of Theatre History, Dramatic Literature, and Dramaturgy at the University of Iowa, where he is also Dramaturg with the Iowa Playwrights Workshop. He has published articles in *The Drama Review*, *Modern Drama*, *Theater*, and *Theater Three* and is completing a book, *The Past's Presence: British Historical Drama since 1956*. He has worked as a dramaturg at the Yale Repertory Theatre, the New York Theatre Workshop, and LaMama, among others.

RICHARD CORBALLIS is professor and head of the department of English at Massey University, Palmerston North, New Zealand. He is the author of *Stoppard: The Mystery and the Clockwork* (1984) and of numerous books, articles, and reviews on Renaissance and modern drama. He has also seved as theatre critic for a number of New Zealand newspapers and journals.

MICHAEL L. COUNTS holds a Ph.D. in Theatre from the Graduate Center of The City University of New York. He is currently Assistant Professor and Director of Theatre at Lyon College, Batesville, Arkansas, where he teaches and directs theatre. He currently serves as Chair of the University/College Division of the Southwest Theatre Association. He is author of *Coming Home: The Soldier's Return in Twentieth-Century American Drama* (1988) and contributor to *American Playwrights, 1880–1945* (Greenwood, 1995).

WILLIAM W. DEMASTES is professor of English at Louisiana State University, Baton Rouge. He is author of numerous articles on twentieth-century drama and theatre, author of *Beyond Naturalism: A New Realism in American Theatre* (1988) and *Clifford Odets: A Research and Production Sourcebook* (1991), and editor of *American Playwrights, 1880–1945: A Research and Production Sourcebook (1995)*. The latter two books are part of a series he edits for Greenwood Press, *Modern Playwrights Research and Production Sourcebooks*, of which the present volume is also a part. He has also authored *Theatre of Chaos* (forthcoming) and edited *Realism and the American Dramatic Tradition* (1996).

DAWN DIETRICH is assistant professor of English at Western Washington University, Bellingham. She has published recent articles on theatre, theory, and postmodernism and is currently at work on a book about American theatre designer Robert Wilson.

KURT EISEN is assistant professor of English at Tennessee Technological University. He is the author of *The Inner Strength of Opposites: O'Neill's Novelistic Drama and the Melodramatic Imagination* (1994) as well as articles in *Comparative Drama*, *Essays in Literature*, *Modern Drama*, and *Studies in the American Renaissance*.

JAMES FISHER is professor of Theatre at Wabash College, Crawfordsville, Indiana. He is author of *The Theatre of Yesterday and Tomorrow: Commedia dell'arte on the Modern Stage* (1992), *Al Jolson: A Bio-Bibliography* (Greenwood Press, 1994), *Spencer Tracy: A Bio-Bibliography* (Greenwood Press, 1994), and the forthcoming *Beyond the Theory: The Early Productions of Edward Gordon Craig (1900–1906)*. He serves as Book Review Editor of the *Journal of Dramatic Theory and Criticism* and has contributed articles to numerous journals, including *Theatre Journal, Modern Drama, The Drama Review, Theater, The Annual of Bernard Shaw Studies, Studies in American Drama, Theatre Research International, Comparative Drama, New Theatre Quarterly, Theatre Symposium, Soviet and East European Performance, The New England Theatre Journal*, and many others. He has been a recipient of a Research Award from the Society for Theatre Research (London), a six-month fellowship at the Newberry Library (Chicago), in 1987–1988 he was named McLain/McTurnan/Arnold Research Scholar at Wabash College, and in 1993 he was selected to deliver the LaFollette Lecture at Wabash College.

WILLIAM J. FREE teaches dramatic literature and playwriting at the University of Georgia. His publications include *Christopher Hampton: An Introduction to His Plays* and articles on Robert Bolt, David Hare, Samuel Beckett, David Storey, Trevor Griffiths, Botho Strauss, Tennessee Williams, dramatic and performance theory, and film. He is Editor of the journal *Text and Presentation* and Artistic Director of the Partly Free Theatre Cooperative of Athens, Georgia.

STEVEN H. GALE holds the University Endowed Chair in the Humanities at Kentucky State University. Among Professor Gale's many books are *Butter's Goint Up: A Critical Analysis of Harold Pinter's Work, Harold Pinter: An Annotated Bibliography, Harold Pinter: Critical Approaches*, and *Harold Pinter: Critical Essays*. Past president of the Harold Pinter Society and coeditor of *The Pinter Review: Annual Essays*, Professor Gale is currently working on a monograph on Pinter's filmscripts.

STANTON B. GARNER, JR. is associate professor of English at the University of Tennessee, Knoxville. The author of *The Absent Voice: Narrative Comprehension in the Theater* (1989) and *Bodied Spaces: Phenomenology and Performance in Contemporary Drama* (1994), he has written articles for *Shakespeare Survey, Studies in Philology, Modern Language Quarterly, Comparative Drama, Modern Drama, Theatre Journal*, and *The Pinter Review*.

C. J. GIANAKARIS is professor of English and Theatre at Western Michigan University. Cofounder and a long-time editor of *Comparative Drama*, he has published nine books, including *Foundations of Drama*, an edition of *Antony and Cleopatra*, and most recently *Peter Shaffer* and *Peter Shaffer: A Casebook*.

His articles and reviews have appeared in *Comparative Drama*, *Modern Drama*, *Theatre Journal*, *JEGP*, *Theater Week*, *Opera News*, *Renaissance Quarterly*, and elsewhere. Professor Gianakaris is also a theatre and music reviewer for newspapers.

WILLIAM HUTCHINGS is professor of English at the University of Alabama at Birmingham. He is the author of *The Plays of David Storey: A Thematic Study* (1988) and the editor of *David Storey: A Casebook* (1992). He has also written articles for a number of books and journals, including *Modern Drama*, *Papers on Language and Literature*, *Modern Fiction Studies*, *Twentieth Century Literature*, the *Journal of Modern Literature*, and the *James Joyce Quarterly*.

CHRIS JONES is assistant professor of Theatre Arts at Northern Illinois University. He is midwestern theatre critic for *Variety*, theatre editor for Chicago's *New City* newspaper, and a frequent contributor to *American Theatre*. His theatre reviews, interviews, and commentaries have appeared in several other newspapers and magazines and on numerous radio stations. He has written and spoken widely on Willy Russell's plays and is also a contributor to Greenwood Press's *Dictionary of State Directors*.

KIM L. JONES-OWEN is assistant professor of English at Ball State University, Muncie, Indiana, where she is Director of the Women and Gender Studies Program. She teaches both English and women's studies courses and writes in the areas of drama and feminist theory.

ILONA KOREN-DEUTSCH holds an M.A. in Theatre and Drama from Northwestern University. She has contributed to the *Cambridge Guide to Theatre* and the *Cambridge Bibliography of English Literature* as well as having written articles for several journals, including *Modern Drama*, *Western European Stages*, *Communications from the International Brecht Society*, and *South African Theatre Journal*.

AMELIA HOWE KRITZER is assistant professor of Theatre at West Virginia University. She has written extensively on Caryl Churchill's work, including the recent *Plays of Caryl Churchill: Theatre of Empowerment*. She is currently working on recovering the plays of early American women and has compiled and edited the forthcoming volume *Plays by American Women 1794–1844*.

DON S. LAWSON is assistant professor of Humanities at Lander University, Greenwood, South Carolina. He has authored and edited numerous studies of modern drama.

COLETTE LINDROTH is professor of English at Caldwell College, Caldwell, New Jersey. She has published articles on modern writers and film directors, including Jean Rhys, Susan Glaspell, Rachel Crothers, Milan Kundera, Stephen Fears, and Spike Lee.

CARLA J. MCDONOUGH is assistant professor in the Department of English at Eastern Illinois University, where she teaches modern drama. Her publications have appeared in *Theatre Journal* and the *Journal of Dramatic Theory and Criticism*. She is currently working on research projects concerning the theaters of Adrienne Kennedy and Maria Irene Fornes.

JOHN E. O'CONNOR is assistant professor of Theatre at the University of North Alabama, Florence. He has presented papers on Howard Brenton's *Bloody Poetry* at the ATHE National Convention in Chicago and on Brenton and David Hare's *Brassneck* and *Pravda* at the Mid-America Theatre Conference in Chicago.

JUDY LEE OLIVA is assistant professor of Theatre at the University of Tennessee at Knoxville. She is the author of *David Hare: Theatricalizing Politics* (1990). She has contributed to *Howard Brenton: A Casebook* (1993), *Contemporary Dramatists* (5th ed.), *Dictionary of Stage Directors* (1993), and has written articles for *Theatre Journal, Theatre Studies, Theatre Three*, and *Theatre Topics*. She is currently editing a new book called *New Theatre Vistas: The Prose and the Passion.*

JANICE OLIVER is assistant professor of English at Southern University, Baton Rouge.

MALCOLM PAGE is professor of English at Simon Fraser University, Burnaby, British Columbia, Canada. He is author of *John Arden* (1984), *Richard II* ("Text and Performance," 1987) and *Howards End* ("The Critics Debate," 1993). He has compiled nine books for Methuen's series "Writers on File," on Arden, Alan Ayckbourn, David Edgar, Michael Frayn, David Hare, John Osborne, Harold Pinter, Peter Shaffer, and Tom Stoppard. He also publishes widely on modern Canadian theatre, is a past president of the Association for Canadian Theatre History, and is Vancouver correspondent for *Plays International.*

WALTER H. PLACZEK has examined how multicultural principles are reflected in contemporary American plays whose primary focus is the educational process. He has also contributed an essay on Irwin Shaw to *American Playwrights: 1880–1945* (Greenwood, 1995).

DAVID IAN RABEY is senior lecturer in Theatre Studies at the University of Wales, Aberystwyth. He is the author of *British and Irish Political Drama in the Twentieth Century* (1986) and *Howard Barker: Politics and Desire* (1989). He is a contributor to Barker's *Arguments for a Theatre* (1989, 1993) and has written articles for numerous journals, including *Critical Quarterly, Essays in*

Theatre, Hamlet Studies, The Listener, Modern Drama, Plays and Players, Studies in Theatre Production, and *Theatre Research International.* As a theatre practitioner, he has directed and/or performed in eight productions of Barker's work; the most recent of these is *Uncle Vanya* (codirector and performer of title role; Theatr Clwyd, Mold, 1994, and Theatr y Castell, Aberystwyth, 1995). He is author of *David Rudkin: Sacred Disobedience* (forthcoming).

SARAH J. RUDOLPH is assistant professor and Director of Theatre at the University of Wisconsin, Marathon County Center, in Wausau, Wisconsin. Her research interests include women's biographical and autobiographical drama as well as contemporary British theatre.

TONY J. STAFFORD is professor of English at the University of Texas at El Paso. He is the editor of *Shakespeare in the Southwest: Some New Directions* (1969) and has written a number of articles on drama ranging from Shakespeare and the Elizabethan and Jacobean theatre to modern British and American drama. He is also a playwright with numerous productions in cities such as Philadelphia, Washington, D.C., Houston, Denver, and Los Angeles. His most recent productions were at the World Premiere Theatre in Eureka, California, in 1993 (*In a Dark Thicket*) and 1994 (*Brandy Stone and the Eighth City*).

STEPHEN WEEKS is lecturer in the School of Drama at the University of Washington, Seattle. He writes on dramaturgy and contemporary British drama.

ROBERT WILCHER is senior lecturer in English at the University of Birmingham. He is author of *Andrew Marvell* (1985) and *Understanding Arnold Wesker* (1991) and editor of *Andrew Marvell: Selected Poetry and Prose* (1986). He has contributed chapters to *Beckett's Later Fiction and Drama: Texts for Company* and *British and Irish Drama since 1960* and has written articles for a number of journals, including *Critical Quarterly, Critical Survey, Journal of Beckett Studies, Modern Drama, Renaissance and Modern Studies, Shakespeare Survey, Southern Review, Theatre Research International,* and *Yearbook of English Studies.*

ISBN 0-313-28759-7

9 780313 287596

HARDCOVER BAR CODE